P9-BZX-164

AUTHOR OF VIVIAN GREY.

Frontispiece "Author of Vivian Grey," after Daniel Maclise, at Hughendon Manor, The Disraeli Collection (National Trust), © NTPL/John Hammond. See the discussion, page 15.

#79717-1/2.

Disraeli

The Romance of Politics

ROBERT O'KELL

UNIVERSITY OF TORONTO PRESS
Toronto   Buffalo   London

©University of Toronto Press 2013
Toronto   Buffalo   London
www.utppublishing.com
Printed in Canada

ISBN 978-1-4426-4459-5 (cloth)

Printed on acid-free, 100% post-consumer recycled paper
with vegetable-based inks

Library and Archives Canada Cataloguing in Publication

O'Kell, Robert, 1939–
Disraeli : the romance of politics / Robert O'Kell.

Includes bibliographical references and index.
ISBN 978-1-4426-4459-5

1. Disraeli, Benjamin, Earl of Beaconsfield, 1804–1881. 2. Disraeli, Benjamin,
Earl of Beaconsfield, 1804–1881 – Criticism and interpretation. 3. Disraeli,
Benjamin, Earl of Beaconsfield, 1804–1881 – Political activity. 4. Authors –
Great Britain – Biography. 5. Prime ministers – Great Britain – Biography.
6. Politics and literature – Great Britain – History – 19th century. I. Title.

PR4087.P6O44 2012   823'.8   C2012-905760-6

This book has been published with the help of a grant from
the Canadian Federation for the Humanities and Social Sciences,
through the Awards to Scholarly Publications Program, using funds provided
by the Social Sciences and Humanities Research Council of Canada.

University of Toronto Press acknowledges the financial assistance
to its publishing program of the Canada Council for the Arts
and the Ontario Arts Council.

Canada Council   Conseil des Arts
for the Arts   du Canada

University of Toronto Press acknowledges the financial support
of the Government of Canada through the Canada Book
Fund for its publishing activities.

Contents

Preface: Fictions of Identity

There have been many biographies that testify to the brutal strength of the tension that can arise between private and public images of the self for those who hold, or aspire to hold, public office. But the life of Benjamin Disraeli offers an exceptionally fine illustration of this relationship within the mind of a politician, not just because of his extraordinary rhetorical command of language, but also because he wrote novels that embody recurring fantasy structures which are similar to the imaginative patterns of his political career – and which he himself referred to as the "Psychological Romance." Disraeli's novels are thus autobiographical, not in a literal sense, but in an imaginative one. As such they serve the purpose of continuously reconstituting or reshaping his sense of identity, by providing rationalizations of the past, and by exploring the dramatic possibilities of the future. The relation between the politics and the fiction is truly reciprocal; each illuminates our understanding of the other. A crucial distinction between them, however, is the matter of plot. The novels are all characterized by conventions typical of romance, and their plot structures often indicate the power of those conventions to sustain Disraeli's sense of himself amid personal and political struggles of terrifyingly poor odds.

The political career, on the other hand, occurs in medias res. For though the life gradually accumulates an outline of gratifying success, political rhetoric is always uttered without the certain knowledge of consequences such as the fantasies of fiction can provide. Thus in accepting Disraeli's warrant to treat the politics as a form of fiction, and the fiction as an expression of politics, I have been concerned to focus upon the rhetorical significance of his language in the novels, tales, pamphlets, speeches, journalism, and letters, drawing wherever possible upon the idiosyncratic images and patterns of repetition that give the individual moments greater explanatory power.

It will be clear from the outset that this is not a typical biography, nor a critical study, such as Michael Flavin's *Benjamin Disraeli: The Novel as Political Discourse* (2005), which interprets the fiction as primarily a forum for political ideas. My narrative follows the emotional intensities of Disraeli's careers rather than the straightforward sequence of events. My hope thereby is to provide some new interpretations of well-known facts, new readings of his novels and tales, and a new understanding of how the fictions and the imaginative shaping of the political career inform one another. For the details, as well as the general outline of Disraeli's careers, I am much indebted to the monumental quarry of a *Life* provided by William Flavelle Monypenny and George Earle Buckle, to the exemplary political biography written by Robert Blake, and to the magnificent volumes of Disraeli's letters, edited first by J.A.W. Gunn, John Matthews, and Donald M. Schurman, and subsequently by M.G. Wiebe, J.B. Conacher, Mary Millar, Ann P. Robson, Ellen Hawman, and Michel Pharand, and still in the midst of publication. I have also relied on the numerous printed memoirs of Disraeli's political contemporaries and benefited from the more recent biographies of the last two decades, notably those of Sarah Bradford (1983), John Vincent (1990), Stanley Weintraub (1993), Jane Ridley (1995), and Paul Smith (1996). My interdisciplinary approach has led to readings of the novels that are essentially revisionist, offering interpretations sometimes directly at odds with the previous orthodox views. That is not to suggest, however, that I have not learned much from Disraeli's other critics and admirers, particularly from the work of Richard Levine, Daniel Schwarz, Patrick Brantlinger, Catherine Gallagher, Rosemarie Bodenheimer, and the others listed in the bibliography.

Acknowledgments

My many intellectual debts to the work of other scholars and critics can best be judged from the notes and bibliography accompanying the text. I wish here to express my gratitude for more personal support. The origins of this study lie far back in a stimulating graduate history seminar taught by Michael Wolff at Indiana University. The discussion there of the intense rivalry between Disraeli and Gladstone led me to the conclusion that in their cases the standard analyses of Victorian politics left much unexplained that might be fruitfully explored from an interdisciplinary perspective. In pursuing that approach ever since I have been most fortunate in having two other mentors from the Victorian Studies Program at Indiana, Donald Gray and Patrick Brantlinger, whose support and encouragement over many years have been so generously given. For similar reasons I must give my special thanks to Mel Wiebe, the former Senior Editor of the Disraeli Project at Queen's University, for granting me most hospitable access to the resources of the Project on numerous occasions, for sharing his encyclopaedic knowledge of Disraeli's careers, and for his helpful comments on a number of chapters in draft form.

Portions of this study were written in the early 1990s, while I was a Visiting Scholar at the Society for the Humanities at Cornell University. I wish to thank Jonathan Culler for that opportunity and also Daniel Schwarz and Peter Bailey for reading and responding to the work then in progress. More recently I have had similar help from Regenia Gagnier, who volunteered to read several chapters in their current form. None of these colleagues, of course, bears any responsibility for whatever limitations this study has.

Through the good offices of the Royal Archivist, Her Majesty, Queen Elizabeth II graciously granted me access to Queen Victoria's correspondence with Disraeli in the Royal Archives, for which I am most grateful. Several other institutions and their staffs have also provided material assistance during the progress of my research, not least among them the staff of the British National Archives and the librarians of the University of Manitoba. I am also especially grateful for several research grants from the Social Sciences and Humanities Research Council of Canada, and I am very pleased to be able to acknowledge the help I have received from Keble College, Oxford, the National Trust, and the Bodleian Library in consulting the Disraeli Papers. At an early stage of the research I was also able to benefit as a visiting scholar from the stimulating environment of the Victorian Studies Centre at the University of Leicester.

My thanks also go to Richard Ratzlaff at UTP for all his support and guidance through the commissioning process. As well, I wish to thank the external assessors, the reader from the manuscript review committee, and the copy-editor, Miriam Skey, for their very helpful suggestions for improving the manuscript. And I want to thank Katie Thorsteinson for her assistance with the Index, as well as the Department of English, two successive Deans, Richard Sigurdson and Jeff Taylor, of the Faculty of Arts, and Digvir Jayas, Vice-President (Research) at the University of Manitoba for providing funds for the illustrations.

My final acknowledgement is the one closest to my heart. My wife, Arlene Young, has been the ideal partner and academic colleague. Her love, encouragement, and patience have been unstinting and I happily confess that this study would never have been completed without them.

DISRAELI: THE ROMANCE OF POLITICS

Introduction

The most striking aspect of Disraeli's life, contemplated in his own day or in ours, must surely be its sheer implausibility. According to all the rules by which the Victorians played the games of society, literature, and politics, Disraeli should have failed to realize his ambitions. Not for lack of talent, of course, but because by the agreed public standards, he started with severe liabilities and he then made almost every serious mistake possible, any one of which should have blocked his path to further advancement. First there was his Jewish heritage, which, though technically dissolved by his childhood baptism in the Church of England, was nevertheless the reason for much animosity and prejudice in the very social and political circles he wished to enter. Then there was the matter of his highly eccentric education outside the institutions designed to prepare those who by virtue of their birth, wealth, or intellect would claim some professional or public role or responsibility. It was an education that left him at the mercy of some very idiosyncratic and romantic notions about religion, history, and politics.

Disraeli soon added to these disadvantages his own series of blunders and indiscretions. Having resisted the safe, but probably too dull, legal apprenticeship arranged by his father, he turned in his early twenties to speculation on the stock market and to puffery of South American mining companies. The result was a debt far beyond his means to repay, and one that would continuously grow and haunt him for many years under the pressure of an extravagant, dandyish life on the fringes of London's aristocratic society. With a mind full of power fantasies and debased romanticism, he wrote and published a jejune novel, *Vivian Grey*, which gained him a lasting notoriety for untrustworthiness and insincerity, because it was in effect a slanderous betrayal of John Murray's confidence and friendship during their attempt in 1825 to establish *The Representative* as a rival to *The Times*. He went on to publish several other novels in the next decade (*The Young Duke, Contarini Fleming,* and *The Wondrous Tale of Alroy*) that only added to the image of intellectual immaturity and imaginative extravagance he had already presented. In the next few years he also carried on, with considerable indiscretion, an adulterous affair with Lady Henrietta Sykes, scandalous details of which seem to have both enlivened his election campaigns (particularly at Taunton in 1835) and shocked the Buckinghamshire gentry in the vicinity of his family's home at Bradenham, near Wycombe.

In his repeated attempts to gain a seat in Parliament, from the summer by-election in Wycombe in 1832 until he finally did so in the general election of 1837 at Maidstone, Disraeli further enhanced his reputation for unprincipled opportunism by adopting a variety of expedient party labels that made him appear far more inconsistent than he actually was. As he stood first as a Radical, then a Radical-Tory, a Tory-Radical, again as a Radical, and finally as a Tory in the successive contests, he was easily characterized by his opponents as a man who could not be trusted. And in turn his displays of mordant wit and savage invective directed at his adversaries may have delighted his partisans and amused the crowds of listeners, but they did little to win the support of sober, uncommitted voters.

The central questions about the early years of Disraeli's careers, then, are how did he survive such crushing political defeats? How did he sustain his sense of his own pre-eminence over so many years of disappointment? And why did he not settle for the private gratifications and smaller measures of success he could easily have had? Disraeli thus stands as a fascinating enigma for those whose curiosity about human nature insists upon more than the clichéd labelling of behaviour and thought with such terms as "genius" and "ambition." In discussing his work, it is best to avoid the usual dichotomy of author and politician, for neither aspect of Disraeli's life is merely an odd or unusual complement of the other. To discuss him as a novelist who happened to succeed in politics, or as a politician who wrote some novels of varying quality, is to misperceive the man. His two careers are so intimately related that neither can safely be interpreted simply as a commentary upon the other, and so the possibility of an interdisciplinary approach becomes almost a necessity.

The evidence for the nature of Disraeli's experience of childhood is disappointingly meagre (only six letters and some fragmentary diaries

pre-date his nineteenth birthday). Robert Blake and other recent biographers[1] have sifted the external information on the circumstances of his
boyhood years, and there is no need to repeat that process here. The
significant fact is that the undoubtedly intelligent, sensitive, and precocious child felt quite alien in his middle-class environment. He seems to
have felt within himself a kind of power which he saw as differenti-
ating him from his milieu. "Power" in this sense is a somewhat vague
word, but it refers to a by-no-means wholly conscious awareness of indefinite possibilities and capacities. Both consciously and instinctively
Disraeli knew himself to be superior to, and different from, even the
most successful people of his acquaintance. He indulged himself in the
unwarranted belief, apparently not fully articulated until later,[2] that he
was descended from an aristocratic Spanish family who had left their
home to escape the persecution of the Jews at the time of the Inquisition;
and further, he insisted that the family name was a mark of pride in that
origin. In reality, however, he was never free of the stigma of racial prejudice his ancestry created in some of the people in the social and political society to which he aspired. Also, he was slight and dark, and well
aware that the cultural standards of beauty and grace were quite the
opposite. In addition, for reasons not altogether clear, Disraeli felt a serious deprivation of familial, and particularly maternal, love. The evidence for this is clear and developed in later chapters that illustrate his
continuing search for substitute forms of that affection. For the moment
it is enough to realize that in both receiving and bestowing affection
he was extremely insecure and defensive. As previously mentioned,
Disraeli was also very haphazardly educated, considering the resources
of his father, Isaac, who did send his two much duller, younger sons,
James and Ralph, to Winchester. Benjamin attended two obscure schools
before resorting to the books in his father's library and the inclinations
of his own mind. Whether the failure to send him to a good public
school was the result of maternal influence or not,[3] it probably rankled
a little in later years. But regret was certainly not a strong feature of his
thinking, and it would seem that Disraeli, though perhaps uncomfort-
able and ambivalent about the academic world he did encounter, had a
lot in common with Vivian Grey, who with more than just compensatory bravado declared that "the idea of Oxford ... was an insult."[4] All of
these things contributed to Disraeli's feelings of alienation and they created tensions within him that remained for a long while essentially unresolved. On the one hand, acceptance of the cultural standards of
value would have meant success in life but a denial of a very large part

of his imaginative self. On the other hand, rejection of those standards would have thrown an intolerable burden upon the inner resources on which he could draw for proof of his singular quality. It would seem that at the core of Disraeli's adolescent personality there was a profound conflict, related to the two opposing senses of himself which he held, and that manifested itself in contradictory desires for recognition of two very different sorts.

This conflict took many forms, one of which was a tension between his enormous pride in his Jewish heritage and his intense resentment of the values of his family, particularly the comfortable accommodation his father had reached with the Protestant Anglo-Saxon establishment. Perhaps more important, however, was the tension Disraeli felt between his related conviction that he was innately superior to other men and his fear that public recognition and acceptance of that pre-eminence could only be forced by a dazzling success that would demonstrate his genius. But from the first, his attempts at gaining such success seemed fraught with personal compromise and hypocrisy. Clearly his Jewish heritage and middle-class upbringing were impediments to such acceptance in class-conscious English society, and so they were part of an identity that would have to be abandoned in the process of either literal or imaginative achievement of it. At the same time, however, Disraeli was always emotionally attached to, and indeed fascinated by, the idea of a pure, innate, unquestioned superiority, the public model of which was the English aristocracy, and the private mythology of which, for him, was the Jewish race.

Perhaps inevitably, given the immediacy with which he felt his powers, the young Disraeli felt that both these desires, for a familial recognition of his precocious but innocent self and for a public acceptance of his superiority, were being thwarted. The family was slow to recognize his genius and the world at large had no reason to admire him. As a result, these perceptions of himself produced considerable frustration. But as most people do, Disraeli neither totally rejected nor totally accepted the criteria for importance and success about him; rather, he lived with the pressure of the certainties and doubts that came with his conflicting desires. In part he did this, again as most people do, by creating fantasies or imaginative constructions that contained in some form the essence of his conflicting senses of himself. What is extraordinary in Disraeli's case is the scale and persistence with which he acted out his fantasies and the way in which, whether they were embodied in his fiction or his political career, they came to help shape the subsequent development of his life.

The process of self-realization, in which his fantasies played so important a role, was marked by a recurrent pattern of assertiveness and passivity, of advance and retreat, that reflected Disraeli's central ambivalence about his identity and the related desires for recognition. The essential struggle, as I have suggested, was one between the claims of "purity" and the claims of "success." He wanted the innate superiority of his pure, innocent self immediately and authoritatively recognized. But once beyond the years of early childhood in which his mother might have satisfied that need, such recognition could only be imagined in terms of a regressive involvement in a substitute relationship, or in terms of established social conventions such as nobility and wealth. Alternatively, Disraeli wanted to achieve the kind of dazzling success that would overwhelmingly demonstrate his genius and compel the arbiters of social importance to grant him appropriate pre-eminence.

The tension between these psychic forces found expression in virtually every dimension of Disraeli's life – emotional involvements, intellectual development, aesthetic perceptions, and religious attitudes – but nowhere more consistently than in the imaginative shaping of his political career and in the fantasy structure upon which his novels rest. This study is an attempt to explore the imaginative relation between Disraeli's fiction and his political career. It suggests that both are imaginative conceptions of the same order that attempt to transcend their creator's ambivalence about himself and so make possible the fulfilment of his ambitions and desires. The predilection for treating the fiction as a form of autobiography and the politics as a form of theatre is ultimately justified not just by the fact that Disraeli did so, but also by the recurrence of the psychological patterns and the persistence of the themes, which give them a status independent of the particular narrative or political moments.

The intention here is not to supplant the traditional interpretations of Disraeli's life and work with a reductionist psychological one. Clearly the novelist had aesthetic motives and the politician practical incentives, and neither can safely be ignored. Nor is it sensible to underestimate the significance of the historical context and literary milieu in which he worked. In Disraeli's case, though, it can be argued that beyond these considerations, the fiction, however consciously organized, represents an embodiment of his fantasies about himself. At its most conscious level the writing of the fiction offered a form of compensation for failure or defeat in imagining transcendent success. At a perhaps less conscious level it served as a means of self-discovery, a way of working out the consequences of his imaginative choices. Similarly the journalism, pamphlets, speeches, diaries, and letters reveal Disraeli's political career to have been a construction whose shape and themes are virtually congruent with those of his fiction. Perhaps not surprisingly, the non-fictional life embodies the same fantasies and they there serve the same purposes. What follows, then, is not just a demonstration either that Disraeli's fiction is a gloss on his politics or that the politics, defined broadly as all those enterprises which attempt to realize social and political ambitions, is an explanation of the fiction. Rather, both are shown to be enactments of the same urgencies and purposes. The political career, like the fiction, is an invention, and seen in the light of their imaginative patterns the fiction and the political career provoke a fuller understanding of the nature and significance of Disraeli's remarkable achievements.

1

The Representative Affair[1]

The first opportunity for fairly evaluating the scope of Disraeli's imagination occurs with the affair of *The Representative*. The correspondence associated with the venture shows quite clearly that Disraeli conceived of it as an opportunity for an overwhelming demonstration of his extraordinary abilities that would catapult him to a position of enormous power within the realm of English political life. As such, the enterprise represents the first major instance of a pattern in which Disraeli flashes out in all the brilliance of unrestrained ambition only to be thwarted in the realization of his fantasy by the more sober judgment of those who actually controlled the power that fascinated him. This pattern, emerging in this very early episode of his political career, subsequently develops into the shaping fantasy of three of his early novels, *Vivian Grey*, *The Young Duke*, and *Contarini Fleming*.

There are a number of puzzles connected with the story of this newspaper, begun in the hope of providing an *engagée* alternative to *The Times* that would strongly support the position of George Canning. One of them is how a twenty-year-old youth came to play such an important part in its founding. When John Murray, the publisher, first conceived the new venture in the summer of 1825, Disraeli was several thousand pounds in debt from speculation in the stock market, and so his position as a financial partner, to contribute one-quarter of the investment, was at best theoretical. Murray, who was to be the newspaper's publisher and principal partner, probably felt that J.D. Powles, the third investor, would be good for anything that Disraeli was not.[2] It was only with the stock market slump of the autumn and the financial panic of December that the money became an issue, and at that moment Powles and Disraeli were both ruined. But from the beginning of the affair Disraeli was at the centre of things.

On 12 September Murray sent Disraeli to Edinburgh to negotiate with John Gibson Lockhart. They envisioned the latter in some sort of managerial role, not precisely editor of the newspaper, but perhaps director of a corporation. Although, as Blake suggests, Disraeli's imagination was running ahead of reality with the fantasies of a seat in Parliament for Lockhart and an "immense" political party or faction, he was not aware that Murray would shortly proffer Lockhart more tantalizing bait, the editorship of the prestigious *Quarterly Review*. Lockhart quickly accepted this position at the same time that he agreed to make a major contribution to the new daily paper. Still, the effusions of Disraeli and Murray to each other at this point contrast sharply with the opinions of Austin Wright, a legal adviser to the publisher. On or about 21 September, Disraeli wrote to Murray. Having assured his chief that Lockhart's astonishment at finding himself confronted with such a young ambassador was very quickly overcome ("in a few hours we completely understood each other, and were upon the most intimate terms"), he goes on as follows:

The Chev[alier] breakfasted here today and afterwards we were all three closeted together. The Chev. entered into it excellently ... He agrees with me, that *M* cannot accept an official situation of any kind, as it would compromise his independence, but he thinks *parliamt for M indispensable*, and also very much to *our interest*. I dine at *Abb[otsford]* today and we shall most probably again discuss matters.

Now these are the points which occur to me.

When *M* comes to town, it will be most important, that it should be distinctly proved to him, that he *will* be supported by the great interests I have mentioned to him. He must see, that thro' Powles, all America and the Commercial Interest is at our beck – That Wilmot H[orton] etc. not as mere undersecretary, but as our private friend is most staunch – That the Church is firm – That the West India Interest will pledge themselves [–] that such men and in such situations as Barrow etc. etc. are *distinctly in our power* – and finally that he is coming to London, not to be Editor of a Newspaper, but the Directeur-General of an immense organ and at the head of a band of high bred gentlemen and important interests.

The Chev. and M, have unburthened themselves to me in a manner *the most confidential, that you can possibly conceive*. Of M's capability, *perfect and complete capability*, there is no manner of doubt. Of his sound principle, and of his real views in life I could in a moment satisfy you. Rest assured however, that you are dealing with a *perfect gentleman*. There has been no disguise to me of what *has been* done – and the *Chev* had had [*sic*] a private conversation with me on the subject of a nature *the most satisfactory*.

With regard to other plans of ours, if we could get him up, we should find him invaluable. I have a most singular and secret history on this subject when we meet.

Now on the grand point – Parliament. M cannot be a representative of a government boro'. It is impossible. He must be free as air. I am sure that if this could be arranged – all would be settled – but it is *"indispensable"*, without you can suggest anything else. M was two days in company with + this summer, as well as +'s and our friend – but nothing transpired of our views. This is a most favorable time, to make a parliamentary arrangemt.

What do you think of making a confidant of Wilmot H. He is the kind of man, who would be right pleased by such conduct. There is no harm of Lockharts coming in for a tory Boro', because he is a Tory – but a ministerial Boro' is impossible to be managed.

If this point could be arranged, I have no doubt, that I shall be able to organise, in the interest, with which I am now engaged, a most IMMENSE PARTY, and MOST SERVICEABLE ONE.

Be so kind as not to leave the vicinity of London, in case M and myself come up *suddenly* – but I pray you if you have any real desire to establish a mighty engine, to exert yourself at this present moment, and assist me to *your very utmost*. Write as soon as possible to give me some idea of your movements and direct to me here – as I shall then be sure to obtain your communication.

The *Chev.* and all here have the highest idea of Wrights *nous* and think it most important, that he should be at the head of the legal department.

I write this dispatch in the most extreme haste.

Ever yrs

BD[3]

This passage shows the sort of momentum the youthful Disraeli could achieve when given the chance. A detached observer might think that the egotistical, aggressive tone borders on impudence, if not effrontery. But Murray did not read it in that light. He had been friendly with Benjamin's father, Isaac D'Israeli, for years and had come to know the son as a result. Disraeli had submitted the manuscript of a novel, "Aylmer Papillon," to him in 1824, and, though he had declined to publish it, this and the favourable impression the young Disraeli had made at some of the publisher's dinner parties led to a certain confidence between them. Then, too, the two years that Disraeli had spent as a law clerk at Messrs Swain, Stevens, Maples, Pearse, and Hunt of Frederick's Place had given him some experience of the world. He served, he said, as the private secretary of the busiest partner, whose correspondence was "as extensive as a Minister's," and he came to know the business of "men of great importance," all of which gave him great facility with his pen and "no inconsiderable knowledge of human nature."[4] Finally, it should be noted that it was to Disraeli that Murray owed his acquaintance with Powles, and that Murray had published some pamphlets written by Disraeli to puff the Mexican and South American mining companies whose stock was currently being issued.

For all of these reasons Murray found Disraeli's youthful brashness a comforting complement to his own rather timorous personality. It is, therefore, not surprising that he would express his enthusiastic admiration for his youthful partner in a letter to Lockhart, dated 25 September. He said that he had "never met with a young man of greater promise … a deep thinker, of great energy, equal perseverance, and indefatigable publication, and a complete man of business." And he added that Disraeli's "knowledge of human nature, and the practical tendency of all his ideas," had often surprised him in one so young, and he went on to assure Lockhart that Disraeli had "a most excellent temper" and that his "mind and heart" were "as pure as when they were first formed." Murray concluded by saying that he could "pledge his honour" and assure Lockhart that Disraeli was "worthy of any degree of confidence" that he might be induced to repose in him, "discretion being another of his qualifications."[5] But, however much confidence in Disraeli's talents Murray had, there were others involved in the affair who expressed some reservations. For example, Wright said in a letter to Lockhart, dated 3 October, "whatever our friend Disraeli may say or flourish on this subject, your accepting of the Editorship of a newspaper would be *infra dig.*" Disraeli, he added, "is a sensible clever young fellow; his judgment however wants sobering down; he has never had to struggle with a single difficulty nor to act in any affairs in which his mind has necessarily been called on to consider and choose in difficult situations … and though he is honest and, I take it, wiser than his father, he is inexperienced and untried in the world, and of course, though you may, I believe, safely trust to his integrity, you cannot prudently trust much to his judgment."[6] Nevertheless, Disraeli continued to be Murray's "right hand" and was busy over the next two months with the details of engaging correspondents and printers. In mid-November he was sent again to see Scott at Abbotsford for the purpose of getting Sir

Walter to reassure some of the *Quarterly*'s "old guard" who were un-happy about the news of Lockhart's appointment as editor of the *Review*, still not officially announced. Things went less smoothly for him this time. For having in poor judgment told Lockhart of John Barrow's discontent with the choice of a new editor (based on Lockhart's reputation for nastiness in *Blackwood's Magazine*), Disraeli soon found both Murray and Lockhart furious. He then had to convince Lockhart of Murray's integrity, and Murray of the harmlessness of the blunder.[7] In this he was successful, as a letter from Murray to Lockhart shows,[8] but his general situation was probably deteriorating. He complained to Murray about some of the *Quarterly*'s "junta of official scamps who have too long enslaved you,"[9] and to Lockhart of the "disgusting thral-dom" they were exerting over the publisher.[10] The ambiguous reference in the same letter to Lockhart to "the agitating and curious scenes which have taken place during these last days" may foreshadow the mystery of Disraeli's sudden withdrawal from the whole project. But ironically, within a week or two of his name for the paper, *The Representative*, being adopted, Disraeli ceased to be connected with the venture. His losses on the stock market may have been part of the reason. Certainly Murray could not any longer have refused to recognize Disraeli's inability to contribute his share. But it may also be that Disraeli had gone too far in his opposition to people such as John Wilson Croker and John Barrow, and that Murray was eventually forced to choose between his flamboy-ant protégé and his experienced supporters.

In manipulating the other principals of the enterprise, it would seem that Disraeli became the victim of his fantasy about his own self-importance. His comments to Lockhart, for example, about "the intrigu-ing, selfish and narrow-minded officials by whom he [Murray] has been so long surrounded," could easily in the end have been his undoing,[11] for the correspondence between Lockhart and Murray, and between Lockhart and Croker, reveals that not only were Disraeli's initial avowals of support from Croker and Barrow unwarranted, but that Lockhart was quite naive about the relationships between Murray and his important contributors to the *Quarterly*. Consequently Lockhart looked foolish complaining to Croker about Barrow's resistance to the appointment to the *Review* not only because the latter two were good friends, but also because he did not realize that Murray in his frustration had lost sight of the distinction between the editorship of the *Quarterly* and that of *The Representative* and was furious with Croker for telling Barrow that the establishment of the newspaper was absurd. Lockhart then made matters worse by writing to Murray about Croker's distressing behaviour (in fact, Croker did not even know about Lockhart's appointment prior to receiving his letter) just as the publisher was regaining his senses and realizing that Croker was not just thwarting him out of pique, as Lockhart suggested, but rather out of wisdom resulting from his own ill-fated attempt to establish *The Guardian* a few years before.

Thus it was that Disraeli's sense of his own power found gratification in creating a complex intrigue out of relatively simple objections, and that he embroiled the others in embarrassing misunderstandings. And when, finally, Barrow's doubts about Lockhart's appointment and Croker's doubts about the prudence of inaugurating *The Representative* were overrun, with Lockhart having arrived in London to edit the *Review* and Murray pushing on determinedly with the newspaper, they must have realized that Disraeli had been indiscreet from the beginning, and that he was responsible for some of the bruised feelings that resulted. This would seem the most likely explanation, for Powles, also insolvent, continued to be associated with the newspaper for several months, and Murray's final comment about Disraeli's role in this affair was that he "had received nothing but the most unbounded confidence and parental attachment; my fault was in having loved, not wisely, but too well." Isaac D'Israeli apparently felt that his son had been treated unfairly by the publisher and Murray's remark was the result of mentioning it to a mutual friend.[12] The later animosity between Disraeli on the one hand and Lockhart and, later, Croker on the other would fit with a sense of betrayal on his part and a resentment of insulting arrogance on theirs, though for the moment, and indeed, even as late as 1830, when he advised his father to apply to Croker about an Admiralty commission for his brother, James, Disraeli did not sense any ill will from him. There is, however, a letter from Lockhart to Murray, dated 14 February 1826, which suggests that this account is correct: "I think Mr. B. Disraeli ought to tell you what it is he wishes to say to Mr. Croker on a business *of yours* … I think, all things considered, you have no need of anybody to come between you and Mr. Croker."[13]

This *Representative* episode in Disraeli's life suggests that at the time he was more than just an egotistical, reckless, and arrogant young man. It is clear enough from his letter to Murray that he revelled in the intrigue and confidentiality of his situation; that he delighted in finding himself treated with dignity by such distinguished persons as Sir Walter Scott, in being able to report the "Chevalier's" agreement with him on crucial matters; and that he was confident that Murray not only trusted

him, but that the publisher could be prodded to act upon his suggestions. But the letter reveals more than this. Whatever Murray thought
he was about, probably the establishment of another successful publishing venture, Disraeli was operating upon a fantasy of much larger
proportions. The rhetoric of his long letter to Murray is astounding. He
imagines that the financial and commercial interests of the nation are
"at our beck," that the Under-Secretary for War and the Colonies is a
"staunch" supporter, that the West-India Interest will "pledge" themselves, and that Government officials such as the Secretary of the
Admiralty "are distinctly in our power." And if Murray will undertake
to arrange a crucial parliamentary connection, Disraeli proposes to
himself "organise ... a most IMMENSE ... and MOST SERVICEABLE"
party. The relationship of all of this to the reality of the moment is not
important. But this is obviously a vision in which the "band of high
bred gentlemen" is devoted to running not just a newspaper, but rather
the country. And in this vision Disraeli as well as Lockhart "is fully
aware that he may end by making his situation as important as any in
the empire."[14]

It is clear that *The Representative* affair gave Disraeli a chance to act
out a fantasy in which he imagined himself possessed of great power
and influence. But in the end that fantasy collapsed. External events,
such as the stock market crash, undoubtedly played some part in his
disappointment, though probably equally important was the offence
generated by his indiscreet attempts to manipulate the other principal
members of the endeavour. The extravagance of his behaviour was a
function of his imaginative over-estimation of his importance to the
success of the venture. With the exception of Murray, the other people
involved clearly held reservations about the young Disraeli's assumptions of self-importance. Their views of him were much closer to that of
his mother, Maria, who wrote a "vigorous and sensible" letter to Murray
protesting against his subsequent anger over the publication of *Vivian
Grey.* In it she described her son as a clever boy but "no 'prodigy,'" and
she accused the publisher of having "formed in his imagination *a perfect
being* and expected impossibilities, and found him on trial a *mere mortal*
and a very very young man."[15]

I

Having been checked in the political fulfilment of his fantasy, Disraeli
turned to the creation of a fictional embodiment of it. *Vivian Grey* (1826)

was instantly successful because its readers took it to be a disguised account of *The Representative* affair and the recent intrigues in John Murray's circle. Consequently, they delighted in attempting to discover the identities of both the author and the characters.[16] But this literalist attempt to relate the work to specific events and people is of little more than curiosity value. The book is, however, worth study of a different kind, for it confirms and develops the emotional pattern of Disraeli's involvement in the events surrounding the publication of Murray's newspaper. The writing of the novel provided an opportunity for compensatory self-justification by enabling Disraeli to reconstruct imaginatively the immediate past and project it upon the future. Somewhat ironically the success of the work in some measure transcended the collapse of the power-fantasy it described. The fame or notoriety he acquired as "the author of *Vivian Grey*" was not the perfect fulfilment of his desire for recognition, but, for the moment at least, it did seem to validate his conception of how he could demonstrate his remarkable talents. The imaginative content of the novel itself, however, reflects no such validation, and, indeed, is true to the author's central ambivalence beneath his alternatively seeking success through a demonstration of his genius and claiming recognition of an innate, unquestioned superiority, the public model of which was the English aristocracy.

Vivian Grey is a hero with neither noble birth nor fortune to distinguish him. But the young, bold, somewhat deliberately Byronic protagonist, sure of his extraordinary power but frustrated by the restraints of established persons, finally resorting to a desperate manoeuvre to achieve his revenge and effect his escape from the consequences of his ultimate failure to manipulate those whom he would surpass, is prototypical of many of the early Disraelian heroes. In this case, the first, adolescent instance of this pattern occurs very early in the novel. The family's situation is comfortable, for the omniscient narrator relates that Mr Horace Grey was for sending his son to Eton, "a place for which, from his temper, he was almost better fitted than any young genius whom the playing fields of Eton or the hills of Winton can remember" (*VG*, 4). Vivian's mother, however, is convinced that public schools are horrible places and so the child is sent to an obscure private establishment. There he asserts himself with "perfect sang-froid" and "a bold front." In no time at all he is "decidedly the most popular fellow in the school ... so dashing! so devilishly good-tempered! so completely up to everything!" (*VG*, 5). His talent is so much admired that his "slight accomplishments become the standard of all perfection ... his opinion the guide in any crisis ... of the little commonwealth" (*VG*, 6). Vivian is not, however, by any means the perfect pupil. He despises the accomplishments of the dull, hardworking classicists and he openly encourages his fellows to resist the rules of the school. Eventually, he is involved in a fist fight with St Leger Smith, another student, over this issue of obedience. Dallas, the headmaster, forbids the boys to put on a play and Smith insults Vivian, who proposes to disregard the teacher. Of course, in the fight the younger, smaller hero more than holds his own until, on the point of victory, he is stopped by an usher. The insolent boldness and wit are then pushed to their imaginative limits as Vivian, in the next term, befriends the previously detested usher, Mallett, to increase the tyranny upon his cowardly "friends" who have abandoned him. And when the boys finally rebel, Vivian defends himself from their revenge by drawing a pistol, but encourages them to gang up on the unfortunate monitor. The episode ends with the "genius" being expelled. The emotional pattern of this one incident is directly related both to that of *The Representative* affair and to the major plot in *Vivian Grey*, but it also informs many other moments in Disraeli's literary and political careers.

Chapter 7 of *Vivian Grey* begins with the implied author discoursing upon the subject of success: "In England, personal distinction is the only passport to the society of the great. Whether this distinction arise from fortune, family, or talent, is immaterial; but certain it is, to enter into high society, a man must either have blood, a million, or a genius" (*VG*, 17). Then Vivian's interest in politics and the engagement of his genius in the ambitious manipulation of the Marquess of Carabas and others swiftly develop into the major theme of the novel. The most striking characteristic of this manipulation is the self-conscious detachment with which it is carried out. Not only is the reader given the benefit of the narrator's awareness, but also of the hero's: "He was already a cunning reader of human hearts; and felt conscious that his was a tongue which was born to guide human beings" (*VG*, 18). Another example also gives away some of the insecurity underneath the repeated assertion of the hero's "sang-froid": "how many a powerful noble wants only wit to be a Minister; and what wants Vivian Grey to attain the same end? That noble's influence ... There wants but one thing more: courage, pure, perfect courage; and does Vivian Grey know fear? He laughed an answer of bitterest derision" (*VG*, 20). But despite the implicit passivity, the dominant tone at the surface of the narrative is one of Vivian's condescending confidence in his ability to lead the marquess into giving him the name and

the influence with which he can take upon himself "the whole organisation of the Carabas party" (*VG*, 38).

The outcome of this venture depends to a great extent upon Vivian's
success in winning Frederick Cleveland to the cause. Despite previous
hostility between Cleveland and the marquess in which the younger man
had publicly triumphed in a pyrrhic way over His Lordship, the latter
suggests him as the man most suitable to lead the new faction in the
House of Commons, and Vivian presumptuously offers to go to Wales
to convince him to leave his exile.[17] Cleveland is explicitly presented as
the very opposite of Vivian in both temperament and training, having
been educated at Eton and Cambridge and there proved that "he possessed talents of a high order." Moreover, in order to perfect his talents,
Cleveland, we are told, has had the "courage … to immure himself for
three years in a German University." And whereas Vivian was "one pre-
cociously convinced of the necessity of managing mankind, by studying
their tempers and humouring their weaknesses," Cleveland, we are told,
"turned from the Book of Nature with contempt" and despite a mind of
"extraordinary acuteness," was "at three and thirty, as ignorant of the
workings of the human heart, as when in the innocence of boyhood he
first reached Eton" (*VG*, 95). This description shows how firmly such
means to "success" are rejected by the narrator. A word like "immure" is
derogatory of both the "German" university and the process of proving
one's talent and acuteness by attendance at such schools. Similarly, the
experience of Eton and Cambridge, we are pointedly reminded, has produced no knowledge of "the human heart."

Nonetheless, though possessed of no fortune, from his connections
and the reputation of his abilities, Cleveland has entered Parliament at
an early age, where his success was eminent. In sharp contrast, Vivian,
who has proved nothing in the formal educational structure, and who
has no connections that he has not created for himself, is dependent
upon his knowledge of the strengths and weaknesses of people's characters for his own advancement. The story has already proved this ability superior in that Cleveland's talents and exertions were quickly
forgotten by the marquess when the previous scramble for power occurred. So Vivian does not dwell upon the logic of his proposal, which
would surely suggest caution on Cleveland's part, but instead plays to
the latter's sense of pique, his desire for revenge, and his frustrated
ambition. The intellectual and emotional opportunism of Vivian's position is shown many times over, but most dramatically, perhaps, in the
following self-reflexive piece of persuasion:

I am not the dupe of the Marquess of Carabas; I am not, I trust, the dupe, or tool, of anyone whatever. Believe me, sir, there is that at work in England which, taken at the tide, may lead on to fortune. I see this, sir; I, a young man, uncommitted in political principles, unconnected in public life, feeling some confidence, I confess, in my own abilities, but desirous of availing myself, at the same time, of the powers of others. Thus situated, I find myself working for the same end as my Lord Carabas and twenty other men of similar calibre, mental and moral; and, sir, am I to play the hermit in the drama of life because, perchance, my fellow-actors may be sometimes fools, and occasionally knaves? If the Marquess of Carabas has done you the ill-service which Fame says he has, your sweetest revenge will be to make him your tool; your most perfect triumph, to rise to power by his influence. (*VG*, 100)

Cleveland, not unlike Lockhart – his prototype in life – is apparently completely taken in by his guest who knows everyone and everything, who is "full of wit and anecdote, and literature and fashion," and who is so "engaging in his manners" and has "such a winning voice" (*VG*, 102). And for the moment, the prospective leader, who is, significantly, "tall and distinguished, with a face which might have been a model for manly beauty" (*VG*, 97), is as much in the control of the young adventurer as are the "fools" and "knaves" of the marquess's circle.

The charm and wit that Vivian displays in captivating Cleveland are also used with deliberate insincerity to manage the affections of virtually all of the other people directly or indirectly involved in the organization of the Carabas interest. The most important of these relationships is that with Mrs Felix Lorraine, the "abandoned" sister-in-law of the marquess. Their first meeting develops into a mild flirtation with Mrs Lorraine quite boldly trying to establish a sense of intimacy between them by revealing her husband's "indifference" to her and her hopes of finding a special "friend" in Vivian. He responds gallantly enough, but this is clearly because he recognizes her "extraordinary influence" upon the household at Chateau Desir. And his response comes in the context of the narrator's extremely uncomplimentary introduction of the lady: "Her complexion was bad, and her features were indifferent ... [her eyes] gazed in all the vacancy of German listlessness" (*VG*, 43). The significance of her aggressive behaviour is not immediately apparent. There is a suggestion that she arranges the departure of the Manvers entourage because she is jealous of Vivian's attentions to the daughter, Julia, and there is a hint of impropriety in her conduct when Vivian encounters Colonel Delmington near the entrance to her rooms late one night. The explicitly sexual motivation of her behaviour is finally revealed, however, when Vivian overhears her disclosures of passion for Cleveland, who, happily married, is disgusted by the siren's advances.

Mrs Lorraine is a very atypical feminine figure in the fiction of the times, and she is one of only two such characters in Disraeli's novels. That this characterization, of a woman for whom sexual gratification and political power are overtly symbiotic, was not a subject of scandal can perhaps be explained by a combination of factors. She is clearly a foreigner and therefore beyond the pale of the customary English charades. Second, Disraeli extends her character beyond, or at least to, the limits of sanity so that her visions of supernatural events undercut the impact of her transgressions, which include proposed adultery and attempted murder. When she attempts to poison Vivian after he reveals that he witnessed her scene with Cleveland, he is so struck by her desperation that he seems to recognize for a moment the implications of his own behaviour:

Oh! my heart is very sick! I once imagined, that I was using this woman for my purpose. Is it possible, that aught of good can come to one who is forced to make use of such evil instruments as these? A horrible thought sometimes comes over my spirit. I fancy, that in this mysterious foreigner, that in this woman, I have met a kind of *double* of myself. The same wonderful knowledge of the human mind, the same sweetness of voice, the same miraculous management which has brought us both under the same roof: yet do I find her the most abandoned of all beings; a creature guilty of that, which, even in this guilty age, I thought was obsolete. And is it possible that I am like her? that I can resemble her? ... It is not so; it cannot be so; it shall not be so! In seeking the Marquess, I was unquestionably impelled by a mere feeling of self-interest; but I have advised him to no course of action in which his welfare is not equally consulted with my own. Indeed, if not principle, interest would make me act faithfully towards him ... But am I entitled ... to play with other men's fortunes? Am I all this time deceiving myself with some wretched sophistry? Am I, then, an intellectual Don Juan, reckless of human minds, as he was of human bodies; a spiritual libertine?

Such a train of thought, with its rationalizations, doubts, and melodramatic qualms of conscience, complicates the reader's response at this point by implying an alternative image of the hero's identity, just below the surface of bravado. The tension of the ambivalence, however, is unstable. In true Byronic fashion Vivian immediately abandons his scruples and resolves to renew the pursuit of his worldly ambitions: "Away with all fear, all repentance, all thought of past, all reckoning of future. If I be the Juan that I fancied myself, then Heaven be praised! I have a confidant in all my trouble … my own good mind. And now, thou female fiend! the battle is to the strongest" (*VG*, 113).[18] Ultimately the effect of this self-reflection is to intensify our anticipation of the mutually destructive battle of wits to follow. What matters in this is her revenge upon Vivian and Cleveland for their rejections by convincing the marquess that they are conspiring against him, and by persuading Lord Countdown to withdraw Cleveland's sinecure. Cleveland and the marquess are then furious with Vivian and the insults of the former lead to a duel in which Vivian by chance kills his rival for power.

The cynical progress of Vivian's political career is entertaining stuff, even today, but when, finally, he can no longer control events and becomes the victim of people he once thought he influenced, his fantasy of attaining power collapses in this patently melodramatic ending to an increasingly improbable plot which admits of no further development. Part 1 closes with the hero recuperating from a loss of consciousness under the sheltering auspices of his doting parents, and with the escape of a European tour. This summary ignores many nuances within the novel's theme, but it identifies the central pattern in which the protagonist attempts to manipulate people in the context of events which will establish his own brilliant career and demonstrate his superiority to all around him. Accordingly, the most significant elements of Disraeli's fantasy are Vivian's contempt for the marquess, whose wealth and position he admires; his winning to his cause of Cleveland, whose talents and accomplishments he would outstrip; and his failure through the deceit of a siren, Mrs Felix Lorraine, whose heart he fancies is captive, first by charm and then by fear. Furthermore, the novelist does not dwell upon his hero's extravagances in proclaiming the moral of the story to lie in the effects of his mis-education, but rather, he absolves Vivian of the responsibility for failure by means of a romanticized plot of revenge and escape.

Not surprisingly, when this novel was published, John Murray took offence at the all-too-thinly disguised portrait of himself as the tipsy, incompetent marquess. And for some time the formerly good relations with the Disraeli family were strained. Lockhart and the others involved in *The Representative* affair were no doubt also equally offended by the bumptious presumption of Disraeli's fantasies, and by the public exposure to ridicule entailed in the various *Keys to Vivian Grey* pamphlets that constituted part of Henry Colburn's puffery of his sensational novel. In the aftermath of his political failure and literary success Disraeli set out in August of 1826 on a three-month tour of the Continent, travelling in the company of family friends, Benjamin and Sara Austen. The latter, excited by the prospect of a literary intrigue, had acted as Disraeli's agent in the transactions with Colburn, for Disraeli had wisely wished to remain anonymous and be represented to the publisher as a man of the world. The letters, written home to his family, from Paris, Geneva, Venice, and Florence, show the young author in his most exuberant high-spirits.[19] They are full of dash and impetuous wit, and they give the impression of a very powerful assimilation of that expansion of knowledge and refinement of taste which such tours were designed to accomplish for the English gentleman. The most immediately striking of his experiences, however, was meeting Lord Byron's boatman, Maurice, in Geneva. There the young Disraeli had the exquisite pleasure of imitating those nocturnal excursions upon Lake Geneva made famous in Canto III of *Childe Harold's Pilgrimage* and absorbing the many anecdotes of Byron's escapades by which the famous Lord's servant now made his living from the English tourists. Perhaps of equal significance from a longer perspective, though, was Disraeli's experience of Italy, particularly Venice, which would eventually play an important role as a setting for some of the fiction. But he did not seem to know that it was the land of his ancestors.[20] Upon his return to England at the end of October, Disraeli, whether from fresh inspiration or the need for money, turned immediately to the task of profiting from his vacation.

The second part of *Vivian Grey*, published in 1827, was obviously a blatant attempt to capitalize upon the notoriety and success of the first two volumes. This sequel, consisting of an episodic and melodramatic account of Vivian's exile of European travels, has so few virtues and so many vices that it has often been dismissed as "trash."[21] But it nevertheless has some significance in connection with Disraeli's fascination with things Byronic. As with the original, beneath the now largely authorial satirical impulse and iconoclastic wit there is a moral pathos at the core of the hero's passive wanderings that destroys his previous claims to "sang-froid." And while in successive vignettes Vivian, as a now perfectly accomplished English gentleman, appears to find acceptance among his touring countrymen in the social circles of the Continental minor aristocracy and the political milieux of various German courts, he is also presented within himself as a tragic victim, first of a forlorn love and then of a hopeless romantic intrigue.

In the former instance, Vivian joins a day's excursion to some ruins near Ems undertaken by a party of friends and young aristocrats of his acquaintance. But while the others simply enjoy the pleasures of the picnic and indulge in the fashion for Gothic medievalism, which the narrator makes the butt of his satirical talents, Vivian falls in love with Violet Fane, whose delicate health is the emblem of her purity and sincerity in contrast to the others' worldliness. When, as the rest of the party takes a more strenuous path back to town, Vivian finds himself alone with Violet, he musters the courage to confess his love to her, and finds it requited, only to have her die in his arms as they kiss for the first time. No doubt readers of any sophistication, then as since, have found this bathos risible. But, as a fantasy, the passage clearly works in a compensatory way to claim for the protagonist an injured sensitivity deserving of our sympathy. This scene had an afterlife of a literary sort in the remarkable courtship correspondence between Robert Browning and Elizabeth Barrett in 1845. Browning, adopting what Elizabeth called "the sphinxine idiom of the *Vivian Grey* argument," interposed Disraeli as a "parallel case" in trying to explain to her both his romantic and poetic intentions while completing "The Flight of the Duchess," a poem usually taken to be an allegory of some sort for the lovers' difficult situation.[22]

In the second instance, Vivian is captivated by the charms of a young and mysterious "baroness" whom he meets at the court of the Grand Duke of Reisenburg, which is dominated by the imposing prime minister, Count Beckendorff. But again, once Vivian has declared his feelings to her and they are seemingly returned, the consummation of their love is thwarted. The baroness cryptically alludes to her unhappy fate and enlists his chivalric assistance. But at the climactic moment of their secret rendezvous the next morning, she is revealed to be the archduchess of the House of Austria, and the romantic encounter with Vivian proves to be but a trifling flirtation on her part – a desperate attempt to escape or forestall the fate of a political marriage to the deformed and mentally deficient Crown Prince. Thus, once again Vivian's heroic fantasies are overcome by the reality of political intrigues over which he has no control, a fact which is emphasized by Vivian's anticipatory reverie and subsequent nightmare, which link his new happiness at being loved by "Sybilla" with the earlier passion for Violet Fane.

However much the plot of *Vivian Grey* embodies fantasies which are
related to Disraeli's recent experiences, it is equally true that the narrative voice of the novel has an imaginatively autobiographical resonance. Daniel Schwarz points out that Disraeli models his "eccentric,
arrogant and delightful narrator" on those of Byron's *Don Juan* and
Sterne's *Tristram Shandy*. Indeed, the intrusive, self-conscious, and play-
ful narrative persona seems at times as much the subject of the work as
is the story he relates. And the presumption of that implied author's
mocking voice undoubtedly gave some Victorian readers as much indigestion as did the details of the roman-à-clef; as Schwarz says, "the
ironic relationship between style and substance" subverts any stable
moral perspective and the work becomes a parody of the Silver Fork
novel it purports to be.[23] Such a technique both licenses and disciplines.
the extravagant fantasies of Disraeli's plots. But even as the intrusions
self-reflexively and arbitrarily turn against the absurdity of the text,
there is an outrageous and aggressive pretension in the wit that would
come to haunt Disraeli's mature accomplishments. *Vivian Grey* was an
indiscretion his enemies never forgot.

II

Like Disraeli's first novel, *The Young Duke* (1831) has a narrator whose
dynamic personality threatens to become the chief interest of the work.
Indeed, the ostensible protagonist often assumes the subordinate status
of a mere moral exemplum for the narrator, who insists upon subjecting
the reader to all manner of manic-depressive digressions upon life. The
"knowingness" of Disraeli's narrative persona is here magnified, to express, on the one hand, a powerful satire on the corruptions and dissipations of the haut monde, and on the other, a poignant sense of lost
innocence and nostalgia. Both of these Byronic extremes are ultimately
ludicrous, but in the process of creating them Disraeli found ample
play for both his corrosive wit and his deepest sympathies. In later editions he would excise many of the solecisms and more outrageous pieces of persiflage, but, as was the case with *Vivian Grey*, the duality of the
original interaction between the teller and the tale is a valuable guide to
Disraeli's social, political, and moral vision.

George Augustus Frederick, Duke of St James, the protagonist of *The
Young Duke*, is an orphan whose patrimony gives him an annual income
of over two hundred thousand pounds. The central theme of the story
concerns his overcoming the effects of an indulgent mis-education which
almost allows his egotism and selfishness to ruin him financially and

morally. The reversals of fortune by which the hero's conscience is fully developed constitute a more interesting novel than might at first seem likely. The plot of the novel is "hardly less improbable" than is *Vivian Grey*'s and the style is "artificial."[24] But despite this, the book has a kind of excitement that keeps the reader skimming forward. This is because the fantasy it embodies offers the author so much more security than does that of *Vivian Grey* that he can confront much more honestly and directly the hero's weaknesses and follies. Despite its superficial removal from reality, the novel has a momentum derived from a plausible internal conflict that is entirely convincing, and because the novel is superficially less autobiographical it is in a sense ultimately more so. The secure position from which the hero begins his growth to maturity is not just a matter of his nobility and wealth, though these are important. Nor is it simply a matter of self-asserted superiority. The most important element of this position is the acceptance of the young duke in England's most distinguished social circle, an acceptance based upon his innate nobility, which is characterized by his "tall and elegant" figure and air of "affable dignity." Indeed, his personal charms are such that, upon his first entrance to society, the Duke of St James, we are told, "was perfectly satisfied with existence, and conscious that he was himself of that existence, the most distinguished ornament."[25]

Among the disagreeable shocks to this young nobleman's initial complacency – the rejection of his amorous proposals by the heroine, May Dacre; the indebtedness incurred through extravagance and gambling; or the hovering scandal of his affair with Lady Aphrodite – none evades the issue of his own responsibility. The terms of May Dacre's refusals, for example, are direct attacks upon his self-indulgent attitudes and he is shown to be incapable and unworthy of the trust and love she finds essential to marriage. He is also clearly responsible for the fact that his flirtations with the already married Lady Aphrodite Grafton have placed his honour and happiness in jeopardy. And in the end, it is his willingness to accept Mr Dacre's good advice on financial matters, and his responsible and generous response to the social and political issues of the Catholic question, that redeem his unthinking, egotistical selfishness. Ultimately, however, this transformation of character is presented less as a result of agonizing self-appraisal than as the inevitable blossoming of his latent nobility. The close of the novel, in which the young duke is united in marriage with the beautiful May Dacre and spends his life "in the agreeable discharge of all the important duties of his exalted station" (350), is perhaps, for modern taste, too simply a case of virtue rewarded, but it acts as a final sanction of the premise upon which the fantasy it embodies is built – that it is impossible that a hero of such "personal distinction," noble, wealthy, handsome, and charming, could have a career "anything but the most brilliant" (*VG*, 17, 47).

Respectively troubled and triumphant, these first two fictions obviously represent Disraeli's fantasies about finding suitable recognition for the dichotomous identities or senses of himself that he felt. In *Vivian Grey* the hero's attempt to demonstrate his superiority is ultimately overwhelmed by the political circumstances and he is forced to retreat to the secure claim of essential purity of heart inherent in his parents' loving solicitude. In *The Young Duke* the hero's innate superiority is established in his nobility, and when that superiority is combined with a regained purity and innocence of true love Disraeli can imagine for him a personal, social, and political recognition of his true distinction.

The next novel, *Contarini Fleming* (1832), contains all of the elements of these psychological patterns that exist in Disraeli's earliest political venture and first two novels. Moreover, it contains a quite explicit thematic development of the nature of the ambivalence Disraeli felt about the alternative forms of recognition he sought and the conflicting awareness of himself that underlay them. Here the ambivalence of the author represents not just a struggle between two opposite identities, but rather a conflict within the conception of each one. In other words, Disraeli's senses of himself were locked in hostile symbiosis. Further, the thematic development of *Contarini Fleming* suggests that while this hostility might conceivably be transcended in future transformations of the related fantasies, the dependency itself could never be dissolved. In *Contarini Fleming*, then, the hero's struggle for success is entangled in guilt over what he feels is his betrayal of his pure, innocent self. Contarini's political success is portrayed as necessitating a hypocritical abandonment of his childhood dream of being loved and admired simply for what he is by nature. Similarly, his search for fulfilment in a private sense, which is imagined in terms of a romance that is clearly a substitute for childhood deprivation of maternal love, is conceived to involve a rejection of the very values of social and political success and a catastrophic exile from the realm in which it could be obtained.

III

Contarini Fleming: A Psychological Auto-biography, was published by Murray in May 1832, a month before Disraeli was to lose the Wycombe by-election in his first attempt to obtain a seat in the House of

Commons. Partly, no doubt, because of the subtitle (actually changed by Murray from the original, "a Psychological Romance"), and partly because the story is told in the first person by the hero, readers have often taken the novel to have a direct correspondence to the experiences of Disraeli's youth. This is to some extent justified even though the physical events of the story only infrequently correspond to anything in the life of the author. The point, of course, is that it is a psychological correspondence they see.

In this novel there are two quite distinct thematic levels of the hero's consciousness, one overt, the other latent. The explicit theme concerns the formation of the implied author's, that is, Contarini's, character: "an ideal and complete picture of the development of the poet" (*CF*, preface to the edition of 1845, ix). The protagonist, we are told, was conceived as a person "whose position in life" is "at variance, and, as it were, in constant conflict with his temperament" (x). This conflict is established in terms of Contarini's unhappiness with the social realities of his family, his education, and the forms of success to which he is presumed to aspire. And with respect to the first of these it is clearly not a material, but an emotional deprivation he feels: "I loved my father dearly and deeply, but I seldom saw him. He was buried in the depth of affairs." His stepmother, too, is a distant presence, for, we are told, though "vigilant in not violating the etiquette of maternal duty," she clearly prefers his two half-brothers with their "blue eyes ... flaxen hair, and ... white visages" so different from his own "Venetian countenance" (*CF*, 5, 6). That Disraeli could now at least partly invert the fantasy of *The Young Duke* and create a hero so obviously beyond the pale of the English ideal must be attributed to the effects of his Mediterranean tour in 1830–1. That tour will be discussed below; for now it is enough to note that his identification with Byron, or rather Byron's reputation, was sufficiently reinforced in that year and a half to swell the expression of his narcissistic delight in his appearance and temperament into something more than mere dandyism. In what follows it is worth remembering that it was Byron who established the English fascination with Venice in the nineteenth century, not only through the direct and indirect associations with *Childe Harold*, *Manfred*, and *Don Juan*, but also through his passionate appreciation of the city's splendour, which so powerfully influenced Ruskin and Turner, and many other travellers of note.[26]

What merit Disraeli's Venetian novel has comes from the tension between Contarini's self-assertiveness and his anxieties. While it purports to be based on the hero's conscious awareness of his own development,

most of the book is about his by no means necessarily conscious search
for affection and security. Thus, on the one hand, in the confidence of
the narrative present time, he claims to experience a "refined and ennobling satisfaction" as he traces "the development of ... [his] own intellect" where "the luminous succeeds to the obscure, the certain to the
doubtful, the intelligent to the illogical, [and] the practical to the impossible." But, on the other hand, in the retrospective past tense, he confesses to having been unhappy and alone: "I had an instinct that I was
different from my fellow-creatures, and the feeling was not triumph,
but horror" (CF, 3, 6). The implicit theme that derives from this material
concerns the discrepancy between the implied author's potential as a
hero and his performance as one. The story, in fact, is a rationalization
of this discrepancy.

   In *Contarini Fleming* the dark, Byronic hero's quest for a realm in
which he could gain recognition of his "poetic" character remains unfulfilled. The explicit struggle between the hero's "position in life" and
his "temperament" is in fact a contest between two mutually exclusive
desires, about both of which Contarini feels ambivalent. The desire to
find a private recognition of his innate, childlike purity and innocence
through romantic absorption in the figure of the substitute mother (represented overtly by both Christiana, his first childhood and adolescent
object of adoration, and Alcesté, his cousin bride) precludes the exercise
of his ambition. When at the very height of his considerable social and
political success, without which he confesses he should find life intolerable, Contarini again meets Christiana as a mature and married woman
who now appears to him as the even more beautiful embodiment of an
innocence and a love he has lost, her presence is a sharp reminder that
he has become an ignorant and selfish "beast" quite unworthy of the
harmony of love and sympathy he really desires: "the presence of this
woman ... amid my corrupt and heartless and artificial life, of so much
innocence, and so much love, and so much simplicity, they fell upon
my callous heart like the first rains upon a Syrian soil ... I recoiled with
disgust from the thought of my present life; I flew back with rapture to
my old aspirations ... and when I remembered what I was, I buried my
face in my hands and wept" (CF, 162). Imaginatively the search for that
affection is shown to be possible only in exile; Contarini abandons his
political and poetic ambitions in his father's northern homeland to visit
Venice, the city of his maternal ancestors. Further, that search is frustrated at the culminating moment by a fate that reflects both the protagonist's feelings of anxiety and guilt about pursuing that desire and

his sense of its inadequacy to complete fulfilment. But, as the quotation also shows, the desire to find a public recognition of his demonstrable superiority in the realm of society and politics involves a denial of his maternal heritage and "true" self. Imaginatively such success seems to necessitate a hypocritical use of power that precludes the possibility of Contarini finding acceptance in terms of his nostalgic ideal.

Vivian Grey is clearly a troubled embodiment of Disraeli's essential power fantasy, for in it the hero's ambitious desire to find a recognition of his demonstrable talents is thwarted by his ultimate inability to control the people and events necessary to his success. *The Young Duke*, on the other hand, embodies a fantasy of acceptance. The hero's innate nobility in the end transcends the selfishly indulgent corruption of his pure heart that threatens to mar his happiness. The young duke's aristocratic heritage is so pre-eminent that the social and romantic acceptance he seeks requires no demonstration of superiority on his part beyond the expression of his natural character. In *Contarini Fleming*, however, the dark hero's heritage is dichotomous. The Protestant, northern realm of his father's life offers the opportunity of fulfilling his social and political ambitions by means of suitable demonstrations of his genius, but it is the Catholic, Venetian realm of his deceased mother that offers the personal fulfilment of unquestioning love. Significantly, in this third novel, the two worlds are conceived to be mutually exclusive. Consequently, Contarini's desire for both kinds of fulfilment becomes the source of his ambivalence about the recognition that either the struggle for "success" or the struggle for "purity" can supply. In effect this ambivalence is a conflict between two opposing senses of himself: his father's son, committed to a worldly success in terms of public recognition of the legitimacy of his ambitions; or his mother's child, committed to a personal happiness in terms of an all-absorbing love that in effect is a recognition of his heart's innate innocence and purity.

The religious dimension of Contarini's ambivalence is by no means incidental. The conflicting potentials of the Protestant and Catholic worlds as realms of fulfilment are shown to be an integral part of his identity confusion. Indeed, the tension between the protagonist's religion by birth and his religion by choice is central to the structure of many of Disraeli's novels. He had first publicly used this motif of religious allegiance as the defining characteristic of his protagonist in *The Young Duke*. In that novel, written at the height of the Catholic Emancipation debate in 1829, his hero is a Protestant by birth whose eventual happiness comes in part as a result of his redeeming advocacy

of the Catholic cause and his subsequent marriage to a Catholic heroine. It is clear now that Disraeli found in the issue of Catholic Emancipation not just a topical setting to exploit, but a disguise for his own
ambiguous feelings about his Jewish heritage. He had, in fact, abandoned the manuscript of *The Wondrous Tale of Alroy* (1833) in order to
write *The Young Duke*, and this is strong circumstantial evidence that his
Jewish heritage was at least at that time a preoccupation directly linked
in his thinking to the Catholic question.

In *Contarini Fleming* the religious dimension of the hero's confusions
about his identity is most obvious in the gothic excesses of Part 3 of the
novel in which Contarini, while on his way to Venice, has two dreams
which blend the political, religious, and erotic elements of his deepest
desires into a supernaturally sanctioned vision of a Messianic destiny.
In the first dream, which occurs in the middle of a terrifying thunder-
storm, Contarini is led into "the vast hall of a palace" where he is welcomed by the president of the council meeting there with much dignity
and the words, "'*You have been long expected.*'" He then enters another
chamber covered with pictures and finds his own portrait paired with
that of Julius Caesar, and his guide repeats, "'*You see you have been long
expected. There is a great resemblance between you and your uncle.*'" As the
dream unfolds, he kneels and prays before a large "irradiated" window
at which the "bright form of a female appeared": "Her fair hair reached
beneath her waist, her countenance was melancholy yet seraphic. In
her hand she held a crucifix. And I said, 'O blessed Magdalen, have you
at last returned? I have been long wandering in the wilderness, and
methought you had forgotten me. And indeed I am about again to go
forth, but Heaven frowns upon my pilgrimage.'" At this the Magdalen
smiles and then responds, "'*Sunshine succeeds storm. You have been long
expected,*'" before she vanishes, leaving Contarini beholding and recognizing the sight of Venice, the home of his maternal ancestors, through
the window (*CF*, 193).

This dream of comforting reciprocal recognitions takes on an even
more mysteriously prophetic significance within the plot when, shortly
afterwards, Contarini stops at a villa and discovers the original painting
of the reproduction that he had seen when he first entered a Catholic
church: "a picture of a Magdalen" with eyes full of "ecstatic melancholy"
kneeling and weeping in a garden (*CF*, 46). At the same time he sees en-
graved in an adjoining banquet temple the words, "*Enter; you have been
long expected!*" (*CF*, 199). In the most melodramatic fashion this villa turns
out to belong to Alcesté Contarini, his orphaned cousin, with whom he

falls in love at first sight. This is the occasion of the second dream or "luminous trance," which occurs while Contarini listens to a Mass in an ancient Venetian church full of his ancestors' tombs, and which relates the original vision to his personal conflict: "I beheld a female figure kneeling before the altar ... I had never beheld so beautiful a being. She was very young, and her countenance perfectly fair ... tinted only with the transient flush of devotion. Her features were delicate, yet sharply defined. I could mark her long eyelashes touching her cheek; and her *dark* hair, parted on her white brow, fell on each side of her face in tresses of uncommon length and lustre. Altogether she was what I had sometimes fancied as the ideal of Venetian beauty" (*CF*, 208, emphasis added). As he falls into a trance, the dream begins with Contarini being saluted by "a long line of Venetian nobles" passing him in procession, and by "the two doges," who "smiled and waved their bonnets." But this gratifying recognition is suddenly interrupted by the appearance of his father, dressed in a northern hunting dress, whose glance of great severity he cannot bear. The scene then transforms into a vision of "the lady of the altar," who stands before him "clinging to a large crucifix, a large crucifix of ebony, the same that ... [he] had beheld in the chapel in the gardens on the Brenta." As he sees tears "quivering on her agitated face," and "would have rushed forward to console her," Contarini awakes to find that no one else has seen the lady in the church (*CF*, 208–9).

The import of these dreams is clearly that in Contarini's imagination Venice offers the reconciliation of erotic and spiritual fulfilment with the gratification of being recognized as the noble descendent of society's most illustrious and powerful family. But, although circumstances seem to confirm this hope, it implicitly involves a denial of his previous existence. Indeed, the ensuing romance with his cousin quickly assumes a melodramatic cast, the initial significance of which lies in the explicit disavowal of his previously demonstrated political success: "'I am entirely Venetian, and have no thought for any other country ... Rather would I be a Contarini amid our falling palaces than the mightiest noble of the most flourishing of modern empires ... I have no father. I have no friend, no relation in the world, except yourself. I have disclaimed my parentage, my country, my allotted career, and all their rights ... I have thrown to the winds all the duties and connections of my past existence'" (*CF*, 217–18). Not surprisingly, in the pages leading up to Contarini's marriage to Alcesté, these denials are shown on three occasions to be mere bravado, masking in their very extremity the profound ambivalence within Disraeli's hero.

The first of these is the continued use of the Magdalen-crucifix motif at the moment of the elopement (virtually an abduction) which keeps Contarini's relationship with Alcesté in the perspective of the emotional substitution it first provided (*CF*, 235). The second is Contarini's reflection on the validity of his Catholic marriage in Protestant law, which also suggests that he has not escaped the original conflict: "I was careful of the honour of the Contarini, and at this moment was not unmindful of the long line of northern ancestry, of which I wished my child to be the heir" (*CF*, 237). A third example, which is at the same time more direct and more ambiguous, is an earlier scene in which Alcesté protests that her engagement to Count Grimani must prevent her from continuing to see Contarini. His response reveals an unabated worldly ambition, which, though it is complicated by the reference to his racial heritage, demonstrates that both sides of the original conflict have taken on a new form: "'Alcesté, you see kneeling before you one who is indeed nothing, if Fame be what some deem. I am young, Alcesté; the shadow of my mind has not yet fallen over the earth. Yet there is that within me, and at this moment I prophesy, there is that within me, which may yet mould the mind and fortunes of my race; and of this heart capable of these things, the fountains are open, Alcesté, and they flow for you. Disdain them not, Alcesté, pass them not by with carelessness'" (*CF*, 228). With this emphasis upon youth and innocence, Disraeli seems to have forgotten that, as the Under Secretary of State in his father's ministry, Contarini had, with perfect cynicism, recently played a key role in European diplomacy. Within the conventions of romance, however, this discrepancy only emphasizes the duality of the protagonist's character.

The clandestine elopement and marriage of Contarini and Alcesté is a variation of the characteristic pattern of frustration, bold expedient, and escape, first seen in the fiction in *Vivian Grey*. This time the conflict would seem to be resolved by the suspension of political activity and the fulfilment of Contarini's need for affection. But the shattering of the domestic bliss with Alcesté's death in childbirth brings forth an exclamation which suggests that Contarini has in fact felt guilty all along about his abandonment of his political career and social success: "'Our house has fallen, the glorious house has fallen ... tell my father he is avenged ... Venice has been my doom'" (*CF*, 250). And although indications of these feelings are suppressed in the period of his idyllic marriage, there is a clear anticipation of them in the previous vision of his father's severity. The word "guilty" does not, however, express the complexities of Contarini's feelings toward his father, for there is an element of anxiety in them as well – really a fear that, despite his longing for affection and a willingness to return it on his part, he will be rejected. This is all made explicit at the end of the novel at the time of his father's death, when it is the parent who takes the initiative for a reconciliation and the responsibility for the estrangement in the first place (*CF*, 354–6).

The effect of this is to sanction Contarini's sense of deprivation from the days of early childhood and to minimize the discrepancy between his conflicting accounts of his own motivations. His consequent search for a new source of affection then reaches its denouement in which his relationship with Alcesté is shown to have been the perfect substitute for the lost original: "There was a packet. I opened it; a lock of rich *dark* hair whose colour was not strange to me, and a beautiful miniature, that seemed a portrait of my beloved, yet I gazed upon the countenance of my mother" (*CF*, 359, emphasis added). The significance of this ideal but impossible (as determined by the plot) resolution of Contarini's conflict should be discussed in terms of events in Disraeli's personal and political life. But, for the moment, it is enough to recognize that within a fictional realm he was describing a fantasy in which a young hero's struggle for political and social power was inextricably linked with what I have called a struggle for "purity" – a state of affectionate, maternally oriented innocence of which he feels deprived. Further, the ending of *Contarini Fleming*, with its vague reference to the once again isolated hero's great political destiny, suggests that the fantasy remains essentially active in the author's mind: "My interest in the happiness of my race is too keen to permit me for a moment to be blind to the storms that lour on the horizon of society. Perchance also the political regeneration of the country to which I am devoted may not be distant, and in that great work I am resolved to participate" (*CF*, 363). Disraeli's third novel is thus not just an explanation of the past in terms of the growth of a poet's mind, but also a valuable key to the future that anticipates the conflicts he will feel in his relationships with women, in his attitudes toward religion, and in his responses to political events.

2

The Byronic Legacy[1]

Contarini Fleming is so markedly different in its range and depth from either *Vivian Grey* or *The Young Duke* that its expression of the complex and ambivalent elements of its author's psychological autobiography should be seen in the context of his impulse to create such a fiction. For while it obtains some parallel relations with events in Disraeli's life before and at the time he wrote his first novel, and also with the tour to Italy he made with the Austens in 1826, there is an equally profound connection with his Mediterranean tour of 1830–1. The former visit to a score of European cities, but most especially to Venice, provided Disraeli with a locale for his romantic fantasies, but it was the latter trip that gave him the confidence to write such a novel about such a hero.

In the late 1820s Disraeli had been suffering from a mysterious and enervating illness, once diagnosed as a "chronic inflamation of the membrane of the brain."[2] More probably it was a nervous condition resulting from fears of failure, with the symptoms of headache, fever, palpitations of the heart, indigestion, and general weakness being psychosomatic ones. In any case the letters written to members of his family while on this second tour contain recurrent and detailed comments on the state of his health, and it is likely that the hope of a complete recovery from the illness was one motive for the trip. And, at least in his own conviction, the warmth of the Mediterranean contributed to just such a result.

The true recovery, however, was one of self-confidence, and the true cause of it was the apparent discovery of an identity, partly real and partly fantasy, strong enough in its conception to survive both criticism and ridicule. From the beginning Disraeli's motives for going on the trip were, in fact, twofold. He had for a number of years been caught up in an enthusiasm for things Byronic, of which the episode with Byron's boatman, Maurice, in Geneva in 1826 and the excesses of *Vivian Grey*, Part 2, are suggestive. This, of course, was a popular fascination, for, as Blake says, "Byron was the symbol of adventure, liberation, romance, and mystery" for a whole generation.[3] But perhaps the intensity of Disraeli's youthful identification was helped by the fact that his father had once met the poet at one of John Murray's dinner parties. In any case, since Disraeli's itinerary in 1830–1 shows a remarkable similarity to that of a tour to Spain, Gibraltar, Malta, Greece, and Albania made by Byron in 1809–10, it is reasonable to conclude that at least in part he wanted to follow the poet's footsteps. The two motives were in all probability linked together in Disraeli's mind. The self-pitying and heroic terms in which he discussed his illness, as well as the path he followed, suggest that he consciously saw himself as fated, like Childe Harold and his creator, to undergo a melodramatic exile. Yet his fascination with the image of Byron led Disraeli to blend the melodramatic heroics of resignation and despair at his own enforced "exile" with the equally powerful imaginative conception of attaining a recognition comparable to that of the obsession with Byron that convulsed not only England, but all of Europe. For the young Disraeli, Byron above all others embodied the social power of the "poetic character."

It is clear that from the outset the Mediterranean tour gave Disraeli a chance to play with identities – a chance to act out his fantasies. At the same time, however, the events and experiences of the tour provided material from which new versions of these fantasies could be fashioned. He grew increasingly nonchalant about his own ability to act with boldness and daring in a variety of social contexts, ranging from the mundane to the dangerous, from the precious to the exotic. His outrageous manner of dressing illustrates this as much as anything does. The flamboyance of his social performances brought him local notoriety, if not fame, which fuelled his fantasies in the same way that his encounters with the masters of Eastern political power did. But Disraeli also acquired a sympathetic knowledge of, and critical insight into, several new cultures, most importantly the Turkish Empire and the biblical home of the Jews. Both of these cultures would henceforth play important parts in both his fiction and his politics, while things Venetian, the enthusiasm of his earlier tour to Italy, would ultimately be the subject of derogatory remarks in the fiction after *Contarini Fleming*. Much of that novel was written while on this Eastern tour, at a distance from his previous social position and from his parents in England, and at a time

before he had had a chance to test his new roles in the more lasting realities to which he would return. So, ironically, at the moment when he
published his melodramatic Venetian dream of self-fulfilment, it had
already been transformed into one more compatible with his current
sense of himself. It must be remembered, however, that the legacy of
the Mediterranean tour was not just self-confidence. Just as the original
Byronic inspiration for it contained an ambivalence, the experience itself proved to be dichotomous. As the following discussion will show,
Disraeli also came to a heightened sense of emotional deprivation, for
which no success seemed capable of compensating. And as a result he
more desperately needed to allay it. These complexities in Disraeli's
sense of himself, and the various roles with which he experimented on
the Eastern tour, became part of the shaping forces in his fiction and
political career upon his return. As has been shown, they are reflected
in *Contarini Fleming*, but they are also present to an even greater extent
in "Ixion in Heaven" and *The Wondrous Tale of Alroy*, and in the social
and political struggles of the next few years.

I

Disraeli arrived at Gibraltar in June 1830 to find that his reputation had
preceded him. Both of the libraries, the Garrison's and the Merchants',
contained copies of *Vivian Grey*, and in a letter to his father, the no longer anonymous author reported the fact with a condescension and wit
undoubtedly tempered by the humiliation that had been inflicted by
English critics: "[it] is looked upon … as one of the masterpieces of the
19th. Centy. You may feel their intellectual pulse from this. At first I
apologised and talked of youthful blunders and all that, really being
ashamed; but finding them, to my astonishment sincere, and fearing
they were stupid enough to adopt my last opinion I shifted my position
just in time, looked very grand, and pass myself off for a child of the
Sun, like the Spaniards in Peru."[4] It is easy to see from such a passage
how Disraeli could have acquired a reputation for cynical opportunism, and to imagine the affectation which some people, for example, the
officers of the garrison at Malta, found so intolerable that they "ceased
to invite 'that damned bumptious Jew boy.'"[5] But many people liked
the young Disraeli and paid him the compliment of repeated attentions. Among these were Sir George Don, the governor of Gibraltar, and
his clever wife. The former "lionized" Disraeli in a way which he would
never have been at home, both at a dinner party and on trips to scenic

places. And with Lady Don there immediately sprang up that quality of friendship expressed in reciprocal flattery and wit for which Disraeli would become famous: "Lady Don was well enough to dine with us, and did me the honor of informing me that I was the cause of the exertion, which though of course a lie, was nevertheless flattering. She is, tho' very old, without exception one of the most agreable personages that I ever met ... To listen to her, you wo[ul]d think you were charming away the hours with a blooming beauty in May Fair, and tho' excessively infirm, her eye is so brilliant and so full of moquerie, that you quite forget her wrinkles." Six weeks later, Disraeli asked his brother Ralph to send Lady Don a copy of *The Young Duke* with the author's compliments inscribed, but a less agreeable, but equally important side of Disraeli's personality is revealed in his account of his aggressive response to meeting the judge advocate at Gibraltar, Mr Baron Field, "who once wrote a book, and whom all the world took for a noble": "it turned out that Baron was to him what Thomas is to other men. He pounced upon me, said he had seen you at Murrays ... but I found him a bore and vulgar, a Storks without breeding, consequently I gave him a lecture on canes, which made him stare and he has avoided me ever since." The truth, Disraeli added, was that "he wished to saddle his brother upon me for a compagnon de voyage, whom I discovered in the course of half an hour to be both deaf, dumb, and blind, but yet more endurable, than the noisy, obtrusive, jargonic judge, who is a true lawyer, ever illustrating the obvious, explaining the evident, and expatiating on the commonplace."[6]

The various roles displayed above – the poseur, the charmed and charming guest, the man of insolent sang-froid – were all staple parts in Disraeli's repertoire when he returned to England and attempted to conquer the social and political cliques of fashionable London. And while these performances were certainly not invented at this late date, there is no doubt that this tour offered him the chance to perfect them. Added to these accomplishments were the courage displayed in numerous meetings with armed robbers in the Spanish countryside and the critical acumen obtained from having seen and judged a variety of cultural artefacts and social milieus. Disraeli waxed discriminatingly, for example, on the subjects of Saracenic architecture, Murillo's paintings, and the "calm voluptuousness" of life at Granada.[7] And he was trenchant on the subjects of social success and the life of military officers: "Here the younkers do nothing but play rackets, billiards, and cards, race and smoke. To govern men you must either excel in their accomplishments – or despise them.

Clay does one: I do the other, and we are equally popular. Affectation tells here even better than wit."[8] This was James Clay, a previous acquaintance whom Disraeli and William Meredith, his sister Sarah's fiancé and his travelling companion, met at Malta. Clay's reputation for wild escapades made Disraeli's family somewhat apprehensive of this friendship, but it continued for many years.

There is one other aspect of Disraeli's genius that was perfected on the Mediterranean tour: his dandyism, which was expressed in the *jeu d'esprit* of daily shocking his audiences with stunningly loud costumes and such props as "a morning and an evening cane."[9] In his diary Meredith had previously commented on his friend's appearance when he came to London to sell the manuscript of *The Young Duke*: "He came up Regent Street, when it was crowded, in his blue surtout, a pair of military light blue trousers, black stockings with red stripes, and shoes! 'The people,' he said, 'quite made way for me as I passed. It was like the opening of the Red Sea, which I now perfectly believe from experience. Even well-dressed people stopped to look at me!'"[10] Disraeli had just met Lytton Bulwer at this time, the spring of 1830. Bulwer's novel, *Pelham*, had been modelled on *Vivian Grey*, and their common admiration of Byron and dandyish fashions led to an intense friendship, which was resumed much to Disraeli's benefit when the tour was over. But before he left London, Disraeli had dined at Bulwer's house, dressed in "green velvet trousers, a canary coloured waistcoat, low shoes, silver buckles, lace at his wrists, and his hair in ringlets."[11] Apparently the invited company were equally impressed by the costume and the conversation.[12] Consequently, it is not surprising to find Meredith reporting from Malta that Disraeli "paid a round of visits ... in his majo jacket, white trousers, and a sash of all the colours in the rainbow; in this wonderful costume he paraded all round Valetta, followed by one-half the population of the place, and as he said, putting a complete stop to all business. He, of course, included the Governor and Lady Emily in his round, to their no small astonishment."[13] Nor is it out of character for him to have set sail on Clay's yacht dressed as a "Greek pirate" in a "blood red shirt with [silv]er studs as big as shillings, an immense [sca]rf for girdle full of pistols and daggers, [a] red cap, red slippers, blue broad striped [...] jacket and trousers."[14] What Disraeli learned from such flamboyancy was that even those who would not take him seriously could be forced not to ignore him. Whether such a strategy helped his cause in any way in the election contests he entered between 1832 and 1837 is debatable, but it is certainly one that he followed.

In a very real sense, however, the experiences of Gibraltar and Malta were but the setting of the stage for the drama of Disraeli's encounter with the Turks. And again the intensity of the experience is reflected in the letters he sent home:

> To lionize and be a lion at the same time is a hard fate ... How shall I con-
> vey to you an idea of all the Pachas, and all the Agas and all the Selictars
> whom I have visited and who have visited me – all the coffee I sipped, all
> the pipes I smoked, all the sweetmeats I devoured. But our grand presen-
> tation must not be omitted ... figure to yourself the largest chamber that
> you ever were perhaps in, full of the choicest groupes of an Oriental popu-
> lation, each individual waiting by appointment for an audience, and prob-
> ably about to wait for ever ... I never thought that I co[ul]d have lived to
> have wished to have kicked my heels in a ministers antichamber. Suddenly
> we are summoned to the awful presence of the pillar of the Turkish Empire
> ... the renowned Redschid, an approved warrior, a consummate politi-
> cian, unrivalled as a dissembler in a country where dissimulation is the
> principal portion of their moral culture. The Hall was vast, built by Ali
> Pacha purposely to receive the largest Gobelin carpet that was ever made,
> which belonged to the cheif [sic] chamber in Versailles and was sold to him
> in the Revolution ... Here squatted up in a corner of the large divan I
> bowed with all the nonchalance of St. James St. to a little, ferocious look-
> ing, shrivelled, care worn man, plainly dressed with a brow covered with
> wrinkles, and a countenance clouded with anxiety and thought. I entered
> the shedlike Divan of the kind and comparatively insignificant Kalio Bey
> with a feeling of awe. I seated myself on the Divan of the Grand Vizier,
> who as the Austrian Consul observed, has destroyed, in the course of the
> last three months *not* in war, "upwards of four thousand of my acquaint-
> ance," with the self-possession of a morning call.[15]

The facet of Disraeli's personality that is most striking in this instance is the determination to place his fascination with and acknowledgment of other people's assumed or demonstrated superiority in the context of his own equal capacities and qualities. In this case, through the meta-phor of the morning call Disraeli imagines himself the peer of the Grand Vizier, while he shapes the destiny of a great portion of the world's population.

Blake argues that the significance of the Eastern tour for Disraeli lies "not ... merely in the effect it had upon his novels and romances," but rather "in the way it affected his attitude in critical issues of foreign and

imperial policy, which, as chance would have it, were to dominate public affairs during his premiership forty-four years later."[16] This is certainly true, but one could add that much of the motivating determination
and the style of his struggle against tremendous opposition that led to
the premiership also grew in the soil of that bizarre encounter with a
very different kind of politics. For undoubtedly, Disraeli's encounter
with the splendours of Oriental life, here embodied in the person of the
Grand Vizier, reinforced his sense of being inherently alienated from
English society. And the proof is in the novels and tales as well as in the
political tracts of the next decade.

There was, however, another side to Disraeli's feelings at this time.
Despite the engrossing pursuit of excitement and notoriety, reflected
again in the "extraordinary effect" of his colourful clothes upon the
"costume-loving" Turks, he was more and more often feeling nostalgic
about his family. Whether out of simple affection or a little guilt at having neglected them, or both, his letters are now usually addressed to
"My Dearest Father" and "My Dearest Sa," instead of with the more
restrained salutations of the earlier ones. And the subject of strayed
letters now crops up with as much regularity as that of his health. But
most significant of all, when he reached the Ambracian Gulf and reflected upon the historical and mythological associations it brought to
mind, he was moved to a sense of himself very different from that of the
social lion: "When I gaze upon this scene, I remember the barbaric
splendour, and turbulent existence, which I have just quitted, with disgust. I recur to the feelings, in the indulgence of which I can alone find
happiness, and from which an inexorable destiny seems resolved to
shut me out ... A thousand loves to all."[17] Thus, somewhat melodramatically, if not self-pityingly, Disraeli felt that his illness, "the great enemy,"
made the intimacy of marriage and a family impossible. Earlier on the
tour he had written from Gibraltar, "Never have I been better, but what
use is this, when the end of all existence is debarred me. I say no more
upon this melancholy subject, by which I am ever, and infinitely de-
pressed, and often most so, when the world least imagines it."[18] And
later, with heroics quite sufficient for the author of *Childe Harold's
Pilgrimage*, he adds, "I wander in pursuit of health like the immortal
exile in pursuit of that lost shore which is now almost glittering in my
sight. Five years of my life have been already wasted, and sometimes I
think my pilgrimage may be as long as that [of] Ulysses."[19] These, at
any rate, were the public mythologies for the extended tour. On the one
hand he felt the promise of salvation in the pursuit of fame and worldly

recognition, while on the other he compulsively imagined himself to be the victim of an enforced exile. And what these home letters demonstrate is that Contarini Fleming's struggle between the purity of a private self and the hypocrisy of a public success closely resembles the author's conflicting attitudes towards innocent domestic affections and worldly experience on his Mediterranean tour.

From a conventional tourist's visit to the Greek islands, Athens, Argos, Mycenae, and Corinth, the three travellers went on to Constantinople, from where Disraeli once again wrote of his hopes of returning to England in the early spring completely cured. Meredith soon left to look at ruins in Asia Minor, while Clay and Disraeli were in the middle of an even more hectic round of masquerade balls and diplomatic dinners. They saw the sultan several times, and Disraeli's remarks on one aspect of the sultan's regime show something of the sympathy for the Turks which would appear in his later foreign policy.[20] Nevertheless, despite whatever political lessons and conspiratorial theories Disraeli was learning for use in the distant future, his response to the news from home was light and ambiguous: "I have just got thro' a pile of Galignanis [*Galignani's Messenger*]. What a confusion! What a capital Pantomime, 'Lord Mayor's Day, or Harlequin Brougham!'" This was a reference to the resignation of the Duke of Wellington's ministry over the issue of Reform, and the subsequent elevation of Henry Brougham to the position of lord chancellor, "a ludicrous turn of events, coming on the heels of his initial truculent refusal of the chancellorship."[21] But English politics was not yet more than imaginatively one side of Disraeli's career, though his inclinations towards an actual involvement were clear enough even at the time of *The Representative* affair.

The next stop on the tour was to have been Egypt, but after meeting up briefly again with Meredith at Smyrna, the other two went to the Holy Land, where Disraeli found himself "thunderstruck" by the "gorgeous" city of Jerusalem, the "wild and terrible and barren" surrounding scenery, and the "severe and savage mountains of Judea." The deep impression made upon his mind by this experience can best be seen, perhaps, in the settings of *Alroy* and *Tancred*, for both are extremely vivid transformations of the reality into what might be fairly termed religious visions. The immediate success was, however, more worldly; he reported that he "made an immense sensation – received visits from the Vicar General of the Pope, the Spanish Prior etc.," and he confessed to being "Never more delighted" in his life. A similar reception awaited him at Alexandria, where the Egyptian partner of an important London merchant followed his instructions to pay "great attention" to the "son of the celebrated author."[22]

Disraeli continued to enjoy the luxurious quality of Oriental life in Cairo, though his letters from Egypt expressed a longing to be home at the scene of the confusion surrounding the Reform Bill, in which he undoubtedly saw an opportunity for genius that "quite unsettled" his mind.[23] But the court of Mehemet Ali seemed particularly brilliant and Disraeli was flattered when the pasha consulted him about the difficulties of establishing a parliamentary form of government in his kingdom. There was, of course, no intention of diminishing in the least his own dictatorial power, but simply that of acquiring advice in an orderly manner, and no doubt, of affecting "all the affable activity of a European prince" as the sultan had done at Constantinople. Monypenny quotes the following excerpt from their conversation in such a way as to imply an obvious absurdity in it: "'God is great!' said Mehemet Ali to the traveller; 'you are a wise man – Allah! Kerim, but you spit pearls. Nevertheless I will have a Parliament, and I will have as many Parliaments as the King of England himself. See here!' So saying, his Highness produced two lists of names … 'See here!' said he, 'here are my Parliaments; but I have made up my mind, to prevent inconvenience, to elect them myself.'"[24] The original account of this incident in *A Vindication of the English Constitution* shows, however, that Disraeli, whatever humour he may have seen in the pasha's resolution at the time, thought that it was a good example with which to bolster his defence of the House of Lords in 1835. The next paragraph begins in complete seriousness, "Behold, my Lord, a splendid instance of representation without election!"[25] The significance to be drawn from Disraeli's anonymous relating of the anecdote lies not just in the flattery of having been thought wise by such a powerful man, but in his obvious admiration of the paternalism of the pasha's use of power. By 1835, of course, Disraeli was committed to shaping his success within the ranks of the Tory party, or at least his version of it, whereas in 1831 that allegiance, however probable, was by no means inevitable.

The return home, which might have been triumphant, was turned into a very sad and agonizing affair by the quite sudden death of Meredith from smallpox on 19 June at Cairo. Sarah, whose expectations of happiness tumbled to ruins at the news, never recovered from the loss. Disraeli recognized immediately what the effect of Meredith's death would be on her and, in great anguish when he wrote from Cairo, said, "Our innocent lamb, our angel is stricken. The joy of our eyes and hearts. Save her, save her. I will come home directly ... I wish to live only for my sister."[26] Quite naturally he did not do this, and, in fact, quickly resumed his previous style of life when he did finally reach England in October. But the same cannot be said of his sister. Sarah's earlier somewhat sceptical affection for her brother was transformed into "a passion bordering upon romance," as she devoted herself to the support of his literary, social, and political struggles.[27] In doing so she was accepting Disraeli's plea that she find in him some substitute for her dear Meredith, and some consolation in his love for her:

> Oh! my sister, in this hour of overwhelming affliction my thoughts are only for you. Alas! my beloved! if you are lost to me, where, where, am I to fly for refuge! I have no wife, I have no betrothed, nor since I have been better acquainted with my own mind and temper, and situation, have I sought them. Live then my heart's treasure for one, who has ever loved you with a surpassing love, and who would cheerfully have yielded his own existence to have saved you the bitterness of reading this. Yes! my beloved! be my genius, my solace, my companion, my joy! We will never part, and if I cannot be to you all of our lost friend, at least we will feel, that Life can never be a blank while illumined by the pure and perfect love of a Sister and a Brother![28]

Disraeli's wish that it might have been his life lost rather than Meredith's brings to mind the myth of Alcestis, especially in the light of *Contarini Fleming*, his "Psychological Auto-Biography." In that myth Admetus, the husband of Alcestis, is to be spared death on the fateful day, if he can find someone to die for him. That moment arrives sooner than expected and, when he cannot, Alcestis gives up her life for his sake. The name of Contarini's Venetian wife, Alcesté, suggests that Disraeli, aware of the possible classical allusion with respect to his feelings about Meredith's death, changed his own role when he came to project the family tragedy into other fictions and blended Sarah's sacrifice of her "life" for his continuing career with his own interior struggle between purity and success (or innocence and hypocrisy).[29] This could be thought a fragile hypothesis on the ground that, when the novel was published in May 1832, Sarah's role as her brother's confidante had hardly begun. But without doubt, Disraeli would have immediately sensed the direction in which her grief was flowing and, in any case, could have presciently anticipated it. As well, his letters of the previous two years indicate his fear that he is fated not to find happiness in love, "the end of all existence," and there can be no doubt that Sarah did come partially to fulfil his need for admiring affection, as a wife, or even a mother, might otherwise do.

II

When in February Disraeli came up to London from Bradenham to launch himself into the 1832 "season," he settled in the fashionable West End and, with Bulwer's help, he began to increase rapidly the number of his acquaintances within the literary and political circles of the capital. At Bulwer's dinner parties over the course of the next year or so, he met such figures of current literary fame as Mrs Norton, L.E.L. (Letitia E. Landon), and Mrs Gore, a variety of minor political or parliamentary men, and "a sprinkling of blues" (i.e., blue-stockings). There, too, he came to know Count D'Orsay, the famous Parisian dandy and friend of Lady Blessington. And he and Bulwer were eventually frequent guests at Lady Blessington's soirées at Seamore Place. The people that Disraeli met were for the most part as eager to make his acquaintance as he was to make theirs; indeed, in some cases more so, for he wrote to Sarah about a typical evening at Bulwer's which included long conversations with Lord Mulgrave and Lord William Lennox: "The soireé last night was really brilliant ... In the course of the evening I stumbled over Tom Moore, to whom I introduced myself. It is evident that he has read or heard of the Y[oung] D[uke], as his courtesy was marked. 'How is your head?' he inquired – 'I have heard of you as everybody has. Did we not meet at Murrays once?' ... A man addressed me by name and talked to me for some time ... I think Geo. Lamb ... evidently a man of distinction, a wit, and a fine scholar."[30] And by April of 1833 he could report (upon returning to town after a week's absence), "My table was literally covered with invitations and some from people I do not know."[31] There can be no doubt that Disraeli was something of a social climber, very much aware not only of every vantage gained, but also of the heights above. He never missed a chance to drop the name of anyone he met whom he considered either important or distinguished. Indeed, his family letters from this time are almost simply lists of his encounters with such socially prominent people as Lord St Maur, Lady Charleville, Lady Cork, and Madame la Marquise de Montalembert, and such political luminaries as Sir Robert Peel and Viscount Castlereagh. Nevertheless, however widespread his acquaintance, Disraeli was, as he knew, by no means moving in the highest of

London's social circles. The truly rich and powerful, if they had heard of him, as they may well have, would have thought him to be "a dandified young bounder" who was trading on the reputation of books of little merit and considerable impropriety.[32] The tone and content of the letters from this period thus show him to be very consciously seeking an increasingly wider social recognition, measured by the social status of the company he kept, and very much aware that his continuing acceptance in the aristocratic and fashionable circles to which he was invited depended on a demonstration of his mastery of the roles of dandy and political wit.

Within a few weeks of coming to London in 1832, having just completed *Contarini Fleming*, Disraeli was at work on *England and France; or a Cure for the Ministerial Gallomania*.[33] Although he informed Sarah that he was "writing a very John Bull book," he was, in fact, not strictly speaking the sole author of it. To Murray, the publisher, some weeks later he protested, "With regard to the authorship of this work, I should never be ashamed of being considered the author. I should be *proud to be*. But I am not. It is written by Legion, but I am one of them, and I bear the responsibility."[34] The truth is that the *Gallomania* was a collaborative effort on the part of Baron d'Haussez, Baron de Haber (both men of suspect political purpose), and the impetuous Disraeli, who was again intoxicated by an intrigue that fed his power fantasies. He told Sarah that his collaborators had provided him with "all the Cabinet papers of Charles the 10th, all the despatches of the Dutch Ambassador, and a secret correspondence with the most eminent opposition member in France," and he boasted, "I am writing a book which will electrify all Europe ... I hope to produce something which will not only ensure my election, but produce me a political reputation ... *This is the greatest of all great se[c]rets and must be confined to our hearth*."[35] Thus, while Disraeli probably wrote most, if not all of the final text of the *Gallomania*, he based it on the conversations and memoranda of his "coadjutors." In the same letter to Murray on 30 March, for example, he said, "at present I am writing a Chap[te]r on Poland from intelligence just received," and in another letter the same day, he pressed the publisher for an agreement on a title for the work on the ground that he was "going to dine with d'Haussez, de Haber, *et hoc genus* ... and must report progress."[36]

Apart from its interest as yet another early example of Disraeli's fascination with conspiratorial intrigues and clandestine sources, the *Gallomania* is chiefly significant for what it reveals of Disraeli's attitude towards Reform. The purpose of the book was ostensibly to attack the

Whig ministry of Lord Grey by exposing, through "a gen[era]l view of
the state of Europe," what the authors considered to be the folly of
British foreign policy.[37] But the subject of Reform became an issue when
Murray asked John Wilson Croker to read the proofs of the book, much
to Disraeli's annoyance. Croker had played some role in thwarting the
young adventurer's ambitions at the time of *The Representative* affair,
though at that time Disraeli put the blame elsewhere. Indeed, as late as
August 1830, he had no hesitation in urging his father to apply to
Croker, whom he was sure would be "delighted to oblige" in the matter
of a naval commission for his brother James.[38] A subsequent letter, written after Croker's refusal, ostensibly on the grounds that he was then a
member of the Opposition and had no influence, was the first indication on Disraeli's part that he sensed anything less than friendship in
the heart of the former secretary: "If Croker really wish to serve my father, he can, whether in or out, because Lord Hill is a creature of the
Duke's, and a whisper from him is enough."[39] Suspicion turned to outright hatred a few weeks before Murray accepted the *Gallomania* when
Disraeli failed to gain admission to the Athenaeum, a club of which
Croker was practically the founder and of which Isaac D'Israeli had
been a founding member. Bulwer, who was a member, had predicted
the failure on the grounds of the members' attitudes towards *Vivian
Grey*, but Disraeli felt that Croker was directly responsible, and he long
harboured a grudge which found expression in the portrayal of the secretary as Rigby in *Coningsby* twelve years later. The immediate point,
however, was that Murray, nervous of the tract's violent rhetoric, wanted a conservative critic's approval.

Originally the manuscript contained a number of expressions of high
Tory sentiment, reflections of the reactionary viewpoints of the Barons
d'Haussez and de Haber. But Disraeli, upon second thought, wanted
them deleted, for he was, after all, at this time courting the electors of
Wycombe as a Radical. And though he was not then quite convinced
of the theoretical merits of extending the franchise, he recognized that
the Whigs were safe on that issue, that the king would if necessary force
the House of Lords to pass the Reform Bill by creating peers, and that
he stood a better chance of being elected to Parliament as an advocate
of Reform than he did by joining the die-hard Tories. Consequently,
when Croker wanted to restore the Tory passages, Disraeli wrote to
Murray: "It is quite impossible that anything adverse to the general
measure of Reform can issue from my pen or from anything to which I
contribute. Within these four months I have declined being returned for

a Tory Borough, and almost within these four hours ... I have refused to inscribe myself a member of 'the Conservative Club.'"[40] Perhaps by threatening to take his publication elsewhere, Disraeli prevailed in keeping the passages out, but even so, the authors did appear to the public to be "enemies of the whole Reform cause." When the pamphlet appeared, Sarah wittily commented: "I long to see you that you may read me many riddles. The principal one is, how you will reconcile your constituents to your politics."[41] Monypenny suggests that the phrase, "the general measure of Reform," indicates that Disraeli's attitude was already close to that which he would soon openly adopt: sympathy with the movement to enlarge the electorate, but deep distrust of the motives of the Whigs in bringing it forward. The *Gallomania* itself, however, places that sympathy within a quite conservative context:

> I have confidence in the genius of the people. I am neither Whig nor Tory. My politics are described by one word, and that word is ENGLAND. I am one of the people, and I am all for the people; but the people is not merely the populace. The divisions in England are in some degree occasioned by the personal distress of great masses of the nation; but the main and most alarming cause is the alliance which party politics have created between the Ministry and the Agitators – between the Government and the enemies of all government.[42]

If such a statement is read in the light of a declaration he made in a letter to Benjamin Austen, "I start on the high Radical interest, and take down strong recommendatory epistles from O'Connell, Hume, Burdett and *hoc genus*. Toryism is worn out, and I cannot condescend to be a Whig," Disraeli's position would seem quite clear.[43] Ostensibly he was claiming a Radical independence and rejecting the Tories, because he felt that the party had gone astray. There is, however, an additional piece of evidence which proves that Disraeli was using the Radical stance very much for his own purposes, and that he had already formulated the idea of reforming the Tory party in the light of past glories into the semblance of a "National" party. Monypenny gives the following passage in a letter from Sarah without comment, and no subsequent historian has remarked upon its significance. It is a continuation of her response to the publication of the *Gallomania*:

> You can imagine the astonishment and consternation of old and young Wycombe. All screwing up their courage to the sticking point ... Huffam

[Disraeli's chief supporter] came over yesterday morning. I do not exactly
know the purpose of his visit. Whether to find out what you were going to
do, or for us to convey to you his feeling. He seemed in a great fright, that
you were going to betray him by proving yourself a Tory after he has for
so many months sworn to all Wycombites that you were not one – what
will happen? I should be sorry to give up *the plan of regenerating and turning them all unconsciously into Tories.* (emphasis added)[44]

This suggests that from the very beginning of his political career,
Disraeli was planning the revival of "true Toryism." Astutely enough,
he realized that the distinction between his ideal and the current reality
of the Tory party would be lost upon the electors of Wycombe in the
heat of the Reform Bill controversy. And thus, for the moment, he chose
to campaign under the banner of that diverse and by no means cohesive
group called the Radicals. Bulwer had already been successful in that
style and, with his help in getting endorsements from several other
Radicals, Disraeli was optimistic about his own chances as one independent of the traditional parties. The next few years would reveal
some flagrant opportunism beneath the variations of his public posture, as he repeatedly tried and failed to be elected. But the foregoing
suggests that there was a thread of consistency in his behaviour, not
recognized because it was at first a secret confided in all probability
only to Sarah. It also suggests that Disraeli's first attempt at electioneering was very much a matter of playing a role, or adopting a political
identity, as an experiment which he hoped would lead to success.

The Reform Act became law on 7 June 1832, and a general election on
the new franchise was expected by the end of the year. Disraeli immediately made plans to be a candidate in Wycombe, despite the fact that
both sitting members were reformers. Then, one of them, Sir Thomas
Baring, unexpectedly resigned to contest a vacancy elsewhere, and as a
consequence there was a by-election in Wycombe on the old franchise.
It appears that Bulwer tried to persuade the Whigs not to contest the
seat, but they declined that suggestion and Colonel Grey, a younger son
of the prime minister, stood as their candidate. Some voters were no
doubt amused that the earl had been the recipient of some extravagant
remarks in the "Dedication" of the *Gallomania*: "My Lord, it has ever
been considered an indubitable characteristic of insanity in men to mistake their friends for their enemies. It is on this principle alone that I
can account for the perseverance with which your Lordship invariably
seizes every opportunity of injuring and insulting our ancient allies,

and assisting and eulogising our hereditary foe" (*Gall.*, vii). In the campaign Colonel Grey was evidently no match for his flamboyant adversary. He made a "brief and stammering speech," admitting that he had never before made a public address. In sharp contrast Disraeli, dressed in the most dandified fashion of "curls and ruffles," poured forth a "torrent of eloquence" for an hour and a quarter. But Disraeli's popularity with the astounded crowd had little effect upon the outcome, and he lost the election 20 to 12, despite the qualified blessing of the Tory *Bucks Herald*.[45] Quite in character he then made a defiant speech "to show that he did not intend to take his defeat lying down," taunted the electors on their hypocrisy, and provoked Lord Nugent, who thought himself personally attacked at one point, to issue a challenge. It was an absurd affair and the duel was prevented when the seconds arranged satisfactory explanations.[46]

III

In August, while he was at home at Bradenham, Disraeli agreed to contribute two short tales to Bulwer's *New Monthly Magazine*. The first of them, "Ixion in Heaven," which appeared from December 1832 to February 1833, was thought very highly of by Isaac. Later critics have echoed that opinion, held mostly on the grounds of the sharpness and the freshness of the satirical style, without discussing the work in any detail. But the structure and thematic content of this modified Greek myth bear parallels to the events surrounding *The Representative*, the publication of *Vivian Grey*, and Disraeli's subsequent life in society too close to be coincidental. Indeed, this short tale is more than just a charming imitation of Lucian, for it sheds light on the extent to which Disraeli's youthful indiscretions continued to haunt the scenes of his ambitious performances, and it has implications for our understanding of the relation between Disraeli's fiction and his political career.

The version of the myth that Disraeli provides as an "Advertisement" to his tale stresses Ixion's despicable behaviour:

Ixion, King of Thessaly ... married Dia, daughter of Deioneus, who, in consequence of his son-in-law's non-fulfilment of his engagements, stole away some of his monarch's steeds. Ixion concealed his resentment under the mask of friendship. He invited his father-in-law to a feast at Larissa ... and when Deioneus arrived according to his appointment, he threw him into a pit which he had previously filled with burning coals. This treachery so irritated the neighbouring princes, that all of them refused to perform the usual ceremony, by which a man was then purified of murder, and Ixion was shunned and despised by all mankind. Jupiter had compassion upon him, carried him to heaven, and introduced him to the Father of the Gods. Such a favour, which ought to have awakened gratitude in Ixion, only served to inflame his bad passions; he became enamoured of Juno, and attempted to seduce her. Juno was willing to gratify the passion of Ixion, though according to other ... [47]

Disraeli's tale begins *in medias res* with Ixion wandering in exile. Upon encountering the voice of Jove, his explanation of the separation from Dia at first hides the truth: "We quarrelled about nothing. Where there is little sympathy, or too much, the splitting of a straw is plot enough for a domestic tragedy. I was careless, her friends stigmatised me as callous; she cold, her friends styled her magnanimous. Public opinion was all on her side, merely because I did not choose that the world should interfere" (Ix., 112). A little of the truth is revealed, however, by Jove's interrogation and Ixion's confession that he was "over head and ears in debt" (Ix., 112). He then admits that he married Dia for money, expecting "a prodigious portion" from her father, but found that "after the ceremony the old gentleman would not fulfil his part of the contract" without his giving up his stud. Although he could not, Ixion says, conceive of "anything more unreasonable," he smothered his "resentment at the time." But when his tradesmen would no longer renew his credit on the strength of the match, and when Dia refused to interfere with her father, Ixion continues, "I invited Deioneus to the Larissa races with the intention of conciliating him. The unprincipled old man bought the horse that I had backed, and by which I intended to have redeemed my fortunes, and withdrew it. My book was ruined. I dissembled my rage. I dug a pit in our garden, and filled it with burning coals. As my father-in-law and myself were taking a stroll after dinner, the worthy Deioneus fell in merely by accident. Dia proclaimed me the murderer of her father" (Ix., 113). This part of the tale can be interpreted as a metaphor for Disraeli's view of his relationship with John Murray at the time *The Representative* was begun. This is not to argue that the tale is simply a fictionalized autobiography of the events in 1825–6 with specific correlations. Such an analysis can prove nothing about what actually happened at the time. But it does seem to reveal how Disraeli felt about those events in retrospect. And, within the known limits of Disraeli's self-interest, it can offer grounds for speculation about the extent of his rationalization of his own behaviour.

In 1825 Disraeli was "over head and ears" in debt, and he did see in the imagined success of the newspaper an opportunity to recoup his losses. The metaphor of betting on a horse must, with the hindsight of 1832, have been an entirely apt one to describe his actual financial circumstances in 1825. In the original myth it is Ixion who promises the bridal gifts, while in 1832 Disraeli's Ixion reverses the commitment, and so the embarrassing fact of the young adventurer's inability to pay his share of *The Representative*'s costs is conveniently neglected. But on the whole Disraeli was being honest in this first part of the tale. It is true that Deioneus, and by the implication of this analysis, Murray, is characterized by Disraeli's Ixion as being first, unreasonable in his demands, and second, unprincipled in his conduct. Ixion puts himself forward as the innocent and injured party. But Disraeli betrays Ixion's habit of speaking with a forked tongue as the latter's description of his father-in-law shifts from "the unprincipled old man" to "the worthy Deioneus." Whether this is irony or inconsistency matters little. Ixion is clearly not speaking the truth at several points, and his character is further demeaned as he relates with a contemptuous sense of rank, how, when public opinion was against him, he "cut" his way "through the greasy-capped multitude, sword in hand," and then as he reveals a callous attitude towards the murder, which though for form's sake he still denies, he obviously committed. The explanation for this remarkably frank characterization of Ixion, and, if the metaphor be granted, portrait of the artist as a young dog, lies in the author's current relationship with Murray.

When Disraeli finished *Contarini Fleming* in February 1832 he was sure it was his best novel, and he took it to Murray because he wanted this serious product of his genius to be launched in a manner befitting it, without the arts of puffery and controversy for which Colburn, his previous publisher, was notorious. Disraeli had in fact been mending his connection to Murray for some time. Upon Bulwer's suggestion he had even written to "the most nervous of God's booksellers" about *The Young Duke*,[48] though in the end he sold it to Colburn for £500. And just before he went on his Mediterranean tour he wrote again to Murray, "I can assure you I leave in perfect confidence both in your 'honour' and your 'impartiality,'" with the hope that upon his return he could again submit a manuscript.[49] Murray replied formally but affirmatively to the request, and subsequently confirmed his readiness in a note to Disraeli, received at Athens in the autumn of that year.[50]

By the time "Ixion in Heaven" was written Disraeli and Murray were on cordial terms, even if their earlier intimacy was never restored.

Murray had recently published both *Contarini Fleming* and the *Gallomania*, and so Disraeli might well have felt the urge to make some reassessment of the earlier events, particularly the portrait of Murray in *Vivian Grey*. It is extremely doubtful that the beginning of "Ixion in Heaven" represents a conscious, open apology to the publisher. But it does represent an admission, perhaps only half-conscious, that Disraeli could see in retrospect that his part in the events of 1825 had been less than commendable, and that his first novel, written with malice afore-thought, contained a piece of character assassination that, however ac-curate, was unjustified. In any case, the structure of "Ixion" (Part 1) is obviously similar in one respect to that of *Vivian Grey*. Jove's invitation to Ixion to spend some time in heaven ("It is evident that Earth is too hot for thee at present, so I think thou hadst better come and stay a few weeks with us") completes the basic pattern of Disraeli's first published novel – of a young hero's plans thwarted by an established figure, fol-lowed by desperate measures and a final escape from the consequences (Ix., 114). This suggests, as did the previous novels, that the autobio-graphical nature of Disraeli's earliest fiction might be best seen as in-volving a psychological or emotional structure, the significance of which transcends any literal correlations with specific persons and events.

The succeeding sections of Part 1 of the tale comprise a flippant ac-count of heavenly society obviously inspired by the social circles in which Disraeli was currently moving. The satirical tone is perhaps best captured by the description of Apollo, "a somewhat melancholy lack-a-daisical looking personage, with his shirt collar thrown open, and his long curls theatrically arranged." When he is asked his opinion of Homer, Apollo replies, playing with his rings, that he does not think much of Homer, who, he claims, was not esteemed in his own age. The present admiration of Homer, Apollo says, is just cant; he was just "a writer of some wild irregular power, totally deficient in taste" (Ix., 120). To such light satirical gossip and open mockery of the prevailing ego-tism, Disraeli added another element, one for which he was himself famous, flirtatious repartee. Ixion, for example, has a conversation with Juno in which, though he affects to laugh at "Destiny," he claims that his present "Fortune" as the guest of Jove is all he desires because he can gaze upon her. When she replies that this seems but a moderate desire, he hints that he is "perhaps more unreasonable" than she imagi-nes and the scene ends with a bold reinforcement of his suggestive words: "Their eyes met, the dark orbs of the Thessalian did not quail before the flashing vision of the Goddess. Juno grew pale. Juno turned away" (Ix., 122–3). This description of life on Olympus as a continuous indulgence in amusement for the witty and daring, regulated by the rituals of dinner parties and soirées, would be of very limited interest, however, were it not for the development of Part 2 of the tale.

Once again in the second half there are emotionally significant elements of plot and characterization with obvious parallels in actual events both current and from the past. Ixion has become much resented by some of the lesser deities for adopting a tone of insolent superiority in ordering them about, which he fancies he is justified in doing as a court favourite. Their detestation of his arrogance is matched by his condescension towards characters and customs that he very recently beheld in awe. *Vivian Grey* contains scenes of similar import in which Vivian's success in establishing himself within the Carabas household is much resented by the "Toadeys" who feel their own small portion of influence threatened by that of the haughty and satirical young man, who thinks himself "quite Lord Paramount" (*VG* [1826], 182). How much of this is based on the attitudes of people close to John Murray at the time is difficult to estimate, although there were certainly some who took a jaundiced view of Disraeli's presumptions. It is even clearer, however, that his popularity in 1831–2 was not a matter of universal admiration. As Blake points out, "His extravagant appearance, his mordant wit, his arrogant demeanour, and his flamboyant conversation" were distasteful to some people, especially those who thought themselves above being devoured by the latest literary lions. Disraeli's Jewish parentage also put him beyond the pale of certain quarters. He was called "the Jew d'esprit," perhaps even by sympathetic company, and "Disraeli, the Jew" by others less so.[51] He was almost always more popular with women. Ixion's flirtations with Minerva and Juno and the resentment of this "mere mortal" by Ganymede and Mercury thus sound a familiar note to readers aware of the corresponding patterns in Disraeli's life – from the flirtatious conspiracy with Sara Austen to publish *Vivian Grey* anonymously to the enthusiastic and probably indiscreet affair with Clara Bolton (wife of the family physician) about the time of the Wycombe by-election; from the resentment of the manipulating youth of *The Representative* business to the hostility towards the literary adventurer of 1832. And whether or not it confirms the motivations of Murray's behaviour in 1825, Mercury's threat of resignation from Jove's court – "really, sire, if Ixion is to go on in the way he does, either he or I must quit" – indicates that at least in retrospect Disraeli felt such a threat from the old guard to be a factor in his withdrawal from the founding of the newspaper.

The most significant aspect of the second part of "Ixion," however, lies in the theme of ingratitude – developed within the tale on two levels, the trivial and the profound, and representing respectively matters of etiquette and moral substance. Jove's initial complaint against his mortal guest is that he keeps him waiting for dinner, an event that throws the god into "a sublime anger" which is further inflamed by the jealous Mercury who describes the discourtesy as lack of respect "little short of celestial high treason" – only a near-sighted exaggeration, for Ixion has been dallying with Juno and is about to seduce her. Again Disraeli makes important changes in the myth. In his version the cloud at Cupid's request envelopes the scene of the lovers' indiscretion, enabling Juno to escape being caught in the act of adultery. In the traditional version, however, Jove uses the cloud to create an imitation of Juno and to trap Ixion in unequivocal circumstances. The modification permits Ixion to adopt an, albeit unwarranted, "tone of bullying innocence" when he is seized by the enraged "King of Heaven" (Ix., 140), and to proclaim an indignant defiance of the god's punishment: "'Celestial despot! … I defy the immortal ingenuity of thy cruelty. My memory must be as eternal as thy torture: that will support me'" (Ix., 141). Allowing that Disraeli was in this case no more consistent in his use of classical allusion than he had been with the Alcestis myth in *Contarini Fleming*, it is clear that the author of Part 2 of "Ixion in Heaven" continues to draw for inspiration upon his feelings about the circumstances behind the publication of *Vivian Grey* as well as upon grievances of a more immediate nature.

The caricature of himself as the drunken, incoherent, and foolish Marquess of Carabas in *Vivian Grey*[52] consolidated Murray's sense of the grievous injury inflicted by Disraeli's ingratitude, as the following excerpt from a letter to Sharon Turner shows: "So my complaint against Mr. D'Israeli's son arises solely from the untruths which he told and for his conduct during, (of which in part I made the discovery subsequently) and at the close of our transactions, and since, and particularly from his outrageous breach of all confidence and of every tie which binds man to man in social life in the publication of *Vivian Grey*."[53] Five months earlier Disraeli had protested to Mrs Murray that her husband "overstepped the bounds … of former friendship, … and he has spoke and is now speaking of me to the world generally in terms which to me are as inexplicable, as they appear to be outrageous."[54] Since *Vivian Grey* had been published a month previously, on 22 April, this is clearly a disingenuous claim not unlike Ixion's response when found by Jove.

Further, the portrayal of Jove as a bad-tempered despot who overreacts to the trivial matter of being kept waiting for dinner, but who has the legitimate grievance of being made a cuckold, has obvious similarities to the position of Murray, who claims in 1826 that Disraeli performed with bad grace in the transactions of *The Representative* and then went beyond the boundary of human decency in the writing of his first published novel. But since Ixion is so clearly guilty of violating the social and moral conventions of this very English heavenly society, Part 2 of the tale continues to represent the reassessment of Disraeli's earlier behaviour that the first part of the story indicated he was undertaking. Apologies in abject humility were not, however, compatible with Disraeli's personality and so, although the characterization of the hero reveals Ixion's arrogance and callousness, the tale does not end on a contrite note. Jove's eternal punishment of the ungrateful mortal, to use the girdle of Venus to bind Ixion to a wheel of the poet Apollo's chariot and hurl him to Hades, is appropriate to both the mythical and the biographical dimensions of the tale's significance: Ixion's crime of illicit love and Disraeli's of poetic injustice. Ixion's final defiance is characteristic of Disraeli's attitude in *Vivian Grey* and of his response to the critical reaction to the novel. It also reflects his response to the rejections he had experienced more recently. The harangue Disraeli delivered to the Corporation at High Wycombe upon his initial defeat in the June by-election is the most blatant example. As Jerman points out, Disraeli "knew that he was the better man, and he saw that he had been outmanoeuvered. It was *Vivan Grey* all over again and his reaction was the same."[55] There was also the matter of his social position at the time. The despotic arbiters of the very highest taste either resented and mocked his claims to attention, or they totally ignored him; and the rejection of his membership in the Athenaeum is perhaps the best symbol of the difficulties he encountered.

Written at Bradenham, during the period of August to December 1832, in the aftermath of his first political defeat, "Ixion in Heaven" represents a significant growth in Disraeli's personality towards the recognition of his "self." *Contarini Fleming* embodies within the character of the hero a conscious conflict between hypocrisy and purity, images of the self which exist in hostile symbiosis. This short tale indicates that the tension in that conflict was noticeably reduced, if only temporarily, as Disraeli committed himself to political action. Given the biographical parallels that the tale carries, the arrogant, callous, and flagrantly immoral character of Ixion implies that at least for a moment

Disraeli in retrospect could accept a partial loss of innocence in the image he wanted to hold of himself. The structure of the tale also indicates that, as the tension of this one conflict lessened, another symbiotic relationship became prominent within Disraeli's personality between ambition and frustration, between success and defeat.

Paradoxically, each time Disraeli's ambition was thwarted, his desire to succeed was ultimately strengthened, even though for a time he might need to escape psychologically or be isolated from the consequences of rash behaviour. Thus Ixion plans to make his fortune in marriage, is thwarted by Deioneus, and murders the old man. But saved by Jove from the wrath of his fellow mortals, Ixion becomes ambitious to conquer heaven. When caught in his seduction of Juno and banished, he proclaims that the very severity of the punishment will support him through eternity. This is a pattern worth keeping in mind as Disraeli struggles for the next five years to enter Parliament and for a much longer time attempts to reach the top of the Tory party, for to some extent it explains his endurance when the odds seemed overwhelmingly long.

The tone of "Ixion in Heaven" confirms what the thematic content and structure of the tale indicate about Disraeli's increasing acceptance of conflicting elements within his personality. His gift for satire is manifested from the beginning of his career as an author. But in *Vivian Grey* the best passages of this type are almost set pieces virtually independent of the plot, while in *The Young Duke* (where they appear as authorial intrusion) this is even more true. Disraeli had attempted a totally satiric work, *The Voyage of Captain Popanilla*, in 1828, but as such it is jejune, for the characters are simply vehicles for the attacks on the abstract principles of Benthamite and laissez-faire economics. In "Ixion in Heaven," however, Disraeli produces a brilliant demonstration of the efficient use of dialogue to reveal the vanity and folly of half a dozen characters. His conscious intention was undoubtedly to do just that, and the success of the satire, never heavy-handed, always witty, and sometimes daring, indicates a control over the subject, the lack of which had led to the excesses that flawed the satiric passages of *Vivian Grey*. This exposure of London's fashionable world also suggests that, though Disraeli was motivated to attempt the satire because he was for reasons of birth, occupation, and temperament excluded from the highest society, he felt himself to be the equal, if not the superior, of all those who played the games of Vanity Fair.

One legacy of Disraeli's Mediterranean tour was indeed a much strong-. er self-confidence, which resulted from the opportunities to experiment with various roles all designed to bring him recognition of one sort or another. As the "author of *Vivian Grey*" he could cultivate his sense of the "poetic character" and taste both the power and the solace of the Byronic pose he so magnificently adopted. His warm reception at virtually every stop, whether the result of his sheer flamboyance, his literary reputation, or the simple courtesy of his hosts, demonstrated how easily his own sense of his importance could be confirmed. And his encounters with the reality of Eastern political life in the persons of the sultan at Constantinople and the pasha at Cairo undoubtedly fed his fantasies of power and political ambitions.

It is clear that upon his return to England, Disraeli continued to exploit the roles or identities he had formed on the Eastern tour. The dandy and wit, the "Radical" politician, and the satirical rebel were all experimental poses adopted in the hope of advancing his social and political ambitions. In their very artificiality they enabled Disraeli to bring different desires and motives together in such a way as to turn, temporarily at least, defeats into victories, if only through the simple act of literal or imaginative defiance.

The social milieu of Lady Blessington's Seamore Place, to pick the most obvious example of the sets Disraeli inhabited for the next ten years, was the perfect one for such a person. Debarred from much of the hypocrisy of the highest *ton* because of the perhaps unjustified scandal of Count D'Orsay's relationship with the countess,[56] its habitués placed more value upon wit than upon rank, and found a lasting source of amusement in the deprecation of dullness, moral or otherwise, wherever found. Sincerity was not a cardinal virtue, for the whole establishment was founded upon a public pretence of financial stability where none existed, and upon the personal conviction of the hostess that "there are so few before whom one could condescend to appear otherwise than happy."[57] Disraeli was thus a member of a social circle in which the one side, the public side, of his personality found ample recognition, in which his past indiscretions were something of an asset, in which his talent for witticisms was appreciated, and in which anyone who from pretension or malice spited him could be satirized with impunity. And "Ixion in Heaven" reflects the real sang-froid that he was beginning to acquire, even though the other side of his personality had not been vanquished.

3

Virtues and Vanities

Previous chapters have shown that Disraeli's earliest fictions and the emerging shape of his political life are to a large extent a function of his fantasies, or imaginative constructions, about himself. Particular embodiments of his imaginative senses of his identity – the roles of the hero, both fictional and socio-political – serve the purpose of compensating for the disparity he felt between his potential and his actual situation. Disraeli's dandyism in the 1820s and 1830s, for example, is an attempt to force by sheer egotism a kind of recognition from people whom he knew would not otherwise accept him. Both the satires of the fiction and the challenge of his social flamboyance are thus psychological equivalents of his defiance on the hustings in the face of his first political defeat. They are attempts by an outsider to turn defeat, real or imagined, into victory.

What Disraeli found confirmed at the fashionable London soirées and in his first election campaign was that the various roles he had perfected on his Mediterranean tour, and brought home to use as means to success, involved certain costs in terms of the sense of himself he could hold while pursuing that success. This is the significance of the imaginative separation of the hero's worlds of private and public fulfilment in *Contarini Fleming*, and, indeed, of that novel's denouement in such sharp contrast to the ending of *The Young Duke*, completed just before the Eastern tour. Both the satire of "Ixion in Heaven" and the extravagance of the dandyism involve a mockery of the values of the very society Disraeli aspires to conquer. These are forms of reservation that enable the author, as both actor and hero, to hold a private conviction of his superiority to those he mocks or offends. Nevertheless, Disraeli found that such roles, in their commitment to a public demonstration of his distinction, demand at least a partial abandonment of his claim to a pure, innate superiority. The reassessment of himself that "Ixion in Heaven" embodies thus involves some willingness to accept the terms of public, social, and political success, even though, paradoxically, the tale ends in a metaphorical defiance of them. That defiance simply reflects Disraeli's frustration with the fact that the present degree of accommodation still ended in failure, as well as his sense of being different in kind from those who were the arbiters of value in the world of the Olympians.

The lesson of his defeat in the second 1832 Wycombe election campaign was that the costs of political and social success would prove too great to bear. Disraeli found himself extremely vulnerable both to the charges of hypocrisy and insincerity that his extravagant roles occasioned, and to the anti-Semitism that his opponents were willing to exploit. He was forced to face the fact that his struggle for success and his struggle for purity were inextricably linked together. On the one hand, it became clear that political success depended not just upon the sincerity and consistency of what he said, but also upon what others perceived him to be. On the other hand, much of his own perception of his essential, primary, pure self derived from his Jewish heritage, a legacy that it was impossible to deny, yet one that was certainly no asset in a struggle for public acceptance in Protestant England.

The central concern of both Disraeli's fiction and his politics in the years after 1832 is to find ways in which to relate the themes of making success out of failure, of claiming and demonstrating superiority, and of reconciling innocence and experience, purity and compromise. *The Wondrous Tale of Alroy*, for example, is concerned with the true and terrible costs of victory for either sense of his hero's identity. *The Rise of Iskander* raises the ultimate moral dimension of the whole issue of identity in an attempt to find a way of escaping the consequences of the author's now dichotomous vision of the relationship between his hero's sincerity and purity. And *A Year at Hartlebury or The Election*, the pseudonymously published novel that Disraeli and his sister wrote together, translates the implications of these exotic Eastern melodramas into the world of English domestic politics. Similarly, the political writings of the period are an exercise on Disraeli's part in redefinition of the self – a matter of sufficient complexity to warrant separate chapters. For the moment, the most important realization is that, by virtue of their fantasy structure, Disraeli's fictions increasingly become a means of self-discovery, an agent of development, rather than simply a form of self-advertisement.

Following his defeat in the Wycombe by-election of June, 1832, Disraeli had spent the summer in London and at Bradenham working on *Alroy* and "Ixion in Heaven." At the same time he went ahead with his plans to contest the impending general election in the same constituency. On the first day of October he issued his address to the voters, now 298 in number. He said that he wore "the badge of no party and the livery of no faction," that he was prepared to support the principle of secret ballots in order to escape the "unprincipled system of terrorism" characteristic of many of the current campaigns, and that he favoured "recurring to those old English triennial Parliaments of which the Whigs originally deprived us." He advocated repeal of the paper duties ("taxes on knowledge") on the ground that "as the people had been invested with power, he wished to see them fitted for its exercise"; he demanded rigid economy in the operation of the government and a general reduction in taxation; and he favoured commutation of tithes to "render the clergy ... fairly remunerated" for their "valuable and efficient" labours. Finally, he supported those changes in the Corn Laws which would "relieve the customer without injuring the farmer"; he attacked the "Gordian knot of complicated blunders" known as Whig foreign policy (which, he said, led to rebellion in Ireland and convulsions in the colonies and left "the farmer in doubt, the shipowner in despair ... merchants without trade, and ... manufacturers without markets"); and he promised to withhold his support from "every Ministry which will not originate some great measure to ameliorate the condition of the lower orders."[1] All of these, except the last, were Conservative in spirit, if not Tory in label, and every one of them is consistent with Disraeli's own later conceptions of Tory democracy. In his expressions of concern for law and order, for the maintenance of the Constitution as he saw it, for the strength of the Church, and for the condition of the poor, Disraeli was no doubt being sincere. But a great many people did not see him in that light and, consequently, the campaign was largely fought on the issue of his person.

In retrospect Sarah's letter, quoted earlier, about the "plan of regenerating [Wycombe] and turning them all unconsciously into Tories," suggests that Disraeli was in fact playing a deeper game than he would openly admit, and that he was shrewdly taking advantage of the paradoxical situation in which a number of Wycombe Tories were willing to give a supposedly Radical candidate their support if it would result in unseating a Whig. This tactic of attempting to unite "opposite extremes against the centre was to be the pattern which he sought to repeat on a national scale twenty years later,"[2] and it was to be transformed into the philosophical foundation of his political novels, *Coningsby* and *Sybil* published in the 1840s. But for the moment it failed to overcome his opponents' tactics of personal disparagement.

Near the beginning of his campaign Colonel Grey charged that his opponents' party had "hired a parcel of drunken brawlers to follow him in his canvass, and to insult those whom he solicited for their votes." Disraeli wittily replied, "Colonel Grey seems to complain of his reception at Wycombe ... and accounts for the want of popular courtesy by the usual story of a mob hired by his opponent. Colonel Grey has been misinformed. I have hired no mob to hoot him. The hooting was quite gratuitous."[3] Although the response amused Disraeli's London friends, it did not block the thrust of other remarks by a Mr Hobhouse (the Whig candidate for Bucks.) and a Dr Mitford (a visiting "reformer" from Berkshire) which were reported in the original account in *The Times*. To cheers and laughter Hobhouse dismissed "Mr. D'Israeli" as "the author of a few miserable novels ... in which he had described either the society in which he lived himself, or a state of society which had no existence," while Mitford remarked that "the only difference between the two counties appeared to be, that in Berkshire they were not troubled by any Jews as they were in Buckinghamshire (Roars of laughter)."[4] The notoriety reflected in a letter from Clara Bolton – "What an extraordinary disturbance you are creating. Every body is telling me of it, yet I cannot discover where all the rows proceed from" – was of little consolation.[5] And it was in vain that Disraeli could extol "the principles of Sir William Wyndham and my Lord Bolingbroke" and maintain, "I have undergone no change. I am as I ever was in motive, principle, and determination ... a Conservative to preserve all that is good in our constitution, a Radical to remove all that is bad."[6] The prevailing reaction to his candidacy among the voters was a prejudice against his Jewish heritage and a belief that he was insincere. Clara Bolton reported in her letter that it was widely thought that he was "playing 'a double game,'" with "no real feeling in any cause ... for the sake of being an M.P.," and that he was but the embodiment of the ruthless, opportunistic hero of *Vivian Grey*. It was also felt by some that the candidacy of this "ambitious Jew scamp for whom nobody cared a straw" was a ridiculously presumptuous challenge to the accepted barriers of class and race. The prejudice against Jews became an important issue in Disraeli's life in the years ahead, but to his credit, even though he felt it to be the most significant factor in his present defeat and declared that the "secret of their enmity was that he was not nobly born," he did not reply in kind.[7]

Instead Disraeli addressed the problem of anti-Semitism, now out in the open but obviously of long-standing personal existence, by returning to the creation of a fantasy in *Alroy*, which, though in some sense an escape, was also a confrontation. Shortly after the publication of this novel Disraeli wrote in his diary: "In Vivian Grey I have portrayed my active and real ambition. In Alroy, my ideal ambition. The P.R. [*Contarini Fleming*] is a developmt. of my poetic character. This trilogy is the secret history of my feelings. I shall write no more about myself."[8] But it is wrong to conclude simply, as Monypenny does, that the only construction that can be placed on this declaration is that "the true aim of the political ambition which was beginning to shape itself within him should be to win back the Holy Land for the chosen people and restore the sceptre to Judah."[9] Rather a comparison between *Alroy* and *Contarini Fleming* confirms a somewhat different sense of the importance of religious allegiance to the problem of Disraeli's personal identity in his life and in his fiction. Both novels reflect an initial isolation of the hero, a sense of expectancy with which his maturity is anticipated, and a sense of guilt which his actions create. But in *Alroy* it is not very helpful to attempt to make the distinction between explicit and implicit themes that illuminates *Contarini Fleming*, for it is clear throughout that the central theme is the ambiguity and conflict within the hero's character. In that regard *Alroy* is the product of a greater degree of conscious awareness of himself on the part of the author. While in its fantasy structure the novel confirms the pattern of early conflict and tension in the author's personality, it also proves that Disraeli was undertaking a reassessment of his behaviour which led him to renewed attempts, in his fiction and in his political life, to establish his sincerity.[10]

In the person of the emotionally autobiographical David Alroy, Disraeli creates a hero who is an ideal, noble, and divinely chosen saviour of his people and who essentially represents a personal defiance of reality parallel to the public postures his creator had recently adopted on the hustings. But, just as there is a deep insecurity underneath the bravado of Disraeli's early political campaigns, there is a fear of failure within the imaginative projection of the ideal. As a mere orphaned youth Alroy impetuously rejects his elders' counsel that the Jews should acquiesce in the public payment of tribute to their Muslim rulers while they privately grow wealthy as the merchant and financial class of the empire. But his defiance quickly gives way to a suicidal despondency over such a shameful destiny: "'What am I? ... A cloud hangs heavy o'er my life ... Ah! worst of woes to dream of glory in despair ... I live and die a most ignoble thing; beauty and love, and fame and mighty deeds, the smile of women and the gaze of men, and the ennobling consciousness of worth, and all the fiery course of the creative passions, these are not for me, and I, Alroy, the descendant of sacred kings, and with a soul that pants for empire, I stand here extending my vain arm for my lost sceptre, a most dishonoured slave!'"[11] The first two chapters of *Alroy* thus describe the familiar pattern of Disraeli's novels in capsulated form. And the same resort to desperate action on the part of the hero first seen in *Vivian Grey* appears again when Alroy murders Alschiroch, the Muslim prince who attacks his sister Miriam, and then must flee into exile to avoid capture and punishment.

The portrait of Miriam as Alroy's devoted sister, who consoles him in his moments of despair, is quite clearly modelled upon Disraeli's view of Sarah. As Alroy realizes that he must escape the consequences of his rash behaviour, he says, "My precious Miriam, what is life? What is revenge, or even fame and freedom without thee? I'll stay" (*Al.*, 19). But the attack upon Miriam was provoked by his own insolence to Alschiroch and the violence is associated with feelings on his part which are undoubtedly sexual in nature: "The Philistine, the foul, lascivious, damnable Philistine! he must touch my sister!" (*Al.*, 18). The killing itself, it is worth noting, is described in terms imitative of Byron: "Pallid and mad, he swift upsprang, and tore up a tree by its lusty roots, and down the declivity, dashing with rapid leaps, panting and wild, he struck the ravisher on the temple with the mighty pine. Alschiroch fell lifeless as the sod, and Miriam fainting into her brother's arms" (*Al.*, 16; cf. *Don Juan*, III, 29). A Freudian critic might see in such a dramatic protectiveness a projection of incestuous feelings suitably disguised and punished. Indeed, the whole novel with its emphasis on Alroy's gaining of his manhood, symbolically through the acquisition of the phallic sceptre of Solomon, and actually through the conquest of Bagdad and its glorious prize, Princess Schirene, must be interpreted as an account of a sexual crisis that has direct relevance to the author's power fantasies. As Disraeli began to scale the heights of social and political success he adopted roles that were designed to bring him specific kinds of public recognition and acceptance. But he saw these poses as expedients that deliberately hid the nature of his true and fundamental private self. As his never failing admirer and, therefore, completely trustworthy confidante, Sarah became for the next few years the one person in whom Disraeli felt he could find not only enthusiastic praise and support for his opportunistic worldly ambition, but also sympathetic understanding and solace of his pure, innate genius. Indeed, until his marriage, when Mary Anne came to fill that role, Sarah increasingly became a mother-substitute figure upon whom Disraeli could project his passionate desires for innocence, and with whom he could identify his purest sense of himself. As was shown earlier, a compulsive wish for this kind of comforting emotional retreat was half the shaping force of *Contarini Fleming*. And with reference to that novel, Blake, at the outset of his biography, links the motif of the substitute mother to a "deprivation" of maternal affection and admiration, which Disraeli with his "intense vanity" and "supreme egotism" felt so profoundly that all his subsequent relationships with women compensated for it.[12]

The plot of *Alroy* embodies precisely the dynamics of such a displacement and its relation to the issue of defining the hero's character. Before he is fully possessed of the supernatural power of the messiah to free the Jewish people, Alroy is twice tempted to abandon the pure identity of his imaginative ideal. The first entirely materialistic suggestion, that he be disguised and pass as Lord Honain's son and so acquire great social success and power in the Muslim world, he rejects to pursue the "eternal glory" of his religious quest. But when, at the emotional climax of the novel, disguised as a deaf-mute eunuch he meets the daughter of the Caliph, Princess Schirene, whose mother was a Christian, Alroy's feverish and agitated response reveals the complexity of his character. Suddenly, seizing the rosary given to him by the Princess and pressing it to his lips, he breaks into ecstatic praise of her beauty: "O more than beautiful! for thou to me art as a dream unbroken: why art thou not mine? Why lose a moment in our glorious lives, and balk our destiny of half its bliss?" The questions immediately provoke the collapse of his "radiant vision":

> "Fool, fool, hast thou forgotten? The rapture of a prisoner in his cell, whose wild fancy for a moment belies his fetters! The daughter of the Caliph and a Jew!
> "Give me my father's sceptre.
> "A plague on talismans! Oh! I need no inspiration but her memory, no magic but her name. By heavens! I will enter this glorious city a conqueror, or die.
> "Why, what is Life? for meditation mingles ever with my passion ... Throw accidents to the dogs, and tear off the painted mask of false society! Here am I a hero; with a mind that can devise all things, and a heart of

superhuman daring, with youth, with vigour, with a glorious lineage, with a form that has made full many a lovely maiden of our tribe droop her fair head ... and I am, nothing.

"Out on Society! 'twas not made for me. I'll form my own, and be the deity I sometimes feel." (*Al.*, 74–5)

This passage is the true climax of the novel, not simply because it reflects most intensely the violent ambivalence in the hero's mind about himself and his situation, although it certainly does that. The opening confession of a long felt need for erotic fulfilment quickly gives way to an expression of social alienation and failure which is then immediately followed by a declaration of his talent and uniqueness. But this too is an unstable mood quickly dissipated by the remembrance of the racial stigma under which he lives with a sense of degrading captivity. The frustration engendered by this thought creates the impulse towards action: "Give me my father's sceptre." But the romantic confidence is subverted by the fear of failure implicit in the alternative of dying rather than conquering, and the initial defiance turns to despair at being "nothing." This conviction reflects the social impotence of the Jew so aptly expressed in the metaphor of the captive and the disguise of the eunuch. Thus the disparity between the knowledge of innate superiority and the lack of recognition breeds the final defiance of sublime egotism.

This entire pattern suggests that the fascinating correlation with events in Disraeli's social and political career is justified and that *Alroy* is indeed part of the secret history of his feelings. The most important point, however, concerns Alroy's and, by implication, Disraeli's motivations. The soliloquy occurs after Alroy has found in the beauty of Schirene and the magnificence of the caliph's palace concrete temptations more persuasive than Honain's abstractions. The tale at this point embodies both literally and metaphorically the impotence of the hero. In the former case it is a matter of disguise, but that fact in itself has thematic significance. Disguise of the hero enters the novel in three places. In the first, on the journey to Bagdad, it is a matter of denying the fact that he is a Jew, which ironically is a fact that would seem to endanger his life, but actually saves him in two separate encounters. The second incident is the visit to Schirene, the significance of which has already been shown. The third action in disguise is also a visit to the princess, after Alroy has conquered the "glorious city," in which she discovers that Honain's slave is in fact a noble and powerful prince. The act of disguise is thus associated with the racial stigma and the impotence of Alroy's position at the moment of temptation, and the fantasy structure works toward the revelation of his ideal, truly heroic identity, as formulated in the penultimate paragraph of this passage. The defiant resolutions thus show that this "true" identity is for him no longer that of the altruistic mystical messiah and that his deepest wish fulfilment would be a worldly recognition of his personal power.

The remainder of *Alroy* is a dramatization of the conflict within the hero's character as to which identity is the stronger: the Prince of the Captivity on a messianic mission to free his people, or the worldly prince of "superhuman daring" in search of an empire and its tribute and willing, if necessary, to adopt the romantic hubris of making himself a deity. The symbiotic relationship between these identities is, however, the most interesting aspect of that dramatization. When Alroy at the height of his messianic mission has completely conquered the Muslim world, Lord Honain comes to deliver formally the city of Bagdad into his hands, acknowledging his "irresistible power," but also stressing the ennobling qualities of his learning, his morality, and his "lineage" (*Al.*, 140). This is obviously an exhilarating fantasy for Disraeli as he lived through the frustrations of political defeat in the summer of 1832, for it clearly represents a transformation of the hero's most hu-miliating captivity into a seemingly limitless victory. It blends the purity of the religious role with a worldly recognition. The reader can see, however, that the fantasy is not the complete victory it might seem. The concluding references to Alroy's "pure and sublime faith" and "sacred and celebrated race" only serve to show how completely those attributes have come to subserve the glorification of the hero's genius. That Disraeli clearly perceives his hero's sin of pride is borne out by the remaining plot.

The marriage of the king and the daughter of the caliph represents the dramatic climax of the novel. Although his fall from grace has already been prefigured astrologically, Alroy is now at the height of his fortunes, and, as the lovers retire to consummate the marriage, the author intrudes to point the moral: "Now what a glorious man was David Alroy, lord of the mightiest empire in the world, and wedded to the most beautiful princess, surrounded by a prosperous and obedient people, guarded by invincible armies, one on whom Earth showered all its fortune, and Heaven all its favour; and all by the power of his own genius!" (*Al.*, 177). The abandonment of any pretence at performing Hebrew rituals, the rumour of Alroy's attendance at a mosque, his alliance with his former enemies, and, finally, his assumption of the title,

"Caliph," and his public display of effete decadence eventually provoke the faithful into a conspiracy against the life of "this haughty stripling" (*Al.*, 181, 183); Alroy's empire is quickly consumed by rebellion and he becomes the captive of his rival. In narrating these events Disraeli's chief concern is the portrayal of the hero's consciousness of what he has done. The conflict between Alroy's two symbiotic selves and their respective commitments to his sister, Miriam, and to Princess Schirene (and all they represent: altruism, innocence, religious and sexual purity versus expediency, hypocrisy, religious betrayal, and self-glorification) is the subject of his thoughts as, alternately despairing and defiant, he awaits his fate in his dungeon cell. It is the question of Alroy's Jewish faith and race that leads to his ultimate act of defiance. When Honain reveals the conditions for Alroy's release, that he should plead guilty to the charge of having had "intercourse with the infernal powers," that he should confess to having "won the Caliph's daughter by an irresistible spell" which at last is broken, and that he should deny his "Divine mission" in order "to settle the public mind," the captive raises no objections. But when Honain adds the final condition of "form," that he will be expected to "publicly affect to renounce our faith, and bow before their Prophet," Alroy leaps into indignation: "Get thee behind me, tempter! Never, never, never! ... I'll not yield a jot. Were my doom one everlasting torture, I'd spurn thy terms! Is this thy high contempt of our poor kind, to outrage my God! to prove myself the vilest of the vile, and baser than the basest?" (*Al.*, 244). The explicit irony, that he has already done this in the service of his own exalted egotism, only serves to prove the complete dichotomy of Alroy's sense of his own identity. In the strength of re-emergent purity he can immediately again assert his own glory and resolve to die a hero for Schirene's sake (*Al.*, 245). But this momentary attempt to join the glorification of his God and the glorification of himself into one destiny cannot succeed; he falls into a trance and is saved from his final temptation by the ghost of the faithful priest, Jabaster. In the denouement Alroy finds consolation in the presence of his pure and holy sister and defies his conqueror's threats of torture even as the sword flashes down to behead him.

In some sense the ending of his life is a triumph for Alroy. He dies forgiven by his God for his sin of pride, comforted by his sister, and secure in the belief that he is ultimately true to his real and primary identity. At the same time, however, it is obviously a pyrrhic victory in that his divine mission to free his people has come to nought, and in that he dies after having completely fallen from the heights of glory. It is not necessary to doubt the hero's sincerity of his return to innocence to recognize that it is an escape from the consequences of a personal failure. But one must also recognize the final act of defiance as an attempt to turn defeat into victory without ever having consciously to admit that defeat. That defiance, even though supported with a sense of righteous purity, leaves the central conflict between Alroy's two senses of his own identity unresolved.

The fantasy structure of *Alroy* shows that Disraeli felt within himself the need both to deny and to affirm his Jewishness, and by implication, the innocence and purity that characterize his hero. The many striking . parallels between the author and his hero – between Disraeli's desire to liberate the Conservative party and Alroy's desire to liberate his people, between Disraeli's recognition that hypocrisy is a necessary ingredient of worldly success and Alroy's betrayal of his faith, between Disraeli's confidential attachment to his sister, Sarah, and Alroy's reliance upon Miriam's recognition of his purest self, and finally between Disraeli's defiant response to political defeat and Alroy's defiant mockery of his conqueror – all suggest that Disraeli did indeed feel in his own early career similar tensions to those he attributes to his hero and that his struggle for "purity" in the context of personal distinction remained an unresolved issue in 1832. It is clear, though, that Disraeli's fictions do not simply serve as an escape through fantasy from the unpleasant social and political realities of his early career. *Alroy*, for example, is a medium for exploring imaginatively the ambivalence Disraeli felt about both of his senses of himself and an imaginative assessment of the costs of choosing either of those identities. Nevertheless, it is a less than satisfactory fantasy because in its attempt to accommodate the conflicting goals of purity and success within the characterization of a less than perfect hero, it cannot permit a complete wish fulfilment and remain honest. The unsatisfactory conclusion of the fantasy did, however, provide Disraeli with the impetus to return in subsequent novels to the subject of his ambivalence about his Jewish heritage in the disguised form of his heroes' concern with Catholicism.[13]

I

The Rise of Iskander, which was published alongside *Alroy* in March 1833, and was probably written in January 1833 shortly after Disraeli's second defeat at Wycombe, confirms that the ending of *Alroy* was for its author an unsatisfactory denouement of the fantasy it embodies. In this short tale the schizoid personality of his earlier protagonist is split into two separate characters who, though allies, are rival heroes. Iskander, born a Grecian prince, has been brought up since infancy in captivity by the Turks. His talents have enabled him to rise in the ranks of the Turkish army to become one of their most illustrious commanders. As the tale opens he is in Athens to exact tribute from the young Nicaeus, prince of Athens, but he reveals to the latter that he is much disturbed at receiving orders to engage a Christian army under the leadership of Hunniades and that he is planning some desperate measure that will prove his loyalty to his secret faith. When he reaches the battlefield in Albania he arranges, at great personal risk, a clandestine meeting with Hunniades at which he promises to betray the Turks and lead his followers back to Epirus, where he will proclaim his country's independence under his true faith and lawful crown. Hunniades's daughter, Princess Iduna, much impressed with this noble hero's courage promises him her prayers and gives him a rosary to wear as a token of their common faith. The plan is completely successful, but just as Iskander frees Croia, the capital of Epirus, and Nicaeus arrives too late to help but ready to congratulate him, news arrives announcing that though Hunniades has defeated the Turks, his daughter has been captured and transported to Adrianople. All of this, however, is but a prologue to the real matter of the tale – the attempt to rescue Iduna and the theme of the contrast between the two heroes.

In the introductory chapters Nicaeus is presented as a young, inexperienced youth, who, though nobly born, is unsuited in temperament and health for action. And though he is possessed of exquisite taste for material and artistic artefacts, he has a weakness of will which leaves him constantly supine, enslaved by the vicissitudes of emotion.[14] He has dreamed of heroic action but in fact submitted to the humiliating rule of the Turks. Iskander, on the other hand, is initially described as being "in the prime of life, and far above the common stature, but with a frame the muscular power of which was even exceeded by its almost ideal symmetry," and as having a "high white forehead ... straight profile ... and oval countenance" (*Isk.*, 216).

The news of Iduna's capture throws Nicaeus into a hysterical fit in which, tearing his hair and flinging himself upon the floor, he reveals that he has long in vain been hopelessly in love with the princess. He beseeches Iskander who has "so much wisdom, and courage ... who *can devise all things*," to help him rescue her (emphasis added; cf. *Al.*, 74–5). Disguised as a Muslem physician and his young assistant the two princes succeed in spiriting away the princess from her tower cell in which she has been languishing before the prospect of being forced to marry the son of the sultan. Iskander, with perfect altruism, attributes the daring plan of escape to his companion so that when their true identities are eventually revealed Nicaeus will gain the credit for it in Iduna's eyes. This intention is thwarted when, being pursued as they flee towards Greece, Nicaeus has a failure of nerve and pleads with Iskander to save the princess even if he is lost. The courageous hero decides, however, to stay behind and hold off their pursuers while the other two reach safety. Unknown to them he performs feats of superhuman daring and not only kills the whole band of Turks, but escapes unscathed himself. Meanwhile the princess, in despair over Iskander's fate, is importuned by Nicaeus to accept him as her lover and husband. When she refuses to entertain such a proposal, the young prince has a fit of rage which is suddenly followed by a mood of what appears to be calm resignation. In fact he has contrived a desperate scheme for forcing the issue, and when they reach a magnificent castle, in fact one of his own, he pretends that it belongs to an absent knight. He then uses the delay in their journey occasioned by the pretext of waiting for their host, to further urge his claim upon her. His statement of this passionate claim quite clearly emphasizes his qualities of innate distinction: birth, rank, youth, beauty, and intelligence (*Isk.*, 283). After she firmly reiterates that she can never accept him, the tale takes on a Gothic quality. Nicaeus locks her in a tower with the threat of carrying her off to Italy if she remains obstinate. By accident "the Lady Iduna" discovers a secret passageway behind a mirror and that same night escapes from the castle. At midnight she comes upon a fountain in a clearing of an olive grove and there encounters the Muslim prince, Mohamed. But Iskander reappears to prevent her recapture. The respective armies of Muslims and Christians decide to engage in full combat the following day and for the moment Iduna is reunited with her father, who has joined forces with Iskander. She relates the story of Nicaeus's villainous persecution to them both just as the prince of Athens arrives in pursuit of his escaped captive.

Having been upbraided by Hunniades for his ingratitude and for his "despicable" and "shameful" behaviour, Nicaeus falls to his knees and begs forgiveness of them all, suggesting, as he does, that the noble Iskander deserves to be the happy recipient of Lady Iduna's love: "'I keenly feel your admirable worth. Say no more, say no more. She is fit wife for a hero, and you *are* one!'" (*Isk.*, 291). Iskander is then left to retire, "bearing with him a prize scarcely less precious than the freedom of his country" (*Isk.*, 293). That freedom is assured the next day by the complete destruction of the Turks, and in the battle Nicaeus is mortally wounded. He dies alone in pathos while the rout is still in progress. Iskander, of course, survives to receive "the glorious congratulations of his emancipated country" and "from the great Hunniades, the hand of his beautiful daughter" (*Isk.*, 296). The tale ends with the glorious and courageous hero being entreated to mount the redeemed throne of the country whose "security," "national existence," and "holy religion" he has secured.

The fantasy embodied in this tale obviously has very different implications than does that of *Alroy*. In this case the heroic Iskander has no internal conflicts. He is true to his real religion and he receives the highest public and private recognition of his courageous and altruistic behaviour. He is clearly an idealization of much more satisfactory dimensions for the author than was the character of Alroy, who represents a projection of both positive and negative traits of Disraeli's personality. In *Iskander* the negative qualities are all embodied in the character of Nicaeus, who displays not only a weakness of will and passivity incompatible with any possible heroism, but also deceit, cowardice, and un-Christian (that is, uncourtly) behaviour in love.

The significance of the fantasy is twofold; in the creation of an active hero, who is not divided within himself, and in the fact that the process of claiming an innate nobility (as Nicaeus does) is completely rejected in favour of demonstrating one's superiority. In this tale true nobility is simply the result of heroic and altruistic action. The hero who thus proves himself noble receives a personal, romantic recognition of his worth, as well as a public political one. *Iskander* is, therefore, the real portrayal of Disraeli's "ideal ambition" and, as such, it also contains a rejection of those elements of his character that, in this tale, he admits are deserving of reprobation.

Alroy, in its attempt to accommodate the conflicting goals of purity and success within the characterization of a less than perfect hero, cannot permit a complete wish-fulfilment precisely because of its honesty. It associates a betrayal of the Jewish faith with the moral collapse of the hero. The unsatisfactory conclusion of the fantasy would thus provide Disraeli with sufficient impetus to reverse its religious dimension in his next fictional projection, as well as to isolate the conflicting elements of the hero's personality in separate characters. Iskander, though like Alroy he embodies the theme of a hidden faith, is in reality a Christian and his success as a heroic figure reflects a new determination on Disraeli's part to engage English politics on its own terms in the hope that he will be rewarded just as paradoxically. But most important, *Iskander* represents a recognition on its author's part that such ideal success and such glorious recognition can only be had through a demonstration of his own nobility. This is one explanation for Disraeli's almost compulsive insistence on his own sincerity in the political campaigns of the next few years. And it is in this particular choice of an ideal identity, of a sense of his "self," that the determination to respond actively to temporary defeat lies. It is, of course, paradoxical that a fantasy that in one sense denies so much of his "self" should enable Disraeli to find him-"self." But such an act of denial does not remove or destroy Disraeli's sense of his Jewishness, nor, indeed, his longing for a recognition of innate nobility. Both of these elements of his personality reappear throughout his career, both in his fiction and in his political ideology.

II

A Year at Hartlebury or The Election, the novel that Disraeli co-authored with Sarah in the fall of 1833, and which they published pseudonymously in the spring of 1834 as "Cherry and Fair Star," translates the themes and motifs of the exotic Eastern tales into the realm of English politics.[15] At issue are the same tensions that inform *Alroy* and *The Rise of Iskander*, though necessarily they are now embodied in quite a different form. It would seem that this novel was never identified with Disraeli in his lifetime, or since, until the discovery of it in 1979 by Professor John Matthews and his co-workers at the Disraeli Project at Queen's University. In retrospect this seems surprising in that the account of the election that it contains bears obvious marks of Disraeli's political ideas and style in the two campaigns at Wycombe in 1832. But those campaigns only achieved widespread public notice much later as material in biographies; moreover, the novel had a very small circulation, and Disraeli was not yet a figure of much importance in London society. Thus, by the time that he used the surname Bohun again in a short story, "The Consul's Daughter" (1836), such a detail was beyond public recall, even though that story is directly related to the novel's plot and theme.

The biographical significance of *A Year at Hartlebury* is twofold. On the one hand, it provides a sense of Disraeli's perspective on the successes and failures of his fledgling political career; on the other, it reflects, even more than do the letters, Sarah's imaginative response to her brother's notoriety. The latter is a matter of both his public recognition and his private indiscretions, and this probably accounts for the blending of social comedy and tragic melodrama in the novel. Sarah seems to have been responsible for the overall structure of this new novel, and it is perhaps not surprising that in its structure and in some of the details of narrative voice, character, and incident *A Year at Hartlebury* is modelled upon Jane Austen's *Emma*. The name "Hartlebury" is clearly a conflation of "Hartfield" and "Highbury," the locations of Austen's novel, and the basic elements of Sarah's story – a young lady, Helen Molesworth, living with a widowed father and receiving the admiring attentions of three young men, the Rev. Arthur Latimer, George Gainsborough, and Aubrey Bohun – are derived from Austen's similar story of Emma Woodhouse courted by the Rev. Philip Elton, Frank Churchill, and Mr Knightley.[16] There is no direct correspondence among these characters in the two works, but the general themes are not dissimilar in certain respects. The arrivals of George Gainsborough and Aubrey Bohun are subject to as much anticipation as that of Frank Churchill, and the heroine in each novel soon finds that there is a mystery to unravel, which leads her to the discovery that all is not as it at first seems, and that men's motivations are more worldly than she realizes. In addition, the principals of the story go on a "pic-nic," which is described as "an exception to all pic-nics": "All returned in the same good humour as they had started" (*Hart.*, 36). The excursion to Bohun Park also differs from that to Box Hill in serving only to stimulate curiosity about the character of the castle's owner, rather than being a critical moment in the life of the heroine.

Sarah's most direct borrowing from Austen's masterpiece is, however, the character of Mrs Escott, "an ancient maiden lady who resided in the neighbouring town" and who was "the last of a family ... who had grown older and poorer in corresponding proportions" (*Hart.*, 14). Like Austen's Miss Bates, Mrs Escott has an indiscriminating curiosity, a love of gossip, a dislike of being anticipated, and a volubility that is daunting to her listeners (*Hart.*, 37). Such debts to Austen's comic genius may well express Sarah's literary ideals, and to the extent that the characterization of Helen Molesworth is to some degree imaginatively autobiographical as well, they may also be a projection of Sarah's fantasies about her life at Bradenham during the time of the Wycombe election campaigns. But Sarah's narrative soon proves to be incompatible with the comedy of manners she has chosen as a model, for in *A*

Year at Hartlebury the theme of Aubrey Bohun's sincerity, in love and politics, is so directly linked to his sexual behaviour that it can only be handled in the conventions of melodramatic romance.

The topic of sexual purity first arises in the story of the beautiful, but wilful orphan, Kate Medley, who, though the beloved of Harry Drewe, "the handsomest young man in the parish," is nevertheless seduced by a stranger, "Mr. Mounteney," with whom she impetuously runs away to India. The point of this "fatal event" in the life of Hartlebury seems to lie in the trite moral of Kate's repentant return, and in Helen's compassionate care for her as she waits for death to release her from a severe, but unspecified illness (*Hart.*, 45–51). This episode is, however, but a prelude to the return to England of the still youthful Mr Bohun, and to his decision to reside in his castle near Hartlebury; the thematic concern with purity and success that had shaped both *Alroy* and *The Rise of Iskander* is now imbedded in the mystery of Bohun's recent life abroad. This mystery arises for the residents of Hartlebury, particularly Helen Molesworth, when it becomes clear that though George Gainsborough has no recollection of Bohun, the latter says that they were acquainted in their travels. But it soon becomes evident to the reader that this mystery has more profound significance than the fact that Bohun was apparently travelling under an assumed name, for the relationship of the two young men is quickly complicated and embittered both by their rivalry for Miss Molesworth's affections, and by some violent past contentions between them.

As was the case in *Iskander*, the two young men seem to divide the autobiographical resonance of the story between them. George Gainsborough, who it will turn out is ruinously in debt to Bohun, is a somewhat narcissistic "young gentleman" whose affectations of gallantry provoke Mr Molesworth to respond upon meeting him for the first time: "'A specimen of the Oriental style, I presume'" (*Hart.*, 20). Bohun is obviously a more Byronic Disraeli, for, though he soon charms the neighbouring gentry with his "air of elegance and refinement," he is initially described in terms that clearly suggest his imaginative ancestry: he combines "a fine poetical temperament" with "a great love of action." This rare combination, the narrator tells us, is sufficient to mark him as "a man of genius," and his "great powers" seem to ensure "a great destiny." What others would call his wasted youth, he defines as "that unbounded pursuit of experience without which no powers are available." And his fortunate lot in life is that a career in which he might "redeem those years that had been wasted," or exercise his acquired

wisdom, was at his command: "As he now gazed upon his rich possessions, and thought about his vast resources, did he grieve that thirty
years of his life had flown away, apparently without producing a result?
No: to sigh over the unchangeable past was not in the nature of Aubrey
Bohun. The exciting present was the world in which he ever lived, and
remorse and regret were phantoms that never disturbed his reveries"
(*Hart.*, 57). This passage is part of the one chapter (14) in volume 1 that
is attributed to Disraeli. In it the allusions to Byron's life are merged
with echoes of Vivian Grey's ambitions, both of which then help shape
the more directly autobiographical elements of the novel that derive
from Disraeli's Eastern tour and the Wycombe elections of 1832.

The power fantasies that are the motive force of Bohun's decision to
contest the local election, for the borough of "Fanchester," can be read
both as another of Disraeli's attempts to formulate an heroic political
identity, and as a defiant compensation for his recent political defeats.
At the simplest level they constitute the same claim that Vivian Grey
makes with respect to the power and influence of the Marquess of
Carabas; for Bohun, with the same ambition and rhetorical skill, has
what Disraeli lacked – the wealth and social position necessary to challenge successfully the influence of the political establishment: "Within
the walls of his castle, surrounded by its massive grandeur and its feudal magnificence, what brilliant and stirring scenes rose before his creative imagination! If he did not with Miss Molesworth exactly project a
tournament, his thoughts were equally chivalric. Devoted vassals rose
up in numbers around him, his willing tools to some great, though as
yet indefinite end. He knew he could work upon men's minds, he felt
he had all those powers of eloquence that could excite and command"
(*Hart.*, 57). In one respect, however, Bohun is shown to be but a reflection of his creator, for the descriptions of Bohun's sensational popularity with the majority of the townspeople, if not the voters, mirrors
almost exactly the effects Disraeli thought he created during the campaigns at Wycombe.

The account of Bohun's first speech at Fanchester, written by Sarah,
contains the inevitable exaggerations of the partisan, but they are chiefly of interest in that they suggest the extent to which she was imaginatively captivated by her brother's notoriety:

He took off his hat – he passed his hand through his curls – he paused a
moment – and then he spoke. The music of his harmonious voice broke on
their astonished ears. He spoke with mildness and with feeling of his re-

> turn to dwell amongst them – of his desire to be their friend. He is inter-
> rupted by vociferous cries of "Bohun for ever". He describes the mutual
> advantages of their friendship. His perfect enunciation aids his powerful
> voice – his tones are audible at the farther end of the street. The crowd
> rapidly increases. He paints with energy the duties of a representative to-
> wards his constituents – the excited people listen in profound silence. …
> He asks what their late members have done for them? – "Nothing," a
> thousand voices respond. He tells them what he will do for them. When
> he pauses, they cry "Go on"; when at last he ceases, they exclaim "We
> must speak to him – we must speak to him." (*Hart.*, 81)

This is, of course, not the account of a close eye-witness to Disraeli's
first speech, for Sarah would not have thought it proper to appear at
such an event. But even the style of the passage indicates that she is trying to visualize and dramatize that success on the basis of what she has
read and heard of it. The intrusive shift from past to present verb tense
and the syncopated sentence structure are an attempt to create both the
impression of immediacy and the interaction between the speaker and
his listeners. But the idealism and decorum of the description act as
such a restraint upon the journalistic impulse as to destroy the authenticity of the representation.

By comparison Disraeli's account of Bohun's second day of cam-
paigning, at the outset of volume 2, presents both the egocentricity and
dramatic flair of the original event in their full intensity. This version of
Disraeli's rhetorical triumph gives the full flavour of the political rough
and tumble of an early Victorian election. The verbal aggression of
Bohun's tirades full of invective and ridicule is matched by the threat
of physical violence, over which the speaker has triumphed by virtue of
his sarcasms and condescension. His sense of power is conveyed in the
ease with which he manipulates the credulous "good people of
Fanchester," in the contemptuous allusion to the present Ministers as
"the saviours of the nation," and in the metaphor of "haranguing the
Benefit Societies, and inoculating them with his new system of politics." That the gratifications of this effrontery are essentially narcissistic is then shown by his delight in finding his listeners "astonished at
his fluency and his fun," finding both "his arguments and his manners
alike irresistible," and by his affectations of nonchalance in smoking "a
pipe of shag-tobacco" (*Hart.*, 101).

A Year at Hartlebury is also of autobiographical interest for the way it
addresses the relation in politics between principles and expediency.

Bohun is certainly opportunistic in telling his agent, Mr Chace: "Agitate ... agitate, agitate. That magic word is the essence of all political success"[17] (*Hart.*, 102), and the narrator's attack on the tyranny of the Whigs is far from disinterested. But it is significant that the charge of his being insincere as a "Radical" opponent of the Government is repelled in the conservative terms of preserving the constitution and the empire and promoting the welfare of the people. Bohun's ambitions and self-interest are declared to be entirely consistent with the principles of his political faith. Thus, we are told, "he had too great a stake in the existing order to precipitate a revolution," and believed that the purpose of the Whigs was "to destroy that happy balance of parties in the state, which in an aristocratic country is indispensible [*sic*] to the freedom and felicity of the mass." Accordingly, getting rid "at any price" of the "political swindlers, who had obtained power by false pretences" and "whose only object had been to root up the power of their opponents," is the necessary prelude to forming a national constituency. Bohun, the narrator says, "was desirous of seeing a new party formed," that would grant "those alterations in our domestic policy which the spirit of the age required," but would "maintain and prosecute the ancient external policy by which the empire had been founded." Bohun, of course, wishes to be the leader of this party (*Hart.*, 105). This description cannot but seem a remarkable projection of Disraeli's career and the policy he would ultimately prosecute as prime minister in the 1870s. But the more immediate significance of so imagining Bohun's triumph is that it depends upon "high lineage," and "splendid fortune," as well as upon "superior talents." While such a fantasy can be interpreted as a simple rationalization of the defeats Disraeli had suffered at Wycombe, it paradoxically also serves within the larger structure of the plot to suggest that sheer genius might be the most important ingredient of success. Bohun's lineage and fortune, it is clear, are not sufficient to guarantee his election, but his rhetorical genius is enough to convince the Tories of Fanchester that they should coalesce with his supporters. After the Whig candidate, the barrister Prigmore, has made a speech "full of the usual commonplaces" and "vague generalities about retrenchment, reform, reduction of expenditure, [and] reduction of taxation," Bohun finds that he has a new opportunity to display his talent:

At this moment Mr. Bohun, who was a perfect master of stage effect, stepped out on the portico of the Rose. An acclamation rent the skies. Individual exclamations were lost in the universal cheer. Nothing was seen but the waving of hats and handkerchiefs and flags, and Mr. Bohun's band of course immediately struck up "See the conquering hero!" … Unhappy Prigmore, never was a man so scarified! It was quite evident that the speaker was himself in a state of almost ecstatic enjoyment. He seemed himself almost intoxicated with his inexhaustible sarcasm. His teeming fancy fired with the maddening shouts of the populace. There is nothing like a good thundering cheer to prompt a man's imagination. Unhappy Prigmore! His friends … had quite piqued themselves on his acid acuteness. Even after Mr. Bohun's first impassioned orations, they consoled themselves by the conviction that his "flowery verbosity" must shrink before the Prigmore powers of ridicule. But alas! what was their disappointment and mortification when they found their desolate champion with a face like an unhealthy lemon exposed to the reckless laughter of the mob … Amid a loud shout of "Bohun for ever", the popular candidate continued, and growing more earnest and impassioned after the retreat of his discomfited rival, he wound up with a peroration whose elaborate gorgeousness made George Gainsborough tremble for its success. (*Hart.*, 113–14)

What is most significant here, in terms of the autobiographical nature of the fiction, is the degree of self-awareness shared by the candidate and the authorial persona. For not only is the speaker "ecstatic" and "almost intoxicated" by his rhetorical success, the narrator is also gratified to answer the opponents' charge of "flowery verbosity" by flaunting the "elaborate gorgeousness" of Bohun's peroration.

It is also Bohun's eloquence on the hustings on nomination day that most impresses Miss Molesworth, who watches his address from the window of a nearby house, and finds that she has "never listened to anything more interesting, or ever witnessed a more captivating spectacle" (*Hart.*, 132). The seductive power of this performance is indicated in the conversation that follows his speech, for when Bohun thanks the ladies for their assistance with his canvass, and asks Miss Molesworth, "How can I ever repay you for all your kindness?" she replies, "By winning! – by winning! – Mr. Bohun: I will dream of nothing but your triumph" (*Hart.*, 133). No doubt the sentiment reflects Sarah's enthusiasm for her brother's cause, and in the fiction that feminine support is given the ultimate significance of determining the political victory. As the contest appears to issue in a tie, Bohun writes to his "dearest Miss Molesworth" as "Your obliged, your devoted, Aubrey" (*Hart.*, 145) to ask that she persuade old Mr Gainsborough to throw over his promise to the Whigs and vote for him. This she does, in the company of Mrs Neville, by exerting no small amount of social leverage and with a good deal of specious logic, insinuating that Gainsborough's promise to support Prigmore against the Tories was "entirely provisional," that he shall have great political influence after Bohun's victory, and that he would suffer a distinct coolness from Bohun Castle and Hartlebury were he not to vote as they wish. Of course, the pressure is too great for the doddering waverer, who has scarcely ceased to bemoan his "awkward situation" before he is whisked off to the poll in Miss Molesworth's "britchka" to cast the winning vote (*Hart.*, 147–52).

The remaining portion of the novel, almost all of which was written by Sarah, is concerned with Aubrey Bohun's romantic interest in Miss Molesworth. The resolution of the plot suggests that Sarah's enthusiasm for her brother's political cause was tempered by a moral disapproval of his indiscretions. In that regard, the reader gains further insight into Bohun's character before the election victory. At four a.m. of the night preceding the final day of the contest, he reflects upon his situation in a Byronic silent soliloquy:

> "'Tis a strange thing this life … It is in vain to struggle against the conviction; there is a destiny which moulds our actions at its will – Aubrey Bohun, Esquire, M.P. for Fanchester. Ha! ha! ha! What would Ulysses, and my comrades say to me, if I offered them a frank which they could not read! Well this is life, this is excitement, and that is all I care about. I feel I live. And yet there is something petty and vulgar in all this bustle, which half disgusts me. I who have played deep for a crown, am now forsooth a candidate for the representation of Fanchester! To be baffled by Capo d'Istrias backed by the resources of an Empire is scarcely shame – but Prigmore! oh! Aubrey!, Aubrey! I fear after all you are but a headstrong boy! No matter, I will not think. Have I not abjured plans for ever? I have now two objects to gain. Neither will keep me long in suspense. Tomorrow I shall know whether my country affords me a career or not: and as for Helen – by the blood of the Bohuns, I am convinced that she has better taste than the electors of Fanchester, and cannot hesitate about my fate. Courage, Aubrey, courage. If I gain her, and gain her I will, what is Fanchester to me. For the rest, if I live I *must* be a great man. 'Tis a consoling conviction!'" (*Hart.*, 141)

The ambivalence of this confession is scarcely less than Alroy's, though in this instance the protagonist's political motivations seem entirely cynical and opportunistic. What is most revealing in the passage, however, is the extent to which the respective contests for love and power are a matter of Bohun's self-reflexive obsession with his own identity as a "great man."

Sarah's continuation of the story works to undermine this opportunistic sense of the self to which Bohun's mysterious past seems to testify. In large measure this is achieved through Helen's consciousness of the difference between the social or political values that have influenced even her behaviour during the election campaign and the personal values that she knows are essential to her happiness. It is the former that discomfort her during the ball at the castle, as she tries with flirtatious badinage, but without success, to penetrate the mystery of Bohun's previous life. But it is the latter that afterwards shape her response to his behaviour. As she attends her neighbour, Mrs Latimer, who has been overcome by a paralytic stroke, Helen has a nightmare that embodies the danger of her moral choices:

> She dreamt that she was at Fanchester. The streets were full of crowds of people, and they all told her that she would be too late. She was going to vote for Mr. Bohun, she looked at the great church clock, it was going to strike, in a minute she would be too late, she felt almost suffocated in the crowd. All of a sudden George Gainsborough was walking by her side; he said he could take her away from the crowd, out of the Town. He said they would soon be at the booth, for it was a private way no one knew but himself, and so on and on they went, and she grew very frightened, and a hollow malicious laugh resounded in her ear, and she turned round, and it was no longer George Gainsborough at her side, but a most malignant looking being who whispered in her ear, "While you are walking here, Mrs. Latimer is dead." (*Hart.*, 166–7)

The fear of the crowd, the idea that she has a vote, and the image of the demonic companion, linked as they are to the accusation of personal neglect, are clearly emblems of Helen's transgressive public enthusiasm in the election campaign. In contrast, her thoughts about friendship and familial love, as her neighbour slowly recovers, suggest a traditional sense of identity and moral relations: "Ah! there is no happiness in this life without the full consciousness of being able to trust those who profess to love you. She dwelt with earnestness on the beauty of truth; beyond her own beloved friends there seemed to be everywhere double dealing and duplicity and mystery" (*Hart.*, 167). The duties and joys of

Helen's private life at Hartlebury with her father are thus shown in the end to be incompatible with Bohun's success in the realm of parliamentary politics. From Disraeli's perspective, Bohun's election at Fanchester leads inevitably to the dazzling triumph of his maiden speech in the House of Commons and an unlimited political future. But, from the perspective of Sarah and her alter-ego, Helen Molesworth, the "or" in the novel's title is finally exclusionary and "The Election" serves ultimately as a metaphor for personal risk.

Sarah's melodramatic final part of the novel simply reiterates the theme of Bohun's unprincipled egotism by revealing both the callous villainies of his Mediterranean adventures, which include the seduction, wedding, and abandonment of the daughter of a Greek bandit, and his bigamous intentions in proposing to marry Helen. His murder on the eve of his return from London, while he is attempting after dark to pursue an assignation with the pretty wife of a rural beer-shop proprietor, is characterized as George Gainsborough's revenge for the earlier seduction of his own betrothed, Alexina, but also as George's desperate act to avoid the embarrassments of his debts and to save Helen from becoming another innocent victim of Bohun's "lust" (*Hart.*, 189). Sarah's conclusion to the novel, which leaves all the other elements of the plot unresolved, shows Bohun to be the author of his own misfortunes and ties his untimely death directly to his lack of personal integrity and sexual indiscretions. Moreover, despite the objections of the family at Bradenham, Sarah left the murder at the end as an unsolved crime. She did consider having George Gainsborough commit suicide, but Disraeli told her that she would only spoil the book.[18] The jury of the magistrates' inquiry thus brings in a verdict of "Wilful murder against some person or persons unknown" and all subsequent attempts to discover the culprit are "absolutely vain," leaving the inhabitants of Hartlebury and Fanchester enveloped in an "impenetrable mystery" as to "the fate of the unfortunate and brilliant Bohun!" (200–1). This was, however, not Disraeli's last word about the relation between politics and love. As later chapters will show, the themes of *A Year at Hartlebury* will be revisited in other of Disraeli's fictions, including a short story, "The Consul's Daughter" (1836) and his last completed novel, *Endymion* (1880).

4

Henrietta: A Love Story

In the spring of 1833, six months before he and Sarah were collaborating on *A Year at Hartlebury*, Disraeli first met Henrietta Sykes, the wife of the third baronet, Sir Francis Sykes. By mid-summer they were deeply involved in an illicit love affair. His love letters to her have not survived, but some of hers are preserved in the Disraeli Papers.[1] They establish that from the very beginning Disraeli cast his mistress in the role of a substitute-mother figure who could not only admire his strengths but also provide him with adoration, sympathy, and encouragement when adversity or despondency threatened. The need for this kind of emotional support was of long standing and had previously characterized his relationship with his sister, Sarah, and his friendship with Sara Austen. It was also closely tied to his sense of his innate, but otherwise unrecognized purity of heart and intellectual superiority. The affair with Henrietta lasted a turbulent three years. In some respects she was not ideally suited for the quasi-maternal role, being not only completely dependent upon her husband for support, but also as Robert Blake says, "basically a passionate, emotional, jealous, highly-sexed woman who wanted a lover" (*Disraeli*, 100). Indeed, her own insecurities proved in the end an unendurable emotional drain upon Disraeli's energies. In the meantime, the progress of their relationship was aided by Sir Francis's own adulterous connection with Mrs Clara Bolton (reputed to be an earlier mistress of Disraeli) and his acquiescence to his wife's, although on one occasion Henrietta had to resort to blackmail to maintain the arrangement. For a while the two couples were frequently seen harmoniously in public together – a rather bizarre gesture to Mrs Grundy – despite the fact that the ladies detested each other. And on at least one occasion the foursome and Mr Bolton, who gossip said received a pecuniary benefit from the proceedings, spent a holiday month together under the same roof at Southend.

By the spring of 1834 Sir Francis had departed on a tour of Europe, not to return until May of the following year, and with his consent Disraeli lived openly with Henrietta in the Sykes's house in London. This was the period of Disraeli's considerable social success in the realm of high fashion and the year during which his debts, already large, became ruinous. It was about this time, too, that Henrietta introduced her lover to Lord Lyndhurst, and there is explicit evidence in the correspondence that they conspired to exploit his Lordship's fondness for her in the hope of furthering Disraeli's political ambitions.[2]

It is not surprising that Disraeli's relationship with Henrietta produced considerable scandal. There was great indignation in Buckinghamshire county society at his bringing Henrietta and Lyndhurst to Bradenham on several occasions to visit his parents and sister, and it was widely held as truth by county residents in July 1835 that Henrietta was the mistress of both men. But the sense of moral outrage was by no means strictly provincial. From the very beginning of the affair there had been threats of social ostracization in London, which Henrietta's letters reflect with fear and trepidation. Lady Cork, for example, for all her friendship, constantly retailed stories of their impending doom. And Henrietta's father and sisters, horrified by the gossip they heard, tried to force her to abandon the affair and put an end to the scandal. But their threats of dragging her home to Norfolk finally drove her to join Lyndhurst and some members of his family on a tour of the Continent in the autumn of 1834.

It is obvious that the notoriety of the whole affair between Henrietta and Disraeli did him a great deal of political harm, especially, it seems, in the area of Wycombe, where he was trying to get elected to Parliament. Some extent of the damage can be inferred from a memorandum of Sir Philip Rose, one of his executors. Writing in 1882 Rose remarked on the indignation aroused in the neighbourhood at the time and stated that Disraeli's scandalous behaviour in the 1830s had been "thrown in … his teeth by influential county people within very recent years" as something that "would never be forgotten and which all D's subsequent career could never obliterate."[3] Another aspect of the political damage occasioned by the affair was that the campaigns at Taunton in 1835 and Maidstone in 1837 were enlivened by stories of Disraeli's huge debts and how they had been contracted in the extravagant and immoral life with his paramour.

Since Disraeli could not have failed to realize the political effects of it, the most obvious question is why he indulged in so flagrant and notorious a display of his relationship with Henrietta. The answer may be complex and very much related to his senses of himself. No doubt, the very publicity of the affair satisfied his Byronic sense of being different. There are even echoes of Byron's words in some of Henrietta's letters. In this respect it was, in its public dimension, an amorous version of *The Representative* affair, wherein he lashed out at dullness with all the brilliance of unrestrained egotism. In its private dimension, however, it is clear that the affair offered him a chance to retreat into a sense of his innate purity. His head "pillowed" on Henrietta's "snowy bosom," he found the innocent bliss of childhood in the unquestioning acceptance of his "true self," and in the rhetoric of Henrietta's passionate adoration and "sincere" protestations of undying love, he found the assurance he craved.[4] Thus, paradoxically, even though it contributed to the frustration of his political ambition, the affair provided some resolution of Disraeli's ambivalence about his identity in that it offered him a role that combined the two kinds of recognition that he sought. This resolution was, however, ultimately inadequate and Disraeli again felt the need to explore the theatrical possibilities of fulfilment in the realm of fiction, where imaginatively he could conceive an ideal identity, one that would finally transcend the forces of scandal, debts, and political compromise or defeat.

The melodramatic conclusion *of A Year at Hartlebury* may reflect some awareness of, or anxiety about her brother's sexual indiscretions on Sarah Disraeli's part.[5] But whether this is so or not, Disraeli continued to feel the psychic tension between the desire for political and social success and the need to claim a pure and innocent self. In that regard, marriage was an explicit concern. The correspondence between them shows that in 1833 Sarah, his father, and even some of his friends were urging Disraeli to marry someone suitable as soon as possible. As his somewhat facetious replies to Sarah suggest, Disraeli felt that he could not afford to marry for love, and for the moment his affair with Henrietta Sykes was all absorbing.[6]

I

"The Consul's Daughter"[7] is a short story, published in Lady Blessington's *Book of Beauty* for 1836, that explicitly reflects all these concerns and, through details of the text, is linked directly to both *A Year at Hartlebury* and Disraeli's next novel, *Henrietta Temple*. Henrietta, the heroine of the story, is the eighteen-year-old child of Major Ponsonby, the British consul at "one of the most beautiful ports in the Mediterranean" (315). The major has aristocratic family connections and is a widower. In "their beautiful solitude" Henrietta has grown up to be a "girl of singular beauty," the "fond child of his affections" and the "cherished companion of his society," who diffuses over their happy home that "indefinable charm, that spell of unceasing, yet soothing excitement, with which the constant presence of an amiable, a lovely, and an accomplished woman can alone imbue existence" (315–16). The devoted daughter, indeed, has shrunk from her father's suggestion, in concern for her future, that she might be more advantageously situated in England: "She could not conceive existence without her father … her sire, her tutor, her constant company, her dear, dear friend." Instead she is mistress of her father's "casino" or "pavilion," where she lives "amid fruit and flowers, surrounded by her birds" and where "she might often be seen at sunset glancing amid its beauties, with an eye as brilliant, and a step as airy, as the bright gazelle that ever glided or bounded by her side" (317–18). This passage resonates with an adolescent's quest for purity and affection in similar terms to those of *Contarini Fleming* and *Alroy*, in that it establishes not only the heroine's devotion to her father, but also the virginal quality of her affections. The roles the father plays ("sire," "tutor," "friend") and the all absorbing bond between them have had no romantic, that is, sexual, intrusions thrust upon them, and to this point the daughter has rejected even the idea of any other claims upon her feelings.

Into this setting comes Mr Ferrers, "a man of an age apparently verging towards thirty" who, in travelling without servants, does not share "the general reputation of his countrymen for wealth." But he is not without interest: "his appearance to those practised in society was not undistinguished. Tall, slender, and calm, his air, though unaffected, was that of a man not deficient in self-confidence; and whether it were the art of his tailor, or the result of his own good frame, his garb, although remarkably plain, had that indefinable style which we associate with the costume of a man of some mark and breeding" (318). It is clear that Ferrers's innate superiority transcends the rather anonymous entrance and the lack of definitive outward signs of his social identity. Reminiscent of the Magdalen scenes in *Contarini Fleming*, when he arrives at the consul's town house his attention is engaged, indeed "monopolised," by a portrait of the daughter: "She stood on a terrace in a garden, and by her side was a gazelle. Her form was of wonderful symmetry; but although her dress was not English, the expression of her countenance reminded the traveller of the beauties of his native land. The dazzling complexion, the large deep blue eye, the high white forehead, the clustering brown hair, were all northern, but northern of the highest order" (319). When Ferrers meets her that evening, "the original of the portrait" proves that "the painter had no need to flatter" (320; cf. *CF*, 46–7), as Henrietta displays "a radiant smile" and "sweet and thrilling voice" in greeting her countryman (321). He, however, seems incapable of being enchanted. He returns his welcome "with becoming complaisance," exhibits "the breeding of a man accustomed to sights of strangeness and of beauty," and retains a "subdued" and "sedate" manner which indicates that he is an "individual whom the world has little left to astonish, and less to enrapture" (321). Similarly, when Henrietta obliges her father's request for a song with a "wild and plaintive air," Mr Ferrers, we are told, "listened with attention and thanked her for her courtesy." He does request the favour of an encore, "but in so quiet a manner that most young ladies would have neglected to comply with a wish expressed with so little fervour" (322). Ferrers is thus presented as a man of wide experience in the world, "a most gentlemanlike personage … very clever and very agreeable," and yet his reserve, it soon becomes apparent, is not simply the expression of ennui, but rather a deliberate passivity. He shrinks from the opportunity of closer acquaintance with his hosts, declining invitations to dinner and being content to appear at the pavilion in the evenings.

Among the drawings in Ferrers's portfolio, which forms the subject of conversation one evening, are some sketches of Lord Bohun's yacht. This young nobleman has often been expected as a visitor by the major and his daughter, but as yet he has not appeared. His "miraculous" reputation as a "great traveller," who at various times has played the roles of "Guerilla chieftain" and "Bedouin robber," has, however, preceded him. When questioned about his knowledge of this "eccentric" man, Ferrers replies, "I never heard much in his favour … I believe he has made himself a great fool, as most young nobles do!" With a sneer he dismisses "romantic" escapades as "Affectations," but then relents somewhat by adding, "Bohun, however, has some excuses for his folly: for he was an orphan … in his cradle" (324).

Some weeks later Ferrers finally, though reluctantly, accepts an invitation to dinner at the special request of Henrietta ("'You do with me what you like'") and from that evening on seems the victim of her charms. And yet it is explicitly stated that "Mr. Ferrers was not her lover." "No act – no word of gallantry – no indication of affection, to her inexperienced sense, ever escaped him. All that he did was, that he sought her society." His reasons for this now constant attention remain unclear, but we are told, "whatever might be his motives ... the English stranger dangerously interested the feelings of the Consul's daughter" (327). This influence is attributed to the "soul-subduing qualities" with which "*nature* had invested" him (emphasis added): "His elegant person; his tender, yet reserved manners; his experienced, yet ornate mind; the flashes of a brilliant, yet mellowed imagination, which ever and anon would break forth in his conversation: perhaps, too, the air of melancholy, and even of mystery, which enveloped him, were all spells potent in the charm that enchants the heart of woman" (327).

With the news (accompanying the arrival of two "gay, noisy, pleasant, commonplace persons ... '*on leave*' from one of the Mediterranean garrisons") that Lord Bohun is rumoured to be coming to the consul's island, Ferrers decides to leave. Before he does, however, he confesses to Henrietta that he would "'willingly compound that the rest of ... [his] existence should be as happy as the last ten weeks ... They have been very happy ... very happy, indeed. The only *happy* time I ever knew ... These ten weeks have been so serene, and so sweet ... because you have been my companion. My life has taken its colour from your character. Now listen to me, dearest Miss Ponsonby, and be not alarmed. I love you! ... Yes, I *love* you ... with a burning heart'" (330). It is at this point in the scene that the mystery of Ferrers's passivity deepens, for he recognizes the disparity between his ardent feelings and his diffident behaviour: "'I am so circumstanced that it is not in my power, even at *this* moment, to offer any explanation of my equivocal position. Yet, whatever I may be, I offer my existence, and all its accidents, good or bad, in homage to your heart. May I indulge the delicious hope that, if not now accepted, they are at least considered with kindliness and without suspicion?'" (330–1). When Miss Ponsonby murmurs in reply, "'Oh, yes! without *suspicion* – without suspicion. Nothing, nothing in the world shall ever make me believe that you are not so good as you are – gifted,'" his reserve is completely broken: "'Darling Henrietta!' exclaimed Mr. Ferrers, in a voice of melting tenderness; and he pressed her to his heart, and sealed his love upon her lips. '*This, this is confidence; this, this is the woman's love I have long sighed for.* Doubt me not, dearest; never doubt me! Say you are mine; once more pledge yourself to me'" (331). Then, promising, "'I shall return to claim my bride,'" and pledg-

ing his "darling" to a "secret" engagement in still more mysterious
terms – suggesting that she may hear things not to his advantage before
he returns – Ferrers departs, leaving with her "an honour *never sullied*":
"'Beautiful being! you make me mad with joy. Has fate reserved for me,
indeed, this treasure? Am I at length, loved, and loved only for myself!'" (331). There are strong verbal and thematic echoes of *Contarini
Fleming* here. "The Consul's Daughter" is clearly a story of a young
man's need to find recognition of his innate superiority and "purity" of
heart in the form of a woman's unquestioning love. As such it embodies
all the ambivalence of Disraeli's struggle with the conflicting claims of
"purity" and "success" demonstrated in his earlier fiction and political
career. The intense way in which that struggle continues to haunt him
in 1835, even as he begins to succeed in formulating a durable political
identity, is shown by the structure of this story.

Lord Bohun arrives to be a guest of the consul and his daughter and
in conversation with them reveals that he knows Ferrers. In response to
their questions he admits him to be "a very agreeable man," one with
"gentle blood in his veins" (333–4), but he insinuates other opinions as
well. To the daughter's spirited defence of her absent lover, Bohun then
adds, "'Oh, I never heard anything particular against Ferrers ... except
that he was a roué; and a little mad'" (334). The comment has its intended effect and produces a "tumult" in Henrietta's mind. Alone she
wonders, "'Could it be so! Could it be possible! Was she, while she had
pledged *the freshness of her virgin mind* to this unknown man – was she,
after all, only a fresh sacrifice to *his insatiable vanity!* Ferrers a roué! That
lofty-minded man, who spoke so eloquently and so wisely, was he a
roué, an eccentric *roué*; one whose unprincipled conduct could only be
excused at the expense of the soundness of his intellect?'" (first and
second emphases added, 335). It is clear that Disraeli is here revisiting
some of the issues of character presented in his sister's conclusion to *A
Year at Hartlebury*, but equally revealing is the comparison with *Vivian
Grey*. While in this instance the issue of the hero's behaviour is presented
solely in romantic terms, the language of the foregoing passage is similar to Vivian Grey's rather more comprehensive introspection after he
has revealed his knowledge of Mrs Felix Lorraine's sexual improprieties
and, as a result, narrowly escaped being poisoned by that desperate
lady. Vivian rationalized his attempted manipulation of her in that he
believes his lack of social position and wealth has "*forced*" him "to make
use of such evil instruments." Yet he is haunted by the paralysing
thought that Mrs Lorraine, "the most abandoned of all beings," is but

"a kind of double" of himself (*VG*, 112): "'It is not so; it cannot be so; it shall not be so! ... But am I entitled, I, who can lose nothing, am I entitled to play with other men's fortunes? Am I all this time deceiving myself with some wretched sophistry? Am I, then, an intellectual Don Juan, reckless of human minds, as he was of human bodies; a spiritual libertine?'" (*VG*, 113). It is not a question that can be comfortably answered, and so, faced with the knowledge that it is too late to recede from his commitments, Vivian sets out to defy the possibility of failure: "'If I be the Juan that I fancied myself, then Heaven be praised! I have a confidant in all my trouble; the most faithful of counsellors, the craftiest of valets; a Leporello often tried and never found wanting: my own good mind'" (*VG*, 113). Such a comparison reveals the consciousness with which Disraeli faced, at least at times, the issues of sincerity and hypocrisy. And it also suggests the degree to which the political and personal dimensions of the tension surrounding those issues and the desire for recognition of his genius are related.

In "The Consul's Daughter" Henrietta refuses to credit the slur on Ferrers's character, largely on the strength of his own mysterious anticipation of it: "She would not doubt him. No desolation seemed so complete, no misery so full of anguish, as such suspicion: she could not doubt him; all her happiness was hope. A gentle touch roused her. It was her gazelle; the gazelle that he had so loved" (335). The gazelle is Disraeli's emblem of romantic love. It is not accidental that here he again associates it with his heroine at the moment when her lover's character is most in question. In Arabic literature the gazelle is a widely used symbol of female beauty, representing grace, beauty of the eye, and exquisite form – a fact Disraeli would undoubtedly have learned on his Eastern tour. It is also used extensively as an emblem of the soul, symbolizing "the persecution of the passions and the aggressive, self-destructive aspect of the unconsciousness."[8]

It is not surprising, then, that the gazelle has additional significance in Disraeli's work, for it becomes a major symbol of ambivalence about romantic love. In *Contarini Fleming* a gazelle is associated with the hero's "eastern bride" and mother substitute, Alcesté, whose death in childbirth leaves Contarini as bereft as did his real mother's death – a fate, it would seem, almost in retribution for the neglect of his successful political career and, in any case, certainly the only imagined result of his quest for purity in love. There the gazelle seems to represent both the desirability and the vulnerability of that love (*CF*, 240 ff. See also ch. 2, n. 28). In *Alroy* gazelles appear in two different contexts and their significance is more explicit, though more complex. In the first instance, while he is on his search for the sceptre of Solomon, the mystical emblem of power for his messianic mission to save the Jewish people, Alroy is on the verge of death by starvation when robbers offer him food in the form of some roasted meat of a gazelle. This he rejects as incompatible with his faith, being forbidden as unclean because the gazelle has a *"cloven"* foot (*Alroy*, 43–4). Later, in Baghdad, when suitably disguised as a eunuch, he meets and falls in love with the half-Christian, half-Muslim Princess Schirene, her pet gazelle is used as a symbol both of her beauty and of the betrayal of the true Hebraic identity his love for her represents (*Alroy*, 68 ff.). The use of a gazelle in "The Consul's Daughter" is, thus, also a sign that the author's theme is once again the resolution of a hero's struggle for purity. But the structure of this tale is rather more revealing of the nature of that struggle, with which Disraeli is so preoccupied in his fiction.

Henrietta, having proved herself loyal to her mysterious lover when his reputation is maligned, must immediately face a more severe test of her purity of heart. Lord Bohun, confessing from the beginning the attractiveness of her charms, soon asks (through a deputy) for her hand in marriage – an event which the major finds extremely gratifying. The prospect of uniting her "eternal lot in life" with the "high birth, high rank, splendid fortune, and accomplished youth" of this noble suitor does not, however, sway his daughter. When she tells Lord Bohun that her heart is "engaged" to Ferrers, he accepts the statement with equanimity and confesses that he has long believed that "the world did not boast a man more gifted" and that it does not now "possess a man more blessed" (338). Her disappointed suitor then departs, assuring her of her lover's imminent return, and the narrator intrudes to point the moral: "Her gentle musings were of him whom she had loved with such unexampled *trust*. Fond, beautiful confiding maiden! It was the strength of thy mind as much as the simplicity of thy heart that rendered thee so faithful and so firm! Who would not envy thy unknown adorer? Can he be false? Suspicion is for weak minds and cold-blooded spirits. *Thou never dids't doubt*; and thou was just, for behold, he is true!" (340, emphasis added). Immediately, Ferrers returns and in the last chapter it is revealed to everyone's satisfaction that it is he who is Lord Bohun, and that the previous events have been but a deliberately staged test of Henrietta's love. This revelation of Ferrers's true identity is accompanied by an extensive explanation, which speaks to both his and the narrator's motives in practising such a deceit. Despite his great fortune and eminent station,

Lord Bohun asks the consul and his daughter to conceive of him as a man with "too dangerous a sensibility; the dupe and victim of all whom he encounters," and "sighing ... to be loved only for his own sake." But having apparently found that love, he was, he says, "haunted," by the suspicion that Henrietta's affection is "less the result of his own qualities, than of her inexperience of life." It was for this reason, he assures them, that he chose "to submit her devotion to the sharpest trial." And only when she has proved to be "truer even than truth," can he announce, "I have come back to claim my unrivalled Bride" (343–4).

The foregoing summary reveals how explicitly "The Consul's Daughter" embodies the theme of the struggle for purity that characterizes so much of Disraeli's earlier fiction. But as a fantasy this story achieves a more complete resolution of the tensions beneath that struggle than do the earlier works. The elements of mystery and the exotic setting provide an isolation from the hero's past and make it the more easily rationalized. The disguise of his true identity both temporarily eliminates the prejudicial evidence of his past behaviour and stresses the innately superior qualities he possesses as grounds for being judged trustworthy in the matter of his affections. Further, both his superiority and purity of heart are established in the most passive, asexual context imaginable. And finally, in anticipation of the climactic revelation of his actual identity, his previous indiscretions are excused on the grounds that he is an orphan and a victim of a corrupt society.

Perhaps nowhere is the nostalgic desire to reconstruct the past more obvious than in the authorial intrusion of the penultimate quotation, where Henrietta's *trust* is apostrophized with the archaic forms of the second-person pronouns (see above and 340). Thus, while the hero's purity of heart is to be accepted by Henrietta on faith despite insinuations to the contrary, he must have tangible proof of hers. Indeed, the elaborate test of Henrietta's love for Ferrers establishes that the author's true concern is to show that his hero's love is dependent upon a reciprocal purity and unquestioning love for, and trust of his true self on the part of the heroine. As such, the story is essentially a fairy tale of which the disguised "prince" and the test of the maiden are appropriate elements. And like a fairy tale, the story ends happily with the past vanquished and the future assured.

"The Consul's Daughter" is undoubtedly a type of wish-fulfilment fantasy in which Disraeli is expressing his hope that Henrietta Sykes loves him "for himself." That his heroine is "a being surpassing the brightest dream of ... purest youth" (343) and the real Henrietta in adoration refers to him as "my child" and signs herself "your Mother" shows clearly enough the origins of this need for "self"-recognition. The choice of Henrietta for the heroine's name and the verbal echoes of *Contarini Fleming* suggest that in writing "The Consul's Daughter" Disraeli was creating a fantasy which asserted once again the import-ance for him of finding both a recognition of his innate superiority, or genius, and a love of his pure self expressed in unquestioning trust.

The conjunction of fiction and biography in this one instance con-firms that the affair with Lady Sykes played an important part in Disraeli's political life in the mid-1830s. The exercise of politics had thrust upon him the necessity of demonstrating his superiority in the face of pervasive doubts about his sincerity. And even though by the fall of 1835 he had in large measure succeeded in the task of formulating a viable political identity, that success was fraught with compromise that left some of the tensions in his perceptions of himself unresolved and, perhaps, stronger. The confidence or hope that he *will* be loved for him-self which informs "The Consul's Daughter" seems to be directly con-nected to the confidence he must have gained in the Sykes affair itself. Superficially it would seem that the audacious visibility with which the affair was consummated would do him nothing but political harm in a society that was rapidly pulling the veil of respectability over public behaviour. No doubt, though, the notoriety and scandal of his conduct fed his desire to act out a role of Byronic defiance of conventional moral-ity and so display his superiority to "the common herd." In fact the affair strengthened his friendship with Lyndhurst, both because his Lordship was fond of Lady Sykes and because he was contemptuous of the hypocrisy of a public morality. And clearly the affair offered Disraeli a form of trust and recognition for which his soul hungered and which he could find nowhere else. It gave him a place to retreat from adversity where the disguises required for political success were unnecessary.

"The Consul's Daughter" should thus be seen as a fictional embodi-ment of a fantasy that in effect asserts Disraeli's need to find a reconcilia-tion of the claims of "purity" and "success" in ideal or unambivalent terms. Yet the confidence it reflects in Disraeli's imagining such an even-tuality does not mean that his psychic life is now untroubled or that his need to work out his fantasies in fiction as well as in politics disappears.

II

Henrietta Temple: A Love Story[9] (1836) is a good illustration of this theme, for again in this work the hero's essential problem is to find an answer to the question, "What is he?"[10] In this case the conflicting possibilities are dramatized in terms of the implications of defining his pure, innocent self in different ways. Although when the novel was published in 1836 Disraeli had achieved considerable fame or notoriety for his "Letters of Runnymede,"[11] which were marked by a continuation of the violent anti-Catholicism of his *Morning Post* articles of the previous year, *Henrietta Temple* begins with a sympathetic and elaborate, if bizarre, delineation of the protagonist's family's Catholicism. This emphasis is so strong that the reader is prepared to see Ferdinand Armine's struggle for happiness ultimately connected with the issue of his faith. Once the Protestant heroine of the novel is introduced, however, the story veers sharply in another direction and the hero's Catholicism is clearly subordinated to what seems to be the larger issue of his filial devotion. The explanation for the remarkable change in emphasis lies in the details of the novel's composition.

The apparent central plot established in the early portion, begun in 1833 but left incomplete,[12] concerns the hero's endeavour to revive the Armine family's fortunes, and the ostensible element of conflict suggested is his disappointed expectations of being heir to the family fortune of his maternal grandfather, Lord Grandison. The development of this conflict depends, however, on an inheritance of a different sort, one that accounts for the early emphasis upon the family's Catholicism. For the second remarkable feature of the first portion of the story is the explicit description of potential ambivalence within the hero's character, which makes any reader familiar with the earlier novels immediately aware that the struggle for purity is not yet exhausted as a theme. From his devoted, pious, and virtuous parents and tutor, young Ferdinand learns "to be sincere, dutiful, charitable, and just; and to have a deep sense of the great account hereafter to be delivered to his Creator," which, combined with "great gifts of nature, with lively and highly cultivated talents, and a most affectionate and disciplined temper," make him "idolised" and "adored" by all who know him. But the narrator, implied author, is quick to interject, "But for his character, what was that? ... Custom blunts the fineness of psychological study ... Nor is it, indeed, marvellous, that for a long time temperament should be disguised" (22, 23). The answer, suggestive of the novel's true thematic concern, is quickly supplied by next describing Ferdinand's fascination for the family portrait of his reckless and flamboyant paternal grandfather, Sir Ferdinand,[13] and by intruding to ask, "Did the fiery imagination and the terrible passions of that extraordinary man lurk in the innocent heart and the placid mien of his young descendant?" (24).

The dramatization of this ambivalence is begun upon the eve of the hero's leaving home to take up his commission as ensign in the Royal Fusiliers. At bedtime on the eve of his departure, both Lady Armine and Ferdinand break down in tears at the thought of their impending separation. Both express their unconditional love for the other: she through "a thousand kisses" asks what she has done "to deserve such misery" and says, "'beloved Ferdinand, I shall die.'" He in response assures her that, "'There is no mother loved as you are loved,'" to which she replies, "'Tis that that makes me mad. I know it. Oh! Why are you not like other children, Ferdinand?'" (47). Although the rationale for the separation is momentarily regained when he says, "'Think, dearest mother, how much I have to do. All now depends on me ... I must restore our house,'" the continuation of this scene emphasizes the innocence demanded of Ferdinand in the maternal relationship and links his filial and religious devotion. Somewhat consoled by her son's promise to write to her by every ship and to send her an emblematic pet gazelle, Lady Armine extracts a final avowal of innocence, "'If I forget thee ... dear mother, may God indeed forget me,'" and she reminds him of her solicitude, "'Mind, you have eight packages ... And take the greatest care of old Sir Ferdinand's sword'" (48, 49–50). This scene, only a small portion of which is quoted here, establishes in two different ways that the struggle for "purity" is indeed the author's chief concern. The mission to restore the fortunes of Ferdinand's house, the invocation of God's witness to his familial and religious loyalty, the mention of the gazelle, and the introduction of the magical phallic sword as the instrument of power, all bring to mind *The Wondrous Tale of Alroy*, which is Disraeli's most explicit and direct treatment of that theme, and which had just recently been published in March 1833.

Moreover, the whole scene itself, in its sentimentality and infantilism, is an idealization of the maternal relationship in which the almost seventeen-year-old hero is literally and figuratively made a "child." It is very close in quality to the scene in *Contarini Fleming* where Christiana smothers the child hero with compensatory maternal affection (11, 15). And the extent to which this scene is a wish-fulfilment fantasy, an idealization of the past, can in part be judged by contrasting it with a poem the adolescent Disraeli wrote and recorded in an early notebook:

The steps within my father's hall, her voice
Sounds in the chambers of my early youth,
The voice of one whose tones my heart rejoice,

Mine & not mine, a melancholy truth!
Ah! thought of woe, ah! memory of sadness
The bitter drop, the very serpent's tooth
Gnawing my highest joy to very madness
And turning my existence which in sooth
Might be the sweet repose of perfect love
Into an anxious & a quivering dream,–
Away with these dread fancies! yon dark grove
Sends forth a being brighter than the beam
That plays upon the terraced walks above
And gilds my Myrrha with its golden gleam.[14]

This is a lament for the incomplete fulfilment he finds in his relationship with his mother. The bitter drop is the knowledge of her divided loyalty, as wife as well as mother, which denies him total absorption. The realm of fantasy provides release from the insecurity which in its intensity turns reality into the madness of a nightmare. The scene in *Henrietta Temple*, however, does provide Ferdinand with total immersion in maternal love. Further, he is recognized as different from other children and loved the more for being so. The depth of Lady Armine's misery is the measure of her affection, an emotion which not only permits but encourages her son's expressions of his love in terms of child-like purity. Given Disraeli's sense of alienation from his own mother, attested to by the poem quoted above, the content of his earlier novels, and the search for a substitute mother so evident in the affair with Lady Henrietta Sykes and his later courtship of his wife, Mary Anne Wyndham Lewis,[15] it is reasonable to see this scene as a wish-fulfilment fantasy which establishes his hero's essential, or at least original, purity and his need to be loved for simply being himself. The first portion of the novel that became *Henrietta Temple*, however, does no more than suggest that in 1833 Disraeli was beginning a story which, like its predecessor *Alroy*, would embody the theme of purity betrayed and perhaps recovered.

When Disraeli took up the little more than embryonic novel again in 1836 he did so largely because he needed money and needed it desperately. In the continuation the hero's debts become the agent of his corruption. At Malta, Ferdinand's innately superior qualities and almost magically acquired accomplishments are immediately recognized, and he instantly becomes the most popular person in the garrison. With his vanity flattered and his expectations of being Lord Grandison's heir increased by a visit to England, he is soon immersed in a life of unwarranted extravagance. The significance of this characterization, however, derives less from the facts of Disraeli's own reception on his Mediterranean tour of 1830–1 or his ruinously expensive social life than from the implied author's *self*-indulgence even as he melodramatically moralizes on the "fatal misery" of debt, that "prolific mother of folly and crime … which taints the course of life in all its dreams": "there are few things more gloomy than the recollection of a youth that has not been enjoyed. What prosperity of manhood, what splendour of old age, can compensate for it? Wealth is power; and in youth … we require power … What, then, is to be done? I leave the question to the school-men, because I am convinced that to moralise with the inexperienced availeth nothing" (61). This intrusion, while it might seem to be a distressing artistic flaw in its combination of high seriousness and flippancy, establishes a pattern of authorial ambivalence – which is often implicit in characterization and plot – with respect to the hero that is in a sense the essence of the novel.

In *Henrietta Temple*, as in *Alroy*, the hero corrupts the mission of his "true" self by indulging his exalted egotism. When Ferdinand learns that his cousin Katherine has inherited the Grandison fortune he determines to marry her, though he feels no love for her. And with no difficulty he succeeds in making the "poor inexperienced, innocent" Katherine love him. Their engagement settled, we are told, "he called for a tumbler of champagne, and secretly drank his own health, as the luckiest fellow of his acquaintance, with a pretty, amiable, and high-bred wife, with all his debts paid, and the house of Armine restored" (65, 66). But it is obvious that the noble and heroic purpose of restoring the Armines's estates and honour, a purpose directly associated with his pure, filial love, comes to subserve the interests of Ferdinand's in-sincere, "false" self. This change is noticed by the narrator who im-mediately intrudes to comment upon the "not … favourable" difference in his "character and conduct," and it is also recognized in the form of nostalgia by Ferdinand himself: "he could not but feel that a great change had come over his spirit since the days he was wont to ramble in this old haunt of his boyhood. *His innocence was gone. Life was no longer that deep unbroken trance of duty and of love from which he had been roused* to so much care; and if not remorse, at least to so much compunc-tion" (70, emphasis added). This third-person passage effectively repre-sents Ferdinand's stream of consciousness, a technique Disraeli frequently uses to link the narrator's and hero's awareness. The passive voice evades the weight of responsibility for his (Ferdinand's) compromise, placing it upon the inevitability of lost innocence rather than upon his own vanity. The same desire to avoid self-indictment is reflected in the almost immediately following tentative denial of the now threatening (because in its contrast it implies guilt) past: "there are moments I almost wish that I had no father and no mother ... and that Armine were sunk into the very centre of the earth. If I stood alone in the world methinks I might find the place that suits me; now everything seems ordained for me ... My spirit has had no play" (71). Clearly here the hero finds both of his previous worlds insufficient, and what he longs for is a realm in which the claims of "sympathy" and success can be reconciled. And the development of the novel from this point on is essentially an elaboration of a fantasy structure related to that end.

The dramatic potential of the hero's rhetorical passivity is established by his rationalizations (which are in effect fantasies) about his identity. He first finds a "wonderful ... providential dispensation" (73) in his fallen circumstances which have led to the "destiny" of being the family's restorer. There is considerable vanity in this claim to innate superiority as one of God's chosen. But the assumption of such significance is an evasion of responsibility which runs counter to the Byronic role he also imagines. "'Conceal it as I will,'" he exclaimed, "'I am a victim; disguise them as I may, all the considerations are worldly. There is, there must be, something better in this world than power and wealth and rank; and surely there must be felicity more rapturous even than securing the happiness of a parent ... Is love indeed a delusion, or am I marked out from men alone to be exempted from its delicious bondage?'" (74). The sharp reversal of values seems to represent both a recognition of his own corruption and a denial of responsibility for it. The exclamation is appropriately the voice of the "devil" because it expresses the inadequacy of the former pure ideal and a desire for a substitute better than the original. As a "victim" of worldly considerations, "marked out" and "exempted" from "rapturous" felicity, Ferdinand is completely passive, and his conception of the love he longs for is a "delicious bondage," that of the child held transfixed by the mother's love (cf. 47).

Ferdinand then postulates that his "wild and restless" grandfather, "while the world ... marvelled and moralised at his wanton life, and ... his heartless selfishness ... was sighing for some soft bosom whereon to pour his overwhelming passion" (75). Given the devout Glastonbury's devotion to Lady Barbara and her son Ratcliffe (Bk 1, ch. 3), a devotion so strong that he considers retreating to a monastery when she dies, and given his justification of his purchase of her grandson's army commission by invoking the memory of "that blessed and saintly being" (42), Ferdinand's identification with Sir Ferdinand and the implication of a want of love in his grandfather's marriage thus becomes a denial of the values of the family and their religion. The rhetorical structure and diction of the spasmodic climax of the exclamation quoted above reveal Disraeli's thematic intentions in this reversal of values: "'O Nature! why art thou beautiful? My heart requires not, imagination cannot paint, a sweeter or a fairer scene ... This azure vault of heaven, this golden sunshine, this deep and blending shade, these rare and fragrant shrubs, yon grove of green and tallest pines, and the bright gliding of this swan-crowned lake; my soul is charmed with all this beauty and this sweetness'" (75). Debased romanticism has scarcely received a more regrettable expression. But the archaic phrasing of the ultimately theological question completes the invocation of "Nature" as an embodiment of the divine and sanctifies the "beauty" which charms the "soul." The "poetic" and spontaneous expression of love of beauty becomes a form of worship. And through such love lies the individual's salvation. The love of beauty in nature is, however, but a paradigm of holiness and purity.

Both the hero's rationale of his essential purity of heart and the narrative *self*-indulgence of the novel's fantasy structure are confirmed in the lengthy authorial intrusion immediately preceding the introduction of the dazzling, beautiful heroine, Henrietta Temple (Bk 2, ch. 4). Love at first sight is defined as "the transcendent and surpassing offspring of sheer and unpolluted sympathy," while "all other is the illegitimate result of observation, of reflection, of compromise, of comparison, of expediency." Apart from the purity of spontaneous love the narrator invokes two additional elements of this emotion, the lover's dependence on the loved one – her beauty is overwhelming and it is her responses, "her joy ... her sigh of love" and "her smile of fondness" which create his "bliss" – and the power of love, the very birth of which (to use the author's metaphor) comes "amid the gloom and travail of existence," to replace the lover's "flaunty ambition." The chief ostensible conflict of the novel is established as "this mighty passion," which makes "revolutions of empire, changes of creed, mutations of opinion ... but the clouds and meteors of a stormy sky," and which rages in Ferdinand's heart when he first sees the "ravishing vision" of Henrietta in the park at Armine (76, 77, 78). Even as he exclaims his "overwhelming ... absorbing ... burning passion" for this "exquisite, enchanting, adored being" (87, 86), he remembers that his parents and cousin are expected home within a week: "Beautiful Henrietta! … what wild … maddening words are these? Am I not … the betrothed, the victim? … I'll cast to the winds all ties and duties; I will not be dragged to the altar, a miserable sacrifice, to redeem, by my forfeited felicity, the worldly fortunes of my race … But this woman: I am bound to her. Bound? The word makes me tremble. I shiver: I hear the clank of my fetters. Am I indeed bound? Ay! in honour. Honour and love! A contest! Pah! The Idol must yield to the Divinity!" (87). As the rapid alterations of mood suggest, the hero's essential struggle is to find an identity compatible with his "dearest desires." Here the alternative to being the romantic "victim" is the role of Byronic defiance so conveniently anticipated in the author's definition of love. The exaggerated language constitutes both a denial of the past and a justification of the future. Since the purity of love transcends all conventions of honour, he is free, though engaged to Katherine, to fall into an "intense delirium of absorbing love" for Henrietta (106).

With some insight into the psychology of guilt, Disraeli then establishes dramatically that his hero's denial of his past and justifications of the present are rationalizations of his ambivalent feelings about himself. One night Ferdinand's dream of Henrietta turns into a nightmare of Katherine's presence so powerful that it continues as hallucination after waking. The reverie-transforming guilt manifests itself not in any recognition of why Katherine might appear "sad and reproachful," but rather in speculation about the "angelic" Henrietta that can only be termed a loss of love fantasy: "What were her slumbers? Were they wild as his own, or sweet and innocent as herself? … Bore anyone to her the same relation as Katherine Grandison to him?" Letters from his mother and his cousin soon replace this imaginatively projected threat to his love with the "dreadful reality" of his actual situation, and images of "his melancholy father, his fond and confiding mother, the devoted Glastonbury," and "all the mortifying circumstances of his illustrious race" rise before him "in painful succession" (107, 108, 109). Although this threat is momentarily fended off with the recurrent wish to be "alone in the world, to struggle with his fate and mould his fortunes," there is no longer defiance in Ferdinand's renewed denial of his family: "He felt himself a slave and a sacrifice. He cursed Armine, his ancient house, and his broken fortunes." Indeed, the appropriateness of the heroic Byronic role with its potential for despair as well as defiance is shown through Ferdinand's ensuing passivity and the confusion of values it reflects. There is in the reference to the "gratification of his own wild fancies" (109) the suggestion that Ferdinand's self-knowledge could eventually embrace his own responsibility for his situation. But that potential is quickly dissipated as he tells Henrietta that he is "the victim of family profligacy and family pride" (111). In this passivity there is no conviction that love conquers all. Indeed, he feels helpless because he lacks the worldly considerations he was so recently willing to forego.

This summary of the first third of the novel establishes that there is both an ambivalence of mood and an ambivalence of values within the character of the hero. Behind his dilemma, of being engaged to one woman and in love with another, and behind the reversals of mood and values it occasions, lies a basic crisis of identity. There is a conflict between two opposing images of the self which he holds; between what he is by upbringing and what he is by nature, between the fair child of duty and filial love and the dark progeny of passionate imagination. Further examination of Ferdinand's passivity confirms the conclusion that with this story Disraeli was creating yet another fictional version of his own struggle for an identity comprising purity *and* success. For his hero the claims of both filial duty and profligate success are enslaving. And neither his defiance nor his self-pity seems capable of altering this. The inescapable imaginative fact is that Ferdinand is an Armine and whichever way he chooses to define his pure, true self, as devoted son or heroic romantic, he incurs the stigma of their poverty. The imagery describing Ferdinand's despair makes the point explicit: "Bound? The word makes me tremble. I shiver: I hear the clank of my fetters" (87). And later the narrator, in describing the hero's thoughts, says, "Nor could he forget his own wretched follies and that fatal visit to Bath, of which the consequences clanked upon his memory like degrading and disgraceful fetters" (109). The image is quite striking in its own right, but it is not the first time Disraeli had used it. His response to Daniel O'Connell's anti-Semitic attack on him at the time of the Taunton by-election – "I admire your scurrilous allusions to my origin. It is quite clear that the 'hereditary bondsman' has already forgotten the clank of his fetter"[16] – shows in comparison that in *Henrietta Temple* Disraeli is indeed again employing the Catholic disguise of the Jewish question in another attempt to create a fantasy which resolves satisfactorily the struggle for purity that still bedevils him.

Disraeli's hero does not, however, simply remain caught between the rationalizations of his dilemma. Accompanying Henrietta on her round of cottage charity, Ferdinand is struck by the "sweet simplicity" of her maternal care and sympathy for the peasants and he is overcome with nostalgia for "the time when he was a happy boy at his innocent home; his mother's boy, the child she so loved and looked after." With a sense of irrevocable isolation from that "sylvan paradise," he reflects upon "his dissipation, his vanity, his desperate folly, his hollow worldliness" and concludes that he cannot admit his beautiful companion into the "sweet and serene society" of that "unpolluted home," not because of "the profligacy of his ancestor," and not because of "the pride of his family," but because of "his own culpable and heartless career!" (114, 115). That Ferdinand's self-knowledge finally comes in the context of so much nostalgia for lost innocence is a measure of how much his passion is a function of his need for solicitude comparable to that which Henrietta has lavished upon the cottagers. The setting Disraeli has chosen is entirely appropriate, for the idealization of the cottagers' life is a function of the absolute trust implicit in the paternalistic tenant society.

That trust is the most important element of the love Ferdinand experiences is readily apparent from the rhetoric of the romantic scenes. The explicit fear of rejection and its attendant helplessness that overwhelms his declaration of passion recalls to mind the scene in *Contarini Fleming* where the hero slips from the fictional recitation of his desperate heroics into a confession of love for Christiana, the now married object of his childhood search for a substitute mother (10–16). That episode ends in Contarini's rage, confusion, "shame" and "irritation" when his passion is rejected and his proposal, that she share his destiny of glory, liberty, and love as an Aegean pirate, elicits only "blank astonishment" and alarm. The imaginative connection is further suggested by one of Ferdinand's earlier moods of Byronic defiance in which he imagines himself "winning Henrietta" and becoming a soldier of fortune: "Why might he not free Greece, or revolutionise Spain, or conquer the Brazils?" (129). In both scenes the extravagant imagery of exile confirms that the crucial issue is the heroine's acceptance or rejection of her suitor. But in *Henrietta Temple* the happy resolution of the anxiety is made possible by the hero's passivity. The significance of Ferdinand's fears is shown by the imagery used to describe his newly found resolution. Once having accepted him Henrietta becomes "the light in the Pharos, amid all his stormy fortunes." The "contest," really between past and future, honour and guilt, guilt and honour, can apparently be abandoned for "the ravishing and absorbing present" of requited love (146–7). The essence of that love is trust and purity, as is reflected by the anxiety of the confession itself – "if you but knew how I have fed but upon … one sacred image of absorbing life" (l44) – and by the implicit regression of Ferdinand's thoughts as he retires for the night. "Ferdinand is within his little chamber, that little chamber where his mother had bid him so passionate a farewell. Ah! he loves another woman better than his mother now. Nay, even a feeling of embarrassment and pain is associated with the recollection of that fond and elegant being … once … the model of all feminine perfection, and who had been to him so gentle and so devoted. He drives his mother from his thoughts. It is of another voice that he now muses" (147). In its thematic bearings this passage is complex, for, even as it works to establish the purity of the new love through infantilism, it recalls the guilt associated with the original betrayal. This is confirmed by the implied loss-of-loved-one fantasy contained in the authorial intrusion which immediately fol-lows: "All nature seems to bear an intimate relation to the being we adore; and as to us life would now appear intolerable … without this transcendent sympathy, so we cannot help fancying that were its sweet and subtle origin herself to quit this inspired scene, the universe itself would not be unconscious of its deprivation" (148). The same fantasy is dramatized within Ferdinand's thoughts in a subsequent chapter as he conjures up "a crowd of unfortunate incidents" ("what if this night she died? … Perhaps she was ill") (162, 160, 162) in her absence. The ob-vious insecurities of these fantasies reveal the fragility of the hero's new identity drawn from his love for Henrietta. Since that identity, with all its felicity, rests upon deceit of his cousin, family, and lover herself, it is not surprising that guilt compounds Ferdinand's insecurities: "were he to dare to reveal the truth … Would she not look upon him as the un-resisting libertine of the hour, engaging in levity her heart as he had already trifled with another's? For that absorbing and overwhelming passion, pure, primitive, and profound, to which she now responded with an enthusiasm as fresh, as ardent, and as immaculate, she would only recognise the fleeting fancy of a vain and worldly spirit" (163). This makes Ferdinand's struggle perfectly clear; however real their consequences, the vanity and egotism that have led to his predicament must be denied as false in order to maintain the purity of the true self for which alone he longs to be adored. This is the essence of the illu-sions of victimization in which he indulges and of the infantilism of his characterization at crucial moments. Indeed, these forms of passivity are essential to the evasion of responsibility for the continued deceits which, paradoxically, he must practise to maintain the innocence of his love. But the limits of this characterization are quickly reached when Ferdinand engages in the climactic deceit of involving his lover in a secret betrothal.

At this moment, the end of Book 3, the novel breaks rather sharply in two. The second half is very different in tone from the passionate lyricism of the first part; it is, on the whole, "an urbane comedy of manners." [17] Ferdinand's deceit is accidentally discovered by Henrietta, the lovers are separated, she becomes engaged to another nobleman, Ferdinand is arrested for his debts, and then the interests of true love are served by the generosity of friends and Ferdinand is reunited with Henrietta, who in the meantime has been discovered to be "one of the richest heiresses in England" (298). Despite the rapidly accumulating improbabilities of plot, this second half of *Henrietta Temple* is by far the best part of the novel and in some respects matches the best of all Disraeli's fiction. In the continuation the theme of sincerity and hypocrisy is absorbed into the new material. Ferdinand at first repeats the rationalizations of the victimized lover that reflect his continuing ambivalence of having both pride in and hatred of his heritage. This is sustained by the ironic fact that it is the dark, romantic qualities of his character, exemplified by his likeness to his grandfather's portrait hanging at Armine, to which Henrietta has been attracted but which now have destroyed his hopes of requited love. And while the ambivalence accounts most satisfactorily for the hero's procrastinations before the inexorable force of time, it admits of no further character development short of the hero's choosing a true self embodying one or the other, but not both, definitions of purity already established. Rather than have his protagonist make this choice Disraeli turns to the exigencies of plot to resolve the artistic and emotional dichotomies. The passivity which previously embodied his ambivalence is now used to begin the resolution or negation of the hero's emotional dilemma. Having in exhaustion and despair verging on madness confessed to the pious Glastonbury that his "heart and resolution have never for an instant faltered" in his love for the "innocent, so truly virtuous" Henrietta (232), Ferdinand collapses. But to the priest's offer of his bed Ferdinand replies in "a faint voice," "'No! let me go to my own room … where my mother said the day would come, oh! … Would there were only mother's love, and then I should not be here or thus!'" (235). And after the necessary arrangements, we are told, "Glastonbury and the stout serving-man bore him to his chamber, relieved him from his wet garments, and placed him in his earliest bed … Ferdinand … did not speak; and it was remarkable, that while he passively submitted to their undressing him, and seemed incapable of affording them the slightest aid, yet he thrust forth his hand to guard a lock of dark hair that was placed next to his heart" (236). In this scene the two identities, involving the purities of filial devotion and passionate romance, become one; the exhaustion of the desperate lover is absorbed by the regression to innocent childhood.

The task Disraeli sets himself in the second half of the novel is to establish this unity in the context of the hero's happiness as a dramatic actuality for him rather than simply an imaginative conception. To this end Ferdinand undergoes the purification of a nearly fatal fever which the attending physician can only attribute to psychic rather than bodily cause. His mother's love for him is re-established in the care lavished upon him during his illness. His cousin generously releases him from his engagement to her when she learns of his love for Henrietta. Katherine and Lord Montfort, Henrietta's considerate fiancé, nobly conspire with Lady Bellair and Glastonbury to reunite the original lovers, and when Ferdinand's arrest for debts prevents that from happening, it turns out to be "the luckiest incident in the world" (433). Lord Montfort finds he is really in love with Katherine, and Count Mirabel proves himself the best of friends by offering to loan Ferdinand the money he has just won at gambling, something which is made unnecessary by the receipt of a similar amount from his cousin. Finally, Lord Montfort offers to win Mr Temple over to the lovers' cause, and the families are united in benevolent approval of it.

In this marvellous conclusion Ferdinand's early extravagances are "but the consequences of his fiery youth," his debts prove trivial before the immense fortunes of the Grandisons and the Temples, and his deceits are but insignificant means to a greater end. Significantly, the tension in the novel's fantasy structure is completely dissolved in the satisfaction of the implied author: "Ferdinand had been faithful to Henrietta. His constancy to her was now rewarded ... Ferdinand Armine had great tenderness of disposition, and somewhat of a meditative mind; schooled by adversity, there was little doubt that his coming career would justify his favourable destiny" (436–7). From this the second half of *Henrietta Temple* may seem distressingly contrived, but it is in fact not so. When Disraeli abandons the hostile symbiosis of Ferdinand's characterization, he frees himself and his hero from the extravagant perturbations of self-absorption and with a completely passive protagonist writes a better novel: Childe Harold becomes Don Juan. The hero's providential destiny is unfolded in brilliantly depicted settings, varying from the drawing rooms of the aristocracy to the depressing surroundings of the sponging-house, and every "improbable" event is founded securely upon realistic characterization, from the compassion, charm, and generosity of the dandy, de Mirabel (modelled upon Count D'Orsay), to the buoyant optimism of the deferential gaoler. Even more impressive is the deft blend of sympathy and satire inherent in the narrative presentation.

What is remarkable, then, about this shift in tone is the extent to which the author has gained control over his material. The stability, which is reflected in the distance between narrator and hero of the authorial intrusions as well as in the elements of plot, characterization, and setting, suggests that the escape from passionate lyricism, manifest in the change from the world of Armine to the world of London, is as much an artistic as an autobiographical one. Compared with those of *Contarini Fleming* and *Alroy,* the other novels in which the struggle for purity is the dominant theme, the conclusion of *Henrietta Temple* represents a complete reversal. Contarini is left in desolation and exile with a vague hope in his future destiny. Alroy is killed for his defiance in the face of defeat. Since it is surely not accidental that Disraeli imagines in the end a blissful Ferdinand Armine as a member of Parliament with the good sense to support a "national" administration, it is reasonable to suggest that the change in this novel reflects a new sense of potential fulfilment in its author. In this regard the nature of the relation between the life and the fiction is important. At the time Disraeli wrote the conclusion in which his hero finds himself with a "beautiful bride ... whom he loved with intense passion" and a "noble fortune, which would permit him to redeem his inheritance," he was probably aware that his love affair with the real Henrietta was finished. Their last recorded meeting was in mid-August of 1836 and the entry of the Mutilated Diary for that year says in part, "Returned to Bradenham at the latter end of August; concluded *Henrietta Temple,*" and the one for the following year specifies that "during the election [of 1837, held in July] occurred the terrible catastrophe of Henrietta [exposed for adultery with Daniel Maclise] exactly one year after we had parted."[18] Still, Disraeli had found in the affair with Henrietta Sykes a kind of acceptance on which his imagination could feed, as witnessed to by the similarity of role he chose in courting Mrs Lewis some years later. Beyond this, the success of the *Morning Post* articles, the *Vindication of the English Constitution,* and the "Letters of Runnymede" had placed Disraeli at the very centre of Lord Lyndhurst's Ultra-Tory circle and brought him some acceptance in the Conservative party at large. He writes in the

Mutilated Diary for 1836, for example, "Establish my character as a great political writer by the *Letters* of *Runnymede*. Resume my acquaintance with Sir Robert Peel. My influence greatly increases from the perfect confidence of L. and my success as a political writer."[19] Disraeli's fame or notoriety largely resulted from his extravagant invective. But, nevertheless, Peel did recognize the genuine merit of the *Vindication* and was undoubtedly flattered by the glorification of himself in Letter V of the Runnymede series as St George, in whose "chivalry alone" lay England's hope of not being devoured by the dragon of Whiggism, and by Disraeli's dedication to him of the collected series when it appeared in July.[20] Peel's response was to invite the author "to dine with a party ... of the late government at the Carlton,"[21] so Disraeli's estimation of his newly won acceptance, if not influence, was not unwarranted.

Previous critics have resisted an autobiographical reading of *Henrietta Temple*. While Blake admits the original inspiration of the novel to have been Disraeli's affair with Lady Sykes, and describes its "authentic ring of personal passion," he finds that the discrepancies between reality and fiction establish that "Armine bears no resemblance whatever to Disraeli."[22] This is also the view expressed earlier by B.R. Jerman: "Except that his heroine takes on the Christian name of his mistress and that Lady Sykes' pet name for him, Amin, is transposed into the family name of his hero, there is, alas, little – too little – autobiography here. Ferdinand Armine in nowise resembles Benjamin Disraeli."[23] But these readings are too literalist in their definition of autobiography. *Henrietta Temple* is indeed an autobiographical novel, not in the sense that historical matter from the author's life gets directly into the fiction, but rather in the sense that the same pattern runs through the life and the fiction displaying there the same needs and motives. As such this novel embodies a fantasy in which Disraeli again returns to the fundamental problem of defining his identity. Here, once again, he adopts the Catholic disguise of his Jewish heritage for the purpose of establishing in his fiction the issue of his ambivalence about himself. The emphasis upon the hero's guilt about betraying his heritage and upon his need to re-establish his essential purity of heart is, in effect, a return to the fundamental issue of *Alroy*. In both novels that need is the basis for the rationalization of ambivalent behaviour and values that characterizes the psychic conflict at the heart of the story. In the first half of *Henrietta Temple* that rationalization of the hero's past and present deceits by means of the exaltation of transcendent love, a process in which both he and the implied author engage, fails to overcome his basic insecurity. This is shown by the loss-of-love fantasies manifest in both Ferdinand's thoughts and the author's intrusions. To the question of his identity the inescapable answer at first seems to be, "a Catholic," the fact of which binds him either to the twin inheritance of poverty and profligacy or to the guilt of self-denial. Disraeli's way out of this twofold emotional and artistic dilemma is a fantasy of acceptance that negates the hero's emotional ambivalence by means of his regression to childlike innocence and that escapes the artistic conflict (which definition of the hero's true self to choose) by means of his completely passive role in a comedy of manners.

Perhaps paradoxically this resolution of the struggle for "purity" and "success" reflects Disraeli's new confidence in eventually being able to transcend the conflicting senses of his own identity. Even as wish fulfilment this fantasy of acceptance is a confident response on Disraeli's part to the question, "What Is He?"[24] The fictional answer, in its simplest form, is that the hero is lovable – so lovable that all his friends, his mother, his cousin, and Henrietta want to ensure his happiness. Further, the character of the love he wishes for – the maternal, unquestioning adoration – comes true for him. As a result, Ferdinand's compelling need to insist upon his "purity" of heart is sanctioned by other people's responses to him. And, while he is a completely passive hero amid the events that lead to his finally being accepted as Henrietta's husband, that resolution entails a destiny of power, wealth, and, by virtue of his wife's nobility, a position among the nation's Protestant aristocracy. Since the corollaries of Disraeli's fundamental doubts about his identity are the questions of whether he will succeed and whether he will be accepted among England's social and political elite, both the tone and content of the concluding fantasy in *Henrietta Temple* show that at least an imaginative confidence pervades his hope, undoubtedly strengthened by the Sykes affair and the recent political recognition, that he can achieve success and be loved for himself at the same time.

Thus while the characterizations, plot, and setting in the concluding portion of *Henrietta Temple* are only superficially autobiographical in a literal sense, the theme of that ending is profoundly so in an imaginative one. And looking at this novel in the context of his earlier ones helps reveal the point of Disraeli's interest in this autobiographical mode of fiction. As both the structure of the fantasies within the characterizations of the heroes and the fantasy structure of the plots themselves show, in embodying the ambivalences of his senses of his own identity in these early novels, Disraeli was able to explore the possibilities of various roles and so to some extent make the fiction serve the function of self-realization. Readers of Disraeli's deservedly better-known novels, the political trilogy of *Coningsby*, *Sybil*, and *Tancred*, and the later ones, *Lothair* and *Endymion*, are aware that from the 1840s on his fiction came to serve other overt political purposes. Yet it can be shown that even as Disraeli attempted to use fiction as a medium for discussing the nature of political parties, the state of the nation, or the role of the Church, he was in significant ways still concerned with both the public and private dimensions of his own identity, indeed, perhaps more compellingly so as the heroic role became realizable in fact as well as fancy. It would not seem to be an extravagant claim, therefore, that a convincing assessment of the artistic quality and significance of his more important novels cannot be made without some awareness of the relation between his continuing use of the autobiographical mode of fiction and the political concerns those works reflect.

5

What Is He? The Crisis Examined[1]

As has been shown, Disraeli's need to work out fictional extensions of the claims of "purity" and the claims of "success" was heightened by the ambivalence he felt about both of these "identities" and by the discrepancy between what he felt himself to be – either innately or demonstrably superior – and what he was perceived to be by the majority of the Wycombe constituents – insincere and opportunistic. The overt anti-Semitism that his opponents exploited, and the flamboyance of his own campaigns had helped to consolidate the issues of his superiority and his sincerity within Disraeli's mind after his defeat in the second Wycombe election. And the fictions, including *A Year at Hartlebury*, bear testimony of that change.

In a similar way, Disraeli's political endeavours in the next few years are a witness to his need to reconcile the disparity between the ideal of an innate integrity and his fierce determination to succeed in fulfilling his ambitions. In effect, this was a need to resolve his own confusions of identity, but it was also a need to negate the discrepancy between his private sense of himself, however defined, and the voters' view of him. When, therefore, he returned to politics in 1833, Disraeli's most pressing problem was to find a political identity that solved both his private and his public dilemmas.

The immediate political problem was to counter the charges of inconsistency, which he knew had played a large part in his previous defeats, and which, one must now suspect, also had a hidden but deep personal resonance. With characteristic energy he sets out to explain his own position – past, present, and future, in the most comprehensive terms. And in laying the ghost of the apparent past insincerity of being both a Radical and a Tory, he finds both a respectable stance on the current issue of reform and the prospect of future heroics. The political identity that Disraeli now begins to fashion is profoundly conservative. But the most interesting aspect of it is that the grand conception of true Toryism which he begins to espouse is in large measure a product of his imaginative senses of himself – of his fantasies about the possible roles of the innately and demonstrably superior person he felt himself to be.

The years of Disraeli's political apprenticeship, 1832–7, are remarkable in several ways, for he remained surprisingly buoyant despite the new electoral defeats at Wycombe and Taunton, the scandal of his love affair with Lady Henrietta Sykes, and the continual harassments that came with his very large debts.[2] Any one of these might have sunk the career of someone less inspired. But it was not simply Disraeli's sense of his own "genius" that kept him afloat; events, both public and private, were more propitious than they seemed. And, although Disraeli had clearly seen the necessity of demonstrating his extraordinary powers to the sceptical public, that was only a partial resolution of his "identity crisis." The fantasy of being immediately recognized as innately superior had lost none of its attractiveness for him, and the tensions of his "struggle for purity," to which that fantasy was connected, had not been vanquished. Yet judging by the evidence of his overtly political writings, Disraeli was quite successful during these years in beginning the vindication of his "English constitution." The explanation for this success lies in part in the distinction between external appearance and internal reality.

During the second Wycombe campaign (the first on the new franchise) Disraeli began to refer with admiration to the principles of "my Lord Bolingbroke."[3] And despite the shifts in emphasis in the next two or three contests, which gained him a reputation for inconsistency, if not insincerity, all of Disraeli's subsequent speeches and political writings from this period reflect the continually deepening influence of Bolingbroke's ideas. In his address of 1 October 1832 to the electors at Wycombe, the attack on the debased nature of the political parties (especially the factious Whigs), the catastrophic view of the country's impending doom, and the rallying cry to form "a great national party" are all obviously resonant with the politics of the Augustan period, whatever their legitimacy in the current context. And more specifically, so are his charges of Whig financial mismanagement and neglect of the agricultural interest, his pride in his independence of party labels, his support of "the true principles … of our admirable constitution," and his advocacy of triennial Parliaments.[4] Disraeli's address to the electors of the county of Buckinghamshire, issued the day after his defeat at Wycombe, appears to be equally derivative, as well as expedient, in that he stresses that he is "the supporter of that great interest which is *the only solid basis of the social fabric*" (emphasis added), that of the farmer.[5] Disraeli withdrew from the contest in Buckinghamshire when he found that he had been anticipated and his next address, in April, 1833, was to the electors of the borough of Marylebone, where in addition to the call for triennial Parliaments and support for the ballot, he stresses a rather different, though equally historic posture of opposition to the Whigs – his independence as "one of a family untainted by the receipt of public money," his "unlimited confidence in the genius of the British nation," and the need for an elevation of the moral condition of the people.[6] So although, as Robert Blake says, Disraeli "trimmed his sails to the prevailing wind" as he moved between rural and urban constituencies,[7] it is also true that his anti-Whig views contain a perspective of a hundred years.

Nevertheless, this was lost upon most of Disraeli's audience, and his enemies were quick to point out the flagrant opportunism, which they thought lay behind his standing consecutively as a Radical, a Radical Tory, a Tory Radical, and again as a Radical. However often he proclaimed his sincerity and consistency, the superficial labels contradicted him. It is clear now, however, that the issue of his insincerity had a profound private as well as a public dimension for Disraeli – that such charges, as well as being politically harmful, were connected with traumas involving his sense of himself going back to his relationship with his mother and his earliest awareness of his Jewish heritage. It is not surprising, therefore, that he felt compelled to dwell upon his consistency rather than ignore it and so minimize it as a political issue. Bolingbroke was also thought by his enemies to be treacherously opportunistic and insincere, a fact that partially explains why he was such an attractive martyr for Disraeli. In any case, Disraeli chose to discuss his sincerity and the title of his next work, *"What Is He?"* published in April 1833 in connection with the expected vacancy in Marylebone, reveals the extent of his defensiveness.[8]

"What Is He?" appears to be much more radical than it actually is, but its significance as a political statement cannot be found in a party label. Although the piece begins with the contention that neither the Tories nor the Whigs can carry on the Government "with the present State machinery," and though it immediately recognizes that a third party has proposed alterations of that machinery, Disraeli does not endorse

the Radicals' position. Rather, he explicitly refers to what "they believe" (16, 17). This is, thus, no more than a renewal of his earlier charges that "Toryism is worn out" and that the Whigs are contemptible.[9] He then goes on to extol "strong Government" based on "public confidence" and to lament the fact that "by the recent change we have deserted the old ('aristocratic') principle of Government without adopting a new one" (17). It is obvious to Disraeli that without an "impelling principle" the Government cannot act, and it is further "evident" to him that without it, public confidence must inevitably decrease and "a public convulsion ... soon occur": "at present Property only is threatened; in a few months it will be a question as to the preservation of Order; another year and we must struggle for Civilisation" (17). The capitalized concern for "Property," "Order," and "Civilisation" is reminiscent of the Tory fears of Walpole's administration and the catastrophic view is similar to that expressed in the cataclysmic language of Alexander Pope, who was a member of Bolingbroke's "Opposition" circle.

Disraeli would seem to be genuinely radical when he next says that he believes it "utterly impossible to revert to the aristocratic principle" and therefore "absolutely necessary to advance to the new or the democratic principle" (18). But again appearances are deceiving. If Disraeli did not quite have the prescience of Lord Grey, to see the Reform Bill of 1832 as "a bulwark of aristocracy,"[10] he did recognize that the bill itself was "essentially aristocratic" in nature and that the composition of the House of Commons was no less so after the general election on the new franchise (18–19). He thought that the intention behind the bill was to "destroy Toryism" and increase the power of the Whigs. And he insisted that "THE ARISTOCRATIC PRINCIPLE HAS BEEN DESTROYED IN THIS COUNTRY, NOT BY THE REFORM ACT, BUT BY THE MEANS BY WHICH THE REFORM ACT WAS PASSED" (19). That is, the Government "deserted" the aristocratic principle when it forced passage of the bill by the threat of creating new peers.

It is important to understand what Disraeli meant by the phrases "aristocratic" and "democratic principles." In his conclusion he refers to the "transition from Feudal to Federal principles of government" that has characterized the last three centuries of European history and that makes him think that restoration of the "aristocratic principle" in England is impracticable (22).[11] So it would seem that by the phrase "aristocratic principle" Disraeli is referring to the idea of government exclusively by the great landowning order, who enjoyed their feudal power to rule under the twin constraints of privilege and responsibility.

In contrast the phrase "democratic principle" is linked to the word "Federal," by which Disraeli seems to be referring to a union of classes or interests that would exercise their governing power in the national interest through the persons of their leaders (22). That those best fitted for leadership by ability, experience, and education would in most cases still be members of the aristocracy is not explicitly stated in this pamphlet, but it is clearly Disraeli's opinion in subsequent works. For the moment, he urges the Tories and Radicals to merge in the formation of a "National Party," which would quickly be able to govern (were the Septennial Act repealed and "Election by Ballot" instituted) with the full confidence of the majority, not of the population, but rather, of those classes and interests now enfranchised (20–1). Disraeli was thus advocating the "democratic" or limited electoral process because he thought that it would replace a Whig oligarchy acting in its own interest with a government acting in the interest of the whole nation.

Yet, having developed this discussion of political machinery and practical remedies, Disraeli ends with a lapse of faith in his own argument. He reverts to the "anxiety, if not … terror" with which a "Statesman must view the present portents" and, as would Thomas Carlyle, he places his hope in "the influence of individual character": "Great spirits may yet arise to guide the groaning helm through the world of troubled waters – spirits whose proud destiny it may still be at the same time to maintain the glory of the Empire and to secure the happiness of the People" (22). Similarly, Bolingbroke, having devoted almost the entire canon of his political writing to attacking the Whig corruption of the political process (and, incidentally, attempting the repeal of the Septennial Act in 1734),[12] in the end placed his hope in the concept of "The Patriot King" whose qualities of individual character would restore or protect the "nation's spirit."[13] Disraeli's choice of imagery may not be anything more than the rhetorical use of a cliché, but it is worth noticing that Bolingbroke also uses the ship of state metaphor in *The Patriot King* when he says that the reign of such a monarch is an occasion that "should be improved, like snatches of fair weather at sea, to repair the damages sustained in the last storm, and to prepare to resist the next" (Bolingbroke, 4:273).

Incidental to his urging the formation of a National Party a few pages earlier, Disraeli inserted one of his set-pieces on insincerity and inconsistency, clearly a defence against the anticipated repetition of such charges against himself: "He is a mean-spirited wretch who is restrained from doing his duty by the fear of being held up as insincere and inconsistent by those who are incapable of forming an opinion on public affairs; and who, were it not for the individual 'inconsistency' which they brand, would often become the victims of their own incapacity and ignorance" (20). And before going on to implicitly assert the logic and rationality of his own ideas, Disraeli adds, "A great mind that thinks and feels is never inconsistent, and never insincere" (20). It is not surprising then that, when he finished reading the pamphlet, Isaac could pointedly ask, "Who will be the proud spirit?"[14] Thus it might be reasonable to claim that Disraeli imagined himself eventually inheriting the heroic role, if not the crown of Bolingbroke's patriot king. After all, the hero of *Alroy* could sometimes feel himself a god[15] and Disraeli did tell Lord Melbourne, when they first met a little more than a year later, "I want to be Prime Minister."[16] It should be remembered, however, that Disraeli's identification with the politics of the Augustan period is the result of an imaginative projection of his own circumstances.[17] Neither his analysis of the past, nor his interpretation of the present can be considered as "the historical truth," for he was writing propaganda, not history. The purpose of drawing attention to the connection between Bolingbroke's and Disraeli's ideas is, then, not just to argue that the latter's actions and political creed in this period were somewhat more consistent than usually allowed, but rather to suggest, as the evidence will soon show more fully, that Disraeli's political career was being shaped as much by an imaginative pattern involving his continuing fantasies of himself as by a rational consideration of his present circumstances. Bolingbroke and the Opposition politics of the eighteenth century were as much a part of those fantasies as they were of the external reality of the 1830s.

I

The next piece of political writing from Disraeli's pen was composed while he was under the influence of his passion for Henrietta Sykes. In the autumn of 1833 he undertook to fulfil a vision that had occurred to him on his Eastern tour and write an epic poem on the revolutionary "spirit of his Time" and so take his place in the tradition of Homer, Virgil, Dante, and Milton.[18] But however "sublime" he thought the conception and the potential results for literature and himself, Disraeli also had the practical motive of earning some money and relieving the pressure of his debts and ruinous expenses.[19]

Book 1 of *The Revolutionary Epick* was published by Edward Moxon in March 1834 and Books 2 and 3 in June. The poem was not a financial success and Disraeli quickly gave it up, as he had promised he would in the Preface should its reception be unfavourable. The fragment of some 3600 of the projected 30,000 lines, nevertheless, gives a very good idea of what Disraeli had in mind. It is obvious that much of his immediate inspiration was drawn from Percy Shelley's works, and there are faint echoes of the poems of Lord Byron and William Blake in various places. But the most significant aspect of the poem's expression is purely Augustan and represents a continuation of the process of political definition reflected in *"What Is He?"* The structure of the poem is very simple. Disraeli imagines "the Genius of Feudalism (Magros) and the Genius of Federalism (Lyridon) appearing before the Almighty Throne (of Demogorgon) and pleading their respective and antagonistic causes." This consumes the first two Books. The "mystical" decree of the Omnipotent gives rise in Book 3 to the birth of Napoleon, "a man … of supernatural energies," who "adopts the Federal or Democratic side," and whose career is then detailed.[20]

Monypenny interprets the poem to represent "the triumph of the 'Federal' side and the apotheosis of Napoleon." This supports his division of Disraeli's personality into two sides, the revolutionary and the conservative. He sees both as genuine aspects of his nature; the former providing the "sympathy with the modern spirit," which makes his conservatism "so sane, so robust, and so fruitful," while the latter, embodying a "reverence for the past, a Semitic feeling for religion," and an "instinct" for "order" and "tradition," is "the front presented to the world in his subsequent career."[21] This is an inadequate and simplistic view of Disraeli's personality, for it misreads both the external and internal evidence and it does not really explain the seemingly incongruous elements of his political and literary careers. Monypenny uses a misquoted excerpt from the Mutilated Diary out of context to establish the *reality* of Disraeli's "revolutionary" sentiments: "'My mind is a revolutionary mind': that was true, and perhaps especially true when it was written and when the *Revolutionary Epick* was conceived. Disraeli had been fascinated by the great drama in which the modern spirit was unfolding itself, and hence we get in the *Epick* the triumph of the 'Federal' side and the apotheosis of Napoleon."[22] But in the Mutilated Diary, Disraeli actually wrote:

The world calls me *"conceited."* The world is in error. I trace all the blunders of my life to sacrificing my own opinion to that of others. When I was considered very conceited *indeed*, I was nervous, and had self confidence

only by fits. I intend in future to act entirely from my own impulse. I have
an unerring instinct. I can read characters at a glance; few men can deceive
me. My mind is a continental mind. It is a revolutionary mind. I am only
truly great in action. If ever I am placed in a truly eminent position I shall
prove this. I co[ul]d rule the House of Commons, altho' there wo[ul]d be a
great prejudice against me at first.[23]

The context of the word "revolutionary" shows that it has no reference to political ideas as such. It demonstrates, rather, that Disraeli is
engaged in an attempt at self-definition of a more private kind, similar
to that already embodied in *The Rise of Iskander*. When he does extend
the attempt into the realm of ideology, having just asserted, "My works
are the embodification of my feelings," Disraeli makes the nature of his
"revolutionary" mind very clear: "The Utilitarians in Politics are like
the Unitarians in Religion. Both omit Imagination in their systems, and
Imagination governs Mankind."[24] He is distinguishing the precise nature of his superiority to other men and attempting to find a role in
which he can enlist his special capacities and power. It is, thus, un-
warrantable to cite this passage as evidence for a revolutionary political
sympathy, the more so given Disraeli's opposition to Whig use of power
in passing the Reform Bill.

Internal evidence from *The Revolutionary Epick* also shows that
Monypenny's analysis overstates the case. The poem begins with a vision of the corrupt earth fallen from the grace of a divinely sanctioned
order, and with the assertion that the regeneration of harmony can only
be achieved by means of Faith and Fealty, the elements of feudalism
that occasion the birth of Loyalty, upon which the fabric of civilization
depends. Magros's defence of the aristocratic principle is no more than
a summary of Augustan social and political theory and, as such, is
marked with nostalgia. Ultimate Power comes from God and the Great
Chain of Being has links within human nature and society: "Thus in
Kings alone,/ And in their delegates, the noble streams/ These royal
sources feed, should Power subsist/ For chosen few its whole exercise;/ Although its sovereign care the multitude/ May rightly claim
and challenge for their own" (*Rev. Epick*, 25–6). Hence the appropriate
use of the organic metaphors and the emphasis on the parallel in
Nature: "Deep in the strata of the human heart,/ The seeds of Aristocracy
are sown/ … Yes! where'er we gaze,/ GRADATION is the spell of
Nature's sway,/ Hence Durability, the power of gods;/ Hence Order,
Happiness, and Life; and hence/ Of parts discordant one harmonious

whole./ And shall a fitter type for man be found/ Than this divine Creation?" (*Rev. Epick*, 25, 36). This and much else in Book 1 is reminiscent of *An Essay on Man*, which it is interesting to note was dedicated to Bolingbroke.[25] But Disraeli's purposes are very different from Pope's. Although Disraeli accepts the reasonableness of the divinely created order and sees its connection with the essence of civilization in the same terms, his real interest is not in the operation of universal reason but rather in the glorification of individualism.

When Disraeli describes the aristocracy the emphasis is placed upon their personal attributes. And the right to power is derived from the individual instance of these qualities. The "Noble that mankind demands … the Man a nation loves to trust," is described as "refined,/ Serene, courteous, learned, thoughtful and brave,/ As full of charity as noble pomp," and he stands as a pledge that "in the tempests of the world,/ The stream of culture shall not backward ebb" (*Rev. Epick*, 27). "Trust" is an important word in these lines. Here and in virtually every other place where Disraeli elaborates his conception of the aristocracy, it is the affective centre of his ideal. This is further suggested when Disraeli adds that the aristocracy is formed, not by its symbols – "the ermined stole, the starry breast, the coroneted brow," but rather by the irresistible "enduring power Genius wields" to mark "the man inspired from the crowd": "He who leads/ Victorious armies; or his subtle soul/ Reveals in stately councils; he who makes/ The Judgment Seat an oracle: the seer,/ That to the anguish of our earthly life/ Pours forth his heavenly balm, and whispers hope;/ The merchant and his thousand argosies,/ Bearing exotic tribute – by such men/ Are nations formed and flourish" (*Rev. Epick*, 38). A superior class, Disraeli argues, is part of the natural order, as native to states as is fragrance to the rose, though it is clear that the manifestations of individual "Genius" include both innate and demonstrated superiority. It is also worth noting that this theory of a hierarchical social and political order founded on trust is the expression of a man whose conflicting senses of his own identity were shaped by a "crisis of trust." It is not surprising, then, that in both the historical and contemporary context, there is a child-parent metaphor behind the idea of the "harmonious" and stable social and political structure that Disraeli extols. But the paternalism (perhaps it should be called "maternalism") in Disraeli's political theories is too well known to need belabouring. The description of "the noble attributes of man" is sufficient to establish their function in the "aristocratic" system: "Learning and Valour, Charity and Faith/ And chief of all, that Social

Discipline,/ Instinctive in the heart of cultured man,/ That prompts the weaker and the poor to view/ In their more able brethren leaders apt/ To guide and aid" (*Rev. Epick*, 37).

In the description of the effects of federalism, as expressed in Book 1, there is further justification for insisting upon a private dimension of Disraeli's political ideology. We are shown "the spectre of a nation, wild and red/ With parricidal gore." The people "wave/ Their flaming torches with a maniac glare,/ In ruin revelling." And amid the "Havoc" "all the charities of life are vanished,/ And all the bands of sweet existence broken" (*Rev. Epick*, 34). France then appears: "o'er her head a flag of triple tint,/ And each an emblem of that nation's state./ Red for their blood and Purple for their shame,/ And white for all their craven cruelty,/ Floats with denouncing spell – EQUALITY" (*Rev. Epick*, 35). Since this is the implied parental (aristocratic) view of the revolution, the language of violence, nostalgia, and guilt might easily lead a Freudian critic to extend the metaphor and see an Oedipal conflict beneath it. But it would seem sufficient to say that such language suggests that the "aristocratic principle," by means of the child-parent metaphor, offers Disraeli a return to innocence, even as, paradoxically, he envisions a paternalistic role for himself. There is further evidence for this idea at the end of Book 1 where Faith and Fealty describe to Magros the ravages of "the monster CHANGE," now explicitly identified with the Reform movement in England (*Rev. Epick*, 43, 44). The image, however clichéd, and despite the poetic licence, is appropriate to innocent childhood's nightmares and fairy tales. It suggests that within the aristocratic point of view, with which Disraeli identifies, there is an element of child-like fear. This in turn would suggest that personal insecurity may well have contributed to Disraeli's sudden shift from the promise of a "National Party" to the "hope" in a modern version of Bolingbroke's "Patriot King" at the conclusion of *What Is He?*

Disraeli's early political ideology, as it begins to be explicitly formulated, is thus personally fulfilling on three different levels. As conscious, explicit, political statement, it provides both an idealistic and a practical base from which to oppose the Whigs. The validity of tarring Lord Grey with Robert Walpole's brush is essentially irrelevant. Disraeli found it plausible and expedient to do so, for charges of corruption and unprincipled behaviour make for effective rhetoric, if not always winning margins. Second, his undoubtedly conscious identification with Bolingbroke, the political martyr, offered Disraeli a heroic and noble defence of his chosen position in what was clearly for the moment a losing cause. Finally, as unconscious expression, the ideology at least temporarily resolves some of the conflicts within his sense of himself by combining the prospect of enormous success with a return to innocence and purity, and by linking the possibility of demonstrating his greatness with the claim of innate superiority.

The fundamental dichotomy between his Jewish and English (or Christian) identities was not so easily absorbed. And however much Disraeli might fancy himself a member of the "natural aristocracy" by virtue of his "genius," he remained extremely vulnerable to the "Jewish question" precisely because, as the unsatisfactory conclusion of *Alroy* suggests, only death could release him from it. *The Rise of Iskander*, in which the hero achieves power while being secretly true to his natural heritage, whether seen as a wish-fulfilment or a fictional statement of intention, consequently presents a parallel with the author's life until such time as Disraeli begins to express his unique version of Judaic-Christian unity. Nevertheless, the expressions of primitive Toryism, which comprise the essence of his political statements, and which are as much the result of romantic projection as rational analysis, have roots deep in Disraeli's psyche. The political ideology, as such, might be said to contain a fantasy structure closely related to that of the novels.

At the end of Book 1 of *The Revolutionary Epick* Magros goes forth to slay the monster, CHANGE, which at the critical moment takes the shape of Lyridon (46–7). At that point the "Genius of Federalism" is described as being "in the service of the devil," further evidence that Disraeli's sympathies lie with the opposing spirit of aristocracy. But it is equally important that Lyridon's account of the development of federalism is inherently the Whig view of human nature and society. Behind the glorification of rationality as the light of civilization, contrasting with the dark storm of savagery, are the ideas of Thomas Hobbes and John Locke. Their emphasis upon the empirical, contractual theory of moral and social order based on an individualist state of nature is the direct opposite of Bolingbroke's insistence upon a divine, natural moral law manifest on earth in the familial origins of society.[26] Lyridon's praise of Solon, who "came to rescue the world from Night like a beacon of a safe port" and "first proclaimed,/ Labour was Property, and Virtue, Worth" (*Rev. Epick*, 67), is thus in context a backward projection of the Benthamite extension of British empiricism that Disraeli condemns in the Mutilated Diary and had satirized years before in *The Voyage of Captain Popanilla*. The very title of that work suggests his early imaginative affinity with Jonathan Swift and Alexander Pope, both

members of the Augustan "Opposition" circle. So when Lyridon attributes the fall of Rome to tyranny ("the sea into which the fountain of
Superstition flows," *Rev. Epick*, 63–4) and to corruption ("the passions
of Asia embodied in Cleopatra" 70), and then goes on to place man's
hope, not in "the heart of noble man" in which there is "a drop inherent
with his Life,/ Tainting his nature with a moral pest" (71), but in
"Knowledge," which is "POWER sharper than the sword,/ And swifter
than the arrow" (73), it is worth keeping in mind Disraeli's mockery of
Benthamism and false Reason in 1828.

The subsequent account of the growth of the female child "OPINION"
(daughter of "PHYSICAL STRENGTH" and "MORAL FORCE" who is
nourished by "Knowledge," "TRUTH," and "HOPE," *Rev. Epick*, 75–6)
and of her role in history prior to being called to "ALBION" is presented
in idealistic terms that partially reflect the youthful Romantics' optimism about revolutionary movements. The tribute to the American
Revolution ends with "Man now/ Lord of himself" and the "dark-
minded" reign of "Force," "Fraud" and "Fear" replaced by the light of
the "glorious Sun":

> But now, with front erect and gaze supreme,
> His Maker man indeed resembles;
> …
> Famine, Disease, and Misery, and Care,
> Have left this equal land: the rich man's curse,
> And harsh command, awake no echoes here.
> God is no more the only test of worth,
> But Labour hath its honour;
> …
>   FLATTERY's fatal brood
> Of pestilential falsehood wither here,
> Where POWER is VIRTUE.   (*Rev. Epick*, 89–90)

The emotive language of this description of how the "Federal Principle"
provides for the flourishing of "HOPE," "AFFECTION," "SYMPATHY,"
"TRUTH," "JUSTICE," "SCIENCE," and "POESY" (90), is clearly at
odds with the rationalist conclusion that "Knowledge" is "POWER"
and "POWER" is "VIRTUE." As such, it points towards one of the central paradoxes of the Romantic movement, which Disraeli has not surprisingly absorbed from his reading of Blake and Shelley. "OPINION's"
praise of "FRANCE" makes the point explicit:

Thou hope of craven Europe! As the flower
Springs from the aloe's ancient breast of thorns,
Thus mid the sorrows of a worn-out world,
Thou risest with thy beauty: full of hope,
And pride, and freshness! ...
... FRANCE! I hail thee now,
Not for the wanton richness of thy soil,
Not for the beauty of thy bright-eyed daughters,
... but I do hail thee,
That REASON in thy land hath found a dwelling,
And built a glorious temple! (*Rev. Epick*, 92)

As Carl Woodring pointed out,[27] there is an inherent contradiction between the intellectual commitment to egalitarian politics that deny the value of the past and the artistic use of organic metaphors that proclaim the roots of the contemporary. The affirmation of "REASON" at this point is thus derivative of Locke's individualism and the contractual theory of government, while the expression of it seems related to the Romantic conception of the One Life and, as such, is essentially antifederalist in impulse.

Disraeli was undoubtedly drawing upon Shelley's *Prometheus Unbound* for part of his inspiration for *The Revolutionary Epick*. The myth of Prometheus, the benefactor of mankind, transcending the evil tyranny of Jupiter and symbolically freeing humanity for a happy existence of love, truth, and virtue by the simple act of willing that there should be no evil, is superficially an appropriate model. But in his eagerness to transfer the myth to the realm of European and British politics Disraeli ignores the essential fact that it is an act of love (of pity and self-awareness) and not "REASON" (or external "Knowledge" and "POWER") that enables Demogorgon to overthrow Jupiter.[28] Disraeli's attempt to blend the two in his depiction of federalism suggests that in reading Shelley he equated the early Godwinian republicanism of the young poet with the thought of the later works. In his haste to recreate the antifeudal principle in action Disraeli ignored or was blind to the implications of reformist and revolutionary idealism that soon became apparent to most of the major Romantic poets. All of this suggests the superficiality of Disraeli's commitment to the spirit of federalism.

Commitment to something is, however, not the same as a recognition or acceptance of it. And though Disraeli may have been an insensitive reader of romantic poetry, he was a very acute observer of post-Reform

Bill political reality. From the outset of his parliamentary career he saw the inevitability of reform and would have no part in the lost cause of opposition to it.[29] A similar pragmatic perspective on the manifestation of the federalist principle lies within the structure of *The Revolutionary Epick*, where the debate between Magros and Lyridon is followed by "THE DECREE OF DEMOGORGON" (Necessity):

> ... what seems Chance to man or higher spirits,
> Is Truth refined to sheer Divinity.
> ...
> In Man alone the fate of Man is placed.
> Lo! where the piny mountains proudly rise
> From the blue bosom of the midland sea
> A standard waves, and he who grasps its staff,
> Nor King, nor deputy of Kings is he,
> Yet greater than all Kings. Unknown indeed,
> Like some immortal thing he walks the earth,
> That soon shall tremble at his tread.
> SPIRITS then seek, for unto him are given
> Fortunes unproved by human life before!   (*Rev. Epick*, 99)

There is no authorial endorsement of Napoleon in this passage, simply a recognition of his inevitable power and a conviction that his career will eventually illuminate divine truth. In Book 3 Napoleon chooses to adopt the principle of federalism, and his conquest of Europe is recounted, ending with his triumphant entrance to Milan and the planting of the tree of liberty. This is as far as Disraeli got with his epic before the disappointing public response forced him to abandon it. But since he had indicated to Sara Austen that "probably it co[ul]d not be completed under 30,000 lines,[30] it is unreasonable to conclude that the one-tenth completed shows Disraeli's acceptance of the ultimate victory of federalism. Two other details also suggest a far different conclusion – the authorial intrusion just before the end of the fragment, which anticipates the Battle of Waterloo, and the fact that Disraeli had requested, and been courteously declined, permission to dedicate his epic poem to the Duke of Wellington.[31] As a consequence, there is no warrant for Raymond Maître's conclusion, in agreement with Monypenny, that "l'opposition des tendances conservatrices et progressistes, reflet de la dualité de son caractère."[32] Rather, it is more plausible to suggest that in this embodiment of the spirits of feudalism and federalism Disraeli is elaborating the ideational basis of his forthcoming alliance with the Tory party. Indeed, it is quite possible that, if the poem had been completed, it would have shown clearly that his intellectual acceptance of the passing of the "aristocratic principle" in "*What Is He?*" did not preclude a wish for its restoration. And though *The Revolutionary Epick* does not support the contention that there is an ideological ambivalence in Disraeli's political stance at this time, it is true that the tension between his desire for acceptance of his innate superiority and his recognition of the necessity of proving his greatness continues to exist in political terms. This is the basis for the dichotomy of the nostalgic indulgence in fantasy and the cynical exploitation of opportunity that distinguishes his political behaviour in the 1830s. In any case, a large part of Disraeli's subsequent political writing, whether journalism or fiction, reflects the conviction that, if it cannot be restored to its original state, the "aristocratic principle" must be regenerated in a new form.

The length of the foregoing analysis might suggest that Disraeli's "epic" poem was of some literary value. To the contrary, the contemporary public's tepid response was justified. Blake is not exaggerating when he describes the effort as "devoid of inspiration" and "destitute of literary merit."[33] In style and thought it is extremely derivative and the result is more rhetoric than poetry. The real significance of *The Revolutionary Epick*, as with the preceding pamphlet, is in the light it sheds on the growth of Disraeli's political ideas in relation to his sense of himself.

II

The earliest expressions of Disraeli's Toryism, as they are found in "*What Is He?*" and *The Revolutionary Epick*, are quite clearly informed by the same terms and needs as are his fictions. In the former pamphlet his call for a "National Party" to govern in the national interest is made in the context of essentially nostalgic reference to the issues and posture of Viscount Bolingbroke's heroic opposition to Whiggery in the early eighteenth century. And that context explicitly manifests the current political opportunity for an as yet unknown genius or "Great spirit" to demonstrate his superiority. Yet that pragmatic necessity is balanced by a rather different idealistic conception when Disraeli turns to the abstract political commentary of his epic poem. There, the true, Conservative political leader is enshrined as a member of the natural aristocracy whose divinely sanctioned grace and power stem from the innate superiority of their personal attributes – their essential genius. So, while in practical terms Disraeli conceived of a political recognition in which the duty of the moment transcended the hero's previous inconsistencies, in theoretical terms he imagined a political recognition in which the paternalism of the eternal hierarchy embodies the innocence and purity of both parties – the rulers and the governed. It is fair to suggest, therefore, that the same tension between the conflicting claims of "purity" and "success" that forms the fantasy structure of the early novels and tales also shapes the development of Disraeli's political thought in the same period. Just as his succeeding fictions reveal a growing ambivalence on their author's part towards both of the alternatively imaginable identities for his heroes, so the formative years of his political career manifest a need on Disraeli's part to find a political identity that would satisfy both his senses of himself. In this respect he had to resolve the discrepancy between what he felt himself to be and what he was perceived to be. In two very real senses this was a matter of expediency.

In the first seven months of 1834 Disraeli became a regularly invited guest at the houses of some of the fashionable aristocratic London hostesses. His letters to his sister at this time describe a constant whirl of social excitement; balls, parties, dinners, and breakfasts followed one upon the other as he was lionized for his wit and extravagant appearance. This social success was largely the result of his literary and personal notoriety as "the author of *Vivian Grey*" and the lover of Henrietta Sykes, and his hostesses tended to be those more concerned with fashion than propriety. But at these houses Disraeli made the acquaintance of a number of politically important men, Radicals of such varying complexion as Lord Durham and Daniel O'Connell, and Tories of such fame as the Duke of Wellington and Lord Lyndhurst. One of the more significant encounters was his meeting with the Whig Lord Melbourne, soon to be successor to Earl Grey. Disraeli's famous remark about wanting to be prime minister is invariably cited for its striking irony, but the most important part of Melbourne's lengthy and astonished response is frequently ignored:

"No chance of that in our time. It is all arranged and settled. Nobody but Lord Grey could perhaps have carried the Reform Bill ... and when he gives up, he will certainly be succeeded by *one who has every requisite for the position, in the prime of life and fame, of old blood, high rank, great fortune*, and greater ability. Once in power, there is nothing to prevent him holding office as long as Sir Robert Walpole. Nobody can compete with Stanley. I heard him the other night in the Commons, when the party were all divided and breaking away from their ranks, *recall them by the mere force of superior will and eloquence*: he rose like a young eagle above them all, and kept hovering over their heads till they were reduced to abject submission. There is nothing like him. If you are going into politics and mean to stick to it, I dare say you will do very well, for you have ability and enterprise; and if you are careful how you steer, no doubt you will get into some port at last. But you must put all these foolish notions out of your head; they won't do at all. Stanley will be the next Prime Minister, you will see" (emphasis added).[34]

It is ironic that Melbourne failed to see that within weeks Lord Stanley would have resigned from the Whig cabinet and that only a couple of months later he himself would be prime minister. But it was equally ironic that his lecture had exactly the opposite effect of what he intended, because it drove straight to the core of Disraeli's struggle for self-definition. In emphasizing Stanley's "blood," "rank," and "fortune," Melbourne was striking, he thought, at the flamboyant upstart's lack of qualifications. Disraeli would certainly have understood the message – that it was important to be a member of the English aristocracy. But although he had no way of answering that argument directly, he was already in the process of redefining nobility by returning to its essence, and of laying his own claim to a position within the "natural aristocracy." Melbourne was thus unwittingly cooperating with Disraeli's imagination when he went on to describe Stanley's capacity for leadership, resting his argument on the personal characteristics of "superior will" and "eloquence." This could only prove to the young man the necessity of what he had already decided upon – an absolutely convincing demonstration of his own power, supported by those same personal qualities. Consequently, Disraeli's desire for recognition of his innate superiority became partially fulfilled in the imaginative or theoretical plane of political ideology,[35] but his actual talents were directed in 1834 toward power and applause wherever opportunity presented itself.

At this time the collapse of Lord Grey's reform ministry was imminent. The event provided Disraeli with a valuable lesson in defining expediency, for the administration's life was prolonged by the Tories, whose leaders, the Duke of Wellington and Sir Robert Peel, chose to support the Whig Government at critical moments rather than risk the possibility of parliamentary chaos.[36] It was obvious that the Tories themselves were not a viable alternative. They could not in practice form an alliance with the Radicals or the Irish faction, and they feared that a dissolution would produce a much less responsible House of Commons. At the same time the Reform ministry, committed to moderate change, was dependent in any direct confrontation with the Tories upon the support of the two most extreme factions. The Government had been embarrassed on various financial matters in 1833, losing a vote on a motion to reduce the malt tax and facing public violence over their taxation policy. In March of that year Lord Durham resigned from the cabinet (partly for personal reasons, but nevertheless disappointed with Whig policy) and Daniel O'Connell's confidence was steadily increasing. The Government amended the Irish Church Bill of the 1833 session, deleting the clause concerning the re-appropriation of increased Church revenues, in the hope of it passing the House of Lords. This angered O'Connell and the other provisions of the bill were opposed by the ultra-conservative Lords in any case. But the Duke of Wellington, even as he castigated Whig policy, allowed the bill to pass the second reading in the Lords in order to keep the Government in office. The Ultras saw this as cowardice. Thus the moderate members of both parties were opposed by the extreme advocates of their respective principles for their obvious resort to expediency.

At the beginning of 1834 the Duke of Wellington thought that the proper government of the country was impossible under the existing circumstances. Despite the fact that O'Connell's motion on the repeal of the union at the beginning of the new session was overwhelmingly defeated, 523–38, the Government introduced another Irish Tithe Bill and when Lord John Russell insisted upon the principle of re-appropriation, four cabinet ministers, including Lord Stanley, resigned. The Government then faced a direct confrontation on the issue from a Liberal private member's motion and the Tories were again caught between the principle of strong, safe government and party consistency. At the critical moment Peel supported the Government's movement of the previous question, which was employed to avoid the direct issue, and it was carried by a margin of fifty-six votes. Peel stood by his deepest convictions in this matter, the necessity of strong government, the defence of the church, and the avoidance of unnecessary factions. But his actions and motives were subject to harsh judgment by those who saw his duty in different terms.

A few weeks later O'Connell and his friends became enraged by the Government's proposal to renew the Irish Coercion Bill. The Irish members apparently thought that their agreement to the Tithe Bill would mean the abandonment of the Coercion Bill, or at least of its clauses forbidding public meetings. Some of the Whig members, anxious to retain the support of the Irish faction at a time when their legislation faced a hostile House of Lords, had worked behind the scenes to obtain the dropping of these clauses and they had told O'Connell confidentially that this would in fact happen. Lord Grey, however, remained unaware of this agreement and chose to ignore the advice which resulted from it. The original clauses were adopted by the cabinet and when the bill containing them was introduced in the House of Lords on 1 July, the result was explosive. O'Connell, convinced that he had been betrayed, revealed the confidence to the Commons, precipitating further resignations from the cabinet and the collapse of the ministry on 8 July.

This was the essence of the exciting political milieu in which Disraeli became caught up during 1834 as he became acquainted with O'Connell and frequented such places as Lady Blessington's Gore House. There, as he told his sister, he frequently met and dined with many of the fashionable and political elite, including Lord Durham and Lord Wilton, who arrived one evening having just had dinner with the king.[37] But the fact that Disraeli now found himself close to the centre of much of the current political manoeuvring does not mean that he was still attracted to the Radical position. Though he described Gore House to Sarah as "the great focus of the Durham party"[38] and was full of speculation about the Radicals' strength ("The Whigs cannot exist as a party with[ou]t taking in Lord Durham; and the King will not consent to it"),[39] it was simply the excitement of intrigue with all its seeming power that fascinated him, as it had done at the time of *The Representative* affair. As a spectator rather than a participant, however, Disraeli could afford to indulge in the wit of detached cynicism. This he did in his next piece of literary work, "The Infernal Marriage," which appeared in the *New Monthly Magazine* from July to October of 1834. Indeed, the writing of that satire offered him not only a chance to exercise his own sense of power in a political situation from which he was in essence excluded, but also the compensatory security of the detached superiority inherent in the satirist's role.

In style and tone Part 1 of "The Infernal Marriage"[40] is similar to "Ixion in Heaven," but in this instance the few allusions that would seem to have a private reference are incorporated into the outward thrust of the satire, which is almost all directed at the political and social

climate of the Reform Bill years. Once again Disraeli resorts to the use
of classical myth, this time in an elaborate extension of the story of
Pluto's union with Proserpine. But whereas in "Ixion in Heaven" the
various elements of plot and characterization within the myth (and
Disraeli's distortions of them) are integral parts of an interior personal
meaning, in "The Infernal Marriage" they serve only as exterior scaf-
folding for the construction of a public allegory.

Part 1 begins with the "elopement" of Pluto, the "Sovereign Power"
of the state, and Proserpine, the "spirit of Reform." In the classical version of this tale it is an "abduction" (cf. 144) and the change might at
first seem to indicate a deliberate ignoring of the coercion used to pass
the Reform Bill. But the description of "the pale and insensible
Proserpine clinging to the breast of her grim lover" during the fearful
passage to hell is the appropriate indication of force used, not against
Reform itself, but in the process of its enthronement (145). Proserpine's
fear of the Furies, Terror, Rage, Paleness, and Death, and her revulsion
at the sight of Cerberus, the watchdog of hell's gates, are clearly meant
to represent the response of Reform to the forces of ultra-conservatism
and the protective agencies of the traditional constitution. Disraeli's
theme, however, is the effects of joining the spirit of Reform with the
Sovereign Power of the state, so this marriage is an inspired metaphor.
His delineation of Proserpine's perverse petulance and wilful hysterics,
which subvert Pluto's judgment and paralyse his authority, is very well
done (though marred by clichés) and may reflect his experience of living with the emotionally turbulent and strong-willed Henrietta, which
he had been doing quite openly since the spring of 1834.[41]

The point Disraeli is making by means of the allegory is that the principle of Reform, once admitted to the constitution, will by its very nature prove to be disruptive. Within the tale the issue requiring judgment
is the presence of a live man, Orpheus, in the kingdom of the dead.
Proserpine in a previous tantrum had persuaded the king of Hades to
banish Cerberus from his post at the gates and the musician had thus
gained entry to the underworld in search of his lost bride. Orpheus explicitly represents Love, the very opposite of the hateful principle upon
which Pluto's realm is organized (160). The Parcae, or Fates, nieces of
the king, who hold the conservative view of the crisis, protest that "'The
constitution is in danger'" and the extremist Furies add, "'Both in
church and state … 'Tis a case of treason and blasphemy.'" Orpheus's
seductive lyre, they claim, has brought chaos to the government's performance of its duty, which is, of course, dispensing punishment: "'The

general confusion is indescribable. All business is at a standstill: Ixion rests upon his wheel; old Sisyphus sits down on his mountain, and his stone has fallen with a terrible plash into Acheron. In short, unless we are energetic, we are on the eve of a revolution'" (159). The Fates, led by Lachesis, take the high Tory line, claiming "the constitutional privilege" of the king's attention and protesting "against the undue influence of the Queen." Lachesis reminds him that she is a "'subject ... who has duties as strictly defined by ... [the] infernal constitution as those of ... [his] royal spouse'" (duties which, she informs the queen, "'I and *my order* are resolved to perform'"), and when she learns of Cerberus's "promotion" she is spurred to lecture Pluto about his responsibilities, concluding with a threat of resignation (161–2). When the king, frightened at this prospect, proposes to recall his protective watchdog and expel the intruder, it is pointed out to him that he has the power neither to do the latter, nor to inflict death upon him. Then Proserpine pleads the lovers' case, asking Pluto to release Eurydice, and Lachesis opposes her: "'Tis the principle ... 'tis the principle. Concession is ever fatal, however slight. Grant this demand; others, and greater, will quickly follow. Mercy becomes a precedent, and the realm is ruined'" (163). The queen in reply argues that since the "State is in confusion" and the Fates have confessed their ignorance of any remedy, the king should follow her as the advocate of "Mercy" and "Concession," and adopt the policy of "expediency": "'Pluto, reject these counsellors, at once insulting and incapable. Give me the distaff and the fatal shears. At once form a new Cabinet; and let the release of Orpheus and Eurydice be the basis of their policy.' She threw her arms round his neck and whispered in his ear" (163). His Majesty, his confidence in the Parcae shaken, and perplexed by the "difficulty" that "had been occasioned by a departure from their own exclusive and restrictive policy," is swayed by his wife: "It was clear that the gates of Hell ought never to have been opened to the stranger; but opened they had been. Forced to decide, he decided on the side of *expediency*, and signed a decree for the departure of Orpheus and Eurydice. The Parcae immediately resigned their posts, and the Furies walked off in a huff. Thus, on the third day of the Infernal Marriage, Pluto found that he had quarrelled with all his family, and that his ancient administration was broken up. The King was without a friend, and Hell was without a Government!" (164).

It is obvious from the foregoing that "The Infernal Marriage" is an allegory of the political environment of the previous three years. The characters and details of the plot in Part 1 do not equate with specific people or events, but it is clear that the arrival of Proserpine in Hades corresponds in a general sense to the passage of the Reform Bill. As the archetypical outsider, whose very presence and poetic talents are so disruptive, Orpheus may also well be seen as a witty and mischievous spirit of the author himself. What Disraeli has done is personify points of view and political ideas with the intention of both mocking their limitations and satirizing those who hold them. The most important feature of this satire, however, is the lack of implied or overt authorial commitment to either of the opposing ideologies. The embodiment of the principle of Reform as the wilful and perverse queen is devastating, but ultimately it is no more destructive of the reader's empathy than the personification of the shades of Toryism in the haughty and pompous Fates and the hideous, inane Furies. The humorous representation of the sovereign power of the state in the character of the pathetic and ridiculous Pluto is also evidence of Disraeli's disinterested, superior stance at the time of writing.

The immediate opportunities for political satire being almost exhausted, Disraeli broadens his scope in Parts 2, 3, and 4 of "The Infernal Marriage" to include the whole social and cultural milieu. He does this by a contrivance of plot wherein Proserpine, falling ill from boredom, is sent upon a convalescent excursion to the Elysian Fields. The remainder of the tale has an episodic structure, which, though it permits the extension of topical commentary, in effect betrays the author's artistic limits. Disraeli has a genuine talent for creating witty repartee and striking argument, such as Jove's snobbish low opinion of Apollo as a possible son-in-law. But when he creates descriptions he frequently falls into clichés and conventions that rest upon superficial sentiment. And when he attempts pictorial satire, the result is sometimes nothing more than cynical or heavy-handed invective, as, for example, when he calls judges "worshipful baboons in most venerable wigs" or describes the lord chancellor as a circus performer "keeping in the air four brazen balls at the same time, swallowing daggers, spitting fire, turning sugar into salt and eating yards of pink ribbon," which, after being well digested, reappear through his nose (174–5). The selling of army commissions or the weaknesses of the judicial system are fine objects of satire, but Disraeli here fails in his intention. The whole episode, in fact, reflects the staleness of an idea that had first occurred to him three years earlier, when he read in *Galignani's Messenger* about the Reform motion and the Duke of Wellington's resignation in November 1830: "What a confusion! What a capital pantomime, 'Lord Mayor's Day or Harlequin Brougham!'"[42] Indeed, this idea occurs frequently in political caricature of the period.

From time to time Disraeli finds a genuine satiric edge again when he interrupts the flow of narration to create a vignette such as the account of the whist game in which Proserpine asks her partner, "'Pray, my dear Tiresias, you who are such a fine player, how came you to trump my best card?'" and the seer replies, "'Because I wanted the lead. And those who want to lead, please your Majesty, must never hesitate about sacrificing their friends'" (184–5). Taken as a whole, though, the remainder of "The Infernal Marriage" is markedly inferior to the first part, despite the fact that the obviously but thinly disguised characters lead the reader to speculate on their identities as actual persons. This attempt at specific personal allusions did not subvert Disraeli's authorial detachment, however. The Titans, who as a group represent the politically displaced Tory aristocratic landowners, are shown to be destructively faction-ridden and consumed by jealousy. And the parasitical condescension of the aristocracy ("a few thousand beatified mortals" whose only occupation is enjoyment) is given some sharp commentary. In particular the sexual morality of high society is the object of mockery: "If a lady committed herself, she was lost forever, and packed off immediately to the realm of Twilight ... Immediately that it was clearly ascertained that two persons of different sexes took an irrational interest in each other's society, all the world instantly went about, actuated by a purely charitable sentiment, telling the most extraordinary falsehoods concerning them that they could devise" (208–9). Disraeli's letters to his sister in this period consistently stress his position as a member of a most fashionable social circle, but in this case, the delineation of condescension and hypocrisy reflects an outsider's point of view. He seems close to biting the hand that feeds him. On the surface this is a further indication of the opportunistic nature of his cynicism, but it also betrays an otherwise hidden social insecurity. It would seem, therefore, that the fantasy of "The Infernal Marriage" as a whole works to put its author back into a securely superior position.

III

On 10 July 1834, at a dinner party given by Henrietta, Disraeli met Lord Lyndhurst, who had been the Tory lord chancellor in the pre-Reform ministries. Though now more than sixty years of age, Lyndhurst retained extraordinary intellectual capacities, but he had a reputation for lax moral standards and reckless conversation, and consequently he did not inspire widespread political trust from his contemporaries. Perhaps not surprisingly, Disraeli and he took an immediate liking for each other, and the young, aspiring politician soon found himself privy to a great deal of confidential information, and with a powerful ally. Lyndhurst in turn undoubtedly saw the political usefulness of the young man's literary talents and within a short time Disraeli became Lyndhurst's unofficial private secretary.[43]

In the meantime, following the resignation of Lord Grey on 8 July, Lord Melbourne had been chosen to form the next Government. The king wanted Melbourne to form a coalition with the Duke of Wellington, Stanley, and Peel. Under royal duress Melbourne investigated the proposal, but the principals all agreed it was impossible and so the Whigs formed another, even more liberal administration. An Irish Coercion Bill and a Tithe Bill passed the House of Commons, the latter drawing violent Conservative opposition. But the House of Lords under the reinvigorated leadership of Wellington, who had recently been elected chancellor of Oxford University, quickly threw out three Government measures in the first two weeks of August: the bill on the removal of Jewish disabilities, the bill on the admission of dissenters to the universities, and the Irish Tithe Bill itself. Perhaps strangely, the cabinet's response to this last action was a fear of the consequences in Ireland, rather than a girding for another constitutional struggle with the upper House.[44] As a result Wellington concluded that the Tory position had gained considerable strength: "I consider the destruction of the House of Lords to be now out of the question and that we have only now to follow a plain course with moderation and dignity to obtain a very great if not preponderating influence in the country."[45] This, however, was not at all Disraeli's mode of conduct. During the parliamentary recess he had been quite ill in retreat at Bradenham, a state brought on, it would seem, by his temporary separation from Henrietta and the contemplation of his bleak financial situation. This could in part account for the poor quality of the latter portion of "The Infernal Marriage," which he was composing at the time and which, he implies, he was not much taken with: "I am quite at a loss how to manage affairs in future as I find separation more irksome than even my bitterest imagination predicted … I have done nothing but scribble one day a third part of *The Infernal Marriage* with which fantasy Colburn pretends now to be much pleased."[46] After being laid up on a sofa for two months with "great pains in the legs and extraord[inar]y languor," he began to feel better. Disraeli ascribed his recovery to "Quiet, diet, and plenteous doses of Ammonia," but the prospect of his return to London probably had no small effect.[47] Within ten days he was back in the thick of political life and plotting a devious course that was neither moderate nor dignified. A letter to Sarah suggests that he was following a pattern reminiscent of Vivian Grey and the hero of *The Representative* affair: "I dined on Saturday with Lyndhurst *en famille* ... I saw Chandos to-day, and had a long conversation with him on politics. He has no head, but I flatter myself I opened his mind a little."[48] Lyndhurst had apparently been telling his new protégé that "the end of Whiggism was at hand," what with the "secession of the Stanley party, the subsequent intrigues ... with O'Connell and the consequent retirement of Lord Grey."[49] The relevant portion of what is called the Bradenham Memo reveals a striking similarity between the role Disraeli currently envisioned for himself and that he had played as John Murray's emissary nine years earlier. Lyndhurst thought that it might now be possible to stop the Whigs from introducing further measures of reform, and so Disraeli was sent to confer with Lord Chandos about organizing an agricultural party that would throw the Government into a minority on an agricultural amendment to the address when Parliament next met. In return for this undertaking, Disraeli reported, Chandos "required for himself the First Lord of the Admiralty" in an ensuing Conservative Government that he anticipated would be led by Sir Robert Peel (Bradenham Memo, 5ff.). But this performance, too, ended with the hero more or less adrift, though not from any exposure of his rashness.

At the very moment that Disraeli was manipulating the Marquess of Chandos into the plot to upset the Whigs the news of Lord Spencer's death arrived. Viscount Althorp's succession to his father's title meant that Melbourne would have to choose a new leader in the House of Commons, although there was no reason why the ministry should not continue in office.[50] On the other hand, there was every reason to think that the Duke of Wellington, despite his recent militancy, would not want to commit himself to a direct confrontation designed to overthrow the Government until he saw what developed. It is not at all surprising, then, that when Lyndhurst approached him with his plan, that the duke "threw cold water upon it."[51] In fact, Wellington seems to have been hopeful, whether from euphoria or astuteness, that the king would send for him, and this is what happened. Using as excuses the prime minister's diffidence about the future of the ministry and the suggestion that Lord John Russell succeed Althorp, an idea he particularly disliked, the king dismissed Melbourne, thinking that the increased strength of the Tories would permit the formation of a Government more in line with his own conservatism. The news was leaked to the

press, where the members of the Whig cabinet learned of their dismissal. Meanwhile Wellington recommended that Peel (who, of course,
knew nothing of the ultra-Tory plans) be brought back from his vacation in Italy to form the next ministry and he and Lyndhurst formed a
caretaker Government designed to keep decisions open for Peel. But
this further alienated many of the Whigs whose eventual support might
be valuable.[52]

Disraeli took it for granted that a general election was in the offing
and that unless he could find a safe seat, his chances of entering
Parliament were slim. His intrigue with Lyndhurst and Chandos was
intended, of course, to catapult him to power. When it fell through, he
took a dim view of the Duke of Wellington's plan of waiting for Peel
and decided to look to his friends for support. Lyndhurst was involved
with Wellington, so Disraeli turned to another aristocratic acquaintance, "Radical Jack":

private
My dear Lord Durham,

   My electioneering prospects look gloomy. The Squires throughout my
own County look grim at a Radical – and the liberal interest is so split and
pre-engaged in our few towns, that I fear I shall fail. At present I am looking after Aylesbury, where young Hobhouse was beat last time and will be
beat this, if he try, but where, with my local influence, your party wo[ul]d
succeed. If you have influence with Hobhouse, counsel him to resign in
my favor, and not of another person, as 'tis rumored he will. At the same
time if Nugent return, he will beat us all. So, my dear Lord, my affairs are
black; therefore remember me, and serve me if you can. My principles you
are acquainted with; as for my other qualifications, I am considered a great
popular rhetor.

   What do you think of the Tories! at a moment when decision and energy
wo[ul]d be pearls and diamonds to them, they have formed *a provisional
government*! "The voice of one crying in the wilderness, Prepare ye the way
of *the Lords*!" Such is Wellington's solitary cry; a Baptist worthy of such a
Messiah as – Peel.[53]

This letter, as the frequency of first-person pronouns indicates, is completely egocentric. It is opportunism wedded to frustration that is the
basis of both Disraeli's appeal for help and his opinion of the Tories.
Durham's reply was sympathetic but unhelpful; he wished him well
but had, he said, no influence that would be of direct aid.[54]

Disraeli felt, therefore, that he had no alternative but to issue another address to the electors of High Wycombe and to stand again as an Independent-Radical with Tory support. Only seven days after writing to Durham, he told Sarah that "The Lord Chancellor is my *staunch friend*, nor is there anyth[in]g for my service w[hi]ch he will not do." And five days later he writes again suggesting that "the Duke is confident" of his chances.[55] Much has been made of Disraeli's inconsistency in trying to be elected first as a Radical, then as a Conservative, and finally as a Radical again. These shifts do not seem, however, to have involved any changes in political ideology, nor do they indicate that he did not have one. His appeal to Durham is very much a request for a personal favour and draws upon their friendly relationship in Lady Blessington's Gore House circle. Disraeli does not claim to be a Radical in the sense of adhering to a radical democratic philosophy, though he obviously felt that he and Durham had some ideas in common. Rather, the self-centredness of his letter indicates that it was recognition of his genius, not his loyalty, for which he was looking. And in turn, even though the Tory leaders were obviously thinking of the party's strength, it is talent that recommends him to them, as is evident from what he tells Sarah a week later: "The Duke wrote a strong letter to Granville S[omerset] – chairman of the Election comm[itt]ee say[in]g that if Wycombe was not insured something else must be found for D. as 'a man of his acquirements and reputation must not be thrown away.'"[56] As for his stance at Wycombe, it was not in essence much different from that of his previous, second campaign there. In fact, in 1834 Disraeli's political ideology was well on the way to maturation and the variations of his public posture were less the result of inconsistency of thought than of frustration at being ever closer to the sources of power yet debarred from a significant role in its manipulation.

On 16 December Disraeli delivered an address in the Town Hall to the electors of High Wycombe. Shortly thereafter it was issued as a pamphlet entitled *The Crisis Examined*.[57] The speech is significant in several respects, the most obvious being its startling similarity to Peel's Tamworth Manifesto, which was approved by the new cabinet and sent to the press the following day.[58] Ten years later, in *Coningsby*, Disraeli would attack Peel's address as "an attempt to construct a party without principles" whose "inevitable consequence has been Political Infidelity."[59] But in 1834, despite his profession of independence, he was much more in sympathy with the Conservative leader's position. *The Crisis Examined* begins, it is true, with an assertion of the author's consistency since the

last campaign, claiming to be influenced "by the same sentiments" he
has ever professed and actuated "by the same principles" he has ever
advocated. But Disraeli quickly turns to the nature of the present "crisis"
and "the course *expedient* to pursue" (24, emphasis added). Under the
heading "Financial Relief" he shows himself to be a stout supporter of
the agricultural interests, whom he finds "more entitled than any other
class to whatever boon the Minister may spare." Though not explicitly
stated, this is partly so because of the landowner's social responsibilities. As a consequence he advocates "at least a partial relief of the malt
tax," opposes direct taxes in principle, and hopes that "the window tax
will soon disappear" (25). He is equally Conservative when, in discussing the issue of "Ecclesiastical Reform," he resists any tampering with
the institution of the Church, preferring Church improvement to Church
reform. The former means, he says, abolishing pluralities and terminating for ever the evil of non-residence as "the value of lesser livings and
the incomes ... of inferior clergy" are increased. Similarly, it is his opinion that the problems of the Irish Church require that "the very name of
tithes in that country" be abolished and the "Protestant Establishment
... be at once proportioned to the population it serves." But he is ada-
mant on the question of re-appropriation in language that foreshadows
the views of Young England and the arguments for the role of the
Church in both *Coningsby* and *Sybil*: "I ... will never consent that the
surplus revenues of that branch of our Establishment shall ever be ap-
propriated to any other object save the interests of the Church of
England, because experience has taught me that an establishment is
never despoiled except to benefit an aristocracy. It is the interest of the
people to support the Church, for the Church is their patrimony, their
only hereditary property; it is their portal to power, their avenue to
learning, to distinction, and to honour" (26). Disraeli can "see no reason
why the surplus revenues of the Church of England in Ireland should
not be placed in the trust of the Prelates ... and lay trustees" for the
purpose of propagating the Protestant faith, but he admits there is "no
chance of tranquility" in Ireland until the people "enjoy the *right ... to be
maintained* by the soil they cultivate" and have "the *consolation* and the
blessing of a well-regulated system of poor-laws" very different from
that "which has recently made all England thrill with feelings of horror
and indignation" (26–7, emphasis added). Thus his support of the agricultural interests and his analysis of the ecclesiastical issue rest firmly
on his feudalistic conception of the fabric of society and his belief in the
value of a mixed constitution.

In the pamphlet's discussion, "Sectarian Reform," the concessions of the Dissenters' claims to registration and marriage rights, as well as the matter of Church rates, might appear to be radical measures, but Disraeli says explicitly that he would grant only those claims that are "consistent with the established constitution of the country" and the maintenance "of the Established Church" (27). So also, in the matter of "Corporate Reform," he believes that "municipalities should be formed upon the model of the mixed constitution which experience has proved to be ... so efficient and so beneficial." Burgesses, he says, should be elected by the inhabitants and "Aldermen should be elected by the burgesses, and serve the office of Mayor in rotation." He is emphatic that mayors and returning officers of boroughs should never be appointed by the Crown, an arrangement which he sees as "part and parcel of the Whig system of centralisation" (28). Nevertheless, despite the Tory principles that lurk behind them, these various proposals amount to a substantial program of safe or moderate reform. They indicate that in practical terms Disraeli accepted the legacy of the Reform Bill itself and that he was convinced that only the redress of legitimate grievances could preserve the institutions of the country and the Conservative principles they embodied from further irrevocable harm.

Sir Robert Peel's Tamworth Manifesto declares an almost identical acceptance of the Reform Bill's "settlement of a great Constitutional question" and a determination to correct "proved abuses" and redress "real grievances."[60] Further, Peel's opinions on the specific issues facing his Government, though more restrained by the responsibilities of office, are remarkably similar to Disraeli's. He proves himself not unfriendly to the principle of inquiry into the matter of municipal corporations, though, since it has already been referred to a commission, he can only promise "full and unprejudiced consideration" of its suggestions (63). As for the position of the non-conformists, he supports the abolition of Church rates and the idea of relieving "the conscientious scruples of Dissenters in respect to the ceremony of marriage." And, though he still opposes their admission as a "claim of right" into the universities, he supports the modification of regulations governing the professions of law and medicine that discriminate against them. On the issue of Church reform, Peel says that he cannot consent to "the alienating of Church property ... from strictly Ecclesiastical purposes," though he favours "an improved distribution of the revenues of the Church" and the settlement of the tithe question "by means of a commutation ... founded upon just principles ... and a mature consideration." And while he evinces "the sincerest desire to remove every abuse that can impair the efficiency of the Establishment," Peel adds that he hopes "to extend the sphere of its usefulness, and to strengthen and confirm its just claims upon the respect and affections of the people" (65–6). From this it is clear that Disraeli's rhetorical question of whether his audience's representative should support a Government prepared to adopt and carry the measures he has just detailed is by no means an absurd anticipation (*Crisis Examined*, 28).

It should be noted that the advocacy of these measures as "the course expedient to pursue" is not merely self-interest. They are "expedient" in the sense that he thinks that, "under the existing circumstances," it is "the duty of an Administration to pursue" them (24). The duty derives from the danger to the constitution brought on by the policy of the Whigs. That policy, as Disraeli sees it, is not the acceptance of the Reform Bill as what Peel calls "a final and irrevocable settlement" ("Tamworth Manifesto," 61–2), but rather as part of a process leading to the dominance of one branch of government and ending not in democracy, but in tyranny: "I will allow for the freedom of the Press; I will allow for the spirit of the age; I will allow for the march of intellect; but I cannot force from my mind the conviction that a House of Commons, concentrating in itself the whole power of the State … would … establish in this country a despotism of the most formidable and dangerous character" (*Crisis Examined*, 34–5). Disraeli supports his conviction with "the historical truth" of the Long Parliament's iniquities, which leave him reluctant to alter the current constitutional powers of the Crown and the Peers. The "expediency" of which he is talking is thus not only that of looking at the future with self-interest, but also that of looking at the past with conviction. As such it happens to be the only practical platform for opposing the Whigs in general and the two sitting members for High Wycombe in particular.

The establishment of such an explicitly reformist program upon such conservative convictions nevertheless raises the problem of consistency and sincerity. The overt basis of Disraeli's consistency, though it has roots deep in his psyche, is his opposition to everything Whiggish. In this instance he attacks as well as defends, and the result is quite astonishing. Many of the Whigs themselves, he points out, have a poor record of consistency, having once been supporters of Prime Minister Canning at the time of his declaration against Reform (29), and further, having been quick to applaud Peel's acquiescence to Catholic Emancipation, an alteration of much greater significance than anything currently proposed (33). But Disraeli's intention is not just to prove that the Whigs are no better than the Tories, for he launches a defence of inconsistency in terms of what is practical: "The truth is ... a statesman is the creature of his age, the creation of his times ... he is only to ascertain the needful and the beneficial, and the most feasible manner in which affairs are to be carried on":

> It is even the duty of public men occasionally to adopt sentiments with which they do not sympathise, because the people must have leaders. Then the opinions and prejudices of the Crown must necessarily influence a rising statesman. I say nothing of the weight which great establishments and corporations, and the necessity of their support and patronage, must also possess with an ambitious politician. All this, however, produces ultimate benefit; all these influences tend to form that eminently practical character ... all I seek to ascertain is whether his present policy be just, necessary, expedient; whether, at the present moment, he is prepared to serve the country according to its present necessities. (32)

What is at stake here is the ability to see what is "just," "necessary," and "expedient" (keeping in mind the conservative principles these words shelter), and in that respect the party distinctions are as sharp as ever. This is not, as a cynical person might think, a fine rhetorical gloss of opportunism and hypocrisy. Rather, it is an indication that Disraeli was beginning to appreciate the ways in which means and ends become entangled in political life.

The last portion of *The Crisis Examined* is an attack upon the Reform ministry. It contains the famous Ducrow simile in which the cabinet is likened to the act of a celebrated circus performer who rides six horses at once but who in turn substitutes donkeys for his ailing steeds and so ends with farce. Such an attack also belies the author's concern for "measures ... and not men" in any sense in which the two are isolated. And the earlier glorification of the character of a statesman is further proof that Disraeli is, in fact, saying that those who see what is "just, necessary [and] expedient" are the better men: "upon the authority of the Whigs themselves, I am justified in believing that nothing can be more *noble* ... more *wise* and more *magnanimous*, than a *bold* adaption of policy to the demands of public opinion" (33, emphasis added). The measures are indeed the measures of the men, and this is a conception completely consistent with Disraeli's previous, essentially Tory political theorizing, however, independently Radical it seems on the surface.

It would appear that in the first half of 1834, as he watched Peel's and Wellington's struggle with their dilemma, which fed his impulse to mock the use of "expediency" in "The Infernal Marriage," Disraeli also began to understand that the protection of one's core principles might require such a choice and that the ultimate satisfaction of one's private interest might be served by acting in the public interest. The inconsistency between *The Crisis Examined* and "The Infernal Marriage" on the matter of expediency reflects the dichotomy between the sincere and the cynical responses of which Disraeli was capable when acting out different senses of himself. In frustration at defeat by a less talented opponent he could strike out with a satirical and compensatory assertion of his own superiority. But in the hope of successfully demonstrating his genius, and with a desperate need to be accepted as one of nature's aristocracy, he could also express himself with ingratiating orthodoxy.

Still, *The Crisis Examined* does represent a real, if temporary advance on Disraeli's part in defining a viable political identity. While the example of Peel's "expediency" might only be a model for cynicism when, in disappointment, Disraeli most needed to claim his own essential purity, it was clearly seen as noblest conviction when he was about the task of demonstrating his superiority. As far as one can tell, *The Crisis Examined* and the "Tamworth Manifesto" were written under independent inspiration, but in a sense the similarity of their political stance is not an accident. Disraeli had learned the first lesson in how to transcend the discrepancy between his private and public worlds, and between his two senses of himself. But, as the intervening events show, the reconciliation of principle and expediency, which is reflected in the complex political identity of the author of *The Crisis Examined*, was extremely fragile. The Chandos intrigue and the letters to Durham and Lyndhurst reveal Disraeli to have been very vulnerable to the seductive promise of his power fantasy – instant success – and when that collapsed, to the need to claim his innate superiority.

Although Lyndhurst had been unable to obtain another Tory nomination for Disraeli,[61] the party managers, under pressure from the chancellor, donated £500 towards the expenses of the third contest at Wycombe.[62] This tangible identification with the Tories undoubtedly contributed to Disraeli's sense of an irrevocably widening gap between his own position and the intellectual radicalism of Lord Durham. Nevertheless, the relationship was important to him, so he sent Durham a copy of *The Crisis Examined* with a covering letter which attempts to mitigate the consequences of their avowed disagreement about the

Whigs with personal admiration and the rhetoric of principle: "As for the opinions contained in these pages, they are those I have ever professed, and I shd. grieve if your L[ordshi]p's junction with the Whigs and my continued resistance to a party who have ever opposed me … sho[ul]d ever place me in opposition to a nobleman whose talents I respect, and who … has only the same object in view with myself, which is to maintain this great Empire on a broad democratic basis, and which I am convinced is the only foundation on which it can now rest."[63] What Disraeli means by "a broad democratic basis" is a federation of just representations from the various segments of society in the form of a mixed constitution involving separate powers and duties for the Crown, Lords, and Commons. He is certainly not implying a faith in the sufficiency of the electoral process or the will of the majority of the House of Commons. And he is clearly at odds in this matter with the opinions of Lord Durham, who had supported the menacing of the Lords and urged the creation of new peers to pass the Reform Bill in 1832.[64] The context of his personal feelings thus suggests that this last phrase of the letter is not an inconsistent or hypocritical allegiance to the Radical position, but only the use of semantic ambiguity to emphasize their common patriotism and to minimize their political differences. In the election of 1834, then, Disraeli is an Independent-Radical only insofar as that label can gather him the support of those voters who are both anti-Whig and anti-Tory. His deepest convictions are profoundly Conservative and his specific platform is remarkably, but not surprisingly similar to the proposed safe-reform program of Peel's Government. With their tangible, financial support and the repeated failure of playing both ends against the middle, Disraeli's application for membership in the Carlton Club shortly after his third defeat (Smith 289, Grey 147, Disraeli 128) is less the marking of "his conversion to the Tory cause" than a formalization of his actual position.[65]

6

Prejudice

Although *The Crisis Examined* (1834) is an attempt on Disraeli's part to define a complex political identity, his behaviour for the next year continued to demonstrate both the strong influence of his power fantasy and the force of his ambivalence about himself. His position as Lyndhurst's confidential secretary tended to reinforce the confusion of fantasy and external political events that marked his response to the fall of Peel's ministry. And, as the Tory candidate in the Taunton by-election of 1835, he succeeded in presenting a coherent political personality only to have an attack upon his religious identity explode that resolution and arouse all the latent issues of his alienation.

When Sir Robert Peel returned from Italy in mid-December, 1834, and set about the task of forming a new ministry, "little sanguine ... as to success," he wrote to Lord Stanley and Sir James Graham, inviting them to join the new Government in the hope of gathering even wider support.[1] Both men felt that their recent association with the Whigs prevented them from accepting office, but they indicated their desire to support the new prime minister. Without them, however, Peel's ministry was so markedly Tory as to seem, even to him, to be "only the Duke's old Cabinet."[2] One noticeable omission was Lord Chandos, who had in the previous month become the leader of "a sort of confederation of counties" or agricultural faction.[3] Chandos was eager to join Peel, but he refused to do so unless he was assured that the Government would recommend the partial or total repeal of the malt tax. Peel, who as his own chancellor of the exchequer had yet to take up the matter of specific duties, could only reply that this would necessitate a property tax equally burdensome to the agricultural interest. And while he said that he would be willing to discuss partial repeal and a substitution at the appropriate time, he could make no binding commitment. Chandos would not budge from the principle and refused Peel's final offer. It is possible that some of his militancy was the result of the Lyndhurst-Disraeli mischief prior to Melbourne's resignation, though the malt tax was an issue with which he had been concerned, if not obsessed, all along. Nevertheless, Chandos's absence from Peel's cabinet was a point of anxiety. And when he brought forward a private motion on the malt tax in the new session, the prime minister, recognizing that a property tax was the only alternative, had to defeat it with resulting bitterness among some members of his own party.[4]

Peel's Government was in trouble from its very beginning. The general election failed to produce a Conservative majority and the only hope of survival lay in obtaining the support of moderates in other parties. But most of the Whigs – though not, it seems, Lords Grey and Melbourne – were keen to turn the ministry out of office, either for the good of the country or their own personal satisfaction. Lord John Russell, now to be their leader in the House of Commons, wanted to oppose the reappointment of the Speaker and the Whigs again found that they had allies in the Radical and Irish factions that had so recently been the source of their embarrassment. Daniel O'Connell, for his part, wanted above all to remove the Orange faction from power in Ireland and was willing to strike a bargain. In return for specific reforms – getting rid of the Protestant influence, the reform of Irish corporations, and restrictions on the Irish Church – he was willing to give up the repeal of the Union for the time being and support a Whig ministry. As a consequence the Whigs, Radicals, and Irish became one force opposing the Tories in what was known (after Russell's residence) as the Lichfield House compact.

The Government was immediately defeated at the opening of Parliament upon the vote to confirm the Speakership. An amendment to the Address was also carried, indicating that the Conservatives could only continue in office as long as they adopted Whig principles and Whig measures. There was one pyrrhic victory for Peel in putting down Chandos's motion on the malt tax; otherwise his efforts were of no avail. He produced a carefully prepared Dissenters' Marriage Bill and an English Tithe Commutation Bill and both were quite well received. Before they could become law, however, the Government was facing continual obstructionism on supplies votes and Russell brought forward a motion on the reappropriation of Irish Church revenues. The issue was debated from 30 March to 7 April 1835 and upon division after division the Tory ministry was defeated, the Radicals and Irish following Russell's leadership. The final resolution of 7 April declared that without the principle of reappropriation no Irish Tithe Bill would be accepted. It passed 285 to 258 and the next day Peel resigned.

Although he had no direct involvement in these events, Disraeli's response to them is important, for it reveals how little he actually knew at the time about parliamentary politics. After his defeat in his third contest at Wycombe he had written to the Duke of Wellington, "I am now a cipher; but if the devotion of my energies to your cause, *in* and *out*, can ever avail you, your Grace may count on me, who seeks no greater satisfaction than that of serving a really great man."[5] Disraeli seems not to have been much taken with Peel. He had, it is true, described him as "a very great man, indeed," after their first meeting in May 1832.[6] But it seems that Peel's response to the extravagant young dandy was one of intuitive dislike, and it appears that there were no further meetings between them prior to 1835. However, Disraeli was certainly privy to gossip. The mocking reference to "such a Messiah as – Peel" in the letter to Lord Durham is no doubt a reflection of both the quarter to which it is addressed and the hearsay of certain social circles. It is, nevertheless, an opinion born of ignorance. A letter to Sarah, sent the day after Parliament met, gives a good indication of Disraeli's sense of his position: "Peel did not speak well; Stanley with great point and power; Burdett, who had written to Lady Blessington, and provised [promised] to vote for Sutton (the Tory Speaker), saying that there was as much difference bet[wee]n Abercr. and him 'as bet[wee]n a nutshell and the dome of St. Paul's,' lost his courage, and sneaked off with[ou]t voting; Henry Stanley, who had promised me to vote for Sutton, voted for Ab[ercromb]y; Sir Chs. Verney and Sulli[va]n, Clayton, and Richard[s] for Sutton."[7] In short, he is not impressed with Peel's leadership, he is picking up information from his friends at Gore House, he identifies with the Tory cause, and he feels very much in the thick of the infighting and has a sense of his own importance as Lyndhurst's protégé. But the limitations of his actual position are clearly shown in a letter to his father five weeks later when he naively attributes "the *malaise* of the Tories" to Peel's alleged domestic difficulties with his wife: "The fact is their chief is bullied by his wife and she is nervous lest he shd. fight and all that."[8] It is perhaps significant that he refers to Peel in this instance as "their chief," but three days later in the context of not seeing "the C[hancello]r since Thursday," says "we expect to win" the vote on the Irish Tithe Bill.[9] In any case, that he would credit rumours about Peel's personal life to the extent of making them the cause of uneasiness within the Tory party proves that he has no conception of the prime minister's real political concerns. Disraeli's egocentricity blinds him to the seriousness of the current situation and corrupts his judgment of the immediate possibilities.

At this point Disraeli became involved in yet another intrigue that offered to fulfil the power fantasy embodied in *The Representative* affair. He described the details in a letter to his father in which he claims to be at the centre of negotiations that might lead to a coalition of Whigs and Tories. He imagines that Mrs Norton, with whom he has recently been "closeted" for two hours, has enlisted him as a secret envoy in an attempt to bring the aristocratic Whig leaders, Lords Grey and Melbourne, together with the Tory leaders, Peel and Lyndhurst. And he reports what he has been told – that Melbourne and his colleagues want "nothing to do with O'Connell *or* the English and Scotch Rad[ical]s," and that they disapproved of Lord John Russell's policy on the Irish Church and his parliamentary strategy of voting against the appointment of the Conservative Speaker of the House of Commons at the outset of Peel's ministry. Convinced that the Whigs "have not advanced a jot," Disraeli concludes with more details about his various conversations during the previous two days and a burst of enthusiasm: "I need not say that we are all in the highest spirits, and that the excitement is unparalleled. I think myself Peel will be again sent for by the King ... That we shall win in the long run and triumphantly I have no doubt. You now know all the secrets of affairs, which not ten people do in the realm and you must burn this letter when read ... I intended to have come down to Braden. to-day or tomorrow but can say nothing of my movements now, as all is on my shoulders."[10]

This very exciting account is full of gross exaggeration. If Lord Melbourne had any serious desire of forming a coalition, it is virtually certain that he would not have availed himself of the services of Mrs Norton. More probably the Whig leader was having difficulty forming a cabinet that would keep power out of the hands of the extremists and exclude Lord Brougham. If indeed he was Mrs Norton's "prompter,"[11] it was undoubtedly with the intention of finding out what the Conservative leaders' attitude would be should he be unable to form a government. If this were done directly and news of it leaked out, it would be a source of great embarrassment within his own party, but Melbourne could easily disavow any connection with Mrs Norton's proposals in the event of premature disclosure. Given Disraeli's reputation, he was ideally suited for the part the Whigs designed for him. In other words, he was probably being pumped for information which, as Lyndhurst's confidential man-Friday, he possessed. As the letter indicates, at this point his old fantasy of creating an important position for himself by manipulating people who already have influence took hold and once again he fell into the role of self-appointed ambassador-at-large. The stress upon his own movements and the time spent in negotiation, the revelling in confidential details, and the last melodramatic assertion, all suggest the compulsive self-aggrandizement typical of Disraeli's fantasies. But once again his egocentricity was the soil for a hope that was doomed to wither as soon as it blossomed. "Insuperable difficulties in the way of an immediate coalition" notwithstanding, Melbourne was eventually able to form a cabinet.

With the change of Government there came another opportunity for Disraeli. When Mr Henry Labouchere, the member for Taunton, was appointed Master of the Mint in Melbourne's new ministry, he had to stand for re-election. The Tory party put up £300 and sent Disraeli to contest the seat, giving him handsome recommendations to the local supporters. He did not really expect to win, but nevertheless the by-election was a huge success. Apart from the fact that he could take comfort in being, for the first time, an official Tory candidate, and one likely to obtain more valuable assistance in the future, Disraeli made a considerable impact on the voters of Taunton and the public at large. The report of an anonymous witness shows that he had lost none of his dandyism and was clearly the most exotic thing that many of them had ever seen:

> Never in my life had I been so struck by a face as I was by that of Disraeli. It was lividly pale, and from beneath two finely-arched eyebrows blazed out a pair of intensely black eyes. I never have seen such orbs in mortal sockets, either before or since. His physiognomy was strictly Jewish. Over a broad, high forehead were ringlets of coal-black, glossy hair, which … fell in luxuriant clusters or bunches over his left cheek and ear … There was a sort of half-smile, half-sneer, playing about his beautifully-formed mouth, the upper lip of which was curved as we see it in the portraits of Byron … He was very showily attired in a dark bottle-green frock coat, a waistcoat of the most extravagant pattern, the front of which was almost covered with glittering chains, and in fancy-pattern pantaloons … Altogether he was the most intellectual-looking exquisite I have ever seen.[12]

Dandyism, as Barbey d'Aurevilly and, after him, Baudelaire have pointed out, is a manifestation of intense egotism, of a desire for "unchallenged sovereignty" within the limits of one's ambition. Dandyism is "an individual and hypercivilised revolt against the rules of a social order which the rebel hates but reveres."[13] As Baudelaire said, it is not simply "an exaggerated love of fine clothes and material comfort. These things, to the perfect dandy, are mere symbols of his own spiritual aristocracy."[14] Disraeli's adoption of an extravagant mode of dress is thus entirely consistent with his personality and his social position. Convinced of his own superiority, yet debarred by his social class and Jewish heritage from the kinds of recognition of his "genius" that would be ultimately satisfying, he found in dandyism a form of self-assertion that did attract a partial recognition of it from the high society he so desperately wanted to join. There were, of course, plenty of models to emulate: Bolingbroke, Brummell, Byron, and D'Orsay had all shown the value of audacity suitably dressed.

If the self-assertiveness expressed in his flamboyant appearance had not altered in the last two years, neither had the need to prove his sincerity. Disraeli's nomination day speech took up the familiar theme of his consistency, for, however easily the essential conservatism of his political position in the post Reform Bill years can be demonstrated in retrospect, it was widely thought and charged at the time that he was in some sense a genuine Radical.[15] In his speech Disraeli maintained that his consistency lay in his constant opposition to the Whigs, whom he looked upon as "an anti-national party" whose policy "must destroy the honour of the Kingdom abroad and the happiness of the people at home."[16] This was so, he said, because the feebleness of the Tory party endangered the constitutional safeguard of a balanced Opposition and seemed to leave "the whole power of the State" in the hands of the Whig majority in the House of Commons. For that reason he claimed to have previously turned to the "independent Reformers" and advocated triennial parliaments and the secret ballot – "to break the strength of the Whigs." But now that the resurgence of the Tory party had renewed the constitutional balance, such measures were no longer necessary. Quite clearly the psychological pattern of Disraeli's responses to events and enactments of his roles holds true. The extraordinary letter to his father is of a piece with the extravagant expressions of his fantasies in the satires and fiction. Again, here, there is a private sense of being different from and better than those he attempts to manipulate. On the other hand, the emphasis in his campaign speech upon his consistency in altruistically pursuing principle through expediency obviously reflects a need to demonstrate his worthiness so that he can be taken in, recognized, and accepted as a member of the political and social elite.

Whether the ideas in the Taunton campaign speech are convictions or rationalizations is difficult to decide. They are probably both. On the one hand, the supposedly Radical measures that Disraeli advocated from time to time can be found in Bolingbroke's opposition to the Whigs a hundred years earlier. On the other hand, Disraeli's adoption of the Radical label in various campaigns was a matter of clear expediency, a matter of increasing his chances of being elected. But even if his explanation of his previous conduct seems to the sceptic to be merely a rationalization, it had the force of conviction for Disraeli now that he had the increased security of official Tory support. This is important because the strength of conviction fuses the conflicting struggle between purity and success into one identity, at least on the political level. The Taunton by-election, when he stands forth as a Tory candidate for the first time, is the moment at which Disraeli is able to combine his claim of purity of motive with a significant measure of public recognition and success. Although he did not win the election (Labouchere 452, Disraeli 282), he could write to Sarah, "The country gentlemen for ten miles round flock to me every day, but I am obliged to decline all their invitations. As for Taunton itself, the enthusiasm of Wycombe is a miniature to it ... It is astonishing how well they are informed in London of all that passes here, and how greatly they appreciate my exertions.[17] And a few days later he could add, "There is no place like *Taunton*, not that I can win this time ... but come in at the general election I must, for I have promises of two-thirds of the electors. I live in a rage of enthusiasm; even my opponents promise to vote for me *next time*. The fatigue is awful. Two long speeches to-day and nine hours' canvass on foot in a blaze of repartee. I am quite exhausted and can scarcely see to write."[18]

With the emergence of a successful political identity with which he could achieve a convincing demonstration of his talent, Disraeli's dandyism gave way to a more profound expression of his spirit. An example of that transition has been preserved by the author of *Pen and Ink Sketches* in his report of the post-election banquet speech Disraeli gave at Taunton:

He commenced in a lisping, lackadaisical tone of voice ... He minced his phrases in apparently the most affected manner, and whilst he was speaking, placed his hands in all imaginable positions ... for the purpose of exhibiting to the best advantage the glittering rings which decked his white and taper fingers. Now he would place his thumbs in the armholes of his waistcoat, and spread out his fingers on its flashing surface; then one set of digits would be released and he would lean affectedly on the table, supporting himself with his right hand; anon he would push aside the curls from his forehead ... But as he proceeded all traces of this dandyism and affectation were lost. With a rapidity of utterance perfectly astonishing he referred to past events and indulged in anticipations of the future. The Whigs were, of course, the objects of his unsparing satire, and his eloquent denunciations of them were applauded to the echo ... he proved himself to be the finished orator – every period was rounded with the utmost eloquence, and in his most daring flights, when one trembled lest he should fall from the giddy height to which he had attained, he so gracefully descended that every hearer was rapt in admiring surprise ... His voice, at first so finical, gradually became full, musical, and sonorous ... The dandy was transformed into the man of mind, the Mantolini-looking personage into a practised orator and finished elocutionist.[19]

The speech itself Monypenny sees as "the first in which we find the main lines of his creed of democratic Toryism firmly drawn." But in fact it was only a rhetorical refinement of the position Disraeli had been developing in the past two and a half years. He believes the Conservative party is the "really democratic party" because it supports the Throne to shield the people from "the undue power of the aristocracy." He is in favour of a hereditary monarchy because the king whose powers and authority are "judiciously limited" is in effect the great leader of the people. And he supports the Established Church because it is devoted to those many people who from lack of wealth and property are otherwise disenfranchised.[20] While his emphasis upon the plight of the people is perhaps unprecedented, there is nothing in this formulation of his ideology that is not derivative of Bolingbroke's ideas and, in particular, the theory of the mixed constitution.

This speech does, however, have another interest. One of the objects of Disraeli's eloquent satire was the current relationship between the Whigs and Daniel O'Connell. And his remarks in this instance suggest an attitude toward Catholicism of quite recent origin. In The Young Duke and Contarini Fleming Disraeli had shown himself to be a sympathetic expositor of the Catholic question in England. But in the letter to Sarah dated 20 February 1835 (previously cited, n. 7), he concluded his description of the Speakership vote with the following remark: "O'Connell is so powerful that he says he will be in the Cabinet. How can the Whigs submit to this? It is the Irish Catholic party that has done all the mischief."[21] This is the first indication of an anti-Catholic animus upon Disraeli's part. His attitude is clearly the result of O'Connell's alliance with his enemies, the Whigs, to thwart what he conceived to be both the public and his private interests. Coming at the moment when he had just declared his commitment to a public identity in the ranks of the Tories, this hostility was to have deep reverberations within the continuing inner struggle of the opposing senses of himself, and, as it became intensified by that struggle, was to affect both the subject matter of his subsequent novels and the political history of England.

In the Taunton festival speech Disraeli mocked the Whigs for obtaining power "by leaguing themselves with one they had denounced as a traitor." In doing so, he was using the language the Whigs themselves had recently employed to describe the Irish leader. The London papers, however, reported a summarized version of the speech in which Disraeli appeared to have himself called O'Connell "an incendiary and a traitor."[22] The volatile Irishman saw the garbled version and, at a meeting in Dublin, produced a savage reply in which he called Disraeli "a vile creature," "an egregious liar," and "a miscreant of ... abominable description." O'Connell then went on to compound the insult by saying that the language, though harsh, was "no more than deserved" and that he could find "no harsher epithets ... by which to convey ... [his] utter abhorrence ... for such a reptile." It was, however, the conclusion of O'Connell's remarks that struck most forcibly at Disraeli's identity, and not just because the Irishman alleged that he had "all the necessary requisites of perfidy, selfishness, depravity, want of principle, &c." to be a Conservative:

His name shows that he is of Jewish origin. I do not use it as a term of reproach; there are many most respectable Jews. But there are, as in every other people, some of the lowest and most disgusting grade of moral turpitude; and of those I look upon Mr. Disraeli as the worst. He has just the qualities of the impenitent thief on the Cross, and I verily believe, if Mr. Disraeli's family herald were to be examined and his genealogy traced, the same personage would be discovered to be the heir at law of the exalted individual to whom I allude. I forgive Mr. Disraeli now, and as the lineal descendent of the blasphemous robber, who ended his career beside the Founder of the Christian Faith, I leave the gentleman to the enjoyment of his infamous distinction and family honours.[23]

These outrageous remarks went to the very core of Disraeli's heart. It was probably the charges of inconsistency and ingratitude (O'Connell had reminded his audience that he had been asked to give Disraeli a letter of support at the time of the first Wycombe campaign) that hurt him the most in the public eye. But the scurrilous references to his Jewish heritage, however limited to his personal character, smacked of anti-Semitism and raised anew the internal struggle between Disraeli's conflicting senses of himself.

Disraeli had every reason to be anti-Catholic in a political sense, for in Ireland, then as now, politics and religion are inextricably bound together. His theory of Conservative ideas placed the institution of the Established Church at the very centre of the social fabric. Peel's Government had fallen on the issue of reappropriating the revenues of that church in Ireland, and it was the support of O'Connell's Irish Catholic faction, whose ultimate aim was repeal of the Union, that had allowed the Whigs to form another Government. But it would seem that O'Connell's abusive attack fanned the flames of Disraeli's hostility into a blaze of religious prejudice that far transcended the personal hatred he felt for the Irish leader. O'Connell's attack struck Disraeli at the very point at which he was most vulnerable. In raising again the issue of his family heritage, it displaced Disraeli's internal struggle from the realm of Tory politics, where at least a partial assimilation of the Jewish identity had taken place, back to the personal one where no resolution seemed possible. It is not surprising, given the motifs of religious identity in *The Young Duke* and *Contarini Fleming*, and given the metaphoric connections among religion, dishonour, and death in *Alroy* and *Iskander*, that Disraeli should respond to his "crucifixion" by issuing a challenge to a duel. O'Connell had previously killed a man in such an encounter and had vowed never to fight another, so the challenge was sent to his son, Morgan O'Connell, who had once before acted in the interests of his father's integrity. The substitution indicates that Disraeli was simply interested in a symbolic restoration of his honour and vindication of his political identity. As the correspondence shows, he was prepared to bide his time to wreak revenge upon the elder O'Connell: "the hour is at hand when I shall be more successful, and take my place in that proud assembly ... I expect to be a representative of the people before the repeal of the Union. We shall meet at Philippi; and rest assured that ... I will seize the first opportunity of inflicting upon you a castigation which will make you ... remember and repent the insults that you have lavished upon Benjamin Disraeli." This letter is for the most part rational and restrained. But just before this passage Disraeli took note of the personal allusions in O'Connell's attack in very different language from that in which he had defended his political consistency in opposing the Whigs.

The violence of Disraeli's anti-Catholic remarks is clearly a function of their juxtaposition to the issue of his Jewish heritage:

> I admire your scurrilous allusion to my origin. It is quite clear that the "hereditary bondsman" has already forgotten the clank of his fetter. I know the tactics of your Church; it clamours for toleration, and it labours for supremacy. I see that you are quite prepared to persecute.
>
> With regard to your taunts as to my want of success in my election contests, permit me to remind you that I had nothing to appeal to but the good sense of the people. No threatening skeletons canvassed for me; a death's-head and cross-bones were not blazoned on my banners. My pecuniary resources, too, were limited; I am not one of those public beggars that we see swarming with their obtrusive boxes in the chapels of your creed, nor am I in possession of a princely revenue wrung from a starving race of fanatical slaves.[24]

This could be considered simply a matter of tit for tat. Certainly Disraeli was ready to give as much as he received when it came to abuse. But there is a difference between the insults of the two men. O'Connell qualifies his onslaught, making it explicitly personal, whereas Disraeli attacks the religion, not just his antagonist. This is shown again when, after having been arrested and bound to keep the peace, Disraeli writes to the electors of Taunton to counteract criticism of his "ferocious" and "vindictive" language: "If in those hot and hurried letters I indulged in expressions which my calmer reason may disapprove, I am sure no candid and generous spirit, whatever may be his party, would scan with severity the words of one who had been subjected, without the prospect of redress, to such unparalleled outrage ... who young, alone, and supported only by his own energies, and in the inspiration of a good cause, dared to encounter, in no inglorious struggle, the most powerful individual in the world who does not wear a crown."[25] This attack on the papacy is, it is clear, simply a renewal of the insult even as the initial instance of it is excused.

There is something strange about this anti-Catholicism on Disraeli's part. While the Lichfield House compact was sufficient reason for a Tory attack on the Catholic faction in the House of Commons, O'Connell seems, as a result of a journalistic inaccuracy, to have uncovered the

flower of a virulent prejudice in Disraeli. Such prejudice does not spring
to life overnight, though the blossoming of it into expression might well
be forced in a traumatic moment. Had his conversion from sympathetic
identification with the Catholic cause to suspicious opposition to it been
simply a form of political manoeuvring, Disraeli's remarks would probably have remained at the level of witticism and personal abuse. He was
too volatile to sustain the dignity and rationalism with which Peel had
fought the charges of betrayal when he was converted in the opposite
direction in 1829. But it is unlikely that Disraeli would have indulged in
the paranoid hatred tinged with self-pity evidenced above unless something more were at stake. It is the way in which Catholicism and
Jewishness are identified with each other in the fantasy structure of the
early novels and tales, and the way in which the issue of religious fealty
is connected in these works to the hero's ambivalent senses of himself,
and, by an extension justified by the compulsively repeated pattern, to
the author's corresponding struggles, which lead one to the conclusion
that O'Connell's attack not only embarrassed Disraeli publicly, but also
threatened privately the resolution of his recent identity confusion.
When Disraeli found the means to achieve the recognition and acceptance he wanted without denying his difference and innate superiority,
he was sufficiently "uneasy in Zion"[26] that upon provocation all the
guilt and ambivalence about purity and superiority on the one hand,
and success and ambivalence on the other, could overwhelm him.

It is not only the evidence of the fiction that supports this idea. The
previously cited entries in the "Early Diary" also reveal that the question of religious affiliation is a vital part within the matrix of Disraeli's
psychological development – that it is connected to his relationships
with his mother and subsequent substitutes, the struggle for both "purity" and "success," and all the forms of self-assertion and self-denial
that are manifested in both the fiction and the political career. O'Connell's
vituperation thus triggered the explosive power of Disraeli's fantasies
about himself, and the resultant violent anti-Catholicism of his political
writings in the next few years, while it should be seen in the light of the
reappropriation issue and the Lichfield House compact, would seem to
be an unconscious and disguised rejection of that part of himself which
threatened to preclude political success at the very time when he had
just established a viable political identity as an official Tory candidate
and triumph seemed imminent.

This is not to suggest that the more obvious explanations of Disraeli's
behaviour are irrelevant, nor that the novels and political life can be

reduced simply to manifestations of his fantasies. Rather, the intention is to assert that the works of fiction and the shape of the political career represent a conjunction of external and internal forces, of public and private motivations, and of conscious and unconscious responses. To recognize such connections is to acquit Disraeli of many charges of hypocrisy and to take the opportunity of explaining much in his life that otherwise seems perverse or illogical. The truth is astounding enough. In the matter of the sudden appearance of anti-Catholic prejudice, for example, Disraeli was neither simply a hypocrite nor an opportunist. The earlier sympathy for Catholics, as reflected in *The Young Duke* and *Contarini Fleming* can be seen as a timely theme, given that "Catholic Emancipation" was a marketable commodity in the 1820s and 1830s. And the incorporation in these novels of the personal religious dilemma in disguised form was an act of deliberate artistic creation. In "The Mutilated Diary" entry for 1833 Disraeli had described *Vivian Grey*, *Alroy*, and *Contarini Fleming* as "the secret history of … [his] feelings." Yet, even so, it is unlikely that Disraeli fully realized at the time the extent to which his fictional writing was a process of self-discovery.

I

The parliamentary session of 1835 was distinguished by the so-called constitutional crisis surrounding the Municipal Corporations Bill. Those who had opposed the Reform Bill of 1832 now saw their worst fears being realized in this new measure of reform. Just as they believed the Reform Bill to have been an attempt to overthrow the political power of the predominantly Tory land-owning class, they now believed that the intent of the new bill was to upset a traditional source of Conservative power by altering the constitution of municipal government. Indeed, the Ultra-Tory Lords' response to the new piece of legislation was so rhetorically violent and so determinedly resistant that it forced into prominence the implicit constitutional changes that they most feared by seeming to bring the House of Lords and the House of Commons into direct and open conflict.

The controversy surrounding the Municipal Corporations Bill gave Disraeli another chance to act out his fantasy of self-importance, and to work in telling ways through men of power. In this instance the ideological issues of the new debate provided an unparalleled opportunity for him to declare himself a principled Conservative, even as he tried to manipulate people and events to his own advantage. The resultant arrangement of Disraeli's needs and ambitions, fantasies and actions, in a staunchly Tory identity was less vulnerable than those he had previously adopted, despite the fact that it was marked by the same desperate overestimation of his role as the earlier unstable arrangements. This is so because he finds an expression of retreat from the collapse of the power fantasy that reinforces the form of his actual political identity.

According to Disraeli, by the time the Municipal Corporations Bill was introduced, Lord Lyndhurst had formed a definite plan for "stopping the movement" (towards democratization) and tried it out upon this measure.[27] Some of the Whigs or ex-Whigs, particularly Stanley and Graham, were anxious to act in accordance with what was acceptable to Peel, but the latter was sufficiently nervous about the principle of a popular constituency and the idea of frequent elections to wish to remain independent and uncommitted in advance. But many other members of the Conservative party were deeply suspicious of the Government's motives, as well as afraid of any excuse for Radical cohesion and of trusting financial matters to the poorer classes. Peel felt that he wanted to "consider what was prudent and safe." He was "more interested in protecting the monarchy and public interests involved in its security" than in developing an immediate party position.[28] When he agreed to the introduction of the bill in the House of Commons it was because he recognized that the time had come to reform the obvious abuses of municipal corporations. He accepted the principle that their revenues should be applied to public purposes, but only apprehensively did he acknowledge that their authority should be under the popular control of an extended franchise. His attempts to amend this last aspect of the measure, however, were not designed to endanger it and he did not argue that the Commons was exceeding its powers in depriving men of their chartered rights. This was the essential issue for most Tories, because the bill would have disenfranchised many who had been voters in parliamentary elections and it would have made the offices of aldermen recurrently elective. It was thus seen as an exclusively factional attempt to destroy the Conservative strength in the corporations. It must be remembered that Peel was again convinced that the Tories could not form an alternative ministry. Many of the Conservative peers, their desires fanned by the sentiments of the king, by the party's increased strength in the Commons, and by the supposed anti-Whig reaction in the country, were more hopeful. Lyndhurst was the central figure in that group.

Initially there seems to have been some inclination to keep the Lords' amendments restricted to what Peel could support, since it seemed to them that he might be returned to office and called upon to propose a similar measure. But when the bill passed second reading in the upper House, it was on the condition that its principle be discussed by legal counsel at the bar of the House of Lords. The Conservative advocate was Sir Charles Wetherell, and his violent argument, which took the better part of two days, excited Ultra-Conservative sensibilities to such an extent that the Tory peers, meeting at Apsley House on 3 August, decided to take evidence against the principle of the bill. The Duke of Wellington objected to this way of proceeding, but he was overruled by the majority present. According to Disraeli, it was about this time that Lyndhurst temporarily took control of the party. He told Sarah, "The Duke has formally resigned to him the leadership of the House of Lords; and there is every probability of his being Prime Minister."[29] Such optimism reflected Disraeli's enthusiasm for Lyndhurst's role in the debate of the previous week and his own sense of being at the centre of the action. In a letter to Sarah, written from the House of Lords, he characterizes the situation as "an awful crisis" where "affa[irs] every hour have assumed a different hue," and he apologizes for not writing earlier by suggesting that to have done so would have misled her and filled her "with wild hopes and fear": "more than once I myself despaired, so hampered are we, or rather have been, by Peels [sic] admission of the principle." The debate, he reported, was "dashing in the extreme" and Lyndhurst had made a "bold and triumphant" speech, "received with tumultuous cheering," that left Melbourne seeming "quite wild and scared."[30] Lyndhurst had attacked the bill as serving the factional interests of the Whigs and "revoking Chartered Rights merely because they were inexpedient." He spoke with such energy and eloquence and stirred such excitement that the Lords voted with a huge majority to take evidence on the arguments of counsel. Moderate Conservatives thought this course likely to lead to crisis rather than compromise, to rejection of the bill rather than amendment of it. And even before the first meeting at Apsley House Peel had told the Tory peers that he completely disapproved of such action and would not be held responsible for it. Now the division between Peel and Lyndhurst was notorious and widely reported in the press.[31]

Ill, disgusted, and angry, Peel suddenly left London and retreated to Drayton. Although he remained out of town for several weeks, his feelings were transmitted to the moderates before the Tory peers met again at Apsley House on the 10th and agreed not to meet the bill with a direct negative, but rather to go into committee. Lyndhurst, who had been

intent upon bringing down the Whig Government, and who in the light
of the king's and Ultra-Tories' support had come to see this as his duty,
now to his annoyance began to find that the necessity of party unity
rendered his "duty" inexpedient. But that was not what his earlier
speech had implied.

During all of this manoeuvring Disraeli was closer to Lyndhurst than
ever. Henrietta, the ex-chancellor, and his protégé had visited
Bradenham together a few weeks before and, incidentally, scandalized
Buckinghamshire society. Lyndhurst's private secretary had "turned
out to be an Ass" under the pressure of the moment, and Disraeli soon
filled his shoes. The excitement and anticipations of these weeks were
so intense that Disraeli at times felt he could not trust himself "to write
about politics," though he did extol the heroic efforts of Lyndhurst to
get up the "counter-project," and tell his sister in the same letter
(11 August), "Tomorrow the war begins in the Lords." This last letter is
of special interest because it reveals how deeply Disraeli has invested
his own hope of getting into Parliament in Lyndhurst's scheme: "He
says there are only three things certain, that the Tories will be in before
we are many moons perhaps weeks older, that Parliamt. will be dissolved and that my seat is secured. I do not choose to Xeamine [cross-
examine] him on this latter score, but I hold him to his voluntary
promise. He says *he has arranged it*. Now as he is very cautious and
chary in promises, and quite to be depended on I indulge the belief that
all is at last right."[32] The "Summary of Political Events for 1835," written at Bradenham in 1836, gives much the same impression of Disraeli's
close, albeit naive, relationship to Lyndhurst:

> Jealousy of Peel. Lyndhurst determines to accept the Premiership if of-
> fered, having recd. hints from Windsor. His plan to make Brougham
> Chancellor – to demand from his party 10 seats in the Commons, which
> were to be given to 10 young men whom he shd. select. I was one, Bickham
> Escott another, Thesiger a third. The Commons to be led by Sir Jas Graham,
> whom he had sounded, and Sir Wm. Follett, in whom he had great confi-
> dence. Peel came up from Drayton and threw him over, and a part of the
> Lords, led by Wharncliffe, frightened at not being supported in the
> Commons, seceded from their engagement at a meeting at Apsley House
> at the end of August or beginning of Septr.[33]

This is a much simplified account of a complex and protracted issue
and shows Disraeli to have once again been caught up in heady fantasies

in which his grasp of political reality was lost among visions of power. There was no chance of a Conservative ministry without a unified party. And Peel, though angry, was hardly jealous; he had the soundest of public motives for his disapproval of what the Ultra-Tory Lords were doing, and a more than sufficient following for his moderate tactics.

Lyndhurst, forced to abandon his plan of forcing an immediate and direct confrontation with the Whigs by rejecting the bill, took up the task of creating amendments that Disraeli called the "counter-project." It is clear that Lyndhurst's intention was still to bring down the Whigs and "stop the movement" by insisting on changes that would be unacceptable to the majority in the Commons.[34] But it is equally clear that Disraeli was so caught up in the Ultra-Tory intrigue that he failed to discern both the extent of Peel's real grievance against his ex-chancellor and the implications of the compromise in the Lords of sending the bill to committee. The outline of Lyndhurst's plan of amendments, which proposed among other things a qualification clause and the appointment of aldermen constituting a fourth of the Town Council for life, were sent to Peel on the 11th of August. He did not approve of them and felt that such antithetical amendments were improper. As a consequence, he let it be known that he "would assume no responsibility in forming a Government if the existing one were broken up by a course to which he had not been a party, and of which he did not approve." Lyndhurst, nevertheless, proceeded to carry his amendments with "crushing majorities," raising the spectre of a constitutional crisis as the bill moved back to the Commons. Meanwhile, an Irish Tithe Bill had passed the lower House only to have its appropriation clause deleted in the Lords.[35]

With less than disinterested naivety Disraeli gave credence to current rumours and expected the Whigs to resign at any moment. On 14 August he tells Sarah that he thinks they will "go out on the Corporations," but a week later supposes they will resign over the appropriation clause. In the event neither was the case. The Government simply decided to withdraw the Irish Tithe Bill. In the midst of these manoeuvres, as Disraeli's gossip indicates, some of the Ultras clearly harboured the hope that, if the Government resigned, Lyndhurst could form a ministry;[36] but the majority, even in the Lords, saw how forlorn that hope was, despite the repugnance with which they viewed the original bill. The Government's intentions with regard to the measure, which by means of the Lords' amendments had indeed become "a Conservative arrangement" and "an entire new Bill," remained a mystery until Monday,

31 August, when Russell, at a meeting of between two and three hundred supporters at the Foreign Office, indicated which of the Lords' amendments he would accept and which he must refuse. That same day he opened the debate in the House of Commons in a temperate and conciliatory manner, conceding much, but rejecting some of the amendments and radically altering the clause about aldermen. Peel, who had suddenly returned for the debate, then took up the task of compromise and, though defending their rights to amend, "as everybody said (some with joy, others with rage), 'threw over the Lords'" by completely abandoning the life tenure provision of the aldermen's clause.[37] Peel's hope was to achieve an amicable settlement and he certainly placated the Whigs. But as Charles Greville reports, "Nothing could exceed the dismay and the rage (though suppressed) of the Conservatives at his speech. He was not a bit cheered by those behind him, but very heartily by those opposite."

When the Tory peers met at Apsley House again on 3 September to consider the amendments to the amendments, "the very existence of the party" seemed at stake.[38] Indeed, the crisis over the Municipal Corporations Bill was less a confrontation between two legislative bodies than one between two factions of the Conservative party. The Ultra-Tories conceived themselves to be defending the essence of the constitution, taking the structure of the corporations to be a microcosm of the larger political realm. As Lyndhurst had argued, "these Corporations were copies – imperfect copies … of the three estates of the realm."[39] Lord Harrowby, however, urged an accommodation with the Commons, saying that the battle of the Houses should be fought on more tenable grounds with a greater issue involving some higher principle. The Duke of Wellington, caught between wisdom and friends, finally urged the politic course of abandoning the aldermen's clause, and that decision was taken. The Commons then acceded to the remaining amendments that the Lords insisted upon, and the "crisis" dissolved. It was the opinion of both Radicals and Ultra-Tories, however, that the storm had done the members of the upper House no good in that it had raised a cry for its reform from those who found its obstruction of the Government's legislation intolerable. Even Lord Howick thought that the Lords would be "swept away like chaff," while Lyndhurst predicted that there was "no chance of the H. of Lords surviving ten years."[40] But that was not the orthodoxy to which the majority of both Tories and Whigs paid lip service: that the independence of the House of Lords had been vindicated.

As Lyndhurst's confidant and unofficial private secretary, Disraeli became very caught up in the Ultra-Tories' reactionary hostility to any kind of reform. Peel's original attempts to amend the Municipal Corporations Bill in the House of Commons had been thwarted by the Whig-Radical-Irish coalition and so Lyndhurst and his colleagues were easily persuaded that they were the last bulwark to the flood of egalitarian democracy. O'Connell's attack on Disraeli after the Taunton by-election had undoubtedly made Protestant high-Toryism the natural safe port, while Lyndhurst's friendship was the course to its entry. These alone would explain the change in Disraeli's ideas about corporate reform from those he had expressed in *The Crisis Examined* (where he urged that burgesses should be elected by the inhabitants and aldermen in turn elected by the burgesses) to an unqualified support of freemen's rights and life-tenure of aldermen. But, as is clear from the correspondence with Sarah and the 1836 summary of political events, the circumstances surrounding Lyndhurst's plan for stopping the "movement" also once again enabled Disraeli to indulge his recurring power fantasy – to envision himself achieving political success by being rewarded with a seat in Parliament and having the confidence of the next prime minister. It is in the light of this fantasy that we should see his eagerness to serve the Ultra-Tory cause by writing a series of pseudononymous articles for the *Morning Post* in August and September.

In his speech advocating the taking of evidence on the principle of the bill, Lyndhurst had characterized the corporations measure as "Whig in its principle – Whig in its character, and Whig in its object."[41] In the *Morning Post* articles Disraeli took up these themes in a strain of "reckless vituperation."[42] His consideration of the principles involved, of the character of the bill itself, and of the purposes it might serve, is completely partisan. The intention is to defend the Tories and attack the Whigs; the result is often rabid journalism. Still, the daily mixtures of topical comment embody four main thrusts that reflect the development of Disraeli's ideas. He is at pains to justify the Ultra-Tory resistance to "Reform"; he attempts to discredit members of the Whig Government; he repeatedly and deliberately exploits the "no Popery cry"; and, finally, he defends the peerage as an institution.

The first of these arguments involves issues of both immediate practical and general ideological concern. Disraeli argues that the Whigs' purpose in bringing forward the Municipal Corporations Bill is "to consolidate their power" and that the Lords' amendments "have eradicated the *party virus*" of it and "baffled the conspiracy to plunder the freemen of England."[43] As was the case in the Reform crisis of 1832, the Tories were convinced in 1835 that the basis of their social privileges and political power was under assault by revolutionary forces. Lyndhurst, for example, considered the Corporations Bill "nearly as important as the Reform Bill" in that he assumed it would make "the new Councils ... Radical," which by influence would "radicalize the Boroughs."[44] With heavy irony and dripping bathos Disraeli predicts the effect of this latest instance of "Gallomania": "The Whigs have previously carved up the old English Counties, and now they are going to Radicalize the old English towns. It is their evident determination to assimilate the institutions of this country to those of France – free and favoured France. Instead of the County and the Borough we shall soon have the *arrondisement* and the commune. The préfet and the gendarmerie follow, of course. Alas, Old England!"[45] In contrast, he claims that the Lords' amendment to retain "the titles and offices, the powers and privileges, of Aldermen" is in "wise sympathy with ancient associations and time-honoured forms, existing authority and vested rights." And, of course, the strength of the Conservative party!

This emphatic defence of concrete Toryism is balanced by one of more philosophic dimensions. The "Whig Reform Act," Disraeli argues, "has filled the imaginations of certain representatives of the Commons ... with the bold but ruinous *project* of destroying the authority of the Upper Chamber, and so monopolising ... the whole power of the State" (emphasis added).[46] The efficacy of this statement stems less from its truth than from the fact that the Government of the day was dependent for its survival upon the Radicals in the House of Commons. This is why the amendments carried by the Conservative majority in the House of Lords could be, and were, projected by extremists on both sides from a party to a constitutional context. Tory insistence on the right and power of the Lords to amend or reject legislation passed by the Commons brought cries for reform of the upper House from the Radicals. In turn, their determination that the will of the majority in the Commons be served, led to charges of despotism and tyranny. Thus Disraeli conjures up, as he had done in *The Crisis Examined* and earlier speeches, the iniquities of the Long Parliament to illustrate the dangers of the country "being governed by the House of Commons alone." The crimes of excessive taxation, fraud, and illegal expropriation, of which he accuses the seventeenth-century members of Parliament,[47] are taken to be real threats of the present time, not just because history would likely repeat itself, but because Disraeli sees the erosion of individual civil liberties in the current Radical position. This is why he extends the debate on the relatively minor matter of a parliamentary investigation of the alleged growth of Orange Lodges within the ranks of the army into a lengthy parallel with that "despotic House of Commons" that had ordered the torture of a reluctant witness.[48] Disraeli's argument is that the freedom and liberties of the people can only be guaranteed so long as the House of Commons is prevented from establishing itself as an oligarchy with supreme power. It follows that the Established Church, the House of Lords, and the monarchy are the guarantors of those liberties and that the Lords in particular have a duty to resist any measures that would tend to place "the whole power of the State" in the hands of one particular interest. That resistance is particularly justi-fied in the case of the Lords' amendments to the Municipal Corporations Bill because that measure is an attempt to consolidate the power of the Whig party, a party which in power has attempted to undermine those institutions that stand in the way of a partisan oligarchy. So runs the first part of Disraeli's argument: it is worth noting that there is little, if anything, new in this position, or the material he uses to support it. But, as Peter Jupp has shown, Disraeli's interpretation of history is based on "extensive reading and a careful synthesis of contemporary conceptual approaches to the past." And, in that sense, history is here a defining element of his political cause.[49]

The second of the argumentative thrusts that distinguish Disraeli's *Morning Post* articles comprises a series of personal attacks on individ-ual members of the Government and their allies. Again, they are not unprecedented, as his mockery of Lord Brougham in "The Infernal Marriage" witnesses. But now, protected by anonymity and prodded by Ultra-Tory passions, Disraeli indulges in personal abuse that would be unthinkable on the hustings or in a work to which he subscribed his name. To begin with mild illustrations, Lord Melbourne is accused of "political profligacy" and "barefaced apostasy," of being "a notorious place-hunter," the "most indolent and inefficient of public men," whose "mind is impregnated with a sort of bastard French philosophy," and who is, "Except Palmerston … the veriest and most thorough political hack going."[50] Disraeli characterizes the public meetings of the so-called PEOPLE as typically no more than the "rump of the Political Union, the debris of that 'aristocracy of blackguards' listening to the brainless brayings of that melancholy ass Attwood."[51] But in general he is content to castigate most of the Radicals for their ignorance and illit-eracy in less violent language: "Hume," for instance, "can neither speak nor write English; his calligraphy reminds one of a chandler's shop, and his letters resemble a butter-man's bill." "Warburton" is "more ignorant even than Hume, but more discreet and consequently less loquacious." Their party is composed of "petty plunderers, would-be Commissioners, and other small toad-eaters ... But the ignorance of Warburton rather staggers even these parasites." "Wakley," on the other hand, "is of a lighter order of mind than the preceding worthies." There is, Disraeli says, "a vulgar vivacity about him which is not un-amusing." He would, he adds, "make an admirable cad or a first-rate conductor of an omnibus."[52]

As the "collision" seems imminent in the latter days of August, Disraeli begins to lose his fancied light touch. In the House of Lords the Whigs cast aspersions on the political past of Lyndhurst, who in rebuttal seemed to get the best of the matter. When Lord Denman renewed the issue (and, as Disraeli describes it, "tried to confirm ... some of the factious exaggerations of his own factious falsehoods, uttered after the miserable inspiration of some of his own bad wine, at some of his own wretched dinners"), he was unable to sustain a single specific charge.[53] Denman's attack on Lyndhurst was, however, enough to bring forth his protégé's scorn. Disraeli claims that Lord Denman is a "remarkable individual for having attained his public eminence despite "the total absence of any qualities which would justify his rise and his appointment." Lord Denman has, he says, "failed decidedly, in everything which he has undertaken," from being "one of the worst lawyers" and "clumsiest advocates" that ever practised to his current position as Lord Chief Justice. But, adds Disraeli, Denman has repeatedly found employment and preferment by the Whigs because he has always been "a violent party man."[54]

The rhetorical artillery of this response is far heavier than required by the threat of the trivial issue at stake – whether Lord Lyndhurst owed "his introduction to public life to 'the Liberals.'" Coupled with the earlier praise of the ex-chancellor, it shows the degree to which Disraeli is identifying himself with his benefactor. It also suggests his continuing vulnerability to charges of political inconsistency, for Denman's most irritating quality is his allegiance to the Whigs, which has brought him success despite his lack of personal ability, while Disraeli, with all his genius, talent, and wit, is still scrambling for recognition and, though he does not know it, is once again on the verge of finding his desire for public recognition and power thwarted.

As the crisis approaches its climax, Disraeli abandons all discretion. The occasion is ostensibly the remarks of the current attorney-general, Sir John

Campbell, upon the Lords' postponement of action upon the Imprisonment for Debt Bill. But it is also the day upon which the Government is to take up Lyndhurst's amendments to the Corporations Bill in the Commons. Having called for Lord Melbourne's "IMPEACHMENT" and proclaimed that the present cabinet's inability to govern the country is something the "first dissolution of Parliament ... will easily rectify," Disraeli proves himself to be a violent party man.[55] His ostensible intent is to mock Attorney General Sir John Campbell's attempts at wit. First Disraeli indulges in insult by calling Campbell a "shrewd, coarse, manoeuvring Pict," but he then goes on with gross vindictiveness:

> Fancy an ourang-outang of unusual magnitude dancing under a banana-tree, and licking its hairy chaps, and winking with exultation its cunning eyes as it beholds the delicious and impending fruit, and one may form a tolerable idea of Sir John Campbell's appearance in the House of Commons on Friday night when he tried to be jocular ... that this baseborn Scotchman, who knows right well that if the tide were, in his opinion, the other way, he would lick the very dust a Lord might tread on – that this booing, fawning, jobbing progeny of haggis and cockaleekie should dare to sneer at the Peers of England – pah! vulgar insolence must have run to seed to have produced this scampish jest.[56]

That Disraeli should defend the Tory Lords in such a manner at the moment when their actions seemed to be precipitating a constitutional crisis is consistent with his position as Lyndhurst's unofficial secretary and his general involvement in the Ultra-Tory plan of resistance to the Whigs' ideas of further reform. But the savage hostility of this attack can in part be attributed to another, more private, political motive.

Sir John Campbell introduced the Imprisonment for Debt Bill with the intention of abolishing imprisonment for debt and replacing it with a "more efficient remedy for creditors" by "personal examination of the debtor as to his property and past expenditure." The bill did not become law until 1837 and only then in a much modified form. But under the provisions of the original bill presented in 1835 "there was no limit to this power of inquiry, and every one was subject to it against whom a judgment was recovered."[57] William Hutcheon attributed Disraeli's savagery to the fact that Lyndhurst was "much alarmed" by this bill, a fact which Campbell records amid speculation about the precarious nature of Lyndhurst's finances and the possibility of a judgment being obtained against him.[58] And it was indeed Lyndhurst who in 1837 approached Campbell to point out the "oppression and extortion which might be practised by the power proposed to be given to judgment creditors" and to insist that "as members of the two Houses were not subject to imprisonment for debt, they ought not to be subject to the inquisition substituted for it."[59] But, as Disraeli's letters from this period show, his finances were in far worse shape than Lyndhurst's. He had at this time virtually no visible earned income and was living an extravagant life with Henrietta Sykes that was supported by money borrowed largely from Benjamin Austen and credit obtained wherever possible. Disraeli was, in fact, constantly being dunned for payments on his loans and debts and his situation was growing steadily more desperate, soon to reach the point of having to evade officers of the law.[60] No doubt, the exemption of members of Parliament from imprisonment for debt was for Disraeli in itself not an insignificant attraction of such a career. The violent response to Campbell's remarks, however, suggests that his concern was more political than financial, that he gave less thought to the possibility of escaping prosecution for his debts than to the danger of having his political career destroyed by publicity about them. His Jewish heritage and his reputation for insincerity, inconsistency, and impropriety were liabilities enough. The Imprisonment for Debt Bill now threatened to render vain what must have seemed his imminent success in transcending them, in that it could, if passed, have enabled his creditors to bring to public scrutiny all the details of his profligacy. So, while this particular scurrilous passage served the Ultra-Tory cause, it was also intended to serve Disraeli's own.

The way in which the two interests are allied and the way in which private motive and public ideology are related can be seen in the continuation of the passage quoted above. Disraeli points out that the subject of the bill has engaged the attention of the Commons for two sessions and that it had there been referred to a committee who examined its details and summoned witnesses. It is thus unreasonable, he argues, to attack the House of Lords and question its "utility" simply because they also want to discuss the principle and the details of the bill.[61] And it is but a short step from this specific argument to abstract Tory ideology. The essence of the issue is the powers, rights, and duties of the House of Lords, which is the most important constitutional question of nineteenth-century British history, and one that would not be finally resolved until the budgetary crisis of 1909.

Another example of the personal element in Disraeli's politics, and the third distinguishing feature of the *Morning Post* articles, is his public exploitation of the "no-Popery" cry. As has been shown, the understandable hostility to the Irish political faction in the House of Commons first grew in the soil of the Lichfield House compact and blossomed into religious prejudice during the row with O'Connell at the time of the Taunton by-election. That anti-Catholicism was related to Disraeli's sense of his own identity, and in 1835 it quickly becomes an integral part of his political convictions. Partly because that prejudice involves an element of self-denial, the political expression of it is both virulent and recurrent. Perhaps the best example of the exploitation of "no-Popery" occurs in the article of 26 August when Disraeli characterizes the Lords' exclusion of the appropriation clause from the Irish Tithe Bill, and the Government's subsequent withdrawal of it, as "a struggle" between "the Protestant Peers of England" and "the Papacy." The bill had been passed in the Commons by a very small majority, "the mere suffrages of the Popish members." In contrast Disraeli extolls the peers' unanimous approval in committee of "every clause which relates to the relief of … practical evils, thus proving the sincerity of their wishes to advance all measures for the benefit … of Ireland." He characterizes Lord Melbourne's refusal at that point to carry the measure any further as an insolent loud clamour, but notes that, in the midst of it, the "clank of his fetter" could still be heard. By depending on "the votes of perjured Papists," the prime minister, Disraeli says, has become "The Slave of O'Connell!"[62]

The invocation of the Lords' struggle for survival as a holy war against the forces of the papacy is continued throughout the whole series of *Morning Post* articles. Again and again O'Connell and the Irish members of the Commons are labelled with the tag, "Popish rebels," and from the first Lord Melbourne is taunted with being "O'Connell's Prime Minister … not the King's."[63] Indeed, it is the alliance between the Irish and the Whigs that calls forth Disraeli's most violent language. On 27 August he pictures the prime minister "crawling in the dust before a Popish rebel," and two days later he refers to Melbourne's attempts to "conciliate O'Connell … by bribing him with the plunder of the Establishment in Ireland" as a "sacrilegious and treasonable connection."[64] The precise nature of that treason is fully elaborated in the article of 28 August. The "arch-conspirators" in the Commons, who would destroy "the authority of the Upper Chamber" and so monopolize "the whole power of the State," "finding that they could not obtain the co-operation of a majority of the British members of the House of Commons in their wicked device, entered into a most infamous and sacrilegious conspiracy with the Popish rebels of Ireland, by whose aid alone they have already upset the King's Government, and by whose continued assistance they propose abolishing the House of Lords, and rooting up the Throne itself."[65] According to Disraeli, then, for the sake of staying in power, Lord Melbourne has engaged in a twofold conspiracy: first with the Radicals who would destroy the constitutional fabric of the country; and then with the Irish Catholics who would destroy its political unity.

Disraeli is correct in pointing out that the majority of the British members of the House of Commons would not support the Radicals' agenda. (Sir Robert Peel's Conservatives actually held a majority of the English seats following the general election in December 1834.) Thus, it is the Whigs' critical alliance with the Irish faction that enables them to bring forward their "destructive measures." From this perspective the Tory opposition to the Whig-Irish coalition is not surprising, even at its most extreme; but it is significant that Disraeli exploits the religious polarization beneath the political issues. For example, in mocking the "desperate but desponding fury" with which a Radical newspaper "raves and rants," he asserts, "It feels, like its doomed faction, that the Popish taint has poisoned the fame and influence of the Whig-Radicals in this Protestant country for ever. In its despair and bewildered cowardice it abjures its friends; it utterly renounces O'Connell and his crew; it exclaims, with frantic ejaculation, 'Get thee behind me, Satan!'"[66] In a similar strain, it is the "indignant and Protestant people of England" who will endure Melbourne's "impotent tyranny no longer" and it is "the House of Lords that at this moment maintains the Protestant cause in this realm."[67] Insofar as the Lords did delete the appropriation clause from the Irish Tithe Bill, this last statement is literally true, but Disraeli's rhetoric, especially the sexual terminology, when discussing the role of the Irish faction in the Commons, confirms that his religious sentiments transcend the immediate political issues at stake, and that Catholicism for him has become an evil force in itself. In this respect the *Morning Post* articles are important because they show how completely Disraeli's anti-Catholicism is absorbed into the rest of his rapidly developing articulation of a Tory political ideology.

The most notable aspect of these pieces of journalism, however, is Disraeli's defence of the House of Lords, which constitutes the fourth argumentative thrust and is of a dual nature. Disraeli justifies the actions of the Tory peers on the specific issues confronting them. But much more importantly, as the crisis develops and the more radical of the Government's supporters begin to ask of what use are the Lords, he defends the upper House in theoretical and constitutional terms. To the Whig charge that the Lords are "opposing themselves to the wishes of THE PEOPLE" by rejecting and amending the legislation from the lower House, Disraeli maintains, "The House of Commons affects to be the representative of The People. 'Tis no such thing. It never was, it never will, it never can be ... The vast majority of the people is unrepresented, and must ever be unrepresented." The House of Commons, he argues, is "the representative of a section of the people, called THE CONSTITUENCY ... that portion of them who are entrusted with the right of electing Representatives ... and thus have a Chamber set apart for the advocacy of their rights and interests, and are established into a third estate of the realm."[68] Disraeli is insistent that the House of Commons is only the representative of the Commons, "those ... who have a right to sit, or vote for representatives" to sit, in that chamber and who "form a favoured section or order of the people." He further points out that the "number of the Commons, like the number of Peers, is purely conventional," that they "still bear a very small relative proportion to the number of the people yet are so numerous and so scattered" that they must "assemble together for the purpose of legislation ... in the persons of their representatives." In Disraeli's view the Peers and the Commons are both privileged orders and both exercise "irresponsible power." The Peers are "invested with the function of hereditary legislation" and the Commons are "invested with the function of hereditary election" to a representative legislative body: "the only material difference between them is that the qualification of one is purely hereditary, while in addition to the hereditary qualification which is enjoyed by that portion of the Commons who are landowners they have also the advantage of a qualification by tenure."[69] According to Disraeli these two privileged orders are in fact established into three estates of the realm; the Lords Temporal and Spiritual, and the Commons, all of whom, according to the constitution of England, play an appropriate role in government under the aegis of the monarch.[70] It follows that the basis of the radical attack on the irresponsibility of the Lords is "the fallacy ... that the COMMONS of England are the PEOPLE of England" and that those who would place all the effective power of the state at the disposal of the Commons are in fact arguing for a despotic oligarchy. The only event in which this would not be the case Disraeli firmly rejects:

Destroy the existing Constitution of England and establish the principle
that no class shall exercise irresponsible power, and universal suffrage follows, of course. Whether a social system under any circumstances could
flourish on such a basis is more than doubtful – that it could be established
in *this ancient realm is morally and physically impossible*. Enough for the present of these sciolists. That they are completely ignorant of the nature of
the British Constitution in particular and of the nature of human society in
general is quite evident. (emphasis added)

The italicized words hint at an emotional as well as an intellectual basis
of Disraeli's theoretical argument. The affective centre of his ideas is
revealed completely in the immediately succeeding lines, when he
takes up the issue of the Radicals' complaint about the rituals of the
conference between members of both Houses.

When they meet the Peers of England, Mr. Hume and Mr. Wakley complain that they must stand and doff their beavers while their Lordships are
seated with covered heads. Why not? …
   If precedence and etiquette, and those forms and ceremonies which the
experience of our *ancestors* have found convenient and decorous, are to be
maintained, and *we are not all at once to sink in the degrading slough of a base
equality*, we are acquainted with no form and ceremony more rational and
fitting than the one of which these ignorant men complain. (emphasis
added)[71]

The stress placed upon the recognition of innate superiority in this concrete situation is parallel to that developed in the abstract exposition of
the theory of the mixed constitution. And since a need for recognition
of his own innate superiority is so marked an element of the development of his own personality in adolescence and beyond, such passages
confirm that Disraeli's Tory political ideology incorporated that part of
his emotional needs, even though the vehicle of its formation was the
result of an alternative determination to demonstrate, not claim, his
superiority.
   From his comparison of the two institutions, the Commons and the
Lords, Disraeli concludes that the peers have every right to exercise
their judgment in the matters before them, and that it is their duty to
both the country and themselves "to strip these measures of their destructive character."[72] In so doing, the peers are only defining and eliminating the partisan purposes of the Whigs and are not in the least less

determined "to improve and ameliorate the institutions of the Empire."
This somewhat anomalous note of disinterested patriotism is accompanied by Disraeli's conviction that the Lords' actions in the present
circumstances "have given ... proof that reform is not necessarily revolution, and that the observance of the sanctity of vested rights is not
incompatible with the establishment of popular franchises."[73] Such
phrases, occurring in the latter portion of the *Morning Post* articles, are
distinct reminders of Disraeli's position in *The Crisis Examined* and the
speeches of the Taunton campaign, where he balances his Tory principles with an advocacy of safe reform very similar to that espoused by
Peel. And the explanation of how a series of propagandistic pieces of
journalism begun in a spirit of extreme ultra-Toryism came to end in
the tones of moderate Conservatism lies in the role played by Sir Robert
Peel in the "crisis" of 1835.

II

When Disraeli began the *Morning Post* articles he was hopeful that Lord
Lyndhurst would emerge from the impending "collision" as the leader
of the Conservative party. The anticipation of another Tory ministry and
its personal rewards was not at all abated by the peers' decision on
10 August to amend rather than reject the Municipal Corporations Bill,
as Disraeli's letter to Sarah on 11 August shows.[74] Lyndhurst's amendments were designed to force the confrontation with the Whigs that had
been postponed by the moderate Peelite majority in the name of party
unity. Peel was for the next several weeks in sulky retreat at Drayton. On
22 August Disraeli glories in the struggle, when he suggests that the
"Whig Ministers want a revolutionary riot to consolidate their power":
"But it won't do. We tell these Gallomaniac apes of everything that is
detestable in the French character that these things will ever be 'managed better in France than in England.' Let the 'collision' be tried, and
as soon as they please. They shall have row enough!"[75] His belief in
the strength of Lyndhurst's hand is reflected when he adds, "We hope,
and we believe, that the Lords will not bate a jot of their amendments
of the Whig Corporations Bill." Two days later Disraeli describes the
peers as "making a triumphant stand for the rights and liberties of
their countrymen" and, as has already been noted, in his anti-Catholic
tirade of the 26th he announces, "The division in the House of
Lords on Monday night realized our proudest anticipations."[76]

Disraeli's sense of his own heroic engagement in a struggle against the imposition of absolute power is reflected not just in the first-person, plural pronouns, but explicitly as well, when he accuses Lord Melbourne of abusing his trust and intending to carry on the government "by the House of Commons alone": "the year will not elapse without some severe ukase being promulgated which will efficiently prevent any criticism of the Press upon ... our new Lords and masters. Yet, while there is time, even if it be the last exercise of our right, and the last fruitless fulfilment of our duty, in the discharge of the noble function of upholding truth and diffusing knowledge, we will attempt to assist our countrymen in clearly understanding what this hitherto third estate of the realm styled the House of Commons really is."[77]

It is, however, in the article published on 31 August that Disraeli reaches the climax of his defiance of the Whigs and their Corporations Bill. With something less than complete candour he insists that "the Peers of England in the most unqualified manner admit its principle," which he defines as "SELF-ELECTION IN MUNICIPAL BODIES SHALL BE TERMINATED BY THE SUBSTITUTION OF A FREE ELECTION BY A POPULAR CONSTITUENCY." The difficulty with the logic of this repeated assertion, that "the principle ... has been thoroughly, completely, unreservedly, and unequivocably admitted by the Peers," and that their Lordships "have never for a moment tampered" with it, stems from their amendments, in particular the provision for aldermen appointed for life from the councils already existing.[78] Disraeli's primary purpose at this moment is, of course, strictly partisan, a fact that is revealed by the structure of his argument. He immediately turns to the "Whig policy" which "is ever to smuggle in laws for the increase and consolidation of the power of their party under the specious guise of advancing the cause of popular amelioration." The principle of the bill, he insists, "advances the popular cause with which the Tories sympathise" while the details "only promote and confirm Whig power," power that "will ever be employed for anti-national purposes." In the next one-sentence paragraph it seems that Disraeli wants both halves of the argument: "Toryism is the national spirit exhibiting itself in the maintenance of the national institutions, and in support of the national character which those institutions have formed." A disinterested observer would immediately see that sympathy with the popular cause, as represented in this instance by the admission of the principle of election by a popular constituency, and the maintenance of national institutions, as represented by the rights of freemen and the privileges of aldermen, are diametrically opposed to each other. But to Disraeli they were symbiotic elements of one philosophy.

"*What Is He?*" and *The Revolutionary Epick* show that, while intellectually Disraeli accepts the inevitably of some further measure of Reform and the growth of the "democratic principle," emotionally he longs for a regeneration of the "aristocratic principle" of government through the persons of great spirits "whose proud destiny it may still be at the same time to maintain the glory of the Empire, and to secure the happiness of the People."[79] Since in 1833 Disraeli equates the "democratic principle" with the "federal" principle of representation of diverse interests, and in 1835 so firmly rejects universal suffrage as the political dimension of the "slough of base equality," it is evident that what he means by "the popular cause" is the satisfaction of legitimate grievances and "the happiness of the People," not any extensive tampering with the political structure. This is consistent with his conviction that the essence of Toryism is "the maintenance of the national institutions" and that the Conservative party has become in itself the "National Party" for which he called in "*What Is He?*" And although it is true that in 1833 he saw the "National Party" emerging from a union of Tories and Radicals, the political marriages of the succeeding two years, including the Whig-Radical alliance and his own with the Tories, result in the conception of his primitive, i.e., structurally and affectively paternalistic Conservatism growing to the embryonic form of Tory democracy manifest in the *Morning Post* articles.

The strength of Disraeli's bond with the Conservative party was a function of several things: of his friendship with Lyndhurst and the scope that gave to his fantasy of obtaining power through the manipulation of others, and of the way in which elements of the Tory philosophy, particularly its paternalism and recognition of innate superiority, acted as surrogates for the satisfaction of his emotional needs. Another not insignificant factor was undoubtedly the Tory emphasis upon traditions and institutions that offered the most patriotic of public identities and a chance to escape his Jewish heritage. All of these things, but especially Lyndhurst's and his protégé's vulnerability to intrigue, ensured that the growth of Disraeli's ideology would in large measure reflect the ideas of the Ultra-Tory faction of the party. His militancy in the *Morning Post* up to 31 August is thus hardly surprising. Having defined Toryism, he again on that date insists upon the necessity of the peers' actions, suggesting that if they were to abandon their amendments to "the Whig Corporation Bill," they would "deserve all their worst enemies wish them": "But will they bate a jot? Not they ... the Peers of England we imagine, would be just and fear not. But in the present instance they may be just without the shadow of apprehension. The nation is with the Peers, not with the Popish majority of the Commons; the people will not back the factious Representatives of a very limited class in this country, and the individuals who form the Popish and factious majority are in the main individuals of a discreditable character."[80] This article is also the one containing the call for Melbourne's impeachment and the outrageous attack on Sir John Campbell. The short item of the next day, confined to an expression of high Tory sentiments and another attack on the prime minister, was probably written on the 31st and its tone suggests an anticipation of the debate in the House of Commons: "if ... Lord Melbourne still retains the reins of power, which he originally obtained by conspiracy ... we deliberately repeat – that the high constitutional process of an impeachment of this weak and guilty man must be the ultimate recourse of an injured and insulted nation."[81] But it was the evening of the day on which this piece was almost certainly composed that Peel came to town and "threw over the Lords."

The Ultra-Tory reaction to Peel's speech was one of intense anger and deep dismay. According to Lord Londonderry, Lyndhurst and his Ultra-Conservative Lords intended to stand firm and in effect reject Peel's leadership of the party. Disraeli's response, however, was quite different. In his *Morning Post* article of 2 September he maintains that the ministers and Radicals "have swallowed every important amendment of the Peers without a struggle, save in one point – the continuance of their worships the Aldermen." He no longer sees the issue as a direct confrontation between the Lords and the Commons, but rather now claims that "the noble efforts of Lord Lyndhurst and his brother peers in favour of the rights and liberties and property of a vast portion of their fellow-subjects are now supported and seconded in the House of Commons even without a murmur ... the great principle of qualification ... is recognised and submitted to ... without a division." Disraeli now argues that there are "only three propositions of the Peers of any magnitude to which the Ministers finally object." The first of these, relating to "the toll-exemption of the freeman," he argues, may be easily settled by compensation; the second relating to "the distribution of Church patronage by the Dissenters," can be managed in "a way not injurious to the Church." In the third case, he claims that "Sir Robert Peel, the leader of the Conservatives of England, combining the qualities of firmness with the desire of conciliation, does not think it necessary to contend for a life tenure of office in the Aldermen, where the humbled Whigs and Radicals offer to give a six year's lease."[82] This explicit recognition of Peel's leadership in praiseworthy terms and his claim of victory, in sharp contrast to the response of the Ultra-Tories, indicate that Disraeli knew from the moment Peel began to speak that the Ultra-Tory dream of a reactionary ministry would not be realized. They also indicate that he knew all along that the "crisis" of the Municipal Corporations Bill involved a struggle between two factions of the Conservative party as much as one between the Tories and Whigs or Lords and Commons. Since Disraeli was not disposed to be on the losing side of such a struggle, he faced something of a dilemma – of choosing between his loyalty to Lyndhurst and the rationality and inevitability of compromise. To his credit as a politician he managed to avoid abandoning either, and he did so in a way that is prophetic of his subsequent career.

In the *Morning Post* Disraeli makes no direct mention, before or after the fact, of the climactic meeting of Tory peers at Apsley House on 3 September, when to those present "the very existence of the party" seemed at stake. In the article of that day, he begins by invoking the spirit of compromise: "it remains for the two Houses, in the points of controversy at present between them, exactly and consistently to guide themselves with a becoming deference to the two principles which they have separately established. This is the only mode by which they can escape a factious imputation." Such language suggests his awareness of the Ultra-Tory rigidity. In loyalty to the leader of the lost cause Disraeli reverts to a last stab at defending the Lords' provision of life tenure for aldermen, but he does so in the most moderate of language. The acceptance of "popular rights," the stress upon the need to remedy genuine grievances, and the commitment to safe Reform, are Peelite in tone and recollective of *The Crisis Examined* and the Tamworth Manifesto, even though the intention behind the idea being defended is extremist. Disraeli's ambivalence is reflected in the continuation of his argument: "shall an Alderman who now holds his authority under the sanctity of a Royal charter – shall he be punished for possessing so high a title, and be turned adrift as if he had committed a high misdemeanour instead of enjoying a high privilege? Why this war upon Aldermen? Why should not the municipal rights of Aldermen be respected as well as the municipal rights of freemen?" While these questions are obviously rhetorical, they do ask for the reader's judgment, an appeal not usually included within the framework of Disraeli's arguments in the earlier articles. Such an interrogative mode is the most passive of his rhetorical structures. Nevertheless, he musters a firm statement of conviction in defence of the Lords, the moderate tone of which is only broken by one last burst of anti-Catholicism ("The vestries are as mute as swine that have had their swill"):

> We trust the House of Commons will follow ... [the Lords'] wise and patriotic example; but if, unhappily, the influence of a fatal connection force the Ministry to refuse their co-operation with the Peers in this great behalf, this we do know, that no consideration in the word will induce the Peers to depart from their resolution, which will be as firmly acted upon as it was deliberately taken ...
>
> Proceed, Peers of England. Proceed in your course – at once wise and courageous, temperate and dignified. Your authority rests upon the confidence and affection of your fellow-countrymen; its recent exercise has doubly entitled you to their respect and support.[83]

The generality of such words as "resolution" and "course" and the juxtaposition of wisdom and courage, temperance and dignity, reflect the new softness of Disraeli's position in contrast to his earlier insistence on not "bating" a jot. And from this somewhat delicate balance he then moves to an acceptance of the inevitable.

Once the Tory Lords had endorsed the Duke of Wellington's commitment to party unity at the meeting on 3 September (abandoning the provision for life tenure of aldermen), and once Lord John Russell seemed disposed to have the Commons accept the remainder of the Lords' amendments, Disraeli finds that the rhetorical excesses of his hostility to the Whigs are no longer serviceable and that the only safe target is the Irish Catholic faction. Disraeli thus concludes the *Morning Post* articles in support of the spirit of compromise on the specific issue that had been the centre of the Lords' opposition to the Municipal Corporations Bill and his final emphasis is on the "wisdom, experience, and moderation of the eminent leader of the Conservatives of England, Sir Robert Peel."[84]

In the more general realm of ideology, however, Disraeli has conceded little or none of his original argument. He attacks the Radicals and their "Brutilitarian allies" now crying for reform of the Lords, and uses their "rebellious nonsense" to reaffirm his belief in the value of a mixed constitution. The definitions of "THE PEOPLE" and the "COMMONS" are brought forward again to answer Russell's error in styling "the King of England one of the estates of the realm." Further, he extols the presence of the Lords Spiritual in the upper House as examples of "the very Peerage for life, for which the Radicals clamour," and he does so on the grounds that "the members must in general necessarily be more distinguished for their talents, their learning, and their piety." In Disraeli's view, "there is not a more democratic institution in the country than the Church."[85] It is significant that the already cited rejection of "universal suffrage" and the defence of precedence and etiquette appropriate to superior, privileged orders (as opposed to "the degrading slough of base equality") occur in the article of 4 September. These things combined, and juxtaposed to the moderate and rational acceptance of the eventual compromise, demonstrate the dichotomy between head and heart, practice and theory, that characterizes Disraeli's position at the end of the crisis over the passage of the Municipal Corporations Bill. This ambivalence also confirms, in part, the hypothesis that the development of Disraeli's political career must be seen whole, that the explanation of the inconsistencies within it can be found in the interplay of private and public motives, conscious and otherwise.

7

Vindication

That Disraeli could at the same time praise the wisdom of Sir Robert Peel's compromise and claim victory for the Lords in the matter of the Municipal Corporations Bill is a mark of his political dexterity, but not necessarily of his insincerity. Both Whigs and Tories asserted that the passage of the bill had proved the independence of the House of Lords. In the last debates Russell himself spoke of "not curtailing the constitutional powers bestowed on either branch of the legislature."[1] So Disraeli's claim that the "principles of the English Constitution have not only rallied, but triumphed," and that the "authority of the Upper House of Parliament ... has during the present session been asserted by its native and essential strength alone," though undoubtedly a rationalization, is a piety of the moment.[2] But it is, nevertheless, a false claim. As Kitson Clark points out, the Lords "had not done what they wished": "They had been forced to pass a Bill which, had they been left to themselves, they would probably not have passed. They had not even kept the amendments that they had made in it."[3] Certainly Lyndhurst's intention of stopping the "movement" with his "counter-project" (the essence of which was the aldermen's clause) had been foiled by the need for party unity. Indeed, in the attempt at gaining Ultra-Tory supremacy "the Lords were forced to be dependent on the views of the Conservative party in the House of Commons, and the Conservative party in that House were ultimately dependent on the views of the people."[4] Although it was not formally recognized, the constitutional change advocated by the Radicals had in part already taken place within the framework of political realities.

That the writing of the articles in the *Morning Post* served not only the immediate political purpose of advancing the cause of Lyndhurst's

faction, but also the psychological one of expressing Disraeli's patriotism as a kind of payment of dues for membership in the Tory party,
might not at first glance be obvious. But both internal and external evidence suggests that this is so. In the fourteen articles reprinted in *Whigs
and Whiggism* the phrase "the Peers *of England*" (emphasis added) occurs twenty-seven times, twelve of those being in the *Morning Post* of
31 August. In addition, the phrase "of England" is used as a modifier in
forty-eight other places, more than half of them in the last week of
August. This could be simply a rhetorical device for attracting the sympathies of the reader as the debate reaches its climax. But the greater
significance of the patriotic invocations in establishing Disraeli's own
sense of his political credentials is confirmed by the structure and content of his next work.

After the session of 1835 Disraeli repaired with Lyndhurst to
Bradenham, where they were joined by Henrietta. There, during the autumn, he composed the *Vindication of the English Constitution in a letter to
a noble and learned Lord*, which was published in December.[5] In essence
this work is an elaboration of the defence of the House of Lords that had
appeared in the *Morning Post*. The doctrine of "the representation in
Parliament of separate estates of the realm and the dependence of the
balance of the constitution on the maintenance of their several rights"[6] is
supported at length by interpretations of the past that comprise an anti-
Whig theory of history. The subtitle, of course, deliberately echoes
Edmund Burke's *A Letter ... to a Noble Lord*. The *Vindication*, however, is
largely a search for political ancestors and, as such, is "a 'vindication' of
Disraeli's own unusual views on the development of English politics,"[7]
whereas Burke's *Letter*, though also an attempt at self-justification, simply reflects in a particularly defensive tone the frustration of a career
spent largely in opposition to the government, and when finally rewarded, attacked for its inconsistency. Despite the differences in their
nominal party allegiance, Burke thinking of himself as a true Whig,
Disraeli may have found this similarity of position a link between them.
But ultimately it was the essentially conservative philosophy beneath
Burke's apologia that attracted Disraeli; the insistence upon the national
interest, the defence of the constitution and the Church, the resistance to
radical change as opposed to reform of real grievances, the distrust of
abstract ideas in the formation of political ideology, and, as a consequence, the hatred and fear of the French revolutionary model.

Disraeli seems to be attempting in the *Vindication* to establish a history of a National Tory party. In 1835, at the moment of composition, he

is committed to recognizing Peel as the leader of that party even though his personal loyalty is to Lyndhurst. Accordingly, "Henry St. John, Lord Bolingbroke is regarded as the founder of a Tory tradition that continues through William Pitt the younger, Burke and apparently Lord Liverpool ... the Duke of Wellington and Peel himself."[8] Robert Blake and others, in particular Richard Faber, have argued quite succinctly that Disraeli's theory of the Tory tradition will not wash;[9] that, in fact, there is no continuous body of Tory doctrine going back to the time of the early eighteenth century, and that the distinction of the 1830s between Tory and Conservative is specious. But Disraeli's claims to distinguished political ancestry ultimately rest upon grounds other than an objective demonstration of continuous descent. If one sees the politics as invention, much as the fiction is invention, what is significant is the way in which the subjective process of identification develops.

In a sense Disraeli does not join the Tories; he adopts them. In "*What Is He?*" he calls for the formation of a "National Party," by definition, a successful party. At the time of writing the *Vindication* his public involvement with the Tories leads him to see them as this National Party. Thus, his ancestors, once found, are "true Tories," though only so in the sense that they have fought for the national interest as Disraeli conceives it. In 1835 it is, of course, the Ultra section of the Tory party that he sees as serving both the national and his personal interests. Despite the political reality of Peel's power within the party, this is not as foolish an identification as it might seem, though the motivation behind it is undoubtedly as much emotional as rational. As Blake has pointed out, the Ultra-Tory policy "corresponded to the actual beliefs of a large section of the political nation" and the "majority of the electorate ... believed in the preservation of the traditional institutions of England, the monarchy, parliament, the Church, primogeniture, the rights of property landed as well as commercial." But however much most people wished to keep things "more or less as they were," it was not altogether clear that the Tory or Conservative party was the one "best capable of achieving that object." Peel's policy of endorsing safe reform was an attempt to demonstrate that it was. The Ultras, however, could not see that "blind adherence to the old constitution" was a "more dangerous ... course ... likely to lead to revolution."[10] In the *Morning Post* articles Disraeli shows himself to be half committed to both policies. As a consequence, the significance of the *Vindication* is threefold. It illustrates Disraeli's awareness of the necessity to convince the present electorate to support the Tories; it shows that, despite the failure of the recent Ultra-Tory intrigue, he feels that the most cogent argument in this respect can be drawn from the past; and it reveals a need on his part to find ideological ancestors whose lives vindicate his chosen political identity.

It has already been noted how conveniently Bolingbroke's reputation fits Disraeli's purposes and fantasies. Henry St John entered Parliament at an early age and by cultivating the friendship of Robert Harley (later Earl of Oxford) he had a meteoric rise to prominence, becoming Secretary of War by the time he was twenty-six years old – this despite his reputation as a rake, completely self-indulgent where women and drink were concerned. Though, along with Harley, he was replaced in office in 1708, two years later he was back in power as Secretary of State for the northern department. Along with other members of the Augustan literary circle, he engaged in a vast propaganda effort to gain support for the Tory cause of ending the war with France. He was instrumental in negotiating the Treaty of Utrecht and in 1712 was created Viscount Bolingbroke. Subsequent to the death of Queen Anne his ambition was frustrated by charges of opportunism, treachery, and insincerity associated with his impeachment following his flight into exile in France. Upon his return to England in 1725 he immediately became the centre of the Opposition circle[11] and the rest of his public life was devoted to attacking the policies of Robert Walpole's Whig government.

In form as well as substance, in style as well as content, there was much in the career of Bolingbroke to attract the Byronic Disraeli. The precise nature of that attraction can be gauged by returning for a moment to Disraeli's first account of thwarted ambition in which his hero, Vivian Grey, demonstrates his own brilliance to the Marquess of Carabas. Claiming that his Lordship has been misunderstood and that the whole difference has arisen from "a slight verbal misconception at the beginning of the argument," Mr Vivian Grey, we are told, "proceeded with the utmost sang-froid; he commented upon expressions, split and subtilised words, insinuated opinions, and finally quoted a whole passage of Bolingbroke to prove that the opinion of the most noble the Marquess of Carabas was one of the soundest, wisest, and most convincing of opinions that ever was promulgated by mortal man" (VG, 27–8). There is a great difference between this fictionalized account of Disraeli's manipulation of John Murray and the high seriousness of his address to Lyndhurst in the Vindication. Yet both are manifestations of the same fantasy in variant forms. The satiric portrayal of Vivian Grey's egotism is evidence that Disraeli is from the first conscious of his fantasy, as he would have to be to reap any practical benefit from it. His relationship with Murray was different from that with Lyndhurst ten years later. He clearly respects both the intelligence and the power of the latter, and it was the lack of respect for the former, so evident in the fictional exposé of *The Representative* affair that made *Vivian Grey* such an insult to Murray. But for all that, and despite the seriousness of the *Vindication*, Disraeli is again in 1835 trying to make his power fantasy come true, as the not so incidental reference to Bolingbroke in the above passage and the details of the Lyndhurst intrigue suggest. In that respect there is another parallel between *Vivian Grey* and the *Vindication* worth pursuing.

The novel was written after the intrigue in Murray's circle had collapsed and, as such, can be thought of as Disraeli's defiant way of coping with the failure to realize his hopes. The *Vindication* is written immediately following the collapse of the Ultra-Tory campaign to bring down the Whig government over the Municipal Corporations Bill. That Disraeli should then turn to the writing of a tract on Tory principles is consistent with the fact that there is no breach with his benefactor in this instance. But as a document that establishes his own credentials, it does illustrate that to some extent fiction and politics serve the same function for him. *Alroy*, which was written immediately following the anti-Semitic attacks and the defeat of the second Wycombe election campaign, is yet a further example of the pattern of fantasy thrust towards power and the self-defining retreat. This pattern in part explains the seemingly discrepant roles played by political practice and political ideology in Disraeli's careers. Indeed, it makes the creation of the sub-genre of the political novel at his hands seem almost inevitable, while it raises no expectations that the political ideas expressed in the novels would ever be acted upon. Rather, the political behaviour would be shaped by variants of the same imaginative conception of the self, symbiotically related to those ideas, but representing in the actual instance the distinction between demonstrating and claiming his superiority to other men.

The *Vindication of the English Constitution* as a vindication of Disraeli's chosen political identity was an enormous success. It may not demonstrate to a historian's satisfaction the existence of a continuous body of Tory doctrine dating from the Augustan period, but it does establish a plausible and respectable intellectual and emotional ancestry for its author. In this regard Burke's position is obvious. More important, however, is Bolingbroke's. The *Vindication* begins where the *Morning Post* articles left off, with an attack on utilitarianism.[12] The Benthamite extension of empiricism is particularly obnoxious to Disraeli because he sees it as the foundation of the Whigs' and Radicals' political ideas. Specifically he disputes the notions that man should act in his self-interest and that a political system can be constructed from abstract principles such as guaranteeing the a priori rights of all men.[13] Bolingbroke's opposition to the bourgeois individualistic values inherent in the policies of Walpole's Whig Government is based upon a similar rejection of Locke's view of men "as equal one amongst another."[14] And, as Isaac Kramnick has pointed out, Bolingbroke equates Locke's "stress on the natural independence of solitary individuals" possessed of natural rights with the Hobbesian view of man's self-interest.[15] Disraeli could thus claim a philosophical parallel between his own opposition to the Whigs and Bolingbroke's attacks on their new socio-economic order, despite the manifest differences in the party in the two periods.

Related to this affinity of anti-Whig postures is a common theory of the origin of government. Bolingbroke argues that the natural state of society is familial and that authority is inherent in it: subordination, order, and union are necessary ingredients of well-being.[16] Further, he claims a divine sanction for this paternalism in that he sees this familial structure as modelled upon God's relationship to man within the Great Chain of Being. Finally, he argues that when this structure proved inadequate to the security of men, they made the natural transition to the form of monarchical government. The kings were chosen for their innate goodness and acquired wisdom but, needing the consent of the governed, they, as well as the leaders who chose them, agreed to a common subjection to law that a posteriori was found conducive to reason and benevolence. That is, Bolingbroke argues that "authority comes from above and knowing what is best for the governed earns public consent."[17] Nowhere does Bolingbroke argue that men enter society to protect rights and property. Perhaps the most significant aspect of Bolingbroke's characterization of the first kings as "philosophical legislators" who succeeded to the authority of fathers of families, as men "wiser and more just than the rest," is the extension of that idea to an insistence that "there were those whose specific function was to govern, and others whose function was to be governed," and that there was "an inevitable division between those destined to lead and those to be led."[18] As Kramnick says, "Bolingbroke suggests that a basic and recurring division runs through the history of mankind between 'the multitudes designed to obey, and ... the few designed to govern.' In paternal government this division is quite obvious, but even at the critical stage of political evolution when natural governments pass into artificial governments, the few emerge, the philosophical legislators, '*men of more genius than the common herd*'" (emphasis added).[19] Bolingbroke's defence of "the special merits and claims of great men and great families" contrasts with "what he considered the liberal's (*sic*) disregard for such distinctions in their *indiscriminate description of 'the people*'" (emphasis added).[20] Further, while Bolingbroke stresses the great man's acquisition of wisdom through education and experience, he also insists that those few inherit their role because in their nature reason predominates in the battle with passion. The potential for leadership is thus in part an innate quality.

Bolingbroke's essay, *On the Spirit of Patriotism*, written as a letter to Lord Cornbury in 1736, is "a plea to the younger generation of the landed and noble classes to recapture the leadership of English political society" and, as such, envisions the aristocracy as the chief "source of natural leadership by rational men."[21] "These are they who engross almost the whole reason of the species: who are born to instruct, to guide, and to preserve: who are designed to be the tutors and the guardians of humankind ... *superior spirits*, men who show even from their infancy, *though it be not always perceived by others, perhaps not always felt by themselves*, that they were born for something more and better" (emphasis added).[22] Such a passage would have enormous appeal to Disraeli. That it in fact did so is obvious from the whole history of the Young England movement in the 1840s. For the moment, however, it is important to see that Bolingbroke's ideas on the origin of government not only offer Disraeli support for his claims of unrecognized genius, but also shape his political ideology. In chapter 5 of the *Vindication* he asserts, "Those great men, who have periodically risen to guide the helm of our government in times of tumultuous and stormy exigency ... looked upon the nation as a family, and upon the country as a landed inheritance." And, Disraeli adds, those great men were of the opinion that "every subject was bound to respect the established Constitution of his country, because, independent of all other advantages, to that Constitution he was indebted even for his life. Had not the State been created the subject would not have existed. Man with them, therefore, was the child of the State, and born with filial duties. To disobey the State, therefore, was a crime; to rebel against it, treason; to overturn it, parricide."[23] Disraeli then goes on to praise the English "commonwealth" and to ascribe its duration to the principle of deference to "reverend antiquity" which has not in the least "checked the progress of knowledge, or stunted the growth of liberty."[24] The passages quoted above and a comparison with his earlier works such as *"What Is He?"* and *The Revolutionary Epick*, show that Disraeli's paternalistic ideas find a form of expression under the direct influence of Bolingbroke's ideas. The emphasis on great men, the ship of state metaphor for government, and the conception of the familial social structure are all directly drawn from his writings. Equally significant is Disraeli's idea of a natural aristocracy, which is also shaped by Bolingbroke's expression of that seemingly universal notion.

This passage from the *Vindication* also illuminates the connection between Disraeli's novels and his political ideas. The middle section, describing the country as a "landed inheritance" stresses both the privileges and the duties of that patrimony. A similar concern on the part of Disraeli's heroes for the entitlements and obligations of their estates is a central theme of *The Young Duke*, *Henrietta Temple*, and *Sybil*, and it is an important motif in virtually all of the novels. When politics serves the same ends as his fiction it seems that Disraeli, convinced of his own nobility and having no actual estates, simply claims the whole of England as his inheritance. The language of the last part of the passage, which extends the logic of the familial conception of society to an insistence that one's socio-political identity and even one's personal identity is dependent upon the constitution, confirms the suggestion that Disraeli finds a partial resolution of his own identity confusion in Tory political ideology. In that light the patriotism of his defence of "the Protestant Peers *of England*" (emphasis added) in the *Morning Post* and the violence of his anti-Catholic and anti-Radical-Whig tirades might well be interpreted as a continuation of the struggle for a viable, secure identity that is manifested in the imaginatively autobiographical early novels.

From this similarity of opinion about the origins of the political structure there follow a host of others about specific institutions, all of which contribute to the coherence of Disraeli's political identity. Bolingbroke's defence of the "special merits and claims of great men and great families," in contrast to what he sees as the Whigs' disregard for such distinctions in their "indiscriminate description of 'the people,'" has already been remarked upon.[25] Disraeli's insistence in the *Morning Post* and again in the *Vindication* that "the Commons" is not "the people," but rather a limited and privileged order forming, like the Lords Temporal and Spiritual, an estate of the realm is undoubtedly derivative of this view.[26] Similarly, although he was a freethinker and a critic of organized religion from a religious point of view (as his posthumously published *Philosophical Fragments* show), Bolingbroke found the Established Church to be a socially and politically useful institution for the purpose of educating people in virtue and morality and encouraging them in obedience and public spirit.[27] This opinion is echoed in Disraeli's defence of the Church as the most democratic of English institutions and the people's true heritage. Bolingbroke sees the peerage as an institution that represents the permanent interests of the nation. He consistently argues that the landed men are the "true owners of our political vessel," and that the Great Chain of Being has its "secular analogy in man's social and political ranks," without which "Distinctions vanish, the social order can be overturned, and havoc ensues."[28] By means of an idealization that reflects the projection of his personal fantasies into the public domain, Disraeli, too, sees the aristocracy as a model of superiority that serves the national interest. Echoing *On the Spirit of Patriotism*, he finds that "hereditary legislators ... have not only a great, a palpable, and immediate interest in the welfare of a country," but also that, by their "ease, and leisure, and freedom from anxiety," they are encouraged to "the humanising pursuits of learning and the liberal love of arts." The aristocracy, he concludes, whose honour (drawn from the "fame and glory of their ancestors") is "a more precious possession than their parks and palaces" and who are trained "from the womb to the grave ... to loathe and recoil from everything mean and sordid," constitute the "choicest elements of a senate." And, further, Disraeli maintains that it is "the peculiar character of the hereditary branch of our legislature [that] has mainly contributed to the stability of our institutions, and to the order and prosperous security which that stability has produced."[29]

The validation of his political identity that Disraeli obtains from Bolingbroke's ideas can also be illustrated by noticing their common perspective on English history. They both see the growth of Parliament's power under the Plantagenets as securing the balance of a mixed constitution and the excesses of the Stuarts' reigns and the Interregnum as destructive of it. Disraeli manages rather more sympathy for Charles I, concluding that the doctrines of divine right and passive obedience, though mistaken, were understandable reactions to the encroachments of the Long Parliament and the destructive forces of religious dissension. This sympathy undoubtedly stems in part from the influence of his father's recent historical investigations into the period.[30] But there is also Disraeli's own eagerness to show that the position of this king, "supported by a considerable majority of his people and nearly the whole of the Peerage," but thwarted by a group of radical (Root and Branch) reformers whose small majority in the Commons depended on an alliance with "Scotch Presbyterians," offers a direct parallel to that of the monarch faced in the 1830s with the Whigs' compact with the "Irish Papists."[31]

Both Bolingbroke in the 1730s and Disraeli a hundred years later see the Whigs as a faction intent upon disturbing the balance of power inherent in the mixed constitution rather than pursuing the "national interest" of maintaining it.[32] Further, they recognize that in their respective eras the constitutional balance has altered and is not totally recoverable. In Bolingbroke's case he sees the change resulting from the growth of new financial institutions such as the Bank of England and the Stock Market, which rapidly accumulate the political power once in the hands of the landed interests. Disraeli also sees the change resulting from the increase of effective power in the hands of the moneyed class, in turn derivative of what is loosely called the Industrial Revolution. For both men the impulse behind these changes is the philosophy of self-interest and so it is not surprising that their common response to that view of society is nostalgia. Kramnick has pointed out that an essential failure of Bolingbroke's long career in opposition to the institutions of Whiggery is reflected in his eventually turning to a non-institutional transcendent appeal to patriotism. *On the Spirit of Patriotism* and *The Patriot King*, while they ostensibly look to the leadership of the future, in reality try to invoke the past. That attempt in itself is a fatalistic recognition of the inexorable momentum of change. Disraeli, too, recognized the inevitability of the "democratic" or "federal" principle as early as *"What Is He?"* and *The Revolutionary Epick*, and he, too, responds with nostalgia, nowhere more apparent than in the *Morning Post* articles and the *Vindication of the English Constitution*. In the final instalment of the former Disraeli says, "We are not ashamed in this cold-blooded coxcombical nineteenth-century to praise the Constitution of England; and if all dared speak as they deem, *the good old times would soon return*, when we were grateful to Providence for our free and famous Constitution as for *the beauteous and fertile land wherein we dwell* (emphasis added).[33] The "beauteous and fertile land" was soon to face the consequences of the most thorough and rapid urbanization and industrialization yet experienced by any nation, but Disraeli's eye is on the nostalgic pastoral. An Englishman, he says, whether he be *"doomed to the plough or destined to the loom,"* is born to "the noblest of all inheritances": the "equality of civil rights." "There is *no station* to which he may not aspire ... *no master* whom he is obliged to serve ... no magistrate who dares imprison him" against the law; and *the soil on which he labours must supply him with an honest and decorous maintenance.*" These, Disraeli claims, are rights and privileges "as valuable as Kings, Lords, and Commons"; and it is only a nation "thus *schooled and cradled* in the principles and practice of freedom," he says, that could maintain such institutions. The conclusion to be drawn is that the English are in politics as the old Hebrews were in religion, "a favoured and peculiar people" (emphasis added).[34] The note of disenchantment, the hint of heroism, the nostalgia for the past, and the implied lament for a lost harmony of God, man, and nature contained in these passages are important ingredients of Disraeli's patriotism. That he should see the typical Englishman as a rustic and again invoke the child of the state metaphor to describe his political existence is indicative of how the nostalgia expresses the sense of innocence lost and the hope of paradise regained. That Disraeli's mind should turn in this context to the allusion to Hebraic purity is remarkably appropriate and suggestive of the future directions of his political thought.

The child of the state metaphor is the explicit rationale of the power of Bolingbroke's ideal monarch: "The true image of a free people governed by a Patriot King, is that of a patriarchal family, where the head and all the members are united by one common interest, and animated by one common spirit."[35] The almost miraculous process of the reestablishment of a free constitution will be begun through the agency of the king's virtue, for as soon as the "Patriot King" is raised to the throne, "corruption will cease to be an expedient of government." In its place "the orders and forms of the constitution" will be restored to their "primitive integrity" and become "real barriers against arbitrary power, not blinds nor masks under which tyranny may lie concealed."[36] According to this simplistic analysis everything depends upon the character of the king. As a consequence, Bolingbroke is at pains to elaborate upon the individual qualities, innate and acquired through education, which must be found in such a monarch: "a warm concern for the interest and honour of the nation"; "decency ... grace ... propriety of manners." The emphasis is to a great extent upon style; the king's character must be like those "of good dramatic or epick writers," drawn from nature, and sustained through the whole piece – with words and actions proper to his character.[37]

Such a conception of the art of politics would appeal strongly to Disraeli, for it offers the opportunity for the very kind of fusion, of claiming an innate superiority and demonstrating a practical one, that is the essence of his Taunton festival speech. As Kramnick points out, politics for Bolingbroke and those in his circle was an elaborate theatre in which the style of the performance was "almost more significant than the deeds done" and public support was the result of noble gentlemen's eloquence and "the compelling aesthetic force of their rhetoric."[38] That Disraeli's dandyism, which had stood him in such good stead among the fashionable elite in London, should give way to the artful, rhetorical, political performance upon the announcement of his official Toryism is thus entirely consistent with his admiration for the principles of Lord Bolingbroke that was so prominent a feature of his Taunton campaign speeches.[39]

By the 1830s it was clear to all concerned that many of the Crown's governmental prerogatives had passed to the leaders of the dominant political party. It is natural, therefore, that Disraeli is concerned less with the character of the monarch than with that essential to the leadership of a national party. Allowing for the possible emergence of "Great Spirits" who would embody the necessary qualities, he stresses the gifts of the natural aristocracy, the peers of England, who in their preponderant Toryism can fulfil a heroic patriotic role. The role that Disraeli envisions for himself is no less heroic, befitting his conception of his own genius that marks him out from "the common herd." Richard Faber points out that Disraeli's interpretation of the past is such that he appears to be using it "purely for propaganda purposes of his own – seeing the past in terms of the present, instead of the present in terms of the past."[40] And many of the already discussed similarities between the opinions of Bolingbroke and Disraeli reveal the latter's interest in identifying the struggles of the 1830s with those of the Augustan period. But nowhere is the process of projecting his own circumstances on the past more apparent than in the description of Bolingbroke in chapter 31 of the *Vindication*. He was, Disraeli says, the "ablest writer" and the "most accomplished orator" of his age, gifted with a "fiery imagination" and a "teeming fertility" of "inventive resources." Where there exists a free parliament and a free press, Disraeli notes, a man with such a "rare union" of talents, blended with "an intuitive knowledge of his race" and "a comprehensive experience of human affairs," would have "the privilege of exercising a constant influence over the mind of his country." Accordingly, "no one was better qualified to be the Minister of a free and powerful nation than Henry St. John." Bolingbroke, Disraeli adds, was opposed to the oligarchic Whigs on principle, as "hostile to genius," and he recoiled from the Tory tenets of the day, which his "unprejudiced and vigorous mind" led him to dread and condemn.

Moreover, because he maintained that "vigilant and meditative independence which is the privilege of an original and determined spirit," Bolingbroke, at the outset of his career, incurred "the common-place imputation of insincerity and inconsistency" until his "sagacious intellect" realized that it was necessary to choose between the Whigs and the Tories and that that was really "a choice between oligarchy and democracy." In joining the Tories, Disraeli tells us, Bolingbroke embraced the national cause and devoted himself absolutely to his party's cause: "in a series of writings, unequalled in our literature for their spirited patriotism, their just and profound views, and the golden eloquence in which they are expressed, [he] eradicated from Toryism all those absurd and odious doctrines which Toryism had adventitiously adopted, clearly developed its essential and permanent character ... and in the complete reorganisation of the public mind laid the foundation for the future accession of the Tory party to power."[41]

With *Contarini Fleming* and *Alroy* in mind we can see from the outset of this passage that the emphasis upon "that fiery imagination,"and "that intuitive knowledge of his race, which creative minds alone enjoy," proves that no one but Disraeli is "better qualified to be the Minister of a free and powerful nation." The common opposition to the Whigs, springing from "genius," and the similar reputations for "insincerity and inconsistency" confirm the complete identification that Disraeli is making between his own role and Bolingbroke's. The conclusive evidence for this interpretation, however, is the sentence, "It is probable that in the earlier years of his career he [Bolingbroke] meditated over the formation of a new party." As the hypothetical phrasing indicates, Disraeli had no evidence of such an idea. It is purely wish-fulfilment, a case of making the present come true in the past, for in "*What Is He?*" and even as early as *Vivian Grey*, he had conceived and fantasized upon such a role for himself. Disraeli's call for a "National Party" and the subsequent transmutation of this into a conviction that the Tories were that truly democratic party is then related to Bolingbroke's embracing of the national cause.

Here it is necessary to distinguish between the political ideas of the two men and the conceptions they held of their political roles. In the *Morning Post* articles and the *Vindication* Disraeli is not simply looking for a previous expression of his own opinions. The political ideas originate with Bolingbroke, and Disraeli, it is clear, finds them in his works. In this respect the influence may be said to move from past to present. But it is equally clear that Disraeli's definition of his own political role derives from his earliest conceptions of his "self" and the development through adolescence of his sense of his personal identity. This passage demonstrates that Disraeli projects his definition of his role in politics backward upon the career of Bolingbroke, seeking to establish a congruency, which, in effect, serves as a vindication of not just his ideas, but his whole political career to date. The ideas he adopts from Bolingbroke are also particularly well-suited to the role he sees for himself beyond the present moment. The noble Lord's influence is thus to a significant degree a function of Disraeli's fantasies and ambitions, even though the similarities to his own career that he finds in that of Bolingbroke quite evidently also shape it in concrete ways. That is, Bolingbroke's career provides both a philosophical vindication of the recent past and a concrete model for present and future heroics. The point was not lost upon Disraeli's contemporaries. In a letter to Sarah he reports: "The sale of the 'Vindication' continues, and, though not quite so brisk, is in daily demand. I received to-day a letter from [Lord] Eliot, which, from its length and the extreme warmth of its feeling, would quite surprise you … He says, among other things, 'In reading your sketch of Bolingbroke I could not help thinking that if opportunities are not withheld, you may become what he might have been.'"[42]

The similarity of the roles Disraeli fancied to those of Bolingbroke's career are also evident in chapter 32 of the *Vindication*, where he suggests a policy for the Tory party in the 1830s that is virtually identical to that he had just described as Bolingbroke's great achievement. Even the language is similar: "First … the *real character and nature of Toryism* should be generally and clearly comprehended: secondly … Toryism should be divested of all those qualities which are adventitious and not essential, and which, having been produced by that course of circumstances which are constantly changing, become in time obsolete, inconvenient, and by the dexterous misrepresentation of our opponents even *odious*: thirdly … the efficient organisation of the party should be secured and maintained" (emphasis added).[43] Even though, ostensibly, he is only proffering advice to Lyndhurst and the other Conservative leaders, with such a statement Disraeli is, in effect, staking a claim to the ideological leadership of the Tory party. In its argument that the Tory party is the National party, that it is the truly democratic party, espousing the common good by supporting the institutions of the country, the *Vindication* is (to use a metaphor with almost literal meaning) Disraeli's self-composed nomination to a position of national prominence within that party. But, as the discussion of the controversy surrounding the Municipal Corporations Bill has shown, the actual leadership of the Tory party had not been either abandoned by Sir Robert Peel or transferred to the care of Lord Lyndhurst. As a consequence, however much Disraeli might feel the compelling force of his essentially Ultra-Tory analysis of the current situation, he had to face the reality that the immediate direction of the party was in the hands of the moderates. A similar recognition had come to him a year earlier, at the time of the third Wycombe campaign, at which time his political statements, embodied in *The Crisis Examined*, showed a striking resemblance to those of Peel's Tamworth Manifesto.

When he agreed to take office in 1834, Peel took on the enormously complicated task of forming a viable Tory party within the context of the inevitable demands for further reforms. He had previously shown himself capable of the necessary degree of compromise in his subordination of his initial private convictions to the much more important matter of the public welfare on the issues of Catholic Emancipation and electoral reform. As early as the *Gallomania* and throughout *The Revolutionary Epick* Disraeli, too, had shown his awareness of the inevitability of reform and of the necessity for compromise with the forces of change. For him *The Crisis Examined* was an attempt, like Peel's, to reconcile expediency with political principle. It was an attempt to set out a complicated political identity and seems now to have been a real advance from the earlier scramble of political disappointment and fantasy that worked to alleviate his resentment of not finding a suitable recognition of his genius. The insistence on a purity of heart and principle within the framework of expediency and compromise, which is the essence of Disraeli's marvellous defence of inconsistency in the name of the national interest, shows an appreciation of the relationship between ends and means appropriate to the successful use of political power. Unfortunately, this advance is not one that Disraeli can sustain in the 1830s. The resolution of his more complicated identity is unstable and explodes in the row with O'Connell. And the involvement in the Ultra's counter-project to the Municipal Corporations Bill, the articles in the *Morning Post*, and the *Vindication* represent a reversion of sorts, an attempt to go back and define, through a different sort of fantasy, a political identity that incorporates in its emotionally patriotic formulation a less vulnerable fusion of the elements of his personal dichotomy.

The standard analysis of the *Vindication* is somewhat vitiated by a recognition of the personal as well as the public dimensions of the work, and by an acknowledgment of the extent to which the ideology it contains is an invention. Blake, for example, is undoubtedly correct in stating that the meaningful organizational continuity of the Tory party dates from the Foxite-Pittite split of 1782–4, and that Disraeli's views of the continuity he saw from Bolingbroke to himself altered as the times demanded. But it is misleading, as Blake and Faber both do, to read the *Vindication* solely as a document concerning "the history of the party which he came in the end to lead"; to conclude only that the details of that history are a function of expediency and that "no continuous body of Tory doctrine exists from the early eighteenth century to the 1830s." Faber also tends to deflect the issue back to the topic of party consistency. Although he does see that Disraeli views Bolingbroke "in terms of his own epoch and experience," and though he does say that Disraeli's debt is "as much imagined as real," Faber still reads the *Vindication* literally, in terms of factual truth, when he says that it is "difficult to establish a regular line of Tory leaders who thought this way."[44] The general point Blake makes looking backwards is more helpful: "No doubt it can be argued that there is *some sort of continuity of ideas – a Tory attitude to political problems* – which can be traced through the eighteenth century to the political struggles in the reign of Charles II when the words 'Whig' and 'Tory' originated" (emphasis added).[45] From this the better conclusion would thus seem to be that Disraeli was less interested in establishing the continuity of Tory doctrine than in proving the validity of a Tory interpretation of history, one founded on a nostalgic and heroic sense of the past. It is, indeed, essential to see precisely what Disraeli finds attractive in Bolingbroke's thought and career in order to understand what function the nostalgic paternalism and the backward projection of the Byronic hero's role ultimately serve.

Faber's assertion that "Disraeli's conception of society was romantic where Bolingbroke's was classical"[46] is also misleading, for his neat distinction between "romantic" and "classical" breaks down in the light of Byron's high estimation of the Augustans and Disraeli's identification with Byron. Whatever the complexities of Disraeli's Romanticism, and they are formidable, it is true that his stress on Romantic individualism is Byronic, as Contarini Fleming's "*Manstein*" illustrates. At times, however, Faber seems to imply only the sentimental sense of "romantic," as, for example, in stating that Disraeli "always realized with a part of himself … that his interpretation of the past was romantic and, up to a point shallow."[47] That Disraeli's imagination idealized the past is quite clear, but such a statement judges that process by the criterion of historical as opposed to psychic truth. All the evidence we have would suggest, however, that the most significant aspects of his political development can best be understood in terms of the latter.

Harold Lasswell, the best known theorist of the psychology of the political process, has argued that the behaviour and ideology of any politician are the result of a rationalization of a displacement of private motives "as they are nurtured and organized in relation to the family constellation and the early self." In other words, the identity of the "Political Man" is created when private motives are displaced from "family objects to public objects" and this displacement is then rationalized in terms of "public interests."[48] Disraeli's political career would seem to be a powerful illustration of this process in that it is quite clear that his earliest fantasies about his identity shape the development not only of his fiction but also of his political career, and in that the resultant role and ideology he adopts are offered to the public as representing the national interest. But though it is interesting to see that the work of the novelist and the politician have roots in common, the real fascination of Disraeli's life lies not in a psychology that one could practise upon it, but in the relation of the two careers, one to another, and the achievements of the man.

Previous chapters have shown that Disraeli's early novels embody a fantasy structure wherein the protagonist attempts to demonstrate his success through superiority and then retreats into an acceptance of his purity. They have also shown that Disraeli's early political career embodies the same pattern. But the most significant point is that the fantasy structures of the successive fictions and the imaginative patterns of the developing political career are interlocked, each influencing the other. In each of *Vivian Grey*, *Contarini Fleming*, and *Alroy*, for example, the hero's power fantasy of achieving enormous success by means of his superior talents proves to be unequal to events or to the conflicting need to appear pure in motive and character. Vivian Grey, whose career is modelled upon Disraeli's involvement in *The Representative* affair, becomes dependent upon his parents' solicitude, the victim of an enervating illness; Contarini Fleming's precocious political achievements give way to a quest for the solace of a substitute mother, the Magdalen transformed into the cousin-bride; and Alroy's messianic mission to save his people ends in death, a punishment for his hubris in neglecting the claims of his true faith and his virginal sister.

In a similar way each of the party intrigues, which are political variations of the power fantasies of the novels, results upon its collapse in an attempt by Disraeli to redefine his political identity. These attempts occur in the context of election campaigns or intra-party struggle and, as such, might not at first seem like retreats into innocence. But it must be remembered that the defence of his consistency, or political purity, is a conspicuous part of both Disraeli's theoretical and pragmatic statements. It should also be noted that in the successive attempts at definition he moves continually closer to a secure identity as a Tory and, beyond that, formulates an increasingly coherent paternalistic ideology. In the third Wycombe campaign, after the first intrigue with Lords Lyndhurst and Chandos has been thwarted, it appears that Disraeli is not retreating but moving forward to an integration of his personal and public identity confusions in a way that is compatible with the political realities he faces. But both the continuing emphasis on consistency in *The Crisis Examined* and his subsequent vulnerability to Mrs Norton's inquiries betray how precarious the growth to moderate, pragmatic politics really is. The Taunton campaign in turn seems to reveal a stable resolution of the identity crisis, but, at the very moment when the senses of innate and demonstrated superiority fuse, the new-found security as a Tory and anti-Whig campaigner explodes in all the guilt of his anti-Catholic disguise of his ambivalence about his Jewish heritage and his impure ambition. It is not until the crisis over the Municipal Corporations Bill that Disraeli finds, through either fiction or politics, an expression of retreat from the collapse of his power fantasies that is sufficiently invulnerable to be the basis of a durable form of his political identity.

The way in which the fantasy structures of the early fiction and the imaginative patterns of the political apprenticeship are connected can be explicitly shown from the chronology of political and literary events. For example, when Disraeli suffered the anti-Semitic abuse of the second Wycombe campaign and was then defeated, he retreated to Bradenham to take up the writing of *Alroy* and so defiantly justify his rejected self with the account of the noble and heroic redeemer of his people. In a similar fashion, upon the collapse of the Ultra-Tory faction's plan for stopping the "movement" in September 1835, he returned to Bradenham with Lyndhurst and composed the *Vindication*, which, ironically, is seen by others as a convincing demonstration of his abilities, which the earlier conspiracies had failed to provide. The *Vindication*, as an embodiment of his patriotic sentiments in a paternalistic theory and history of government, can be seen in psychoanalytical terms as fulfilling personal emotional needs that have been displaced into the realm of politics. But as a demonstration of his superior qualifications for leadership, it gains him the greatest degree of recognition yet achieved. Lyndhurst and others, even Peel, praised the work. Monypenny explicitly recognizes its assertive value: "The *Vindication* gave Disraeli what his fugitive efforts could never have given him, a recognised position as a political writer and thinker, and it not only helped to fix and clarify his own ideas, but, in appearing at a moment when party boundaries were shifting and principles in a state of flux, it from the first exerted no inconsiderable influence over the development of political thought."[49] The actual degree of influence is perhaps here exaggerated, but enough notice was taken of the *Vindication* to make it seem in Disraeli's eyes to have won him a significant place among the Tory leaders. It is, however, the language of a letter from his father that confirms the work's value in establishing Disraeli's identity. Isaac sees its publication as a noble "political birth" that has gained his son "a positive *name* and a being in the great political world" which he had not previously had because his "genius ... was apt in its fullness to run over." He also lauds his son's acquisition of *"a perfect style,"* and tells him that should he ever succeed in getting into Parliament his "moral intrepidity" and "rapid combinations of ideas" will throw out "many 'a Vindication' in the brilliancy and irresistible force of [his] ... effusions."[50] Such approval and recognition of Disraeli's genius could not help but magnify his achievement in his own eyes and, as a consequence, it would not be surprising if Disraeli found Lord Eliot's comparison of him to Bolingbroke quite apt.

There was, however, the more contemporary identification with Byron, and also with Shelley, that was still shaping Disraeli's sense of himself in the period just before his first success in being elected to Parliament. Earlier chapters have shown just how intense was his adolescent fascination with the author of *Childe Harold's Pilgrimage* and how closely he modelled at least the first part of his own eastern tour on the itinerary taken by Byron in 1809. His interest in Shelley's poetry as a source for his own ideas has also been remarked upon here and by others.[51] It is thus not entirely surprising that in 1837, when Disraeli decided to write another novel in the hope of alleviating the pressure of his debts, he should turn for inspiration to the most controversial of the Romantic poets. Critics have pretty much written off *Venetia*[52] as a bizarre, idiosyncratic potboiler of little, if any, literary value. Sarah Bradford has described it as the least autobiographical of his novels.[53] Certainly the idea of projecting the lives of Byron and Shelley backward into the years of the American Revolution and giving Shelley, in the character of Marmion Herbert, a career in exile as a revolutionary general seems in retrospect a most implausible displacement, which is not in the least rescued by the allusion to Scott's hero or the implicit nod to other historical fictions in the name Plantagenet Cadurcis. Indeed, the emphasis in *Venetia* on Lord Cadurcis's childhood and the subsequent reckless scandals of his adult life, in the form of direct parallels with the details Byron's life, renders the displacement futile in anything but, perhaps, a legal sense.

Venetia does, however, have an imaginatively autobiographical interest quite distinct from its tributes to the Romantic poets. The fantasy structure that shapes the story of the eponymous heroine's life has direct connections with the plot of *A Year at Hartlebury or the Election*, the novel written by Disraeli and his sister three years earlier, and it also anticipates the similar fantasy that controls the denouement of *Tancred; or the New Crusade*, a decade later. In all three cases the central element of the fantasy is the threat to the heroine's purity posed by the reckless and immoral behaviour of the antagonist. In the earlier work, as chapter 3 has shown, it is Lord Bohun's lack of integrity, his unprincipled egotism, and his predatory lust, both during his Mediterranean adventures and since, that precipitate the melodramatic response to his bigamous interest in Helen Molesworth, who within the political context of the plot is a character in large part derived from Sarah Disraeli's enthusiastic support of her brother's ambitions. In *Venetia* the heroine's relationship to Cadurcis begins in their childhood, when the troubled and soon orphaned boy is welcomed by Lady Herbert to Cherbury, her secluded estate, as a brotherly companion for her young daughter. Their growing affection for one another is explicitly described as that of siblings. But when Cadurcis grows up to assume the notoriety of the Byronic excesses of his entrance into society, he finds his desire to marry Venetia thwarted by the obstacle of Lady Herbert's objections to his dissolute character, which is soon further revealed in the episode of Lady Monteagle's hysterical infatuation for him and her husband's challenge to a duel.[54] Even late in the novel, in the scenes set in Italy after Lady Herbert has been reconciled with the husband and he and Cadurcis find themselves on terms of intimate friendship, the theme of innocence and purity betrayed re-emerges in the incest motif, as Cadurcis revives his hope of marrying Venetia. The language at this point, albeit clichéd, is strongly indicative of the connections with both the earlier and later fictions.

Cadurcis tells Venetia that he will not have their hearts "polluted by the vulgarity of fame" and that he wants her to feel for him as she did when they were children. She replies, "'I think it will be much better for me never to marry ... You can live here, and I can be your sister. Will not that do?'" Cadurcis then importunes her with claims of his constant love through innocent childhood, passionate youth, and detached manhood, but the result is less than reassuring. As he tells her that she is the only being who exercises any influence over him and explains it as springing from "some deep and mysterious sympathy of blood, which he cannot penetrate," he slips into emotional blackmail and Byronic extravagance:

> The world has called me a libertine; the truth is, no other woman can command my spirit for an hour. I see through them at a glance. I read all their weakness, frivolity, vanity, affectation, as if they were touched by the revealing rod of Asmodeus. You were born to be my bride. Unite yourself with me, control my destiny, and my course shall be like the sun of yesterday; but reject me, reject me, and I devote all my energies to the infernal gods; I will pour my lava over the earth until all that remains of my fatal and exhausted nature is a black and barren cone surrounded by bitter desolation. (442–5)

Coming as it does with reminders of his profligate life, Cadurcis's claim on the pure affections of Venetia is fraught with hypocrisy, even as it is constrained by parental scepticism. Nevertheless, despite the desperate volatility of his emotions, Venetia's reluctance to respond to his expressions of ardour is delineated only in the formal promise she has made never to marry without her father's and mother's consent. And within the fantasy of the pure love they shared, the threat posed by his intervening sexual immorality is disposed of when, in a reformulation of Shelley's death, both Cadurcis and Herbert are drowned together in a storm in the Gulf of Spezzia. In the novel's denouement Venetia marries Plantagenet's cousin, George, who has now succeeded to the title, and who has, all along, proved his devotion to her in the purity and delicacy of his feelings, even as he tried to ameliorate the conduct of his tempestuous relative.

The tension in *Venetia* between the claims of the "siblings'" pure love and the "pollution" of the "libertine" is one that will continue to shape the emotional dynamics of love relationships in Disraeli's later novels. As later chapters will show, it appears in a minor key in *Coningsby* and *Sybil*, and as a much stronger element in *Tancred*. As such it is a testimony to the fact that the Byronic legacy had continuing power within the imaginative shaping of Disraeli's political career even as that became a more realistic enterprise.

8

Young England / *Coningsby*[1]

When in the general election of 1837 following Victoria's accession to the throne, Disraeli finally succeeded in being elected to the House of Commons, his chances of ultimately achieving a dazzling political eminence were quite slim. For one thing, as the letters to his solicitor, William Pyne, show, Disraeli's financial situation had become precarious. Throughout the spring of 1837 he was repeatedly in danger of being arrested for debts and only some extraordinary legerdemain and considerable luck prevented him from suffering that public disgrace. For another, Sir Robert Peel had by then gained firm control of the Tory party. Lords Lyndhurst and Chandos and the Ultra-Tory faction could no longer be seen as offering any hope that, by some conspiratorial "dishing of the Whigs," their young literary protégé would find himself catapulted to a position of real power and influence. Moreover, Disraeli's flagrant and notorious display of his relationship with Lady Henrietta Sykes was still the subject of current gossip, for, although the lovers had finally parted the previous autumn, there occurred during the election campaign itself "the terrible catastrophe" of Henrietta being exposed by her husband for her adultery with the painter Daniel Maclise.[2] If one adds to these impediments Disraeli's reputation as "the author of *Vivian Grey*," which in polite and decorous circles was one of dubious integrity, and the often explicit anti-Semitism that marred his early campaigns at Wycombe and Taunton, there would be ample justification for concluding that the beginning of his parliamentary career was anything but auspicious.

That Disraeli, with a characteristic, if foolhardy, sense of drama, then chose to make his maiden speech on the subject of the validity of some Irish elections and to speak after his great antagonist, Daniel O'Connell, had just sat down is, perhaps, not surprising if one considers the traumatic impact of his "crucifixion" in the Taunton campaign three years earlier. But it was, all the same, a stroke of good fortune that the Irish radicals showed their customary lack of restraint in transforming the occasion into a bitter and factious row, for their discourtesy made him a celebrity and gained him some sympathy when, if he had been heard, the rhetorical extravagance of his speech would have elicited nothing more than contemptuous bemusement. Nevertheless, the issue of whether or not he had failed in his first attempt to catch the ear of the House immediately became Disraeli's central preoccupation. As the letters to Sarah, and later to his wife, Mary Anne, show, he was for the next few years compulsively concerned with the impact of his speeches.

Disraeli's most successful contribution to the 1837–8 session was that directed against the Corn Laws on 15 March. The next day he wrote a long letter to Sarah, which revealed his chief concern. He told her that "very unexpectedly" he had risen and made, "not merely a very good speech" but by far, and "by all sides agreed, the very best speech of the evening." This, he added, "is always a great thing to achieve, as then nobody else is talked of." He was heard, he said, with "the greatest attention and good humor" and, having succeeded in all his points, sat down "amid loud cheers," including some from Sir Robert Peel and other members of the Conservative front bench. He then went on to list the more than dozen other members of the House who had cheered him during the speech or congratulated him immediately afterwards, before mentioning the especially significant comment that Lord John Russell had made to a mutual friend, "a most brilliant speech … the best thing he had heard for a long time." Disraeli concluded his letter by saying that it was impossible to enumerate all those who had offered him their congratulations afterwards at the Carlton Club.[3]

Such a letter reveals several things about Disraeli's sense of himself and his situation. The inherent narcissism makes it clear that the most important issue is the extent to which he has succeeded in demonstrating his talent or genius. Because Sarah was at this time his only real confidante, it is not surprising that he should have so freely expressed his feelings of gratification to her. But it is surely remarkable (*The Times*'s or Jem's accounts notwithstanding)[4] that nowhere in the letter does he mention the subject of the debate or anything he actually said. Indeed, such matters seem entirely peripheral to his sense of triumph. Further, the emphasis upon the names of the important men in the party who shook hands with him, "Graham, Goulburn and Harding[e], and good old Herries," is indicative of both his need to find acceptance among the ranks of the powerful and his hope that in a significant way he has done so. Disraeli knew, however, that such acceptance was not based on any appreciation of his innate superiority to other men and that it would require recurrent demonstrations of his talent. Thus, five weeks later he again writes to Sarah in a similar vein: "I made a most brilliant and triumphant speech last night. Unquestionably and agreed upon by all hands the crack speech of the night, and everyone who spoke after me, either for or against, addressed himself to me; but of this you cannot judge by the reports … I write in a great hurry. The whole day has been passed in receiving compliments on my speech; but Sir Jas Graham, who was in the house, was really most warm; but of all this when we meet."[5]

By the spring of 1839, when it seemed that the Whigs would soon be out of office, Disraeli began to think that his performance in the House of Commons was paying significant dividends. In February he was one of "some 25 gentlemen" invited to dinner at Sir Robert Peel's and he told his sister that the party's leader talked to him a good deal.[6] A week later he reports that when he rose with several others at the same time to speak on Thomas Duncombe's theatrical entertainments motion, "the house called for me, and [I] spoke with great effect and amid loud cheering and laughter."[7] And undoubtedly even more satisfying was the reaction to his speech in early March on Irish corporations in which he not only spoke against the Government, but also deviated from official Conservative policy: "I was listened to in profound silence and with the utmost attention. Peel especially complimented me, sore as he was at the Conservative schism, and said 'D[israeli] – you took the only proper line of oppos[iti]on to the bill' – but Sir H[enry] Hardinge, a sharp critic spoke to me earnestly after the debate, and said with many other things, that I had now entirely got *the ear of the House* – and had overcome everything."[8] Two other letters from this period reflect much the same tone. The first describes the reaction to his speech on Lord Russell's scheme for the foundation of a central Education Board: "I had not time yesterday before post to receive the congratulations of my friends which came thick as the autumnal leaves of Vallombrosa. How strange that nearly in despair at the end of the session I should have made by universal consent the best speech on our side on the most important party question." In the second letter he tells Sarah that after the speech he went up to the Carlton Club to find that his fame and the rumour of his success had preceded him and that both friends and foes were anxious to extend their hands and congratulate him on "one of the best speeches of the session."[9] Then, on 12 July, Disraeli made "a most capital speech on Chartism" that drew extensive comment from both *The Times* and the *Morning Herald*.[10] And on 8 August he made another, on the Constabulary Report then in committee. Writing to Sarah, he says: "It made great effect, quoting all the pages and names with[ou]t any documents."[11] This was followed the very next day with an extensive speech evaluating the whole session, which he reports to Sarah with an obvious sense of great accomplishment: "I made a most effective speech last night: by very far the most able I have yet made. The complete command of the house I now have is remarkable. The moment I rose perfect silence, O'C[onne]ll part[icul]arly attentive, members running from the lib[rar]y and all hurrying to their seats."[12]

Robert Blake has suggested that Disraeli, in his desire to be seen to succeed, may have overestimated his success in his first few sessions as a Member of Parliament. In one sense this would seem to be true; in another it is not. The paradox lies in the faction-ridden nature of the House of Commons itself. Despite his frequent triumphs in making the best speech of the night, there is no evidence that Disraeli gained any dominant or preponderant influence over other members' opinions in these first two years. They might appreciate engaging rhetoric, but they were committed to intransigence on most points at issue. Yet Disraeli's eagerness to recount the approbation of established parliamentary figures reveals the extent of his ambition. Both the gratifications of receiving compliments from important men and the use of such phrases as "complete command of the house" are indirect reflections of the unabated power fantasy that his early novels had embodied so fulsomely. This is important, for it explains Disraeli's "mortification" and sense of being thwarted in the fulfilment of his dream when the Tories returned to office.

When, for example, at the opening of the 1840 session Peel invited Disraeli to a caucus of the principal members of the Conservative Opposition – sixteen in all, of whom Mary Anne proudly boasted, "Dizzy was the only one who had not been in office" – he undoubtedly interpreted this "signal proof of confidence" as an indication that he was at last recognized as deserving a place in Peel's inner circle.[13] Moreover, Disraeli continued during the sessions of 1840 and 1841 to speak "with great effect" from his chosen place in the House directly behind Sir Robert and to gain the party leader's praise for his efforts.[14] After his speech on the question of parliamentary privilege, for example, he reports to Sarah, "Since Tuesday I have done nothing but receive congratulations about my speech ... Ld Fitzgerald just told me that since the good old days of Canning, he had never heard so brilliant a reply ... I never heard more continued cheering – the house very full, about 1/2 pt 10 when I sat down, a prime hour and EVERY man of distinction there ... It is in vain to give you any account of all the compliments, all the congratul[ati]ons, the shaking of hands etc. etc. which occurred in the lobby ... from Robt Peel downwards, there is but one opinion of my great success."[15]

In March 1841 Disraeli was again invited to a dinner party at Peel's house, having just a few days earlier attended a "most recherche party" at Prince Esterhazy's, where the guests included "the Duke, Peel, and Stanley," and where "Mary Anne had a long convers[ati]on with Sir Robt."[16] It would hardly be surprising, therefore, if Disraeli began to see himself as an ever more important member of the party. The intensity of his desire for Peel's approbation that is so explicit in his correspondence undoubtedly reflects his anxiety as well as his ambition in this regard, but he obviously takes great pride in both his acceptance among the party's elite and his demonstrated success in furthering the Conservatives' cause. In this regard, it is significant that in his speech of 14 May 1841, on the Sugar Duties Bill, Disraeli concluded with a "spirited defence of Peel against charges of factionalism." By the time of the 1841 election he clearly thought himself to be at the very centre of the Tories' strategic manoeuvres, for in early June he forwarded a confidential, anonymous memorandum to Peel purporting to convey Lord Russell's opinions and intentions with respect to the impending dissolution.[17]

Never being one to underestimate his potential, Disraeli may well have felt some chagrin when, in July 1841, the editor of the *Morning Herald* relegated him to the relatively minor position of Paymaster of the Forces while speculating upon the details of Peel's forthcoming cabinet appointments. Disraeli's assertive defence of Peel's propriety in a letter to Sarah shortly after his election undoubtedly concealed a hope that he was destined for a more important role in the new Government: "As for all these editorial figments and newspaper on dits they are manufactur'd for Country cousins. Peel *never opens his mouth* and very properly: until he is entrusted with the task of forming a government, it would be the height of arrogant impertinence in him to appoint any of his colleagues ... Of course, there can [be] no rational doubt about the official positions of two or three individuals: such as Lord Stanley, the Duke of W[ellingto]n and Ld. Lyndh[urs]t: all the rest will remain in obscurity until partridge shooting."[18] For the next five weeks Disraeli remained in a state of heightened anticipation of a promotion to office. He repeatedly assures Sarah that though there is "no news ... all things look very well." In the middle of August he reports, "As for rumours, such a thing as an *on dit* is not heard of – but I suppose 'tis the pause before the earthquake."[19] By the 24th, however, there is a distinct sense that the critical moment is at hand, when he writes to Mary Anne from the Carlton Club: "I am obliged to go down to the House. There is to be an amendment of non-confidence in the Government moved on the Address. I have seen Lyndhurst but *nothing* said." And again he writes to Sarah: "There is no news of any kind; all about appointments in the papers moonshine." But then there is a clear indication of his frustration in the note of 2 September to Mary Anne: "I can't stay at this infernal club, and shall walk on to Crockford's for change of scene."[20]

Such an interpretation of Disraeli's situation is consistent with both his sense of his recent successes and with the tone of his appeal to Sir Robert once it was apparent that no summons to office was forthcoming: "I confess to be unrecognised at this moment by you appears to me to be *overwhelming*; and I appeal to your own heart – to that justice and that magnanimity, which I feel are your characteristics – to save me from an *intolerable humiliation*" (emphasis added).[21] The concrete nature of Disraeli's frustrated expectations is fully revealed, however, in a letter he wrote to his sister the next day: "All is over; and the crash wo[ul]d be overwhelming, were it not for the heroic virtues of Mary Anne, whose ineffable tenderness and unwearied devotion never for a moment slacken. I must and ought to console myself for any worldly mortific[ati]on in the poss[essi]on of such a wife – but it was principally to honor her that I aspired to this baffled dignity." His hopes, he adds, were not "a fool's Paradise," for they were "shared by the wise" – "Lynd[hurs]t was stupified at the catastrophe and at all times expected more than I ever anticipated."[22] After his election Disraeli had spent the first half of August in Buckinghamshire, much of it, it seems, in the company of Lord Lyndhurst. And whatever expectations of office he had on the basis of his own recent parliamentary performances were clearly heightened in sanguine conversations with his former co-conspirator and benefactor.

When he returned to London in mid-August, however, Disraeli was disagreeably surprised to discover that he was reputed by Lord Stanley, F.R. Bonham (the party agent), and others to have been indulging in "a great deal of abuse of the party leadership" and to be the author of "a somewhat insolent letter of advice to Peel," which had appeared in *The Times* on 2 August under the pseudonym, "Pittacus."[23] Bonham had written to Peel about "the most extraordinary and bitter abuse less at the Carlton than elsewhere (I hear) on the part of Disraeli who is the Psittacus [*sic*] of the Times, and of whom you will doubtless hear more."[24] Despite the fact that the letter in *The Times* ended, "Oh, Sir, recollect what Pitt would have done in your position," the political pun, if not the classical allusion, may have been lost on Bonham. On the other hand, the transformation of a sage into a parrot looks rather like a deliberate witticism at Disraeli's expense. Realizing the probable consequences of being maligned as a troublemaker, Disraeli immediately wrote to Peel protesting his innocence;[25] but, despite this denial, it is not inconceivable that Disraeli was, in fact, the author of the offending document. More likely he was the victim of his own reputation and of the prejudice with which he was regarded by some of the most influential Tories. Not surprisingly, this sense of victimization, which seems like an ironic realization of the fantasies embodied in his early novels, was uppermost in his mind when he wrote to Peel extending his claim to official recognition. For having mentioned his exertions and expenses on behalf of the party, he insisted that there was one "peculiarity" in his case on which he could not remain silent: "I have had to struggle against a storm of political hate and malice, which few men ever experienced, from the moment, at the instigation of a member of your cabinet, I enrolled myself under your banner; and I have only been sustained under these trials by the conviction, that the day would come when the foremost man of this country would publickly testify, that he had some respect for my ability and my character."[26]

In his reply Peel placed an astonishing misinterpretation upon these assertions. He assumed that Disraeli was claiming that he had been promised a position in the new government, and he observed bluntly that "no member of the Cabinet ... ever received ... the slightest authority" to make such an offer. Moreover, he went on to expatiate in two more paragraphs about the imprudence of this alleged offer of promotion and the integrity of his own principles in rendering "justice" to the many claims of preferment he had received.[27] What Disraeli had actually said was simply that he had joined the Conservative party at the instigation of a member of the Cabinet, and he quickly sent the prime minister a dignified clarification correcting his misconstruction and insisting that he had hoped for parliamentary office, not as the fulfilment of a promise, but only as a "recognition of party service and parliamentary ability."[28]

Blake argues that Disraeli's failure to obtain ministerial office in Peel's 1841 Government is in no way surprising.[29] If one considers Peel's situation and the nature of the Conservative establishment, that conclusion seems fully justified. Only one member of the new cabinet, the Duke of Buckingham, had not previously held office. And only one, William Gladstone, was not a member of the titled orders. Once Peel had satisfied the claims of territorial and party influence, he had very little discretionary power of appointment, even outside the Cabinet, and his assertion of that fact in his answer to Disraeli was no exaggeration. But Peel's evasiveness in responding to Disraeli's special plea seems all the more significant in that light, for he betrays his own discomfort and sense of injustice in the legalistic and formal tone with which he mistakes Disraeli's motives and converts the supposed indiscretion into a promise of office, which he then pompously discredits. One further point deserves notice. In explaining the constraints of his position, in which he had far more colleagues with claims upon the party than offices to fill, Peel assures Disraeli that were this not the case, he would be glad to avail himself of his "offer of service." This would become an important matter later, during the Corn Law debate in 1846, when Disraeli vehemently denied that he had ever made "an application for office." But for the moment it is enough to notice that this exchange of letters shows that Peel and Disraeli held very different views of what had transpired between them.

Disraeli, of course, could not contemplate the limitations of Peel's situation with any sympathy. The "crash" of his expectations was "over-whelming" and humiliating precisely because he could not imagine that his genius and demonstrated talents did not override the claims of all but the noblest and most distinguished of the aristocracy. Hence, about the positions of Stanley, Wellington, and Lyndhurst there could be "no rational doubt," but the rest were negotiable and would "remain in obscurity until partridge shooting." This suggests that Disraeli had a very unsophisticated and highly romantic notion of current party politics, one that accords with his own egocentricity and is consistent with his previous roles within the Ultra-Tory faction; but one that also suggests that his four years' experience in the House of Commons had not in the least diminished the intensity of his fantasy of heroic individualism first manifested in *The Representative* affair sixteen years earlier, and since embodied in *Vivian Grey*, "Ixion in Heaven," *Iskander*, and *Alroy*.

When the parliamentary session of 1842 began, Disraeli was in a mood of some desperation, feeling "solitary" and "utterly isolated":

"Before the change of Government," he said, "political party was a tie among men, but now it is only a tie among men who are in office."[30] He decided, however, to create an overwhelming, practical, and solid demonstration of his talents with a speech about the consular establishment. And that speech, for which he spent several weeks preparing and memorizing an astonishing mass of factual information, was an enormous success. It was an attack on Palmerston's administration of the Foreign Office. In part its effect upon the House of Commons was magnified because Palmerston, without much success of his own, replied "with great pains & with as much effort as if he were answering Peel."[31] In addition, Palmerston made the mistake of saying that he hoped his antagonist would soon obtain office – thus insinuating that there was some disappointment on that score – and Disraeli was able to make a "most happy" retort, full of sarcasm, about the Whig minister's own *"unprecedented"* career in seven successive administrations. Thus Disraeli appeared to everyone to have "broken lances with Palmerston and rode away in triumph," and he could, as a result, justly feel that the effect of his success would be permanent and that his position in the House was "sensibly altered."[32] Indeed, he now found himself "with[ou]t effort the leader of a party – chiefly of the youth, & new members," and was much sought after as a spokesman by those who had motions of their own to put forward, or who, like Sir Richard Vyvyan, had some dissident plan for obstructing Peel's Corn Law Bill.[33] But while he was immensely gratified by these signs of power and influence, Disraeli took care to avoid any collaboration that would overtly place him in a position antagonistic to the prime minister – even going so far as to absent himself on occasions when an attack on Peel was in the offing and he might from others' malice be presumed a silent partner in it.[34]

The party of youth that began to form around Disraeli was, of course, the embryo of the Young England movement, a *partie carrée* composed of George Smythe, whom Disraeli had known for at least ten years, Lord John Manners, whom he had met the previous year, and Alexander Baillie-Cochrane, who was a Cambridge friend of both Smythe and Manners. It seems that during the 1842 session the first two, discovering in him a common sympathy for many of their own views on society and politics, increasingly looked upon Disraeli as their spiritual and intellectual leader. While Smythe and Manners were very much contrasting personalities, the former being a brilliant but wildly extravagant and somewhat deliberately Byronic figure and the latter a good-natured and very idealistic and gentle devotee of lost causes, they shared a nostalgic perspective on the Tory party, the Church, the monarchy, and the general progress of recent political events that was the antithesis of the "liberal utilitarian spirit of the time" and that seemed to harmonize with the views Disraeli had espoused and expressed in the *Vindication of the English Constitution* seven years earlier.[35]

The shape of Manners's and Smythe's idealism was largely formed in their undergraduate years through their friendship with Frederick Faber, who, as their eloquent idol, impressed them profoundly with the spirit of the Oxford Movement and all of its enthusiasms – lofty ideals of chivalry and divine kingship, noble views of feudalism, and a passionate hope of revivifying the Church of England. The essence of the bond that brought Young England's foursome together, however, was patriotism. Their conception of that was in part derived from their revulsion at the battle of warring factions that early nineteenth-century society seemed to have become and from their desire to restore what they conceived to be an ancient social harmony. To this end Bolingbroke's definition of patriotism as a quality founded in great principles and supported by great virtues offered them a heroic role in the process of such restoration.[36] Only through the nobility of character in great men and the performance of their privileged duty could such harmony be established. In that respect Disraeli's earlier identification with Bolingbroke and the Opposition Circle politics of the early eighteenth century now clearly became transformed into a conscious adoption on Young England's part of the role that Bolingbroke had urged Lord Cornbury and his circle of young aristocrats to play in the reform of the Tory party and the country. Inherent in this posture is the idea that the Conservative party in the hands of Peel and his moderate policy is unequal to the task of addressing the nation's most pressing problems.

It was in Paris during the fall of 1842 that the parliamentary identity of the Young England movement took shape. Both Smythe and Baillie-Cochrane were also there, and the letters they wrote to Manners in London provide a "fascinating commentary" upon the role that Disraeli was beginning to envision for them all.[37] Once again he had become absorbed in a world of high fashion and his letters to Sarah are full of reports of social encounters with dukes, duchesses, princes, counts, ambassadors, and influential politicians. In this heady atmosphere, and with a sense of recent parliamentary triumph, Disraeli began to imagine the possibilities of obtaining real political power and to conceive of forming a party rather similar to the "most immense ... and serviceable" one proposed by the youthful protagonist of *The Representative* affair when he wrote to John Murray from Scotland in September 1825. Something of the precise nature of the fantasy in its latest form can be gauged from Smythe's letter to Manners, dated 19 October 1842: "*Most private*. Dizzy has much more parliamentary power than I had any notion of. The two Hodgsons are his, and Quinton Dick. He has a great hold on Walter and 'The Times.' Henry Hope (who will come in soon) is entirely in his hands. He was in Paris, and I had an opportunity of judging." Smythe went on to assure Manners that Cochrane's alarm at "the extent of Dizzy's influence" was but an anxiety that it might soon swallow the intimacy of their friendship. In Smythe's view, though, "to be of power, or fame, or even office," they could not have their party swell too much, or be "too *liés* with Disraeli": "You see, Kok does not know him well ... and is jealous of his throwing us over. But even if he did, it is always better to *be in a position* to be thrown over, than to be *nothing at all*."[38]

What is quite extraordinary is the explicitly manipulative quality of Disraeli's vision. The comparison with *The Representative* intrigue is apt, both because he seems to be as vulnerable as ever to his adolescent power fantasy and because the issue of his sincerity, or lack of it, clearly remains his greatest liability. As Smythe's letter indicates, Cochrane was not the most disinterested observer of these events, but his reservations throw even more light upon the nature of the relation between Disraeli's imagination and external reality. Cochrane felt that no man could indulge in the "contemplation of self-aggrandisement" in the way Disraeli seemed to be doing "without at last, in the words of Thiers, 'prenant ses voeux pour des réalités.'" Disraeli's head, he said, was full of "great movements, vast combinations, the importance of numbers, cabinet dinners, the practice of dissimulation! in fact of the vaguest speculations, the mere phantasmagoria of politique legerdemain."[39] And if Disraeli returned to England in the "hope and expectation" of finding himself at the "head of a large party," who would "intrigue against the Government," Cochrane feared that it would all end in "disappointment and much injury to all parties concerned." From these expressions of concern one could draw a portrait of either Disraeli's naivety or cynicism. The full extent and implications of his egocentricity are best revealed, however, not by such a distrustful witness, but in his own words.

The greatest triumph of his visit to Paris was the personal relationship that Disraeli established with King Louis Philippe. Having obtained an audience with the king through General Baudrand, with whom he had become familiar at dinner parties and soirées, he seized the opportunity of enlightening His Majesty upon the current state of English politics. Disraeli's point of view was exactly the reverse of the one he had expressed in the *Gallomania* ten years before, but it harmonized perfectly with the king's desire for an Anglo-French alliance and was consistent with the attacks on Palmerston's "anti-commercial" foreign policy, which Disraeli maintained was more responsible for England's economic distress than were the Corn Laws. After the initial royal interview he wrote a lengthy memorandum to the king in which he outlined a plan for "restoring the understanding between France and England."[40] Having mentioned at the outset his own qualifications, as one with "that knowledge of the actors and motives of the political world of England which years of thought and action and intimate intercourse with the chiefs of parties can alone give," and having flattered "the genius of a great Prince, eminently fertile in resource and strengthened by an unprecedented experience of life," Disraeli proposed a threefold course of action.

First, he suggested that on the opening night of the next Commons' session, "an influential member who has the ear of the House" should give notice of a motion calling for a comprehensive debate on the state of relations between England and France, a debate that would "produce a marvellous effect ... teach men to think ... give principles to that vast majority who must be led ... afford an opportunity to a great section of the Opposition to repudiate the late policy of Lord Palmerston," and "echo in every Cabinet in Europe." Second, he proposed, that since Peel's Government could not always depend on the presence of some forty to fifty "agricultural malcontents" within the ranks of the Tories, to organize a party of Conservative members, who, "full of youth and energy and constant in their seats, must exercise an *irresistible control* over the tone of the Minister. Sympathising in general with his domestic policy, they may *dictate* the character of his foreign, especially if they appeal to a conviction which at the bottom of Sir R. Peel's heart responds to their own" (emphasis added). The third measure that Disraeli advocated was "the comprehensive organis[atio]n of the Press of England in favor of the F[rench]. and E[nglish] alliance." Rather than depend upon the pages of any single journal, which would then become "only an organ" without authority, he proposed to "speak in journals of every school of politics, and sound in every district." And offering either to undertake or supervise this task, he confided to the king, "It is with a machinery of this description that the ideas of a single man, acting upon latent sympathies wh: only require developement, soon become the voice of a nation."

The most interesting aspect of this memorandum is the light it sheds upon the ways in which fantasy and external reality are connected in Disraeli's mind. His success in catching the "ear of the House" and attacking Palmerston during the previous session is combined, for example, with his paternalistic conception of the political process and becomes the basis for imagining that his voice will soon "echo in every Cabinet in Europe." And the political power conjured up by such words as "exercise an irresistible control" and "dictate the character of his foreign [policy]" is certainly not less than that of the most influential and ruthless cabinet ministers. Disraeli is, in effect, proposing to exploit the divisions within the Conservative party and blackmail the prime minister. Such a plan recalls to memory both Vivian Grey's manipulative advice to Frederick Cleveland and Contarini Fleming's daring threats to achieve the containment of Russia – not to mention the Ultra-Tory intrigues surrounding the Municipal Corporations Reform Bill of 1835. Moreover, Disraeli's confidence that the "Press of England" can be orchestrated to present a pro-Gallic view that will become "the voice of a nation" clearly rests upon an overestimation of his success as the anonymous author of the *Morning Post* articles (1835), the letters of Runnymede (1836), and his more recent sallies in *The Times* as "Atticus" and "Laelius."

To look at the memorandum to Louis Philippe simply as a public document is to miss its significance. For in that light it appears to be the euphoric posturing of a naive, sublime egotist. It is, in fact, not just a piece of advice to the king, but also a fantasy embodying its author's conception of his own potential. Cochrane's witty appraisal of Disraeli's performance in Paris is much to the point: "Disraeli's salons rival Law's under the Regent. Guizot, Thiers, Molé, Decazes, and God wots how many *dei minores* are found in his antechamber, while the great man himself is closeted with Louis Philippe at St. Cloud, and already pictures himself the founder of some new dynasty with his Manfred love-locks stamped on the current coin of the realm."[41] But just as the protagonist of *The Representative* affair, and "the author of *Vivian Grey*," embodied in *The Young Duke* a compensatory alternative to his adolescent alienation in the form of a fantasy of acceptance, so in this version of his recurrent power fantasy he embodies a similar compensation for, and a retreat from, the failure to gain a seat in Peel's cabinet in 1841. In this case, however, the fantasy succeeds in blending the external and internal realities of public and private identities by taking the shape of an heroic political role that was, no doubt, derived partly from the experience of being accepted in the aristocratic social and political circles of Paris, and partly from finding some wider recognition of his demonstrated talents in the House of Commons.

The true significance of the memorandum lies, not so much in its optimistic impracticality, but rather in the way it implicitly shows how Disraeli's political career takes on the character of a fiction, one in which he conceives of himself as the protagonist of a political novel engaged in a heroic struggle. And in another, equally significant respect the memorandum illuminates Disraeli's role within the Young England movement. It more than confirms Cochrane's suspicions of his manipulative intent and reveals that, from the very formation of the group, Disraeli was thinking in terms the others, Smythe perhaps excepted, would have found the antithesis of its professed ideals. Most historians of the period have focused upon the nostalgic paternalism of Young England's cherished notions about the Church, the aristocracy, the people, and the condition of England in the 1840s. But it is clear now that Disraeli was also thinking of their potential as the tail that could wag the dog on British foreign policy, a subject that, he knew, was more likely to realize his ambitions than national holy-days, the imprisonment of Don Carlos, or the repeal of mortmain. In this light Manners's diary entry, "Could I only satisfy myself that D'Israeli believed all that he said, I should be more happy: his historical views are quite mine, but does he believe them?" and Smythe's witticism, "Dizzy's attachment to moderate Oxfordism ... is something like Bonaparte's to moderate Mahomedanism," are suggestive of the hidden discrepancies of intention between Disraeli and his disciples.[42]

The issue of his character was, in fact, still the most important aspect of Disraeli's position both within the Young England group and within the Conservative party at large. In a letter to Lord Strangford the Duke of Rutland wrote: "It is grievous that two young men such as John and Mr. Smythe should be led by one of whose integrity of purpose I have an opinion similar to your own, though I can judge only by his public career. The admirable character of our sons only makes them the more assailable by the arts of a designing person."[43] Disraeli would not necessarily have known about the opinions of Manners's father, though he was well aware that many of those within the Conservative establishment still looked upon him with jaundiced eyes. Yet we should recognize that however much as a political outsider he felt the necessity of

intrigue and manipulation, Disraeli was equally and genuinely attracted by the purity of Young England's motives and ideals, perhaps
best exemplified by Lord John Manners's generous nobility. But the real
political issue was an internal one; the tension of his ambivalent desires
for recognition of his innate superiority and of his demonstrated success had not been vanquished. Indeed, the Young England movement
intensified that ambivalence precisely because for Disraeli it both manifested the ideology of true Toryism and shrouded the gratification of
his ambition.

Such a recognition of the mixed nature of Disraeli's imaginative conception of himself, and of his role in Young England, has implications
for our understanding of the novel in which he immortalized that
movement. For, though *Coningsby; or the New Generation* has been widely accepted as a "manifesto of Young England," the structure, plot, and
characterizations of that novel might more plausibly be considered a
reflection of the author's ambivalence than an aesthetic failure to wed a
polemical and satirical essay on politics to a frivolous and adolescent
romance. To see, for example, the sharp contrast between the idealized,
but passive and insipid, Coningsby and his equally idealized, powerful
alter-ego, Sidonia, as a dichotomous fantasy about the respective costs
and rewards of "purity" and "success," or to see the marvellous resolution of the romantic-political complication of the plot as a form of
wish-fulfilment, is to suggest that there is a close affinity between this
first novel in the "political trilogy" and Disraeli's earlier fictions. In particular, a careful analysis of *Coningsby* might well vitiate the usual claims
that Disraeli had by 1844 found in the politics of the 1840s a significantly new inspiration and purpose for his fictions. Rather, the politics
of "the New Generation" would seem to be the politics of nostalgia in
two senses; however much *Congingsby* is a political novel in a literal
sense, it clearly embodies a truly brilliant and witty, but reciprocal displacement of personal motives and public objects. As Disraeli became
caught up in Young England, he not only conceived of propagating
their ideals through the medium of fiction, he also wanted to create an
ideal embodiment of the political protagonist. Harry Coningsby should
thus be seen as more than a tribute to George Smythe's lost innocence.
And the novel that bears his name might be considered less "A
Dissertation Upon Parties" than a bildungsroman that extends, but
does not transcend the imaginatively autobiographical mode of fiction
that Disraeli had developed in the previous decade.[44]

I

Coningsby; or, the New Generation, written in the autumn and winter of 1843–4, has traditionally been seen as the first example of a subgenre, the political novel, and, as such, part of a trilogy that is overtly propagandist in conception. Further, most critics, of whom Robert Blake is the most eloquent and representative, have agreed that Disraeli's "trilogy," made up of *Coningsby*, *Sybil*, and *Tancred*, "is quite different from anything he had written before" and that "a wide gulf separates them from his silver fork novels and historical romances of the 'twenties and 'thirties."[45] This view has been largely derived from Disraeli's retrospective statements of intention, first in his preface to the fifth edition of *Coningsby* in 1849, and later in the general preface to the 1870 collected edition of his novels, wherein he claims to have adopted "the form of fiction as the instrument to scatter his suggestions" about the "derivation and character of political parties; the condition of the people which had been the consequence of them; and the duties of the Church as a main remedial agency."[46] There is, of course, some validity for this post hoc authorial perspective. The world of Tadpole and Taper clearly reflects Disraeli's disenchantment with the Conservative party of the 1840s, and the portrayal of Young England's characters and ideas in *Coningsby* at least partially reflects his involvement in that movement.

But *Coningsby*, which is significantly subtitled: by the "author of 'Contarini Fleming,'" also reflects the relation between Disraeli's private and public lives and is, I think, more concerned with the development of a compensatory, ideal, heroic, political identity than it is with the contemporary state of political parties. The structure of the novel confirms this claim, for the careful reader can see that although *Coningsby* is, in fact, part fiction and part tract, the portion of it that takes the form of political essays is very much subordinate to the bildungsroman in which Harry Coningsby, Esq., finds the sources of his fulfilment. Yet, in resolutely attempting to elucidate the message of the *roman à thèse* which they take the novel to be, most critics have rested heavily upon those essays – chapters 1 and 7 of Book 1, chapters 1 and 5 of Book 2, and, to a lesser extent, chapter 4 of Book 5. The message is, of course, there. But the reason it becomes a critical synecdoche is perhaps that few readers of *Coningsby* have read all or even some of Disraeli's early novels and that most have an imperfect understanding of his political thinking in the 1830s. Because there seems to be no appreciable distance between the authorial voice and Disraeli's own, it is easy to conclude that the novel is indeed little more than a "manifesto of Young England."[47] The difficulty with this argument, however, is that, as the novel progresses, the voice of the essayist is increasingly subsumed in the romance of Coningsby's private *and* public self-fulfilment. Far from the implicit assumption of most previous critics, that the romance is merely an illustrative embellishment of the narrator's political philosophy, the essays seem, rather, to form a context for the romance, which, once established, carries on with its own momentum in Books 6 through 9. Thus, to overcome one's reluctance to treat the work as fiction is to be forced to the conclusion that there is a strong continuity between it and Disraeli's early works, from *Vivian Grey* and *The Young Duke* through *Contarini Fleming*, *Alroy*, and *Henrietta Temple*.[48]

For all the emphasis upon the duties of the "New Generation," *Coningsby* is, in essence, a fiction that looks retrospectively upon the period of the formation of Disraeli's Tory ideology in the 1830s, replacing the actuality of his struggle to transcend his alienation from the establishment – the basic terms of which were his Jewish heritage, his literary improprieties, and his reputation for insincerity – with ideal versions of the past as it should have been. As much as anything else, it is a romance of fictional wish-fulfilment, so purified that elements of the author's internal conflicts are projected upon characters other than his nominal hero rather than embodied in him as had been the case with Vivian Grey, Contarini Fleming, David Alroy, and Ferdinand Armine. This is the most plausible explanation of the insipid and almost completely passive character of Coningsby and of the bizarre projection of supernatural powers on to his alter-ego, Sidonia. Lest this notion seem extreme, it should be remembered that the fictional split personality is also a feature of two of Disraeli's other works, *The Rise of Iskander* and *Tancred*, and that the central theme of both is also the conflict between principle and expediency, or altruism and betrayal.

While the discussion of politics in *Coningsby* is an expression of this theme, it might be said to serve four aesthetic functions. First, it creates a topicality designed to enhance the matter of the actual fiction. Second, and more important, it creates the vacuum that Disraeli's hero is ultimately to fill: "No one had arisen," we are told, "either in Parliament, the Universities, or the Press, to lead the public mind to the investigation of principles; and not to mistake, in their reformations, the corruption of practice for fundamental ideas" (Bk 2, ch. 4, 103). Third, both in satirical and expository terms, the political analysis helps to define by contrast

Coningsby's true nature. Fourth, the political ideology itself works to shape the thematic impact of the romance's controlling fantasy. The first two of these functions are quite obvious and require little comment, but both the matter of characterization and that of the fantasy seem more complex.

II

Coningsby is initially presented in terms similar in some respects to those that describe both the Duke of St James and David Alroy. Like them he is an orphan, and his situation is given a melodramatic cast. He is clearly in the clutches of the "sinister," "dishonest," and innately vulgar Rigby (Bk 1, ch. 1, 2–3); Lord Monmouth's tyranny has occasioned Mrs Coningsby's cruel fate of estrangement and death; and the moral is explicit in the narrator's intrusion: "the altars of Nemesis are beneath every outraged roof, and the death of this unhappy lady, apparently without an earthly friend or an earthly hope, desolate and deserted, and dying in an obscure poverty, was not forgotten" (Bk 1, ch. 2, 9). But in thus establishing the exemplum of poetic justice, the implied author is led a step beyond the limits of his heroic conception. For, when Coningsby's tears fail to impress his grandfather in their first interview, the authorial voice intrudes once more: "How often in the nursery does the genius count as a dunce because he is pensive ... The school-boy, above all others, is not the simple being the world imagines. In that young bosom are often stirring passions as strong as our own, desires not less violent, a volition not less supreme. In that young bosom what burning love, what intense ambition, what avarice, what lust of power; envy that fiends might emulate, hate that man might fear!" (Bk 1, ch. 3, 21).

It does not take an astute critic to realize that this passage, with its increasing intensity and emotional violence, quickly becomes tangential to the characterization of Coningsby. In doing so, it casts an autobiographical reflection, given what we know of Disraeli's adolescence, that collapses whatever aesthetic distance might have been presumed to exist between the author and his narrator and that suggests the nature of the creative inspiration which shapes the novel. Coningsby, who is, of course, devoid of "avarice," "lust of power," "envy," and "hate," finds an early recognition, as Disraeli did not, of his preeminence and nobility in the form of adulation from his schoolboy peers following his heroism in saving Oswald Millbank's life. But what is equally striking is that at the time of his initiation into the realm of social and political action (in Book 3), the narrator describes Coningsby's feelings in terms virtually identical to those of the internal struggle that characterizes the protagonists of *Contarini Fleming* (1832) and *Henrietta Temple* (1836).

Coningsby's "pure and innocent" heart, we are told, "not withstanding all his high resolves and daring thoughts, was blessed with that tenderness of soul which is sometimes linked with an ardent imagination and a strong will" (Bk 3, ch. 1, 117). And, although his "noble aim" demands "absolute, not relative distinction," he feels in his isolation the need for a companion for his heart as well as for his intellect (Bk 3, ch. 1, 118–19). In short, he longs for a heroic role in which the struggle for "purity" and the struggle for "success" are blended and the two made manifest by the recognition of his own genius. For example, immediately following the delineation of the hero's aspirations, the author turns to an account of Rigby's feeblemindedness ("he told Coningsby that want of religious Faith was solely occasioned by want of Churches"). This suggests that Disraeli's satirical portraits are primarily designed to define by contrast his protagonist's character: "His deep and pious spirit recoiled with disgust and horror from such lax, chance-medley maxims" (Bk 3, ch. 2, 131–2). Similarly, the point of the portrait of life at Coningsby Castle is to establish the hero's true sensibility. The other guests, however distinguished and graceful, are caught up in an artificial world of questionable motives, dubious propriety, and studied effects the very opposite of his innocent spontaneity and tender affection.

Coningsby, rather like the Duke of St James in *The Young Duke* and Ferdinand Armine in *Henrietta Temple*, is ultimately accepted as a hero because of his innate, natural superiority. Action on his part is superfluous and unnecessary, as is, indeed, stressed by the fact that the only active demonstrations of his heroic sensibility occur when he saves Oswald Millbank from drowning at Eton and when he solaces the actress, Flora. The point of the fantasy is that he is accepted for what he is – noble and pure of heart – and not for what he does. That is why his rewards of political preferment, marriage to his true love, and enormous wealth have the miraculous quality of wish-fulfilment. It is also why Disraeli's characterization, with its emphasis upon the youth's nobility, innocence, virtue, and sensibility, can justly be seen in part as a compensatory version of the potential political protagonist. The very traditional quality of the ideal – grandson of a marquess, hero of Eton, Cambridge undergraduate – was for the author, however, a denial of a large part of his imaginative self.

The other side of Disraeli's ambivalence is embodied in the characterization of Sidonia, which in psychological terms might be said to represent the projected ideal of his other, alienated self. As a member of the Jewish race, Sidonia, too, is innately superior, but his acceptance among the social and political elite is based upon his demonstrated superiority. Ultimately, it is not just his enormous wealth or his dazzling intellect but rather his power and success in exerting political control over the whole of Europe that gains him his welcome. It has been suggested that Sidonia is modelled upon Baron Salomon de Rothschild, with whom Disraeli had become familiarly acquainted during his marvellous visit to Paris in the fall of 1842.[49] But there is no real similarity, other than their Jewishness and wealth, between Sidonia and his alleged model, so it is more sensible to argue that de Rothschild was merely the match that set Disraeli's imagination on fire. Sidonia was "descended from a very ancient and noble family of Arragon," who, "strange as it may sound ... secretly adhered to the ancient faith and ceremonies of their fathers – a Belief in the unity of the God of Sinai, and the rites and observances of the laws of Moses" (Bk 4, ch. 10, 220–1). Disraeli maintained that his own ancestors on his father's side of the family were aristocratic secret Jews expelled from Spain in 1492, and he included this highly romantic but false account of his origins in the memoir with which he prefaced his father's collected works in 1849.[50] Moreover, the theme of a secret religious allegiance is an important feature of both *Alroy* and *The Rise of Iskander*, and what I have earlier termed "the Catholic disguise of his Jewish heritage" is embodied in *The Young Duke*, *Contarini Fleming*, and *Henrietta Temple*.

It is worth noting, too, that Sidonia constantly speaks with Disraeli's voice. Virtually all of his political opinions are taken, often word for word, from Disraeli's earlier expressions of his creed in the *Morning Post* articles of 1835, his early pamphlets, the *Vindication of the English Constitution*, and *The Revolutionary Epick*. For example, Sidonia tells Coningsby: "'It is not the Reform Bill that has shaken the aristocracy of this country, but the means by which that Bill was carried'" (Bk 4, ch. 11, 236). By 1844 this may have become something of a Tory cliché, but in *"What Is He?"* (April 1833) Disraeli had written: "The aristocratic principle has been destroyed in this country, not by the Reform Act, but by the means by which the Reform Act was passed."[51] Further, Sidonia's elaborate justifications of Hebrew superiority were to be repeated both in *Tancred* and in Disraeli's anomalous chapter on the Jewish question in his political "biography" of Lord George Bentinck in 1852.

Despite the obvious sincerity of the latter statement of Disraeli's views, some critics would argue that the extravagant characterization of Sidonia is satirical. But it seems as much mistaken to judge the absurdity of his accomplishments by the test of verisimilitude as to restrict oneself to a literal definition of autobiography. It is clear that the twofold essence of Sidonia's character, in both respects contrasting sharply with that of Coningsby, is that he is an outsider and that he is powerful. Consequently, he should be interpreted as an equally idealized counter-assertion upon Disraeli's part. Perhaps the conclusive proof of this ambivalence is the allegorical steeplechase in Book 4, chapter 14, where Coningsby mounted on the best of his grandfather's stud, aptly called "Sir Robert," comes in second behind Sidonia in his gorgeous Arab "of pure race," again symbolically named "The Daughter of the Star" (Bk 3, ch. 1, 127 and Bk 4, ch. 14, 259). In showing that the outsider, the alienated Jew, is equally "pure" and, indeed, superior to his nominal protagonist, Disraeli adopts an imaginative posture of defiance rather similar to that of taking up *Alroy* immediately after his defeat in the second Wycombe campaign of 1832, a campaign in which he was the victim of marked anti-Semitism. The most important aspects of Sidonia's characterization, however, go well beyond such obvious compensation and confirm my claim that Disraeli's identity confusion manifested itself not only as a tension between conflicting views of himself but also as ambivalence within each one.

The ostensible political lesson that Sidonia teaches his youthful protégé concerns the inspirational potency of heroic individualism. Coningsby is, of course, an apt pupil, for, as an adolescent, he had indulged in "visions of personal distinction, of future celebrity, perhaps even of enduring fame." Thus Sidonia preaches to the converted when, in discoursing upon "'the Spirit of the Age,'" he extols the "'influence of individual character'" (Bk 3, ch. 1, 124ff.). It is a doctrine of elegant simplicity. Power residing in institutions, whether nobility, monarchy, church, or Parliament, brings opprobrium upon them (Bk 4, ch. 13, 249–50), but truly "'great men ... prophets ... legislators ... conquerors,'" can control or create "'a vast public opinion'" and are "'Divine'" (Bk 3, ch. 1, 124–5). For the present the "'age does not believe in great men, because it does not possess any,'" but the "'Spirit of the Age is the very thing that a great man changes.'" According to Coningsby's alter ego, the function of institutions is subsidiary: "'From the throne to the hovel all call for a guide. You give monarchs constitutions to teach them sovereignty, and nations Sunday-schools to inspire them with faith'"

(Bk 3, ch. 1, 124–5). The hope of "'an age of social disorganisation'" is in "'what is more powerful than laws and institutions,'" in the regeneration of a sense of "'community'" based on "'national character'" and "'public virtue'" (Bk 4, ch. 13, 250–1). Perhaps most important, such a reconstruction of society can occur not from "'any new disposition of political power,'" nor from "'material'" or "'purely rational'" calculations. Sidonia insists that that attempt has failed: "'Man is only truly great when he acts from the passions; never irresistible but when he appeals to the imagination ... Man is made to adore and obey; but if you will not command him, if you give him nothing to worship, he will fashion his own divinities, and find a chieftain in his own passions'" (Bk 4, ch. 13, 252–3).

This statement, with its division between mechanical and organic theories of society, its rejection of materialism, its doctrine of hero worship, and its fear of unregulated human nature, is so obviously resonant with the ideas of Carlyle that critics have often surmised that Disraeli was here borrowing directly from him. There is, however, no conclusive evidence that Disraeli had read Carlyle's works. When one recognizes that all of the elements of this political theory had found expression in *The Revolutionary Epick*, published in 1834 (considerably earlier than Carlyle's major works), the most sensible conclusion would seem to be that such ideas were, as much as their antithesis, a part of the spirit of the age, which found its most forceful expression in Carlyle's prose.

The attraction of Sidonia's political theory resides in its simplicity and seemingly magical quality. Among the most enchanting things he tells Coningsby are his convictions that "'Great men never want experience'" and that "'To believe in the heroic makes heroes'" (Bk 3, ch. 1, 127). Such notions recall *The Wondrous Tale of Alroy* in which the youthful, indeed adolescent, protagonist, empowered by his altruistic faith in his role as the spiritual leader of the Hebrew people, finds that his exertions result in almost miraculous conquests. But the point of such a comparison is not just a matter of the inherent egocentricity. The implicit assertion of Hebrew superiority in *Alroy* is matched in *Coningsby* by Sidonia's similar belief (given the sanction of "fact" by the implied author) that the Hebrews, along "with the Saxons and the Greeks," are "in the first and superior class" of the human species and as an "unmixed race of first-rate organisation are the *aristocracy of Nature*" (emphasis added, Bk 4, ch. 10, 232). Perhaps the intrusion of the authorial voice here is significant, for *Alroy*, though begun in 1829, was completed in 1833, only a year before Disraeli's first explicit advocacy of a natural aristocracy in *The Revolutionary Epick*. Thus, Sidonia's simple notion, however circular, of faith in one's own destiny as the motivating and creative source of the heroic sensibility, might be said to confirm the suspicion that there was a more than casual connection between Disraeli's egocentricity and the Ultra-Tory, paternalistic ideology he formulated in the 1830s from his understanding of Lord Bolingbroke's ideas. In any case, Sidonia's ideas, when seen in the context of their first expression, confirm that Disraeli was drawing his inspiration for *Coningsby* as much from his experiences in the 1830s as from his circumstances in the 1840s.

As the collapse of the heroic fantasy in *Alroy* establishes, the imaginative links between Disraeli's egocentricity and his ideology were the issues of altruism and sincerity. The characterization of Sidonia suggests that the tension between "purity" and "success," between altruism and expediency, that distinguished David Alroy continued ten years later to be an ambivalence within the formulation of the political ideal expressed by Sidonia and espoused by Coningsby. Although Sidonia's political theory embraces a nobility of character and an altruistic vision of an organic community, his political practice is a sanction of very different values. For one thing, his true self remains largely hidden; though he is, we are told, "affable and gracious," it is "impossible to penetrate him," and the dichotomy between his surface candour and underlying secrecy is expressed in explicit terms. Moreover, juxtaposed to Sidonia's sense of himself as the alienated outsider, looking upon life "with a glance rather of curiosity than content" and perceiving himself as "a lone being," are the compensatory gratifications of clandestine power derived from communications with "secret agents," "political spies," and "all the clever outcasts of the world." The "catalogue of his acquaintance," we are told, "would throw a curious light on those subterranean agencies of which the world in general knows so little, but which exercise so great an influence on public events ... The secret history of the world was his pastime. His great pleasure was to contrast the hidden motive, with the public pretext, of transactions" (Bk 4, ch. 10, 230–1). The content of this fantasy, in contrast to the ideals of Young England, is obviously manipulative and subversive, but it is the implied author's subordinate reference to "subterranean agencies" that suggests the imaginatively autobiographical links.

Perhaps more substantial than the contrasting gratifications of alienation from society and of engagement in its affairs is Sidonia's inconsistency on the Jewish question. For, however much he believes in the superiority of the Jewish race as a "fact," he puts the argument against anti-Semitic prejudice and discrimination in purely pragmatic and ex-pedient terms. When Coningsby suggests that it would be easy to re-peal any law embodying "so illiberal" a conception, Sidonia replies: "'Oh! as for illiberality, I have no objection to it if it be an element of power. Eschew political sentimentalism. What I contend is, that if you permit men to accumulate property, and they use that permission to a great extent, power is inseparable from that property, and it is in the last degree impolitic to make it the interest of any powerful class to oppose the institutions under which they live'" (Bk 4, ch. 15, 262–3). He then goes on to assure his protégé that the Jews "'are essentially Tories'" and "'Toryism ... but copied from the mighty prototype which has fash-ioned Europe.'" This opinion is supported by a very egocentric account of the way in which the intellectual and political affairs of Russia, Spain, France, and Prussia are all interconnected through his financial ma-nipulations, and by the narcissistic conclusion that "'the world is gov-erned by very different personages from what is imagined by those who are not behind the scenes'" (Bk 4, ch. 15, 265). To explore fully the implications of this vision for Disraeli's later political career, especially his involvement in foreign affairs, is well beyond the scope of this chap-ter. But it is important to recognize that the characterization of Sidonia does contain a conspiratorial theory of politics that gives a legitimacy to the kind of secret manipulation and intrigue that is the antithesis of the ideals Disraeli has traditionally been thought to have been propounding in this "manifesto of Young England."

On the other hand, however extravagant a creature, Sidonia also rep-resents, through the conception of his "natural aristocracy" *and* his dem-onstrated success, an attempt to blend the conflicting claims of altruism and expediency. While the justification of his identity rests upon his un-deniable genius, the rationalization of his conduct rests upon his in-disputable power. For this reason Sidonia, as much as Coningsby himself, can be seen as part of the heroic fantasy of wish-fulfilment, the content and scope of which, in comparison with those of *Alroy* and *Henrietta Temple*, reflect Disraeli's increasing confidence in his sense of himself.

III

To appreciate fully the continuity of Disraeli's fiction, it is essential to examine the way in which politics in an ideological sense supports *Coningsby*'s central theme of heroic individualism. In *Contarini Fleming*, the conflicting worlds of the hero's public and private fulfilment are conceived to be mutually exclusive. Contarini finds erotic fulfilment of his purest feelings in the love of his cousin, Alcesté, who is explicitly portrayed as a mother substitute. But this expression of the true self necessitates an exile from the realm of political success in his father's world and from what he feels is the hypocritical behaviour essential to it. The contrast between the two worlds is presented as a dichotomy between Catholic and Protestant cultures in such a marked manner that the use of the religious motif must be seen as a reflection of the author's ambivalence about his Jewish heritage. Sidonia, the exemplum of demonstrated success, is an exile from the possibility of erotic or romantic involvement. Indeed, his emotional impotence confirms that the tension between "purity" and "success" that is the essence of the earlier works continues to exist in Disraeli's imaginative shaping of *Coningsby*. Though it is true that this characterization partially resolves the political expression of that tension by means of the notion of a natural aristocracy, it is also true that the unsatisfactory explanation of Sidonia's emotional aridity is that he "notoriously would never diminish by marriage the purity of his race" (Bk 6, ch. 2, 334–5). But the fact that the religious dimension of Sidonia's character is both part of the attempted resolution of the conflict between altruism and expediency and part of the renewed expression of that tension's power is suggestive of the continuing complexity of Disraeli's own attitudes towards his Jewish heritage, essentially a hostile symbiosis capable of producing both pride and despair.

The passage describing Sidonia's emotional deprivation is in the voice of the implied author. The conception of romantic love it contains is, not surprisingly, perfectly consistent with that inherent in the earlier fictions and with what we know of the emotional currents of Disraeli's own involvement with Henrietta Sykes and with his wife, Mary Anne. Clearly, the disconcertingly strong emphasis upon the consolatory nature of love – with its "profound sympathy," softening of "sorrows," counselling in "cares," and support in "perils" – is a vision in which "the lot the most precious to man" is to find in unquestioning acceptance the antidote to frustrated genius and fear of failure (Bk 4, ch. 10, 229). With respect to Sidonia, the effect of the passage is to deny any such vulnerability, a denial that is later confirmed in the plot by his immunity to the passionate advances of the Princess Lucretia and his purely avuncular affection for Edith Millbank. The Princess Lucretia, who later marries Lord Monmouth and conspires to cheat Coningsby of his inheritance, is somewhat like Mrs Felix Lorraine in *Vivian Grey*. In their treachery, both seem to display the dangers of unromanticized sexual passion. But the main point is that, through the portrayal of Sidonia, the imaginative conflict between love and power that was the mainspring of the plot in *Contarini Fleming* continues to exist in *Coningsby*.

The alternative, a vision in which love and power are blended, was for Disraeli an equally compelling fantasy. It finds its expression in the almost miraculous unfolding of Coningsby's destiny, and, not surprisingly, that expression bears comparison with the earlier novels. When, for example, Coningsby first visits Millbank, he is fascinated by a portrait of a beautiful young woman. He later finds out, upon opening a box of his father's papers held in trust for him and discovering there a locket containing the same likeness, that this woman is his deceased mother. This use of the portrait-locket-mother detail, while admittedly a romance convention, is clearly a repetition of that in *Contarini Fleming* where at the conclusion the hero discovers in the same way that his Magdalen-cousin-bride was physically identical to his deceased mother. Moreover, in *Coningsby*, Edith Millbank, while not literally the hero's sister, is, as the daughter of the man who first loved his mother, nevertheless an imaginative variant of Miriam in *Alroy*, whose devotion to her brother is the emblem of his purity of motive. The variations of the fantasy elements are, of course, important in that they ultimately permit the marriage of Edith and Coningsby, but the similarities are equally so in that they imaginatively confirm the purity of that union.

The structure and diction of the story make much the same point. When Coningsby realizes at the ball given by the Baroness S. de R-d. in Paris that the beautiful young woman he has fallen in love with is none other than the girl who had so charmed him at Millbank, we are told she had "a face of sunshine amid all that artificial light." His conversation with her recalls the "high, and pure" ideas which bind him in friendship to her brother. Yet juxtaposed to this scene is a long passage that reiterates Sidonia's indifference to the heart's affections as "one of those men ... who shrink ... from an adventure of gallantry" with "neither time nor temper for sentimental circumlocutions," and who "detested the diplomacy of passion" and found its "studied hypocrisies ... wearisome" (Bk 6, ch. 2, 331–4). This sharply contrasting vision of love as a social game strongly reflects precisely the sort of ambivalence the subject occasions in Disraeli's earlier fiction, the more so since the following chapter begins with Coningsby's "agitated slumber" in which he is "haunted" by dreams of a "beautiful countenance that was alternately the face of the mysterious picture, and then that of Edith," and from which he awakes "little refreshed; restless, and yet sensible of some secret joy" (Bk 6, ch. 3, 337).

The presence of the mother motif, soon elaborated as "fanciful speculations which connected Edith and the mysterious portrait of his mother," is sufficient to establish this development of the plot as an extension of the imaginative shaping not only of *Contarini Fleming* but also of *Henrietta Temple*, in which Ferdinand Armine is similarly haunted in dreams by the apparently conflicting claims of his pure, filial devotion to his mother, associated with the family's restoration, and of his equally pure passion for Henrietta. The depth of the imaginative connection between *Henrietta Temple* and *Coningsby* is also suggested, however, by the voice of the narrator, who intrudes at this point in the latter work to philosophize upon love: "Ah! what is that ambition that haunts our youth, that thirst for power or that lust of fame that forces us from obscurity into the sunblaze of the world, what are these sentiments so high, so vehement, so ennobling? They vanish, and in an instant, before the glance of a woman!" (Bk 6, ch. 3, 337). This passage has a strikingly similar theme to that in Book 2, chapter 4 of *Henrietta Temple* where the narrator intrudes to say that to behold a beautiful being and sense the bliss of love is "to feel our flaunty ambition fade away like a shrivelled gourd before her vision; to feel fame a juggle and posterity a lie." The difference in language between the two would seem to reflect that as a protagonist, Coningsby embodies none of the guilt occasioned by hypocritical or calculating motives that characterizes Ferdinand. Yet, despite this purification of the hero in *Coningsby*, the most convincing evidence of the close affinity with *Henrietta Temple* can be found in the very much related characterizations and plots.

Among the obvious instances of such similarity are Coningsby's alternations between a sense of his innate helplessness and a resolution to confront his destiny with Byronic defiance (Bk 8, ch. 4, 435ff.). His changes of affect are less reckless, but in despair at thinking Sidonia is his rival for Edith's love, he, very much like Ferdinand Armine (and David Alroy, too), confesses, "'I am nothing.'"[52] Also, like Ferdinand, he sees himself as a victim of his hereditary position, thwarted in love by his grandfather's actions.[53] Further, Coningsby responds to the threat of failure, just as does Ferdinand, by denying the reality of his circumstances and living for the pleasures of the enchanting moment. In Edith's presence, he wishes that the party should never end: "All mysteries, all difficulties, were driven from his recollection; he lived only in the exciting and enjoyable present" (Bk 6, ch. 8, 358).[54] And just as Ferdinand procrastinates leaving Henrietta to return to Bath, so Coningsby thinks of postponing his departure for Cambridge (Bk 6, ch 8, 358, 359).[55]

All of these relatively minor details suggest the true nature of Coningsby's imaginative ancestry. But perhaps more convincing evidence of the affinity between the two works is the plot contrivance in both whereby the lovers are separated by rumours of their respective engagements to others – Coningsby to Lady Theresa Sydney, Edith to Lord Beaumanoir, Ferdinand to his cousin Katherine, and Henrietta to Lord Montfort. Moreover, in both novels the hero is then shown to be completely altruistic and lovable, and the disentanglement of the romantic complication is occasioned by the intervention of a circle of his friends who gladly conspire to remove all obstacles to his felicity. Both Coningsby and Ferdinand are completely passive protagonists in the unfolding of these events. This is not to argue that this plot mechanism is more than the hackneyed convention of the romantic comedy of manners; but rather, that it is significant that the pattern of wish-fulfilment in the two works is identical.

IV

Having recognized the parallels between *Henrietta Temple* and the first volume of Disraeli's "trilogy," it is instructive to look again at the relation between the politics and the romance in *Coningsby*. The argument that the political ideology serves to define an ideal identity or role of heroic individualism can best be sustained by the description of Coningsby's "noble ambition" at the moment he moves from adolescence to manhood, which, we are told, "must be born in the heart and organised in the brain, which will not let a man be content, unless his intellectual power is recognised by his race, and desires that it should contribute to their welfare. It is the heroic feeling; the feeling that in old days produced demi-gods ... without which political institutions are meat without salt; the Crown a bauble, the Church an establishment, Parliaments debating clubs, and Civilisation itself but a fitful and transient dream" (Bk 5, ch. 1, 274). This is strong stuff; but, as the rhetorical flourish of the passage implies, a full appreciation of Disraeli's use of the political theme requires further analysis of the ideology itself. In this respect, the ambivalence of Disraeli's role in the Young England movement is worth recalling, especially the suspicious anxieties of Alexander Baillie-Cochrane and the grandiose plans revealed in the lengthy memorandum Disraeli wrote to King Louis Philippe in which he embodied his plans for an Anglo-French alliance.[56] As has been shown, this was more than the euphoric posturing of a naive egotist. For all its sublime egotism, that memorandum is really a fantasy embodying Disraeli's conception of his own potential, though it certainly confirms Cochrane's worst fears of his manipulative schemes. But this is not to deny that Disraeli was equally and genuinely attracted by the purity and nobility of Young England's motives and ideals and, in particular, that he shared the others' conception of patriotism as the antidote to the class divisions and social disruptions that seemed to characterize nineteenth-century society.

Indeed, the essence of Coningsby's new Toryism, derived largely from Bolingbroke's *On the Spirit of Patriotism* and *The Idea of a Patriot King*, is trust. And it is clearly a reflection of Disraeli's identification with Bolingbroke, which involved a perception of their similar political roles. The vision that compels Coningsby is that of the necessity of undertaking the heroic struggle to restore the ancient solidarity of the governed and the governing classes. Most of the elements of that vision Disraeli had expressed as early as 1834 in *The Revolutionary Epick*. But the struggle now requires a modern "demi-god" because in the current state of affairs all of the political institutions, monarchy, Church, Lords, and Commons, have become debased by either the Whigs' "Destructive Creed" or the Conservatives' "Political Infidelity." The only weapons that the ideal political protagonist has at his command are the conviction of his own genius and the power to influence public opinion. Here Disraeli steps beyond the Tory orthodoxy of the *Vindication*, where he had argued that Parliament was the constitutional representative of the estate of the Commons, and the monarchy and Church the representatives of the people. Coningsby, echoing Sidonia, tells Oswald Millbank that "Representation need not necessarily, or even in a principal sense, be Parliamentary": "'a principle of government is reserved for our days … Opinion is now supreme, and Opinion speaks in print. The representation of the Press is far more complete than the representation of Parliament. Parliamentary representation was the happy device of a ruder age … but it exhibits many symptoms of desuetude. It is controlled by a system of representation more vigorous and comprehensive; which absorbs its duties and fulfills them more efficiently'" (Bk 7, ch. 2, 374–5). This "polity," Coningsby argues, "'is capable of great ends and appealing to high sentiments.'" The means by which it is to "'render government an object of national affection'" is the symbolic restoration of the power of the sovereign, who is both to lead and yet be restrained from arbitrary action by public opinion (Bk 7, ch. 2, 375).

As a political theory, this argument is based entirely upon subjective qualities. When Oswald Millbank objects that "'public opinion may be indifferent. A nation may be misled, may be corrupt,'" Coningsby urges in reply a faith in the "national character." He then goes on to justify that conception in terms of individual nobility: "'If a nation be led to aim at the good and the great, depend upon it, whatever be its form, the government will respond to its convictions and its sentiments.'" In short, the political ideology that Coningsby advocates depends for its efficacy entirely on the integrity or the purity of the hero. In such a conception there is a noticeable detachment from the constitutional focus of government. Coningsby goes on to assure Oswald that "'true wisdom lies in the policy that would effect its ends by the influence of opinion, and yet by the means of existing forms'" (Bk 7, ch. 2, 373, 375). The idea that these "forms," the monarchy, the Church, and Parliament, are but "means" to the "ends" of "the good and the great" throws an entirely new light upon both the consistency of Disraeli's later political practice and the satirical portrait of the Conservative party's expediency. Indeed, from such a perspective, the latter has a cogency very much related to Coningsby's destiny.

It is clear that Disraeli's satirical treatment of the Conservatives' "Political Infidelity" in abandoning the constitutional forms that should support the cause of true Toryism is not implicitly a defence of those institutions for their own sake. It is their symbolic power to effect the heroic vision that interests Coningsby and, by implication, Disraeli. Thus, at the climax of the novel in Book 7, chapter 3, the central issue is Coningsby's purity. At this point, his political ideology and his love for Edith are blended into one theme. The essence of the climax is Coningsby's resolution to defy his grandfather and to refuse to be the family's Conservative candidate at Darlford. Lord Monmouth's aim in returning Coningsby to Parliament is overtly selfish; he believes that such expedient support of the Conservative cause will result in a dukedom for himself and the revival of a family barony in his grandson's name. Coningsby, however, confesses that he has "'for a long time looked upon the Conservative party as a body who have betrayed their trust; more from ignorance ... than from design; yet clearly a body of individuals totally unequal to the exigencies of the epoch, and ... unconscious of its real character'" (Bk 8, ch. 3, 431). In contradicting his grandfather's pragmatic cynicism by demanding political "faith," he does, admittedly, seem to shift the basis of his thinking and refer to the "rights and privileges" of the Crown, the Church, and the House of

Lords as if they were political ends in themselves. But his final words in this scene revert to the conception of trust, or social harmony, at the centre of his ideology: "'What we want, sir, is … to establish great principles which may maintain the realm and secure the happiness of the people. Let me see authority once more honoured; a solemn reverence again the habit of our lives; let me see property acknowledging, as in the old days of faith, that labour is his twin brother, and that the essence of all tenure is the performance of duty'" (Bk 8, ch. 3, 434). The blending of this nostalgic ideal with the rather practical assessment of the new social conditions under which a political leader must operate is by no means the least significant aspect of Coningsby's thinking. It not only embodies the ambivalence of Disraeli's role in Young England but also foreshadows the most controversial aspects of his later career. For this reason, it deserves more respect in our analyses of the Victorian political dilemma than it has received. But equally important to this study is the linking of the hero's public and private fulfilments.

Coningsby's first reaction to his grandfather's news is a vision of the strife and anguish that his rival candidacy to Millbank's would cause him: "The countenance of Edith … rose to him again. He saw her canvassing for her father, and against him. Madness!" (Bk 8, ch. 3, 428). In other words, the fantasy is so constructed that the abandonment of his political faith would entail an alienation of his love. In this respect, Disraeli's choice of words is important. Near the end of the previous chapter, when Edith has just heard the rumour that Coningsby is engaged to marry Lady Theresa Sydney, the implied author summarizes Coningsby's feelings: "he passed a sleepless night, agitated and distracted by the manner in which she had received him … His affection had never for a moment swerved; it was profound and firm … whatever were the barriers which the circumstances of life placed against their union, they were partakers of the solemn sacrament of an unpolluted heart" (Bk 8, ch. 2, 425–6). Quite apart from the fact that this passage closely resembles a description of Ferdinand's love for Henrietta, the phrase "an unpolluted heart" suggests the true motivating power and the ultimate shape of Disraeli's romance. For, when in double despair that both his political prospects and his personal happiness have been irrevocably damaged, Coningsby is suddenly seized with a heroic conception of his identity. Having compared himself to Caesar, "he thought of Edith in her hours of fondness; he thought of the pure and solemn moments when to mingle his name with the heroes of humanity was his aspiration, and to achieve immortal fame the inspiring purpose of his life. What were the tawdry accidents of vulgar ambition to him? No domestic despot could deprive him of his intellect, his knowledge, the sustaining power of an unpolluted conscience" (Bk 8, ch. 4, 438–9). The language is indicative of the theme. From this it is obvious that the defining quality of the ideal political identity embodied in the characterization of Coningsby is purity of heart, conscience, and ambition. The shape of the fantasy is a testimony to the fact that such purity, at least in the realm of this romance, which is indisputably the realm of the author's imagination, guarantees a transcendent success. The plot is, however, not without further complications. Before Coningsby finds himself possessed of that success, he is temporarily disinherited and plunged once more into profound gloom. At this moment, the implied author's language in describing his hero's thoughts has an anomalous extravagance that dissolves the screen of fiction and confirms again the imaginatively autobiographical nature of the romance: "Nothing is great but the personal," the narrator says: "The power of man, his greatness and his glory, depend upon essential qualities. Brains every day become more precious than blood." Then Coningsby's conviction of power in the midst of his despair is described as a "revelation" in language that resonates with Disraeli's own ambitions. Just as in the authorial intrusion in Book 1, chapter 3, the narrator's reference to being prepared for "infinite suffering," "a bitter inheritance" of "obscurity," "struggle," "envy," "hatred," "prejudice," "criticism," and "hostilities" steps beyond the limits of Disraeli's characterization of his hero. As, indeed, does the imagined result of his hero's struggles: "but the dawn would break, and the hour arrive, when the welcoming morning hymn of his success and his fame would sound and be re-echoed" (Bk 9, ch. 4, 480–1). But the real significance of the passage lies in both its explicit and contextual egocentricity, for it is clear that here the issues of party ideology are absorbed in the destiny of a heroic role. Thus, Coningsby's election to Parliament in absentia, his reunion with Edith accompanied by the tangible blessing of Millbank's generosity, and his ultimate inheritance of his grandfather's fortune from the grateful Flora can legitimately be seen as the completion of the fiction's central fantasy of acceptance, one in which the melodramatic delight of revenge in destroying Rigby's venomous, self-serving career is combined with the gratifications of an otherwise universal recognition of the hero's genius. In the end, the links between purity and power, love and success, sustain the claim that *Coningsby*, very much like Disraeli's earlier fictions, is chiefly concerned with his conflicts of identity; that politics, while an integral part of the work, is essentially a motif within the genre of the "psychological romance." As the ensuing discussion will show, that "romance," however quixotic the struggles of Young England, was to be a shaping force in Victorian politics as well as the continuing inspiration of Disraeli's novels.

9

Sir Robert Peel and the Apotheosis of Young England

The publication of *Coningsby* and the writing of the next novel, *Sybil*, must have confirmed what Disraeli had known for some time: that there was no brilliant future for him within the ranks of the Conservative Government led by Sir Robert Peel. The tension between his ambition and his frustration at this time is typically expressed in remarks he made to his constituents at Shrewsbury at the end of August 1844: "There is no doubt ... that all men who offer themselves as candidates for public favor have motives of some sort. I candidly acknowledge that I have, and I will tell you what they are: I love fame; I love public reputation; I love to live in the eyes of the country; and it is a glorious thing for a man to do who has had my difficulties to contend against."[1] This tension can also be seen in his justification of his independence. For in the same speech he claims that he "supported the Conservative Party as long as they kept to their principles," and only voted against them when they "deserted those principles." And he also explicitly insists, in response to "sneers and taunts," that he had "never asked Sir Robert Peel for a place."[2] The defensive tone of this re-iterated denial suggests that by 1844 Disraeli was very conscious of the fact that his character and conduct were increasingly viewed with hostility and suspicion by those sympathetic to the prime minister.

But previous to this Disraeli seems to have been quite naive about the "official" responses to his actions. In the parliamentary session of 1843 the members of Young England had twice opposed Peel's Irish policy, and Disraeli had also, on 15 August, risen directly after Peel to criticize the Government's failure to support Turkey in her attempts to resist Russian encroachments upon her empire. The British Government's policy Disraeli described as "uncertain and superficial, and founded in

ignorance," one that made them "the laughing stock of Europe."[3]
Whatever the merits of his views (made to seem quite far-sighted by
later developments in the Crimea), Disraeli's Turkophile interests were
no doubt much excited by the confidential conversations on the topic
he had had with King Louis Philippe in Paris the previous winter and
in which he had so gloried.[4] The connection of this topic to his fantasies
of his own heroic role in English politics is worth noting, not just for the
later developments of the Eastern question, but also in that this speech
was the first instance of his sarcastic personal attacks on Peel's character: "I remember some time since to have made an inquiry of the right
hon. gentleman with respect to the interference of Russia in Servia, an
inquiry couched, I believe, in Parliamentary language, and made with
all that respect which I feel for the right hon. gentleman, and to which
the right hon. gentleman replied with all that explicitness of which he
is a master, and all that courtesy which he reserves only for his supporters!"[5] Disraeli's "difficulties" were thus to some degree of his own making. But some indication of their real extent, and of the prejudice held
against him, can be seen in the private correspondence of the period.

Shortly after Disraeli's speech, Sir James Graham, the Home Secretary,
commented on this rebellion in the party ranks in a letter to John Wilson
Croker, characterizing "D'Israeli" as the puppeteer of Young England:
"I consider him unprincipled and disappointed; and in despair he has
tried the effect of bullying. I think with you, that they will return to the
crib after prancing, capering, and snorting; but a crack or two of the
whip well applied may hasten and ensure their return. D'Israeli alone
is mischievous; and with him I have no desire to keep terms. It would
be better for the party, if he were driven into the ranks of our open
enemies."[6] And when Disraeli naively asked Graham for a minor government post for his brother James, Graham, although he sent a polite
letter of refusal, wrote to Peel: "His letter is an impudent one and is
considered by me doubly so when I remember his conduct and language in the House of Commons towards the end of the last session."[7]
The prime minister in turn replied to Graham: "I am very glad that Mr.
Disraeli has asked for an office for his brother. It is a good thing when
such a man puts his shabbiness on record. He asked me for office himself, and I was not surprised that being refused he became independent
and a patriot. But to ask favours after his conduct last Session is too
bad. However, it is a bridle in his mouth."[8] And later Peel also put down
some of the opposition to his Maynooth Bill and Corn Law measures as
"disappointed ambition and the rejection of applications for office."[9] As

I have shown, Disraeli disputed Peel's interpretation of the correspondence between them in 1841, but his defence of his actions before his
constituents at Shrewsbury in 1844 suggests that he anticipated that he
might be challenged on that score. What is clear is that each man nursed
a grievance against the other. And the acute sensitivities of both men
are revealed in the somewhat hypocritical exchange of letters between
them when Peel deliberately omitted to send Disraeli the party's circular letter at the beginning of the 1844 session. Disraeli immediately
complained that in important respects he had supported Peel's commercial and foreign policies and that his specific remarks had been no
more critical than those made by others. But he then went on to observe, "with frankness, but with great respect," that the explanation for
his own lack of spontaneous "hearty good-will" could be found in
Peel's "want of courtesy in debate" which he had had "the frequent
mortification of experiencing" since his "*accession to power*" (emphasis
added). Whatever the effects of Peel's reserve, these words reveal more
than Disraeli intended, for they recall both his feelings and the occasion
of his "humiliation" in 1841. The prime minister merely replied, however, that the "tenor" of Disraeli's recent observations on "the conduct
of the Government" had given him an "honest doubt" whether he was
entitled to send the usual circular, but that it gave him "great satisfaction to infer" that his "impressions were mistaken" and his "scruples
unnecessary."[10]

For the moment these half-conciliatory letters seemed to close the
open breach between them. But sarcasm, like salt, adds zest to the mixture and can be addictive. Disraeli had discovered that Peel, with his
peculiar stiffness and probity, was an easy victim to that rhetorical ag-
gravation, and he therefore soon began to flavour his speeches liberally
with it. Even the very able speech on Ireland, in which he supported the
Government against Lord John Russell's motion of censure, contained
some genial sarcasm when he complimented Peel on having removed
"most effectually" the Whig prejudices of his "very eminent" secretar-
ies of state, Lord Stanley and Sir James Graham, both of whom had left
Lord Grey's ministry in 1834 to join the Conservatives.[11]

The speech on Ireland is of particular interest, not just because the
issues that Disraeli discussed continued to haunt the Conservative
party throughout his career, but also because its trenchant eloquence
gained him a new measure of respect in the House of Commons. Even
Gladstone and Archbishop Manning would praise it twenty-four years
later during the Irish Church Disestablishment debates.

> I want to see a public man come forward and say what the Irish question is. One says it is a physical question; another a spiritual. Now it is the absence of aristocracy; then the absence of railroads. It is the Pope one day; potatoes the next. Consider Ireland as you would any other country similarly situated. You will see a teeming population which, with reference to the cultivated soil, is denser to the square mile than that of China; created solely by agriculture, with none of the resources of wealth which develop with civilisation; and sustained, consequently, upon the lowest conceivable diet, so that in the case of failure they have no other means of subsistence upon which they can fall back. That dense population in extreme distress inhabits an island where there is an established church which is not their church (loud cheers from the Opposition); and a territorial aristocracy the richest of whom live in distant capitals. Thus you have a starving population, an absentee aristocracy, and an alien church (renewed cheers from the Opposition), and in addition the weakest executive in the world. That is the Irish question.[12]

Whether it was just "heedless rhetoric," or whether, what he called his "historical conscience" carried him further than it was wise for a Tory to go,[13] Disraeli did not evade the imperatives of his vision. Since revolution was impossible, it was, he said, the duty of an English minister "to effect by his policy all those changes which a revolution would effect by force."[14] In 1844 Disraeli thus seemed both more alert to the reality of Ireland and more courageous in advocating changes in English policy for governing it than did his colleagues. They should, he argued, "get rid of all those institutions which they had forced upon that country," for the government of Ireland "should be on a system the reverse of England and should be centralized" with a strong, "pervading executive" and "an impartial administration."[15]

This speech showed again Disraeli's recognition of public opinion as a decisive force in politics: "All the right hon. baronet would have to do would be ... to create public opinion instead of following it; to lead the public, instead of always lagging after and watching others."[16] Disraeli clearly understood that speeches in Parliament duly reported in the newspapers were only a partial and limited means with which to shape public opinion. The success of *Coningsby* had taught him as well, that the novel offered peculiar and remarkable advantages to a person of imaginative genius with that ambition, for not only did fiction easily accommodate both the revision of history and topical political comment by means of discursive digression. It also offered unique opportunities for satire, parody, and melodrama which spoke loudly to the newly emerging political constituencies within the middle classes. And Disraeli, better than anyone else at the time, including Dickens, understood that the creation of public opinion in his favour was not simply a matter of persuading others of the truth and wisdom of his own ideas, but also of destroying the credibility of his opponents' views.

In 1844 the members of Young England had made a considerable stir in parliamentary circles by their resistance to Peel's enforcement of party discipline with threats of resignation over the Factory and Sugar Duties Bills. Disraeli gained great applause in the Commons by declaring on the second occasion that he had no intention of "changing [his] ... vote within forty-eight hours at the menace of a Minister."[17] There was even wide speculation that the Government might be defeated on the amendment to the Sugar Duties Bill, causing the prime minister to write to the Queen to warn her of the danger. Her Majesty, much relieved when Peel's ministry survived by twenty votes, then wrote to her uncle Leopold, king of the Belgians: "we were really in the greatest *possible* danger of having a resignation of the Government *without knowing to whom to turn*, and this from the recklessness of a handful of foolish *half* 'Puseyite,' half 'Young England' people."[18] It was really the publication of *Coningsby* in May 1844, however, that first brought Disraeli's ideas about true Toryism to the consciousness of large numbers of people outside the immediate circle of parliamentary politics. And it was the enormously popular reception of *Coningsby* that reinforced the lesson of Peel's vulnerability that Disraeli had learned in the Commons. Although his sarcastic wit had long been his invitation to many scenes of social and political triumph, Disraeli now found that in both politics and fiction his satirical portraits were the perfect complement to his fantasies of heroic achievement: he could defend his political principles while slaking his growing thirst for revenge, and all the while bask in the warm light of his fame and notoriety.

The summer and fall of 1844 brought Disraeli further evidence of his growing social standing as well as of his political and literary importance. In early July he reported to Sarah that he and Mary Anne had enjoyed their visit with the Walters at Bearwood and had attended the Waverley Ball. But the real "coup," he said, was the invitation to preside at the literary meeting of the Manchester Athenaeum in October, though perhaps he was equally gratified by the Duke of Buckingham's invitation to commemorate the majority of the Marquess of Chandos, on 10 September at Stowe.[19] In that respect one notable feature of

Disraeli's life at this time is that the social, literary, and political elements of his senses of private and public identity are fused. In late August, for example, Disraeli spent three days with his constituents at Shrewsbury. In letters to Mary Anne reporting his success he makes much of his audience's sympathy for his first separation in five years from the woman who was "a perfect wife as well as a perfect companion": "Frail says *my domestic character does me a great deal of good at Shrewsbury.*"[20] Similarly, the next day he reports on the enthusiasm for his candidacy generated at "a capital meeting": "Taylor the Maltster in the chair. His speech proposing your health a miracle of rhetoric. He said being your husband was a very good reason why I was fit to be member for Shrewsbury. Indeed the feeling for you here is beyond all imagination. Everybody enquires after you: high & low. Taylor's speech gave me a good opening about our first separation & the wedding day, wh: is now known all over Shrewsbury. The effect was very great."[21] But as well as describing the political effect of the image of chivalric domesticity, Disraeli also commented on other aspects of his attempts to shape his public persona: "It is understood I find that I am *the tradesmen's member* – so I don't trouble myself much about the pseudo aristocracy & less about the real. The Lawrences, Groves, Taylors, Lees, are the men. They quite approve as to the attack on the Government, but a little alarmed in some quarters I find about Popery, Monasteries, & John Manners. This I shall quietly soften down."[22] In the conclusion of his remarks to his constituents, in which he had defended his own integrity and excoriated the Government's desertion of its principles, Disraeli expresses his sense of satisfaction and control of his political situation: "What might have injured me, I have now turned to good account. The feeling of the people is genuine and may be depended on. They seem all of them quite to appreciate my start this year, both literary and political."[23] Just as did the explicit denials of place-seeking, these comments by implication acknowledge that Disraeli's hope is still that, with careful management of his opportunities, his literary fame and social acceptance can transcend the doubts about his political loyalties and personal trustworthiness.

The evening meeting of the Manchester Athenaeum on 3 October 1844, with Disraeli in the chair, certainly gave substance to that hope and was by all accounts every bit as successful as the members of Young England could have wished. *The Times* reported that 3176 tickets to the "grand soiree" were sold and that, including guests, more than

3200 ladies and gentlemen were in attendance at this "most brilliant and magnificent spectacle."[24] Disraeli, Manners, and Smythe all gave speeches that were enthusiastically received and later published in pamphlet form for a wider audience. In praising Manchester's enthronement of "Intelligence" in place of "Force" Disraeli prided himself on his conception of "knowledge" as like "the ladder in the patriarch's mystic dream" upon which "the great authors" are the "angels ascending and descending on the sacred scale, and maintaining, as it were, the communication between man and Heaven."[25] Lord John Manners, in turn, raised a number of Young England's favourite themes. He deplored the political rancour of the time, and its distinctions of class and party. And he urged the value of recreation and amusement in the lives of working men. But, most important, he spoke of the need for a new understanding of history: "I rate highly the good which may accrue to this country from having its past history not a mere record of the kings who reigned and the battles they fought, but the history of its inner life, the habits, thoughts, and tastes of its people, the real aims and objects of its governors laid faithfully before us, because I am every day more and more convinced that half the mischief which is done to a country like this by its legislators and rulers is done from a misunderstanding of its past history."[26]

In the context of an earlier, similar speech to the Athenic Institution at Birmingham on 26 August, in which he had deplored the decay of feudalism and the "unhappy separation of the classes which now existed" – "two classes of society, and two only – rich and poor,"[27] Manners can be seen here to adumbrate the themes of *Sybil*, some of whose scenes and settings are clearly based on the observations of Disraeli's extended visit in the North following the triumph at Manchester.

George Smythe's speech in turn prophesied an "auspicious destiny" for literature, now free of patronage and class limitations, and it exceeded the rhetorical sublimities of those of Manners and Disraeli.[28] But as Charles Whibley notices, it has a special interest because Smythe took the occasion to eulogize George Canning as a "statesman" who had been sacrificed to the "absurdities," the "barbarities," and the "vulgarities" of "party warfare."[29] Smythe asked his listeners to remember "the fate of our last great man ... how his views were thwarted, his spirit cowed, his heart broken – how he was hasted to his grave," for then they would understand how, through calumny and misconstruction – through such men's envy, and the insults of men yet smaller, he

[Canning] must have "pined for some such neutral ground" as that of this Manchester meeting. Smythe then suggested in conclusion that "in the prospect of a happier hour, of advancing toleration" such as this meeting afforded, there were few among them, "now that 15 years have passed over his grave," who will hesitate to exclaim with him – "'Oh, for one hour of George Canning.'"[30]

Much of this extended apostrophe the naive listener might interpret as a simple invocation of Young England's nostalgic idealism. But, as Smythe's references to "an adventurer ... born to no hereditary fortune," "a caballer and intriguer," the victim of "calumny and misconstruction" make clear, the knowing would have recognized it as a defence of Disraeli and it should, I think, be read as particularly addressed to him, "the Cid and Captain" of Smythe's "every sympathy."[31] The heroic image of George Canning had been near the centre of Disraeli's sense of his own political identity for a long time, certainly ever since the attempt in 1825 to establish *The Representative* as a newspaper supporting Canning's policies. And more recently, Canning's struggles with the Duke of Wellington and Sir Robert Peel had been an important part of the revisionist history of Toryism provided in Book 2, chapter 1 of *Coningsby*. But, as neither Smythe nor Disraeli could quite foresee, this identification with Canning on Disraeli's part would soon play a much larger and crucial role in his own struggle with Peel in 1845, and in the ensuing friendship with Lord George Bentinck, upon which so much of his success depended.

The evening at the Manchester Athenaeum ended as a complete triumph for all the members of Young England, but especially for Disraeli, who was given nine rounds of applause and thanked profusely for presiding over the event. Again his "domestic character" added to his popularity, and Mary Anne, too, was cheered three times, before the speeches gave way to the merriment of dancing "until a late hour" before a full military band. But even in Disraeli's ritual acknowledgments of such praise, the issue of his conduct and character seems particularly alive. It was, he said in reply, "the greatest distinction that man could receive when he received the approbation of a refined community of his fellow citizens." And he went on to add that "far from believing that he was entitled to it, all that he would say, was, that he was determined to endeavour to deserve it." They had, he said, conferred upon him "an honour and an obligation that when he returned to his home, he should cherish – which in public life, he should often recur to for animation and support – which he never should forget – and which, he trusted, might inspire him to conduct that would never forfeit their regard and their respect."[32] The sense of gratification and the optimism with which Disraeli here looks to the future were undoubtedly reinforced during the remainder of the autumn, while the Disraelis extended their visit in the North and stayed at the country houses of several of Young England's sympathizers, Lord Francis Egerton at Worsley Hall, W.B. Ferrand at Bingley, and Pemberton Milnes at Fryston.

It was at this time that Disraeli absorbed much of the detailed knowledge of industrial conditions that informs his portrayal of them in *Sybil*. And while at Bingley, where the Ferrands were experimenting with garden allotments for industrial operatives, he made a speech that also indicates the direction of his thoughts while writing that novel:

> We are asked sometimes what we want. We want in the first place to impress upon society that there is such a thing as duty ... we are anxious to do our duty, and, if so, we think we have a right to call on others, whether rich or poor, to do theirs. If that principle of duty had not been lost sight of for the last fifty years, you would never have heard of the classes into which England is divided ...
>
> We want to put an end to that political and social exclusiveness which we believe to be the bane of this country ... It is not so much to the action of laws as to the influence of manners that we must look ... But how are manners to influence men if they are divided into classes – if the population of a country becomes a body of sections, a group of hostile garrisons?[33]

Such a passage makes manifest the profoundly conservative nature of Disraeli's view of society, for he is clearly not proposing an amalgamation of the classes in any radical sense, but rather a reciprocal, intimate, moral relationship between persons of inevitable social distinctions. And this harmonizes completely with the intent of the allegory embodied in *Sybil*.

The pinnacle of Disraeli's social successes during the parliamentary recess was undoubtedly the lavish party given by the Duke of Buckingham on the evening of 17 January 1845 as a culmination of the Queen's visit to Stowe. The guests comprised the cream of Buckinghamshire society – aristocracy, gentry, and many persons of eminence, in addition to various members of the government. This was the first occasion on which Disraeli and Mary Anne were presented to Her Majesty, and, perhaps it is not surprising that the occasion seems to have been mutually fascinating. Mary Anne's letter to Bradenham with an account of the affair captures the flavour of their reciprocal interest and excitement. She described how, after the Queen had retired, the evening became one of "joy and triumph" to them: "Sir Robert Peel came to us, shaking hands most cordially, and remained talking for some time, then Lord Nugent, introducing his lady, Col. Anson, Sir James Graham, Lord and Lady de la Warr, Lord Aberdeen." These gratifying conversations were followed by that of the duke, who "almost embraced Dizzy, saying he was one of his oldest friends," and who then offered Mary Anne his arm and took her "all through the gorgeous splendid scene," up and down the supper room, with everyone making room for them. The only other lady so distinguished by their host that evening, she noted, was the Queen. After this, she said, she retired to a sofa with the duchess, who told her that "her Majesty had pointed out, saying *There's Mr. Disraeli.*'" The conclusion of this social triumph was that "the Duchess invited [her] ... to luncheon the next day to see the Queen's private apartments."[34] After such an evening it would hardly be surprising were Disraeli to have felt that he had at last achieved a significant measure of the acceptance and recognition to which he had long felt entitled.[35] And certainly the events of the last seven months, from the publication of *Coningsby* to the Duke of Buckingham's embrace at Stowe, could not but have confirmed his desire and intention to demonstrate his superiority in the House of Commons to those who had, by attempting to keep him in his place, left his abilities unrecognized and his ambitions unfulfilled. In other words, Disraeli's desire for revenge was more than a matter of getting even: his own success, it would seem, must be the proof of others' errors.

When the parliamentary session of 1845 began, Disraeli took the first occasion (20 February 1845) to continue his sarcastic attacks on the members of the Government, and particularly the prime minister. The issue, initially, was the matter of the Home Secretary's interception of Giuseppe Mazzini's letters in 1844, justified by Sir James Graham as a means of preventing a general war in Europe. Thomas Duncombe, the Radical MP, now claimed that his own letters were being similarly opened and Disraeli supported a motion calling for a committee of inquiry into the matter. He first complimented Graham as the "great master of analytical narrative" in having "traced the other night the vast and precise consequences of the non-interception of the letter of Mr. Mazzini." "For," he said, "since the celebrated narrative of the *House That Jack Built* never was detail so consecutively precise." But he quickly went on to mock Peel's defence of the Government's actions, noting that although "the right hon. gentleman ... displayed an unusual warmth ... it by no means follows that the right hon. gentleman felt it (Laughter)":

The right hon. Baronet has too great a mind, and fills too eminent a position, ever to lose his temper; but in a popular assembly it is sometimes
expedient to enact the part of the choleric gentleman. The right hon. gentleman touched the red box with emotion. (A laugh.) I know from old experience that when one first enters the House these exhibitions are rather
alarming, and I believe that some of the younger members were much
frightened, but I advised them not to be terrified. I told them that the right
hon. baronet would not eat them up, would not even resign; the very
worst thing he would do would be to tell them to rescind a vote. (Loud
cheering and shouts of laughter.)[36]

The very structure of this passage reveals the adversarial relationship
between Peel and himself in Disraeli's mind. And the false civility of
excessively repeating "the right hon." gentleman or baronet shows, at
least implicitly, that the real issue is one of Peel's integrity. Disraeli's
own claim to superiority is, of course, here embodied in the momentary
reduction of the prime minister to an ogre in a fairy tale and in the nonchalance of his worldly advice to the inexperienced. Despite the obvious ridicule and these signs of rivalry, Disraeli went on to deny that
he was motivated in his opposition to the Government by personal feeling or a hostile spirit, claims which brought laughter from the
Opposition and ironic cheers from the front bench.

In his reply the following day Peel indicated clearly that he felt
Disraeli was being hypocritical and that he found such hypocrisy as
difficult to bear as the insinuations of expediency and dissimulation on
his own part. While Disraeli, he said, undertook "to assure the House
that my vehemence was all pretended, and warmth all simulated, I, on
the contrary, will do him entire justice – I do believe that his bitterness
was not simulated, but that it was entirely sincere ... The hon. gentleman has a perfect right ... to support a hostile motion ... but don't let
him say that he does it in a friendly spirit (Cheers)." This would have
been a sufficient reply, but Peel thought he could enhance its effect by
quoting four lines of poetry:

Give me the avowed, the erect, the manly foe;
Bold I can meet, perhaps can turn the blow;
But of all plagues, good Heaven, thy wrath can send,
Save me, Oh, save me, from a candid friend![37]

In most circumstances this would have been a crushing blow. But the
well-known lines that Peel quoted were written by George Canning.

And, as Robert Blake points out, those opposed to Peel had not forgotten that "his relations with Canning had been the most controversial episode in his career." His enemies argued, indeed, that in withdrawing his support of Canning in 1827 and engaging in a factious opposition, Peel had pushed "the great man" to his premature death. This was ostensibly because Canning favoured Catholic Emancipation, a measure that Peel denounced while Canning was prime minister but carried himself two years later when he returned to office as Home Secretary.[38]

As the analysis of Disraeli's novels makes clear, the Catholic question had a special significance for him in that his treatments of it embodied his ambivalent feelings about his Jewish heritage. The continuing power of that ambivalence, about both Judaism and Catholicism, in Disraeli's imagination is suggested by a letter he wrote at this time to Dr Robert Mackenzie. In it he repeated his mistaken beliefs about his Sephardic ancestry: "My grandfather's father was a Lara; the descendant of one who emigrated from Spain to Italy at a remote period. He, (as well as his son,) vacillated for a length of time between Judaism & Catholicism; but late in life he was touched with remorse, & invented & assumed the name of D'Israeli."[39] Not surprisingly, therefore, as the developments of his political career reinforced his sense of struggling against prejudice and persecution, the heroic image of George Canning lovingly fostered by Young England now carried an explosive symbolic power for Disraeli. And Peel's assumption of probity and moral superiority was, he knew, vulnerable to the charge of having betrayed first Canning and then his party in his rise to power. So when Duncombe again raised the matter of the opened letters in the Commons a week later, Disraeli again supported him and in doing so he turned the issue of his own trustworthiness into one of Peel's integrity. The speech was a masterpiece of rhetorical control. He accused the prime minister of using "innuendo and imputation" – "the insinuation of base motive and the allegation of factious conduct," to prevent his Conservative followers from having "fair discussion on questions not of a party character." He described this as a "system" of "tyranny ... as degrading to those who exercised it as to those who endured it." The essential point of this attack was that Peel had abandoned the principles of the Tory party and adopted the practice of the Whigs. Speaking as one "sent to swell a Tory majority – to support a Tory Ministry," Disraeli for a while pursues this theme in a genial tone that almost belies the serious accusation which is offhandedly treated as gossip:

The right hon. gentleman caught the Whigs bathing, and walked away with their clothes. (Much cheering and great laughter.) He has left them in the full enjoyment of their liberal position, and he is himself a strict conservative of their garments. (Continued cheers and laughter.) I cannot conceive that the right hon. gentleman will ever desert his party; they seem never to desert him. There never was a man yet who had less need to find new friends. I therefore hope all these rumours will cease. I look on the right hon. gentleman as a man who has tamed the shrew of Liberalism by her own tactics. He is the political Petruchio, who has outbid you all.[40]

This tone of ingenuous banter conveys, among other things, Disraeli's sense of control. It is clear that he understands perfectly how to make his point known, and his superiority felt, by amusing his audience with witty metaphor and allusion. And it is obvious, as he subsides into "feigned humility," that he knows how to exploit contrasts in preparing his devastating conclusion. Two years later *Fraser's Magazine* published a description of Disraeli's oratorical technique, which Monypenny astutely uses to convey the sense of drama on this occasion. His ordinary speaking voice was apparently quite monotonous and his manner was usually marked by diffidence. But when he chose to make a special point he exquisitely managed the inflexion of his voice to effect the irony or sarcasm intended: "In conveying an innuendo, an ironical sneer, or a suggestion of contempt, which courtesy forbids him to translate into words – in conveying such masked enmities by means of a glance, a shrug, an altered tone of voice, or a transient expression of face," he was "unrivalled."[41] Much of the effect of Disraeli's attacks came, however, from his coolness in delivering his devastating sarcasms. While his listeners were convulsed with laughter and his victims were writhing in mental agony, he remained completely impassible and detached from the tumult. He was a most dangerous antagonist in debate because he left his opponents little to grasp by way of defence or counter-attack. And "the moment the shouts and confusion ... subsided, the same calm, low ... distinct and searching voice" continued to pursue his ideas while he prepared "to launch another sarcasm, hissing hot, into the soul of his victim."[42]

The conclusion of this direct attack on Peel is one of the most succinct examples of Disraeli's parliamentary technique. It perfectly demonstrates his ability to disguise his malice until the climax of his speech and to make a premeditated attack seem to arise casually from another topic. Initially, the subject of this peroration seems to be the obstreperous

behaviour of the Young England members and the prime minister's
power to maintain party discipline.

> If the right hon. gentleman may find it sometimes convenient to reprove a
> supporter on his right flank, perhaps we deserve it – I for one am quite
> prepared to bow to the rod; but really, if the right hon. gentleman, instead
> of having recourse to obloquy, would only stick to quotation, he may rely
> on it, it would be a safer weapon. It is one he always wields with the hand
> of a master; and when he does appeal to any authority, in prose or verse,
> he is sure to be successful, partly because he never quotes a passage that
> has not previously received the meed of Parliamentary approbation, and
> partly and principally because his quotations are so happy. The right hon.
> gentleman knows what the introduction of a great name does in debate –
> how important is its effect, and occasionally how electrical. He never re-
> curs to any author who is not great, and sometimes who is not loved – Can-
> ning, for example. That is a name never to be mentioned, I am sure, in the
> House of Commons without emotion. We all admire his genius. We all,
> at least most of us, deplore his untimely end; and we all sympathise
> with him in his fierce struggle with supreme prejudice and sublime medi-
> ocrity – with inveterate foes and with candid friends. (Loud cheering.)
> The right hon. gentleman may be sure that a quotation from such an
> authority will always tell. Some lines, for example, upon friendship,
> written by Mr. Canning, and quoted by the right hon. gentleman! The
> theme, the poet, the speaker – what a felicitous combination! (Loud and
> long-continued cheers.) Its effect in debate must be overwhelming; and I
> am sure, if it were addressed to me, all that would remain would be for me
> thus publicly to congratulate the right hon. gentleman, not only on his
> ready memory, but on his courageous conscience.[43]

The effect of this speech was, in Monypenny's words, "stupendous."
The House was in an uproar for some time as "the thunders of cheering" prevented the next speaker, Sir James Graham, from making himself heard.[44] And when Peel finally rose to reply he was still visibly
shaken: Disraeli noted, "As for P., he was stunned and stupefied, lost
his head, and vacillating between silence and spleen, spoke much and
weakly. Never was a greater failure."[45] In its written form it is easy to
appreciate the mastery of Disraeli's retaliation. The feigned humility,
the extended extravagant compliment behind which lurks an insult, the
seemingly casual mention of Canning's name, the insinuation of Peel's
insincerity, and the mordant exclamation all lead inexorably to the

mock capitulation and the culminating accusation of complete hypocrisy. And the ultimate result of this is a demonstration of Peel's lack
of power, his inability to quash the ambitious upstart in his ranks. But
however great the immediate impact of this attack, it was really just a
skirmish on the fringe of a not very important issue, and its long-term
effect would not have been so great in establishing the theme of Peel's
perfidy had Disraeli not taken every occasion to renew the charge.
Ironically both Peel's ideas on domestic policy and events beyond his
control played right into Disraeli's hands.

Although the majority of Tory and Conservative members in the 1841
Parliament were representatives of the agricultural interest and accordingly espoused protectionism, Peel had only cautiously adopted that
policy in the early 1840s, not on the ground of principle, but rather for
pragmatic considerations. In 1842 his plan was to secure reciprocal
commercial treaties, but that proved unworkable and over the next few
years he gradually changed his mind about the value of protective tariffs on agricultural products. By 1845 he was, indeed, persuaded by
both the theoretical and practical arguments put forth by Richard
Cobden and those urging a complete repeal of the Corn Laws. Peel kept
his "conversion" a close secret, hoping to delay the announcement of
his new convictions until such time as a dissolution was appropriate
and he could campaign openly as a supporter of free trade. In the meantime he was in a difficult position, for the majority of his own party,
pledged on principle to the ascendancy of the landed interest, would
see any further weakening of the Corn Law duties as a betrayal of their
constituents and the Tory party. Thus, when in the middle of March
1845 Cobden again spoke powerfully against the Corn Law,[46] Peel
found himself unable to answer his argument. Sidney Herbert (one of
two cabinet ministers who knew of Peel's convictions – the other being
Graham) replied in Peel's stead, but in so doing he remarked that it
was "distasteful to the agriculturalists to come whining to Parliament
at every period of temporary distress."[47] Disraeli voted with the
Government to defeat Cobden's motion calling for an inquiry into the
effect of the Corn Law on agriculture, but he obviously sensed the implication in the Government's response: that for them Protectionism
was at best an expediency, not a policy designed to defend a vital interest of society.

When the matter was reopened a few days later, Disraeli took the opportunity to attack Peel again. Granting that Protection might be an
expedient, but a necessary one, he argued that it was not a matter that

could be settled by reference to theory and dogma. Rather, he pointed out, Cobden's alternative to Protection was unrealistic, for it wrongly assumed that if England dispensed with tariffs, other countries would immediately follow her example. But whatever the merits of the argument, on either side, Disraeli was more interested in the matter of Peel's attitudes towards his Protectionist supporters. He wittily characterized Peel as a jaded lover who had abandoned the previous object of his affections and was now trying to ignore her recriminations and avoid an embarrassing scene. Observing that "Protection appears to be in about the same condition that Protestantism was in 1828," he reiterated the charge of Peel's apostasy, and bitterly condemned the Government's policy. He would, he said, prefer that measures to establish free trade be proposed by the "hon. Member for Stockport" (Cobden), not by "one, who through skilful Parliamentary manoeuvres, has tampered with the generous confidence of a great people and of a great party." And then, addressing the prime minister directly, he added: "Dissolve, if you please, the Parliament you have betrayed, and appeal to the people, who, I believe, mistrust you. For me there remains this at least – the opportunity of expressing thus publicly my belief that a Conservative Government is an Organised Hypocrisy."[48]

While the reference to events in 1828 might suggest that Disraeli had long harboured a hostility to Peel, the reckless tone and note of suppressed bitterness in fact reflect a new sense of opportunity. The prime minister professed, at least publicly, to be puzzled by Disraeli's inconsistency, noting in passing his offer of support in 1841 and his praise on several occasions since. But neither the naive nor the cynical view accounts satisfactorily for Disraeli's behaviour. Blake is probably right in suggesting that in writing *Coningsby* and *Sybil* Disraeli came to realize the incompatibility of his ideas and Peel's pragmatism, and to feel the futility of hoping for preferment within the Conservative party led by Peel, Graham, and Stanley.[49] Certainly such feelings seem warranted by the reactions to Disraeli revealed in the private correspondence of the leading Conservatives. But the writing of *Coningsby* and *Sybil*, and the public reaction to them, had another, equally important effect. They gave Disraeli not so much a platform for specific political action as a basis for establishing a more successful political identity. In that regard, the significance of Disraeli's attacks on Peel at the opening of the 1845 session of Parliament is threefold. In his own eyes and those of his supporters, they first enable him to shed temporarily the question of his

1 Benjamin Disraeli, 1852, by Sir Francis Grant PRA (1803–78), The Disraeli Collection (National Trust), © NTPL/John Hammond. See the discussion, page 346.

2 Benjamin Disraeli, 1873 (b/w photo), by W. and D. Downey (fl. 1860–1905). Private Collection / Avant-Demain / The Bridgeman Art Library. See the discussion, page 427.

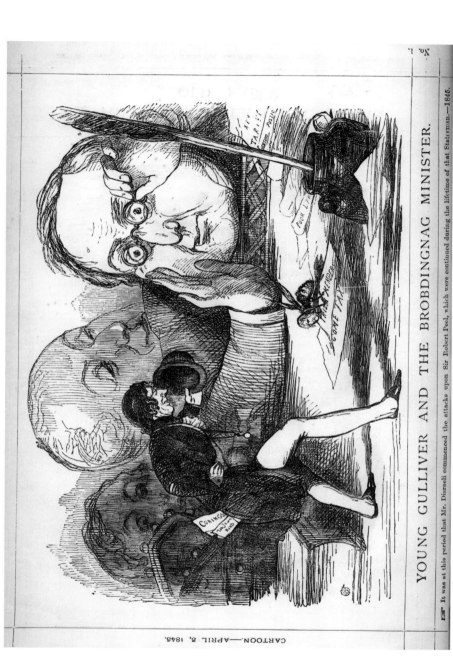

3 "Young Gulliver and the Brobdingnag Minister" (April 5, 1845). Cartoon 1, *Benjamin Disraeli: Earl of Beaconsfield, K.G. In Upwards of 100 Cartoons from the Collection of "Mr. Punch."* Punch Office, 85 Fleet Street, London. 1878. See the discussion, page 240. Figures 4–14 are also printed from this book.

THE RISING GENERATION—IN PARLIAMENT.

PEEL. "*Well, my little Man, what are you going to do this Session, eh?*"

D——LI (the Juvenile). "*Why—aw—aw—I've made arrangements—aw—to—smash —aw—Everybody.*"

☞ At this time Sir Robert Peel had resigned the Conservative leadership in the House of Commons, which was assumed by Lord George Bentinck, assisted by Mr. Disraeli.—1847.

No. 3.

4 "The Rising Generation – in Parliament" (January 30, 1847). Cartoon 3, *Benjamin Disraeli*. See the discussion, page 300.

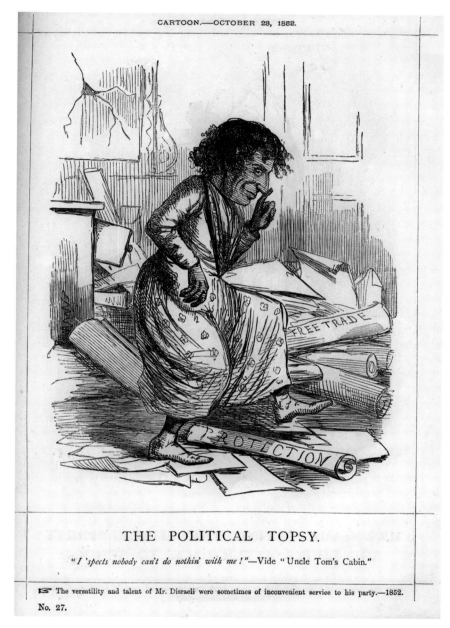

THE POLITICAL TOPSY.

"I 'spects nobody can't do nothin' with me!"—Vide "Uncle Tom's Cabin."

☞ The versatility and talent of Mr. Disraeli were sometimes of inconvenient service to his party.—1852.

No. 27.

5 "The Political Topsy" (October 23, 1852). Cartoon 27, *Benjamin Disraeli*. See the discussion, page 340.

THE ASIATIC MYSTERY.

☞ Mr. Disraeli moved for a Royal Commission to enquire into the grievances of the Natives which had led to the mutiny in India.—1857.

No. 33.

6 "The Asiatic Mystery" (August 8, 1857). Cartoon 33, *Benjamin Disraeli*. See the discussion, page 452.

DRESSING FOR AN OXFORD BAL MASQUÉ.

"The question is, is Man an Ape or an Angel?" (A Laugh.) *Now, I am on the side of the Angels.* (Cheers.)"—Mr. DISRAELI'S Oxford Speech, Friday, November 25.

☞ In addressing the Oxford Diocesan Society in a speech having reference to the policy of the Conservative Party towards the Church, Mr. Disraeli made the above declaration, which gave rise to much comment.—1864. No. 43.

7 "Dressing for an Oxford Bal Masqué" (December 10, 1864). Cartoon 43, *Benjamin Disraeli*. See the discussion, page 366.

THE DERBY, 1867. DIZZY WINS WITH "REFORM BILL."

MR. PUNCH. *"Don't be too sure; wait till he's* WEIGHED.*"*

☞ The first division on the Reform Bill in Committee resulted in a majority of 21 for the Government in a full House.—1867.

No. 54.

8 "The Derby, 1867. Dizzy Wins With 'Reform Bill'" (May 25, 1867). Cartoon 54, *Benjamin Disraeli*. See the discussion, page 345.

FAGIN'S POLITICAL SCHOOL.

"*Now, mark this; because these are things which you may not have heard in any speech which has been made in the city of Edinburgh.* (Laughter and cheers.) *I had—if it be not arrogant to use such a phrase—*TO EDUCATE OUR PARTY. *It is a large party, and requires its attention to be called to questions of this kind with some pressure. I had to prepare the mind of Parliament and the country on this question of Reform.*"—MR. DISRAELI'S Speech at the Edinburgh Banquet.

☞ Mr. Disraeli had asserted that no Party could lay claim to a monopoly of Liberal principles—hence
the Government were quite at liberty to deal with the Reform question.—1867.

No. 58.

9 "Fagin's Political School" (November 9, 1867). Cartoon 58, *Benjamin Disraeli*.
See the discussion, page 353.

THE CONSERVATIVE PROGRAMME.

"Deputation below, Sir.—Want to know the Conservative Programme."

Rt. Hon. Ben. Diz. *"Eh?—Oh!—Ah!—Yes!—Quite so! Tell them, my good Abercorn, with my compliments, that we propose to rely on the Sublime Instincts of an Ancient People!!"* [See Speech at Crystal Palace.

☞ A great Conservative demonstration was made at the Crystal Palace in recognition of the growing unpopularity of the Government. Mr. Disraeli refrained from committing his Party to a definite programme.—1872.

No. 70.

10 "The Conservative Programme" (July 6, 1872). Cartoon 70, *Benjamin Disraeli*. See the discussion, page 446.

"MOSÉ IN EGITTO!!!"

☞ Mr. Disraeli extorted the admiration of the country by purchasing for £4,000,000 on behalf of the Government the shares in the Suez Canal held by the Khedive of Egypt.—1875.

No. 81.

11 "'Mosé in Egitto!!!'" (December 11, 1875). Cartoon 81, *Benjamin Disraeli*. See the discussion, page 447.

"NEW CROWNS FOR OLD ONES!"

(ALADDIN *adapted*.)

☞ The Bill for adding to the Royal Titles that of Empress of India, though pressed forward by the Government, was scarcely approved by the country.—1876.

No. 85.

12 "'New Crowns for Old Ones!'" (April 15, 1876). Cartoon 85, *Benjamin Disraeli*. See the discussion, page 452.

A BLAZE OF TRIUMPH!

☞ By the Anglo-Turkish Convention, the British Government contracted to defend the Empire of the Turks in Asia; conditionally upon the adoption of a reformed Administration and the cession of the Island of Cyprus,—which is now garrisoned by British Forces.—1878.

No. 103.

13 "A Blaze of Triumph!" (July 27, 1878). Cartoon 103, *Benjamin Disraeli*. See the discussion, page 486.

THE "PAS DE DEUX!"

(*From the "Scène de Triomphe" in the Grand Anglo-Turkish* BALLET D'ACTION.)

☞ Lords Beaconsfield and Salisbury, in reward for their labours as Plenipotentiaries at the Congress, were installed as Knights of the Most Noble Order of the Garter.—1878.

No. 104.

14 "The 'Pas de Deux!'" (August 3, 1878). Cartoon 104, *Benjamin Disraeli*. See the discussion, page 488.

EARL OF BEACONSFIELD, K.G.

PHOTOGRAPHED AT OSBORNE BY COMMAND OF H.M. THE QUEEN,
JULY 22ND 1878.

BY JABEZ HUGHES, RYDE, I.W.

15 Benjamin Disraeli, 1st Earl of Beaconsfield (1804–81) photographed by Jabez Hughes at Osborne House, Isle of Wight (b/w photo) by English Photographer (19th century). Private Collection / The Bridgeman Art Library. See the discussion, page 447.

16 "The Earl of Beaconsfield 1877" after Von Angelli, Hughendon Manor, The Disraeli Collection (National Trust), © NTPL/John Hammond. See the discussion, page 488.

own trustworthiness. Indeed, his revenge upon Peel was the more gratifying for embodying a projection, and a deflection, on to Peel of the issue of his own political hypocrisy. But the attacks on the prime minister are also the most effective yet demonstration of Disraeli's rhetorical superiority to those who merely by virtue of their birth, wealth, or education claimed a position in public affairs. By the summer of 1845 he could rightly feel that he did in fact have "the ear of the House" and that he was recognized on all sides as a figure of considerable importance. Finally, and equally so, the attacks on Peel were central to Disraeli's political identity, because in their substance they were in part another expression of the altruistic purity of motive and nobility of purpose that had been crucial, conceptual elements of his Tory political and social ideology for more than a decade.

It would seem, however, that from the beginning of 1845 Disraeli did indeed understand that his own subsequent success in the Tory party necessitated the destruction of Peel's Conservative ministry. The third occasion of his attacks on Peel that spring, the Maynooth Bill to endow permanently the Roman Catholic seminary in Ireland with £30,000 per year, shows more explicitly than the previous ones had done that he had formed the intention of ruining Peel. Given Disraeli's obvious sympathies with "Holy Church" and the "old faith" in *Sybil*, it might well be thought that he should have supported the grant to Maynooth. Lord John Manners and George Smythe were more consistent with their Young England enthusiasms in voting for the measure. But Protestant feeling in England was strongly against the bill, and Disraeli, perhaps from genuine ambivalence, though more likely from expediency, opposed it, distinguishing sharply in either case between faith and clericalism. Arguing that the Maynooth Bill embodied a principle against which the Tory party had always struggled, Disraeli said that he did not think "the gentlemen who were now seated on the Treasury bench" were morally entitled to bring forward such a measure. And after characterizing the provision of the bill as "meagre" and "miserable," he urged the Catholic gentlemen of the House not to accept such a "boon" from an "individual whose bleak shade fell on the sunshine of ... [their] hopes for more than a quarter of a century" and from one whose hands were "polluted."[50] It may be that the use of this adjective, so closely allied to the definition of the hero's identity in both *Henrietta Temple* and *Coningsby*, is an unconscious sign of the link between Disraeli's ambivalent sense of his own identity and his nasty characterization of

Peel. Certainly the implication of the temporal allusion to the ministers "now seated on the Treasury bench" was conscious and deliberate, for the peroration of this speech leaves no doubt whatever about his hope and intentions:

> Let us in this house re-echo that which I believe to be the sovereign senti-ment of this country; let us tell the people in high places that cunning is not caution, and that habitual perfidy is not high policy of state. On that ground we may all join. Let us bring back to this house that which it has for so long a time past been without – the legitimate influence and salutary check of a constitutional Opposition. (Cheers.) That is what the country requires, what the country looks for. Let us do it at once in the only way in which it can be done, by dethroning this dynasty of deception, by putting an end to the intolerable yoke of official despotism and Parliamentary im-posture. (Loud cheers.)[51]

Disraeli was not the only one to impugn Peel's character in this debate. Macaulay, who supported the bill, attacked him with equal violence and bitterness: "Did you think ... when you went on, session after ses-sion, attacking those whom you knew to be in the right, and flattering all the prejudices of those whom you knew to be in the wrong, that the day of reckoning would never come? That day has come ... you are do-ing penance for the disingenuousness of years."[52] It might, of course, be expected that the Whigs would have a jaundiced view of Peel's actions in taking the initiative in a variety of measures that they felt were more properly their own prerogative. But the important point is that Disraeli's assaults on Peel's character and motives found sympathetic ears among both disgruntled Whigs and uneasy Tories well before the crisis re-sulting from the famine in Ireland placed the prime minister in a polit-ical and moral bog from which he had no power to extract himself.

I

Despite the unpopularity of the Maynooth Bill, which manifested itself in the shape of more than 2000 petitions to Parliament, Disraeli esti-mated that the Government was in a stronger position at the end of the 1845 session than it had been four years earlier. Even the disenchanted Tories for the most part supported Peel's measures and there seemed little chance of a strong opposition from the Whigs to the prime min-ister's policy of gradual, liberal reforms. The ministers' position was,

Disraeli later admitted, "aggrandized and confirmed by a conviction then prevalent" that they were "the only body of men then competent to carry on affairs."[53] In 1852, of course, this is said with telling irony; but in the summer of 1845 Disraeli seems to have had little anticipation of a dramatic change in Parliament.

After the success of the publication of *Sybil* the Disraelis enjoyed finding themselves now regularly invited to the houses of London's social elite. In one week, Disraeli told Sarah, they had been to a "most recherche party" at Landsdowne House, "a gigantic ball" at Lord Salisbury's, "a colossal fete" at Ashburnham House, and "an assembly at Lady Palmerston's."[54] What made these invitations a "great social revolution" was the fact that Mary Anne was also invited, and this seemed to reflect an awareness of Disraeli's new political importance rather than just a curiosity about his notoriety. The reference in the letter, however, to the fact that some of his correspondence with his sister is being kept secret from Mary Anne is a clear indication that Disraeli has not entirely escaped from his embarrassing past. Sarah, of course, was his confidante of longest standing and there are several indications in the correspondence of these years that Mary Anne resented the continuation of their filial intimacy. Nevertheless, the reasons for such secrecy were compelling. Because Sarah had shared the fantasies of the early years and believed in her brother's genius when others did not, her intimate appreciation of his struggles and triumphs had special meaning for him. Sarah also knew some of the details of Disraeli's financial escapades and the resulting debts, which, apparently, had not all been confessed to Mary Anne or repaid, but which, with his greater political and social success, were an even more threatening source of embarrassment. On 6 September, as the Disraelis prepared to set out for an extended vacation in France, he wrote to his sister from the Carlton Club indicating that on the following Monday he would send her a private dispatch (i.e., unknown to Mary Anne) with all of his instructions about how to manage the letters that would arrive during his absence.[55] It is possible that Disraeli's taste for clandestine intrigues was perversely gratified by such domestic duplicity, but his next letter, on 8 September, suggests the concrete motive for his caution: "I think it *quite impossible* that any unpleasant letters can arrive. You must howr. use yr. discretion. The moment we are settled, we will write & apprise you when you are to commence yr. duties … You can understand the pang it costs me to leave England with[ou]t seeing you, but there was no alternative. To this very moment my affairs occupy me."[56]

The next letter to Sarah, dated 17 September, reports that they have crossed the channel to Boulogne and then settled near Cassel to enjoy the seclusion of the rustic surroundings. Disraeli, perhaps encouraged by finding *Sybil* advertised in the windows of shops in Boulogne – as good holiday reading – immediately began to write the opening chapters of another novel, *Tancred; or, the New Crusade.*[57] But this project was put aside when after two months the Disraelis moved to Paris for the remainder of their trip and Disraeli found himself at the centre of intense speculations about Sir Robert Peel's response to the crisis in Ireland.[58]

By the autumn of 1845 it had become apparent that a famine was likely to develop in Ireland where the blight known as "the potato cholera" had destroyed the staple of the Irish peasants' diet, and at the same time very wet weather had destroyed a significant portion of the grain crops in England.[59] Justly alarmed at the horrifying prospect of four million or more people threatened by starvation, Peel proposed to repeal the Corn Law as one drastic measure to cope with the impending emergency. But, as Blake has pointed out, the logic of Peel's actions is somewhat obscure. Most of the Irish peasants lived in such extreme poverty that the anticipated reduction in the price of bread from Peel's proposal would have made no difference to them. Moreover, instead of immediately suspending the Corn Law by Order in Council, as he could have done, Peel wanted to proceed with a bill that would gradually reduce import duties to zero over a period of three years. Peel's *Memoirs* show that he had, in fact, long been convinced by Richard Cobden's arguments that the Corn Law should be abolished, and that he found it repugnant to disguise that conviction in the language of a "temporary expedient."[60] Yet, at the same time, he knew that he had no electoral mandate to come forward as an advocate of repeal on economic grounds, and that to do so would be seen by his party colleagues as a betrayal of their principles. It was thus only on the grounds of responding to the emergency that Peel could honourably justify his measure for repeal.[61] This argument did not, however, persuade all of Peel's colleagues, and after a flurry of cabinet meetings in November, he resigned as prime minister on 6 December, when Lord Stanley and others gave him notice of their own resignations should the Government proceed with a measure for permanent repeal of the Corn Law.

There was a hiatus in affairs of almost two weeks at this point, while Lord John Russell attempted to form a Government, but ultimately failed when it became clear to him that Lord Grey and his Whig friends would not accept Lord Palmerston as a cabinet colleague. Russell was then, in Disraeli's words, relieved of his false, premature position when he "endured the mortification of confessing to his sovereign his inability to serve her, and handed back with courtesy the poisoned chalice to Sir Robert."[62] Disraeli's mocking use of this courtly image undoubtedly reflects his cynicism about Peel's conscious adoption of a chivalric posture in resuming office. The Duke of Wellington wrote to John Wilson Croker on 28 December: "there is no doubt but that Sir Robert Peel went down to Windsor on Saturday the 20th with the firm determination, if so required, to become her Majesty's Minister again; and to enable Her Majesty to meet her Parliament, even if he should stand alone, rather than oblige her to seek for a Minister among the Radicals!"[63] And then in reply to Croker's expressed doubts about Peel's re-formed cabinet, Wellington wrote again the following day to say that "a movement of enthusiasm induced Sir Robert Peel, when sent for, to determine, before he saw the Queen, that if required he would stand by her, even alone if necessary, to enable her to meet her Parliament, rather than reduce Her Majesty to the necessity of calling upon Mr. Cobden and others whose names I have no right to indicate as his associates, to serve Her Majesty as her Ministers." He then added as further assurance that he had "participated in this movement," and had at once "consented to give ... [his] assistance to the Queen in her difficulties."[64] The heroism of this romance was designed to lessen Croker's sense of Peel's perfidy – an important matter, for Croker, one of the founders of the *Quarterly Review*, was still writing the political essays for that most influential of Conservative voices. Croker had, in fact, written to Peel two weeks earlier in alarmist terms that evoked the horrors of the French Revolution: "are the Landed Interests, and ultimately the aristocracy, and the monarchy, to be handed over to the fierce democracy of the *League*? ... such a triumph ... will drive – indeed it seems, has driven the League mad – and the Landed Interest and their advocates are already designated to public vengeance as 'murderers' ... in all this dreadful catastrophe ... black as the whole horizon looks, I cannot persuade myself that *even yet, you* could not save us. If you can't, we are all lost."[65]

Much the same fear characterizes Henry Goulburn's reply to Peel's cabinet memorandum on 30 November: "the party of which you are head is the only barrier which remains against the revolutionary effects of the Reform Bill ... But if it be broken in pieces by a destruction of confidence in its leaders ... I see nothing before us but the exasperation of class animosities, a struggle for pre-eminence, and the ultimate triumph of unrestrained democracy."[66] It is thus hardly surprising that amid the encouragements of Wellington, the hysteria of Croker, and the fears of his colleagues, Peel should adopt a chivalric interpretation of his political position. But it is one of the many exquisite ironies of the time that it was Disraeli who, in the letters of "Runnymede" in 1836, had first characterized Peel as St George defending England from the dragon of Whiggism.[67]

To a significant extent Peel's determined chivalry in 1845 was the cover for unpleasant political realities. He was fully aware that his conversion to agricultural free trade would be interpreted by the landed interests as a betrayal of Tory principles, and he knew that a bill to repeal the Corn Law should logically be the work of a Whig ministry.[68] But he also felt compelled to take some decisive action to forestall the twin calamities which seemed impending; starvation, disease, and violence in Ireland (and even, perhaps, England)[69] and the likelihood of political radicals gaining control of the government.[70] So even though Peel knew that some members of his cabinet were not convinced that opening the ports to foreign grain would ameliorate the Irish situation,[71] he could not resist the logic of his own argument. Since he knew that even a temporary suspension of the duties on corn would compel an early reconsideration of the principle of Protection, he required the urgency of the impending crisis to sanction *his* determination to proceed with repeal. His sense of that urgency was undoubtedly sincere, and he repeatedly urged his colleagues to commit their support on that basis, but the contrasting emphases on the larger question of Protection in the cabinet memoranda of late November 1845 make it clear that strategic political considerations were also a shaping force in his thinking, particularly after Lord John Russell's open letter to *The Times*, 22 November, advocating immediate complete repeal. The irony of the situation would seem to be that the very intensity of Peel's scruples combined with his sense of duty to lead him to a course of action that left him peculiarly vulnerable to charges of being unscrupulous.[72]

In Paris, meanwhile, Disraeli was quick to resume the gratifications of his intimacy with the king of France. He mentions in letters to Sarah, to Baron Lionel de Rothschild, and to Lord John Manners, that the king had sent for him the day after his arrival, and to the last of these correspondents he reports that he is immersed in "a political atmosphere of fever heat," conversing with "none but Ministers and Ambassadors, of all parties and all countries, and all equally distracted."[73] But the extent to which the crisis of Peel's Government gripped Disraeli's imagination is best revealed in the lengthy letter he wrote to Lord Palmerston on 14 December.[74] By that time he knew that Peel had resigned and that Russell was trying to form a Whig administration. Mentioning first that on Friday he had had a "private conversation" with M. Guizot about the "intelligence" from London, Disraeli goes on to tell Palmerston about his extensive conversation with the king the next evening, the chief point of which was the likelihood of a Whig administration, and consequently of his "Lordships accession to office." It is clear from what follows that Disraeli once again believes that he has an opportunity to play a crucial role in the development of momentous affairs, for he takes upon himself that task of diminishing the king's apprehensions about Palmerston's coolness to France and her interests: "being not unfamiliar with the subject, it was in my power to discuss it in all its bearings, & to make those representations to the King, and enter into those explanations & details, wh: were desirable. I impressed on his Majesty with delicacy, but witht. reserve, that your Lordp was our first foreign Minister who had taken the French intimacy as an avowed element of our national policy." Indeed, Disraeli reports that in his conversation with the king, he even went so far as to speak for Palmerston's intentions: that if "frankness and decision were not wanting" on the part of the French government, "I felt sure that yr. Lp would never take a litigious view of the policy of France, but rather would assist in any fair development of its influence wh: had for its object to popularise the throne & satisfy the public."[75]

Just as he had done on his previous visit to Paris in 1842, Disraeli is here indulging his ambition and his sense of his own importance. The similarity of the occasions is further shown when he comes to express the true "purpose" of his letter: "It is this. I suspect, from many circumstances, that a sort of cry of affected terror will be raised in England … against yr Lordsp, sure to be re-echoed here, wh: may add to the embarassments of your Govmt., I doubt not, sufficient without it. Do not you think some means might be devised to terminate this for ever?"[76] What Disraeli suggests in answer to his apparently rhetorical question is that when Parliament reconvenes "it would not be difficult to arrange something wh: wd. elicit a satisfactory exposition" of Palmerston's new policy and real sympathies. And he even adds that, were he present, he would be "very happy to assist … in this respect." His behaviour in thus becoming his "Lordship's" unsolicited agent in Paris and in (he fancies) furthering the Whigs' cause might at first seem puzzling. But the strategic and personal nature of his motives is fully revealed when he continues his conditional anticipation: "but if the Parlt. be summoned speedily, I do not think I shall be tempted to quit this agreeable residence; especially as *the great object of my political career is now achieved*" (emphasis added).[77]

Such candour to the foe reveals how deeply Disraeli had come to desire Peel's destruction. In that light, too, his insistence to Guizot, the king, and all his correspondents of the moment, that Peel's triumphant return to office was "highly improbable," seems to be as much wish-fulfilment as hasty judgment.[78] In the letter of 17 December to Lord John Manners (by which time he has heard a rumour that the Whigs had "resolved to decline the enterprise"), he dwells obsessively on Peel's character, as he sees it: "I think it is a false famine; & the question is not ripe eno' for his fantastic pranks. He is so vain, that he wants to figure in history as the settler of all the great questions, but a parliamentary constitution is not favorable to such ambitions; things must be done by parties, not by persons using parties as tools; especially men with[ou]t imagination or any inspiring qualities, or who rather offer you duplicity instead of inspiration."[79] It would thus seem that for the moment Disraeli's gratifications at Peel's discomfiture were almost equal to those of his own social success and ambitious fantasies. But what the events of Disraeli's second Parisian visit also suggest is that the long-standing tension between principles and pragmatism in Disraeli's own mind became completely focused on, or projected upon, the issue of Peel's motives during the famine crisis and the ensuing Corn Law debates. The symbiotic, but only half-conscious relationship between altruism and expediency, which had been so characteristic of Disraeli's own political identity, found an extraordinary resonance in Peel's explanations of his determination to act on the repeal of the Corn Law in 1846.

It is not just that in terms of political power Peel played into Disraeli's hand. It would seem, too, that at some level of awareness Disraeli recognized his antagonist's dilemma as his own. And, in effect, the vitriolic condemnations of Peel's betrayal of his Tory principles became the means by which Disraeli purified his own twofold expediency – the desire for revenge, and the ambition for office. In an imaginative projection, Disraeli was in his own eyes able to prove that Peel was as unprincipled as he had ever been accused of being, and that Peel's assumption of a moral superiority was unfounded. That such a conjunction of historical events and personal political exigencies should have offered Disraeli this opportunity just after the Young England movement became defunct is one of those profound ironies that tempts historians to interpret coincidence as fate. Palmerston, of course, had not been fooled by Disraeli's expression of diffidence. In his reply to that extraordinary letter he shrewdly remarked that, whatever may be the allurements of Paris, he thought Disraeli would "hardly refrain" from being in his place on "so curious and interesting an occasion" as the opening of the new session of Parliament.[80] With Peel back in office, that session (which opened on 22 January 1846) presented Disraeli with the necessity and the opportunity of renewing his assaults on the integrity of the prime minister.

10

Sybil: Two Nations, or One?
An Allegorical Romance[1]

The popularity of *Coningsby; or The New Generation* when it first appeared in May 1844 was undoubtedly part of what prompted Disraeli to begin immediately writing another "political" novel. But part of his motive must also have been his realization that the enormous success of *Coningsby* derived less from any appreciation of his reflexive attempt to define the proper contemporary role of heroic sensibility than from the widespread conviction that he had produced a "manifesto of Young England" and, not so incidentally, another sensational roman à clef.[2] Disraeli knew, however, that in *Coningsby* his "romance" had run away with his theme before he had fully developed the social implications of his political views. And while it was true that in part the work could still be seen as a satirical treatise on the shortcomings of Sir Robert Peel's conservatism, Disraeli's intention in writing *Coningsby* had been much broader and deeper than such notoriety acknowledged. The writing of another novel thus became a pressing matter: *Sybil; or, the Two Nations* was completed and published within a year (May 1845), despite the author's hectic political and social life.

Because of its prominence in the subgenre known as the social-problem novel, *Sybil* has attracted more serious critical comment than the rest of Disraeli's fiction. But this commentary has often reflected equally serious misreadings, for *Sybil* has generally been assumed to be Disraeli's most typical novel when there are important respects in which it is his least typical work.[3] And despite the similarities of its romantic plot with the earlier works, it is only when these differences between *Sybil* and the other novels are perceived that the force of Disraeli's social vision in the 1840s can be fully understood.

What is missing from *Sybil* and present in almost every other of Disraeli's novels except his last, *Endymion* (1880), is the central, imaginatively autobiographical fantasy about the ambivalent nature of his protagonist. For the moment, though, in 1844 that recurring fantasy embodying a conflict between altruism and expediency had reached a most satisfactory fictional resolution in *Coningsby* with the romance of Harry Coningsby and Edith Millbank. And in Disraeli's private life it had also temporarily lost some of its urgency. As the leader of the Young England coterie, as the confidant of the king of France, as a successful orator in the House of Commons, and as a popular novelist, Disraeli had in his own eyes gained a considerable measure of acceptance and recognition among England's social and political elite.

Sybil also differs from most of the other novels in that so much of it is derived from a variety of printed materials, including several parliamentary blue books.[4] These sources are significant discoveries that illuminate Disraeli's artistic methods, in particular the ways in which he seemed careless of factual detail and often conflated material from several sources to augment the emotional impact of his story. But the scholarly interest in Disraeli's numerous sources for *Sybil* has proved to be a mixed blessing, for the efforts to show that the descriptions of such things as the effects of the New Poor Law or the rick-burning incidents are inaccurate only reinforce the notion, far too prevalent, that social-problem novels are themselves merely historical documents, if somewhat unreliable ones. Indeed, the question of Disraeli's accuracy in conveying the "historical truth" is largely irrelevant to a critical appreciation of his purposes as a politician and novelist. However much he intended to propagate the knowledge of social conditions that he had obtained from his reading of parliamentary papers and from his travels to England's industrial regions, in writing *Sybil* Disraeli was much more importantly attempting to write propaganda in the form of an allegorical romance.[5] And the second charge often laid against Disraeli – that in *Sybil* he has no sensible solution for the social problems he exposes – needs to be re-examined in the light of that allegorical romance's meaning.

I

In the general preface to the 1870 collected edition of his novels, Disraeli maintains that *Coningsby*, *Sybil*, and *Tancred* form "a real trilogy" because they treat of the same subject: "The origin and character of our political parties, their influence on the condition of the people of this country, some picture of the moral and physical condition of that people, and some intimation of the means by which it might be elevated and improved, were themes which had long engaged my meditation."[6] He said as well that in beginning *Coningsby* he intended to treat all three – the character of political parties, the condition of the people, and the duties of the Church – but found "they were too vast for the space ... allotted," so that only the first was adequately dealt with in that work (General Preface, xiv). This has led most critics to assume that this "trilogy" is the result of careful planning in which each volume deliberately treats a separate topic, and that *Sybil* is primarily concerned with the second of Disraeli's avowed interests, the condition of the people. Accordingly, his artistic and political purpose has been judged to be transparently that of exposing the discrepancies between the lives of the two nations, the rich and the poor. And his success as a social novelist has been qualified not only by citing inaccuracies of factual detail, but by interpreting the marriage of Egremont and Sybil as a symbolic failure because the revelation of her nobility destroys the reconciliation of the classes that their union is supposed to represent. In this light Disraeli stands convicted of imaginative "tommyrot."[7]

Much more cogent is Patrick Brantlinger's argument that *Sybil* is pervaded by ironies, not the least of which is that the idea of the "Two Nations" is a "dangerous illusion," and clearly seen to be so by Disraeli. Although it is an idea that startles Egremont out of his complacency and edges him towards responsible political thought, it is worth remembering that the concept of the "Two Nations" is expressed by the atheist and utopian radical, Stephen Morley, and it is ultimately exposed and discredited by Egremont as a "false doctrine" which only sustains the heroine's prejudice. However sharp the contrast between the scenes of luxury and the scenes of destitution – those at Mowbray Castle versus those in the room of Warner, the handloom weaver – it is not unwitting ambiguity that informs Disraeli's demonstration that the poor are, as Brantlinger says, "not at all a united nation confronting the rich," but "rather a congeries of quarreling factions." Brantlinger is also quite right when he says that "Disraeli points to the diversity of the class system as a refutation of the two-nations theory held by his Chartist characters."[8] Indeed, the ironies and satire in *Sybil*, which encompass both the rich and the poor and demonstrate on the one hand the recent "felonious origins" of the "Venetian oligarchy" and on the other the naivety of working-class political and social consciousness, are quite deliberate. And the conclusion that Disraeli simply fails in "his attempt to weld Toryism and Radicalism together" would seem to be a reading that misinterprets Disraeli's compassion for the face of distress as a radical political sympathy, and mistakes his Tory social conscience for a reformist ideology.

Such a confusion seems to rest primarily upon the novel's central paradox, that the "symbolic" marriage of the "working-class girl" and the aristocratic hero is unconvincing in the light of her revealed nobility. However, the truth is that though Disraeli fully acknowledges the legitimacy of the people's grievances in his "social" novel, he has no "political" sympathy with their cause whatever. *Sybil*, in fact, reflects his actual position in the House of Commons debates on the Chartist petitions.[9] This is also consistent with the theory of the "mixed constitution," which he had advocated publicly since 1835. Accordingly, he considered the proper political representation of "the People" to be the duty of the aristocracy and the Church. And he argued that the true interests of the aristocracy and the true interests of the people are identical and demand a social harmony based upon mutual trust and the acceptance of their respective positions and duties within society. Thus the error of looking for a Tory-Radical compromise where none was intended is in part based upon our Whiggish assumptions about what the work as a realist social novel ought to be arguing, and upon our limited sympathy for Disrael's conception of Toryism.

While it is ultimately true that Disraeli is less interested "in making us feel sorry for the poor" than in proving them "to be mistaken,"[10] the connection between his melodramatic evocation of pathos among the working class and his rejection of Chartism is both stronger than has yet been granted and by no means the antithesis usually implied. Disraeli's illustration of the "condition of the people" goes, and is intended to go, beyond the quality of their material existence. In the General Preface of 1870, he writes that in 1845 he had been attempting "some picture of the moral and physical condition" of the country's people and "some intimation of the means by which it might be elevated."[11] His claim that this improvement had "long engaged" his meditation is borne out by the fact that as early as 1833, in an election address to the electors of the borough of Marylebone, he had stressed the need for an elevation of the moral condition of the people. Moreover, in *Sybil* the "condition" that Disraeli is trying to illustrate is "the degradation of the multitude," both physical and moral, a process that was, he felt, the result of the oligarchic Whigs' addiction to "the triple blessings of Venetian politics, Dutch finance, and French wars" (Bk 1, ch. 6, 25). The short revisionist and conspiratorial "history" of England in Book 1, chapter 3, makes his concerns explicit: the principle of Dutch finance "to mortgage industry in order to protect property[12] ... has ended in the degradation of a fettered and burthened multitude ... Nor have the demoralizing consequences ... on the more favoured classes been less decided ... It has introduced a loose, inexact, haphazard, and dishonest spirit ... ruthless of consequences and yet shrinking from responsibility ... It has so over-stimulated the energies of the population to maintain the material engagements of the state, and of society at large, that the moral condition of the people has been entirely lost sight of" (Bk 1, ch. 3, 23–4). Such a passage makes it clear that Disraeli saw the physical distress of the working population as intimately related to their moral and spiritual condition. And it is also clear from this passage that he saw both of these aspects as in turn closely connected to the lack of proper leadership among their social superiors. It is thus hardly surprising that Disraeli's intimation of how "the moral and physical condition" of the people could be elevated involved a regeneration of not only concrete political and social responsibility, but also a spirit whose essence is religious.

Oddly, perhaps the least-satisfactorily discussed aspect of *Sybil* is Disraeli's very obvious yet important use of a religious motif.[13] This is the more surprising given the presence of the allegorical "Baptist" and "Bishop" Hatton brothers presiding respectively over the secular heaven and hell of the novel. It seems that in the haste to decry the inefficacy of the supposedly interclass marriage of Charles Egremont and Sybil, critics have forgotten that Disraeli would have recognized from the outset that she was not a representative working-class heroine. Indeed, since the plot works from the beginning to deny the simplicities of polarized class antagonism and to reveal Sybil's aristocratic ancestry, it is surely more plausible to argue that Disraeli attached a rather different symbolic value to the concluding marriage: the wedding of sensitive but secular leadership to the spirit of piety and devotion that provides a divine sanction for the political settlement of true Toryism.

At the moment of her first appearance, at twilight amid the ruins of Marney Abbey where she sings "the evening hymn to the Virgin," Sybil is dressed in "the habit of a Religious," though the revelation of her physical beauty suggests that she is not in fact a nun. Egremont's first glimpse of her "countenance ... impressed with a character of almost divine majesty" comes soon after his discussion with the stranger (Sybil's father, Walter Gerard) about the spirit of community and the moral commitment that had marked the administration of the monasteries prior to their dissolution. But it also comes immediately after Stephen Morley's pronouncement of the existence of the two nations, "THE RICH AND THE POOR." The juxtaposition of Morley's bitter claim and Sybil's seraphic presence is so theatrical as to be clearly intended as an epiphany. In other words, the ultimate inadequacy of the secular class dichotomy and the religious nature of Disraeli's alternative are surely embodied in Egremont's response to Sybil's piety and beauty (Bk 2, ch. 5, 77–8). His "conversion" from the aristocratic life of idle hedonism, which is brilliantly portrayed with all its decadent complacency in the opening "Derby" chapters, to an existence imbued with conscientious compassion for the less fortunate is, in part, a matter of his innate character: "a physiologist would hardly have inferred from the countenance and structure of Egremont the career he had pursued, or the character which attached to him. The general cast and expression of his features when in repose was pensive: an air of refinement distinguished his well-moulded brow; his mouth breathed sympathy, and his rich brown eye gleamed with tenderness. The sweetness of his voice in speaking was in harmony with this organization" (Bk 1, ch. 5, 38). But Disraeli's concern is equally to establish Egremont's need of a vocation. His "native generosity of heart," we are told, is matched by a mind "worth opening" and "conscious that he wanted an object ... ever musing over action, though as yet ignorant how to act" (Bk 1, ch. 5, 40–1).

The process of Egremont's conversion is initiated by means of a series of schematic contrasts in the first few chapters of Book 2. His intelligence, sensitivity, and compassion, for example, are enlarged by his encounters with the "iron selfishness," the greed, and the cruelty of his elder brother, Lord Marney, and with the obsessive stupidities of Sir Vasavour Firebrace. Lord Marney is a petty domestic tyrant whose only idea of public policy is to suppress all discontent with stringency and severity. His "brother magistrate," the absurd Sir Vasavour, imagines that the salvation of the country depends entirely on the restoration of baronets' rituals and privileges. Equally striking is the contrast of settings provided in chapter 3. The rural town of Marney is situated amidst a "merry prospect" in "a spreading dale, contiguous to the margin of a clear and lively stream, surrounded by meadows and gardens, and backed by lofty hills, undulating and richly wooded." This "beautiful illusion" is juxtaposed to the ugly vision of the town itself, mostly "wretched tenements" and "squalid hovels" surrounded by filthy open drains and putrid dung-heaps, where "penury and disease fed upon the vitals of a miserable population" (Bk 2, ch. 3, 60–3). Such a generalized description at this point in the novel ensures that the reader too can begin the process of conversion, from the simple delight in the malicious satire of the *beau-monde* to sober reflection on what appears to be another nation. Significantly, it is here that the narrator tells us that the "Holy Church at Marney had forgotten her sacred mission" and that the "harrowed souls of a Saxon peasantry" found religious consolation instead in "conventicles" bearing names such as Sion, Bethel, and Bethesda – "names of a distant land, and the language of a persecuted and ancient race" (Bk 2, ch. 3, 63).

For the moment his remark about the "mysterious power" of these Judaic allusions may seem to be only one of Disraeli's idiosyncrasies. But the narrator's reference to "Holy Church" is picked up in the next chapter as Egremont wanders over the ruins of Marney Abbey, musing upon the causes of rick-burning, an instance of which had occurred the previous night at the abbey farm. The details of the ruins are lovingly described by the narrator as he nostalgically evokes the time of the monks' lives there with its true hospitality, profound devotion, and sacred charity (Bk 2, ch. 4, 67–8). It is this reverie of past and present, implicitly Egremont's as well, with its sense of impending social calamity, that is disturbed by the dramatic encounter in the graveyard with the mysterious strangers – the one, frank, manly, and vigorous; the other, pale, pox-marked, and intellectual. Disraeli's thematic assertion of the need for a religious revival is thus amply established before the moment of Egremont's epiphany, when he sees the radiant "Religious … with a character of almost divine majesty" singing the hymn to the Virgin in the Lady's Chapel (Bk 2, ch. 5, 77–8).

II

In the ensuing chapters of Book 2, the unfolding of the two strands of the plot, those of secular temptation and moral obligation, offers some important hints about Disraeli's allegorical romance. Lord Marney's calculated plan to marry his younger brother to an heiress, the eldest daughter of the Earl de Mowbray, is clearly undercut from the outset by Egremont's thoughts about the strangers he had met at the abbey ruins, who were from Mowbray, and especially by his feelings of "sweet perplexity" about the identity of the "beautiful Religious" with which chapter 6 ends. Much more obvious is the narrator's exposure of Lord Mowbray's shoddy family history, which reveals that in the space of seventy years Mowbray's father, John Warren, rose from being a club waiter and valet to the ranks of the nobility by means of speculation, sharp financial practice, marriage, and borough-mongering. This account of the earl's plebeian origins and false Norman pedigree is juxtaposed with the revelations in chapter 8 about the identities of the mysterious strangers, who, though apparently of humble yeoman stock, are attempting to regain their lost lands. In the best tradition of gothic romances, this sudden clarification is accompanied by further mystery. The reader learns that Walter Gerard's name is the same as that of the martyred last lay abbot of Marney Abbey from whom the "holy trust" of these lands was apparently seized. And, as the reader remembers from chapter 3, this plunder was perpetrated by Egremont's and Lord Marney's ancestor, Baldwin Greymount, who, much as John Warren had latterly done, rose by despicable means from being a confidential domestic servant to a peer of the realm apparently of Norman descent. In contrast, Gerard implicitly claims a more honest pedigree when he tells his young companion, Stephen Morley, "my fathers fought at Azincourt," and when his daughter refers to their name as that of "the good old faith" (Bk 2, ch. 8, 97). At the same time Gerard reveals that, with the aid of a mysterious man named Hatton, his father had once obtained a "writ of right" to the lost lands, but that it had disappeared along with Hatton in the confusion of affairs at his death. This chapter concludes with their return to Mowbray, where Sybil lives in a convent, and with the indication in their farewells that Morley is in love with her although he has no religious faith.

Given the emphasis placed upon the corrupt genealogies of Lord Marney and the Earl of Mowbray,[14] and given the details of Walter Gerard's claim to be the heir to the lost estates of an ancient family, probably of Saxon roots, it is difficult to see why the theme of dispossession is not recognized more widely as the structural framework of the novel. And given the limits of Sybil's characterization, confined initially almost entirely to her tedious religiosity, her striking beauty, and her filial devotion, it is equally difficult to imagine that Disraeli intended her to be a representative, that is, typical working-class heroine. Part of such a reading may come from Gerard's active role among the Chartists and from his and Sybil's talk about restoring "the people to their land" (Bk 2. ch. 8, 96), but most of it derives from the sheer vitality of the working-class world Disraeli does depict, and from the mediating role

Sybil plays amid the scenes of working-class misery and popular agitation. She certainly sees herself as the moral representative of the people. But even readers who see the emblematic quality of Sybil's character often fail to recognize the intent of the allegory of which she is a part. Daniel Schwarz, for example, describes Sybil as "an *emblem*, within the novel's dialectic, for the potential of the Church," and he recognizes that Disraeli wishes her "to represent the spiritual values that England requires," but he does not take his own insight seriously enough to overcome his assumptions that the novel is an exposure of the "Two Nations," and that the concluding marriage is a failed attempt to bridge the "schism between rich and poor."[15]

To understand the full meaning of Sybil's emblematic role, it is essential to see the significance of other characters in the larger allegorical romance. Inevitably this brings one to Disraeli's peculiar ideas about Christianity and Judaism, and to his feelings about Roman Catholicism. One such emblematic figure is Aubrey St Lys, the new vicar of Mowbray church. His name literally embodies his true nobility, saintliness, and purity – the lily, of course, having a rich symbolic value within both Catholic and Anglican liturgies of the Resurrection and the Annunciation, as well as heraldic resonance with French royalty and nobility.[16] But the pronunciation of his name, clearly "sin-less" (by comparison with that of Disraeli's favourite Tory philosopher, Henry St John, Viscount Bolingbroke, whose family name is pronounced "sinjin"), also makes it clear that he is more than a character within a realistic social context. Disraeli presents St Lys as a man who has accepted a divine mission, although his talents would have justified a richer ecclesiastical or secular preferment. Prior to his arrival, the narrator says, "the frigid spell of Erastian self-complacency fatally prevailed" in the magnificent and beautiful church built centuries earlier by the monks of Mowbray. Indeed, though the building is so glorious as to be appropriate as an episcopal seat, the congregation has dwindled almost to "zero." And so, instead of a bishop, Mowbray received "a humble vicar ... who came among a hundred thousand heathens to preach 'the Unknown god'" (Bk, 2, ch. 11, 125).

Part of St Lys's mission is to be an agent of divine consolation, charity, and mercy for the destitute and dying. This is effectively dramatized in his conversations with Lord Marney about the cruelly low wages paid to his agricultural workers, and in the piteous scenes in the room of Warner, the handloom weaver. There his timely intervention adds both a spiritual sanction to Warner's honesty in the face of starvation and an

institutional corroboration of Sybil's private charity. But the most interesting aspect of St Lys's presence in *Sybil* is his theological influence on
Egremont's thinking. Their conversation, recorded at the end of Book 2,
chapter 12, begins with St Lys blaming only the Church for "all that has
occurred," claiming that the Church deserted the people, thus degrading them and endangering itself. His lament at first passes for a typical
piece of Tractarian or Young England nostalgia for the medieval past
where "religion undertook to satisfy the noble wants of human nature,
and by its festivals relieved the painful weariness of toil." In the past, St
Lys claims, the "day of rest was consecrated, if not always to elevated
thought, at least to sweet and noble sentiments" and "the whole
Christian population" found "in the presence of God," that they were
all "brethren." And, he reminds Egremont, "under its splendid and almost celestial roofs amid the finest monuments of art that human hands
have raised," the church "shared equally among all its prayer, its in-
cense, and its music; its sacred instructions, and the highest enjoyments
that the arts could afford" (Bk 2, ch. 12, 129). Certainly this emphasis
upon the "essentially spiritual" existence of all art would have sounded
an alarmingly Puseyite tone in the ears of Disraeli's readers. Before addressing that issue, however, it is important to see that St Lys's exaltation of a community based upon the union of all people under God and
made literally harmonious by religious forms and ceremonies, is a direct alternative to the secular community of human purpose based upon
"co-operation" and "association," which was advocated by Stephen
Morley, the author of the "Two Nations" paradox (Bk 2, ch. 5).

Disraeli's admiration for St Lys's Tractarian mystical aesthetics is, no
doubt, genuine, but he is well aware (as who was not in 1845, a few
months before Newman's formal defection) of the political dangers of
Tractarian ideas. Egremont directly addresses the Romish tendencies
when he protests that the people of England associate such forms and
ceremonies "with an enthralling superstition and a foreign dominion"
(Bk 2, ch. 12, 130). St Lys's response is crucial to our reading of Disraeli's
allegorical intentions, for it not only defuses the paranoia about the
"Romish system," but also provides the theological basis for the concluding marriage of a Protestant hero and a Catholic heroine. St Lys
argues that, "as the only Hebraeo-christian church extant," the Church
of Rome must be respected, for even its intervening excesses should not
"make us forget its early and apostolic character, when it was fresh
from Palestine and as it were fragrant from Paradise." Palestine and
Paradise are in apposition because the Judaic and Christian religions

are one, the latter form being the fulfilment of the former. St Lys points out that the apostles succeeded the prophets and that "Our Master announced himself as the last of the prophets" who were in turn "the heirs of the patriarchs." As a consequence, St Lys argues, the rituals they have been discussing are the products of a continuity far older than the establishment of the Church of Rome: "The second Testament is avowedly only a supplement ... Christianity is completed Judaism, or it is nothing ... the order of our priesthood comes directly from Jehovah; and the forms and ceremonies of His church are the regulations of His supreme intelligence ... I recognize in the church an institution thoroughly, sincerely catholic: adapted to all climes and to all ages" (Bk 2, ch. 12, 130–1). These claims bear a close relation to Sidonia's emphasis upon the genius of the Jews in *Coningsby*; they are also an anticipation of the great Asian mystery which is the putative climax of Disraeli's next novel, *Tancred; or, the New Crusade*.

It is clear that St Lys speaks for his author – Disraeli used almost identical arguments both in speaking in the House of Commons on the subject of Jewish disabilities and in his biography, *Lord George Bentinck* (1852): "Who can deny that Jesus of Nazareth, the Incarnate Son of the Most High God, is the eternal glory of the Jewish race?"[17] The lesson that Egremont thus learns is that a recognition of the true "Hebraeo-Christian" catholicity of the Church renders the distinction between Protestant and Catholic merely perversely political. *Sybil* thus embodies a very old Disraelian theme, for the marriage of Protestant and Catholic protagonists is a central feature of *Henrietta Temple* (1836), *Contarini Fleming* (1832), and *The Young Duke* (1831). Earlier I have argued that in his fiction Disraeli disguised his ambivalence about his Jewish heritage in this recurring Catholic motif, partly because the Catholic issue was of much stronger public interest than the matter of Jewish disabilities. In *Sybil* Disraeli is able to integrate the reality and the disguise so that the individual question of religious identity comes to serve his vision of an ideal relation between religion and politics, between church and state. And in *Sybil*, to a degree greater than in his earlier works, the realm of private fantasy embodied in the romance of Egremont's pursuit of Sybil is successfully integrated with the realm of public debate about the condition of England.

III

Like Carlyle, Disraeli sees the social and economic crisis of the 1840s as a symptom of a moral collapse. This view expresses itself in the very

structuring of *Sybil*. Many critics have remarked upon the juxtapos-
itions of scenes of aristocratic wealth and working-class poverty, but the
structuring is more complex and ideational than that formula of simple
contrasts suggests. For example, immediately after Egremont's conversation with St Lys, Disraeli presents the pathetic scene in Warner's
room, where the weaver is struggling valiantly to finish a task which
may bring the price of a meal for his ill and starving family on the verge
of eviction. Here the theme of dispossession is renewed in Warner's
reverie about why workers like himself were driven from their "innocent and happy homes" and "country cottages" to face life in cellars and
squalid lairs "without even the common necessaries of existence" (Bk 2,
ch. 13, 134). It is perfectly clear, even to him, that the laissez-faire argument that "the interests of Capital and of Labour are identical" does not
address the moral issue in the fate of "the race whose only property is
labour," and who, though "innocent," have lost their "estates." Even
though the metaphor lies in Warner's nostalgic imagination, the linking
of his sense of dispossession to Walter Gerard's leaves Disraeli open to
the charge of mangling the factual truth. But perhaps he is not so guilty
of distorting the psychological one, for victims of other people's greed
or indifference no doubt felt the truth of such metaphors as much in the
1840s as at any time before or since. In any case, Disraeli's purpose here
is also to create the first meeting between Egremont and Sybil in a moment of mutual charity that Egremont later describes as a "mission of
grace" (Bk 3, ch. 5, 198), and then to complicate his romantic desire with
her disgust for the owners of Marney Abbey.

The stagecraft involved in making his hero's identity a central concern of both the plot and the theme is typical of the method in romantic
novels in general and Disraeli's in particular. But Egremont lacks the
intense ambivalence about himself that is characteristic of virtually all
of Disraeli's earlier protagonists from Vivian Grey to Harry Coningsby.
In *Sybil* Disraeli makes the question of identity one of public vocation,
just as he attempted to do in *Coningsby*. In the earlier novel, however,
the conflict between altruism and expediency is partly projected outward onto other characters such as Sidonia, and partly subsumed by
the magic and purity of Coningsby's reciprocated love for Edith
Millbank. By contrast, Egremont's ambitions are completely dissolved
in his duty, and his political career emerges with the unassailable sanction of being a religious vocation.[18]

The first evidence that Egremont conceives of his political career as
a "mission of grace" is a small but intrusive detail. When (he having
returned to London and taken up his seat in Parliament) his mother

asks him to accept a birthday present from among her possessions, Egremont chooses a picture that reminds him of Sybil and the "portrait of a female saint" which she had placed "over the mantle-piece" of her father's cottage. His choice is "the portrait of a saint by Allori: the face of a beautiful young girl, radiant and yet solemn, with rich tresses of golden brown hair, and large eyes dark as night, fringed with ebon lashes that hung upon the glowing cheek" (Bk 4, ch. 2, 244). Then, three chapters later, when Gerard and Morley arrive at his rooms as Chartist delegates in their canvass of MPs, the portrait is mentioned again in a way that indicates its real symbolic importance, not just as an icon of romantic memory, but also as one of guiding spiritual force:[19] "Egremont was seated in his library, at a round table covered with writing materials, books, and letters … his parliamentary papers and piles of blue books. The room was classically furnished. On the mantlepiece were some ancient vases, which he had brought from Italy, standing on each side of that picture of Allori of which we have spoken" (Bk 4, ch. 5, 266). This description is meant to confirm for the reader the transformation that Egremont has undergone, from being a languorous aristocrat who stood for Parliament "at the instigation of the family" and from "no feeling of his own" (Bk 3, ch. 2, 177), to an energetic representative of the people's interests, who in his new vigour can only mock those of his own class who think of politics as a game of social intrigue, where all the "power, patronage, and pay" are reserved for a small circle of self-indulgent, vapid, noble society (Bk 4, ch. 3, 248). An example of this is his forthright attack on Lady St Julians and Lady Firebrace, who think that they can govern the world by their "social influences": "'asking people once or twice a-year to an inconvenient crowd in your house; now haughtily smirking, and now impertinently staring, at them; and flattering yourselves all this time, that to have the occasional privilege of entering your saloons and the periodical experience of your insolent recognition, is to be a reward for great exertions, or if necessary an inducement to infamous tergiversation'" (Bk 4, ch. 3, 250).

This transformation, which is actually a realization of his innate character, takes place during the period of his earlier sojourn (in disguise as Mr Franklin) as a neighbour of Gerard and his daughter in Mowedale. Central to Egremont's new understanding of "the condition of the people" is his visit to Trafford's model factory. Here the true "baronial principle" has been revived in the practice of industrial feudalism to create an idyllic village where the moral and physical well-being of the whole population is the result of the proprietor's paternal, loving concern. At the centre of this community, whose every detail has been designed to foster the "domestic virtues," lies a "gothic church," which "Mr. Trafford, though a Roman Catholic, had raised and endowed" (Bk 3, ch. 8, 211–12). It is to this church that Egremont pays a visit when Lord de Mowbray and his entourage suddenly arrive to inspect Trafford's factory. The symbolism of the action is clear, for any other retirement would just as easily have preserved his incognito. But clearly Egremont wishes specifically to deny his association with the spirit of secular grandeur and the unwarranted differentiation of rank embodied in the "pretension," "pride," and "condescension" of the de Mowbrays (Bk 3, ch. 8, 213–16).

At the same time Disraeli reinforces the previous strong hints in his theme of dispossession. First, the narrator comments that after his tour of the works, Lord de Mowbray was "profuse of praise and compliments ... His lordship was apt to be too civil. The breed would come out sometimes. Today he was quite the coffee-house waiter. He praised everything: the machinery, the workmen, the cotton manufactured and the raw cotton, even the smoke" (Bk 3, ch. 8, 214–15). A moment later, as the conversation of the luncheon party turns to the subject of Sybil's beauty, Lady Maud de Mowbray is so astonished to learn that Sybil is Gerard's daughter that she twice in one sentence refers to him as that "so very aristocratic-looking ... person" she had seen in the factory (Bk 3, ch. 8, 216). Finally, after the de Mowbrays' departure, Gerard tells Egremont (Franklin):

> "A year ago this earl had a son – an only son, and then his daughters were not great heiresses. But the son died and now it's their turn. And perhaps some day it will be somebody else's turn. If you want to understand the ups and downs of life, there's nothing like the parchmounts of an estate. Now master, now man! He who served in the hall now lords in it; and very often the base born change their liveries for coronets, while gentle blood has nothing left but – dreams; eh, master Franklin?" (Bk 3, ch. 8, 218–19)

The chapter in which this passage occurs follows immediately upon those in which Morley, in quest of Gerard's lost family documents, tracks down the brother of the mysterious Hatton at Wodgate. And it immediately precedes that in which Gerard remarks to Morley upon the strangeness of his meeting Lord de Mowbray face to face: "'He offered me money when it was over ... I would not look at it. Though to be sure, they were perhaps my own rents, eh?'" (Bk 3, ch. 9, 223). It is a fine point, but Disraeli seems to use the habitual colloquial interjection as a verbal echo to link this conversation to the earlier one with Egremont, for it has previously been used sparingly. In any case, it is clear that only by ignoring her obvious symptoms of good breeding and neglecting the more intrusive elements of the dispossession theme can a reader interpret Sybil to be a working-class heroine, or be truly surprised at the revelation, or rather, confirmation of her nobility.

Just as important to an understanding of Disraeli's intentions in the first half of the novel is an awareness of how Stephen Morley's ideas are undercut. Apart from the several references to his lack of religious faith, there are some dramatic incidents which demonstrate that within the larger allegorical romance his ideas are a foil for Disraeli's main thesis. On the way to Wodgate he stops in a colliery village where, in the local pub, he explains his "principle of association" and the advantages of cooperative living to the miners grumbling about tommy shops. But Mr Nixon's pithy comment, "Sir ... you speak like a book," in conjunction with the narrator's summary of abuses of children's employment in the mines and the specific grievances of the men, is a devastating, contemptuous retort to Morley's assertions of the people's "rights" and "power" (Bk 3, ch. 1, 168). Morley seems more sensitive when he next intervenes at Diggs's tommy shop to assist the young boy injured in the brutal crush (Bk 3, ch. 3, 186–7). He does this by threatening to expose Diggs and his son in the *Mowbray Phalanx* as "oppressors of the people," unless they carry the boy to a warm bed in their house. But such sympathy is, perhaps, suspect, for it is arguably a hollow victory for a radical journalist to buy a moment of forced kindness with his silence.

Disraeli is much less ambiguous when he has Morley reject as "unnatural" the example of Trafford's altruistic concern for his workers' domestic virtue. He argues that "the irresistible law of progress" demands that the "domestic principle" should be replaced: "'In the present state of civilization and with the scientific means of happiness at our command, the notion of home should be obsolete. Home is a barbarous idea; the method of a rude age; home is isolation; therefore antisocial. What we want is Community'" (Bk 3, ch. 9, 225). Apart from the fact that Gerard and Sybil both disagree with Morley, the reader is also guided by the narrator's previous endorsement of Trafford's views: he had "imbibed" a "correct conception of the relations which should subsist between the employer and the employed" and, having "deeply ... pondered" upon his possible influence, he "knew well that domestic virtues are dependent on the existence of a home" (Bk 3, ch. 8, 210–11).

The results of Trafford's efforts speak for themselves; in his village there is cleanliness and order, crime and drunkenness are unknown, the people are well-clad and the "moral condition of the softer sex" has been "proportionately elevated" (Bk 3, ch. 8, 212). Finally, Morley's claim to the reader's intellectual sympathies is completely destroyed in the last chapter of Book 3. Here Disraeli descends to comic pathos in using the affections of Sybil's "Saxon" bloodhound, Harold, to indicate both her fondness for the still-disguised Egremont and Morley's violent intentions. But in having the utopian, secular rationalist driven to attempted murder by his sexual jealousy, Disraeli is undermining all of the ideas, including that of the "Two Nations," which that utilitarian frame of mind has produced.[20] In effect, Morley is shown not to be wicked, but perverse, for he has developed a materialist conception of human nature which ignores the very aspects of it that Disraeli sees as fundamental to humanity's morality and happiness.

IV

The development of Disraeli's religious allegory does not depend solely upon the overtly sincere emblematic elements of his romantic plot. It also comprises parodic elements, which in effect are illustrations of the antithetical, or Satanic, view of society. The most obvious of these parodies are the scenes in Wodgate (otherwise known as "Hell-house Yard") and the investiture of Dandy Mick into a trades union. In the former, "Bishop" Hatton presides over a secular hell in which all of the principles of Christian civilization have been inverted. Wodgate has no Church, no government, no magistrate, no schools; and the working population of this "most hideous burgh" exists amid "gutters of abomination" and "pools of filth," in a state of complete degradation and "savage instinct."[21] It is ironic that in Wodgate, "Labour reigns supreme," for the manufacture of ironmongery is carried on in the form of a pre-industrial guild. And equally so, the masters form a "real aristocracy" which earns its privileges. As the very name of the town indicates, Disraeli intends here to illustrate the perverse consequences of such forms when inspired by pagan rather than Christian values. This is also the function of the Satanic sacrament of marriage in which the bishop, Tummas tells Morley, "'sprinkled some salt over a grid-iron, read 'Our Father' backwards, and wrote our name in a book'" (Bk 3, ch. 4, 194). Equally obvious in its purpose is Sue's statement of their creed: "'He believes now in our Lord and Saviour Pontius Pilate who was crucified to save our sins; and in Moses, Goliath, and the rest of the Apostles'" (ibid.). Disraeli's wit, it should be noted, is deadly serious, for embodied in the Dantesque infernal scenes of grotesque physical deformities, horrifying punishments, and the incessantly compelled motion of the files is the central vision of life governed not by love and charity, but by fear and violence.

The same inversion of religious values is the most salient characteristic of Dandy Mick's induction into a trades union. The torch-lit procession in "mystic robes" and "secret masks," the blindfolding before being thrust kneeling into the presence of the "SEVEN," the skeleton, the marshals with swords and battle-axes, and the mystic rhymes are all kin to the diabolic rituals in gothic fiction. Further, the demonic impact of the scene is enhanced by the use of such religious language as "prayer," "Hymn," "neophyte," and "sacred volume"; for what Mick Radley is required to swear in the name of "Almighty God" is his willingness to "execute with zeal and alacrity" whatever "chastisement ... assassination ... and demolition" is imposed as his task. Disraeli thus satirizes the notion that such unholy "Brethren" could be furthering the "common welfare" (Bk 4, ch. 4, 254–7).

Again it is worth noticing that Disraeli's control of the episodic structure continually reinforces the central religious allegory. The trades union initiation is followed by the chapter in which Egremont is at work in his study beneath the inspiring picture of the saint by Allori discussed above. Then immediately following is the symbolic, seemingly chance meeting between Egremont and Sybil in Westminster Abbey. That scene begins with the narrator discoursing on the general purifying and elevating influence of sacred buildings and then protesting the "mean discipline and sordid arrangements," which "injure and impair the holy genius" of the abbey by confining the public to small portions of the building. Although on his first visit Egremont had felt "as if the Abbey were in a state of siege" and had been outraged to find "iron gates shutting him out from the solemn nave and the shadowy aisles," it has become his favourite habit to retreat there from the "dull" debates in Parliament to listen to the "celestial symphony" of the organ. A similar delight, the narrator suggests, brings Sybil to stand just before the Poets' Corner, against "the iron grating that shut her out from the body of the church," looking "wistfully down the long dim perspective of the beautiful southern aisle" (Bk 4, ch. 6, 267–9). Just as Egremont comes forth from the choir his eye catches, but does not immediately recognize, "the symmetry of her shape and the picturesque position which she gracefully occupied; still gazing through that gate, while the light pouring forth through the western window, suffused the body of the church with a soft radiance, just touching the head of the unknown with a kind of halo" (Bk 4, ch. 6, 270). Because of its representation of a national Church in need of reclamation, and of a figure of saintly piety excluded from the centre of that Church – albeit in part from her own prejudice and naivety – this scene ought to be recognized as the core of Disraeli's allegorical romance of secular politics and spiritual devotion.

But many readers focus instead upon the ostensible realism of class distinction in Sybil's rejection of Egremont, once she learns his true identity: "'the gulf is impassable … utterly impassable'" (Bk 4, ch. 8, 286). To do so is to mistake the contrivance of plot for thematic concern. The narrator, who can be taken as a reliable guide to Disraeli's views, describes Egremont's momentary despair in terms of Sybil's "prejudices and convictions more impassable than all the mere consequences of class" (Bk 4, ch. 8, 287). This contrasting comparison suggests that what Sybil must give up in recognizing and accepting Egremont's true nobility and moral vocation is not only her false dichotomy of the "Two Nations," but also the fanatical exclusivity of her "old faith." This is the reason that within the allegory both Trafford and "Baptist" Hatton are Catholics, the former a model of ecumenical charity, the latter a master of deceit, who profanely rationalizes his own scheming fantasy of marrying Sybil and producing a noble son as a "glorious vision" of restoring an old Catholic family to its former greatness (Bk 4, ch. 10, 296).

"Baptist" Hatton's acknowledgment to Gerard that "'on every principle of justice … Mowbray Castle is as much yours as the house that is built by the tenant on the lord's land'" (Bk 4, ch. 9, 292), his courtesy to "Lady Sybil," his reflection that he has deprived her of "a principality," and his fantasy of restoring her to "the rank she would honour," and thus assuaging the "sharp pangs of conscience" and achieving through marriage to her "the secret ambition" of his life (Bk 4, ch. 10, 295–6) all cast an ironic light on Sybil's subsequent claims to be "a daughter of the people" (Bk 4, ch. 15, 324). The point of such irony is not, however, to undermine her moral identification with "the people," but to show that her conception of them is as mistaken as are her notions of the aristocracy. It does this in part by making it clear that the accidents of her humble birth and education are as confining as those of Egremont's nobility. The shape of the allegorical romance is, therefore, that of their mutual transcendence of these limitations through their reciprocal powers of inspiration. Just as Egremont admits that her beauty has been master of his spirit, so Sybil comes to acknowledge that his love determines her fate.

Unfortunately, the simplicity of this romance tempts the reader to oversimplify Disraeli's depiction of social class.[22] The process of Sybil's re-education discredits the view that Disraeli intends merely to expose the social reality of the two nations. Egremont calls her idealistic notions of the people's strength and integrity, "fallacious fancies," and he insists that her dualistic "phantoms," the oppressors and the oppressed, are not an accurate representation of either human nature or society. Further, he predicts that the ideals of the Chartist Convention will end in factions, betrayal, and violence. Of course, Sybil's experiences in London soon confirm these lessons, for she soon learns that the world is "a more complicated system" than she had previously thought; that "characters were more various … motives more mixed, the classes more blended" than she had imagined. She also begins to see that the feeling of the rich towards the poor was not that "unmingled hate and scorn which she associated with Norman conquerors and feudal laws," and she ascribes the "want of sympathy between Wealth and Work in England" to mutual ignorance between the working and more prosperous classes (Bk 5, ch. 1, 337–8). It is in this frame of mind that she reads Egremont's speech from the debate on the National Petition and begins to realize the power of moral commitment wedded to secular position: "Yes, there was one voice that … had dared to express immortal truths: the voice of a noble, who without being a demagogue, had upheld the popular cause; and pronounced his conviction that the rights of labour were as sacred as those of property … who had declared that the social happiness of the millions should be the first object of a statesman" (Bk 5, ch. 1, 339). Egremont's speech is an echo of the one Disraeli made on the subject of the Chartists' petition on 12 July 1839. There he argued that the real causes of the Chartist movement stemmed from the pernicious effects of the Reform Bill, which had created a powerful new class with political rights but no corresponding social duties. Under the old constitutional arrangement, he insisted, political rights were entrusted to "a small portion of the nation" on the condition that "they should guard the civil rights of the great multitude." But with the transfer of those social duties to a centralized government, as for example in the administration of justice, the public employment of labour, and the distribution of relief to the destitute, the working poor sensed that their civil rights had been invaded: they were taught that the destitute must "not ... look for relief to those who were their neighbours, but to a distant Government stipendiary"; they were taught that "the unfortunate labourer ... had no legal claim to relief – that the relief he should receive must be an affair of charity."[23] Egremont's sympathetic response to the cause of the labouring poor, without any belief in the mechanism of the charter, is thus a mirror of Disraeli's. And it is with Egremont's convictions to support her that Sybil learns that her father has become entangled in a conspiracy against the state. At the same time she finds that Morley, the utilitarian idealist and advocate of moral power, has been reduced by the exigencies of his "indecent" passion for her to the "pollution" of slander, blackmail, and blasphemy (Bk 5, ch. 4, 352–8).

The implications of such knowledge are dramatized in the ensuing search for her father through the slums of Seven Dials, which is both literally and figuratively a descent to the underworld. The full impact of Disraeli's ironic use of class in the novel is felt here, for although the narrator describes the houses, population, costume, manners, and language of this district as "of a different state and nation to those with which the dwellers in the dainty quarters of this city are acquainted," the emphasis is not upon poverty. Indeed, the impression conveyed of the life in the streets is one of vulgar, but fascinating vitality: "They were plunged into a labyrinth of lanes ... where the dog-stealer and the pick-pocket, the burglar and the assassin, found comrades for every enterprise; and a market for every booty ... A multitude were sauntering in the mild though tainted air; bargaining, blaspheming, drinking, wrangling; and varying their business and their potations, their fierce strife and their impious irreverence, with flashes of rich humour, gleams of native wit, and racy phrases of idiomatic slang" (Bk 5, ch. 6, 365). Disraeli's point is that this is a world of complete moral depravity, so much so that he knows he is challenging the middle-class boundaries of innocence and purity (and even the limits of what is acceptable in fiction) by having Sybil traverse it. After all, she is not only confronted by thieves and a half-naked, drunken woman with "brutality stamped on every feature," she is "overwhelmed with shame and terror" when she finds herself invited to enter a brothel (Bk 5, ch. 6, 368). That such a descent into humanity is an integral part of Disraeli's allegorical theme is shown by the way she is protected from the entirely plausible fate worse than death. In chapter 4 of Book 5 when Morley, having already sneered at the power of "the Holy Virgin," nevertheless attempts to force Sybil to foreswear her love for Egremont in the name of the Holy Virgin, by all the saints, and by her hope of heaven, she "became white as the marble saint of some sacred niche" (Bk 5, ch. 4, 357). But when she faltered, "a burning brightness ... suffused the cheek of Sybil," causing Morley to rush out frantically and abandon her in the extremity of her fears for her father's safety. She then sets out upon her search, which takes her into the criminal underworld, with the courage and faith inspired by prayer and with "a conviction of celestial aid" (Bk 5, ch. 5, 359). That celestial aid appears in the form of the good and presumably sober Irishman who hears her cry of alarm, "'O! holy Virgin aid me!'" and who, replying "'that's a blessed word to hear in this heathen land,'" undertakes to guide "a sister in Christ" to her true destination (Bk 5, ch. 6, 368).

In this paradigmatic encounter Sybil is both a victim rescued and an agent of redemption. This episode reveals as well as any in the book how Disraeli furthers his political allegory by blending the conventions of realism and romance. Much the same point can be made about the often remarked upon shifts from the scenes of poverty to scenes of wealth. But in juxtaposing the incidents in Seven Dials to the grand ball at Deloraine House, Disraeli is as much interested in the moral comparison as the theatrical contrast. This is made explicit by the double perspective. The members of the *beau-monde* are shown to be every bit as morally depraved as are the denizens of the criminal slums, both by the selfish intrigues that consume their thoughts and by the conversations of the destitute and homeless vagrants lying in the darkness of the park opposite the brilliantly lit mansion, of whom the noble guests are completely unaware. By such means Disraeli is constantly making the point that "the degradation of the people" is the result, not of economic circumstances, but of immoral leadership. In other words, his social and political satire of both upper and lower classes is an integral part of his illustration that the lamentable "condition of England" is a symptom, not a cause, of moral depravity.

V

Readers who are dissatisfied with the conclusion of *Sybil* have good grounds for their discontent, even though Disraeli cannot justifiably be convicted of the imaginative "tommyrot" of converting his "daughter of the People" into an aristocrat. Sybil's identification with the "People" is largely a moral one. And the theme of Gerard's dispossession is so strong throughout that there is a constant ironic light cast upon her naivety about social class. Nevertheless, the conclusion seems unsatisfactory because the exigencies of the romance plot become too intrusive. Like the wish-fulfilment fantasies of some fairy tales, the climactic scenes of the riot at Mowbray Castle dispose of all the characters who stand in the way of the symbolic consummation Disraeli has in mind. Lord Marney, Walter Gerard (who was convicted and jailed for his Chartist conspiracy), and Stephen Morley ("the Apostle of Community") are all dispatched in violent deaths which are the consequences of their moral errors. Disraeli thereby denounces the selfish indifference of the aristocracy, the temptation to use violent means for the redress of grievances, and the distortion of love in the motives of abstractly rational utopian thought. But in so abandoning the balance of genres that has characterized his novel thus far, he disappoints the reader intent on realism by seeming to undermine the public significance of the symbolic union he has laboured to create.

Seen as the completion of a religious allegorical romance, however, the conclusion of *Sybil* is less troubling. Disraeli's view of the Chartist movement, for example, is revealed by the delightful irony that the "Chartist Apostle," Field, succeeds in converting the illiterate "Bishop" Simon Hatton to the belief that, by leading an insurrection of the "Hell-Cats," he will be the liberator of the people (Bk 6, ch. 6, 435–6). But as such he is really a parodic disciple of the Antichrist, as is suggested by the image of him mounted on "a white mule, wall-eyed and of hideous form," brandishing "a huge hammer" (Bk 6, ch. 6, 436). In the end the "Utopia of Toil" brings destruction to every place he visits. Disraeli turns the "Bishop" into a ridiculous figure, clamouring for fire with which to destroy Trafford's idyllic factory, but he is finally consumed in the flames of the conflagration of Mowbray Castle ("the funeral pile of the children of Woden," Bk 6, ch. 12, 485–6) that his own besotted followers set. By contrast, St Lys reappears and is described as a check to Chartist violence as he uses every opportunity to preach sermons on the theme of "Fear God and honour the King" (Bk 5, ch. 10, 394; Bk 6, ch. 9, 453). In the midst of the riot at Mowbray Castle, St Lys rallies the honest workmen of Mowbray "in the name of God," and he combines with Sybil to rescue Lady de Mowbray and her daughters from the murderous mob and its "deed of darkness" (Bk 6, ch. 12, 477–8).

The extensive ironic use of religious epithets and allusions ("Bishop *Simon*," "Baptist," "Apostle," "Hell-Cats") in contrast to the saintly imagery of the devout struggles of Egremont, Sybil, and St Lys, indicates that Disraeli wants to represent the consequence of conceiving England to be Two Nations as an infernal version of the Gospel. And given this inversion, the climactic and penultimate episode must also be read symbolically. When Egremont, in command of a troop of yeomen, arrives to rout the mob, his valorous, melodramatic rescue of Sybil, literally from the hands of a band of drunken ruffians, is, in effect, the deliverance of the Church from the imminent moment of its desecration:

> One ruffian had grasped the arm of Sybil, another had clenched her garments, when an officer covered with dust and gore, sabre in hand, jumped from the terrace, and hurried to the rescue. He cut down one man, thrust away another, and placing his left arm around Sybil, he defended her with his sword … Her assailants were routed, they made a staggering flight! the officer turned round and pressed Sybil to his heart.
>
> "We will never part again," said Egremont.
> "Never," murmured Sybil. (Bk 6, ch. 12, 486)

Disraeli's resolution of the dichotomy of the Two Nations is, thus, to wed the compassionate secular leadership of true nobility to the spirit of piety and devotion in a pure Christian faith.

The political implications of this resolution are suggested in the denouement, when, after the marriage of Egremont and Sybil, both of whom have succeeded to their titles, the narrator endorses the allegory's harmonious vision of One Nation: "There is a whisper rising in this country that Loyalty is not a phrase, Faith not a delusion, and Popular Liberty something more diffusive and substantial than the profane exercise of the sacred rights of sovereignty by political classes" (Bk 6, ch. 13, 492). Clearly, a society based on common loyalty, faith, and liberty would subsume the potentially divisive distinctions of wealth, class, and religious practice, which would then cease to corrupt the aristocracy and degrade the people.

The vision of society expressed in *Sybil* is thus consistent with the ideals of Young England embodied in *Coningsby* and with the characteristic ideas of Disraeli's ideological commitment in the 1830s to the theory of the mixed constitution, wherein in a society conceived as organic in nature, the true representatives of the people are the aristocracy and the Church. *Sybil* is, however, very different from *Coningsby* and Disraeli's earlier novels because there is an allegorical rather than a psychological romance blended with the sympathetic and satirical material derived from his own "observation" of life.[24] The reader of *Sybil* who notices the religious intent of that allegorical romance cannot but conclude that Disraeli achieved his later stated purpose of examining both "the condition of the people" and "the duties of the Church as a main remedial agency."[25] But the contemporary response to the novel, like much recent criticism, did not focus on the latter intention as often as the author might have wished. This may in part be because the exigencies of the allegorical romance are often in conflict with the claims of plausibility and truth which are supposed to inform the social-problem novel. On those grounds it might be better to conclude that because its religious theme strikes the social realist as unworldly and impractical, *Sybil*, not *Coningsby*, should be considered Disraeli's "manifesto of Young England."[26]

11

Rhetoric, Principles, and Expediency: The Corn Law Debate of 1846 and the Politics of Protection

Sir Robert Peel's conversion from Protectionism to free trade and his decision to repeal the Corn Law need to be seen not only in the context of Chartist agitations and the campaign of the Anti-Corn Law League, led by Richard Cobden from 1838 onwards. His reversal of policy needs to be seen, as well, in the light of the practical exigencies the Government faced with the growing unemployment and extreme poverty in England's industrial centres during the "hungry forties," and with the agricultural crisis that rapidly developed in 1845 with the failure of the potato crop in Ireland and the grain crops in England. In Ireland there was such widespread distress among the peasants that more than a million people died of starvation and another million or more emigrated to America. In England, meanwhile, there were frequent insolvencies among the farmers and desperate conditions among the agricultural labourers and their families. As was mentioned earlier, Peel had been convinced for some time that repeal of the Corn Law was justified on rational, philosophical grounds, but he also felt that immediate action on his part could only be justified by the unfolding emergency.[1] The political problem he had was twofold: he knew that even immediate and total repeal would not avert the catastrophe in Ireland, and he knew that most members of the Conservative party would not support such a change.

Chapter 3 of *Lord George Bentinck* is exclusively devoted to the events of the opening night of debate in the new session of the House of Commons in 1846. The pervasive irony and sarcasm of Disraeli's account of Sir Robert Peel's speech on that night reveal, even in retrospect, the extent to which he anticipated and recognized that the prime minister's dull probity and his own sardonic wit were the perfect symbiosis of the moment. The prime minister's speech, he reports, was "not distinguished by that clear conception ... lucid arrangement, and ... prudential management" which were characteristic of his general style. Rather, though elaborate, it was "confused and ... even contradictory." Peel initially had the full attention of all of his listeners when he announced that his opinions on the subject of Protection had changed, for his confession led the more "credulous bosoms among his former supporters ... to ask themselves what vague surmise could be more horrible than the reality, and why he should wish to be heard previous to condemnation, when his vindication was an aggravated avowal of the offence of which he was accused." But, although his audience was "on the tenters" for the promised explanation of the Government's resignation, Peel then began "a lengthened, not to say wearisome discussion, replete with figures," of the tariff alterations of the last four years and all of their effects. The "bewildered" members of the House, Disraeli mockingly adds, found themselves "listening once more to lucid narratives of the price of flax and wool ... some dissertation on domestic lard, the contract price for salt beef for the navy, and the importation of foreign cattle," so that they "almost began to believe ... that the huge vagaries of December were but a hideous dream, and that instead of defection and perfidy, the great conservative party were only going through that gradual process of decomposition and destruction to which ... they had become accustomed, and which, judging from their demeanour, it would seem they rather liked."[2]

By Disraeli's own retrospective account it seemed that, after Lord John Russell had followed the prime minister with his "authentic statement of Whig disasters," the debate might well collapse, much to the advantage of the Government, for the house "was tame and dispirited" (55). But judging from what followed, it is certain that Disraeli had made thorough preparations for the renewal of his attack on Peel and that he was ready to speak on the opening night of the session. Disraeli's speech was a rhetorical masterpiece, not only because his displays of premeditated and spontaneous wit revived the listless spirit of revolt in the Tory ranks, but because he turned each point in Peel's "vindication" into a liability. At the outset Peel had explicitly raised the question of the motives and principles of his own conduct during the parliamentary recess. Disraeli slyly acknowledged that there was indeed a difficulty in finding an historical comparison to "the position of the right hon. gentleman":

The only parallel which I can find is an incident in the late war in the
Levant [between Turkey and Egypt] ... I remember ... when the existence
of the Turkish Empire was at stake, the late Sultan, a man of great energy
and fertile in resources, was determined to fit out an immense fleet to
maintain his empire. Accordingly a vast armament was collected. It consisted of some of the finest ships that were ever built. The crews were
picked men, the officers were the ablest that could be found, and both officers and men were rewarded before they fought. (Much laughter.) There
never was an armament which left the Dardanelles similarly appointed
since the days of Solyman the Great. The Sultan personally witnessed the
departure of the fleet; all the muftis prayed for the expedition, as all the
muftis here prayed for the success of the last general election. Away went
the fleet; but what was the Sultan's consternation when the Lord High
Admiral steered at once into the enemy's port! (Loud laughter and cheers.)
Now, sir, the Lord High Admiral on that occasion was very much misrepresented. He, too, was called a traitor, and he, too, vindicated himself.
'True it is,' said he, 'I did place myself at the head of this valiant armada;
true it is that my Sovereign embraced me; true it is that all the muftis in the
empire offered up prayers for my success; but I have an objection to war. I
see no use in prolonging the struggle, and the only reason I had for accepting the command was that I might terminate the contest by betraying my
master.' (Tremendous Tory cheering.)[3]

There are a number of inaccuracies and fabrications in this account.
For example, the sultan had died just as the fleet left the Dardanelles,
and it seems that the "Capitan Pasha," as the admiral was called, decided to put his fleet under the protection of his nominal enemy because he feared that the new sultan, a boy of sixteen, could not prevent
the Government of the Porte from falling into the hands of conservative extremists. And, in any case, the sultan's original plan of landing
Turkish reinforcements at "Beyrout" had been rendered hopeless by
the decisive defeat and complete routing of the Turkish army in Syria
by the Egyptian forces encamped at Aleppo.[4] The very subject of this
brilliant, extended parallel – "the late war in the Levant" – is, however,
pregnant with implications, for this anecdote is not merely a reflection
of Disraeli's exotic imagination. Indeed, the parallel suggests, as other
elements of the speech and future events will confirm, that there is
a much closer connection between Disraeli's next novel, Tancred; or,
the New Crusade (1847), and the politics of 1846 than has yet been
recognized.

Many of Disraeli's alert listeners would have realized that the structure of this set-piece perfectly paralleled the structure of recent events in England as perceived by the Tories. For both Peel's claim that he had been misrepresented and the Tories' sense of his apostasy are directly echoed and emphasized in the text: "Now, sir, the Lord High Admiral on *that* occasion was very much misrepresented. He, *too*, was called a traitor, and he, *too*, vindicated himself" (emphasis added). Thus the identification of the prime minister with the Lord High Admiral is complete and congruent before the latter confesses his seemingly idealistic, but actually base motives.

At this point the parallel embodies Disraeli's damning indictment of Peel's behaviour, for the Lord High Admiral's acknowledgment, "true it is that my Sovereign embraced me," captures the tone and spirit of Peel's insistence in his speech upon his personal obligation to rescue the Queen from her constitutional difficulties, when in December 1845 Lord John Russell had found that he could not form a Whig government. Even more cogently, the Lord High Admiral's explanation of his action captures the egocentric quality of Peel's peroration, in which he had said: "I will reserve to myself the unfettered power of judging what will be for the public interest. I do not desire to be the Minister of England; but while I am Minister of England I will hold office by no servile tenure (loud cheers); I will hold office unshackled by any other obligation than that of consulting the public interests and providing for the public safety."[5] The final climactic phrase of Disraeli's historical comparison makes the central issue one of Peel's trustworthiness. But in Disraeli's view that issue is directly related to the prime minister's egotism, upon which he had been sarcastically commenting in his letters from Paris. The connection between the two is explicit, for example, in the letter he wrote to Lord John Manners, in which he berated the vanity and ambition that, lacking inspiration, had led Peel to "duplicity."[6]

In a very real sense, then, Disraeli's renewed attack on Peel was a dramatization of his previous judgement. It is marvellously ironic, of course, that this performance involves the complete, but half-real, half-fictional transposition of each other's virtues and vices. It is Peel, not Disraeli, whose words are "rich in egoistic rhetoric"; it is Peel, not Disraeli, who misappropriates for himself a heroic role; and it is Peel, not Disraeli, who stands impugned as untrustworthy. And conversely, it is Disraeli who claims to represent the interests of the Conservative party; and it is Disraeli who stands forth as the man of principled integrity and the defender of the "sacred cause of protection": "my idea of a great statesman is of one who represents a great idea – an idea which may lead him to power, an idea with which he may connect himself, an idea which he may develop, an idea which he may and can impress on the mind and conscience of a nation. That, sir, is my notion of what makes a man a great statesman."[7] Disraeli knew that Peel's conversion to free trade had an explosive power within the Conservative ranks far beyond that of any previous contentions, partly because those in the landed interest foresaw an immediate threat to their prosperity and an ultimate threat to their influence, and partly because Peel's previous change of heart in 1829 on the question of Catholic Emancipation was still remembered by many of the same people as the blackest apostasy. Thus when Disraeli charged Peel with betrayal of his party, he wanted to sound the historic- ally resonant note of Protestant fervour. For that reason, Peel's "courtly language" and emphasis upon his confidential relationship to his sover- eign was the most exquisitely ironic of the transpositions just mentioned, for it enabled Disraeli to undercut the prime minister's vindication with withering sarcasm: "why does he tell us that he has exercised authority and occupied high office under four sovereigns? Because it is a recom- mendation to say, 'This man is able and experienced; the grandfather of our present Sovereign trusted him; a regent and a king trusted him; a king in a revolution trusted him; a Conservative Sovereign trusted him: – he must be wise, able, experienced.'"[8] This particular passage has not been cited in recent biographical extracts of this speech, but it is import- ant, for it shows clearly how Disraeli insists that trust is the essence of all political virtue and the legitimate basis of all political power.

From this principled position Disraeli is able to sustain the onslaught of irony and sarcasm throughout the rest of his reply, first scorning "this great statesman, who talks with a sneer of an ancient monarchy and a proud aristocracy," and then condemning Peel's expedient inconsis- tency by pointing out that he had once "opposed Catholic Emancipation against arguments as cogent as any which the gentleman of the League can now offer, in spite of political expediency a thousand times more urgent than that which now besets them." But it is the mocking rhetoric undermining Peel's character that carries the weight of the argument:

always ready with his arguments and amendments; always ready with his fallacies, ten thousand times exploded; always ready with his Virgilian quo- tations to command a cheer – the moment that an hon. and learned gentle- man [Daniel O'Connell] was returned for the county of Clare, then immediately we saw this right hon. gentleman not ashamed to recall his arguments, not ashamed to confess that he was convinced, but telling us, on the contrary, he should be ashamed if he had not the courage to come forward and propose a resolution exactly contrary to his previous policy."[9]

Given the subtlety and moderation of Disraeli's use of religious affiliation in *Sybil*, and given the significance of the Catholic motif in much of his previous fiction, the exploitation of extreme Protestant sympathies inherent in this comparison of Peel's actions in 1829 and 1846 might well seem little more than expediency itself. But the ambivalence of Disraeli's posture is more complicated than that interpretation allows.

As earlier chapters have shown, Disraeli habitually distinguished between the matter of individual Catholic faith, which he sympathetically portrayed, and the matter of Catholic politics, which he violently rejected. The earlier analysis of *Henrietta Temple*, for example, demonstrates, in the light of its author's vitriolic "No-Popery" in the *Morning Post* of 1835, the central relation of that ambivalence to the conflicts of Disraeli's sense of his identity in the 1830s. No doubt, the medievalizing enthusiasms of Young England, combined with his recent social and parliamentary successes, softened the antithesis for a while, but it is likely, nonetheless, that the antagonism with Peel in 1845 and 1846 revived some of its force. That would seem to be the implication of Disraeli's transposition of their respective virtues and vices whereby Peel and his colleagues are caricatured as "'imps of fame'": "Throw your eyes over the Treasury bench. See stamped on every ingenuous front 'the last infirmity of noble mind.'"[10] In any case, Disraeli concludes this assault on the prime minister by making principles of consistency and loyalty: "Let men stand by the principle by which they rise, right or wrong. I make no exception. If they be in the wrong, they must retire to that shade of private life with which our present rulers have often threatened us ... Do not, then, because you see a great personage giving up his opinions – do not cheer him on, do not give so ready a reward to political tergiversation." Above all, Disraeli argued, you should maintain a demarcation between parties, for the independence of party helps to maintain "the integrity of public men, and the power and influence of Parliament itself."[11] Disraeli's emphasis here upon the party structure of parliamentary government transparently attempts to inflate Peel's intention to abandon Protection into a constitutional issue, but the real effect is to reinforce the Tories' sense of his betrayal, a prerequisite for forcing Peel to resign once again.

Among those in the Tory ranks who most intensely felt betrayed by Peel was Lord George Bentinck, the second son of the Duke of Portland. When Disraeli had first attacked Peel in personal terms in 1845, intimating that the Government might defect from the policy of Protection, Bentinck had in private "violently condemned the unfounded attack" and "impugned the motives of the assailant."[12] And it was precisely because Bentinck had trusted Peel implicitly and absolutely that he now found the prime minister's conduct "dishonourable."[13] Bentinck was well known for his nobility of spirit and his personal courage, and he had, indeed, that "reputation for unbending rectitude that wins the confidence of men." But he was also possessed of a categorical habit of mind and a violent temper that made him "fiercely intolerant of anything like deception."[14] No doubt it was for this reason that the Sir Robert Peel that Bentinck saw after the opening of Parliament in 1846 was not the same gentleman he had previously admired. It does not follow, of course, that because Disraeli was (in Bentinck's eyes) right about Peel's apostasy over the Corn Law, his own motives were pure and disinterested. But it would seem that the transposition of vices and virtues that characterized Disraeli's assaults on Peel also took place in Bentinck's mind, for in the collaboration that followed the attempt to establish a third parliamentary party to resist Peel's proposals, Bentinck seems never to have doubted Disraeli's altruism and sincerity of purpose.

The cynical interpretation of their relationship is that it was a coalition of convenience, that Bentinck, being inexperienced as a speaker, recognized the value of Disraeli's ability in parliamentary debate, and that Disraeli, being unscrupulous, exploited and manipulated Bentinck's friendship to further his own political ambitions. There is some truth in these assertions, but Disraeli's relationship with Lord George Bentinck was far more complex than such cynicism allows. The bond between them grew out of circumstances more private than public, more psychological than political in any ordinary sense. The extraordinary sympathy between the two men, ostensibly so different in background – parentage, education, wealth, social position, and personal habits – arose primarily from each man's peculiar sense of himself and recognition of a similarity in the other. Much of the evidence for this is inferential, but not, I think, ambiguous. Beneath the surface of a life open to disparagement and censure, both men harboured a sense of idealism and purity of motive. And thus each man had an intuitive understanding of the other's rhetoric and views, and came to a recognition of the other's true qualities, no doubt projected in part from his own experience. On the one hand, Bentinck certainly knew that his devotion to horse-racing and his intemperate, vehement character were much criticized by persons of real or supposedly stringent probity. His acerbic cousin, Charles Greville, for example, though obviously motivated by jealousy, catches the flavour of such criticism in his famous memoirs. Acknowledging Bentinck's "indefatigable activity ... intelligence and penetration" in the matter of the "Running Rein" scandal of the 1844 Derby,[15] Greville characterizes Bentinck in less flattering terms:

> "Lord George" is a very great man and I suppose presents himself to the world as the Grand Enemy of every sort and degree of roguery, the Personification of turf honor and honesty! ... What humbug it all is, and if everybody knew all that I know of his tricks and artifices what a rogue he would be thought! ... He has made for himself a peculiar code of morality and honor, and what he has done he thinks he had a right to do; that the game at which he plays warrants deceit and falsehood to a certain extent and in a certain manner. He cannot but know that if all the circumstances relating to Crucifix, by which he won so much money, were revealed they would be considered disgraceful and dishonest; but he no doubt justifies them to himself.[16]

This passage reverberates with parallels to what an unsympathetic critic might say of Disraeli's behaviour in the 1840s. The emphases on trickery, deceitfulness, money, and psychological rationalizations, all suggest the underlying resonances that shaped Disraeli's and Bentinck's relationship. Such resonances were complex as well as reciprocal; Disraeli, well aware that his reputation was his greatest liability, instinctively understood Bentinck's sense of patriotic virtue and duty, and his indignation that he should be thought to be merely serving his private interest in defending the Corn Law. For Bentinck, Peel's decision to modify the duties on corn was an expedient "dishonourable to Parliament,"[17] and hence his own defence of Protection was a matter of principle in both substance and form. And in Bentinck's eyes, because Disraeli was right about Peel's apostasy, it naturally followed that he and Disraeli shared the honour, the principles, and the duty which compelled him to a parliamentary resistance to the government for which he knew he was unsuited.

When Bentinck first asked Disraeli for assistance in expressing the Protectionists' case, he no doubt did so only from the desire to use his rhetorical skills, having himself no experience in debate despite the fact that he had sat in Parliament since 1828. But their immediate sense of the complementary nature of their respective positions soon deepened to an appreciation of each other for the reasons suggested above. Disraeli was certainly adept at the conspiracies of Opposition. Indeed, his earlier role as Lord Lyndhurst's unofficial confidential secretary in the Ultra-Tory schemes of 1835 seems in retrospect to have been the perfect apprenticeship for the relationship he now enjoyed with Bentinck. In that respect, *Lord George Bentinck* is an extremely interesting work, for it embodies the conventions of biography, autobiography, history, and fiction in one narrative to a degree that is surely unique. It has been noticed and often remarked upon that the book contains a curious displacement of Disraeli's role in the events described. Throughout he refers to himself anonymously in the third person, usually with suggestions or explicit avowals of his own subordinate position and contribution. This might be interpreted as merely the conventional modesty of the intimate biographer. But the anonymity is very intrusive, and so this modesty might otherwise be interpreted cynically as a compensatory device by which to deny implicitly the charge frequently made then and since, that Disraeli was manipulating Bentinck for his own advantage. The psychological interpretation can be extended to suggest that this retrospective enhancement of the subject and effacement of the author reflects the natural and inevitable idealization and guilt that Disraeli would have felt upon Bentinck's sudden death in September 1848, which was widely thought to have been precipitated by overwork and exhaustion.

The real nature of Disraeli's relationship to Bentinck is, however, revealed by the ways in which the characterization of the biography approximates that of Disraeli's novels, particularly in *Coningsby* and *Sybil*. In a very real sense Disraeli's Bentinck is the apotheosis of the Young England hero: noble, principled, sensitive, energetic, and courageous. And as such he is also an expression of Disraeli's most romantic sense of his own potential. Disraeli began by noting that Bentinck's political career was "peculiar" in that "he had sate in eight parliaments without having taken part in any great debate, when remarkable events suddenly impelled him to advance and occupy not only a considerable but a leading position in our public affairs."[18] In the portrait that follows, with such details as his "courage," his "lofty spirit," his "mastery of details," his "quick apprehension and ... clear intelligence," it is clear that Disraeli draws upon the idealizations of his previous fictional heroes. But the link between Lord George Bentinck and Harry

Coningsby and Charles Egremont is even more explicit in the reference to Bentinck's sense of duty and devotion which "impelled" him to "relinquish all the ease and pleasure of a patrician existence" to work "eighteen hours a day." The extent to which Disraeli also identifies his own character with Bentinck's is revealed in the references to the "circumstances of great difficulty," the "contrarieties and prejudices" against which he must struggle. Indeed, the profound ambivalences underlying Disraeli's sense of his own position find expression in the explicit denial that Bentinck worked for "a vain and brilliant notoriety" and in the claim that, "sustained only by his own resources," he altruistically sought to advance "principles, the advocacy of which ... was sure to obtain ... only contention and unkindly feelings." It would seem from this that life does indeed imitate art; that Bentinck, with his "original, vigorous and self-schooled intelligence," offered Disraeli exactly what the fiction had recently done, a paradigm for demonstrating the triumph of purity of motive over expediency, principle over ambition.

This theme embodied anew in *Lord George Bentinck* has a dramatic urgency and an authenticity which serve to make the work Disraeli's best fiction; the ultimate imaginative autobiography in which psychological romance and political realism are perfectly blended. This is evident in the reiterations of Bentinck's character: "His eager and energetic disposition; his quick perception, clear judgment, and prompt decision; the tenacity with which he clung to his opinions; his frankness and love of truth; his daring and speculative spirit ... even the fierceness of his hates and prejudices; all combined to form one of those strong characters who whatever may be their pursuit must always direct and lead." And as befits the hero of a romance, the idealization extends to Bentinck's appearance: "Nature had clothed this vehement spirit with a material form ... in perfect harmony with its noble and commanding character. He was tall, and remarkable for his presence; his countenance almost a model of manly beauty; the face oval ... the forehead lofty and white; the nose aquiline and delicately moulded; the upper lip short. But it was in the dark-brown eye that flashed with piercing scrutiny that all the character of the man came forth: a brilliant glance ... acute, imperious, incapable of deception or of being deceived."[19] Although most of this description would fit any of the protagonists of the earlier novels, this passage seems to be atypical of the fiction prior to *Sybil* in one respect. The Disraelian hero is here completely purged of his youthful passivity and ambivalence. In the midst of his political vocation Bentinck is eager, energetic, decisive, tenacious, daring, fierce, and strong. As such he is clearly the worthy object of Disraeli's extravagant admiration. But the most telling detail of the passage, and the one that makes both their relationship and the autobiographical impulse of the work most clear, is the final phrase, "incapable of deception or of being deceived." What seems to be a tribute to Bentinck here becomes a defence of the author, for if the subject and "the writer" enjoy the warmth and candour which is amply illustrated throughout, it follows that Bentinck's probity and friendship are a warrant for Disraeli's integrity. Thus, given the tension between principle and expediency in Disraeli's attacks on Peel, this idealization of Bentinck's powers suggests that their relationship embodied in Disraeli's eyes something more than an intensification of the patterns from the past. What Disraeli needed to do was escape the liability of his reputation. And, though obviously the political exigencies of the Protectionist cause and Peel's dilemma were real, the relationship with Bentinck offered Disraeli a chance to combine the gratifications of power and the definition of principled success in a way that the Young England movement never had.

Disraeli's role in the debates upon the Government's resolutions and the resultant Corn Law Bill reveals, however, that he remained extremely vulnerable to cynicism about his reputation and integrity. Psychiatric literature and political history abound with cases and examples of men who in the moment of their success betray a compulsion to confirm their antagonists' most serious doubts. It would seem that something like this compulsion, having to do with his own sense of his identity, underlay the ironic climax of the Corn Law debate in which the moment of Disraeli's psychological triumph over Peel was quickly followed by what many have considered the most disgraceful incident of his public career.

When on 15 May the protracted discussion of the Corn Law reached its final moments, Disraeli again resorted to personal invective to define Peel's apostasy. At the conclusion of a speech of almost three hours' duration, recapitulating all of the arguments in favour of Protection for agriculture and against Free Trade, he turned to the fact that, since 1841, the Tories had trusted Peel to represent the Protectionist cause, and that, in leading the party and the Government, Peel had accepted that trust. Disraeli recalled that a year earlier he had said that it appeared to him "that protection was in about the same state as Protestantism was in 1828," and then he added: "I remember my Friends were very indignant with me for that assertion, but they have since been so kind as to observe that instead of being a calumny it was only a prophecy. But I am bound to say, from personal experience, that, with the very humble exception to which I have referred, I think the right hon. Baronet may congratulate himself on his complete success in having entirely deceived his party."[20] The rhetoric here is not one of indignation. Rather, in its humour and complexity, it gives the impression, frequently noted at the time, that Disraeli was playing with his victim. Accordingly, after some reference to Peel's "Machiavellian manoeuvres" and an extended ironic simile comparing the conversion of the Peelites to free trade to that of Charlemagne's conversion of the Saxons, who were "converted in battalions, and baptized in platoons," Disraeli goes on to say a word in "vindication of the right hon. baronet" (Laughter). He acquits the right hon. gentleman of ["foregone treachery"], "of a long meditated deception, of a desire [un]worthy of a great statesman – even of an unprincipled one – to give up all the opinions by which he rose to power," because upon reflection it seems that "the right hon. gentleman" has always "traded on the ideas and intellects [i.e., intelligence] of others" (Cheers). Indeed, Disraeli adds, "His life has been a great appropriation clause" (Renewed cheers and laughter.) "He has been the burglar of others' intellects" and there has never been a "statesman who has committed petty larceny on so great a scale" (Cheers).

To this Disraeli adds, "The right hon. gentleman tells us he does not feel humiliated … But I tell the right hon. gentleman, that although he may not feel humiliated, the country ought to feel humiliated" (Loud cheers). And then, mocking the idea that Peel would dare to appeal to the people of England on "a fantastic scheme of some presumptuous pedant," Disraeli reaches his own peroration:

> I have that confidence in the common sense and common spirit of my countrymen to believe that they will no longer endure the huckstering tyranny of the Treasury bench, or of the political pedlar who bought his party in the cheapest market and sold them in the dearest. (Laughter and cheers.) … I know, Sir, that we appeal to a people debauched by public gambling – stimulated and encouraged by an inefficient and shortsighted Minister. I know that the public mind is polluted with economic fancies; a depraved desire that the rich may become richer without the interference of industry and toil. I know, Sir, that all confidence in public men is lost. But, Sir, I have faith in the primitive and enduring elements of the English character. It may be vain now, in the midnight of their intoxication, to tell them that there will be an awakening of bitterness; it may be idle now, in the spring-tide of their economic frenzy, to warn them that there may be

an ebb of trouble. But the dark and inevitable hour will arrive. Then, when their spirit is softened by misfortune, they will recur to those principles that made England great, and which, in our belief, can alone keep England great. Then, too, perchance they may remember, not with unkindness, those who, betrayed and deserted, were neither ashamed nor afraid to struggle for the "good old cause" – the cause with which are associated principles the most popular, sentiments the most entirely national – the cause of labour – the cause of the people – the cause of England.[21]

Disraeli's use of such strong language to characterize Peel's role in public affairs was extreme even by the lax standards of the House of Commons in that period. *The Times*, indeed, refused to use the words "polluted" and "depraved" in reporting the speech, presumably because of their highly charged sexual connotation. "Unpolluted" is, however, a word that Disraeli frequently uses in his novels to convey the threat of contamination to sexual innocence or purity of motive. Harry Coningsby, for example, thinks of his love for Edith Millbank in these terms: "His affection had never for a moment swerved; it was profound and firm ... whatever were the barriers which the circumstances of life placed against their union, they were partakers of the solemn sacrament of an unpolluted heart." And shortly thereafter, we are told, when he is seized with a heroic conception of his identity, "He thought of Edith in her hours of fondness; he thought of the pure and solemn moments when to mingle his name with the heroes of humanity was his aspiration, and to achieve immortal fame the inspiring purpose of his life. What were the tawdry accidents of vulgar ambition to him? No domestic despot could deprive him of his intellect, his knowledge, the sustaining power of an unpolluted conscience."[22] Such examples suggest again the extent to which Disraeli was projecting his own fantasy of wickedness onto Peel, and also the extent to which in the transposition of the political debate, he had attached all of Peel's reputation for probity and honour to the principles and patriotism he claimed for himself.

I

When the prime minister rose to speak a short while later in the climactic debate on 15 May, he clearly felt compelled to respond to Disraeli's onslaught, but he would not, he said, insult the House and the country by bandying "personalities." Instead, in referring to the "venomous attacks of the member for Shrewsbury," he said that, if Disraeli had entertained this opinion of his character for so long, it was a little surprising that he should have been ready in 1841 "to unite his fortunes with mine in office, thus implying the strongest proof which any public man can give of confidence in the honour and integrity of a Minister."[23]

If ignored, such a retort would probably have had little impact. But Disraeli was very sensitive to the issue of his own character, for he knew that many people were deeply suspicious of his integrity, and many others were prejudiced against him as a Jew, however Christianized. And there was, of course, good ground for some suspicions: Disraeli had first come to public notice in the 1820s as a flamboyant dandy and the author of some jejune, trashy, and very indiscreet novels. In the 1830s he had added to this reputation of immaturity and insincerity the burdens of the scandalous adulterous affair with Lady Henrietta Sykes, and of the crushing series of debts, run up to pay for his extravagant style of life on the social fringes of the Tory aristocracy. In addition to all of this, in his first five election campaigns he had at least nominally presented himself variously as a Tory, a Radical-Tory, a Tory-Radical, and again as a Tory, while between elections he had indulged his powers of wit and invective with Ultra-Tory conspiracies and rabid journalism. Moreover, this lurid political past had been dredged up in the Commons only a week earlier, on 8 May, by John Arthur Roebuck, the Radical member for Bath, who had raised the whole issue of Disraeli's consistency by referring to his allegedly Radical campaigns in 1832 and 1833. Disraeli had replied at great length, "very much annoyed," he said, that he should be obliged to defend his motives and consistency with another elaborate explanation.

Thus, when Peel raised the question of his antagonist's consistency and, by implication, of his motives, Disraeli immediately followed by violating the rules of the House and begging an indulgence to speak again to refute the "insinuation" made about his character. This reply is too long to quote in full, but the emphatic reiterations of Disraeli's denials ("I never shall ... make an application for any place"; "I never asked a favour of the Government"; "I never, directly or indirectly, solicited office") suggest that he knew the question was damaging, and that he must insist that his attacks on the prime minister were not motivated by merely personal feelings of disappointment: "I do most unequivocally, and upon my honour, declare that I never have for a moment been influenced by such considerations in the House."[24] The obsessive quality of Disraeli's denials would suggest, even in the absence of concrete evidence, that there is something problematic in this defence of his motives. The repeated reference to the rumours about his past behaviour suggest a defensiveness and a vulnerability to public opinion as might be occasioned by a guilty conscience. Indeed, the usual interpretation of this speech is that in a moment of panic Disraeli simply lied to the House, fearing that his reputation would otherwise prove a liability to the cause of Protection in the division about to follow.

The facts seem to warrant such a conclusion, for Disraeli had indeed written to Peel appealing for recognition as the Government was being formed in September 1841. In that letter, after mentioning the four election campaigns he had fought for the Tory party, Disraeli referred to the peculiarity of his case, that he had had "to struggle against a storm of political hate and malice, which few men ever experienced," and that he had only been sustained under these trials by the conviction that someday Peel would reward these efforts: "I confess," he concluded, "to be unrecognised at this moment by you appears to me to be overwhelming; and I appeal to your own heart – to that justice and that magnanimity, which I feel are your characteristics – to save me from an intolerable humiliation."[25] As noted above, Peel's feeling of humiliation, or lack of it, had been a focus of Disraeli's attack earlier in the evening. And in his explanation to the House, Disraeli followed very closely the tone and content of both Peel's answer to his letter in 1841 and his own subsequent note of clarification. Peel had replied, "I must ... observe that no member of the Cabinet ... ever received from me the slightest authority to make to you the communication to which you refer. Had I been consulted by that person, I should have at once declined to authorise a communication which would have been altogether at variance with the principle on which I have uniformly acted in respect to political engagements."[26] Disraeli immediately wrote back to correct Peel's "misconception," denying that he had meant to intimate that a promise of official promotion had been made to him. He then insisted that it was "utterly alien from ... [his] nature to bargain and stipulate on such subjects" and that parliamentary office, in his view, "should be the recognition of party service and Parliamentary ability."[27] "Not to be appreciated," he concluded, "may be a mortification: to be baulked of a promised reward is only a vulgar accident of life, to be borne without a murmur."

In retrospect it is possible, I think, to have some sympathy for Disraeli's claims. His interpretation of the events in 1841, both then and since, was undoubtedly warped by the egocentric intensity of his ambitions and disappointment, but, as M.G. Wiebe suggests, the events of 1841 and 1846 are open to another interpretation than has usually been given them.[28] During the fortnight between his election and the formation of Peel's cabinet in 1841, Disraeli had spent a good deal of time in the company of his friend and political patron, Lord Lyndhurst, perhaps the most indiscreet man ever to hold public office. When Disraeli had first allied himself formally with the Tories in 1834, Lyndhurst may well have intimated to him that his services to the party would eventually be recognized when they returned to power. And more recently, after Peel's victory, Lyndhurst had apparently encouraged Disraeli to think that it was certain that he would be included in the cabinet, or given some other important office; at least he did not discourage him from thinking so, which, given the history of their previous conspiratorial Ultra-Tory intrigues, amounted to the same thing. It is significant in this regard that in 1841 Disraeli does not immediately solicit office, but waits to hear from Peel or someone in authority, as though it is just a matter of time – as though he expects a previous understanding to be fulfilled. This is also the import of his letters to Sarah and notes to Mary Anne during this period, to whom he reports that he has heard nothing yet, and that the newspaper speculations about ministerial appointments are "moonshine."[29] As shown in chapter 8, Disraeli was himself quite naive about such matters, and apparently innocent of the inner workings of the party. In his "explanation" of 1846 he thus describes Lord Lyndhurst's opinions as a communication which he (Disraeli) took to originate with Sir Robert Peel, a conclusion that he soon realized was a "misconception." In other words, it seems that in 1841 Disraeli thought that Peel fully understood and would recognize that he had legitimate claims on the patronage of the party. And when it finally became obvious that no preferment to office was forthcoming, Disraeli naturally saw himself as a wronged party, even as he wrote to Peel asking to have his services recognized. This too is the significance of Mary Anne's letter to Peel reminding him of the contributions to the party's success that she and her husband have made.[30] Accordingly, it is only when Peel sends his somewhat frigid reply, disclaiming any promise that Lyndhurst has made, that Disraeli realizes that the prime minister has no knowledge of the (mis)understanding upon which he has based his calculations. And to Disraeli's chagrin it appears that he and Lyndhurst have created a "fool's paradise" between them, and that he has indeed just solicited office in a most inopportune way.[31] But the distinction he makes, between appreciation and reward, in his second letter to Peel in 1841, suggests that he did not in his own mind see himself as initiating an application for office, certainly not any specific office, but rather as only expressing his "mortification" at not being appreciated for his extraordinary abilities.

In such a reading of the events of 1841, in which it is Disraeli who feels himself the victim of a misplaced trust, the emphatic denials of his explanation in the House of Commons in 1846 are not quite the "reckless mendacity" they seem,[32] but rather an insistence upon the understanding behind his support of Peel's party between 1834 and 1841. Moreover, this was not the first time he had made such denials, for he had been challenged on the issue of his disappointment of office during a meeting of his constituents at Shrewsbury in 1844. And it therefore seems unlikely that in 1846 Disraeli had either forgotten the terms of his correspondence with Peel or acted from a sense of panic. His insistence upon his own honourable, if mistaken, understanding of the situation in 1841 seems, instead, a declaration that he is prepared to move the issue of public trust to a personal level if Peel pursues the question of political motivation. This may well be why the prime minister, even though he had the correspondence of 1841 to hand, chose not to read the exchange of letters to the House of Commons as a means of refuting Disraeli's assertions and utterly destroying his credibility, even with the Protectionists. Disraeli had, after all, been close enough to Lyndhurst and to Tory policy in the past five years to have some devastating ammunition about unseemly political patronage, should he care to use it. Even George Smythe's recent appointment as Under-Secretary for Foreign Affairs, a position for which he was manifestly unsuited, could be construed as a purchase of silence. Peel may well have considered, therefore, that adopting the dignity of moral probity and ministerial decorum was the best policy, for it would leave Disraeli vulnerable to the gossip and innuendo that any ambiguity would foster. And whatever Disraeli might insist with regard to the solicitation of office for himself in 1841, his letters to Lord Stanley and to Sir James Graham in 1842 and 1843, asking for a minor place for his brother James, though perhaps a trivial matter, could not be truthfully denied. The second of the letters to Graham is, in fact, quite interesting for what it reveals about Disraeli's feelings. In expressing both his own reluctance to perform this "domestic duty" of acting on his brother's appeal for help, and his anticipation of another rejection, Disraeli is, in effect, disavowing the request that he seems to be making. But even more striking are the references to his "exemption" from the "obsolete notions" of patronage, which still "linger in the country," and to the "more correct conception of the nature of party connections, & the value of party services," for these phrases, in their defensive, perhaps even sarcastic bitterness, imply that Disraeli interpreted the events of 1841 in precisely the way that Wiebe has suggested.[33]

Graham and Peel, however, saw the matter in an entirely different light. Graham thought that Disraeli's letter was "an impudent one," and told the prime minister that since "to have bantered him on the subject of party ties would have been degrading," he had sent a "a civil, but flat refusal." Peel, in reply, said that he was "very glad that Mr. D'Israeli has asked for an office for his brother": "It is a good thing when such a man puts his shabbiness upon record. He asked me for office for himself and I was not surprized that being refused he became independent and a patriot."[34] Such phrases as "degrading" and "such a man," and Peel's use of the antique spelling of Disraeli's name are signs of the prejudicial disdain for him held by the leaders of the Conservative party. It would thus hardly be surprising if Disraeli came to the conclusion that it was prejudice that deprived him of office in 1841. Indeed, W.F. Monypenny even speculates on the basis of anecdotal evidence that Peel did in fact want to offer Disraeli a place in his cabinet and was dissuaded from doing so by Lord Stanley or other members of the Conservative establishment.[35] But whatever can be said on Disraeli's side of the affair, it is clear in an objective sense that he had written to Peel soliciting some tangible recognition, and that his insistence that he had never asked a favour of the Government was belied by the letters he had sent to Lord Stanley and Sir James Graham, asking for a job for his brother.

Certainly the general impression among the Government's supporters in 1846 was that Disraeli had lied to the House in a futile attempt to defend the consistency of his actions and the purity of his motives. In Whig and Peelite circles this was merely a confirmation of the prejudices that already existed and of the opinion that Disraeli was completely untrustworthy, unprincipled, and opportunistic. What is more interesting is that Disraeli's "lie" was clearly the subject of some comment among the Ultra-Tories and Protectionists. Several of the Tory newspapers, for example, refer in editorials to the matter of Disraeli's explanation in ways that make it clear that, though they welcomed his advocacy of their cause, they did not find his denials convincing. *John Bull*, for example, a journal that had previously castigated Peel's actions earlier in the session as "treacherous and dishonest" (Saturday, 28 February 1846), referred in its issue of 16 May to "the tolerably plain intimation which the Right Hon. Baronet gave, that the Hon. Member for Shrewsbury has been an *unsuccessful* applicant for place," and then the editor continued: "If so, all we can say is, that he has been less fortunate than the Hon. G. SMYTHE. They used to bark in couples; but ever since the Hon. Member for Canterbury found his way to Downing-Street he has been one of the 'dumb dogs' of the Treasury Bench." The *Morning Post*, by comparison, was not so subtle, and was therefore more problematic for Disraeli. In the issue of Monday, 18 May 1846, the editorial comment, ostensibly supporting his denial of Peel's insinuation, is phrased as an ultimate form of hypothetical conditions: "If it were absolutely true that Mr. DISRAELI had been a place-hunter, would Sir ROBERT PEEL cease, in virtue of that fact, to be a cowardly apostate? If it were an incontrovertible fact, that, in 1842 Mr. DISRAELI offered his services to Sir ROBERT PEEL, would that circumstance prove Sir ROBERT PEEL's policy to be other than destructive of the best interests of England?" And having reiterated that "Mr.DISRAELI ... flatly contradicts Sir ROBERT PEEL's statement," and that he "utterly denies that he sought office at the hands of Sir ROBERT PEEL," the editorial concludes that with respect to the opposing assertions of the "two honourable gentlemen," they "do *not* know that the testimony of any betrayed party can be adduced in proof of the worthlessness of Mr. DISRAELI's solemn asseveration." Because such strong language is combined with a logically weak conclusion, thus implying more than is being said, some of the newspaper's readers may well have found the defence of Disraeli unconvincing. That said, however, it must be remembered that the *Morning Post* was completely committed to the Protectionists' cause, and it was in general a vehicle for the expression of Ultra-Tory extremities. The tone of its political columns was frequently that of rabid prejudice, righteous indignation, and hatred, as was evidenced by Disraeli's own anonymous, scurrilously patriotic articles at the time of the Municipal Corporations Reform Bill in 1835. It is not surprising, then, that the *Morning Post* should use categorical language in defending Disraeli. The editor described "the brilliant and impressive peroration of his noble speech," while claiming that Sir Robert Peel's summation "displayed even more than the usual proportion of grave effrontery, mixed with cunning and stupidity."[36] And five weeks later, when he referred to the prime minister as "the Right Hon. Betrayer of his party,"[37] he rejoiced that the government of this "dishonest politician" had been overthrown on the Irish Coercion Bill: "One thing, however, seems sure," he gloated, "that the dishonest pseudo-Conservative Government is knocked on the head, and of that we are right glad, because we abhor dis-honesty."[38]

Whatever effect it had on the *Post*'s readers, this emphatic reiteration of Disraeli's denials, coupled with such moralistic claims for honesty, must have seemed fraught with danger to Disraeli in the aftermath of his explanation to the House of Commons. Moreover, the *Morning Post* was not the only newspaper to dwell at length on the matter of his denials. The *Standard*, in the issue of 16 May, also contained a sympathetic comment so elaborate as to question by implication Disraeli's veracity. Of course, not all of the press was by any means that supportive. The Whig and Peelite newspapers were openly critical of Disraeli, and some journals indulged in anti-Semitism. For example, in noticing that "Mr. D'Israeli" complained that Peel was "too irritable" in the face of "his own unmerciful castigation," the *Nonconformist* remarked, "only a Jew could be capable of such cool impudence."[39] The *Spectator*, very sympathetic to Peel, suggested that Disraeli's obstructive behaviour was motivated by "personal malice and factious ends," and claimed that the public viewed "with unmitigated disgust the personalities now current in Parliament."[40] This was quite restrained in comparison with the *Observer*, which used the full contempt of unsavoury metaphor to assail Disraeli's motives. Characterizing Disraeli as wanting again to have "his bark and his bite" at the prime minister, the editorial writer described Peel's insinuation as "a stunning kick as must ever render the assailant an unworthy associate for the nobler dogs even of his own pack." The *Observer*'s conclusion was that all of the "venom" and "vituperation" of the "honourable member for Shrewsbury" was attributable to his failure to receive office, and that the country, having "laughed at and despised the effect," could take its leave of "this high-minded advocate of political purity."[41]

This comment, perhaps better than any other, expresses the public, and perhaps even the private burden of Disraeli's "lie" to the House of Commons, for the very words such as "trust" and "purity," which Disraeli had so often used to express his personal and political ideals in his fiction, are here used against him with contemptuous scorn and sarcasm. And the issue of his untrustworthiness did not seem to lose its public interest very quickly, even after the defeat of Peel's ministry. As late as 15 August 1846 *Douglas Jerrold's Weekly Newspaper*, fancying itself topical, interjected this quite anomalous comment into an item about Army discipline: "Mr. Disraeli has discovered the phrase – organized hypocrisy. It is his own. The cock in Esop, scratching the dunghill, had not a greater right to his discovery; (nor possibly a greater right to crow over it.) And when Mr. Disraeli – having served his country as prime minister – shall be carried to Westminster Abbey, with six dukes at least for pall-bearers – the phrase 'organized hypocrisy' – so say his political sponsors, O'Connell and Hume – may serve for his best epitaph."[42] But, however annoying such remarks might be, Disraeli's notoriety now brought with it a measure of power and influence. The relation between the two is best shown in the editorial comment of *The Times* anticipating the passage of the Corn Law Bill in the Lords: "In the House of Lords there may be much bitterness of invective, as there doubtless is much bitterness of feeling; but there will be no one to point the shaft of allusive sarcasm, to watch the shifting features of the galled victim, to search his tenderest sensibilities with the rambling antithesis, and rouse the hottest exultation of his triumphant foes. There may be many declaimers, but there will be no DISRAELI."[43] In such a recognition Disraeli doubtless took much satisfaction, perhaps precisely because it does suggest the real power of combining talent and expediency.

How much of all this commentary Disraeli actually read is unknown. But in focusing on the climate of opinion following the climax of the Corn Law debate, I have established the grounds for suggesting that his actual or objective political position was complicated by a psychological burden, with both public and private dimensions, which was created by the intense scrutiny of his motives and actions in attacking Peel. In that regard the matter of the "lie" to the House of Commons is more complicated than has yet been granted. To call it a moment of "reckless mendacity" caused by "panic," as does Robert Blake,[44] does not pay sufficient attention to the context of the debate or to the psychological features of the antagonism between Disraeli and Peel. The key point is that over the course of the previous year Disraeli had struggled to create a complete separation of his political identity from that of Peel; to insist that the prime minister was in every respect the antithesis of the principled advocate of the noble constitutional cause that Disraeli claimed to be. Of course he was motivated by malice, at least to the extent of enjoying his revenge, for, as the very language of the debate indicates, Disraeli was intent on imposing the same humiliation on Peel that he had felt from the prime minister's neglect of his abilities in 1841. But there was a larger issue, too; the one of his ambitions. In 1846 Disraeli knew that as long as Peel led the Conservative party, he would gain no preferment. The proposal to repeal the duties on corn gave him a policy, and a principle, upon which to attack Peel. And by the time the debate reached its conclusion, Disraeli had become the most powerful advocate of the landed interests. True, Lord George Bentinck was the nominal leader of the Protectionist party, once it was formed, but he depended heavily upon Disraeli's rhetorical skills to sustain the debate. Over the course of the spring Bentinck and Disraeli had become inseparable allies and warm personal friends. As a consequence, at the moment when Peel made his insinuation, Disraeli (however the vote on the Corn Law Bill turned out) had just established a new political combination with considerably more promise than the enthusiasms of Young England had ever supplied. It must have seemed to Disraeli that only a categorical denial of having solicited office under Peel could maintain the separation of political identities he had successfully created, but which Peel's intimation threatened to collapse. As the comments in the newspapers show, Disraeli's denials did far more damage in that respect than silence would have, for his position among the Protectionists was by no means secure.

II

Disraeli's friendship with Lord George Bentinck continued to deepen and flourish in the weeks following the climax of the Corn Law debate in the Commons. Interestingly, the image of a heroic George Canning once again played a significant role in Disraeli's evolving sense of his political identity. As previously shown, Disraeli's identification with Canning went back to the days of *The Representative* affair in 1825, and in recent years it had been reinforced by the enthusiasms of Young England and by the episode of the "candid friend."[45] On one level this identification was derived from the public political issue of Catholic Emancipation, and, in that regard, it embodies Disraeli's long-standing ambivalence about religious matters. He can disparage Peel both for his factious opposition in 1827 to Canning's Catholic sympathies and for his subsequent apostasy in abandoning Protestantism in 1829. But, as I have shown, Disraeli's ambivalence about the Catholic issue, manifest in both the politics and the fiction, was to some degree a disguise of his feelings about his Jewish heritage. Hence it is not difficult to see how the identification with Canning is, on a second level, derived from essentially private issues.

Canning, to some extent like Disraeli, grew to maturity without the advantages of wealth and established position. Like Disraeli, too, he had literary interests and entered politics determined to force a recognition of his extraordinary abilities through the sheer brilliance of his rhetorical skill. In part this accounts, too, for the fact that Canning was widely distrusted, though the obvious expediency of his joining the Tory party to enhance the prospects of his ambition was no doubt the major factor. Finally, the private aspect of Disraeli's empathy also reflects the fact that Canning had had to overcome the stigma attached to his mother's career on the stage. Earl Grey's opinion, that it was "axiomatic that no son of an actress should become Prime Minister of England," is only the most succinct expression of a widely shared prejudice;[46] and, doubtless, Disraeli felt the parallel to his own struggle against the pervasive anti-Semitism he encountered.

In all of these respects there is clearly a resonance between Canning's political career in the 1820s and Disraeli's in the 1840s. The most significant feature of the psychological reinforcement, however, was the fact that Lord George Bentinck was Canning's nephew, and he had served as private secretary to his uncle when he was prime minister in 1827. It is difficult to know just how explicitly the subject of Canning's tragic demise strengthened the initial relationship between Bentinck and Disraeli. But arguing retrospectively, from Disraeli's keen appreciation of Queen Victoria's feelings after the death of Prince Albert, it seems likely that his intuitive understanding of Bentinck's nostalgic perception of his uncle's political heroism contributed in some large measure to the growth of this remarkable friendship born of the Protectionist exigency in 1846.

The account of affairs at this time in *Lord George Bentinck* shows that while the Corn Law Bill was being considered in the House of Lords, Disraeli and Bentinck considered themselves co-conspirators bent on revenge:[47] the danger, in their view, was that the Government would quickly bring the session to an end and prorogue Parliament once their Corn Law measure was law. "Was it probable," in any case, Disraeli asked, that "those who were conspiring their overthrow would be richer in their resources or more felicitous in their expedients than at the present moment, when vengeance, ambition, the love of office, and the love of change, all combined to advance and assist their wishes?"[48] The difficulty was that, for the moment, the only legislative instrument with which to answer the question, "How was Sir Robert Peel to be turned out?" was the Irish Coercion Bill, which was designed to suppress the various acts of violence provoked by the famine by suspending habeas corpus, introducing military tribunals, and instituting a curfew. Bentinck and most of the Protectionists had supported this bill when it was introduced in the Commons on 13 March as a supposedly urgent measure.

Disraeli now persuaded Bentinck that the Protectionists should reverse themselves and oppose this "anti-murder bill" (as Bentinck referred to it), on the grounds that it could only be justified by "some dire emergency" incompatible with the Government's delay in bringing it forward for second reading on 8 June.[49] Disraeli knew that the coalition that had supported Peel in the Corn Law debate was unstable, and that the Irish Coercion Bill would produce an entirely new combination of separate interests in opposition, each with its own reason for rejecting such a measure. The difficulty was that the Whigs would not put Peel's ministry in jeopardy until the Corn Law Bill had passed the Lords, and so Disraeli and Bentinck were obliged to follow a strategy of procrastination and bedevilment.

Bentinck resolved to speak "early and strongly," very much aware that, as he said to Disraeli, "It may be perilous, but if we lose this chance the traitor will escape."[50] His speech was an intemperate affair, full of violent imagery impugning the prime minister's character, and claiming that the Government was now supported only by "his forty paid janissaries, and some seventy other renegades, one half of whom, while they support him, express their shame of doing so."[51] In his climax Bentinck revived the allegations of Peel's apostasy over the policy of Catholic Emancipation in the late 1820s, but he did so in extremely melodramatic and personal terms: "I have lived long enough, I am sorry to say ... to remember with sorrow – with deep, and heartfelt sorrow – the time when the right honourable baronet chased and hunted an illustrious relative of mine to death."[52] The allusion was to Peel's refusal to support Canning's initiative on Catholic Emancipation in 1827 and to Peel's subsequent statement in the Commons in 1829 (when he was himself proposing a similar measure). This was interpreted to mean that he had in fact changed his opinions on the subject as early as 1825. In Bentinck's view Peel stood on both occasions "convicted ... [now] by his own verdict, of base and dishonest conduct ... inconsistent with the duty of a minister to his sovereign."[53] In his peroration Bentinck insisted that the country would not forgive twice "the same crime in the same man," and that "atonement should be made to the betrayed constituencies of the empire."[54] The word "atonement," used, as it is, three times in conjunction with "treachery" and "dishonour" in the final few sentences of Bentinck's speech, seems to carry a special emotional charge for the Protectionists in so far as it embodies their sense of justified out-rage and their lust for revenge. The full significance of the word for Disraeli does not, however, emerge for some months, until it is seen in the context of his characterization of his hero in his next novel, *Tancred*.

What was apparent at the time was that the prime minister felt that both the profligate rhetoric and the substance of Bentinck's accusations originated with Disraeli. For much of his long speech in his own de-fence, Peel laboured through the maze of documents relating to his role in the Catholic Emancipation debates of the late 1820s, particularly the correspondence with Lord Liverpool and Canning, arguing that the charge of his duplicity was spurious, if not malicious. But on the matter of his conduct over the Corn Law, the case was, he thought, even less ambiguous for any dispassionate judge. In defending himself against what he termed, the "odious ... aspersion" that "has been sought to be cast upon" him (the curious indirection of the phrase expressing the displacement of the source), Peel explicitly claims an altruistic motive both for his actions and for those of his colleagues and friends. Those with whom he is "connected by official ties," he characterizes as "acting from as pure and conscientious a sense of public duty as ever influ-enced any member of this house"; and those whom Bentinck had de-scribed as "paid janissaries and renegades," he insists are "gentlemen engaged in public service – gentlemen exercising their free right of judgment on public matters."[55] That Peel so dwells on the honour and integrity of gentlemen, and on the purity of his colleagues' motives, implies by contrast the invidious self-interest he attaches to Disraeli. But the thrust of Peel's vindication cuts deepest in his final, insistent denials that he has ever desired "to rob others of credit to which they ... were entitled," that he ever wished "to interfere with the settlement of the question by the noble lord opposite [Lord John Russell]," or that he had been "influenced by any desire" to fortify his own power, court popularity, or gain distinction or advantage of any kind. Such an "im-putation" to him of "motives so base" would, he said, "be as foul a calumny as a vindictive spirit ever *dictated* against a public man" (em-phasis added)[56] The account of this climactic moment in *Hansard* differs from that in *The Times* in a small but significant way. Since *Hansard* is subject to correction, it reflects the speaker's intentions as shaped by his editorial discretion, whereas the account in *The Times* is that taken down by reporters in the public gallery of the House of Commons. Discrepancies of phrasing are, therefore, not uncommon, especially at the most raucous moments of debate. In this case, the context of

Disraeli's subsequent speech makes it obvious that Peel did indeed use the word "dictated," thus implying that Bentinck had been manipulated into being the voice of Disraeli's personal malice. Upon reflection, Peel changed "dictated" to "directed," perhaps to avoid provoking further assaults, or to be seen for the record to be using more gentlemanly language. On the other hand, *Hansard* does print the words of his denial that were drowned out by the loud cheers of his supporters: "that I have been influenced in this course *by any impure or dishonourable motive* ..." (emphasis added).[57]

Clearly Disraeli could not ignore this contrast between "the positive purity" of Peel's conduct,[58] and his own "foul calumny." That this occasion should have produced such a challenge to Disraeli's integrity in precisely the terms that had bedevilled him for years – those of altruism and expediency – is not surprising. That Disraeli's counterattack would self-consciously betray the impact of Peel's accusation seems inevitable, given the nature of their previous encounters. Disraeli's defensiveness is immediately evident in the way he fastens upon the word "dictated." Quoting the prime minister's culminating accusation against him in full, Disraeli adds: "The vindictive imagination of a political opponent dictated this calumny! Why, I find it in the reports of the debate in this house, I find it in the minutes of his own [Peel's] parliamentary explanations; and he who described that imputation as the foulest calumny of a vindictive imagination was describing the conduct which he had himself professed."[59]

The subject was not, however, closed by this attempt to project the charge back upon its author. When Disraeli next turned to vindicate Bentinck's provocative language, he again referred to the imputed collusion between them: "Sir, when I heard the language of my noble friend, who spoke without any previous communication with myself (a laugh); I mean, of course, as to any particular expression he used ... " At this point he was sufficiently interrupted by the mirth of the "hon. gentlemen opposite" to be forced to acknowledge the "mare's nest" they seemed to have found in his claim. This seems to have been another instance of his denials only confirming the suspicions of his detractors. In this case, however, Disraeli was well-prepared (perhaps even suspiciously so) to refute the charge against his noble friend, that Bentinck had taken an unprecedented licence with parliamentary language in using the phrase, "paid janissaries."

Linking Bentinck's sense of outrage to the mood of Charles James Fox in an earlier era, Disraeli promptly argues, in Fox's words, that "delicacy and reserve are criminal where the interests of England are at hazard," and he then cites two precedents from earlier times for the offending words: one from a peroration by Fox and one from a speech of Mr Grenville.[60] Fox, who was well-known as a great, but intemperate orator, may well have been the chief source of Bentinck's rhetoric, for Disraeli also quotes in his friend's defence another passage in which Fox assaults his enemies that resonates with the attack on Peel: "The whole compass of language did not afford words sufficiently strong to mark the contempt he entertained for their conduct – their impulsive avowal of political profligacy, as if that species of treachery were less infamous than any other. – It was not only a degradation of a station, which ought to be occupied only by the highest and most exemplary honour, but they forfeited by it all claim to the character of gentlemen, and were reduced to a level with the meanest and basest of the species."[61] Such emphases upon treachery and dishonour are no more than the clichéd discourse of all political crises; but what is interesting and significant in this debate is the way both sides try to revitalize the merely conventional phrase, "honourable gentlemen," and give it a literal meaning by which their opponents can be condemned. In that regard, both Disraeli and Peel find themselves vulnerable: Peel unusually so, by virtue of what seemed to the Protectionists his deception of them over the Corn Law; Disraeli typically so, by virtue of his previous notoriety and his present motives.

The centre-piece of Disraeli's obviously self-reflexive vindication is therefore the simple task of proving that Lord George Bentinck is a gentleman: a man who has been "most unwillingly" pressed into prominence, who has "never aspired to more than the reputation of a high-spirited and honourable English gentleman," a man who "has not sought nor wished to occupy any office," and who on this occasion has justifiably expressed himself with "unusual warmth" and "the racy vigour of his brave honesty."[62] The structure of this vindication reveals much about Disraeli's sense of himself and his political strategy at this time. By demonstrating his familiarity with the specific precedents for Bentinck's violent words, he identifies himself closely with the feelings they convey. But then by emphasizing Bentinck's reluctant, disinterested, pure, and humble involvement in the present crisis, Disraeli shows that the attack on the prime minister comes not from the imagination of a vindictive spirit, but from the offended judgment of an *honourable* gentleman (emphasis added). In short, Disraeli here moves to dissociate himself from his own reputation and to claim for his actions the integrity of his noble friend. There are even echoes in this present association between them to the time of Disraeli's earlier *Vindication* and the political principles he then espoused. The allusion to Bentinck's pride in once having filled "the humblest situation of a political career near to a great Minister" (as private secretary to his uncle) recalls Disraeli's service as an unofficial confidential secretary to Lord Lyndhurst in 1835. But the *Vindication of the English Constitution in a letter to a noble and learned Lord* was written in the hope of defining the political principles of the Conservative party and of demonstrating the value of Disraeli's support for that party, not just to Lyndhurst, but also to Peel. Nevertheless, the obvious implication of Disraeli's emotional attachment to Bentinck in these terms is that Peel had betrayed the principles of the party he led, principles that are now defined and embodied in Disraeli's own actions and words.

Disraeli was not, however, content with his defence of Lord George Bentinck's rhetoric and his own motives, for he now turned to the substance of Peel's supposed apostasy on the matter of Catholic Emancipation. He set out to prove what Bentinck had claimed a week earlier: that Peel had withdrawn his support from Canning's ministry in 1827 over the issue of Catholic disabilities, even though he had changed his mind about that issue in 1825, and had so informed Lord Liverpool at the time. The basis of Disraeli's proof was a correspondence of the accounts in *The Times* and the *Mirror of Parliament* for the debates of 5 and 6 March 1829, in which the then Secretary Peel was reported as having said that he had told the prime minister, the Earl of Liverpool, in 1825, that "the time was come when something respecting the Catholics ought, in my opinion, to be done."[63] Noting that this passage did not appear in the report of *Hansard*, Disraeli alleged that Peel had deliberately omitted the sentence in the corrected account, and so suppressed the damaging admission it contained. Further to this charge, Disraeli pointed out that in an apparent reply to Peel's speech in 1829, Sir Edward Knatchbull had explicitly referred to this change of opinion on the Home Secretary's part.

In the peroration of this culminating attack on Peel, Disraeli reverts to the inspiriting image of George Canning, which serves, not only to "vindicate" Bentinck's words, but also simultaneously to indict the prime minister for his apostasies, to affirm his own integrity, and to define the legitimacy of his own ambitions.

I am not surprised that closely connected with Mr. Canning as he was, my
noble friend should have expressed himself as he did. The feeling to which
he gave utterance is shared by all who have had intercourse with Mr.
Canning. I never saw Mr. Canning but once, when I had no expectation of
being a member of this house, but I can recollect it but as yesterday when
I listened to the last accents – I may say the dying words – of that illustrious statesman. I can recollect the flash – the lightening flash – of that eye,
and the power of that imperial brow! But, Sir, when shall we see another
Mr. Canning – a man who ruled this house as a man rules a high bred
steed, as Alexander ruled Bucephalus (a laugh) of whom it was said that
horse and man were alike proud. I thank that hon. gentleman for his
laugh. The pulse of the national heart does not beat as high as it once did.
I know the temper of this house is not as spirited and brave as it was, nor
am I surprised when the vulture rules where once the eagle reigned (Loud
cheers). The right hon. gentleman once said that Ireland was his great difficulty. I ask the right hon. gentleman ... whether, if he had acted with
frankness to Mr. Canning in reference to his communication with Lord
Liverpool in 1825, Ireland would have been his great difficulty? (Cheers).
This the right hon. gentleman must feel at the present moment, when we
are about again to divide on an Irish question – a division which may be
fatal to the endurance of his power – he must feel that it is a Nemesis that
dictates this vote and regulates this decision, and that is about to stamp
with its seal the catastrophe of a sinister career. (Loud and continued
cheering.)[64]

The intent of this peroration was clearly to reinforce at that crucial
moment, just before the division, the Protectionist members' sense of
the prime minister's betrayal of them. Disraeli's masterful control of
rhetoric is again apparent in the manner in which his sarcastic reference
to Peel's elaborate explanation gives way to the simplicity of his own
personal anecdote. Yet the subject of Canning's tragic heroism is complex, for it not only raises the memory of Peel's earlier "apostasy," but
also embodies the complicated matter of Disraeli's long-standing identification with Canning. In descanting on Canning's "dying words"
and "the power of that imperial brow" to rule the House of Commons,
Disraeli is clearly trying to establish the legitimacy, indeed, the nobility,
of his own ambitions. To suggest, as he does, that he was as a mere
youth inspired by Canning is to imply a degree of consistency in his
own actions and a purity in his own motives since. This prepares the
way for the culminating image in which Disraeli explicitly transforms

himself from the malevolent opportunist adduced by Peel's charge of "dictation" into an agent of fate and poetical justice. The last phrase, in which Nemesis stamps with its seal "the catastrophe of a sinister career," is no less effective for being manifestly unfair to Peel. By it Disraeli succeeded in reducing the whole issue of the Corn Law debate, and that of the Irish Coercion Bill, to the single question of Peel's disloyalty to his party – defined as those in the landed interest.

To such serious charges, the prime minister felt obliged to respond, and on 19 June (after a search of his ministerial papers at Drayton) Peel gave a lengthy explanation of his correspondence and relations to both Lord Liverpool and Mr Canning in 1825 and 1827, showing that his views on the Catholic question had remained consistent and opposed to the liberalization of the law. Moreover, with respect to 1829 and the controversial passage attributed to him, he was able to show that the accounts in the *Mirror of Parliament* and *The Times* were not independent at all, but in fact came from the same source – *The Times*'s reporter in the gallery of the Commons. And in conclusion Peel noted that there were four other accounts of his speech in four other morning newspapers, the *Herald*, the *Chronicle*, the *Post* and the *Journal*, none of which included the notorious sentence. Peel also defended himself against the charge of "suppressio veri" by pointing out that the note attached to the account in *Hansard* was only a matter of indicating that he had authorized the reprinting of the speech, originally published by Mr Murray, the bookseller. Thus Disraeli's proof collapsed to the inference that could be drawn from Sir Edward Knatchbull's reply in 1829. The account of this reply in the *Mirror of Parliament* iterates the charge of Peel's duplicity in 1825 and 1827 (while other newspaper accounts do not), but in any case it is unclear whether in fact Sir Edward had heard Peel's speech in 1829, or was responding to the version of it he had read in *The Times*. Having thus undermined the base of the allegation against him in logical terms, Peel turned to consider the emotional import of Disraeli's peroration: "The hon. Gentleman concluded his speech by a passionate representation of his veneration and affection for the memory of Mr. Canning ... One would have supposed that he had devoted all the energies of all his intellect to magnify the praises of Mr. Canning, and that he had submitted to some great personal sacrifice on account of his devotion to Mr. Canning."[65] The implication of this comment is clearly that Disraeli's words embody a fantasy of heroic identification that has no warrant in reality. And Peel, whose sense of personal and public probity is so strong, can see nothing in these words but insincerity, opportunism, and hypocrisy: "Why, Sir, if he has those feelings, they are to be held in honour; but if the hon. Gentleman is parading these feelings of veneration for the memory of Mr. Canning for the mere purpose of wounding a political opponent, he is desecrating feelings which, when sincere, are entitled to esteem and respect." The expression of this suspicion is, of course, deliberately ironic. In the last paragraph, Peel reiterates the phrase, "the hon. Gentleman," eight times as he questions Disraeli's motives. One can imagine that he had difficulty in preventing a note of sarcastic emphasis from spoiling the discrepancy between the literal and insinuated meaning, between the form and the content, of his address. Obviously, whenever it is applied to a political opponent, the phrase "honourable Gentleman" carries ironic possibilities. But here, as was the case earlier with Disraeli's use of "the right honourable baronet," it is the insistent repetition, when other forms such as "the honourable Member for Shrewsbury" are possible, that betrays the sarcastic intent or moral indignation of the speaker.

After Peel sat down, Lord George Bentinck rose to insist that the quarrel was really between himself and the prime minister, and that his "hon. Friend, the Member for Shrewsbury," had done no more than defend him against the allegations in Peel's first reply. He then went on to repeat at some length all of the charges he had previously made, quoting extensively from Peel's speeches in the 1820s to justify his accusation of perfidy. But given the effect of the prime minister's careful explanation, this would have been anticlimactic. Perhaps so, too, was John Arthur Roebuck's return to the question of Disraeli's motives shortly afterwards, for the members of the House had several times before heard his set-piece on Disraeli's inconsistencies and "vituperations," which he said were based solely upon the mortifications and spite of disappointed ambition. But with one memorable image Roebuck caught the obsessive brilliance of Disraeli's revenge on Peel: "unfortunate still in the attainment of his object, he did not gain his place, and then he chose to deal in that species of vituperation of which they had heard so many specimens. He was a sort of Paganini playing upon one string; he could only play upon the right hon. Baronet."[66]

Such an image embodies perfectly the contrast between Peel as the emblem of the stalwart English gentleman and his tormentor, who, however entertaining in his witty displays of rhetoric, was seen as essentially foreign, and therefore alien to the virtues of his victim. Roebuck obviously thought that nothing could be further from the sensibility of an English gentleman than that of an Italian musician or a political adventurer. But though the image wonderfully captures the prejudicial view of Disraeli, it would have made little difference to the outcome at this stage of the debate. Though a few subsequent speakers tried to return to the substance of the Coercion Bill, for most of the Tory members the lines of disagreement were firmly drawn, and the fundamental issue was still Peel's apostasy in repealing the Corn Law. And when the division was called, on 25 June (as soon as the House of Lords had reported the passage of the "Corn Importation Bill"), Peel was in a minority of 73 because more than 70 Protectionists voted with the Whigs, the majority of whom, as Greville reports, were animated "by mere hostility to the [Prime] Minister."[67]

No doubt there was much bitterness on both sides, and much was said privately about Disraeli's role in the whole affair. Even before the final vote, *The Times*, in an editorial on 20 June, had commented upon the spurious quality of Disraeli's and Bentinck's antagonism to the prime minister: "[they] have left these broad and admitted facts, and betaken themselves to a critical argument on a few doubtful, if not apocryphal expressions ... Nothing can be more perilous, more endless, more unsatisfactory, than such an investigation. A somewhat unprofitable chapter in the 'curiosities of literature' is the only possible result."[68] And in explicitly stating that "the controversy is a literary one," the writer of the editorial left no doubt that Disraeli's fantasies were shaping his political postures: "Nothing is more hazardous than the attempt to make great discoveries in a field open and familiar to all. You may as well look for lions in the Green-park, or ostriches in Trafalgar-square. Mr. DISRAELI knows the term by which we usually express the imaginary wonders sometimes hatched by a lively or a perverted curiosity. He and Lord G. BENTINCK have certainly found an article of this fictitious and transient interest" (ibid.). Also indicative, perhaps, of the kind of comments made about Disraeli in private, especially in Whig and Peelite circles, is the remark Greville had noted in his diary the day before: "The real reason why so many of Canning's colleagues refused to serve under him in 1827 was that they had a bad opinion of him, and would not trust him. They knew of his intriguing, underhand practices, and ... they would not consent to his assuming that powerful and responsible post."[69] Disraeli's deliberate identification with Canning was thus not entirely unproblematic. And Greville's comment precisely describes the problems Disraeli now faced even within the Protectionist wing of the Conservative party. It was widely assumed that Disraeli was manipulating Bentinck for his own ends, using him as a stalking horse for his own ambition. Even many of those most happy to have Peel's "apostasy" avenged were by no means tolerant of Disraeli's new prominence in Protectionist affairs. In its immediate form, then, Disraeli's problem was that of simultaneously denying and yet forwarding his ambitions. That this inner ambivalence was perceived, and seen to have public implications, is suggested by the vulgar motif of "the Jew and the Jockey," which now surfaced in private correspondence as well as in *Punch* and other venues of public satire.

The phrase itself is the heading on page 103 of volume 3 of *The Croker Papers: The Correspondence and Diaries of ... John Wilson Croker*, not indeed published until 1884, after Disraeli's death. The rationale for it is the juxtaposition on that page of two letters to Croker, written in January 1846. The first of these, from W.B. Baring, reports:

> There was a *blow up* – I use the term of my informant – at the Stanley dinner, between the two leaders in Lords and Commons. Stanley made a nice speech, recommended forbearance from strong language and agitation. Lord G. took it as a rebuke to himself, and spoke angrily. D'Israeli poured oil and calmed the waves; but this looks like a want of cordiality. It is better, however, that it should be so than that the reports spread by your opponents should be true. I do not wish to see the weaker nature of Stanley moulded by Lord G. and his Jew.[70]

The second letter, from J.G. Lockhart, refers to the same episode, but suggests more directly that the underlying issue in the political gossip about the event was Disraeli's manipulation of Bentinck, much as first overtly charged by Peel near the beginning of the previous session: "I hear there was a very hot little *scena* at a late Carlton Club dinner between Stanley and Lord George Bentinck; but they were pacified ere they parted. Still, the Jockey's complaint was of *dictation*, and that word indicates, I should think, a course of thought." Such a judgment from such a quarter seems to echo the scepticism about Disraeli's behaviour among the principals of the *Quarterly Review* circle at the time of *The Representative* affair twenty years earlier. But it also makes clear that a great many political observers in 1846 were content to take the most reductive and least flattering view of Disraeli's actions.

In *Punch* Bentinck is repeatedly characterized in the cartoons of 1846 and 1847 wearing a jockey's helmet, an obvious allusion to his obsession with the turf, and to the sobriquet by which he was known in unfriendly circles. The best satirical example of the motif is perhaps the cartoon of 12 September 1846, showing Disraeli and Bentinck winning a political sack-race: "Great Holiday at Mr. Punch's Park." But there were many other such allusions, including, for example, the cartoon and vignette entitled "The Protectionist Don Quixote" (*Punch*, 3 October 1846), with its suggestion that Disraeli had become "dizzy with ambition" and therefore was unwilling to continue playing Sancho Panza to Bentinck's Don Quixote. Similarly, the illustrated vignette, "A Master I Had, &c" (*Punch*, 27 March 1847) offers a dialogue in which "Disraeli" repeatedly offers the ostensibly subservient response, "Yes, my Lo-ord" to a series of questions posed by "Bentinck" but then alters the tone to a triumphant and gleeful, "yes, *my* Lo-ord," when he finally assures him that he has "made out" his patron's "speech for the House." The scene ends on a note of deflation as "Disraeli" is then dismissed and sent off to find his supper. The point of the satire is thus, not only to expose Bentinck's dependence on Disraeli, and so confirm the charge of *dictation*, but also to squash the vaulting ambition of the social parvenu.

Disraeli's relationship to Bentinck was, of course, more complicated than such satirical thrusts imply. As Robert Blake points out, Disraeli would certainly have realized that Bentinck's temperament was unsuited to any long-term leadership of the Protectionist party. And he would clearly have understood as well, that it was both expedient and necessary to shield himself from the sort of prejudiced contempt expressed so forcibly in Baring's letter, by supporting Bentinck's all too reluctant claim to the leadership in the Commons. On the other hand, Disraeli's idealization of his noble friend, attested to so fully in *Lord George Bentinck*, continued to find warrant in fact, for Bentinck was so committed to the Protectionist cause that in 1847 he sold off most of his promising racing stud to devote all of his energies to politics. In that regard, he proved to be an assiduous student of economic issues and made striking progress in overcoming the awkwardness of manner in public speaking that had seemed his natural state. In addition, he proved intensely loyal to Disraeli in the face of the ugly prejudice against him, and ultimately he voted in favour of Lord Russell's Jewish Disabilities Bill, much as it was against his personal inclination to do so.[71]

What Disraeli himself refers to as "the crisis of my affairs" during 1846 involved other dimensions than the political agitation against Peel's Government. The "long-distracted" complications of his numerous and very large debts began once again to wear an urgent aspect. Disraeli had been trying to raise a considerable sum of money ever since the summer of 1845, when he had apparently entertained the idea that his growing fame as a politician and his accomplishments as a popular novelist made the reprinting of his fiction a lucrative prospect.[72] There were at least two difficulties in such a project, however. One was that the re-appearance of the very early novels, *Vivian Grey* and especially *The Young Duke*, in their original form – full of youthful extravagances – would only give his detractors further damaging evidence of his indiscretion.[73] For this reason he sought to regain the copyright of these novels even as he tried to negotiate the terms of a collected edition. The more serious problem, however, was the direct pressure from his creditors. The substantial debts that Disraeli had acquired as a young man by speculating on South American mining stocks had grown ever larger from his inability to repay them, from the costs of maintaining his dandyish style of life in the 1830s, and from the expenses related to his election contests. Blake estimates that by 1846 Disraeli's debts amounted to between £15,000 and £20,000 (probably the equivalent of two million dollars in today's currency). This was, of course, an age of unregulated interest rates and a great deal of financial sharp practice, so that debtors were often victimized by the necessity of renegotiating their obligations. In any case, the surviving correspondence for this period suggests that Disraeli was constantly scrambling for money to keep his creditors at bay, and that in the midst of the political crisis in the spring and summer of 1846, when the debates over the Corn Law and Irish Coercion Bill were at their most intense, he was negotiating with lawyers, publishers, and creditors to arrange expedients that would avoid unwelcome publicity. It would seem, too, that his creditors were well aware that Disraeli's increased fame and political prospects gave them ever more leverage in that regard, and ironically, the very success of bringing down Peel's ministry posed a great personal danger, for were it to result in an immediate dissolution of Parliament, he would lose his immunity from prosecution for debt. But, paradoxically, even at the most critical phase of these financial negotiations, Disraeli was formulating a grand scheme to convert himself from being a representative of a borough (currently Shrewsbury) to a county member for Buckinghamshire, a plan that would entail a more than modest purchase of land. This is the real import of his asking Philip Rose at this time to be his confidential agent and "man of business."[74] It was undoubtedly with great relief that he realized that there would be no immediate dissolution that fall, and that by December his solicitor, Richard Wright, had finally arranged a settlement of the most pressing debt, more than £10,000 owing to Robert Hume and others.

Indeed, the anxieties of his precarious financial situation must have seemed manageable (perhaps even trivial) to Disraeli in the light of his first invitation, after the parliamentary session was over, to visit Belvoir Castle, the home of the Duke of Rutland, Lord John Manners's father. The duke had previously been deeply suspicious of Disraeli's character, and this invitation was clearly a recognition of his contribution to the Protectionist cause and the defence of the landed interest. Disraeli's gratification is reflected in the letter to his wife that he wrote on his arrival: "Nothing cd. be more delightful than our voyage to Belvoir, and nothing more amiable than G. [Granby, the duke's elder son]. The scene, the weather, the castle on its wooded crag flushed in the sun – Coningsby to the life – we arrived in our fly and were received by six servants bowing in rows."[75] This is truly an emblematic moment, but satisfying as it was for life to thus imitate art, the political romance still contained the tensions associated with the antithetical versions of the self that found such heightened rhetorical expression in recent events, but which also informed the structure of both the politics and the fiction from the very outset of Disraeli's public careers. The force of those tensions can frequently be caught in the private correspondence, especially the letters to Sarah and Mary Anne. For example, the letter to his sister that announces that he has settled "the long litigated affair of Hume," goes directly on to say, "We dine today with the Lionels" [the Rothschilds].[76] At the literal level this is merely endearing family news. But such a juxtaposition of the scheming debtor and the dinner companion of aristocratic bankers, even in a short note written in obvious haste, is also an association that perfectly exemplifies the sustaining and recuperative powers of Disraeli's psychological romance.

Tancred and the Politics of Identity: Principles, Expediency, and Trust

When in September 1846, after the parliamentary session had concluded without a dissolution, and after the glorious visit to Belvoir Castle,
Disraeli repaired once again to Bradenham. He did so intending to take
up the "abortive MSS" of the previous year, which was ostensibly a
continuation of the Young England novels.[1] That he told his friendly
and obliging creditor, Thomas Bailey, that he intended to "work very
hard upon it,"[2] and that, indeed, *Tancred; or the New Crusade* was finished in the short space of four months, indicate that the project was of
some personal urgency, probably both for the income it might bring,
and for the release of ideas and emotions it would provide. As the
manuscript and the correspondence show, Disraeli had done little more
than re-establish the "new generation" theme of *Coningsby* and *Sybil* in
the person of the young Tancred, Lord Montacute, before he had abandoned this new story, and become caught up in the "political atmosphere of fever heat" produced by the crisis of the Irish famine and the
possibility of Sir Robert Peel's return to office. The manuscript is on
folded folios, giving four pages to each. In folio 42 there is a clear break
in the narration, with notes toward an eventual resumption taking up
pages 3 and 4. In the printed text of the novel, this break occurs at the
end of chapter 6, Book 1, volume 1.[3]

When he resumed work on the novel, almost a year later, Disraeli's
fame and notoriety had been significantly increased by his role in the
Corn Law debate and the resignation of Peel's ministry after their defeat on the Irish Coercion Bill. It would, therefore, not be unusual for
the intervening experiences, and the transformations of identity they
contained, to shape the form and structure, and perhaps even the theme
of the continuation of this third political novel. Such a recognition

might prove helpful in overcoming the problems of taste and interpretation that have shaped the critical response to the novel ever since it first appeared in March 1847. Both favourable and unfavourable assessments of *Tancred* have generally followed a separation of matter and manner. On the one hand, the ideas of the novel are discussed as being either profound or naïve, while quite distinctly the manner, including plot, characterizations, and setting, are treated as either fascinating or deplorable.

Those in the circle of Disraeli's close friends praised *Tancred* for its vivid characters and depictions of oriental scenes, and they enthused as well about his success in portraying a hero of spiritual values. Lord John Manners, for example, said that it was "charming as a novel, wild as a romance, picturesque as an illustrated book of travel, and profound and soaring as a theological speculation."[4] The members of the family, Isaac and Sarah in particular, were also much impressed with the book, especially its treatment of the Jewish motif. Indeed, Isaac's compliments were very effusive, and could not but confirm Disraeli's sense of having successfully vindicated his familial and cultural heritage. It was, his father said, "a work for its originality and execution without a rival; faultless in composition, profound in philosophy, and magical in the loveliness of its descriptions."[5]

For the most part, however, Disraeli's contemporary readers, though usually captivated by the early scenes of social satire, found that the second half of the novel was, at its best, a descent into a "prolonged travelogue," and more frequently a "bizarre and incoherent," "strange phantasmagoria" – "a mere mystification."[6] Not a few readers took offence at Disraeli's dismissal of all that was progressive, liberal, and enlightened in the Victorian culture, and many were appalled at the implications of his arguments for the innate superiority of the Hebrew race. Richard (Dicky) Monckton Milnes, for example, in rejecting the idea of "the essential and inalienable prerogative of the Jewish race, to be at once the moral ruler and the political master of humanity," concluded that he must "distrust the fitness of such a man [as the author] to take a prominent part in the direction of the affairs of a nation which he so little esteems and understands."[7]

Most subsequent critics have tended to follow this separation of a slightly opaque novel of ideas from its dramatic embodiment in a completely implausible Bildungsroman. Very influential in this regard, for example, were Monypenny and Buckle, who, having sketched the story and characters of the novel in their previous chapter, then provided a lucid summary of Disraeli's views on the Jewish race, on the role of the Church of England, and of the relation between them in his mind.[8] To be fair, it should be noted that in outlining the bewilderment of previous critics, Monypenny and Buckle do acknowledge that, though *Tancred* did its author a disservice by increasing the "distrust already existing in many minds," and though it "hindered and delayed public recognition of the real seriousness of his political ideas and of the lofty nature of his patriotism," it offered those who "penetrated deep into the spirit of the novel … more of Disraeli's message to his age than … any other of his works."[9] Most modern critics, even the most astute, have found, however, that a consideration of this message does not prevent them from concluding that the novel is deeply flawed.

In his chapter "The Trilogy," Robert Blake, for example, makes some cogent discriminations among the ideas that constitute Disraeli's philosophy, but he admits that "it is not easy to disentangle the novels as novels from their 'message.'" *Tancred*, he believes, is only a "vehicle for Disraeli's own highly idiosyncratic views on race and religion," most of which appear to be derived from his father's *The Genius of Judaism* (1833).[10] In Blake's view Disraeli's conception of regenerating English life remains "indistinct and cloudy," and consequently "it cannot be said that he gets very far" in "propagating his theory" because he "has no idea what to do with his hero" once he gets him to the Holy Land. Blake argues, indeed, that after the supposedly climactic, but "regrettable" scene on Mount Sinai, over which "it is kinder to draw a veil," the book becomes "chaotic" – essentially just "a series of paradoxes on the theme of race and religion." On this basis Blake dismisses the next two volumes of the novel, which, he concludes, "trail off into a wild Oriental phantasmagoria" that, "suitably cut [would] make an excellent film scenario."[11] As literary criticism, this is not very helpful, for, whether from a desire to protect Disraeli from the consequences of his own indiscretions, or from a mere embarrassment of taste, Blake chooses to avoid any discussion of the details, structure, relationships, and narrative point of view in the second half of the novel.

In a somewhat similar way, Richard Levine's discussion of *Tancred* takes it to be "a vehicle for Disraeli to present more clearly his views of the Hebraeo-Christian Church."[12] Hence Levine also sees the fiction solely as a means to give the reader "the theoretical foundation of religious thought upon which men like Eustace Lyle in *Coningsby* and Aubrey St Lys in *Sybil* can erect their practical applications of … religious medievalism."[13] Once again this description and analysis of

Disraeli's ideas is illuminating, particularly in so far as Levine shows how radically English culture would need to be redefined in order to make Disraeli's vision of a harmonious nation real. But it is significant, that when he tries to provide a sketch of Tancred's "adventures" in the Holy Land, Levine offers an inaccurate, reductive, and very misleading summary, which distorts the import of events within the story.[14] Moreover, he then explicitly builds his own argument about Disraeli's intentions on the basis of "the assumed later marriage between Tancred and Eva," and the symbolic value of "this pyramid of marriages" within the three Young England novels. The ending of *Tancred* is, however, far more problematic than this allows, and such a reading beyond the text is unwarranted.

The most ambitious literary treatment of *Tancred* to date is that of Daniel R. Schwarz, who astutely links Tancred's new crusade both to Disraeli's early works, *The Voyage of Captain Popanilla*, *Contarini Fleming*, and *Alroy*, and to the genre of Victorian spiritual autobiography.[15] Schwarz also sees some continuity between *Tancred* and the previous two novels, *Coningsby* and *Sybil*, when he suggests that its "implicit premise" is likewise that a prophetic voice could arouse the moral sensibilities of a new generation of aristocratic leaders. Yet, ultimately, he too, along with Blake and Levine, is troubled by the discontinuity created by the extravagantly melodramatic plot, which turns the story into a "clumsy metaphor for the discovery of the divine within oneself."[16] In Schwarz's view, too, the second half of the novel "dissolves into a spiritual myth of Sisyphus" and Tancred becomes not the heir to, but rather "a ludicrous parody of … those biblical heroes to whom God and his angels spoke."[17] The "progressive dubiety" in each of the three novels' endings, Schwarz argues, "demonstrates Disraeli's disillusionment with Young England as a political movement," and "his frustration with his failure to obtain political power."[18]

The difficulty with this latter argument is that the specific political context does not support such an interpretation of Disraeli's feelings, and, indeed, suggests the opposite. However much Disraeli might have idealized Young England, he also saw the movement in pragmatic terms, and he clearly felt some ambivalence about the tension between principles and expediency that his role as leader of the small group embodied. But nothing could be more clear than his gratification in reporting to Mary Anne from the Carlton Club that Peel's ministry had resigned: "All 'Coningsby' & 'Young England' the general exclamation here. Everyone says they were fairly written down."[19] And the sense of personal triumph that underlies Disraeli's account of arriving at Belvoir Castle for a visit a week later has already been noted. It is, therefore, wrong to conclude, as Jane Ridley also does, that when Disraeli sat down at Bradenham to resume work on the manuscript of *Tancred* in mid-September, he was disillusioned or frustrated.[20] It is true that the Young England movement had by then been subsumed by the Corn Law debate and the growth of the Protectionist party. But Disraeli's letters show clearly that "Young England" was also now congruent with his own identity. The reputation that he is happy to accept – of having "written down" Peel, and hence of meriting the favour of the Tory aristocracy – is in his eyes a substantial accomplishment that gives him more power than he has ever had. If the pun can be forgiven, in both pragmatic and personal terms Young England had proved to be a smashing success. *Tancred* cannot, therefore, reasonably be seen as some form of defence against a sense of failure in Disraeli's political life, though it could well embody an imaginative exploration of the future's potential to transcend the all too pyrrhic victory over Sir Robert Peel and thus to realize even higher ambitions.

Whether or not such essentially autobiographical connections are considered, most modern critics of *Tancred* have seen the novel itself as a failure. Typical is Paul Smith, who, in his otherwise astute brief biography, says that "the promise of the novel's sparkling opening ... is sadly belied by the pilgrim's guide to the Holy Land which follows. Tancred is no more than a vapid vehicle for his creator's ideological obsessions ... The novel runs downhill to an unsatisfying conclusion."[21] An exception to the trend would be Nils Clausson, who, though he resists autobiographical and political readings of the novel, has more recently argued that our misreadings of Disraeli's achievement result from our failure to see that he was working within the genres of "the quixotic or ironic *Bildungsroman* ... and, even more relevantly, the historical romance."[22] Clausson points out that in structure and theme *Tancred* has interesting parallels with Scott's *Waverley* and he notes that Tancred is presented with much the same ironic narrative detachment as informs the characterization of Scott's hero. Schwarz, on the other hand, also believes that there was a failure of realized intent, when he argues that "Disraeli must have felt that he had not dramatized the enduring spiritual principles on which a revived Church could be based, and that *Tancred* did not provide an alternative to utilitarian rationality and objectivity."[23] But in this case the sense of failure is not Disraeli's, and Schwarz is incorrect when he adds that Disraeli "would have seen with regret" that his novel "vacillates erratically from its political moorings to its concern with faith, subjectivity and imagination." To the contrary, as his correspondence shows, Disraeli seems to have been very proud of his accomplishment in *Tancred*, and it continued to be his favourite of all his novels for many years. For example, in a much later letter to an American journalist, Robert Carter, he commented: "I never venture to offer any *literary* criticism on anything I have ever written, tho' I do not shrink, and have not in my late preface, from fully stating or discussing the political or religious views involved. But as you have given me yr opinion about 'Tancred' & asked mine, I will venture to observe, that throwing aside 'Lothair' of wh: I wish not now to speak, I have never written anything that entirely fulfilled my purpose, & satisfied me, except 'Tancred.'"[24] More frequently the critics' sense of *Tancred*'s failure is ostensibly aesthetic, and derives largely from an inability to see any meaningful pattern in the seeming confusions of the latter half of the work. But it may also derive from an embarrassed reluctance to explore the autobiographical significance of such a trashy, fantastic, and adolescent narrative. Thus, for example, Edward Said, in his generally perspicacious and rewarding study *Orientalism*, is confident that,

> the failure of ... *Tancred* can easily be ascribed to its author's perhaps over-developed knowledge of Oriental politics and the British Establishment's network of interests; Tancred's ingenuous desire to go to Jerusalem very soon mires Disraeli in ludicrously complex descriptions of how a Lebanese tribal chieftain tries to manage Druzes, Muslims, Jews, and Europeans to his political advantage. By the end of the novel Tancred's Eastern quest has more or less disappeared because there is nothing in Disraeli's material vision of Oriental realities to nourish the pilgrim's somewhat capricious impulses.[25]

There is a core of truth within this judgment. And Said's general point, that *Tancred* displays the features of Orientalism – a Western construction of attitudes toward the East – is worth reiterating. Even his specific assertion that the novel is "steeped in racial and geographical platitudes" is not one to bring objection. Disraeli's memories of his Grand Mediterranean tour in 1830–1 had been refreshed and nourished by newspaper accounts of the war in the Lebanon in the late 1830s and early 1840s. And when he first conceived the outline of the novel in 1845, he made a point of reading memoirs, political correspondence, and travel books written by Westerners just returned from the Middle East.[26] There is still, however, a critical tendency here to reduce the novel to a mere travelogue heightened by the author's imagination.

This standard view of *Tancred*, exemplified above, that it is a not very successful, completely implausible, and largely incoherent conclusion to the trilogy of novels written to propagate the ideas of the Young England movement, results from a failure to examine the work closely, and to see how precisely the fiction and the politics are related. *Tancred* is in fact a fiction well within the genre of the psychological romance that defines Disraeli's previous works, and there is a political element in the result that ties this novel very directly both to the crisis of Tory politics surrounding the repeal of the Corn Law in 1846, and to the earlier conflicts of Disraeli's public and private senses of his identity in the years of his political apprenticeship, his adolescence, and his childhood. The central theme in both the politics and the fiction is one of trustworthiness, and Disraeli's ambivalent sense of his political identity is reflected in the plot and characterizations of the novel. More precisely, the internal conflict between principle and expediency in Disraeli's political life, and his ambivalence about each of them, appear in *Tancred* in the form of antithetical characterizations of the protagonists and in a romance plot structure, which, in psychological terms, are projections of Disraeli's fantasies about his identity. The previous chapter indicates how Disraeli attempted in 1846 to establish his position as the principled advocate of a noble cause, and then how the crisis of the Corn Law debate undermined this claim at the very moment of his success. It also shows that the climate of opinion in the newspaper commentary of the day intensified the issue of Disraeli's integrity in ways that had both public and private significance for him. What can now be shown are the imaginative parallels between the politics and the fiction, which demonstrate that the ostensible theme of the novel (the sanction for a revivified Judaic-Christian faith) becomes subsumed in a psychological romance designed to explore, and perhaps to justify, the motivations and actions of Disraeli's recent political behaviour.

The ways in which *Tancred* is a continuation, however unsatisfactory, of the Young England novels, *Coningsby* and *Sybil*, are quite straightforward. The new novel begins by re-establishing "the new generation" theme of heroic sensibility in the person of Tancred, Lord Montacute, who, like Harry Coningsby, rejects the easy path of political preferment, but does so in order to pursue the sanctions for a new religious faith that were adumbrated to Charles Egremont by Aubrey St Lys as part of the religious allegory in *Sybil*. Much of the first two books of *Tancred* consists of the same malicious satire of the *beau monde*, particularly its complacent and selfish materialism, its moral corruption, and its intellectual fatuity as were exposed in the two earlier works. Moreover, as a deliberate reprise, Coningsby and Edith, Egremont and Sybil, Sidonia, and other members of Young England are briefly introduced, though it is clear that, except for Sidonia, they have no direct bearing on the story about to unfold. There is, however, a noticeable difference of tone and perspective, for the protagonists of Young England are presented in *Tancred* with a considerable authorial distance which conveys the ironic realization that the zeal of Young England has found a comfortable accommodation to the realities of social and political success.[27]

Tancred is also, however, a continuation of the themes and fantasies of Disraeli's much earlier fiction, in particular those of *Contarini Fleming*, *The Wondrous Tale of Alroy*, and *The Rise of Iskander*. As the earlier chapters have shown, these works, and others such as *The Young Duke* and *Henrietta Temple*, are imaginatively autobiographical in that they embody in their fantasy structures the tensions and conflicts of Disraeli's personality. The central theme of all these works is that of defining a heroic identity from conflicting forces – those of a need to claim an innate superiority and integrity of character, and of a need to force a recognition of achievement from an alien establishment by whatever means are expedient. It is clear, however, that the core of Disraeli's personality contained not just a simple tension between these claims of what I have labelled "purity" and "success," but also a profound ambivalence within each conception about the costs of maintaining it.

As shown earlier, this psychological tension manifests itself in Disraeli's political career as the rival claims of altruism and expediency. The former, the need to claim a superior integrity, is the shaping force of the paternalistic Tory ideology that Disraeli adopted in the 1830s, and of the subsequent defence of constitutional principles in the name of Young England. The latter, the need to demonstrate his success, underlies Disraeli's opportunistic fondness for intrigue and manipulation, as well as his susceptibility to theories of clandestine government. Moreover, both the politics and the fiction of the early years make it clear that the conception of principled altruism was for Disraeli directly related to the question of religious identity, and that the ambivalence he felt about the relative costs of altruism and expediency was in part a function of his ambiguous position as a Christianized Jew in a society rife with prejudice. *Tancred* is a romance in which these elements mingle.

When he first began the novel in the fall of 1845 Disraeli no doubt intended to pursue the implications of the religious allegory embodied in *Sybil* by sending his eponymous hero to the Holy Land to gain divine sanction for the doctrine of "theocratic equality" as the basis for a renewed Judaic-Christian faith. But the crisis over the repeal of the Corn Law, in which the questions of principle and expediency were so sharply dramatized, first by Disraeli's characterizations of Peel and then by the incident of the "lie," led Disraeli to explore again, as he had done before in the fantasies of fiction, the ambivalences he felt about the conflicting claims of purity and success. The shape that this exploration of values takes in *Tancred*, I would argue, reflects not Disraeli's thematic incoherence, but rather his desire to assess the possibility of reconciling principled and expedient behaviour in political life. Accordingly the dynamics of the romance plot embody the relation between altruism and expediency through the relationship of the two protagonists, who are, in effect, aspects of a split personality. Tancred, the only son and heir of the Duke of Bellamont, is the personification of nobility, altruism, and faith, while the Emir Fakredeen, a prince of the Lebanon (whom Leslie Stephen called "a Syrian Vivian Grey"),[28] is portrayed as a completely egocentric, ambitious opportunist, who lives in a swirl of schemes and lies designed to extract him from his crushing debts and to gain him political power over a unified Syrian kingdom. Disraeli had used this narrative agency of a split persona once before, in a short tale, *The Rise of Iskander*, whose fantasy structure bears a strong similarity to that of *Tancred*: essentially that of two antithetical romantic rivals (one strong and courageous, one vacillating and weak) of ostensibly differing religious faiths, who engage in military escapades and rescue the heroine from captivity.

In *Tancred*, Fakredeen's schemes, first to capture and ransom and then to befriend the English nobleman of whom he is so deeply in awe, suggest a recognition on the author's part of the ways in which principles, and those who hold them dear, can be exploited by men of base motives in the pursuit of their personal gratifications. Similarly, Tancred's high-mindedness suggests altruism's vulnerability to that exploitation, while his transformation, from a pilgrim seeking the word of God on Mount Sinai to a man who plans to convert the whole of the civilized world by conquering it with Arabian cavalry, suggests the author's understanding of the way in which the high ideals of a principled cause can feed extravagant power fantasies to the point of being self-consuming.

The imaginatively autobiographical nature of *Tancred* can also be seen in the way the work reflects Disraeli's special attachment to his sister. It is clear from their correspondence that Sarah played a very special role in his imaginative as well as his practical life. From the days of his adolescence on, she was the intimate confidante of Disraeli's most intense ambitions, the constant admirer of his genius, and the delighted observer of his every social and political triumph. Because she lived at Bradenham with their parents, she was shielded from most of her brother's sexual indiscretions, but she certainly knew a good deal more about the embarrassments of his debts than did his father, his wife, his lawyers, or perhaps even his creditors. Not surprisingly, then, she could also be on occasion a gentle but cogent critic of his scrapes and imbroglios, though never to a third party. Because of her complete loyalty and their childhood and adolescent intimacy, and perhaps as well because of her isolation from the corruptions of London society, Sarah became for her brother a symbol of what was best in his Judaic heritage and what was ideal in personal relations.

Both the literal and symbolic features of this familial bond are embodied in *Tancred* in the relationships between the two protagonists and the heroine, Eva, daughter of Adam Besso, the chief banker and agent of Sidonia in the Middle East. Fakredeen, the emir of Canobia, was orphaned as an infant and has been raised as a foster-brother to Eva. But his adolescent romantic attachment to her has been thwarted by her engagement to her cousin, so that their intimacy ostensibly remains that of siblings. It is quite obvious that the dynamics of their relationship are in large measure modelled on those of Disraeli and his sister, for Eva shares knowledge of, even if she doubts the wisdom of, her foster-brother's many schemes to evade his debts, and of his endless "combinations," by which he dreams of gaining political power amid the quarrelling factions of Lebanon. Moreover, Eva and Fakredeen spend considerable time discussing the matter of his shifting religious identities. Indeed, in a single scene of some half-dozen pages, Fakredeen claims to be first a Christian, then a Muslim, and finally a Hebrew, the last provoking her amused and amazed indignation at his effrontery. By comparison it is worth recalling the tone of the letter to Disraeli from Sarah in April 1832, when he was attempting to be seen as both a Tory and a Radical amidst the Reform Bill controversy: "I long to see you that you may read me many riddles. The principal one is, how you will reconcile your constituents to your politics."[29] In Fakredeen's relations with Eva there is also a manipulative and exploitive element, as, for example, when he pleads with her to persuade her father to loan him money, or when he uses her fondness for him to engage her in unknowingly deceiving his chief creditor, Scheriff Effendi, about her father's sanction of his plans. This may well be a distorted reflection of the role Sarah played in Disraeli's financial affairs. The correspondence certainly shows that both his father, Isaac, and his wife, Mary Anne, were kept in the dark about the true extent of his debts, and that, at least in the case of the latter, Sarah was instrumental in intercepting letters that contained embarrassing revelations about his misrepresentations in that regard.

Tancred's relationship to Eva is, by contrast, one of purest altruism. Admittedly, it is tinged with erotic interests that make the two protagonists sexual rivals from the outset. But the romantic element of Tancred's interest in Eva is clearly tied to her sympathies for his religious quest. And her purity of mind is the more obvious for the comparison with the young women Tancred had met in London before his departure to the Holy Land. In the first instance Tancred falls under the charming influence of Lady Constance Rawleigh. Lady Constance, the narrator remarks, was "clever": "she talked like a married woman, was critical, yet easy; and having guanoed her mind by reading French novels, had a variety of conclusions on all social topics ... These were all new to Tancred, and startling. He was attracted by the brilliancy, though he often regretted the tone, which he ascribed to the surrounding corruption from which he intended to escape, and almost wished to save her at the same time." Lady Constance recommends "The Revelations of Chaos," the latest work on evolution (the title is a parody of Robert Chambers's 1844 *Vestiges of Creation*): "'everything is explained by geology and astronomy ... It shows you exactly how a star is formed; nothing can be so pretty! A cluster of vapour, the cream of the milky way, a sort of celestial cheese, churned into light, you must read it, 'tis charming.'" At this point, Tancred quickly regains the urgency of his crusade: "'What a spiritual mistress! ... I must get out of this city as quickly as possible; I cannot cope with its corruption.'"[30] Before he manages to do so, however, he becomes infatuated with the Countess of Bertie and Bellair, who *is* married, but who, under the guise of sympathy for his desire to visit Jerusalem, conducts herself with such flirtatious impropriety as to call her marital fidelity into question. Only when Tancred learns that she is "the most inveterate female gambler in Europe," and a notorious speculator in railway shares, does he extricate himself from her sighs and set sail. By contrast, Eva is for Tancred the embodiment of spiritual purity, as, in the setting of her garden at

Bethany, she discusses with him the doctrines of the Expiation and Atonement and so dissolves the basis for any prejudicial distinctions between Christians and Jews.

Given the insistence with which Lord George Bentinck had demanded that there be "atonement" for Peel's betrayal of his party in 1846, it is perhaps significant that Disraeli makes the Christian "doctrine of the Atonement" the crux of his discussion of the Jewish question in *Tancred*. And in that regard it is also worth noting that in Jewish theology "atonement" is a purification of the sinner and a reconciliation with God through the process of confession, repentance, ritual, and acceptance of God's grace. In Christian theology, by contrast, though it is among the most complex and debated of doctrines, the "Atonement" refers to the sacrificial death of Christ as the specific agency of mankind's redemption. In having Eva and Tancred discuss the apparent differences of their two religions, Disraeli's intent, it is clear, is to remove the stigma attached to the Jews ostensibly on the authority of the Gospels. When Tancred attempts to justify the "penal" state of the Jews by claiming it is "'the punishment ordained for their rejection and crucifixion of the Messiah'" and naively cites the self-inflicted curse of the multitude, "Upon our heads and upon our children be his blood,"[31] Eva, like many a biblical textual scholar since, points to the inadequacy of that as any proof of divine intention, and raises the complementary issue of the diaspora. And when Tancred turns to the theme of "the Expiation" as the essence of the Christian scheme, an idea she characterizes as full of "mystery, power and solace," Eva responds: "'Now tell me: suppose the Jews had not prevailed upon the Romans to crucify Jesus, what would have become of the Atonement?'" This implicitly perverse rationalization, in effect, felix culpa, is then carried to its logical extremity when Tancred describes the Crucifixion as "'pre-ordained by the Creator of the world for countless ages,'" and Eva then replies that there can surely be no inexpiable crime in so fulfilling God's will.[32] The conclusion to the argument is that the Jews, far from being the objects of Christian persecution, should be worshipped as the saviours of the human race. Both the extravagance of Eva's final assertion; "'Why, if you believed what you profess, you should kneel to us!'" and the tone of paradoxical syllogizing throughout, were deeply offensive to many of Disraeli's more serious readers, who resented what they regarded as his flippancy over matters of faith.

It would seem, however, that the liberties that Disraeli takes with the doctrine of the Atonement are designed primarily to undermine the

religious rationalizations of what was in reality a largely secular prejudice against the Jews in Victorian England. We should remember that
Disraeli's hero is naive in more than one way, as the remainder of the
novel plainly shows, and that elsewhere Disraeli had offered other,
more cogent reasons for religious and social tolerance; though he does
repeat the argument from *Tancred* in the anomalous 24th chapter on the
history of the Jewish race in *Lord George Bentinck* in 1852.[33] But, though
Disraeli sincerely believed in the fundamental continuity of the Judaic
and Christian faiths (as adumbrated, for example, in *Sybil*), it would be
wrong to take these arguments in *Tancred* as a serious attempt at theological disputation on Disraeli's part. Rather, the whole discussion of
the Atonement here seems to resonate with the motif of innate purity
and demonstrated success that were so marked a feature of his previous political and literary careers. It is reasonable, of course, to see Eva's
arguments for the superiority of the Jewish race to all others simply as
a compensation for the unpleasant reality of the anti-Semitism which
Disraeli could not ignore. But her use of the "Atonement," with its associations of purification and redemption, as part of that claim may
also reflect Disraeli's more private fantasy of reconciling the two idealized conceptions of heroism that will inevitably continue to shape his
destiny – those of Tory nobility and racial identity. The discussion of the
Jewish question in *Tancred* thus works not just as a defiance of prejudice, or a revolt against conventional political wisdom,[34] but also as a
reclamation of purity and principle – on the hero's part, and on the
author's. The integration of faiths towards which the plot moves is thus
in both public and private spheres the secular and spiritual at-one-ment
the religious doctrines prescribe. And as a fiction of identity *Tancred* is a
novel about the reintegration of the self.

In that regard, Tancred's dependence upon Eva's powers of confirmation is then extended later in the novel when she nurses him back to
health, after he has received the "doctrine of theocratic equality" from
the angel of Arabia on Mount Sinai[35] and lies fevered and apparently
dying, either from his vision or his previous wounds, amid his Arabian
captors in the desert. The relation of this fictional dependency, and its
associated purity of spirit, to Disraeli's affections for his sister is a matter of contextual, rather than direct, evidence. Disraeli's detailed knowledge of the Holy Land, and hence of the specific settings of this novel,
was gained on his Grand Tour of the Middle East as a young man, in
1830–1. It was on that trip that William Meredith, Sarah's fiancé, tragic-
ally contracted smallpox and died suddenly in Cairo just as they were

preparing to return home in the summer of 1831. As I have shown, the anguish felt by Disraeli on his sister's behalf led to an intensification of their mutual devotion that became, as Sir Philip Rose said, "a passion bordering upon romance."[36] And *Alroy* (1834), the first of Disraeli's fictions to use the Middle-Eastern setting, and the one he described as portraying his "ideal ambition,"[37] contains the most intensely devotional brother-sister relationship of all his novels. Tancred and Eva in many ways echo the theme of religious purity established earlier in the love of David Alroy for his sister, Miriam, and which in turn reflects the idealizations and intense poignancy of Sarah's devotion to Disraeli and of his to her.

In a very real sense, then, *Tancred* is autobiographical in that it embodies in its characterizations the ideas and feelings that are significant in Disraeli's earlier life, not just the years of his political apprenticeship, but clearly also those of his adolescence and youth. But the specific relation of the novel to events in 1846 becomes clear when the shape of its plot is examined.[38] The Young England theme of noble altruism is firmly established in the first two books through Tancred's rejection of both a secular career and the delights of society. In so far as people tended to read Disraeli's novels as a key to his character, such a disavowal of conventional ambition may serve as an imaginative defence against the cynical charge of his being a mere "political adventurer," a view that was certainly widespread, even within the Protectionist party. In the novel, the purity of Tancred's principles is best illustrated by the dismissal of the bishop whom his parents have asked to dissuade him from his folly of going to Jerusalem. One should note that it is the narrator who embodies Tancred's caustic judgment of this unfortunate prelate: "Placed in a high post in an age of political analysis, the bustling intermeddler was unable to supply society with a single solution. Enunciating second-hand, with characteristic precipitation, some big principle in vogue, as if he were a discoverer, he invariably shrank from its subsequent application, the moment that he found it might be unpopular and inconvenient. All his quandaries terminated in the same catastrophe; a compromise. Abstract principles with him ever ended in concrete expediency."[39]

If, however, the plot of *Tancred* is examined from the perspective of Fakredeen, the active as opposed to the passive protagonist, there is a startling similarity in the structural dynamics of the fantasy to the expediencies of the role Disraeli played in the Corn Law debate. To summarize briefly: Fakredeen, deeply in debt and consumed by power fantasies, schemes to arrange various political "combinations" and to capture and ransom the noble Tancred. But he finds himself so awed by Tancred's altruism that he imagines that he could assume a similar identity through the osmosis of intimate friendship. For a while it seems that the two friends can share the religious crusade that has motivated Tancred from the outset. But their plans become increasingly strategic and pragmatic, ending in their decision to visit the Ansarey, a mysterious tribe in the mountains to the north who are essential as allies if the whole of the Near East is to be conquered and converted. When, however, they visit Astarte, the queen of the Ansarey, in her remote mountain fortress, Gindarics (a version of the Krak des Chevaliers, built by the Crusaders), they discover that this tribe are the descendants of the Greeks who inhabited classical Antioch, that they still worship the Olympian gods, and that Tancred bears a remarkable resemblance to the statue of Apollo in their temple. At this point, Fakredeen thinks he sees an opportunity for a personal alliance with the queen. He indulges in a fantasy of establishing "the Gentile dynasty of Fakredeen and Astarte"[40] ruling over an independent Syria, and he betrays his noble friend and their great cause by repeatedly lying to the queen about Tancred's plans and his own identity. He tells Astarte, who appears to have fallen in love with Tancred, that the Englishman is already engaged to the Jewess, Eva, and that Tancred's ambitions are only the worldly ones of establishing himself as the monarch of Syria. This is, of course, but a projection of Fakredeen's own selfish ambition and of his previously confessed desire to marry his foster-sister. When the queen's jealousy proves explosive, and she imprisons Eva, who has been captured by the Ansarey while on her way to her wedding at Aleppo, Fakredeen dissembles and claims to be a long-time enemy of the Besso family. He pleads for the privilege of executing his "more than sister," but then in her dungeon cell he confesses all his villainy to her and they escape, returning to her father at Aleppo. Meanwhile, dismissing Fakredeen as a "vile intriguer," Tancred resolves to defend the queen's domain from the invading Turks sent to avenge Eva's capture. This he does in heroic fashion, before being forced to flee to the eastern desert, still the symbolic setting of his original plan. Back in Jerusalem Tancred once again meets Eva, who, apparently still unmarried, consoles him for the loss of his faith in the possibility of regenerating the whole world, and to whom he suddenly declares his ardent love. Meanwhile, Fakredeen seems to have disappeared.

By comparison, at the beginning of 1846, Disraeli, hopelessly in debt, schemes to overthrow Peel's Government, but finds, when the parliamentary session begins, that there is the great cause of Protection and the landed constitution to fight for. In the course of the debate his friendship with Lord George Bentinck considerably strengthens his vision of himself as a principled advocate of a noble cause, although it is clear that his personal ambitions are but subsumed in it. In the exigencies of the struggle, it is also clear that the so-called venomous attacks and vituperation heaped upon the prime minister involve a projection of his own reputation for inconsistency and insincerity on to his victim. At the climax of the debate he finds that he must in desperation so categorically deny that he ever sought office under Peel that others believe his statement to be a lie. His motive in making such a claim was perhaps to save the noble cause of Protection which he has endangered by his excess, perhaps, paradoxically, to save his ambitions by denying them. It is important that other than the prime minister and his close cabinet colleagues, Sarah was the one person who knew for certain that Disraeli had not told the whole truth in disclaiming both his willingness to serve under Peel and his applications for favours, for she had shared by letters his earlier mortification. Hence, I think it is important that Eva plays a confessional role for Fakredeen and a consolatory one for Tancred in the fictional, imaginatively recreated version of these events.

The full congruency of the fiction and the politics has been amply demonstrated in the detailed analysis of the ways Disraeli's sense of himself as a principled person was entangled in 1846 with his antagonism to Peel and his friendship with Lord George Bentinck. But I would not argue reductively that the fictional exploration of the relation between altruism and expediency ends with an unequivocal rejection of the latter. The narrator's attitude towards both Tancred and Fakredeen is too ambiguous to support that conclusion. Rather, I would note that Tancred is portrayed sceptically, as amusingly naive throughout the book, and that his crusade is several times on the verge of being described as absurd. This can be attributed in part to the regressive fantasy structure of the plot, which, as the comparisons with *Alroy* and *Iskander* suggest, has its origins far back in the grandiose daydreams of Disraeli's youth or childhood.[41] As Tancred himself explicitly fears, and wishes to deny, his quest is a mere boyish fantasy. But it is equally significant that Fakredeen is also an essentially comic figure for the narrator, who repeatedly suggests his fondness for this scoundrel whose pathos is always equal to his villainy.

Disraeli has often been given credit for great originality in his portrayal of Fakredeen. Lady Blessington, for example, considered him "one of the finest conceptions ever painted." "Never," she said, "was there so true a portrait of a misapplied Genius, and an unprincipled mind. With what wonderful skill have you managed this character forcing your readers to love, while they cannot esteem him."[42] Mary Millar has pointed out that Fakredeen was seen by many of Disraeli's friends to be a portrait of George Sydney Smythe, whose friendship with Disraeli was characterized by what she calls "the double game" of his conspiratorial assistance and anonymous betrayals.[43] But the nature of Disraeli's imaginative genius in transforming life into literature, and vice-versa, is more fully revealed by noticing the literary and historical source of this characterization. In Eliot Warburton's *The Crescent and the Cross* there is a chapter on the mountain tribes of the Lebanon, which contains the embryonic conception of Disraeli's second protagonist and his obsessions. In Warburton's account, the emir "Fakreddin ... wanted but honesty and singleness of purpose" to convert "the populace of a thousand villages into a people." But when he sought to ally himself with the Christian European nobility, he found that his popularity tempted him into the pleasures of a "voluptuary" and he "forgot the cause he had come to plead." And when "at length, he did return to the mountain, all his energies and resources were dissipated in selfish schemes of policy, and building fantastic palaces."[44] The lack of honesty, the inability to sustain a worthy purpose, the dissipation of energies, the indulgence in pleasure, the selfish schemes, and the grandiose dreams of this account are all incorporated into Disraeli's characterization of his Fakredeen. Yet the dramatized result also reflects the imaginative projection of Disraeli's own experience, including the friendship with Smythe, so that the one world becomes a metaphor for the other in this imaginatively autobiographical novel. This is not, however, the extent of Disraeli's debt to *The Crescent and the Cross*. In Warburton's chapter, "The Jew," there are a number of direct allusions, to the diaspora and other elements of Jewish history, both real and legendary, that are reflected in Eva's discussion with Tancred. And there are also depictions of interiors and landscapes in Warburton's account of his adventures to which Disraeli seems to owe more than a casual debt of inspiration for similar scenes in *Tancred*. For example, Disraeli's picture of Besso's house in Damascus obviously draws upon some of the details given in Warburton's description of a Hebrew's house to which he had been invited. And Disraeli's description of the approach to Fakredeen's castle, Canobia, is similar to Warburton's account of his mountainous journey through a region formerly controlled by the emir Bescheer.[45] Disraeli had met Warburton in the late spring of 1845, when he invited him to one of his literary breakfasts.[46] And reading *The Crescent and the Cross*, recently published by Colburn, was obviously a catalyst to Disraeli's intention to write a sequel to *Sybil*, which had also just appeared under Colburn's imprint on 9 May.

The most interesting aspect of Disraeli's characterization of Fakredeen is, nevertheless, the dynamic of his friendship with Tancred, which has already been outlined. There are a number of passages in the book that suggest the psychological identification of these two protagonists, but the crucial and most explicit one is very near the conclusion, describing Tancred's state of mind before he meets Eva again: "Tancred passed a night of agitating dreams. Sometimes he was in the starry Desert, sometimes in the caverned dungeons of Gindarics. Then, again, the scene changed to Bellamont Castle, but it would seem that Fakredeen was its Lord; and when Tancred rushed forward to embrace his mother, she assumed the form of the Syrian goddess, and yet the face was the face of Eva. Though disturbed, he slept, and when he woke, he was for a moment quite unconscious of being at Jerusalem."[47] The confusion of identities in this dream is both complex and suggestive. For one thing, it was Fakredeen, not Tancred, who visited the "caverned dungeons" of Gindarics. For another, Fakredeen momentarily seems, as heir, to have assumed the title of Tancred's father, though the immediately following Oedipal transformation of mother into lover suggests that the father is just conveniently missing. In any case, this account of Tancred's dream makes it tolerably plain that Disraeli fully intended to present Tancred and Fakredeen as alter-egos. And so, too, the curiously ambiguous image of the substitute mother is deliberate, for that is a recurring motif in both the life and the previous fiction. Certainly, the psychological nuances of the transformations in this dream (Tancred to Fakredeen, and mother to lover) would sustain the claim that Tancred, as much as Fakredeen, is imaginatively Eva's sibling.

As Daniel Bivona has also discussed from a different overall perspective,[48] the incestuous relationships intimated in this dream may be the key to the thematic resolution of the novel's plot, which differs significantly from that of *The Rise of Iskander*. In the earlier tale, written in 1832, the rival protagonists are presented as antithetical versions of a persona. Niceus, the weak and vacillating Greek prince is killed, while the noble and courageous Iskander lives victorious in love and war. By comparison, the protagonists of *Tancred* are in the end shown to be symbiotic versions of one self. And while, in the narrative terms expected of the romance genre, the conclusion of *Tancred* would seem to be as inept and inconclusive as almost all previous critics have claimed,[49] it does indirectly acknowledge this symbiosis. Tancred declares his passion to the startled Eva, who protests that their bonds to others are a taboo to such feelings. At this point she is clearly not just referring to her previous engagement. There is but a single ambiguous demonstrative pronoun in her protest, "'There are those to whom I belong; and to whom you belong,'" and she explicitly refers to their different religious faiths. Tancred's reply, "'I kneel to a daughter of my Redeemer's race,'" and his inspiration that their "united destinies shall advance the sovereign purpose of … [their] lives," would then seem to intimate a typical ending to a Disraelian novel in which religious differences are dissolved in a vision of the future in which love and power are blended. But it is then, just as Eva's head falls upon Tancred's shoulder and they embrace, that the lovers are disturbed by a commotion. The final sentence of the novel is, "The Duke and Duchess of Bellamont had arrived at Jerusalem."[50] As everyone cannot but notice, this does stop things *in medias res*. But given the emergence of the incestuous component of the fantasy at this point, it is hard to imagine a more definitive conclusion to the romance than the arrival of the hero's parents.

If, however, this ending is seen in the light of the mixture of narrative modes of which all novels partake, the arrival of the duke and duchess at Jerusalem involves to some degree a precipitous deflation of the fantasy and a return to the criteria of realism that implicitly controlled the social satire with which the novel began. In these terms the conclusion of the work is ambiguous and deliberately so, for if *Tancred* is to have any value as a social novel, Disraeli cannot leave his eponymous hero permanently estranged from his position in England as heir to the Bellamont title and estates. Yet, at the same time, the imperatives of rationality embodied in realism would in 1847 render unthinkable a marriage between the heir to an English dukedom and a Syrian Jewess. Thus, while the very presence of the Duke and Duchess of Bellamont in Jerusalem may imply some hope of reconciliation between them and their son – and hence between their worldly concerns and his spiritual values, Disraeli, by stopping short of realizing Tancred's vision of "united destinies" in a symbolic marriage, chooses to leave the reader in a state of momentous indecision. As a consequence there is a temptation to read beyond the text. Bivona, for example, has cleverly argued that the ending of the novel is a forecast of England's imperial destiny by interpreting the duke's and duchess's "move to the Middle East" as the "final step in the process of incorporation and displacement" that marks all three novels in Disraeli's "trilogy."[51]

At the end of December 1846, Disraeli confessed to Lady Londonderry that Tancred had "turned out a much more troublesome & unmanageable personage" than he had anticipated.[52] This recently resumed correspondence with the marchioness was habitually carried on in an elaborately courtly and chivalric mode, expressing his humble gratitude for the gracious condescension of her patronage. His letters to her were always designed to gratify her taste for authentic and preferably slightly malicious gossip about other members of fashionable society, particularly the aristocracy. In this case, he passes on tidbits about Lord George Bentinck (who had just paid a visit to him at Bradenham), Lord Brougham, Lord Aberdeen, Lord Lyndhurst, and Lord and Lady Jersey. In this context the impulse to tell her about his difficulties with Tancred is perfectly natural, for Lady Londonderry had an interest in literary news as well. But it does indicate that, as he approached the conclusion of his fantasy, his thoughts were also focused upon the world of the real aristocracy.

As a novel, *Tancred* thus works as a form of mediation between the realms of Disraeli's imagination and of his rational awareness. The ostensible theme of a religious integration of Christianity and Judaism is imbedded in a romance structure that carries a theme of personal integration as well – in effect it becomes an exploration of the tension between principle and expediency as the shaping motivations of honourable political behaviour. In thematic terms, the ambiguous conclusion of the religious motif and the incorporation of the "vile intriguer" into at least the dreams of Young England suggest that by 1846 Disraeli had realized that, although it was admirable to act on principles, and to be seen to do so, success in politics necessarily involved some manipulation and intrigue. *Tancred* is an embodiment of that realization, and, as such, it is more than an Oriental phantasmagoria or an impenetrable Asian mystery.

13

Leadership

In the two years immediately following the defeat of Sir Robert Peel's Government in 1846, the Protectionists under the leadership of Lord Stanley in the House of Lords and Lord George Bentinck in the Commons assumed the role of the official Opposition to the Whig ministry of Lord John Russell. Disraeli cast himself in the role of Bentinck's lieutenant as they struggled to form a coherent and disciplined party out of the least talented, least intelligent remnants of the old Tories, for the most part men more addicted to fox hunting than to politics. From the very beginning the enterprise was fraught with difficulty. As Robert Blake points out, these men, mostly landed squires and sons of the aristocracy, had little, if any, professional interest in politics and were animated mostly by the prejudices and convictions of their class.[1] The summer election of 1847 had left the balance of power much as it was. Lord John Russell's Whig minority ministry was sustained by the jealous rivalry in the split Opposition, and there seemed little that could be pursued in the way of an active Protectionist policy in the immediate future.

Then in December 1847, as a response to the election of Baron Lionel de Rothschild as a Liberal member for the City of London, Lord Russell introduced a bill for the removal of Jewish disabilities. The Government's argument for such legislation was, of course, based upon the principles of religious freedom and toleration. But Disraeli's eccentric and more controversial views on the relation between Judaism and Christianity, which had been published at length in *Tancred* the previous spring, inevitably became the focus of debate from the Protectionist benches. His repeated claim, that Christianity was but completed Judaism, and his emphasis upon the fact that their saviour was born a Jew, offended almost all of those who sat behind him. Consequently, Bentinck now found himself in a difficult position. As he indicated privately, he didn't "care two straws" about the Jews, and "heartily wish[ed] they were all back in the Holy Land."[2] But this was mostly the expression of his frustration, for he had voted for their emancipation in 1830 and 1833 on the principle of religious liberty, and he now also felt compelled by loyalty to support his co-conspirator.[3] Thus, even though there was no advantage in doing so, Bentinck spoke and voted in favour of Russell's bill, which in any case had an easy majority in the Commons, but was sure to be defeated in the Lords. When the whips conveyed to him that his actions had given "dire offence" to many of the Protectionist members, Bentinck, already frustrated by the difficulties of his position and appalled by the religious prejudices and bigotry of his followers, immediately resigned as leader.[4]

It was not known at the time that Disraeli (with some help from Bentinck) had collaborated with Lionel de Rothschild on the writing of a pamphlet, *The Progress of Jewish Emancipation Since 1829*, which had been published anonymously on 15 January 1848. But it was in any case unthinkable that a party that had, in Bentinck's words, "degenerated into a 'No Popery' 'No Jew'" affair, and that could "muster 140 ... [against] a Jew Bill" but could not claim "much above half those numbers on any question essentially connected with the great interests of the empire," would then turn to Disraeli as its leader in the Commons, even if it were acknowledged that Lord Stanley would continue to lead the party as a whole from the House of Lords.[5] It is not surprising, therefore, that the session in 1848 showed the Protectionists in the Commons to be confused and divided. Lord Granby, the eldest son of the Duke of Rutland, tried briefly but ineffectually to serve as leader, and thereafter things were left to the whips acting under Stanley's direction. Bentinck and Disraeli continued to speak when needed, but without any concerted support from the other members, and it was only at the end of the session that there seemed some possibility, at Disraeli's suggestion, of patching up the quarrel between Bentinck and Stanley. Then, in September, Bentinck died suddenly of a heart attack, leaving the question of the Protectionist leadership in the Commons even more acute.

Bentinck's death presented Disraeli with several serious problems, the first of which was the loss of friendship and the support in Parliament of his closest ally. But there was also a private, practical matter of great delicacy. Disraeli had decided that he should try to represent the constituency of his home county, Buckinghamshire, rather than a borough such as Shrewsbury, where election contests were likely to be corrupt, expensive, and hotly contested. To do this he needed to be a landowner, and so in the months just before his death, Bentinck had undertaken to enlist his two brothers' and his father's help in arranging for the purchase of an estate in Disraeli's name. But the financial arrangements were still pending. His sudden death was thus a blow to Disraeli in both emotional and financial terms, though, as it turned out, Bentinck's brothers carried through with the original scheme that enabled Disraeli to complete the purchase of Hughenden in 1849. Their motives in doing so were essentially strategic, rather than personal: to enable Disraeli to play the high game in public life as the man most able to defend the interests of the aristocracy and the landed interest.

The political consequences of Bentinck's death were not so easily or so quickly overcome. Many in the party, including Lord Stanley, were prejudiced against Disraeli and considered him too disreputable for the post of leader of the party in the House of Commons. Disraeli fully understood just how deep the antipathies went, but he also knew that for him it was now or never. He also understood that were he to be seen conspiring to grasp the leadership, it would only reinforce the perception of him as an opportunist and adventurer. His strategy was thus to let others make his claim and to organize support within the party and in the press, wherever he could behind the scenes. To bolster his confidence and gain an explicit affirmation of the legitimacy and wisdom of this course, he several times over the next few months made a pilgrimage down to Brighton to consult his friend, Prince Metternich, who was living there in exile and retirement. Metternich's advice was to see the blow of Bentinck's death, not as a defeat, but as a challenge and opportunity. It was, he said, Disraeli's duty to keep fighting for the political cause of conservatism, and he assured him that, as a man of principles and action, he would eventually come to power.[6] In his letters to Metternich at this time Disraeli also reports on the arts of social persuasion that obviously bear on the question of the leadership. On 30 October, for example, he writes from Wimpole, the "beautiful chateau" of Lord and Lady Hardwicke, that he and his wife, Mary Anne, have been staying there along with Lord Stanley, John Wilson Croker, and Samuel Wilberforce, the bishop of Oxford, whom Disraeli describes as a very young man with great abilities.

For several months the question of the leadership was discussed behind the scenes. Disraeli deliberately kept out of the way, though he certainly received advice and support from some quarters. But things came to a head at Christmas, when Disraeli received a letter from Lord Stanley, dated 21 December. In that very long letter, Stanley reviewed the problem of the leadership, saying that he must write "with an absence of reserve which nothing short of the critical state of our affairs would justify." He acknowledged that there was no one else in the party who had Disraeli's skills as a debater and that the latter's "powers of mind" and "ability" would always give him "a commanding position in the House of Commons" and "a preponderating influence" in the Conservative party. But he went on to say that he believed that making Disraeli the formal leader of the party would not receive "a general and cheerful approval" on the part of those with whom he would have to act. And so, Stanley said, he paid him "the much higher compliment" of thinking that he had both the "clearness of perception" to see this, and the "manliness of character" to acquiesce in "the feeling of the party." He further suggested that Disraeli should be satisfied with "the real eminence" of his position and give his support to "a Leader of abilities inferior to ... [his] own, who might command a more general feeling in his favour." Stanley went on to say that he therefore proposed to ask the elderly J.C. Herries, a man of some financial and commercial experience, but without any great powers of debate, to become Leader in the House of Commons. He said this would give Disraeli "an opportunity of greatly serving the party, and also of establishing a strong personal claim on them for the future," if he could but offer Herries the "support of which he will stand greatly in need."[7]

It does not take a genius to see that Lord Stanley's compliments were pure flummery. Herries was a 68-year-old mediocrity, quite incapable of real leadership, and Disraeli knew full well that the party needed him at this juncture as much as he needed them. His reply to Stanley was a masterpiece of firm civility and made it perfectly clear that, though he was gratified by the frank manner of the letter he had received, he had no intention of waiving his claims to recognition. What is particularly interesting about the reply, though, is the way Disraeli, in defining the role of Leader, subordinates all particular political issues to the larger constitutional question.

My dear Lord,

... The office of the leader of the Conservative party in the H. of C. at the present day, is to uphold the aristocratic settlement of this country. That is the only question at stake, however manifold may be the forms which it assumes in public discussion, and however various the knowledge and labor which it requires. It is an office which, in my opinion, would require the devotion, perhaps the sacrifice, of a life; and however great his qualities for its fulfilment, would not be wisely undertaken by any man, who did not possess, not only the confidence, but even the warm personal regard of those with whom he acted in political connection. If you had been in the House of Commons you could have fulfilled this office, and dark and difficult as I deem our future, I would have acted cordially under your banner, because I am sure it would have led always to honor, if not to triumph ... Honor, and personal feelings, stronger than any public consideration, attached me to George Bentinck ... But I am now free from all personal ties; and I am no longer disposed to sacrifice interesting pursuits, health, and a happy hearth, for a political career, which can bring one little fame, and, even if successful in a vulgar sense, would bear me a reward which I now little appreciate.

... I am not insensible, especially in this age, to the principle of duty – but in the present distracted state of parties, it is my opinion, however erroneous, that I could do more to uphold the cause to which I am attached, that I should have better opportunities of reviving the spirit, and raising the general tone of feeling among our friends throughout the country, by acting alone and unshackled, than if I fell into the party discipline, which you intimate.[8]

One would have had to be very imperceptive indeed not to see immediately that Disraeli acting "alone and unshackled" would mean trouble. But for the moment, Stanley persisted in his plan of asking Herries to assume the position of leader, in the hope, as he put it in a letter to Charles Newdegate, one of the whips, that "Disraeli will have the good sense to acquiesce in, and aid, the arrangement": "I have never seen, of late years, any reason to distrust him, and I think he will run straight; but he would not be acceptable as Leader."[9]

Herries would soon decline Stanley's suggestion on the ostensible grounds of his own doubtful health. Meanwhile there was a well-coordinated effort by Lord Henry Bentinck and others of Disraeli's supporters to convince Lord Stanley that he should recognize the necessity of the time and try to persuade "the awkward, crotchety fellows" who objected strenuously to the party being led by a person whose background, character, and reputation they took to be disreputable. Henry Bentinck's letter to Disraeli of 2 January 1849 gives a good sense of how the strategy unfolded. It was proposed, he said, to "collect in Town a small conclave of 14 or 15 of the most influential *fighting* men – no mutes – on Saturday next" and have them draw up and sign a petition to Lord Stanley, urging him to "be himself the means of bringing over to their views" all those in the party who might be likely "to throw difficulties in the way." Bentinck also suggested that Disraeli should write a letter in which he indicated that he would "not accept the Post" unless he were "assured of the ardent support etc. and a clear understanding" on several points, notably on the endowment of Catholic clergy and Catholic education and on "the Jew Question." With regard to the former, Bentinck suggested that Disraeli should agree to work with "Mr. Henley & Mr. Bankes" to find a course that would "best accord with the feelings of the entire Party," while in the case of the latter, Bentinck urged Disraeli to assure his colleagues that he would not consider it proper to use the power of the party to "further a measure obnoxious to them," but to claim the right of individually following his own conscience with "unfettered discretion." Bentinck thought that "something of this sort that c[oul]d be shown about w[oul]d bring over great numbers."[10]

Disraeli was completely caught up in the sense of intrigue. He reported to his wife, Mary Anne, who was at Hughenden: "Lord H. will not hear of Stanley's project. He is going to get the Duke of Newcastle to write to Stanley – & Trollope is to ride over to Granby for the same object. He impresses on me the importance of getting Mandeville to do the same … I wish you wd. send me by post Stanleys [sic] letter & copy of my answer, that I may show them, & the others, to Mandeville before he writes."[11] Two days later, in another letter to Mary Anne, Disraeli reports that he has been down to Brighton to see "Professor" Metternich, and the following day adds: "I have not been able to leave the house for an instant. Phillips has just gone – having set immense machinery to work … Affairs get more complicated and exciting every moment. This morning brings *another letter from STANLEY!* He seems at my feet – but the difficulties are immense … An idea has just crossed me on wh: I shall act. It is to make Delane my confidant & ask his advice. I think some articles in the 'Times,' done with discreet thunder, might do the business."[12] For whatever reason, *The Times* did not print any articles on the leadership question in January, though other papers were not at all shy of the subject. On 16 December the *Morning Chronicle* had called Disraeli "the *de facto* leader of the Protectionists in the Commons despite the failure of the party 'magnates' to bestow on him any external sign of the fact." And two weeks earlier, *The Express* (28 November) had wondered in print, "What is Mr. Disraeli to do?" and answered that since the party as a whole would not follow him, he must find a "prime puppet in the dizzy show" to do for "a sham chief to head the party whom ... he in reality leads."[13]

Towards the end of the first week in January the issue of the leadership seemed to be gaining some momentum and one can sense the tension in Disraeli's notes to his wife. On the 9th, for example, he writes: "My dearest Love, I am harassed to death – Herries has come up! Just arrived. There is to be a Congress at Burleigh [the seat of the Marquess of Exeter] next week, where Granby is going, & where I suppose they must settle something. I have been with Delane all this morning. Nothing can be more difficult than my position – & it requires the greatest tact & discretion to manage it." The next day, on the verge of departing London for Hughenden, he adds: "nothing, as it turned out, c[oul]d. be more opportune than my visit, &, I hope, more discreet than my departure. For having set every wheel at work, it is just as well that I sh[oul]d. be off the scene when everyone is on it."[14] The crisis did not, however, come to a speedy resolution. For the next three weeks groups of the party's magnates and other vested interests assembled in various combinations to discuss the leadership without being able to effect a decision. Despite the fact that Disraeli had the support of many powerful men, there was clearly a violent reaction on the part of others to the idea of his leadership. In his letters to his wife, Mary Anne, and to his sister, Sarah, Disraeli reports with great delight the successes of gaining adherents to his cause, but that in itself suggests the strength of the opposition to him and the prejudices behind it.[15] And when, on 29 January, he writes to Lord John Manners, there is an explicit recognition of the strength of the opposition in the way that he characterises his situation in noble terms that would appeal to his idealistic friend: "With respect to the great question, nothing will induce me to attempt the task unless it is with the general wish & consent of the whole party: for nothing but that unanimous feeling cd. sustain me in the terrible struggle wh:, as you well know, I have long seen looming in the distance bet[wee]n. the aristocratic & democratic principles." Most of the letter is, however, focused on the personal strategy of the more immediate contest. Disraeli knows that he cannot be seen to be manipulating people and that, as a consequence he needs to keep out of the way, for much of the time "in the country as quiet as possible," and since in town, avoiding the Carlton Club. Yet he knows, too, that he needs to be as informed as possible about the strength of the campaign, about which he gives Manners the details: "I have received the adhesion, unqualified and complete, of every shade of Church Party ... Saturday there was a meeting at the National Club ... & ... it was unanimously resolved ... that I was the man, & that if I accepted the office, I had a right to expect an unreserved confidence ... I am told Inglis was present & Walpole. Will you believe it, that Plumptree [sic] is going to support me!"[16] The National Club was an Ultra-Protestant organization. Sir Robert Inglis had been a leader of the opposition to the Maynooth grant funding a Catholic seminary in 1845; Spencer Walpole was an important member of the party and would later twice serve as Home Secretary in Conservative ministries; John Pemberton Plumptre was known for his hostility to the emancipation of the Jews.[17] And while Disraeli might insist to Manners, as he had done to others, that he had "literally not entered into the intrigue" and was keeping out of the way, some influential party members were nonetheless suspicious. For example, William Beresford, the other party whip, wrote to Lord Stanley about what he saw as a "deep intrigue carrying on in the Party to force Disraeli on us as our Leader."[18] The depth of resistance to Disraeli's leadership can be gauged by a retrospective passage in the autobiography of Sir William Gregory, written almost fifty years later: "It was in vain that the squires and aristocracy kicked at the supremacy of one whom they looked on as [a] mountebank; in vain their gorges rose at being directed by a Jew."[19] The physical imagery here suggests a revulsion that no amount of letter writing was likely to overcome.

Finally on 31 January, only a day before Parliament was to meet, Disraeli met with Lord Stanley, who this time suggested that the party be led in the Commons by a triumvirate. Disraeli's brief and hurried report of that meeting in a note to Mary Anne reflects his sense that he is at last gaining control of the situation.

MOST CONFIDENTIAL

A proposition that the party shd. be led by myself, Granby, & Herries *with equal power*; that I shd., or rather must, be, the real leader; that this would remove all jealousies for the moment; & that when Granby was called to the Upper House, soon to be anticipated, I shd., of course, become the only leader, & every jealousy & distrust wd., by that time, have been removed.

Very friendly & cordial.

Says it is all over with the party if I retire.

Refused – but at his request left it open, as he has not yet even consulted Granby.[20]

Disraeli never withdrew his refusal to act as a member of the proposed triumvirate, an arrangement that was in any case ludicrous and unworkable. Indeed, the *Morning Chronicle* sarcastically described it as "obviously borrowed from the idea of the Abbé Sieyes: it is Cambacéres [*sic*], LéBrun [*sic*], and Bonaparte over again."[21] But, with Stanley's obvious cooperation, Disraeli moved an amendment to the Address on the first night of the new session that was identical to the one Stanley moved in the House of Lords. And that same night he made a very fine speech in tribute to Lord George Bentinck, which gained lavish praise from the Ultra-Tory *Standard*, a newspaper that had previously been opposed to him. The terms of what Disraeli called their "manifesto of recantation" were as significant as its timing: "we freely acknowledge our late prejudices against the member for Buckinghamshire, and as freely acknowledge that by his conduct and genius during the struggle of the last three years, closing with his splendid triumph of Friday, these prejudices have been overcome."[22]

Having gained the de facto leadership in the Commons of what would eventually be considered once again the Conservative party, Disraeli's formidable task in the sessions to come was to wean that party from the lost cause of Protection and yet continue to uphold the "aristocratic settlement" of the country. In that regard, the immediate focus of his efforts was to devise a more equitable scheme of taxation that would lessen the burdens on landowners, but there were other issues that soon claimed his attention. Both the Jewish Emancipation Bill of 1849 and the no-popery agitation of 1850 in response to the so-called papal aggression left no doubt that religious prejudice was still a force to be reckoned with in English politics. After a failure to form the Government in 1851, Lord Stanley (after 1851, 14th Earl of Derby) did finally succeed in forming a Conservative ministry in 1852, and in that Government Disraeli was appointed chancellor of the exchequer. The most notable feature of that appointment, apart from the personal triumph of having overcome all of the obstacles to his success, was that it infuriated William Gladstone, who by this time was a complete convert to Peelite, small "l" liberal, economic doctrine, and who was convinced that it was his special destiny to reform the fiscal and monetary policies of British government. Gladstone was also jealous of Disraeli's interest in foreign affairs and of his attempts to shape public opinion in patriotic support of Conservative values. Thus, the stage was set for the great political rivalry that would come to dominate Parliament for the next thirty years. In assessing that rivalry and the many strange twists that it took, such as Disraeli's "dishing the Whigs" over the 1867 Reform Bill, and his Government's extensive social legislation between 1874 and 1880, perhaps we should keep in mind the French politician Guizot's remark to Disraeli in 1849: "I think your being the Leader of the Tory party is the greatest triumph that Liberalism has ever achieved."[23] It would be twenty years before Lord Derby would give up the overall leadership, leaving Disraeli in sole charge of the gradually reconstituted Conservative party. In the interval there were three Tory administrations in which Disraeli held the post of chancellor of the exchequer – 1852, 1858, 1867 – but it was by no means inevitable until after his extraordinary control of the debate on the Reform Bill of 1867 that he would become prime minister in any subsequent Conservative Government. That Reform debate, more than any other issue in the intervening years brought the tension between principles and expediency in his career back into sharp focus. Persons of self-conscious probity continued to think of him as a "political adventurer," lacking any settled convictions, and willing to exploit whatever political opportunities came his way. Sir William Gregory, for example, who had been on the fringes of Young England in its early days but had followed the Peelite course in 1846, thought that there was "no more flagrant instance of unscrupulousness in the annals of public men of this century than Disraeli's conduct in 1867 in respect to the Reform Bill." His "disreputable manoeuvres" in proposing household suffrage, after having defeated Russell's bill with moderate restrictions the year before, were, in Gregory's view, like his speeches, "admirably adapted to the exigency of the moment and to the intention of 'dishing the Whigs.'" But such expediency is condemned in extreme language: "There was never a more profligate act, or one which more lowered the character of the great and respectable country party." And this was clearly a view that did not diffuse over time, for in retrospective summary Gregory concludes: "That he was a man of immense talent not even his greatest enemy can deny; but even I, his personal friend, must confess that from his entrance into public life until his last hour he lived and died a charlatan."[24]

Such a view reveals sympathy and prejudice to be ostensibly compatible, but it is not a fair assessment of Disraeli's career, because it ignores the sometimes complex relation of means and ends in politics, which often includes the equally significant moral relation of motive and action. In that regard Disraeli's behaviour in the leadership crisis of the late 1840s is open to other, more generous interpretations. In reply to Stanley's attempt to talk him out of pressing his claim to the leadership in the Commons, for example, Disraeli was clearly up to the game and willing to bluff in playing his hand. But such an opportunistic insistence upon his own claims does not necessarily imply Disraeli's lack of principle. Indeed, as Blake points out, Disraeli's defence of the "aristocratic settlement," by which he means, not an oligarchic power, but the whole hierarchy of legal, religious, and social institutions with their reciprocal duties and obligations among all ranks and orders of society, is "the key to Disraeli's policy for the rest of his life."[25] It is, moreover, entirely consistent with the vision of true nobility embodied in his Young England novels, and with the concept of the mixed constitution that he had espoused and defended in the 1830s. In such a territorial constitution, the owners of estates are but trustees of the land, and political representation is not based upon individual rights. Indeed, by this light the greatest danger to the welfare of the people is that the radical forces of democracy will undermine those institutions that alone guarantee the stability of society, which is in turn necessary to individual happiness and liberty.

Disraeli's correspondence covering the years when he was for the first time a cabinet minister, as chancellor of the exchequer in the short-lived Derby Government of 1852, and then leader of the Conservative opposition in the House of Commons for a prolonged period of difficult and unsettled party politics, reveals Disraeli's own sense of his ambitions and frustrations at a time in his career when he is stretched to the utmost in first struggling to sustain a weak Government and then attempting to wean the fractious Tories from their hopeless attachment to Protectionism. In office Disraeli found the weight of his responsibilities overwhelming, and yet he admits that he loves the work, despite its often intractable difficulties. The sense of full engagement is palpable in the letters, as he comments on the strategies, both great and small, by which he governs the preparations for the battle on his second budget. At one moment, he contemplates the possibility of a coalition with the Peelites, even imagining "an inkling of sympathy" between himself and Gladstone.[26] This brief fantasy is, of course, soon replaced with the outright jealousies and hostilities occasioned by the latter's ferocious assault on Disraeli's December budget, which resulted not only in the fall of Derby's Government, but also, somewhat anticlimactically, in frosty squabbles over the furniture at 11 Downing St and the chancellor's official robes.

When Disraeli was appointed chancellor of the exchequer and Leader of the Government in the House of Commons, it was his "humble duty" to write to the Queen to keep her informed of parliamentary business. Although she was at first suspicious of both Disraeli's character and the policy of the new Government, she was soon captivated by the novelistic style of his letters, entertained by the précis of personalities, and pleased to be for the first time privy to the thrust and counter-thrust of the actual debates. In the very first of these letters, for example, Disraeli told her: "Mr. Villiers opened the proceedings, terse & elaborate, but not in his happiest style. He called upon the House to contrast the state of the country, at the beginning of the year, & at the present moment. But he cd. not induce the House to believe that 'all now was distrust & alarm' … The great speech on the opposition side was that of Sir James Graham: elaborate, malignant, mischievous. His position was this: that Lord Derby, as a man of honor, was bound to propose taxes on food, & that if he did so, revolution was inevitable. Mr. Walpole followed with great taste & moderation, confining himself to the constitutional question, & avoiding the statistics, wh: Sir James introduced[.]"[27]

The Queen's sense of having a new, more intimate sense of her Parliament was also the result of the fact that Disraeli was often sending her brief bulletins directly from the front bench of the House of Commons while tumultuous debate was still in progress: "House of Commons, 6 o'ck – Monday The Chancellor of the Exchequer, with his humble duty to Your Majesty, informs Your Majesty that Lord John Russell has withdrawn all further opposition [to approving the estimates], & that the prospects are now quite serene. Mr. Secretary Walpole has given notice of introducing the Militia Bill on Monday next."[28] A week later Disraeli writes at "midnight" to tell the Queen that there has been an "unexpectedly animated" debate on "the Ballot," but that "It does not seem probable that Ld. John Russell will rise" and so "the C[hancello]r. of the Ex[cheque]r counts on a good division." Then, after the vote has taken place, he adds the result: "For 144 / Against 246," and can't resist adding as well, "Sir Robert Peel voted for the Ballot[.]"[29]

Since Lord Derby's Government did not command a majority in the House of Commons, it is natural enough that the subject of Disraeli's correspondence with the Queen was often, as he put it, any potential "disturbance in the progress of Yr. Majesty's business,"[30] but it is a noticeable feature of his letters that in making Victoria his confidante with respect to personalities and issues, he plays on her annoyance with obstructionism and her fears of radicalism and instability. And by repeatedly flattering her sensibilities and by implying or stating his care to alleviate these irritations and fears, he tries to enlist her sympathies for the cause of Conservatism.

In Opposition to Lord Aberdeen's coalition Government, Disraeli reverted to the characteristic patterns of earlier struggles, even as he tried to forge new means of the Conservatives' regeneration. His youthful fantasy of shaping public opinion through the power of the press was reborn in the establishment of *The Press* weekly newspaper, a venture for which Disraeli committed himself to both financial and journalistic contributions. Disraeli had for some time felt that the party was badly served by the Ultra-Tory expostulations of the *Morning Herald* and the *Morning Post* and so the intention was to make *The Press* an organ of progressive conservatism that would over time generate a broader public support. The leading articles were published anonymously and Disraeli kept the authorship of his contributions confidential, even to the point on one occasion of criticising his own speeches. But Lord Stanley's hand-written annotation of his copy of each issue at Knowsley identifies the contributors and on that authority we know that Disraeli wrote ten of the first eleven leaders.[31] They reveal him to be as addicted as ever, under the cover of anonymity, to personal invective and extreme political rhetoric. The attack on Lord Aberdeen in the fifth number is typical:

> His mind, his education, his prejudices, are all of the Kremlin school. Now that he is placed in a prominent position, and forced to lead English gentlemen, instead of glozing and intriguing with foreign diplomatists, not a night passes that his language or his demeanour does not shock and jar upon the frank and genial spirit of our British Parliament. His manner, arrogant and yet timid – his words, insolent and yet obscure – offend even his political supporters. His hesitating speech, his contracted sympathies, his sneer, icy as Siberia, his sarcasms, drear and barren as the Steppes, are all characteristic of the bureau and the chancery, and not of popular and aristocratic assemblies animated by the spirit of honour and the pride of gentlemen.[32]

As time passed, however, much of Disraeli's journalistic effort in overseeing *The Press* was expended in trying to find a credible opposition to the Whigs' handling of the Crimean war, the most difficult part of which was trying to predict the outcome of the diplomatic manoeuvres of the European powers. As he had done in the 1830s and 1840s, Disraeli again succumbed to the seductive appeal of clandestine intrigue and sexual politics, when he sent Lord Henry Lennox "on a secret mission to Paris" to charm the empress and get "authentic news" from Princess

Lieven, "the great focus and fountain of all political intrigue ... once Aberdeen's Egeria, & ... still his faithful friend."[33] As the coalition Government's inept prosecution of the war in the Crimea unfolded in 1854, Disraeli found himself more and more frustrated with the limitations of his own situation and Lord Derby's diffident leadership of the Conservative party. One letter in particular, that to Lady Londonderry on 7 August, captures Disraeli's exasperated sense of the political opportunity being missed. (Square brackets here indicate material crossed out.)

> There are a thousand things wh: ought to be done wh: are elements of power, & wh: I am obliged to decline doing, or to do at great sacrifice. Whether it be influence with the Press, or organisation throughout the country, everyone comes to me, & everything is expected from me. Tho' so many notables & magnificoes belong to the party, there never was an aggregation of human beings, who exercised less [polit] social influence. They seem to disregard, or to despise, all the modes & means of managing [p] mankind. As for our Chief, we never see him. His House is always closed; he subscribes to nothing, tho his fortune is very large; & expects, nevertheless, everything to be done. I have never yet been fairly backed in life. All the great personages I have known, even when what is called "ambitious," by courtesy, have been quite unequal to a grand game. This has been my fate, & I never felt it more keenly than at the present moment, with a confederate always at Newmarket & Doncaster, when Europe, nay the world, is in the throes of immense changes, & all the elements of power at home in a state of dissolution. If ever there were a time when a political chief shd. concentrate his mind & resources on the situation, 'tis the present. There cannot be too much [coura] vigilance, too much thought, & too much daring. All seem wanting.[34]

It would, in fact, be several more years before the Conservatives could be seen as an alternative to Aberdeen's coalition. Lord Derby's lack of enthusiasm for the political battles of 1854 and 1855 was not, however, just a failure of nerve. Disraeli could see that, without the prospect of a new and stronger electoral mandate, the Conservatives would just inherit the weaknesses of the current Government without the power to implement new policies.

By the late 1850s, though, Disraeli's hard work was paying off. It was widely recognized that, while his earlier reputation might still be a liability in some Tory circles, he was nevertheless indispensable to the

Conservative's cause. He was now a mature and seasoned politician, very much at the tactical centre of his party's struggles in the House of Commons, both in Opposition in 1857 during such important debates as those on divorce and the Indian rebellion, and then as chancellor of the exchequer in a minority Government again in 1858–9, seeking an alternative to the East India Company's powers of governance, and attempting a measure of further parliamentary reform at home. Although Lord Derby was again the prime minister, the day-to-day burden of the Government's existence fell chiefly on Disraeli in the Commons. It is thus not surprising that the letters from this period, especially those to Derby, Lord Stanley, and Disraeli's Conservative colleagues in and out of the cabinet, reflect the considerable stresses and strains of planning policy and executing the strategies of debate. Through it all Disraeli emerges as a man of more tact than he has generally been given credit for, and as a politician who, whatever the Conservative impulses of the moment, while fighting for legislative majorities in a hostile House, always understood that they were caught in the midst of larger social, cultural, and political transformations. In hindsight it is instructive and sometimes amusing to see his struggles with recalcitrant colleagues, but it is equally interesting to see in his letters the anticipations of Disraeli's later policies on reform and foreign affairs. These often reflect a pragmatic yet idealistic wisdom about the Conservatives' need to be progressive in an age of political and cultural movement.

The best illustrations of Disraeli's skilful management of the Conservative cause at this time are his letters to and about Lord Stanley and Sir Edward Bulwer Lytton. In the former instance Disraeli had to exercise the most delicate diplomacy, for Stanley was a most reluctant and skittish member of his father's cabinet and it required the utmost in tact and encouragement in communicating with Stanley himself, Lord Derby and the Queen to keep him on side. As Disraeli well knew, Stanley's allegiance was the key to avoiding others' defections from the party. Moreover, Stanley had the capacity for mischief, such as, for example, the letters (signed "M.P.") he had sent to the press in late 1853 and early 1854 criticizing Prince Albert.[35] Almost as challenging for Disraeli was the task of persuading Bulwer Lytton to stay in the cabinet and stand for re-election in 1858. Bulwer and Disraeli were old friends from their silver-fork novel days, but the former's matrimonial difficulties left him vulnerable to threats of blackmail from his perhaps understandably distraught wife and to some very questionable medical and legal advice about what to do in response. Under the stress of trying to cope with the situation, not the least of which was his wife's public denunciations of him during the 1858 election campaign, Bulwer became convinced that he was dying, and Disraeli had the delicate task of supporting his colleague while talking him out of this delusion.

Perhaps the most frustrating and certainly the most annoying aspect of Disraeli's position in office in 1858 was that of settling matters of patronage, which, echoing the catechism of the *Book of Common Prayer*, he wittily described in one of his letters to Stanley as "the outward & visible sign of an inward & spiritual grace – and that is Power."[36] There was not only the problem of both legitimate and dubious expectations to deal with. Not being the prime minister, Disraeli frequently found himself at the mercy of cabinet colleagues with whom he did not see eye to eye about the merits or urgency of individual claims. On a few occasions he was obliged to write letters of an overtly didactic sort to either claimants or colleagues, but even so he managed the issues of patronage as skilfully as he did those of legislative debate. It is thus fair to conclude that 1857 to 1859 are the years in which Disraeli, as Lord Derby's trusted chief lieutenant, shows the energy, commitment, and maturity that would soon firmly establish his own claim to the leadership of the Conservative party.

Throughout this period Disraeli is constantly concerned to strengthen and consolidate the party. This is certainly reflected in his letters to Sir William Jolliffe, his parliamentary whip, and in the influence that Ralph Earle, his young, new, and very able private secretary, was having on Disraeli's correspondence with his colleagues. And at one point, Disraeli was even willing, for the good of the party, to subordinate his own interests, as when he wrote in extraordinarily generous terms to Gladstone (25 May 1858) to overcome their mutual suspicions and urge that his arch-rival accept Lord Derby's offer of a position in the Conservative cabinet. This was the third of such overtures to Gladstone on the part of Lord Derby, each time with Disraeli's full concurrence. Disraeli's generosity did not, however, extend to giving up his positions as chancellor and leader in the House, so Gladstone could see that there would inevitably be incompatibilities of policy between them, and that, despite the letter's flattering remarks about his "shining qualities" and the "commanding position" he would inherit, he was in fact being asked to serve under Disraeli's leadership in the House of Commons. Gladstone's reply was a model of politeness, but its assertions of candour were full of reserve and caution. The formal syntactical coherence was a striking counterpart to Disraeli's impetuous sentiments and the difference of style eloquently reflected their anti-thetical personalities, which would dominate Victorian politics for the next twenty years.[37]

When the Derby-Disraeli Government was defeated in the election of 1859 and Lord Palmerston again became the prime minister, it was of an ostensibly Whig, but actually quite conservative ministry. Indeed, even as the election was still in progress Disraeli had contacted Palmerston privately to see if he would consider taking up the leader-ship of the Conservative party. This would seem to have been an en-tirely pragmatic move, motivated by the need to find some stratagem by which the Conservatives would have a working majority in the Commons – in this case by the addition of twenty or thirty members who would, it was assumed, follow Palmerston's lead. As in the case of the various overtures to Gladstone, it reflects the shifting relation be-tween fantasy and pragmatism in Disraeli's thinking. As early as 1854 he had indulged the hope that he might be the leader of the next Conservative ministry, but, in the context of the actual parliamentary struggles and the current state of his party, Disraeli could very clearly see the limits of his position, the need for compromise, and the neces-sary subordination of his own desires to the common good.

By the mid-1860s it was clear that some further measure of electoral reform and extension of the franchise was both inevitable and urgent. In so far as Disraeli believed that a Conservative Government was in-herently likely to do less damage to the traditional institutions of the country, his "profligate" behaviour in combining with disaffected Liberals to defeat Lord Russell's Reform Bill in 1866, only ultimately to pass a far more reaching one of his own in the next session, can be seen as an action based on conviction as well as expediency. Blake's cogent account of the passage of the 1867 bill makes it clear, however, that Derby, Disraeli, and their colleagues had no very clear vision of what they were specifically intending to propose as they assumed office. The vision often attributed to Disraeli, of challenging the middle-class Whig-Liberal-Radical coalition by means of an alliance of the urban working classes and traditional rural Conservative supporters, how-ever prescient in a general sense, was not evident in the day-to-day compromises of the amending process by which Disraeli demonstrated his mastery of the House of Commons. Certainly the adoption of house-hold suffrage in the final bill was sheer pragmatic improvisation, a mat-ter of keeping control of the government and taking credit for the reforms in the eyes of the newly enfranchised voters.[38]

Not surprisingly, Disraeli's responses to the exigencies of the Reform Bill debate were given a sinister cast by those most upset by the turn of events, including some staunch Tories. Lord Cranborne thought that the Conservative success had been "purchased at the cost of a political betrayal which has no parallel in … Parliamentary annals" and Robert Lowe claimed that Disraeli's conduct merited "the contempt of all honest men and the execration of posterity."[39] Such, too, was the tone of articles that appeared that autumn in the *Edinburgh Review* and the *Quarterly Review*, respectively the most influential voices of the Liberal and Conservative points of view. The latter was, in fact, written by Cranborne, who, along with Lord Carnarvon and General Peel, had resigned from the cabinet in early March 1867 and subsequently voted against the bill in its later stages.

Equally distressed was Gladstone, who had been outmanoeuvred in his attempts to amend the bill and so deprive Disraeli of his initiative. Indeed, so despondent was Gladstone at his humiliating "smash" that he briefly contemplated a retirement from the leadership of the Liberals in the Commons. The antagonism between Gladstone and Disraeli was of long standing. Gladstone's animus against Disraeli went back as far as the vituperative attacks on Peel during the Corn Law debate in 1846, and his feelings first took the form of a personal rivalry for power in 1852 when he set out to demolish both the rationale and specific details of Disraeli's first budget as chancellor of the exchequer. And though in 1859 there had been some speculation that Disraeli might willingly make room in the cabinet for Gladstone to be chancellor within a Conservative ministry led by Derby, it was clear by 1867 that the parliamentary rivalry was a permanent feature of their relations and that Disraeli saw Gladstone as the chief threat to his success. Disraeli's correspondence with Derby and others, as the Reform Bill evolved to its curious result, repeatedly focuses on Gladstone's hostile intentions and the need to thwart his hope of wrecking the bill and defeating the Conservatives on a motion of confidence. Yet the complexities of the Reform Bill debate cannot be reduced to simple personal jealousies. Gladstone was no doubt sincere and altruistic in his fear of provisions that would enfranchise the "residuum" of the working class, those below the level of respectability and moral responsibility, even if that fear chiefly took the form of suspecting that Disraeli was reckless enough to do it. And on the other hand, Disraeli was less concerned with the expansion of the franchise itself than with its effects on the balance of political power. He was willing to accept a quite radical redundancy of Liberal voters in the boroughs as long as the Conservative strength in the counties could be protected. Even within such a pragmatism, however, as Maurice Cowling has emphasized, there was no intention on the part of either Conservatives or Liberals to alter the "existing political structure," that is "the situation in which gentry, aristocracy and the respectable classes continued to be responsible for the conduct of English political life." The Reform Bill debate was, in short, not about creating a "democratic" constitution, but about the best way of enhancing the support of the status quo: "What Gladstone wanted was the enfranchisement of a literate, independent, non-conforming element – the skilled labour of the country which would warm to guidance from forward-looking, educated Whig-Liberals under his own leadership, and carry the more advanced and literate working-men along with them into a future replete with free trade, commercial prosperity, removal of religious disabilities and increasing regard for the public interest."[40] Disraeli, on the other hand, was convinced that even the large extension of the franchise created by Grosvenor Hodgkinson's household-suffrage amendment, would not threaten the Conservative strength, partly because the effects would be greatest in the Liberal urban boroughs, partly because many of those ostensibly enfranchised would neither register nor pay the rates making them eligible to vote, and partly because redistribution under Tory control would do much to guard the party's interests. It is important, however, to recognize that if Disraeli's policy was one of "consistent opportunism"; his success in taking the progressive wind out of Gladstone's sails in 1867 was partially the result of the latter's failure to keep the factions of the Whig-Liberal-Radical coalition together.[41]

Disraeli's success with the Reform Bill left no doubt that he was the heir to the leadership of the Conservative Party in the event of Lord Derby's retirement. And by the end of January in 1868 it was clear that Derby's ill health from devastating attacks of gout would soon prevent him from continuing as prime minister. The formal change came towards the end of February with Derby's resignation and the Queen's choice of Disraeli as his successor. As he famously told those who congratulated him, he had "climbed to the top of the greasy pole."[42]

14

On Top of the Greasy Pole:
The Disestablishment Crisis of 1868

It was Gladstone's sense of the Liberals' failure in the 1867 Reform Bill controversy, with its inevitable feelings of frustration, that largely shapes the continuation of the personal political rivalry between him and Disraeli at the core of the Irish Church Disestablishment debate in 1868. When poor health forced Lord Derby to retire as prime minister and Disraeli succeeded him "at the top of the greasy pole" in February 1868, Gladstone's jealousy was intensified all the more. Just as it had galled him to see Disraeli become chancellor of the exchequer before him in 1852, he now was deeply chagrined to see his flamboyant rival attain the highest political prize, a position for which he felt himself far more qualified. The "Gladstonian temper of the moment" was brilliantly caught by a journalist writing in the *Pall Mall Gazette*, who compared the Liberal leader to King David puzzled by "the prosperity of the wicked and the scornful": "That the writer of frivolous stories about *Vivian Grey* and *Coningsby* should grasp the sceptre before the writer of beautiful and serious things about *Ecce Homo* – the man who is epigrammatic, flashy, arrogant, before the man who never perpetrated an epigram in his life, is always fervid, and would as soon die as admit that he had a shade more brain than his footman – is not this enough to make an honest man rend his mantle and shave his head and sit down among the ashes inconsolable?"[1] But even with the burden of public satire added to his mortification, Gladstone knew in his own mind that in both intellectual and moral terms he was the better man. With such a conviction, it was undoubtedly easy to conclude that Disraeli was in fact unfit for the office of prime minister, and indeed dangerous to the welfare of the country. Such, it would seem, was the extremity of Gladstone's opinions when Disraeli's Government was formed.

A confidential memorandum in the Disraeli Papers, dated 1 March 1868 and signed "J.L." [James Lowther] is entitled "Legislation for Ireland."[2] It would appear to be a discussion paper for the cabinet meetings of 2 and 3 March, outlining both the general goals and the specific proposals that the new ministry should adopt with respect to the perpetual grievances and disturbances that had characterized life in Ireland throughout the century. Although the discussion of the "Celtic characteristics" and "peculiarities of race," which are alleged to be the source of the real evils of Ireland, is not very percipient, the memorandum raises the issue of the Irish church in the light of the general aims of pacifying the people and improving their economic condition. Lowther at first argues forcibly that, though the question is encompassed with difficulties, "the basis of any settlement must be religious equality," which can only be established in two ways; "by a general endowment of all religious denominations," or "by abolishing the Established Church and applying the Revenues to general secular purposes in which all denominations might participate." The first of these choices, he takes to be impracticable because "the general spirit of the age is opposed to it," because "the Catholic Bishops have repudiated any endowments," and because "the English dissenters are altogether opposed to it." He thus goes on to suggest that a general disestablishment might be accompanied by a partial endowment of parsonages and glebe lands available to all the denominations on a voluntary basis, and that a commission would need to be established to deal with the ecclesiastical revenues. Since this was a more complicated matter than could be dealt with immediately, Lowther suggests that "something should be done to show the good will and the intentions of the Government": "the Ecclesiastical Titles Act ... should be repealed in a generous spirit ... a Charter might be given to the Catholic University, or some other Catholic College of importance; and perhaps, some modification might be made in the national system of Education, so as to render it more in accordance with the denominational system of England." He then concludes with some warnings about the importance of ascertaining the opinion of the Holy See upon the question of endowments, and about the danger of conducting negotiations through either "English R.C. Ecclesiastics" ("of whom the Irish Priesthood are very jealous") or "Irish Ecclesiastics," whom, he says, it would be "still more objectionable" to employ.

Lowther's warnings were well-founded, for, ironically, Disraeli's optimism that the new ministry might be able to begin the process of

ameliorating the Irish situation was in large part based on his recent
acquaintance with Henry Edward Manning, archbishop of Westminster,
who was anxious to·take the lead in furthering Catholic interests, and
who had first made overtures of cooperation to Disraeli the previous
spring. On 13 April 1867 Manning had first written to Disraeli, ostensibly to show his disapproval of the Fenians' violence, but also to encourage the adoption of "a large and adequate policy for Ireland."[3] A
few weeks later he wrote again to request an interview for himself and
the rector of the Catholic university in Dublin, who had been authorized, he said, by Cardinal Cullen "to treat with Government ... the chief
object of desire" being a charter, or a "fairer, more just recognition of the
only Catholic University in Ireland."[4] And then on 21 May, with the
interview still in the offing, Manning assured Disraeli, that, though no
one except the rector, Dr Woodlock, was aware of these communications with the chancellor of the exchequer, he was "able to say of ...
[his] own knowledge, that any favourable proposal from Govt. on the
subject of the Catholic University would not only encounter no opposition, but would be assisted." He then went on to add: "I believe I may
say that this includes the granting of a Charter ... I can add that the
'Chief' I conferred with is in the front: and he fully recognizes the need
of removing the Catholic Education of Ireland from the turbulent region of politics. I told him that letters from Ireland show me how loyal
and leading men are growing weary of waiting for these measures
which are ... practicable and even easy, if men would make the religious welfare of Ireland the object of united action."[5] As the correspondence continued, Manning frequently expressed his personal
concern and sympathy to Disraeli for the stresses and strains of the
on-going parliamentary struggle. In retrospect this is important, and
more than just the form of addressing a busy man, for such assurance
as the archbishop is providing – based as it is on personal sincerity and
confidential knowledge – seems calculated to give Disraeli the impression that he has the secret support of the Catholic hierarchy.

This impression was undoubtedly strengthened by another request,
on 29 July, for a second interview, and by a letter in August telling Disraeli
that the opposition of the Irish MPs to the idea of granting a charter did
"not represent the sense and desire of Cardinal Cullen, or of the Irish
Bishops."[6] In the same letter Manning alerts Disraeli to the fact that the
Irish bishops will meet in September or October and that "their cooperation ... [with] any proposal the Government may frame ... is obviously
essential to success." A request for a third interview, in early December,

to discuss "certain subjects of much importance" is accompanied by an expression of mutual regret over the death of Lady Gainsborough and by a hope that "Mr. D'Israeli's health is fully re-established."[7] Then, on 22 December, Manning reports that he has received a letter from Cardinal Cullen "on the subject of our last conversation," the matter of which he wishes to communicate at Disraeli's convenience.[8] That meeting at the end of December was followed by Manning's suggestion of another in mid-January, and by yet another appointment on 20 February.[9] In the letter dated 15 January, Manning tells Disraeli, "I have been reading with great assent a passage in a speech of yours [on Irish affairs] in 1844." Thus the general effect created by Manning's initiatives led Disraeli to conclude that he could depend upon the archbishop's support and personal friendliness in bringing the Government's Irish policies to fruition. Certainly nothing could be more suggestive in that regard than Manning's letter of congratulation when Disraeli became prime minister, for in it he remarks on the "kindness and consideration" he has received from Disraeli, and on the "happiness" he feels in seeing him placed "as first Minister of the Crown." Moreover, in adding expressions of his "sympathy" and "best wishes," Manning "trusts" that Disraeli will have "health and life" to carry out the legislation on Ireland that they have previously discussed. It is true that these wishes are prefaced with mention of Manning's political neutrality and his nearly forty years of friendship with Mr Gladstone, which do seem ominously intrusive notes in such a letter. But the overall impression was, nevertheless, reassuring.[10] As a result, Disraeli showed Manning a printed draft of the Government's proposal on the subject of the Catholic university in Ireland, even before it was discussed in cabinet. Though it only gave a charter without endowment, Manning was convinced that the charter once given would bring money in due time, and consequently he became a go-between, conveying Disraeli's plans to Cardinal Cullen and urging that they be accepted.[11] Lord Mayo, the Irish Secretary, introduced the Government's policy in the House of Commons on 10 March, claiming, perhaps innocently, that there had been no prior negotiations over the university charter with the Catholic Church, and the next day he invited the delegated Irish bishops to submit their views and suggestions on the proposed measure. It was soon apparent that the bishops' objections to the charter were not solely concerned with the lack of an endowment, but also that they were strongly opposed to vesting the election of the chancellor and the academic control of the institution in a senate and convocation whose majority would be laity.

In the crisis that quickly developed, Manning continued to negotiate at what he took to be the centre of the controversy. On 14 March he wrote to Cardinal Cullen: "*Confidential*. I have just now had an interview with Mr. Disraeli. I feel no doubt that he sincerely intends to carry his proposal. But his hope of carrying it is satisfying the Irish Bishops. Mr. Fortescue last night declared that if the Catholics in Ireland accepted the plan he would not hinder it. I think I can say that will be Mr. Gladstone's line."[12] In the light of subsequent events, this last sentence carries a terrible irony. But for the moment Disraeli was again reassured by Manning that if there were some modifications in the governance clauses, Cardinal Cullen thought the charter ought to be accepted. On 15 March the archbishop wrote a long letter to Disraeli, urging a conciliatory policy toward the Catholic faith in Ireland and refuting the various allegations contained in Mr Horsman's violently anticlerical attack on Irish bishops and priests, which had been issued in the House of Commons three days earlier. And then the next day, the 16th, he left a note for the prime minister, along with a copy of his recently published pamphlet on the subject of Ireland. In that note he repeated what he had told Cardinal Cullen: that "if Government can content the Irish Bishops," Mr. Fortescue and his friends "will not hinder the passing of the *Charter*." And his final suggestion was that "it would be both important and grateful to the Irish if the Archbishop of Cashel, and the Bishop of Clonfert were to come over & discuss the details."[13]

That same evening Gladstone announced in the House of Commons his intention to submit resolutions calling for the disestablishment of the Irish Church. This was not entirely unexpected, for there had been rumours of some dramatic move on the part of the Opposition for several weeks. A confidential memorandum in Disraeli's hand, written before the parliamentary session began, is quite explicit in its anticipation of Gladstone's action and the Government's response to it. In Disraeli's view "the Prot[estant] feeling of the country" was "every day more developing itself & comprehending that the struggle … [was] really bet[wee]n Prot[estantism] and Popery," and, further, he felt that no Protestant church would eventually stand, if this attack were to succeed. He did admit that after a pending inquiry "considerable modification in the temporalities of the An[glican] Ch[urch] in Ireland" might be expedient, but he was also of the opinion, that "any proposition tending to the disestablishment, or disendowment, of that Ch[urch] ought to be reserved for a new Parliament."[14] This memorandum goes a long way towards defining the Conservatives' strategy both in the

current debate and in the subsequent election that fall. Disraeli understood that Irish Church Disestablishment was going to be the crucial
issue for the Conservative Government, and it was his hope that any
attempt to deal with it could be postponed until there had been an election on the recently reformed franchise. That he chose to identify "the
struggle" as one between Protestantism and popery indicates that he
had no intention of permitting the clergy to have academic or administrative control of the proposed new Catholic university.

As soon as Gladstone announced his resolutions, the situation changed
completely with regard to the interests of the Catholic hierarchy. There
was now the prospect of very significant change in the position of the
Catholic Church in Ireland, should Gladstone and the Liberals come to
power. Manning ceased immediately to have any communication with
the Conservatives, and the Irish bishops, not in any case conciliatory,
adopted a posture of intransigence on the terms of the proposed charter.
Disraeli would soon claim that he had been "stabbed in the back," for he
thought he had a commitment of support from Manning and Cullen,
and it would be some years before he would accept any other interpretation of events. Manning, on the other hand, claimed that he immediately
found himself in the most awkward of positions. As he later admitted,
he disagreed with the policy of the Irish bishops on the question of the
charter, but could not risk telling Disraeli so, for fear of damaging his
own laboriously cultivated relationships with the Irish episcopate and
quite possibly damaging both his and the Catholic Church's influence in
shaping Government policy. He chose, therefore, to be silent and withdraw, even though it meant giving the impression of having acted in bad
faith. Manning's claims of innocence and misunderstood integrity need,
however, to be seen in the light of other events. Certainly, he was as fond
of secret negotiations and as susceptible to theories of clandestine government as was Disraeli, and hence he was often peculiarly vulnerable
to charges of deceit and manipulation.

In this particular instance, Manning's claims of political neutrality are
somewhat problematic, in that it would seem to have consisted of a
desire to support whichever party offered the best terms. But, as he
himself noted, his long-standing personal friendship with Gladstone
was inseparable from his involvement in political questions. In the period of late 1867 and early 1868, while he was establishing his confidential relationship with Disraeli, Manning was also continuing to write
regularly to Gladstone, urging the Liberal leader to adopt his views on

both the Irish church and education questions. For example, his letter to Gladstone on 15 January echoes sentiments sent to Disraeli the same day. Then on 11 February he wrote another, most remarkable letter to the Liberal leader that shows very clearly that his neutrality is not non-involvement. He began by complaining about the distribution of patronage to Protestants and Orangemen, which, he said, had produced "a despair of obtaining anything from Parliament, and a willingness to listen to bad counsels." He then said that Ireland was becoming republican, and, even amongst the clergy, increasingly showing "a calm, and reasonable preference for the civil and religious equality of America rather than the irritating and impoverished inequalities of the United Kingdom's spreading." The real point of the letter, however, was to urge the Liberal leader to adopt a specific policy towards education in Ireland. He encouraged Gladstone to find a way of gaining the confidence of the Irish, who, he said, were looking to him, but added a warning: "Unless the denominational system is maintained in all its integrity, and extended to Ireland, there will be a split with those whose support is now with you."[15] The allusion to Gladstone's parliamentary strategy and strength implies a distinct political preference, and one suspects that Manning's many avowals of being "Yours faithfully" to Disraeli are either contingent upon his usefulness, or perhaps a punning reference to his own religious devotion.[16] Equally revealing of his sense of opportunity is his letter to Cullen, in reply to the cardinal's expressed anxiety about dividing the endowment of the Church of Ireland among other denominations. This was after the Disestablishment resolutions had been carried in the House of Commons. Manning writes, on 21 May: "Late events have placed me in a difficulty as regards Mr. Disraeli, and I have not liked to communicate with him. I will take care that your Eminence's suggestion as to the Irish Church Endowments shall reach Mr. Gladstone."[17] In short, Manning was playing both ends against the middle, which, as a strategy for promoting his church's interests, had obvious advantages as well as dangers.

The most significant moment of Manning's interventions in 1868, however, was that of 11 March, when he sent Gladstone an advance copy of his pamphlet, *Ireland: A Letter to Earl Grey*. Apparently it was sent to all the leading statesmen of the day, but Manning did not deliver Disraeli's copy until the 16th, the very day of Gladstone's announcement in the Commons.[18] This very substantial "letter" argued that Ireland could only be pacified and contented by five radical reforms: the repeal of all penal statutes against the Catholic Church; the equality of that church with other denominations; the creation of a denominational system of education; the disestablishment of the Protestant Church of Ireland; and the settlement of the land question, giving tenants permanent tenure. In claiming that the civil law must yield to the "higher jurisdiction" of the divine law, itself resting upon the "natural law of God," Manning was focusing upon what he took to be the only hope of restoring social order in Ireland; but his eloquent example, "A starving man commits no theft if he saves his life by eating of his neighbour's bread so much as is necessary for the support of his existence," seemed to many to be hardly less than a justification of the Fenian violence he had previously condemned. Gladstone, however, seems to have read the pamphlet in a more persuasive light, and it may well be that it acted as a catalyst in bringing him to decisive action. For some time Gladstone had privately been convinced that the Church of Ireland could not be upheld as an establishment, but, just as he would later do over the issue of Home Rule, he waited for public opinion to mature before announcing his conversion to such a policy. The archbishop's influence in this direction was neither new nor sudden. Indeed, his efforts went back many years, but, in Vincent McClelland's words, "it is not unlikely that Manning's pamphlet to Earl Grey finally convinced Gladstone that the time was now ripe for Disestablishment."[19]

This view is not incompatible with recognizing other political motivations. The Duke of Argyll (who, as Gladstone's "dearest and most intimate friend," was credited with some authority in the matter), explained to Lord Shaftesbury's mother-in-law that Gladstone introduced his resolutions because "there was really no other way of getting Dizzy out of office!"[20] Such political expediency is not quite as reductive and disillusioning as Shaftesbury took it to be, for, as a corollary of his mortifications at Disraeli's success, Gladstone was rapidly developing a conviction that it was his divinely sanctioned "mission to pacify Ireland."[21] In summary, Gladstone's behaviour reflected a mixture of private and public concerns that well illustrates Harold Lasswell's formula describing the way in which public political postures or ideologies embody a displacement and rationalization of private motives.[22] That this process could be complex, and to some degree self-conscious is given eloquent testimony in this case by the elaborate explanation of his motives and actions that Gladstone shortly produced as *A Chapter of Autobiography*, an essay originally intended to be an election pamphlet, but ultimately not published until November, when the fall campaign results were complete. What needed to be explained in Gladstone's apologia was how the conservative, indeed Tory defender of religious establishments, and author of *The State in Its Relations with the Church* (1838), "came at the time of the Maynooth debate in 1845 to believe that a foolish defence of the Irish ecclesiastical establishment would do the Church more harm than good, but that an act of disestablishment must await its most propitious moment."[23] As was consistently the case, Gladstone insisted here that his policy towards Ireland must endorse only those actions which were within the limits of safety and prudence. And, thus, just as was the case with his antagonist, Gladstone's actions reflect a mixture of principle, pragmatism, and expediency.

Much the same could be said of Manning's behaviour. Disraeli clearly felt that the archbishop had betrayed him at the most critical, defining moment of the parliamentary session. Yet the prime minister was not naively innocent of Gladstone's intentions, nor unaware of the fact that the real struggle over the relative positions of the Protestant and Catholic Churches in Ireland could at best be postponed until a new Parliament had been elected. Eventually he and Manning would come to a more just appreciation of their negotiations in 1868, but for the next few years Manning maintained that events had simply been taken out of his hands, and Disraeli interpreted the archbishop's excuses as lame hypocrisy. In that regard the elegant letter that Manning wrote after Disraeli had resigned, and the title "Viscountess of Beaconsfield" had been conferred on Mary Anne Disraeli as a symbol of her husband's services, is a revealing document:

> Being now assured of the mark of confidence bestowed upon you by her Majesty, I hope I may break the silence which events have forced upon us to express my sense of the graceful manner in which your arduous services are acknowledged in the honour bestowed on Mrs. Disraeli. If not unfitting on my part I would ask you to convey this expression of my respect to her.
>
> I have felt that a ravine, I will not say a gulf, opened between us when the resolutions on the Irish Church were laid upon the table of the House. I regretted this as I had hoped to see the scheme of the Catholic University happily matured; but with my inevitable convictions as to the Irish Church I felt that, I ought not to trespass upon your kindness: which I can assure you I shall remember with much pleasure. On Wednesday in next week I go to Rome until the middle of March, & as I may hardly have the pleasure of seeing you, I cannot refrain from writing this note.[24]

On the surface Manning seems merely to be seizing the occasion of the gratifying announcement to re-establish communication with Disraeli. But the diplomacy is self-destructing, for there is too much left unsaid that lies just beneath the surface of the text, and that transforms the apparent simplicity into a subtlety that could well give further offence. Even though the letter expresses Manning's regrets over the failure of the university charter, and his pleasure in remembering the prime minister's kindness, it must necessarily elide the unpleasant facts; that Her Majesty's "mark of confidence" is a predication of Disraeli's electoral defeat on the issue of the Irish Church, and in consequence of Gladstone's conversion to Disestablishment, which Manning had so long and so assiduously promoted. The letter must also necessarily elide the failure of Manning's diplomacy over the university charter. His expression of regret is not an apology. And while in all probability he could not have brought the Government and the Irish bishops to a compromise over the academic powers of the clergy, Manning's intense desire to mediate between them, and his assurances of Cardinal Cullen's support, could not but give Disraeli the impression, when these negotiations collapsed on the very day of Gladstone's resolutions, that the archbishop had been less than candid about his role in these events.

By phrasing the matter of his regret as a suggestion that he wishes to deny (that a "gulf" has opened between them), Manning magnifies his "inevitable convictions" as the basis of his feeling that he "ought not to trespass upon … [Disraeli's] kindness." This ostensibly compelling scruple has the effect of negating the expression of regret; but that cannot be avoided, because the hidden truth is that Manning's withdrawal and the failure of the proposed university charter reflected other considerations. His desire not to expose either the extent of his negotiations with the Government, or his contrary views to those of the other Irish bishops, was in part based upon the more compelling desire to maintain his position of power and influence within the Catholic hierarchy. There was also the possibility that Gladstone and the Liberals would offer a charter that was more attractive to the Catholic Church as soon as they assumed office.

Manning's subsequent description of the "strait" he was in at this time implies that he knew Disraeli would feel betrayed, but that he preferred this imputation on his character to the risks inherent in any candid explanation. In closing his letter to Disraeli with the reference to the pleasure he takes in remembering the prime minister's kindness, and to the pleasure-denied of not expecting to see him before leaving for Rome, Manning assumes the civilities of friendship. But it was an expression of sentiments that he could hardly expect to be reciprocated. And it may well be this insensitivity to Disraeli's feelings that led the former prime minister to be so explicit when in the spring of 1870 a deputation of Catholics, including the Duke of Norfolk and Sir Charles Clifford, called at Grosvenor Gate to discuss a pending motion on Catholic convents:

> Mr. Disraeli said … that it was impossible for him to give any help to Catholics in matters affecting their political interests; that, when in office, he had made certain propositions; and that on the score of those proposi-tions certain Catholic leaders had given him an undertaking of support; but that undertaking had not been observed, but had been betrayed … and, in fine, that he no longer possessed the confidence of the Party in Catholic questions. The Duke and Sir Charles withdrew, but he followed them to the head of the stairs and said it was to Archbishop Manning he particularly referred, and that he wished what he had said to be commu-nicated to his Grace.[25]

This same letter by J. Pope Hennessy corroborates the handwritten note among the Disraeli papers to the effect that Disraeli had indeed referred to this "betrayal" as being "stabbed in the back."[26] Meanwhile, Manning, who was in Rome for the Vatican Council, was soon informed of Disraeli's views. He immediately wrote another letter of explanation, outlining the various attempts he had made through intermediaries to explain that the negotiations in 1868 "were entirely taken out of … [his] hands by the Bishops." He also insisted, that, had he "been left free to act," these negotiations "would have been successful," that he "had never ceased to regret the failure of … [his] efforts," and that Disraeli's impressions and judgment of the matter were therefore "erroneous."[27] It is ironic that the same issue – of a charter for a Catholic university in Ireland – would precipitate a rupture of Manning's friendship with Gladstone in 1873. And this ravine did indeed become a gulf when, after his electoral defeat in 1874, Gladstone published his intemperate attack on the Vatican decrees resulting from the Council of 1870. More immediately, five days before Manning sent his explanation from Rome, Disraeli took his own literary revenge upon the archbishop in the satir-ical portrait of Cardinal Grandison in his next novel, *Lothair*, which appeared to great public anticipations on 2 May 1870.

In the debate on Gladstone's resolutions, which took place at the end of March and beginning of April 1868, Disraeli's Government clearly

felt embattled. The prime minister's first inclination was to meet the
Liberal attack by enlarging the issue, and placing the matter of the Irish
Church amid the larger question of all religious establishments. By thus
invoking threats to the safety of the Church of England, the Conservatives
hoped to be able to rouse the Protestant feeling of the country to their
defence. And, as it turned out, once Gladstone had carried his resolutions in the Commons, this was to be their strategy of the ensuing election campaign in the late summer and autumn. Once again, however,
Disraeli's policy was to be a curious mixture of expediency and principles. The immediate exigency was to prevent Gladstone and the Liberals
from gaining the power and patronage of office prior to the forthcoming
election on the new franchise. Accordingly, the chief accusations lev-
elled by Disraeli's supporters were that Gladstone's resolutions were
destructive in that they would only fan the flames of political agitation
and religious bigotry in Ireland, and that they were ill-timed, purely
party measures, designed to dislodge the Conservative Government
even before their subsidiary Reform Bills for Scotland and Ireland could
be passed.[28] However much he might acknowledge the need to reform
the temporal abuses of the Church in Ireland, Disraeli had for many
years believed, as one of the strongest elements of his conviction, that
the union of church and state embodied in the Established Church was
a bulwark of the English constitution, including the rights of property
and the freedom of individuals.

If *Sybil* is read as a religious allegory symbolically representing that
same union of church and state as the ideal form of a harmonious society, then Disraeli can certainly be said to have held this view for more
than twenty years before Gladstone, somewhat paradoxically, made it
the crux of their political rivalry. Moreover, in a number of speeches on
the present and future state of the Church delivered earlier in the decade,
Disraeli had anticipated the arguments he used in the debate of 1868. In
these speeches he described the Church as the conscience of the state,
providing a sanction of civil authority and "the means of lofty and virtuous government, by the aid of which we may prevent government
from degenerating into a mere machinery of police."[29] The Church was,
therefore, not only "the sanctuary of Divine Truth," but also "our best
security for that civil and religious liberty of which we hear so much,
and which we are told is opposed to its institution."[30] In short, for
Disraeli the Church was a "national," not a "clerical" corporation,
whose duty through education, spiritual guidance, and public worship

was to sustain and enhance the welfare of the people.[31] In his view there was nothing incompatible between the endowed property of the Established Church committed to maintaining a standard of truth and the people's right to a complete freedom of religious faith.

In opposing Gladstone's resolutions in 1868, Disraeli clearly saw himself as defending a national institution that had been under attack for a long time. That, indeed, had been the focus of his speech "The Present Position of the Church" in 1861: "During the last session of Parliament alone a series of Bills was introduced, all with various specific objects, but all converging to the same point – an attack upon the authority of the Church ... Our charities are assailed; even our Churchyards are invaded; our law of marriage is to be altered; our public worship, to use the language of our opponents, is to be 'facilitated.' Finally, the sacred fabrics of the Church are no longer to be considered national."[32] He thus interpreted the assault on the Irish Church in 1868 as a wedge to force the destruction of the Established Church in England. And the unnatural strength of the Opposition coalition on this issue he took to be prima facie evidence that there was a conspiracy at work to use Irish Church Disestablishment to further a multitude of heinous ends: "the crisis of England is now fast arriving. High Church Ritualists and the Irish followers of the Pope have been long in secret combination, and are now in open confederacy ... I know the almost superhuman power of this combination. They have their hand almost upon the realm of England. Under the guise of Liberalism, under the pretence of legislating in the spirit of the age, they are, as they think, about to seize upon the supreme authority of the realm." Such a vision of danger calls for a patriot to thwart it, and Disraeli was insistent that so long as, by "favour of the Queen" he stood as her prime minister, he would oppose it "to the utmost of ... [his] ability." He linked that opposition directly to the policy of "the right hon. Gentleman who is their representative," a policy, he said, that, if successful, "would change the character of this country ... deprive the subjects of Her Majesty of some of their most precious privileges," and "dangerously touch even the tenure of the Crown."[33] In defining his role in the crisis in such heroic and chivalric terms, Disraeli was in effect realizing that "Vindication of the English Constitution" which had been his chosen political identity since first joining the Tory party under the patronage of Lord Lyndhurst in the mid-1830s. It was for him not solely a matter of civil and religious freedoms, but also involved both the rights of private property and the Protestant identity of the country with its doctrine of Royal Supremacy. Disraeli thus repeatedly characterizes Gladstone's resolutions as a "vast and violent step," designed to subvert the entire social fabric. The extremity of the case in Disraeli's view is embodied in a letter he wrote to the Rev. Arthur Baker defending his views. There he denied any intention of casting a slur upon the High Church party, but repeated his conviction that there was a "secret combination" between an "extreme faction in the Church ... and the Irish Romanists." He described the Liberation Society, with its "shallow and short-sighted fanaticism," as "a mere instrument" in the hands of this confederacy, which he believed was working to establish a "spiritual despotism" that would dissolve the union between church and state. But he assured Baker that he would use his "utmost energies to defeat these fatal machinations."[34]

This compelling fantasy of a conspiratorial opposition, however much it might be derided as the product of a "heated imagination,"[35] is a very significant element of Disraeli's political thinking, and hence of his subsequent strategy. While it was undoubtedly precipitated in part by the recent experience of secret negotiations with Manning over the Catholic university, such a fantasy has roots far back in Disraeli's earlier imaginative life. It bears an obvious connection, for example, to the clandestine theory of government outlined by Sidonia in *Coningsby*, and it is related to the power fantasies of Disraeli's early political journalism, particularly those embodied in the writing of *England and France; or a Cure for the Ministerial Gallomania* and the similarly anonymous articles in the *Morning Post*. It is, of course, a happy characteristic of paranoia that the mystery of the unknown seems to confirm the suspicion of hidden danger and evil. But equally important here is the sense of heroism that is derived from the conviction of thwarting a conspiracy. As the Disestablishment crisis unfolds, Disraeli's sense of his role is that of being called to defend the very unity and liberty of his country – that most noble of political causes – against the insidious forces conspiring to subvert them. It is interesting that this "psychological romance," embodied now in the role of prime minister, is once again shaped by Disraeli's ambivalence towards Catholicism, that disguise of his own self-divisions which was so evident in the early novels and journalism. As much as he believes his own Irish policy to be one of justice and conciliation, and while he thinks that Gladstone's will only exacerbate violent animosities, Disraeli is also convinced that the papacy remains secretly and constantly at work upon the destruction of the Royal Supremacy and the project of "sacerdotal tyranny."[36]

I

It is ironic that Disraeli's sense of his political duty, following the Commons's adoption of Gladstone's first resolution by a majority of sixty, bears a close resemblance to the chivalric posture for which he criticized Sir Robert Peel in 1846. Queen Victoria was in any case much distressed by the Liberals' policy and anxious not to have a change of ministers. And in a "Most Confidential" letter to Disraeli, Lord Derby had previously reported that Her Majesty had spoken to him "in most unreserved terms of condemnation of Gladstone's motion and conduct." Similarly, Gathorne Hardy, the Home Secretary, had written to say that he was "much struck by the dread the Queen expresses of Gladstone and his scheme," which she thought was in conflict with her Coronation Oath.[37] But Disraeli had already made a point of emphasizing to Her Majesty the constitutional dangers and political results he anticipated from Gladstone's "uncompromising, violent, & elaborate proposition." In a letter, dated 23 March, he had told the Queen that "Mr. Gladstone has mistaken the spirit of the times, & the temper of the country," for the "abhorrence of Popery, the dread of Ritualism, & the hatred of the Irish" have long been "smouldering in the mind of the nation." Accordingly, he anticipated that the "religious sentiment" would soon develop itself and end in the "violent mistrust of the multitude." In the boroughs, he thought, there would be an earnest revival of "the no-Popery cry," while in the counties the clergy and gentry would rally round "the sacred & time-honored principle of Church & State." And it was, he concluded, "perhaps, providential, that this religious controversy shd. have arisen to give color to the character and a form to the action, of the newly enfranchised constituencies."[38]

The immediate concern was to forestall any expectation that the Government would resign. Well before the vote on the first of Gladstone's motions, Disraeli had intimated that his strategy would be to maintain office until such time as an election could be held on the new franchise.[39] The implications of Disestablishment were so great, he thought, that the issue should be put to the country as a whole. He therefore proposed, if pressed, to challenge the Opposition to produce a direct want of confidence motion in the face of the threat of an immediate penal dissolution upon the old registration. This arrangement was made formal in an interview and two subsequent exchanges of letters with the Queen just before and immediately following the Government's defeat on the first resolution.[40] But there was a difficulty with such a strategy, for Disraeli

adopted this course without the full sanction of his cabinet. He rightly
sensed that several of them (Gathorne Hardy, the Duke of Richmond,
the Duke of Marlborough, Lord Malmesbury, and perhaps others) would
have preferred to resign and had no appetite for continuing as a minority Government in a hostile House of Commons. Thus, when presenting
as a fait accompli Her Majesty's assent to his plan ("to dissolve this
Parliament as soon as the public interests will permit")[41] Disraeli seemed
to some on both sides of the question to have infringed upon the political neutrality of the Queen. Although in his formal letter to the Queen
Disraeli had explicitly raised the alternative of an immediate resignation, and although she had explicitly rejected it in her reply, it looked to
those members of the Opposition who were eager to replace the ministry, as though Disraeli were clinging to office by giving his Irish policy
the sanction of royal preference. Indeed, the radicals in the Opposition
assailed Disraeli's tactics as an outrageous breach of privilege, John
Bright going so far as to accuse the prime minister by implication of a
"very high crime and a great misdemeanour against his Sovereign and
against his country."[42]

Not surprisingly, the unsympathetic press took up this cry as a favourite political theme in the following months. In an essay that was
ostensibly a review of John Bright's *Speeches on Subjects of Public Policy*,
for example, the *British Quarterly Review* expatiated on the old theme of
Disraeli's political inconsistency, and the author accused the prime
minister of being willing to say or do anything in order to "retain the
only object of his public life – political power."[43] More influential, however, were two quite scurrilous articles in *Fraser's Magazine*; "The
Caucasian Administration and the Irish Difficulty" (April 1868), and
"The Caucasian Administration in Trouble" (May 1868), both of which
Gladstone noted in his diary as part of his daily reading as soon as they
appeared.[44] These articles were written by Abraham Hayward, who
published a whole series of similar attacks upon Disraeli in *Fraser's*
from 1867 through 1869.[45] In the former, Hayward attempts to convict
the prime minister of "political roguery" by quoting extensively from
Vivian Grey and *The Revolutionary Epick* to illustrate the dishonesty and
opportunistic want of principle that he finds in Disraeli's whole career.
In the latter piece he attacks what he terms "Mr. Disraeli's fancy for re-
kindling bigotry," by reviewing the church and state argument in the
light of the "Maunday Thursday" letter to the Rev. Arthur Baker. And
he tries to expose the hypocrisy of "the Disraelite complaint of personality" by recalling the attacks on Sir Robert Peel in 1846 and the role

Disraeli subsequently played in the Protectionist cause. Although the May article appeared just as the debate on Gladstone's resolutions was resuming at the end of April, it anticipates the Liberal objections to Disraeli's account of the Queen's role in sanctioning the Government's actions:

> What language is too strong to describe the conduct of a man who, in his capacity of prime minister, tries to fix a stigma on an honourable competitor, and thereby deprive him of the royal, if not national, esteem and confidence, by an utterly groundless charge of complicity in a non-existing plot for undermining The Altar and The Throne? ... Setting aside any objections to such measures in themselves [the charter for a Catholic university and the scheme of concurrent endowment], can any one help seeing the utter dishonesty and trickery of the proposal of them by a man who was trying to destroy a loyal adversary by imputing to him a treacherous league with Popery? Has or has not Mr. Disraeli whispered his "heated imagination" charge in the ear of royalty?[46]

With respect to his own cabinet, Disraeli was, of course, simply trying to avoid trouble, and so he had cast the decision to remain in office in terms of their chivalric duty "as gentlemen," who, "whatever the mortifications" they might experience, "were bound" to stand by Her Majesty and "secure at least a fair trial" for the constitutional principle of Royal Supremacy under ministers favourable rather than inimical to it.[47] But in thus reporting to the Queen the substance of the Lord Chancellor's remarks, Disraeli was moving well beyond the precedents of "his humble duty" to convey the decisions of the cabinet to Her Majesty. In his biography, Blake provides an excellent discussion of the way Disraeli, from the moment of taking office, set out to gain the friendship of the Queen with an enchanting mixture of chivalric romance and political gossip.[48] And there can be no doubt that she was greatly entertained by the novelist's dramatic flair in his correspondence, and much flattered by his many compliments. But most of all she was delighted to be his confidante. Never before had she been privy to the personalities and discussions in the cabinet, and never before had she received notes scribbled in haste from the floor of the House of Commons in the heat of debate. She declared, indeed, "'that she never had such letters in her life ... and she never before knew *everything*.'"[49]

Gladstone's darkest suspicions of Disraeli's character were, no doubt, reinforced by reading the articles in *Fraser's Magazine*, but, by the time

the vote on his first resolution was taken, Gladstone was at least ambivalent about the prospect of an immediate change of ministers.
Having at the outset of Disraeli's premiership "considered a good deal
the personnel of ... [his] party with a view to contingencies," Gladstone
had by 23 April apparently decided that his own coalition of Whigs,
Liberals, Irish, and Radicals was only united on the one immediate
issue, and was therefore a poor basis for a new ministry.[50] With much
evident relief Disraeli wrote on that day to Gathorne Hardy, conveying
information he had just received on the present state of affairs:
"Gladstone, instead of wishing to upset us, has no Cabinet ready, & tho'
sanguine as to his future, is at present greatly embarrassed. He wishes
to build us a golden bridge, and if we announce a bona fide attempt to
wind up, he would support Bills to extend the time of registration."[51]
Such optimism failed to take into account how galling Gladstone found
his situation, but that feeling was clearly reflected when, after the vote
on 30 April, he proposed to take the Commons's order of business into
his own hands with a motion to prevent discussion of Ways and Means.
The frustration of temporary impotence was also evident when, in
Hardy's words, Gladstone attacked the Government on 5 May "in a
white heat with an almost diabolical expression of countenance."[52] The
Liberal leader thus had really no option but to pass his other resolutions, bring in an Irish Church Appointments Suspensory Bill (that
would not pass the Lords in any case), let Disraeli wind up the parliamentary business as quickly as possible, and await the verdict of the
general election, which, he anticipated, would give him a sound working majority for a new Liberal government. This proved, however, to be
an accommodation that gave him much distress.

The earliest date for a dissolution on the new franchise was, it turned
out, mid-November, and during the intervening months there were a
quite extraordinary number of vacancies in the hierarchy of the Church
of England, a matter on which Gladstone felt intensely jealous of his
rival's power. Moreover, given Disraeli's conviction that the forthcoming election was to be a great "Protestant struggle," it is not surprising
that the prime minister conceived of this church patronage in political
terms.[53] The difficulty was that, despite his oft-stated views about the
importance of the Church as a national institution, Disraeli was singu-
larly uninformed about the qualifications of the most important clergy.
He saw the Church as rather crudely divided into parties and factions;
High vs. Low, ritualists vs. rationalists, Romanisers vs. evangelicals,
etc. And in the light of the conspiracy among ritualists and Romanists

which he perceived behind the call for Irish Church Disestablishment, he determined to strengthen the "Protestant" cause by appointing clerics known chiefly for their staunch support of the Conservative party and for their zealous antipathy to Catholicism. Apart from the task of finding suitable candidates, there were two difficulties with this strategy: first, that, given the internecine nature of Church politics, such appointments were likely to offend as many people as they pleased; second, that the Government's Church patronage required the sanction of the Queen, and Her Majesty was much better informed than her prime minister about the merits of individual clergymen. Moreover, the Queen quite properly took the issue to be the welfare of the Church as a whole, rather than the strengthening of one portion of it, and she was thus alert to the implications of the first difficulty. As a consequence there soon developed what might be termed a tussle of wills over each succeeding Church appointment.

The subject of ecclesiastical patronage first arose for Disraeli within a week of Gladstone's announcement of his intention to pursue Irish Disestablishment. And with respect to such patronage the tension between temporal and spiritual concerns is apparent from the outset. On 21 March Disraeli wrote to Lord Derby, reporting that he had been told by a "person of authority" and "a social friend of Gladstone's" that the Liberal leader's "present violent courses are entirely to be attributed to the paralytic stroke of the Bishop of Winchester." It was "strange," Disraeli said, "that a desire to make Bishops should lead a man to destroy Churches!"[54] The witty remark points the reader both to the distinction between conjunction and causality, and to the intense excitability for which Gladstone was well-known. The possibility of making such a clerical appointment was but a spark to the explosion of a larger and long-standing political jealousy. It is therefore ironic, especially in the light of the many subsequent vacancies, that the death of this particular prelate did not occur immediately. It was not until some months after the general election that the bishop of Winchester resigned his see for reasons of failed health, at which time Gladstone was able to recommend his successor. But only a week after writing to Lord Derby, Disraeli was called upon to fill a canonry at Worcester. The Queen wished, on the basis of her personal regard for him, to prefer the Rev. Charles Kingsley to this position, and the Prince of Wales was equally eager to have his first tutor, Mr Birch, appointed. But Disraeli took exception to both of these suggestions, noting with regard to the former that, though he was anxious to please Her Majesty, "the appointment of

Mr. Kingsley, just now, would be seriously prejudicial to Mr. Disraeli." The Queen's description of Kingsley as a man of "liberal and enlightened" religious views was certainly no recommendation in her prime minister's eyes, and so he suggested the names of two Oxford clerics, both described as "sound Churchmen, of temperate views," but more noted for their attachment to the Conservative party. Of these the Queen chose the Reverend Dr Wynter, president of St John's College, who, with "ten sons, all unprovided for," had obvious need of a patron.[55] But the political qualifications were clearly foremost in the prime minister's mind, when he wrote to a High Church friend the next day: "My dear Beauchamp, I have appointed your friend to the vacant Canonry. I had no idea before of the numerical power of the Clergy."[56]

When less than a month later the bishop of Hereford died, Disraeli wrote immediately to the Queen informally suggesting that Dean Wellesley at Windsor be appointed to succeed him, and that she should then prefer the Hon. and Reverend Grantham Yorke to the vacant deanery. Mr Yorke, he assured her, was an entirely suitable candidate for such royal preferment: a hard-working clergyman in the largest parish of Birmingham, known for his devotion to his duties, and a man of "very temperate" opinions, whose appointment "would not offend the High Ch:, would satisfy the Low, but would rejoice all temperate & earnest supporters of Church & State." He was also, Disraeli said, "from his appearance & manners ... a gentleman not unworthy of being placed in somewhat intimate relations with Yr Majesty."[57] This "arrangement" did not, however, please the Queen, who had no intention of agreeing to the rustication of Wellesley, her most trusted adviser on ecclesiastical affairs. And, though it is only speculation, this would appear to have been Disraeli's motive in making the suggestion, for the dean of Windsor did not meet any of the prime minister's political criteria for ecclesiastical promotion, however much he might deserve it.

On 3 May Disraeli then sent the Queen a list of five additional names to be considered for the vacant bishopric. Of these the first was "Dr. Atley, Vicar of Leeds," who was being recommended as "a right-minded & sound Churchman" on the advice of Spencer Walpole, the previous Home Secretary under Lord Derby. Disraeli observed as well, that Dr Atlay had taken the chair at the meeting of Leeds on the Irish Church, and "so he cannot be very high." This suggests that Disraeli was recommending a person of whose reputation he had no personal knowledge, a suspicion strengthened by the fact that he misspelled his name. Of the others on the list, two were admitted to be High Church: Christopher

Wordsworth, canon of Westminster, was portrayed as "learned and eloquent as a divine. A capital scholar. Rather high, &, perhaps a little too controversial," while Dr Leighton, the warden of All-Souls was described as "High Church, but quite sound." Another of the candidates, Dr Cookson, master of St Peter's College, Cambridge, apart from his academic pursuits, was described as "a stout Conservative" who was "firm & moderate in his religious views and opinions." The fifth man, Dean Goulburn was only cursorily referred to as "an Oxford man" – an allusion to the traditional balancing of episcopal appointments between graduates of the Oxbridge universities.[58] It would thus seem that initially Disraeli was willing to recommend High Church candidates for preferment, provided that they were politically "sound." He was certainly getting advice to that effect, for in addition to Lord Beauchamp, others such as Gathorne Hardy and the bishop of Oxford, Samuel Wilberforce, were urging him not to let his fear of ritualists stand in the way of a fair distribution of honours. Cairns, the Lord Chancellor, was, however, just as eager to recommend Low Church candidates, for he was convinced that there was considerable public uneasiness about Wilberforce's influence in the matter of Church patronage – "a feeling which was due, no doubt, to the appointment of the Bishop's chaplain, Dr. Woodford, to succeed Atlay at Leeds."[59]

In the next two months, there were only a couple of minor posts to dispose of, and the prime minister was able to comply with at least one royal preference by making Mr Birch a canon of Ripon.[60] But by August, when the dean of Ripon died, Disraeli was caught in the exigencies of the pending election – "the great Protestant struggle," the success of which depended upon the shaping of public opinion. He thus felt strongly that he must strengthen the Protestant cause through some explicit mark of sympathy for the evangelical party in the Church. Accordingly, he recommended "Dr. McNeile of Liverpool" (actually canon of Chester) for the vacant deanery. In Disraeli's words, McNeile was "a shining light of the Protestant party," a man who was "gaining golden opinions all over England by his eloquent, learned, & commanding, advocacy of the Royal Supremacy," and whose words at this moment of "national excitement" would "influence opinion." Perhaps anticipating the Queen's displeasure, he added as a further explanation of his controversial choice: "The present Government has been accused, tho' unjustly, of favoring the High Ch: party."[61] When Her Majesty nevertheless demurred, asking him to consider the ill feelings that would be aroused by appointing a man who had "chiefly rendered himself conspicuous by his hostility to the Roman Catholic Church," Disraeli replied that he had anxiously and deeply considered his recommendation before making it, that he had consulted the Lord Chancellor, who was very strongly in favour of it, and that the claims of Canon McNeile were such that if he were now passed over, "a higher preferment might fall to him." In short, Disraeli was translating his sense of the political exigency into a choice of the lesser of two evils, at least as seen from the Queen's preference for moderate and liberal appointments to what she referred to as "a high dignity in the English Church."[62]

The real political considerations in Disraeli's mind are shown, however, when in the same letter he goes on to say that there is "no hope of conciliating the Roman Catholics" and that the "Protestant party in the Church consider that they have been neglected ... by the present Government." The preferment of Canon McNeile would remedy this, he argues, and be an encouragement to this "very powerful, very energetic" party. And while he says that he quite enters into the Queen's "general views" on this proposition, "distinguished" by her "wise and just appreciation of affairs," he adds that he fears there is a danger that "the Protestant feeling of the country ... may not be enlisted on the side of the Ch: of England." Such a letter reflects the polarization in Disraeli's thinking that was, perhaps, the inevitable consequence of the success of Gladstone's Disestablishment resolutions. It also shows the peculiar effect of this election, turning as it did on the question of religion, for Disraeli's electoral strategy is to claim an identity of interest between his ministry and the Church of England, the constitution, and even the monarchy itself. It is understandable that those of Liberal persuasion might well be tempted to deplore this patriotism as the last refuge of a scoundrel, but it seems clear enough that such a strategy was based upon his conviction that there was a conspiracy of subversive forces at work to undermine these institutions. His reference to Archbishop Manning's influence "being omnipotent" at this juncture is surely significant in this regard, for it suggests that Disraeli began to see the issue of Church patronage as a means of thwarting that conspiracy. The extent to which the events unfolding in 1868 took the form of such a political romance in his mind is ultimately revealed by the publication of *Lothair* in 1870, but for the moment the imaginative shape of his political life was formed by a struggle for power whose result was still uncertain.

The very great danger in Disraeli's definition of his political identity as the defender of Church, constitution, and monarchy was, as his enemies foresaw, that he would compromise the Queen's political neutrality. This danger is nowhere more manifest to us now than in the nature of their remarkable correspondence. In sharing his thoughts with the Queen as he did, Disraeli inevitably made her the confidante of his party's political strategy, as well as of his Government's public policy. At times of elections it is never easy to maintain the distinction between them, but in this case the difficulty was exacerbated by the quite unprecedented opportunities for Church patronage during an election focused upon a religious issue. A crucial document in this regard is the letter, marked "*Secret*," that Disraeli wrote to the Queen on 21 August, while she was vacationing in Switzerland. The letter begins with the assurance that his reflections on the rapidly ripening state of affairs in England are based upon a mass of authentic information "of obvious truth and intelligence" received by the prime minister every day from "trusty agents" and casual correspondents. In England, he says, "the great feature of national opinion, at this moment, is an utter repudiation by all classes, of the High Church Party":

It is not only general; it is universal. It is not only the inhabitants of towns, but every farmer is against them, & a very large proportion of the gentry, & all the professional classes.

If the Irish Church fall, it will be owing entirely to the High Ch: party, & to the prejudice wh: they have raised against ecclesiastical institutions.

One of the most remarkable circumstances, at this moment, is the almost universal report by the agents, that the new County Constituency of £12 qualification, turns out highly conservative, tho' universally opposed to the High Church.

Mr. Disraeli speaks on this subject entirely without prejudice, the bias of his mind from education, being brought up in a fear of fanaticism, being certainly towards the High Church, but he has no sort of doubt as to the justness of his present conclusions, & it is his highest duty to tell Yr. Majesty this.

Nevertheless, the Church, as an Institution is so rooted, & the doctrine of the Royal Supremacy so wonderfully popular, that if the feeling of the Country be guided with wisdom, Mr. Disraeli believes, that the result of the impending struggle, may be very advantageous, & even triumphant to the existing constitution of the country.

Speaking under ordinary circumstances, it would be, in this rapid age, almost impossible to foretell the result of a general Election, that will, even now, not take place for nearly a quarter of a year. But Mr. Disraeli has no doubt, from all that he observes, & all that reaches him, that it will be a

great Protestant struggle – & that if the government of the country temper-
ately, but firmly & unequivocally, enlist that Protestant feeling on the side
of the existing authority the institutions of the country will be greatly
strengthened, & the means of governing proportionately facilitated.

But if not thus guided, & even unconsciously controlled, the Protestant
feeling will take a destructive, instead of a conservative, form; & those,
who may have the honor & happiness of being Yr. Majesty's servants,
must prepare themselves to meet embarassments [sic] & difficulties of no
ordinary character.[63]

Although he is careful here to refer to "the existing constitution" and
"the existing authority," and thus to stay within the bounds of propriety, the context strongly implies that the advantage and triumph
Disraeli foresees as a consequence of his policy is more narrowly political. His desire to "unequivocally enlist the Protestant feeling," which
can be "even unconsciously controlled," is based upon the assumption
that hostility to the High Church party can be translated into political
action through the deliberate manipulation of Church patronage of the
kind represented by the preferment of Canon McNeile. And this assumption, or conclusion, as Disraeli calls it, is justified by the paradigm
of the secret and confidential information that is available to the prime
minister, a vision of political power with obvious resonance to his early
political adventures, such as *The Representative* affair and the publication of the *Gallomania*, as well as to his role in the Young England movement of the 1840s.

II

Events would soon prove that Disraeli, no doubt remembering the
no-popery agitation of 1851, overestimated both the power of the clergy
to influence voters' opinions and the extent to which the public would
identify the fate of the Irish Church with any threat to English institutions. In any case, the Queen was not persuaded by Disraeli's letter, for
she saw a more immediate danger in the very strategy he proposed –
that the preferment of "Ultra Evangelical" partisans, whom she described as "narrow-minded" and illiberal, would bring the Church as a
whole into public disfavour.[64] But her desire to appoint men of moderate religious views, while ostensibly apolitical, had the disadvantage
from the Government's perspective of usually favouring their political
adversaries, since Broad Churchmen tended to be Gladstonian Liberals.

In this regard, the role of Dean Wellesley is worth noting, for though his views were very close to the Queen's preference for clever, sensible, liberal-minded men who had distinguished themselves in the performance of their religious duties, he did advise Her Majesty that it would be unreasonable to expect Disraeli to accept men whose political loyalties were known to be to the Opposition. Thus, while he was not at all sympathetic to Disraeli's purpose, in both his specific recommendations and strategic advice to the Queen, Wellesley strove to find a compromise between ecclesiastical and political considerations. This is the more striking in the light of his great personal distaste for what he later described as Disraeli's "utterly unprincipled" conduct in Church affairs.[65]

While the effects of McNeile's appointment, to which the Queen had most reluctantly agreed, were still being debated, the bishop of Peterborough died, and the controversy over Church patronage was immediately renewed with yet greater intensity. Once again, in a letter also marked "*Secret*," Disraeli set forth his views on the whole question and its relation to the impending election. In the face of public meetings and outspoken journalism protesting the influence of the High Church ritualists, especially that of the bishop of Oxford, whom he described as "more odious in this country, than ArchBishop Laud," he thought it a matter of "civil prudence" to make another evangelical appointment – "some man of learning, piety, administrative capacity, & of views, tho' inevitably decided, mild & temperate & conciliatory in their application."[66] Consequently, he put forth the names of Canon Champneys of St Paul's and Archdeacon Hone of Worcester, neither of whom, though Low Church, had the "strong individuality" that had caused the stir in the case of McNeile. In their justification Disraeli added that, though such appointments would not please the "sacerdotal school," nor even satisfy the "philosophic," they would be "received with respect alike by Ritualist & Rationalist; and with confidence & joy by the great body of Yr. Majesty's subjects." The Queen, however, thought that neither man was sufficiently distinguished for such promotion and, on the eve of Disraeli's attendance at Balmoral, she sent him a note again objecting to any "ultra Protestant" or "extreme Evangelical" appointments. This seemed to be a successful prelude to their subsequent conversations, for she noted in her journal, on 20 and 22 September, that Mr Disraeli was agreeably "anxious to make good, liberal and moderate" church appointments.[67] But another, somewhat different, view of Disraeli's state of mind can be gleaned from the letter he posted to Lord Derby from Perth, as he journeyed north:

I wish I could consult you about the Bishop ... These questions, within the last few months, have become so critical and complicated ...

I think the deanery of Ripon has been a *coup*. I was really surrounded by hungry lions and bulls of Bashan till that took place, but, since, there has been a lull, and an easier feeling in all quarters – strange to say – among all parties. Probably they were all astounded.

Oh! for an hour of confidential talk in St. James's Square! There are priests now, and men of abilities, who are as perverse as Laud, and some as wild as Hugh Peters![68]

This was an allusion to the publication of a letter by the dean of Chichester, Walter Hook, announcing that, in his indignation over McNeile's appointment as dean of Ripon, he would oppose the sitting local Tory candidate, Lord Henry Lennox. Disraeli had written on 9 September to the bishop of Oxford about this mortifying conduct, and Wilberforce had replied two days later that he was himself astonished by it, for he thought that the "vast body of sound Churchman" were entirely with the prime minister "on the great question of the day." The bishop's reply did, however, contain a warning that Disraeli seems not to have taken sufficiently to heart:

I should not tell you all that I believe to be the truth if I did not add that there is at this moment a jealous and an alarmed watchfulness of your administration of Church patronage – men who through the long period of Palmerston's administration held their fidelity in the barrenness of an ostracised position are soured by seeing or thinking they see those who, by steadfastness of principle and quietness of action, have the greatest influence amongst Churchmen passed over for unknown men or men of the long-patronised minority.

I had an earnest entreaty lately from the diocese of Peterborough that I would bring this matter before you, with the assurance from laymen and clergy that the character of the appointment to that see would determine two seats.[69]

As Blake noticed, the Queen was receiving advice that was much the same in its general import from Dean Wellesley. Disraeli's "mistake," he said, was to think that the people would put down ritualism "through the instrumentality of the Puritanical party." In the dean's opinion, Disraeli's evangelical appointments would not gain him more votes than he would lose "from the moderate party."[70]

Nevertheless, in his answer to Wilberforce's letter, sent from Balmoral on 28 September, Disraeli maintained the basis of his conviction that the election would be a great Protestant struggle. He assured Wilberforce that "the chief Minister of this country, if he be ignorant of the bent of the national feeling at a crisis, must be an idiot. His means of arriving at the truth are so multifarious." He was, he said, certain that "the long pent-up feeling" of the nation "against ultra-Ritualism" would "pronounce itself at the impending election." Thus it was that, in his desire to gain political advantage from the situation, Disraeli, although he knew almost nothing of the man, at first resisted the Queen's suggestion that Dr William Magee, the moderately evangelical dean of Cork, would be a good appointment for the bishopric at Peterborough. To his surprise, however, Lord John Manners, "the highest Churchman in the Cabinet," also suggested the eloquent Magee as a perfect symbol of "the *unity* of the Church." Even so, Disraeli complained to Montagu Corry, his private secretary: "One objection to Magee is, that his appointment would give us nothing, and that is a great objection."[71] But for lack of a suitable alternative, Disraeli eventually acquiesced to the Queen's wish, preferring Champneys instead to the vacant deanery at Lichfield, and appointing Professor Henry Mansel dean of St Paul's. The combination of these appointments seemed to please all the contending factions of the Church, and Disraeli, perhaps following Wilberforce's advice, came round for the moment to a somewhat more balanced view of such patronage. In the next two months he would suggest or agree to several High Church preferments: Francis Leighton, warden of All Souls, and a friend of Wilberforce, became a canon of Westminster; William Bright, at Lord Beauchamp's request, was given Mansel's chair at Oxford and made canon of Christ Church; and Robert Gregory, probably on the recommendation of Gathorne Hardy, was appointed a canon of St Paul's.

The ironic coincidence of the election and Church patronage had, however, not yet reached its climax. On the night of 27 October, the archbishop of Canterbury, Charles Thomas Longley, died, creating what the editors of *The Times* (and no doubt many others) thought to be "the strange fate" which made Disraeli "the adviser of the Crown with respect to the highest office in one of the greatest Churches of Christendom." And in giving their advice to the prime minister, they could not resist a touch of sardonic reflection for their readers: "It scarcely, perhaps, entered distinctly even into the visions of Vivian Grey to nominate an Archbishop of Canterbury, but there is sometimes more incongruity in facts than in dreams. We trust, however, that while the Government will avoid selecting one who has displayed a decided sympathy with any of the parties in the Church, they will at the same time endeavour in these critical times to obtain a Primate of energy and courage."[72] The Queen, no doubt anticipating even greater disagreement about this appointment, immediately took the initiative and suggested that Archibald Tait, the bishop of London, would be the only fit choice for the appointment to Canterbury. Her confidential box crossed with Disraeli's containing his suggestion of the bishop of Gloucester, Charles Ellicott. Not surprisingly, both found the other's choice a matter for despair. The Queen, taking Dean Wellesley's opinion, thought that Ellicott, though "amiable," was an "insignificant" and overtalkative man, lacking the dignity and sophistication required for such a position.[73] Disraeli, on the other hand, saw Bishop Tait as the antithesis of his desire: he was a Broad Church liberal, whom Disraeli characterized as "obscure in purpose, fitful & inconsistent in action, & evidently, tho' earnest & conscientious, a prey to constantly conflicting convictions" – at once courageous with respect to colonial bishops, but compromised over the issue of religious sisterhoods. And with what could not but be a comparison to Gladstone, Disraeli added: "there is in his idiosyncracy a strange fund of enthusiasm, a quality which ought never to be possessed by an ArchBp. of Canterbury, or a Prime Minister of England." The "most dangerous feature" in Bishop Tait's character, in Disraeli's view, was, however, "the peculiar influence wh: Neology has had upon his mind": "one wh:, while it fascinates, disheartens, him, and which is likely to involve him in terrible, & perhaps fatal, embarassments." Disraeli thus concluded that Tait had "forfeited the confidence of the High Church and the Evangelicals," and was only looked up to "with curious & unquiet hope by the Romanising, or the Freethinking, Clergy."[74]

In a letter to Lord Derby, appealing for advice, Disraeli maintained that his Church policy was "to induce ... the two great and legitimate parties to cease their internecine strife, and to combine against the common enemies: Rits and Rats." Accordingly, he said that he wanted neither a High Churchman nor an evangelical for archbishop, but that the persons among whom he must choose were very few. Derby replied that he could not agree with Her Majesty that Tait would be a popular or judicious selection, but that Ellicott, though sound, had "a foolish voice and manner" and was said "to be entirely under the influence of the Bishop of Oxford."[75] Neither Derby nor Disraeli had met the bishop of Gloucester, though the prime minister's correspondence with him seemed to discount the alleged influence of Wilberforce. Meanwhile, Dean Wellesley's advice to the Queen was a model of propriety. He seconded her preference for Bishop Tait, but advised her not to insist upon that appointment, or force the prime minister against his convictions, for, he said, "it would not be fair to him in his position." Rather, he suggested, Disraeli would have to make other suggestions, and he canvassed the merits of the various possibilities. Among these comments Wellesley expressed his regret that "Mr. Disraeli appears to have taken up such exaggerated prejudices respecting the Bishop of Oxford," which he attributed to the former's correspondence with the bishop of Gloucester, who, it seems, had fallen out with his former friend.[76] A week or so later, Disraeli again wrote to Lord Derby, still bemoaning his lack of suitable choice: "Harold Browne [bishop of Ely] is offered as a compromise. But what do I gain by Harold Browne?" He went on to indicate that he was prepared to give up the suggestion of Ellicott, but significantly he added that "the Bishop of Oxford is quite out of the running, so great is the distrust of him by the country." That was, he said, "the great fact, that has come out of the canvass of England." Thus, without any strong alternative to the Queen's choice, the conclusion to which he was driven was that he would have to accept the bishop of London as Primate, and attempt to countervail "his neological tendencies" by raising John Jackson, the "orthodox and Protestant" bishop of Lincoln, to London.[77]

The ground for such a concession had been laid in Disraeli's letter to the Queen, dated 4 November. Having objected so strongly to Bishop Tait's qualifications to lead the Church, he concluded in terms of gracious conciliation, confessing to "the infinite pain" that would be caused by seeming to differ "from a Sovereign to whom he is not only bound by every tie of personal devotion, but whose large, & peculiarly experienced, intelligence he acknowledges and appreciates, and whose judgment on many occasions would have more influence with him, than that of all his colleagues":

> All he desires is, that his views should be placed before Yr. Majesty, & that they shod. be considered. Whatever Yr. Majesty's final judgment under such circumstances, he is disposed to believe the best: nor is there anything, that he would more deprecate, than that Yr. Majesty should ever, on any subject, give a constrained assent to any of his counsels. That would cause a cloud between Yr. Majesty & himself, than which nothing could be more injurious to the satisfactory government of Yr. Majesty's realm.

His idea of the perfect relations between the Sovereign & Her Minister, is, that there shod. be, on Her part, perfect confidence; on his, perfect devotion. In the blended influence of two such sentiments, so ennobling & so refined, he sees the best security for Yr. Majesty's happiness, & the welfare of the Realm.[78]

Such a flattering and chivalric interpretation of their respective positions and powers did not, however, weaken Her Majesty's resolve. Indeed, it seems to have stiffened it, for in her reply she reiterated her view that Bishop Tait was "the proper Person – indeed the only proper Person – to succeed the late ArchBishop." To this she added: "Under no circumstances, however, cd. the Queen approve of the promotion of Dr. Ellicott"; and she indicated that, should the prime minister still object to the bishop of London, there were several other bishops, Ely, Lincoln, and Lichfield, that she would "more gladly see ... promoted than the Bishop of Gloucester."[79]

This correspondence regarding the appointment of the new archbishop of Canterbury illustrates the relations between the prime minister and the Queen at this particular moment in the evolution of parliamentary democracy. As his other letters show, despite the flattering chivalric romance of his ideal, Disraeli found the whole matter extremely vexatious in its practical bearings. George Buckle in his continuation of Monypenny's *Life of Benjamin Disraeli*, reports as well, for example, that in the midst of the controversy Disraeli emerged from an audience with the Queen in a state of "great excitement ... telling [Lord] Malmesbury 'Don't bring any more bothers before me; I have enough already to drive a man mad.'"[80] What is interesting, however, is the interplay of fiction and reality amid his struggle for the power of Church patronage. It is clear enough that Disraeli's intention is to exploit every preferment for Conservative advantage, whether through the personal influence of the appointed person, or through the public reaction to that person's religious affiliation within the Church. In that regard there seems to be a large element of miscalculation, which is really wish-fulfilment or fantasy, in Disraeli's anticipation of the likely effects of such patronage. The "great Protestant struggle" never materialized in the terms Disraeli forecast, and his fear of a ritualist-papal conspiracy did not find much resonance in the mainstream of public opinion. Moreover, despite his new sense of the "numerical power of the Clergy," it would seem that, in England at least, individual clergymen, even when they took leading roles in public meetings, had relatively little influence on the undecided or indifferent voter. And while there was certainly strong clerical feeling about McNeile's appointment as dean of Ripon, it would seem again to have followed party lines. For although it pleased the evangelicals and offended the Broad and High Churchmen, the preferment seems to have had little effect upon voters outside the Church. Also significant is the fact that, in his attempts to persuade the Queen of his view of the relation between Church patronage and the election, Disraeli, however strongly he felt, never went beyond the conception of his role as her adviser in such matters. Conversely, the Queen was most careful, even in her most insistent phrases, to put the matter in the form of granting her approval of the prime minister's suggestions. The uncertain balance of constitutional powers in Church preferments was thus maintained by two factors: the Queen, though she found Disraeli's letters in general most reassuring, was in this instance much better informed about the merits of individual clergymen than he was; and he, though convinced of the exigency in Church politics, was ultimately unwilling to risk Her Majesty's displeasure, or any serious disruption of their otherwise remarkable relationship. That there were elements of conscious manipulation in Disraeli's correspondence with the Queen is obvious; but, at the same time, it seems probable that the chivalric romance in which he formulated that relationship was also an emblem of his most deeply held political principles.

This chivalry did not, however, prevent Disraeli from pursuing every practical advantage to his cause. On the eve of the election he requested that the Queen confer a number of baronetcies upon supporters of the Conservative party. General Grey, having been commanded to do so in her name, replied immediately that the Queen felt that such a distribution of honours, "avowedly for the purpose of influencing Elections," would be a dangerous precedent because it would convey "the appearance of *Partisanship*." Having pointed out that she had refused Lord Russell's wish to make several peers when he left office, Grey added that Her Majesty thought that it would be "a still more inconvenient precedent, and even a dangerous one, were a Minister, appealing to the country against an adverse House of Commons, and staking his Ministerial existence on the issue of the elections, to claim, as if it were a right, established by precedent, the power of trying to influence those elections by the distribution of Honours, as a proof, at such a critical moment, of the Sovereign's favour and support."[81] At the same time, Grey assured Disraeli that the Queen was anxious to afford him "every constitutional proof" that he possessed "her confidence in conducting public affairs," and that she was willing to confer baronetcies on those whose names had before been submitted to her once the elections were over. As the results of various contests came in over the next ten days, Disraeli could see that a majority for the Government was at the best uncertain. And so inevitably, where the precedent was established, the Church appointments subsequent to that of the archbishop of Canterbury continued to reflect his immediate political considerations. On 20 November he told the Queen that "the High Church party are much enraged with the Episcopal appointments, and are endeavouring in consequence, injuriously to influence the County elections," and he urged that the preferment of Mr Gregory of Lambeth, "a High Churchman, but staunchly Conservative," would be "well-timed." In the light of such candour, it is hardly surprising that Dean Wellesley, in acknowledging that Mr Disraeli had behaved well toward Her Majesty in all these Church appointments, nevertheless regretted that "he has not some more fixed principle about them than the mere political bias they may have one way or other."[82]

Paradoxically, in the seemingly pragmatic concession and compromise of accepting Tait as the new archbishop of Canterbury and appointing Jackson bishop of London, there lurked, beneath the surface of his rational motives, some elements of Disraeli's darkest fantasy. This can best be seen in Disraeli's attitude to Wilberforce. Although in his second letter to Derby on the subject Disraeli had ruled the bishop of Oxford "out of the running" for the Primacy on the grounds of the country's distrust of him, it was very widely recognized, both within the Church and without, that Wilberforce was eminently suited by both experience and temperament to be bishop of London. Nearly all of the newspapers anticipated his promotion, and his expectations were naturally raised when Tait expressed his earnest desire that Wilberforce would succeed him.[83] The fact that Disraeli passed over this obvious preferment, which even Lord Derby had recommended to him, caused great anger and resentment among not only the bishop's close supporters, but also those who took a professional or a disinterested view of the Church's welfare.

Among those who were most critical of Disraeli's choice for London was Dean Wellesley, who in a private conversation with Wilberforce unburdened himself of his official moderation and restraint. Disraeli, he told the disappointed bishop, had been "utterly ignorant, utterly unprincipled," and it was only the prime minister's hostility to him, he added, that had prevented Wilberforce from being offered the see of London: "You cannot conceive the appointments he proposed and retracted or was overruled ... he had no other thought than the votes of the moment; he showed an ignorance about all Church matters, men, opinions, that was astonishing, making propositions one way and the other, riding the Protestant horse to gain the boroughs, and then, when he thought he had gone so far as to endanger the counties," he went "right round and proposed names never heard of"[84]

Whatever the merits of the argument, it is clear from his obsessive indiscretions, including mentioning the names of the unsuccessful candidates proposed by both the Queen and the prime minister, that Wellesley had for some time harboured an intense dislike of Disraeli. It would hardly be surprising if, given the invidious comparisons of the dean's confidences, the bishop's self-esteem was somewhat injured, though he had until then affected to bear his disappointment stoically. The disparity between reason and feeling in Wilberforce's comments on the situation[85] seems somewhat forced, especially in light of the fact that Dean Wellesley's expressions of disgust came in the context of other violent sympathies of an anti-Disraelian cast. The week before that conversation Wilberforce had been a guest of the Marquess of Salisbury at Hatfield, Viscount Cranborne having succeeded to the title upon the death of his father. The nature of the political climate he found there, as the results of the election unfolded, can be seen from a note in the bishop's diary: "Rode with Lord Salisbury. His high-minded views. He said he would not oppose Gladstone as a Minister, but only on any particular measure on which he differed." And Wilberforce reported again to Sir Charles Anderson, that Salisbury was "full of high patriotic views" and that "Bob Lowe" was there for two days with "prognostications for the future of England" that were "enough to make the flesh creep."[86] Whether conscious of it or not, the bishop in his disaffection was being led back into the Liberal camp, where, despite his difference of opinion on the Irish Church, his sympathies really lay. Thus, a month later he was again invited to Hatfield when the other guests were Gladstone and Cardwell, and his diary and correspondence record the extent of his political conversion: "Gladstone as ever; great, earnest, and honest; as unlike the tricky Disraeli as possible"; "I have very much enjoyed meeting Gladstone. He is so delightfully true and the same; just as full of interest in every good thing of every kind, and so exactly the opposite of the mystery man"; "he [Gladstone] always impresses me ... with the sense of his perfect honesty and noble principles."[87]

Upon their departure from Hatfield, Wilberforce had the great satisfaction of sharing a railway compartment with Gladstone and reflecting on the Liberal leader's "rectitude of purpose and clearness of view" as he was on his way to Windsor Castle to accept the Queen's commission to form a new ministry. That somewhat naive impression would eventually be complicated when a few months later the bishop received an overture from Lord Lyttelton, Gladstone's brother-in-law, that seemed suspiciously like a bribe. Lyttelton's letter quite explicitly linked preferment to the anticipated vacancy of the bishopric at Winchester with the desirability of Wilberforce's public support of Gladstone's Irish Church Bill. To the bishop's credit, after much anxious reflection, he held his ground of conscience, and Gladstone appointed him to Winchester anyway, when Bishop Sumner resigned in failing health. But for the moment, at the end of 1868, Wilberforce thought that the politics of Church patronage were an entirely Disraelian evil.

The bishop was not alone, however, in his sense of his unmerited neglect. As soon as Archbishop Longley's death was announced, for example, the dean of Chichester, Walter Hook, wrote to Wilberforce's friend, Anderson: "My dear Sir Charles, – Oxford for Canterbury. Do write to me, and say whether we can do anything. He may refuse the place, but it *ought* to be offered to him."[88] Most knowledgeable observers and most of the press, as I have indicated, thought that the more likely promotion for the bishop of Oxford was to London, but Hook's speculation and Anderson's response point to another aspect of Disraeli's decision to prefer Jackson instead of Wilberforce to that see. For coincident with Longley's death, after a month's illness, there was a public announcement that Wilberforce's daughter and her clergyman husband, Henry Pye, had been taken into the Church of Rome. Wilberforce, his family, and friends had known of, and been much oppressed by, this conversion since late August, and the delayed proclamation of it at the end of October excited some dark suspicions of a papist intrigue. In a later note to the bishop's son, Reginald, Anderson wrote: "I feel sure that Manning kept Pye as a bagged fox, and turned him out at this particular time to prevent S.O. [Samuel, Oxon.] from going to Lambeth. At all events the fact of Archbishop Longley's death and the defection of the Pyes appearing side by side in the newspaper [the *Guardian*] is remarkable and more than suspicious when one knows the creeping slyness and unscrupulous crafts of Romish tactics."[89] Although there is no consistency in the two conspiratorial views, and though allowance should be made in this case for the great pain and anguish felt by Wilberforce and his friends, this is, ironically, precisely the sort of suspicion that Disraeli entertained of Manning. And, as Standish Meacham points out, the Pyes' conversion put an end to any possibility, however slight, that Wilberforce would be promoted to London: "Disraeli was reported by Sir Edward Hamilton, Gladstone's private secretary, to have remarked on the subject later: 'How could I? His daughter by some strange malignity turned Papist just at that moment. The father's appointment would probably have cost me several seats at the General Election.'"[90] This comment implies that Disraeli fully appreciated Wilberforce's claims to preferment, even though, in the midst of the election, he felt he could not but react to the evangelical animosity toward the bishop. Disraeli was, of course, aware that Manning was Wilberforce's brother-in-law and that the bishop's brothers, Henry and Robert, had previously converted to Roman Catholicism. But what Disraeli did not know was how firmly Wilberforce himself rejected the appeal that Catholicism had made to his family. The bishop's diary and letters in the period from late August to early November reveal him to be in the deepest constant "pain" over the loss of his daughter and son-in-law. In August he wrote in his diary: "It seems as if my heart would break at this insult out of my own bosom to God's truth in England's Church, and preference for the vile harlotry of the Papacy." And just as the conversion was about to be made public in October, he wrote two very poignant letters on the same day to his son Ernest. In the first, he said, "I feel as a man may feel who has fallen down a precipice and is lying smashed. I am utterly prostrated in mind and body, but, God helping me, I will not yield." In the second letter the pain he feels is expressed even more poignantly: "I am for ever needing to discipline my spirit not to feel unkindly to one who has robbed me of my only daughter in blood and brought reproach on the Church I have, however imperfectly, ever endeavoured to serve. As to the Papistry itself, I only more than ever see it to be the great Cloaca into which all vile corruptions of Christianity run naturally, and loathe it."[91] The double irony of these sentiments from Disraeli's perspective, had he known of them, would have been that the second of these letters was written from Hawarden Castle, where the bishop found Gladstone to be a noble and consoling friend.

III

The complex matter of Disraeli's neglect of Wilberforce's ambitions to succeed Tait as bishop of London involves much misunderstanding and not a little perversity. It is symptomatic of the whole question of Church patronage and its supposed relation to electoral politics in the mid-Victorian decades. In the exigency forced upon him by Gladstone's resolutions, of defining the election almost exclusively in terms of Disestablishment and its implications, Disraeli clearly overestimated both the political effect of clerical appointments and the public's susceptibility to extreme Protestant fears that the Church of England was in danger. In the result, which left Gladstone and the Liberals with a clear parliamentary majority, Disraeli's failure to have his own way with the more significant preferments was not the crucial political issue it seemed to him at the time. The Queen's interventions, though they restrained Disraeli's zeal, did not, it seems, adversely affect his political prospects. Indeed, they may well have brought him more credit than was his due, for his ignorance of Church personalities beyond his own diocese was a serious limitation on his perspective. Disraeli's view, however, was shaped, not just by partisan considerations, but also by the several strains of the continuing psychological romance with which he invested his position as prime minister. In that regard, it is clear that Archbishop Manning's influence was never far from his mind, and that he was still peculiarly vulnerable to conspiratorial interpretations of government that had marked earlier stages of his career. But in defining his role as nothing less than the defence of the realm and the thwarting of a threat to undermine the monarchy and the constitution, Disraeli was also expressing part of his conception of true Toryism. The chivalric romance in which this ideal is phrased may thus legitimately be seen as an extension or development of the ideology, or historical fulfilment, conceived many years before in the Young England novels, however much it also seems to be a rationalization of more immediate and narrow political purposes.

15

Lothair: The Politics of Love, Faith, and Duty

On 8 December 1868, John Patrick Crichton-Stuart, 3rd Marquess of Bute, then twenty-one years of age, was formally received into the Roman Catholic Church.[1] Although the conversion was not publicly announced until Christmas, it had been anticipated in fashionable circles for some months, as is shown by a note from Montagu Corry to Disraeli, dated 22 September of that year: "He [Lord Bute] is going to Baronscourt next month, it is evident rather as a claimant of his bride than as a suitor. Evidently the whole matter is already arranged. But still, I fear, that his joining himself to the 'scarlet woman' – and soon too, is equally certain. Fergusson says that no ingenuity can counteract the influence which certain priests & prelates have over him, chief among them being Monsignore Capel. The speedy result is inevitable, & the consummation is only delayed till he has won his bride."[2] Although Bute's conversion lacked the ecclesiastical significance of Newman's in 1845 and Manning's in 1852, it nevertheless seemed of momentous import to a great many people that a young nobleman of such wealth and influence should just then abandon his Protestant heritage. Many newspapers commented with hostility on what *The Times* labelled the "defection," one, indeed, going so far as to suggest that "this perversion ... [was] the result of priestly influences acting upon a weak, ductile, and naturally superstitious mind."[3] To Disraeli the event must have seemed yet another ominous confirmation of Archbishop Manning's malign influence, for in the aftermath of his electoral defeat he took the incident as the seed of a new novel, which throughout 1869 he wrote under such great secrecy that not even the trusted Corry knew of it until the announcement of its forthcoming publication.

Lothair appeared on 2 May 1870 to public anticipation the like of which had not been seen since the days of Byron. There were rumours to the effect that the author had received the enormous sum of £10,000 for the copyright. Advance subscriptions ran to over 4,000 copies, and sales were so brisk that the publisher, Longmans, could not keep the book in print. Some 15,000 were sold in a matter of days, and eight editions were called for in the next few months. Mudie's Select Library was reported on the day of publication to be "in a state of siege" by "real subscribers, and representative footmen," while Appleton, the American publisher, sold 25,000 copies in three days and had disposed of 80,000 copies by October. A novel by a former prime minister was bound to create a sensation in any case, but the reception of this one was certainly enhanced by the news that the setting was contemporary and that many of the characters were drawn from the models of prominent persons. The fashionable world was simply entranced; and, much as Dickens's *Pickwick Papers* had done many years before, *Lothair* took on the dimensions of a cultural mania. Horses, songs, ships, dances, a perfume, and a street were named after the hero and heroine, and Dizzy's new novel was the literary topic of the social season.[4]

Despite this huge popular success, however, the political world was full of misgivings about Disraeli's return to fiction. As Monckton Milnes reported, "His wisest friends think that it must be a mistake, and his enemies hope that it will be his ruin."[5] It is thus hardly surprising that there was political bias in many of the reviews, a good number of which, as Henry James remarked, were written in the light of either a partisan sympathy or "a deep aversion to the author's political character."[6] But whether it was seen as "a profound study of spiritual and political forces at a supremely important moment in the history of modern Europe," as a profane "outrage" that fosters prejudice and "sins alike against good taste and justice," or merely as an amusing, but frivolous "romance of the peerage," in Disraeli's day, *Lothair* was universally interpreted as an allegory of the times.[7]

Disraeli's theme is the threatening encroachments of the Roman Catholic Church upon England's Protestant realm, which here manifest themselves in the attempt to convert an orphaned young English nobleman of enormous wealth. The eponymous hero is obviously modelled upon the Marquess of Bute, though the story of his conversion is but a match to light the author's imagination. In a literal sense at least, most of Lothair's adventures seem to bear only a superficial connection to actual incidents, and the chief similarity between the story of Disraeli's innocent and somewhat unworldly protagonist and that of the far more eccentric and studious Bute, is the author's desire to expose the conspiratorial techniques of the Catholic priesthood in furthering the interests of their church. In the portraits of Cardinal Grandison and Monsignor Catesby, Disraeli clearly has the satisfaction of revealing the subtleties and sophistications he believes were practised by Archbishop Manning and Monsignor Capel upon both the young marquess and himself. And upon this evidence of his malicious satire, Disraeli has sometimes been thought to have finally declared in *Lothair* his irrevocable hostility to the Roman Catholic religion, the more so in the light of his Protestant strategy in the 1868 election campaign.

But the novel has also been read as an expression of Disraeli's sympathy for Catholicism. For all the paranoia in his anticlerical portraits, Disraeli dedicated *Lothair* to his closest Catholic friend, His Royal Highness, the Duc d'Aumale, which he would scarcely have done were the book meant to be considered an attack upon the Catholic faith. Going beyond this single inference, Buckle noticed that Disraeli was "at once attracted and repelled by Rome": however much he felt "the bondage which she imposed upon the spirit of man," the "historical tradition and … sensuous and ceremonial worship" of the Catholic Church "appealed strongly" to one side of his nature.[8] And more recently David Painting has made a similar case for Disraeli's fascination with the aesthetic beauty of Catholic rituals, which, at least in his fictions, he always acknowledged.[9] As earlier chapters have shown, however, Disraeli's interest in Catholicism went far deeper than that, and involved fundamental ambivalences at the core of his identity. For this reason, if no other, *Lothair* must be read in the light cast by the earlier novels.

There have also been disagreements about the nature of *Lothair* among modern critics. Robert Blake argues that it is "perhaps the best of all Disraeli's novels," and he follows J.A. Froude in valuing its "perfect representation of [the] patrician society in England," which, though it had lost its purpose and claim to endurance, was still in the brilliance of full bloom. The chief difference between this and the portraits of the aristocracy in the earlier works is thus a matter of tone – what Froude calls "the mellow calmness of matured experience."[10] Daniel Schwarz, more searchingly, emphasizes the distance between *Lothair* and the Young England novels, and sees in the differences between them a "radical" departure from the original theme of moral and political regeneration. Indeed, in the later novel Schwarz sees a significant further progression of the cultural "dubiety" manifest in *Tancred*, for in *Lothair*, he believes,

"Disraeli tentatively and dispassionately explores major nineteenth-century epistemological positions." The effect, he suggests, is akin to a morality play, an "ideological *Pilgrim's Progress*," in which the hero, being "a kind of educated Everyman," tests and is wooed by characters who espouse various "moral, religious and political positions."[11]

Although there is considerable merit in these interpretations, neither Blake nor Schwarz takes sufficient notice of the very strong continuities between *Lothair* and Disraeli's earlier fiction. Schwarz does acknowledge, as has Richard Levine, that *Lothair* seems to be "an effort to clarify, if not rewrite, *Tancred*" (132), and he also indicates the general relevance of recent political events, particularly the issue of Irish Church Disestablishment, to the novel's religious theme. But once again in *Lothair*, as was the case with *Coningsby*, *Sybil*, and *Tancred*, the connections with politics and the recurrence of religious motifs are more complex than mere background. Disraeli's recent political life and his long-standing ambivalence about Catholicism so inform the fantasy structure of *Lothair* that it, too, for all the wild extravagance of its plot, can be said to fall within the genre of the psychological romance.

In so arguing one must understand the reciprocal nature of Disraeli's autobiographical fiction: on the one hand, the novels are a means of rationalizing the past and reshaping the formative experiences of his identity; on the other, they are a way of keeping the question of identity open by exploring imaginatively the possibilities of further commitment. In the case of *Lothair*, the fantasies of the allegorical fiction serve at once both to deny that the events of the recent past are definitive, and to assert that heroic possibilities still exist. That Disraeli's protagonist should again be, in the words of two contemporary reviewers, a perfect "goose,"[12] with so little character as to appear "unpleasantly like a fool,"[13] is entirely, if paradoxically, characteristic, and thus still further evidence of the unity of his fiction. As the earlier works clearly demonstrated, the passivity of the ambivalent hero in Disraeli's novels is a function of both the author's conception of an innate superiority and his experience of the detachment necessary to success. As with *Tancred*, it is a mistake to see the strength of *Lothair* only in what Buckle calls the "splendid pageant of English aristocracy," and to neglect the melodramatic excesses of the ensuing travelogue as a mere embarrassment or artistic failure. Froude did not exaggerate much when he suggested that *Lothair* "opens a window into Disraeli's mind, revealing the inner workings of it more completely than anything else which he wrote or said."[14]

The difference in tone between this novel and the earlier ones bears a somewhat paradoxical relation to the imaginatively autobiographical material it contains. The "mellow calmness of matured experience" that Froude remarks on (218) pervades the satire as well as the romance, and it is obviously a function of Disraeli's age and political success. But it is also a guide to his satirical purpose, and hence to the self-reflexive features of the text. In *Lothair* Disraeli minimizes the didactic role of the authorial persona, who formerly provided definitive ideological and historical perspectives on the political or social issues of the story. In its place he depends much more than before upon the dramatic effects of dialogue to reveal his satirical thrust. Whereas in the earlier novels such self-revelation was largely confined to the more fatuous of the secondary characters, in *Lothair* even the central antagonism of the hero and villain is developed through dialogue which reverberates with ambiguity and unconscious ironies. No doubt Disraeli understood the value of this strategy in treating a topic as explosive as that of papal intrigue. But it is interesting that in this novel the technique displayed to some advantage in *Tancred* has been fully matured and even the hero and his idealisms are presented through self-devastating ironies.

When *Lothair* appeared it was immediately noticed that it had a generic ancestry. In a letter to the *Scotsman* Professor John Stuart Blackie identified Disraeli's new novel as a *Tendenz-roman* of the type initiated by Goethe's *Wilhelm Meister* – an illustration of the effects of prevailing contemporary intellectual forces on the character of a vulnerable young man – and this letter was subsequently used by the publisher as a promotion for later editions.[15] But Disraeli's intention is also implicit in the motto from Terence (*Eunuchus*, Act V, Sc. 4, l. 940) with which Disraeli introduces the text: "Nosse omnia haec, salus est adolescentulis" (To know all this, is salvation to a young man).[16] The classical warning against harlots obviously embodies the anxiety revealed in the clichéd depiction of the Catholic Church as "the scarlet woman" in Corry's memo in the fall of 1868. But the ironic source also suggests that within the realm of fiction Disraeli perceives his hero's temptation as a comedy of thwarted intentions, for this particular line, spoken by the slave, Parmeno, not only refers to his supposed stratagem for revealing the sordid reality behind the attractive appearance of whores, but also points indirectly to the self-interest that is often disguised as altruism.[17]

As a result, the motto prepares the reader for the intentional ironies in Disraeli's portrait of an ineffectual, love-struck youth. From the outset of the story the idealizations of Lothair's situation as the heir to fabulous wealth and noble estates are undercut by the gentle but worldly sarcasms of the narrator and the naive protestations of the hero. For example, the pure domesticity of the ducal family who befriend Lothair as a college friend of their eldest son, Bertram, is given a narcissistic tint that hints at the complicating deflations of realism:

> The Duke, though still young ... had a high sense of duty, and strong domestic feelings. He was never wanting in his public place, and he was fond of his wife and children; still more proud of them. Every day when he looked into the glass, and gave the last touch to his consummate toilette, he offered his grateful thanks to Providence that his family was not unworthy of him.
>
> His Grace was accustomed to say that he had only one misfortune ... he had no home. His family had married so many heiresses, and he, consequently, possessed so many halls and castles, at all of which, periodically, he wished, from a right feeling to reside, that there was no sacred spot identified with his life in which his heart, in the bustle and tumult of existence, could take refuge ... The daughters loved Brentham, and they loved to please their father; but the sons-in-law, though they were what is called devoted to their wives, and, unusual as it may seem, scarcely less attached to their legal parents, did not fall very easily into this arrangement [of yearly visits]. The country in August without sport was unquestionably to them a severe trial: nevertheless, they rarely omitted making their appearance, and if they did occasionally vanish, sometimes to Cowes, sometimes to Switzerland, sometimes to Norway, they always wrote to their wives, and always alluded to their immediate or approaching return. (ch. 1, 2–3)

This last detail resonates with a chapter in Trollope's *Framley Parsonage* (1860), where the youthful and self-indulgent Lord Lufton escapes the boredom of English society and the complications of his romance by going salmon fishing in Norway with a party of his friends. These friends, we are led to infer, are in the habit of making this excursion for six weeks at the end of the London season. If the allusion is deliberate, it suggests that Disraeli may have consciously taken Trollope's comic realism as a model for his own more mellow narrative tone.

Equally interesting is the way Disraeli brings out his hero's initial naivety. Lothair, having been raised by "a rather savage" uncle in Scotland, finds at Brentham his introduction to "refined society" and the pleasures of drawing-room flirtations, after-dinner smoking, and morning croquet. Life there is, indeed, such a continuous enchantment of domestic happiness that, after an acquaintance of a fortnight, Lothair seizes an opportunity to ask the duchess for her permission to marry her youngest daughter. When the astonished duchess immediately protests that Corisande is but "a child," whose character is not yet formed, Lothair unconsciously betrays his own immaturity. To the suggestions of the duchess he replies "with much decision" that he has no wish to travel, and no wish to enter the world, characterizing the one society party that he has attended in London as a disgusting "mass of affectation, falsehood, and malice." And when the duchess protests again that she meant rather "knowledge of the world, and that experience which enables us to form sound opinions on the affairs of life," he adds, "Oh! as for that … my opinions are already formed on every subject; that is to say, every subject of importance; and, what is more, they will never change." Far from recognizing the ironic effect of declaring his shallow certainties, Lothair goes on to muse aloud upon his altruistic intentions, once married to Corisande, to build churches and schools: "'I think we agree on all the great things … Her Church views may be a little higher than mine, but I do not anticipate any permanent difficulty on that head … Then, as to churches themselves, she is in favour of building churches, and so am I; and schools, there is no number of schools I would not establish. My opinion is, you cannot have too much education, provided it be founded on a religious basis. I would sooner renounce the whole of my inheritance than consent to secular education'" (ch. 5, 15). This sententious bravado only leads Lothair on to a further display of his limited intellectual grasp of the world. He tells the duchess that he is sure Lady Corisande would sympathize with his plan to devote the rest of his energies to "the extinction of pauperism," which he fancies is "not an affair so much of wages as of dwellings." The solution to what he describes as "the terror of Europe, and the disgrace of Britain," lies, he believes, simply in providing proper lodgings for the working classes. Consequently, he proposes to build 2,000 cottages on his estates, the designs for which (somewhat like Dorothea Brooke in *Middlemarch)* he has all ready (ch. 5, 15–16).

Disraeli's intention is not just to mock his naive hero, but rather to show that the innocence and altruism of his young protagonist are dangerous limitations. For when the duchess, with explicitly maternal solicitude, again urges him to see more of the world, and replies that his idea of "a perfect society" (being married as he proposes, paying visits to Brentham, and having them reciprocated) is a "fairytale," he still asks, "'Does your Grace see any objection to my speaking to your daughter?'" The humour of this witless persistence is, however, qualified by the poignant loneliness of the orphan, who clearly is searching for a substitute mother as much as for a bride (ibid., 16–17).

The first five chapters of *Lothair* thus seem to establish Disraeli's theme as that of the typical Bildungsroman – the discovery and enlisting of the hero's capacities. This is soon supplemented with the equally important matter of recognizing the real limits of ideals, in a world in which those very ideals leave him vulnerable to exploitation by agents of zealous and possibly malign or sinister purpose. For example, as a youth Lothair is easily manipulated by the conventions of courtly language which others use for ulterior purposes. In that regard, the portrait of Cardinal Grandison is both subtle and sophisticated, for through the dramatic process of dialogue Disraeli creates a highly ambiguous character, one whose motives seem to encompass for the reader both the possibility of sincerity and the suspicion of cynicism. Even in the latter part of the novel, when the cardinal seems implicated in a monstrous and absurd conspiracy to entrap Lothair, it is not possible to be certain that his behaviour stems from hypocrisy, for Disraeli leaves open the extent to which Grandison's actions and words express political expediency, pious convictions, or delusions of faith.

At several points in the story Grandison claims that he has taken his trust as one of Lothair's guardians with scrupulous responsibility. Having been appointed to that office before his own conversion to Rome, he has, as he himself later suggests, been careful not to impose his religious views upon his ward. Rather he has contented himself with insisting upon the exact educational provisions of the deceased father's will (in the hope that Oxford would mitigate, if not subvert the prejudices of his childhood), and with guarding the value of the inheritance which Lothair will come into on his twenty-first birthday. Previous to going up to Christ Church the youth has in fact been raised entirely by his other guardian, the Scottish uncle of extreme Presbyterian faith. But the cardinal is quick to seize the opportunity of meeting Lothair at the soirée arranged by Mr Putney Giles and his socially ambitious wife, Apollonia. And Disraeli is at his sardonic best in describing the success with which Grandison insinuates himself into the good opinion of those whom he meets:

Nothing could exceed the simple suavity with which the Cardinal appeared, approached, and greeted them. He thanked Apollonia for her permission to pay his respects to her, which he had long wished to do; and then they were all presented, and he said exactly the right thing to everyone. He must have heard of them all before, or read their characters in their countenances. In a few minutes they were all listening to his Eminence with enchanted ease, as, sitting on the sofa by his hostess, he described to them the ambassadors who had just arrived from Japan, and with whom he had relations of interesting affairs. The Japanese Government had exhibited enlightened kindness to some of his poor people who had barely escaped martyrdom. Much might be expected from the Mikado, evidently a man of singular penetration and elevated views; and his Eminence looked as if the mission to Yokohama would speedily end in an episcopal see; but he knew where he was, and studiously avoided all controversial matter.

After all, the Mikado himself was not more remarkable than this Prince of the Church in a Tyburnian drawing-room, habited in his pink cassock and cape, and waving, as he spoke, with careless grace his pink barrette. (ch. 8, 30)

The satirical effect of this passage is achieved by incorporating in one voice the different gratifications and perspectives of several participants in the scene: that of the amused, detached and invisible observer, that of the enthralled hostess and her guests, and that of the suave cardinal himself. By such means Disraeli suggests that Grandison's graceful and worldly manners are an instrument of personal and political power, and that his social engagements are but the means of policy. This is evident in the fact that these pleasantries of the evening are merely the prelude to accomplishing his real purpose, the serious conversation with Lothair, after which he immediately effects his escape without the usual formalities of leaving. But the real nature of the cardinal's concerns is outlined in a conversation between Monsignore Berwick and Lady St Jerome (another zealous convert to the Catholic faith) in the next chapter. Berwick, who is described as "the greatest statesman of Rome," explains to her that though in his opinion the time is ripe for establishing a Catholic hierarchy in Scotland, the cardinal for the moment prevents it in order to pursue a larger campaign in England and Ireland:

"The original plan was to have established our hierarchy when the Kirk split up; but that would have been a mistake; it was then not ripe. There would have been a fanatical reaction. There is always a tendency that way

in Scotland: as it is, at this moment, the Establishment and the Free Kirk
are mutually sighing for some compromise … But we are thoroughly
well-informed, and have provided for all this. We sent two of our best men
into Scotland some time ago, and they have invented a new Church, called
the United Presbyterians. John Knox himself was never more violent, or
more mischievous. The United Presbyterians will do the business: they
will render Scotland simply impossible to live in; and then, when the crisis
arrives, the distracted and despairing millions will find refuge in the bosom of their only mother. That is why, at home, we wanted no delay in the
publication of the bull and the establishment of the hierarchy."

"But the Cardinal says no?"

"And must be followed. For these islands he has no equal. He wishes
great reserve at present. Affairs here are progressing, gradually but surely.
But it is Ireland where matters are critical, or will be soon." (ch. 9, 37–8)

This vision of an ultramontane conspiracy to convert all of Britain by
means of secret agents bent on sedition comes, it should be noted, not
just from the English experience of finding Ireland ungovernable, nor
just in addition from the impact of notable conversions to the Catholic
faith, or from reports that the Vatican's Office of Propaganda had considered "the question of Scotland" in early 1868.[18] It comes as well from
Disraeli's experience in the prime minister's office, which, through the
intelligence reports of secret agents, had fed his old fantasies about
clandestine powers subverting the diplomacy and safety of every realm
in Europe. *Lothair* is, in fact, riddled with such fantasies about the
power of sinister secret societies at work to shape the political destinies
of Protestants and Catholics alike. And in the course of the novel they
are expressed in ever more improbable events. The nature of paranoia
is such, however, that the secret, the mysterious, and the unknown only
confirm, and never dispel, even the most tenuous of suspicions. Thus,
in analysing this process, the reader finds that the precise relation between fact and fantasy becomes almost impossible to ascertain. Not
surprisingly, the imagined realm of Disraeli's novel is one where Fenian
agents, papal ambassadors, and Italian patriots are at once the perpe-
trators and victims of secret plots, and in such a world the exaggerations of his paranoid fantasies are given some plausibility through their
dramatized relation to actual historical or contemporary events, such as
the "Papal Aggression," the Risorgimento, and the Fenian outrages.

Although the development of Lothair's religious sensibility takes
place in London and at the St Jerome's estate, Vauxe, the process whereby

he is drawn into the ambiance of the Catholic faith has similarities to the experience of Lord Bute during his years as a student at Oxford. As a shy and studious schoolboy at Harrow, Bute had developed a passionate interest in Eastern Europe and the Holy Land, and in the summer before going up to Oxford, he went at the age of seventeen, and rather in the spirit of Disraeli's Tancred, on a "veritable pilgrimage" to Palestine. There, hoping to find the sanction for his spiritual life, this "thoughtful and religious-minded" youth visited "the Holy Places of Jerusalem" and reflected upon those of his ancestors among "the myriads of devout and holy men, saints and warriors, who had made the pilgrimage before [him]."[19] Thus, when he arrived at Christ Church he found himself thoroughly estranged from the usual dissipations and diversions of the other undergraduates, and much more interested in the subjects of comparative religion and the history of the Christian church than in the prescribed studies of the college. These private readings, reinforced by the experiences of another Eastern pilgrimage in the summer of 1866, would ultimately lead him to the conviction that the schism of the Reformation, particularly in England and Scotland, was to be regretted.

When, during the Christmas vacation of 1866, Bute declared his hope of soon joining the Catholic faith, there was immediate consternation among both his guardians and the officials of the Lord Chancellor's Court. And upon his return to Oxford for the Hilary term, there was a storm of opposition among the college authorities at Christ Church, who, fearing contagion in their midst, denounced the decision and set out to pressure Bute into at least postponing any action until he had reached his majority. This promise they were able to extract, but it was of little avail, for Bute had gained some intimate Catholic friends in the family circle of Mr Scott Murray, and there he fell under the influence of the eloquent and personable Monsignor Capel, the Murrays' chaplain. Throughout the year Bute's thoughts continued to be focused on the form of his faith, and by Christmas of 1867 his correspondence with Murray reports every instance of "going over" that has come to his attention.[20] Then on consecutive days in the Trinity term of 1868, two of the undergraduates, one of whom Bute knew well, met almost sudden death in fatal accidents, and the experience gave a melodramatic funereal fright to those concerned with the state of their souls. Monsignor Capel decided to take up residence in Oxford to be near Lord Bute and his friends, so as to offer them sympathy and spiritual guidance. When it soon became apparent that several of these young men were contemplating a conversion to Rome, the dean of

Christ Church, Dr Liddon, "issued a peremptory mandate prohibiting the under-graduates of the House from making [Capel's] … acquaintance." The monsignor reported to Murray, however, that this was "a clear case of shutting the stable door after the horse had been stolen. All those who *want* to know me, I think, already do."[21] He also reported, a little later, upon Bute's state of mind: "Bute is in admirable dispositions, and during the month of May has been leading the life of a true Christian. The long delay has tried him much: yet his spiritual progress since last summer has been extraordinary. I am simply amazed at some of the things he has told me. May our dear Lord be eternally blessed for all He has done, and is doing, for this soul so dear to Him."[22] It seems clear from all of this that Monsignor Capel took his role to be that of Bute's spiritual guardian, whose specific task was to ensure the youth's ultimate conversion. Such is also the import of a much later account in which Capel added further details of the process that unfolded over the summer and fall of 1868, while Disraeli's "great Protestant struggle" was unfolding: "A course of reading was suggested, I seeing him [Bute] from time to time. Newman's pathetic hymn, 'Lead, kindly light, amid th' encircling gloom,' was often on his lips. In the course of time he was fully convinced that the true Church is an organic body, a Divine institution, the source of all spiritual power and jurisdiction, and the channel of sacramental grace, under the Vicar of Christ, the Bishop of Rome."[23] Monsignor Capel's efforts went, however, beyond the one noble instance, and are attested to not only by Bute's formal conversion in December, or by the hysteria of his Presbyterian trustee, Sir James Fergusson, who seems that year to have told everyone who would listen that his ward was "on the verge of turning Papist."[24] In a letter written shortly after his acceptance into the Catholic Church, Bute wrote to Mrs Scott Murray of Capel's "most extraordinary success at Oxford," the result of "the perpetual physical and mental toil" of receiving converts, preparing others, and "awakening a great many." Capel, he said, had, "partially at least, sanctified the congregation, and reclaimed the wandering," and in general he had given the mission "an infusion of life" by daily hearing confessions and renewals of baptismal vows, holding Communions and High Masses and preaching sermons to immense audiences "among whom were a vast number of Protestants, *several Dons* and the *President of Trinity College!*"[25] Such is the indefatigable presence that Disraeli takes as a model for his Monsignore Catesby, who takes on the task of daily steering the thoughts of the innocent young Lothair toward the one "true Church."

Monsignore Reginald Catesby is first introduced at Vauxe as the descendent of an ancient English family who for many generations had in "a spirit of triumph, made every worldly sacrifice for the Church and Court of Rome." A man of "considerable abilities," who has been "trained with consummate skill," he is described as having both a "determined will" and winning manners. There is a suggestion that he is a Jesuit, for the narrator adds, "he was as well informed in the ways of the world as he was in the works of the great casuists" (ch. 15, 59–60). In conjunction with the naivety of the young hero, such a characterization allows Disraeli to suggest what he takes to be the pernicious, yet ultimately futile subtleties of the clerical intention. The seemingly casual, but relentless pursuit of the potential convert by the cardinal, the monsignore, and Father Coleman is dramatized as a form of psychological seduction that exploits the young lord's desire for a religiously sanctioned heroic role.

Central to this drama is Lothair's appreciation of the sensuous beauty of the Catholic rituals to which he is gradually introduced. The erotic quality of the powerful identifications thus engendered, which is so reminiscent of the earlier novels embodying the Catholic motif, is then made explicit. As Lothair finds himself attracted to the St Jeromes' beautiful and pious niece, Clare Arundel, he begins to meditate on two great ideas: "the reconciliation of Christendom and the influence of architecture on religion." And while Miss Arundel urges him to devote some of his enormous wealth to the building of a Catholic cathedral in the centre of London, Monsignore Catesby is ever ready to share his knowledge of the Gothic style: "To hear him expound the mysteries of symbolical art, and expatiate on the hidden revelations of its beauteous forms, reached even to ecstasy. Lothair hung upon his accents like a neophyte" (ch. 16, 62). And once the London season has begun, Monsignore Catesby, we are told, "looked after Lothair, and was always breakfasting with him without the necessity of an invitation," with the intention of drawing the youth into his confidence and thereby gaining the means to steer him more effectively (ch. 21, 82–3). The crucial event in this regard is the cardinal's staging of a ceremonial dedication "at the Jesuits' Church" to the idea of regenerating "Christendom." This is ostensibly to be an ecumenical occasion, but in fact the cardinal, we are led to believe, conceives "the restoration of Christendom" (ch. 28, 124) as a single European state under the spiritual and temporal power of the papacy. Just how impolitic and compromising it might be for Lothair to attend this ceremony is suggested by the appearance of what are later described as "insidious and calumnious paragraphs" in the newspapers, commenting upon rumours of the young lord's impending conversion (ch. 44, 219). But despite, or perhaps because of, the continuous efforts of the cardinal, the monsignore, the St Jeromes, and Miss Arundel, Lothair begins to resist their sense of his moral obligation. And, on the evening in question, he escapes the monsignore's impositions of this "duty" (described ironically as "a wonderful performance") by impetuously gratifying his desire to visit Belmont, the home of his third Egeria, the mature and mysteriously exotic Theodora Campian, who, perhaps because she is married, proves to be an even more inspirational figure for the easily infatuated young protagonist (ch. 30, 143–7).

The subtle but insistent efforts of the clerical "invaders" (ch. 34, 171) then focus upon the opportunities offered by the occasion of celebrating Lothair's majority in magnificent fashion at his principal estate, Muriel Towers. Disraeli now dramatizes the threat of a religious conversion in the rivalry between the cardinal and the Anglican bishop (a satirical portrait of Samuel Wilberforce, bishop of Oxford) who both scheme during the festivities to arrange some symbolic ritual of allegiance that will have definitive significance. Once again the Catholic party are frustrated in their attempt to thwart Lothair's participation in any Protestant devotions, and they are finally outmanoeuvred by the bishop when an "unexpected" diocesan deputation of archdeacons and rural deans comes forward during the formal birthday reception to present Lothair with "a most uncompromising address" and to beg him to accept "a bible and prayer-book richly bound, and borne by the Rev. Dionysius Smylie on a cushion of velvet" (ch. 47, 241). The essentially comic effect of this clerical melodrama is then succinctly captured in the responses of the various witnesses: "The habitual pallor of the Cardinal's countenance became unusually wan; the cheek of Clare Arundel was a crimson flush; Monsignore Catesby bit his lip … The great body of those present, unaware that this deputation was unexpected, were unmoved" (ibid.). But the final climactic interview between Lothair and his Catholic guardian again raises the serious issues dividing the Christian faith, and does so once again in the context of what role Lothair can conceive religion to play in the life of civilization. Having dismissed the Church of England as merely a creature of Parliament, the cardinal responds even more forcibly to Lothair's regret that the Church of Rome seems to "have placed itself in antagonism with political liberty":

"I cannot admit," replied the Cardinal, "that the Church is in antagonism with political freedom. On the contrary, in my opinion, there can be no political freedom which is not founded on Divine authority; otherwise it can be at the best but a specious phantom of license inevitably terminating in anarchy. The rights and liberties of the people of Ireland have no advocates except the Church; because there, political freedom is founded on Divine authority; but if you mean by political freedom the schemes of the illuminati and the freemasons which perpetually torture the Continent, all the dark conspiracies of the secret societies, there, I admit, the Church is in antagonism with such aspirations after liberty; those aspirations, in fact, are blasphemy and plunder; and if the Church were to be destroyed, Europe would be divided between the Atheist and the Communist." (ch. 48, 251)

This speech is a perfect example of the dramatic effect of dialogue mentioned earlier, for while on the one hand it embodies the sincere convictions of a Catholic about the primacy of that faith, it simultaneously posits to a Protestant reader some propositions about politics in relation to "the Church" that seem tendentious and casuistical. To Disraeli's credit as a novelist, he does not attempt to settle this argument by logical means. The cardinal, finding that his late ward is "not in that ripe state of probation which he had fondly anticipated," merely recommends that Rome should be the first destination of Lothair's projected travels, hoping apparently that there he would find the historical setting, the refined civilization of the church, and the friendly presence of the St Jeromes conducive to a more pious state of mind.

Lothair's resistance to "the Popish plot" (as his friend Hugo Bohun calls it, when referring to what the bishop deems those "insidious and calumnious paragraphs which had circulated during the last six months"; ch. 44, 218–19) is shown to be a reflection of his infatuation with the "divine" Theodora, whose humanistic ideals and sentiments seem to constitute an entirely new religion whose form of ritual is classical beauty and whose dogma is political freedom. Schwarz, in discussing Lothair's passivity as a sign of his desperate need to be loved, quite rightly observes that the seemingly central issues of the novel, involving his choice between Anglicanism and Catholicism and his involvement in revolutionary Italian politics, are dramatized almost solely in terms of his sexual attraction to the three women who seem to have no personalities independent of the values they represent. For Schwarz it is sadly Lothair's "libido," rather than his intellect, that determines the values he embraces, and thus the forlorn orphan finds that the "maternal" Theodora, who "combines the role of surrogate mother and fantasy lover," has the power to rescue him from the ecclesiastical battle for his soul.[26] It is, however, also worth considering the narrator's attitude towards the seeming pathos of Lothair's behaviour, for a focus upon just the ideas of the novel may prevent the reader from seeing the significance of the fiction's fantasy structure.

Theodora's gentle dissuasions of Lothair's ardour present a constant reminder of the youth's emotional naivety and innocence, which stand warrant for his idealism and integrity. But at the same time the satirical comedy of his encounters with secular society, much of it reflecting his immediate perspective and experience, represents not just Disraeli's cynical amusement, but also his protagonist's maturing intellectual development. Among the best of these set pieces in which the perspectives of narrator and hero seem to merge, is Lothair's encounter with the Oxford professor who is Colonel Campian's guest for dinner:

> The Oxford Professor … was quite a young man, of advanced opinions on all subjects, religious, social, and political. He was clever, extremely well-informed, so far as books can make a man knowing, but unable to profit even by that limited experience of life from a restless vanity and overflowing conceit, which prevented him from ever observing or thinking of anything but himself. He was gifted with a great command of words, which took the form of endless exposition, varied by sarcasm and passages of ornate jargon. He was the last person one would have expected to recognise in an Oxford professor; but we live in times of transition … The Professor, who was not satisfied with his home career, and, like many men of his order of mind, had dreams of wild vanity which the New World, they think, can alone realise, was very glad to make the Colonel's acquaintance, which might facilitate his future movements. So he had lionised the distinguished visitors during the last few days over the University, and had availed himself of plenteous opportunities for exhibiting to them his celebrated powers of exposition, his talent for sarcasm, which he deemed peerless, and several highly finished picturesque passages, which were introduced with extemporary art … Like sedentary men of extreme opinions, he was a social parasite, and instead of indulging in his usual invectives against peers and princes, finding himself unexpectedly about to dine with one of that class, he was content only to dazzle and amuse him. (ch. 24, 95–6)

Professor Goldwin Smith, who had left Oxford in 1868 to help establish Cornell University in Ithaca, New York, was quick to protest in a letter to Longmans that he was the intended victim of this ridicule, which he termed "the stingless insults of a coward."[27] But the protest was fruitless and, when the letter was made public, it only served to stimulate the sale of the novel to the extent of requiring a new edition. In any case, Disraeli had good reason to pillory Goldwin Smith, for the professor had been the anonymous author of much nasty and personal invective directed at him in the *Morning Chronicle* twenty years earlier.

Ultimately, however, this identification is less significant than the fact that the authorial voice at the beginning of the scene gives way to a dialogue in which Lothair quietly triumphs over the noisy and intrusive scholar. When, in discussing university reform, Disraeli's professor suggests that he "would get rid of the religion" because "Universities have nothing to do with religion," Lothair succinctly replies, "I thought Universities were universal ... and had something to do with everything."[28] And when the professor then expatiates on the historical efficacy of plots and conspiracies, which he describes as "great principles in violent action," Lothair takes pleasure in sympathizing with Theodora's disagreement: that for her such "action" has always proved to be "an experience of wasted energies and baffled thoughts" (ch. 24, 98). The use here of the verb "baffle" is a reliable guide to Disraeli's intention in this scene, for repeatedly, in both the fiction and his political speeches, this word signals the speaker's superior wisdom. Thus their harmony, when Lothair suggests in a teasing tone that he and Theodora should for once "enter into a conspiracy together ... join in a happy plot" and contrive to visit the private gardens at Blenheim on the next day, is but the occasion of enabling her to explain to him the obligations and fulfilments of duty that come with his great wealth (ch. 25, 99–100). The idealism of his consequent inspiration is captured in the classical terms of his reverie upon her beauty, for (no doubt remembering that her profile had been used as the official image of "La République française" on the five-franc piece of 1850; ch. 8, 33) he recalls, as he gazes upon her in the railway carriage back to Oxford, that "he had read of such countenances in Grecian dreams: in Corinthian temples, in fanes of Ephesus, in the radiant shadow of divine groves." The excursion to Blenheim palace, that extraordinary Palladian monument to military and political power, has, therefore, been the perfect occasion for instilling a historical sense of the relation between private wealth and public duty, and between personal feeling and political commitment. As a result, the repressed and sublimated sexuality in the romance of Lothair's identity is not quite as destructively dissociated from the question of his values as a focus upon the novel's metaphysics might imply. Rather, however melodramatically, Disraeli's blend of romance wish-fulfilment, satirical impulse, and realistic detail shows that the idealistic commitments of late adolescence and early maturity are a function of emotional and aesthetic experience, as well as of intellectual choices.

The turning point of the novel occurs, fittingly, once Lothair is empowered to act on his own behalf. Shortly after the morning conversation with the cardinal about the political role of the Catholic Church, Lothair visits Theodora in her suite of rooms and learns more of her passionate commitment to the cause of liberating Rome from the "debasing thraldom" of the papacy. From this point on, the historical context of the rest of Disraeli's story is not the English domestic politics of reform, but rather the revolutionary war with the papal states, during which it briefly seemed in 1867 that the pope might again be forced into exile. Upon finding that Theodora is a powerfully symbolic leader of the movement, and that Garibaldi's republican forces are again ready to launch an insurrection, but lack the funds with which to do so, Lothair declares his own commitment in terms of his newly claimed, mature identity:

"I am the right person for you to appeal to, the only person ... For I owe to you a debt that I never can repay ... Had it not been for you, I should have remained what I was when we first met, a prejudiced, narrow-minded being, with contracted sympathies and false knowledge, wasting my life on obsolete trifles, and utterly insensible to the privilege of living in this wondrous age of change and progress. Why, had it not been for you I should have at this moment been lavishing my fortune on an ecclesiastical toy, which I think of with a blush. There may be, doubtless there are, opinions in which we may not agree; but in our love of truth and justice there is no difference, dearest lady. No; though you must have felt that I am not, that no one could be, insensible to your beauty and infinite charms, still it is your consummate character that has justly fascinated my thought and heart; and I have long resolved, were I permitted, to devote to you my fortune and my life." (ch. 49, 258–9)

This ironic turn of events depends upon the uncompromising terms in which Lothair rejects his former religiosity. The dichotomy of past and future, of narrow-minded prejudice based upon false knowledge and the experience of living in a wondrous age of change and progress, seems irreconcilable. Accordingly, the great project of building a Catholic cathedral is reduced to an "ecclesiastical toy," which he is embarrassed to remember. Yet the claim of sudden maturity is belied by the chivalric form of the new commitment, which is not to the cause of change and progress, but to Theodora herself as the heroic embodiment of altruism. The sublimation of forbidden eroticism within the fantasy of chivalric devotion is thus explicitly a part of the empowerment of the self that Lothair now envisions. This is a pattern central to most of Disraeli's fictions, and equally important, I would argue, in the shaping of his political career.

The motif of Theodora's literal and symbolic power continues to generate the plot of the novel as Monsignore Berwick, the most powerful minister of the Vatican, acknowledges that the revolution, which only recently had seemed lifeless and penniless, has suddenly been revitalized by the infusion of "unlimited credit" and the recruitment of a general to lead the insurgents. Berwick's view, however, is that the assault on the papacy is an international affair, in which "the secret societies" of Europe, particularly the "Mary Anne associations" of France, are playing a crucial role. The myth surrounding these "essentially republican" associations, he reports, is that they were founded by a woman, and that "Mary Anne" has now returned and will soon issue orders to her adherents which must be obeyed. Thus, amid all the diplomatic complications of whether France might again interfere in the affairs of Italy to save the Holy See, the matter reduces, in Berwick's opinion, to a struggle between "the Church and the secret societies" (ch. 50, 259–66).

Once again the elements of fantasy are given the sanction of historical and pseudo-historical events, for the existence of these clandestine forces is then given a fictional reality when Lothair, now enlisted in the republican cause as Captain Muriel, finds himself escorting Theodora to a meeting with the Princess Colonna and her brother, who are, it seems, leaders of the "Madre Natura."[29] There they discuss the possibility of a secret treaty with the French Emperor, the terms of which would guarantee the security of his throne from renewed republican unrest in return for his promise not to interfere again in Rome. In urging Romolo Colonna to undertake this dangerous mission to Paris, Theodora is so passionate on behalf of "Rome and freedom" that she implies that should diplomacy fail, Colonna ought to assassinate the French emperor. But it is Theodora who is mortally wounded at Viterbo, in the first of the battles between Garibaldi's forces and the papal troops. She lingers before death long enough to explain to Lothair her fear that "another, and a more powerful attempt" will be made "to gain ... [him] to the Church of Rome," and to extract from him a solemn promise never to enter that communion (ch. 59, 304). Her fears then seem prophetic as he is seriously wounded in the next day's fighting at Mentana and in the confusion of the battle carried unconscious back to Rome.

The next ten chapters of the novel (chs 61–70) constitute a renewal of "the Popish plot" in terms that seem ever more implausible. Lothair is nursed slowly back from the brink of death, through delirium, to fragile health by Clare Arundel, who, along with other expatriate women, has become a sister of mercy for the wounded papal troops. Overwhelmed by his suffering, which is more than physical pain, Lothair finds that Monsignore Catesby has reappeared to devote "his whole life, and the inexhaustible resources of his fine and skilled intelligence to alleviate or amuse the existence of his companion" (ch. 61, 314). Soon the young Englishman gains welcome "solace in the beautiful services of a religion which he respected." And gradually he finds himself again absorbed into a world defined entirely by Catholic rituals and daily visits to beautiful churches and chapels. When this begins to seem claustrophobic, Lothair discusses his situation with Cardinal Grandison, who has just returned to Rome, and who undertakes to show the young Englishman more of the eternal city, and to introduce him to such eminent officers of the Vatican bureaucracy as the Cardinal Prefect of the Propaganda. Through all of this Lothair is troubled by a mysteriously pious attitude toward him on the part of his friends and all others whom he meets. In a number of these encounters there are vague and seemingly ambiguous references to his recent experience, which he does not fully understand, but which allude to his rescue from the battlefield. Catesby refers at one point to the "Annunciation," but will not discuss the topic further (ch. 61, 313). The very superstitious Princess Tarpeia-Cinque Cento refers to a "manifestation" which leads her to "cherish" his "favoured life"; and other Roman ladies sink to the ground in an "obeisance offered only to royalty" when they meet him (ch. 63, 323).

The mystery comes to its crisis when Lothair is persuaded to attend a service of thanksgiving at the "Jesuit church of St. George." Catesby reports that "the Holy Father" has commanded Miss Arundel to offer thanks "to the Blessed Virgin ....for the miraculous mercy vouchsafed to her in saving the life of a countryman" (ch. 65, 334). And though

Lothair feels anxious about the propriety of his presence at such a service, out of gratitude to the "angelic" Clare he agrees to attend it. Catesby then tells Father Coleman of Lothair's decision "with a look of saintly triumph": "'It is done at last. He will not only be present, but he will support her. There are yet eight and forty hours to elapse. Can anything happen to defeat us? It would seem not; yet when so much is at stake, one is fearful. He must never be out of our sight; not a human being must approach him'" (ch. 65, 335–6). The purpose of this Jesuitical manipulation is only revealed by the ceremony and its aftermath. When Lothair arrives at the church in the company of Catesby, he is taken to the sacristy, where he finds himself welcomed by the most powerful cardinals of the church: "had this been a conclave, and Lothair the future Pope, it would have been impossible to have treated him with more consideration" (ch. 66, 338). He is then drawn into the elaborate procession and given a lighted taper to carry to his prominent place amid the pomp of cardinals, prelates, and priests. Afterwards, as they leave the church, Lothair finds that many persons in the crowd fall upon their knees, ask a blessing from him, and kiss the hem of his garment (ch. 66, 340). The meaning of this elaborate ceremony is revealed the next morning in the newspaper of the Vatican, which claims that Lothair, having enlisted as "a volunteer in the service of the Pope," was wounded at Mentana while courageously fighting for "the sacred cause" (ch. 67, 342). This official account then describes his rescue through the mysterious appearance of "a beautiful woman, with a countenance of singular sweetness and yet majesty," who informed Miss Arundel of his desperate condition (ch. 67, 343). The account goes on to report that the Holy Father and the Consulta of the Holy Office have concluded that Lothair's life has been saved by the divine intervention of the Blessed Virgin; and that this miracle is attested to, according to the Cardinal Prefect, by the supporting witness of two priests and a porter who saw a halo about the head of this woman (who seemed to appear and vanish by magic), and by the report of children who said that this same woman gave them flowers (a rose and a lily), which she promised would never fade (ch. 67, 343–5).

Lothair reads this account of his role in the recent celebration of this miracle "with a continually changing countenance, now scarlet, now pallid as death; with a palpitating heart, a trembling hand, a cold perspiration, and at length a disordered vision" (ch. 67, 342); and at its conclusion he feels that he is "sinking into an unfathomable abyss" (ch. 67, 345). His despair at being the victim of "a great and unceasing and triumphant conspiracy" soon gives way, however, to anger and an "agony mixed with self-contempt":

> He felt all the indignation natural to a sincere and high-spirited man, who finds that he has been befooled by those whom he has trusted; but summoning all his powers to extricate himself from his desolate dilemma, he found himself without resource. What public declaration on his part could alter the undeniable fact, now circulating throughout the world, that in the supernatural scene of yesterday he was the willing and principal actor? Unquestionably he had been very imprudent, not only in that instance but in his habitual visits to the church; he felt all that now. But he was lorn and shattered, infinitely distressed both in body and mind; weak and miserable; and he thought he was leaning on angelic hearts, when he found himself in the embrace of spirits of another sphere …
>
> Whatever happened he could never return to England, at least for many years … He would go to America, or Australia, or the Indian Ocean, or the interior of Africa; but even in all these places, according to the correspondence of the Propaganda, he would find Roman priests and active priests. He felt himself a lost man; not free from faults in this matter, but punished beyond his errors. But this is the fate of men who think they can struggle successfully with a supernatural power. (ch. 67, 346–7)

Although presented in the third-person, this passage is in effect an interior monologue in which Lothair contemplates the image of himself as the pathetic victim of a Satanic conspiracy. In conjunction with the preceding scene, it is an uncompromising attack upon the whole papal hierarchy, for it displays the Catholic Church as involved in a pious fraud. Accordingly, the Vatican and its servants are apparently willing to fabricate miracles, and to manipulate and exploit the superstitions and piety of the innocent faithful in order to further the temporal power of the pope.

Disraeli does not, however, let the matter rest there. Lothair clings for a moment to the hope that Cardinal Grandison, "his father's friend, an English gentleman, with an English education, once an Anglican, a man of the world, a man of honour, a good, kind-hearted man," is not a part of the conspiracy (ch. 68, 347). When Lothair then confronts the cardinal with the "indignation," "alarm," and "disgust," he feels for this monstrous fabrication, Disraeli is able, through the ambiguously dramatic dialogue, to pursue further the subject of his hero's naivety, and at the same time permit the opposite view of the situation to be heard. The reader is thus given a choice of two conclusions: either the cardinal is sincere but deluded in his own protestations of belief, or he is deliberately deceitful, willing to use any means, including direct lies, to further the spiritual and political ends he has in view. To Lothair's accusation that the account in the "official journal" is "'a tissue of falsehood and imposture,'" the cardinal replies calmly that there is really no evidence for Lothair's conviction that he fell at Mentana while fighting "against the Holy Father," and that, given his recent delirium, it is probably a "'hallucination'" (ch. 68, 349). As to the rest of the statement, the cardinal maintains that its truth has been "'established by evidence so incontestable, by witnesses so numerous, so various, in all the circumstances and accidents of testimony so satisfactory,'" indeed, "'so irresistible,'" that "'controversy on this head would be a mere impertinence and waste of time.'" And when Lothair remains unconvinced, Grandison urges him to remember that he is in "'the centre of Christendom, where truth, and where alone truth resides.'" He also reminds Lothair that "'Divine authority has perused this paper and approved it,'" so that he feels entirely justified in concluding that "'this great act has been accomplished, in a manner which can admit of no doubt, and which can lead to no controversy'" (ch. 68, 350–1). Most gratifying of all for the cardinal, however, are the political consequences of Lothair's conversion, which will amount to nothing less than an English Counter-Reformation: "'the Secret Societies have received their death-blow; I look to the alienation of England as virtually over. I am panting to see you return to the home of your fathers and reconquer it for the Church in the name of the Lord God of Sabaoth. Never was a man in a greater position since Godfrey or Ignatius. The eyes of all Christendom are upon you as the most favoured of men'" (ch. 68, 351). Apparently all that remains to convert Lothair into the "champion and regenerator" of Christendom is that the Holy Father should himself receive the young lord "into the bosom of that Church." This is, of course, a most ironic vision of the "New Crusade," the more so since the cardinal's grandiose fantasy casts a derisory heroic stature upon the agent of his plans. But such a technique is a masterful way of handling the explosive issues of religious fanaticism and Protestant prejudice in fictional form, for at the crucial moment it escapes what would here be the inevitably destructive authority of narrative omniscience. And in so reducing the politics of the Catholic Church to such an anticlerical climax, Disraeli is able to leave the faith itself virtually untarnished as an object of the reader's sympathy.

This distinction between Catholic dogma and Christian devotion continues in the remainder of the novel, and is illustrated in part in Disraeli's characterization of Lord St Jerome and his niece. After Lothair has encountered the ghostly spirit of Theodora in the Coliseum and once again collapsed, it is Lord St Jerome, who in his anxiety for his countryman's welfare, insists that he be attended by an English doctor, and then removed from Rome. Significantly, St Jerome is described as "devout, and easy in his temper," but also as "an English gentleman" with "a fund of courage, firmness, and common sense" at the bottom of his character that "sometimes startled and sometimes perplexed those who assumed that he could be easily controlled" (ch. 70, 358). Similarly, though Clare Arundel is easily drawn into her aunt's zealous participation in the priestly plan to convert Lothair, her piety and devotion are always treated as genuine manifestations of her spiritual commitment. And this authorial perspective is represented by Lothair's continuing friendship and his gift of a special crucifix as a remembrance of her "Christian kindness" when she subsequently enters a convent, even though he thinks that decision "barbarous and unwise" (ch. 83, 432–3 and ch. 87, 454).

One also sees the same crucial distinction when, near the end of the novel, the cardinal tries to persuade Lothair that he should attend the pope's "'Oecumenical Council ... the greatest event of this century ... greater, in its consequences to the human race, than the fall of the Roman Empire, the pseudo-Reformation, or the Revolution of France'" (ch. 84, 434–5). To this instance of the cardinal's habitual hyperbole Lothair remains unmoved. Though he clearly retains an interest in the possibility of an truly "oecumenical" church, it is clear that he and Grandison differ on the meaning of that term. Where Lothair wishes for a reconciliation among the differing forms of Christian belief, the cardinal anticipates the withering of heresy and the imperial triumph of Rome. When Lothair asks whether it is true that the Vatican Council has been arranged to declare "the infallibility of the Pope" (ch. 84, 435), the cardinal, in yet another example of ambiguously significant dialogue, responds in almost apocalyptic terms.[30] He says that the Catholic Church is "'not only a human and historical witness of its own origin, constitution, and authority, it is also a supernatural and divine witness, which can neither fail nor err.'" When the church "'oecumenically speaks,'" he adds, "'it is not merely the voice of the Fathers of the world; it declares what "it hath seemed good to the Holy Ghost and to us."'" Then, addressing Lothair as "'my child,'" the cardinal goes on to discuss the meaning of the separation of church and state, insisting that where it exists, either from "'royal edict, legislative enactment or revolutionary changes,'" society is no longer "'consecrated,'" and is, indeed, in danger of having all morality perish. Secular political leaders, he argues, "'are urged on by an invisible power that is anti-Christian, and which is the true, natural, and implacable enemy of the one visible and universal Church.'" According to Grandison, the "'coming anarchy is called progress, because it advances along the line of departure from the old Christian order of the world,'" which was founded on "'the sacrament of matrimony, the spring of all domestic and public morals.'" In his view the next step in this devolution is to establish national education without Christianity, while his ominous conclusion is that "'Secret Societies'" are hurrying the civil governments of the world (mostly the governments who disbelieve in their existence), to "'the brink of a precipice, over which monarchies and law and civil order will ultimately fall and perish together'" (ch. 84, 436–7).

Whatever the degree of sincerity in its didactic purpose, and despite its melodramatic reduction of history into a simple binary opposition, this passage effectively captures the quite prevalent Victorian habit of rationalizing faith and its imperatives. But although Disraeli was willing to defend the Anglican establishment in much the same way, he here uses the cardinal's words ironically to define the threat posed by the Catholic Church to the English constitution. In Disraeli's view that threat extends from the individual sacrament of marriage to the security of the realm. And, as was the case with the Young England novels, it is in this link between the private and the public dimensions of politics that Disraeli's allegorical romance gains its coherence.

By this point in the story, however, Grandison's ideas no longer pose any real danger to the hero's convictions and faith. Immediately upon his escape from the Sicilian villa where he was held a captive guest, Lothair had written from Malta to his man of business in London, directing him to "take all necessary steps" to contradict the account of his conversion and to counteract its consequences. Mr Putney Giles in consequence has endowed two new Anglican churches on his Lordship's estates, subscribed generously in his name to various Anglican charities, and arranged for newspaper paragraphs that reassured the world that the "unfounded and preposterous account of the conversion" had been a calumnious libel (ch. 80, 409–10). The point of the cardinal's final attempt at persuasion is thus simply to show that he always has larger goals in view and that no temporary disappointment can deflect him from his proselytizing mission.

When, at Malta, Lothair again encounters Mr Phoebus, the exquisite pantheist-artist-connoisseur, the narrative is immediately released from Disraeli's obsession with the papal "conspiracy," and the authorial persona again assumes the voice of the satirical rationalist who is enraptured by the extravagances of wit and beauty to be found in the world of nature's aristocracies. On Phoebus's Greek island Lothair finds that Theodora's political idealism has been subsumed in the religion of nature and the worship of beauty, for Phoebus, a secular materialist devoted to sensuous aesthetics, has erected the statue of the "divine Theodora" (first seen at Belmont) at the centre of the sacred grove of Daphne, site of frequent peasant processions and an annual religious ceremony dating back to classical antiquity. But this is but mere prelude to their trip to the Holy Land where Lothair paradoxically encounters both the apotheosis of his own religious vocation and the subject of his political and social duty.

The former is the Syrian, "Paraclete," who on the Mount of Olives inspires him with a discussion of "'the truth first revealed to man amid these everlasting hills ... that God made man in His own image.'" In what is obviously a resumption of the argument outlined in *Sybil* and *Tancred*, the Syrian offers Disraeli's protagonist a synthesis of the Judaic and Christian faiths that must have seemed familiar to Victorian readers of the 1860s:[31]

> "In My Father's house are many mansions," and by the various families of nations the designs of the Creator are accomplished. God works by races, and one was appointed in due season and after many developments to reveal and expound in this land the spiritual nature of man. The Aryan and the Semite are of the same blood and origin ... Each division of the great race has developed one portion of the double nature of humanity, till after their wanderings they met again, and, represented by their two choicest families, the Hellenes and the Hebrews, brought together the treasures of their accumulated wisdom and secured the civilisation of man. (ch. 77, 396–7)

When Lothair raises the subject of those who trust in councils as the only foundation for the church, the Syrian scornfully dismisses such claims and asserts the primacy of his ancestors' direct faith: "'the first Council was held more than three centuries after the Sermon on the Mount. We Syrians had churches in the interval ... I bow before the Divine decree that swept them away from Antioch to Jerusalem, but I am not yet prepared to transfer my spiritual allegiance to Italian Popes and Greek Patriarchs.'" Rather, he asserts the primacy of his direct faith: "'We believe that our family were among the first followers of Jesus, and that we then held lands in Bashan which we hold now ... So I am content to dwell in Galilee and trace the footsteps of my divine Master; musing over His life and pregnant sayings amid the mounts He sanctified and the waters He loved so well'" (ch. 77, 397).

At Paraclete's invitation Lothair goes to visit the north of Palestine, where he finds the "scenes of miracles that softened the heart of man, and of sermons that never tire his ear." For a while he dreams of "settling for ever on the shores of these waters," and rebuilding the culture of their vanished happiness while pursuing "researches" in this "cradle of pure and primitive Christianity" (ch. 79, 403). But this reverie is broken by the urgent intrusion of more worldly concerns.

Lothair's awareness of his particular public obligations comes through news from England. His friends Bertram and St Aldegonde, who have also been in Jerusalem, receive word that the Irish Church Disestablishment crisis is reaching its climax in Parliament, and that their respective political parties require their immediate return. And on the way back to Jerusalem to join them, Lothair encounters the general who had commanded the revolutionary troops at Mentana, who also urges upon him a renewed sense of responsibility: "'were I you, I would return home and plunge into affairs. That was a fine castle of yours I visited one morning; a man who lives in such a place must be able to find a great deal to do'" (ch. 79, 407). This conjunction of Lothair's private inspiration with the subject of his public obligations comes in the context of having read Corisande's letters to her brother, where he finds in their "earnest and lively" pages, "a picture of a mind of high intelligence adorned with fancy and feeling." As he reads her account of his own adventures and the rumours they occasioned, he is gratified to find himself described as the friend "who always most interested me, and seemed most worthy of your affection" (ch. 78, 399), and he reflects despondently upon the experience of the world that has separated him from the woman whose love would make him happy.

The conclusion of the novel, in which Lothair returns to England and the complications of his romantic life are disentangled, thus assimilates, in terms typical of Disraeli's psychological romances, the subjects of faith, love, and duty, which together resolve the crucial question of the hero's real identity. He finds to his relief that the St Jeromes are glad to see him again, and that the denizens of the fashionable world have long since forgotten his "scrapes and misadventures," being "so engrossed with themselves that they never missed anybody" (ch. 81, 415). For the most part, however, Disraeli's satire has now lost its edge, and the remaining comedy is very gentle. The duke and duchess find that their anxiety over Bertram's desire to marry Euphrosyne Cantacuzene (sister-in-law of the painter, Mr Phoebus, and the daughter of a Greek merchant) is easily dissolved when they learn that the Cantacuzenes are "people of high consideration," not only fabulously wealthy, but also the descendants of the Greek emperors (ch. 85, 442). Similarly, Lothair's jealousy of Lord Carisbrooke and the Duke of Brecon evaporates when it turns out that Corisande has refused them both. Finally, the misunderstanding about Clare Arundel's bejewelled golden crucifix is dispelled when Lothair explains to the duchess that it was "a homage to her great goodness ... when ... [he] was ill at Rome," and that he has long known of her intention to take the veil (ch. 89, 461–2).

The final scene, in which Lothair and Corisande are joyously united in love, is clearly intended to represent the completion of the hero's growth to maturity. This is conveyed symbolically by their exchange of emblematic gifts – the pearls bequeathed by Theodora to "Lothair's Bride" and the rose from Corisande's garden (ch. 89, 465–7). And that maturity is explicitly the focus of the conclusion to the novel from the moment Lothair returns to London. In the same chapter that details the actions he previously took to counteract the rumours of the conversion, Mr Putney Giles describes his meeting with his noble client on the day following his arrival: "'I never knew a man so unreserved, and so different from what he was when I first knew him, for he never much cared then to talk about himself. But no egotism, nothing of that sort of thing: all his mistakes, all his blunders as he called them.'" And to his wife's curiosity about how Lothair now looks, he adds: "'Very well; never saw him look better. He is handsomer than he was. But he is changed. I could not conceive in a year that anyone could be so changed. He was young for his years; he is now old for his years. He was, in fact, a boy; he is now a man; and yet it is only a year. He said it seemed to him ten'" (ch. 80, 409–10).

This transformation, although it incorporates all of Lothair's experience abroad, seems to have reached its climactic, empowering moment in the inspiring dialogue with Paraclete in Jerusalem. That conversation is crucial to Lothair's development, for it not only dismisses the pontifical claims of authority, but also, as Bogdanor suggests, it "combats both Phoebus's Aryan 'Pantheism' with its attendant anti-Semitism ... and also the illusions of science which purports to prove man's insignificance."[32] From this it is clear that Paraclete's discussions play much the same role in *Lothair* as do those of Eva in *Tancred*, Aubrey St Lys in *Sybil*, and Sidonia in *Coningsby*, for in each of these novels the protagonist is taught that to have a true understanding of his faith, Christians must comprehend the power of its Semitic origins. This theory of race, which was drawn from Isaac D'Israeli's *The Genius of Judaism*, Blumenbach, and other sources, is also the theme of the anomalous twenty-fourth chapter of *Lord George Bentinck*. And so, for all its differences of perspective and tone, *Lothair* has profound similarities to Disraeli's Young England novels of the 1840s.

Because of the obvious way in which *Lothair* is a *roman à clef* with its fictional portraits of Lord Bute, Cardinal Manning, Goldwin Smith, and many other members of England's fashionable society, it is tempting to read the novel simply as a compensatory fantasy. For in having Lothair resist the blandishments of "Popery," and return home to marry the staunchly Church of England heroine, Disraeli would seem to be wishfully denying the import of Bute's conversion. In that regard it is worth noting that Lord Bute's engagement to the youngest daughter of the Duke of Abercorn, to which Corry had referred in his memorandum of 22 September 1868, was broken off by her parents as a result of Bute's impending conversion to Catholicism. And in 1869 and 1870, when Disraeli was writing the novel, the question of Bute's marriage, as an eventuality attracting great public curiosity, was entirely uncertain. As proof, however, that fact is often stranger than fiction, and that in this case there were unusual bonds of sympathy in the relation between the two, when Lord Bute did marry Gwendolen Mary Anne Fitzalan Howard, the eldest daughter of Lord Howard of Glossop, on 16 April 1872, Archbishop Manning conducted the ceremony, at which many Protestants were present; Monsignor Capel said the nuptial Mass and preached the sermon; and the witnesses signing the register were the Duke of Cambridge, the Dukes of Northumberland and Argyll, and Mr Disraeli. The father of the bride, who was the second son of the Duke of Norfolk, had been until 1868 MP for Arundel (see note 42, below).

There is, however, another, less literal sense in which *Lothair* can be seen as an allegory of the times. Just as all of Disraeli's earlier novels were imaginatively autobiographical, so in this one, too, he transforms the conflicts of his personal experience into the fantasy structure of a psychological romance concerned with defining a representative hero's identity. And very much in the way that *Tancred* embodies a disguise of Disraeli's concerns in the Corn Law debate, the allegorical romance of *Lothair* is a disguised form of the recent political crisis over the disestablishment of the Irish Church and the ensuing election campaign of 1868. However, as a representative hero, Lothair is not simply an alter ego for his author, for in this case, the imaginatively autobiographical transformation is complicated by the degree to which Disraeli, as prime minister, legitimately sees himself as a personification of the English constitution. Disraeli's identification with Lothair thus involves the symbolic representation of the Protestant realm through Lothair's position in the landed aristocracy, and this political synecdoche controls the whole of the allegorical plot. Accordingly, at the outset of the story, Lothair's interest in the possibility of an ecumenical rapprochement between Catholics and Protestants can be seen as an expression of Disraeli's hope, as he took office in February 1868, that his government would be able to adopt an Irish policy of conciliation. The same metaphoric relation would then identify Lothair's plans to build a Catholic cathedral as an emblem of the ministry's plans to grant a charter to an Irish university. Such an interpretation suggests that there is an important connection between literal and symbolic sources of inspiration in the resultant fiction. Disraeli and his readers would have been well aware, for example, that upon the death of Cardinal Wiseman, his friends had established a fund with which to build a Catholic cathedral as "the most fitting Memorial to the first Cardinal Archbishop of Westminster." Manning, the new archbishop, was expected to press forward with this memorial to his predecessor, but much to the disappointment of those who revered Wiseman, he merely secured the necessary land and left the building to his successors. His reason for doing so, he said, was that he wished to concentrate all his efforts and resources upon the rescue and education of children from the poorer districts of England's cities. But there were some who suspected that Manning's motives and ambitions were less altruistic. Thus, though the characterization of Cardinal Grandison is plainly a satirical portrait of Archbishop Manning, Disraeli exploits the ambiguities in the behaviour of his model not only to further his theme, but also to gratify the curiosity and prejudices of his readers regardless of their persuasion.

Whether, as seems likely, Manning's pamphlet on the Irish question was the catalyst that caused Gladstone to act, or not, the Opposition leader's resolutions on Disestablishment placed Disraeli's Government in direct opposition to the hierarchy of the Catholic Church. In the debates on those resolutions, Disraeli chose to focus upon the threat he thought they posed to the English constitution and to the people's civil liberties. In the allegory of the novel, this change is represented by Lothair's involvement in the Italian campaign against the forces of the papacy. The emphasis at this point in the novel upon the secret societies reflects not just the secret intelligence that Disraeli and his cabinet ministers were receiving about the Fenians during 1867 and 1868, or the confidential assessments of their election prospects by political agents, but also his long-standing conviction that such secret and clandestine forces did in fact have considerable influence in the affairs of Europe. The strongest thematic links between the republican forces of the novel and the position of Disraeli's Government are, however, the subjects of constitutional freedom and national unity. In that respect the turning point of the struggle is in reality the Government's defeat on the Disestablishment resolutions in the House of Commons, while in allegorical terms that defeat is marked by the death of Theodora and the wound sustained by Lothair on the battlefield at Mentana.

Lothair's struggle for life, his ambivalent involvement in the rituals of the Roman Church, and his escape from what he feels is an entrapment in religious superstition, are all elements of an imaginative displacement of the Government's position in the 1868 election campaign. Central to Disraeli's sense of that political struggle was his conviction that the alliance he saw between ritualists and Romanists amounted to a conspiracy designed to disestablish, not just the Irish Church, but ultimately the Church of England as well. Perhaps understandably, his view of Gladstone's role in this struggle was somewhat paranoid. The leader of the Opposition, whatever the justifications of his desire to defeat the Government and so assume the office of prime minister himself, was clearly allied in the debate on the Irish Church with the hierarchy of the Catholic Church. It is, therefore, an interesting feature of the psychological transformations involved in the political allegory of the novel that Lothair's absorption in daily visits to Roman churches, his introduction to the most powerful of the cardinals in the Vatican bureaucracy, and the intimation that his "conversion" is of personal interest to the Holy Father, are details that seem to be derived from Gladstone's experiences in Rome during the winter of 1866.

Gladstone had been in close contact with Manning before his trip to Italy and the archbishop had taken care to warn the Vatican in several letters that they should show their distinguished English visitor every possible consideration and thus mitigate the possibility of his becoming a dangerous opponent.[33] Manning's concern to win Gladstone's support for the pope's temporal power, couched as it is in terms of the company he should keep in Rome, the kindness to which he would be susceptible, and the potential of his extreme hostility, thus seems to anticipate the elements of Grandison's attempt to convert Lothair from an opponent of the papacy into its heroic "champion and regenerator." Moreover, there are other points of comparison; for Gladstone's very great enthusiasm for visiting churches and hearing sermons during his eleven-week stay in Rome, rather than seeing the more typical tourist attractions, was sardonically remarked upon. In his account of this trip, for example, John Morley reported: "I have been told by one who saw much of the party during the Roman visit, that Mr. Gladstone seemed to care little or not at all about wonders of archaeology alike in Christian and pagan Rome, but never wearied of hearing Italian sermons from priests and preaching friars."[34] So, too, Gladstone's diary records his visits to dozens of Catholic churches, including the well-known "Gesu," the chief Roman Jesuit church: "In aft. from Pal. Bolognetti saw the Pope's arrival & departure from the Gesu wh as a demonstration was a total failure."[35] And, of course, the diary also records Gladstone's many meetings with influential cardinals and monsignori at the Vatican, and it contains a long memorandum detailing the conversation in the first of his two audiences with the pope.[36]

Gladstone's behaviour in Rome was clearly the subject of some public speculation and misunderstanding, for it was soon reported in the European press, perhaps maliciously, that Gladstone had been discussing politics with the pope, including, it was said, the possibility of Ireland as a sanctuary for His Holiness should the political situation in Italy require his withdrawal from Rome. This was very much the focus of the extract from the *Corriere Italiano*, reprinted in *The Times* under the heading "The Pope and Mr. Gladstone": "The conversation concerning Italy having ceased, they spoke of the Church in Ireland, and the Pope warmly recommended his well-beloved flock to Mr. Gladstone, then, smiling, added, 'If I should one day or other quit Rome, although Ireland is far removed from the centre of Christianity, I should not disdain to select it for my domicile. Malta, a town almost entirely commercial, now that the revolutionists have taken to accusing my poor priests, cannot have my sympathies.'"[37] The circulation of these erroneous reports gave "grievous offence," and consequently Gladstone found it necessary to publish a refutation of this rumour (in both English and Italian) in the official journal of the Vatican, and to have the fact of his denial reported in *The Times*.[38] One further, though by no means unique, or even atypical detail of comparison with Lothair's experience is that on 10 December 1866, Gladstone caught a severe chill and while confined to bed for a week with headache, fever, and a sore throat, was attended by Dr Topham, an English physician resident in Rome. It is, of course, impossible to recapture the full extent of the gossip about Gladstone's personal eccentricities and embarrassments among his cynical political opponents in London. But from these details of comparison, it would seem that in making Lothair a hero representative of the English constitution (and not just his alter-ego), Disraeli found amusing creative inspiration in the threat posed by ultramontane plots to a constitutional Opposition as well as to a constitutional Government.

In any case, the great Protestant struggle of the election campaign is given general allegorical shape in Lothair's attempt to evade the papal schemes for his conversion. Disraeli's own sympathies with the High Church seem to be embodied in the genuine solace that Lothair receives from the beauty of Catholic rituals when he is ill, while Disraeli's determination to thwart Archbishop Manning's "universal" influence, and to counteract the dangers of Ritualism with Low Church patronage, is transformed into Lothair's escape from the clutches of Grandison's power. Accordingly, the miracle fabricated to promote Lothair's "conversion" is a symptom both of Disraeli's profound suspicions about Manning's motives and sincerity – exemplified, for example, in the matter of the (un)timely conversion of Bishop Wilberforce's daughter and son-in-law (see ch. 14) – and of the fantasy that gave the question of religious allegiance such exaggerated force in the election of 1868.

A minor detail that is perhaps also indicative of the imaginative link between the issue of Church patronage and the plot of the novel concerns a metaphor from Disraeli's letter to Lord Derby, 18 September 1868, commenting upon the preferment of the ultra-Protestant Canon McNeile: "I think the Deanery of Ripon has been a coup. I was really surrounded by hungry lions and bulls of Bashan till that took place, but, since, there has been a lull, and an easier feeling in all quarters."[39] The allusion is to Psalm 22, the language of which is echoed in the Crucifixion scenes of the New Testament. The detail in the novel that resonates with this heroic sense of combatting the dangers of ritualism is Paraclete's statement (quoted above) that he is "'not yet prepared to transfer ... [his] spiritual allegiance to Italian Popes and Greek Patriarchs'" and that his family "'were among the first followers of Jesus, and that we then held lands in Bashan which we hold now'" (ch. 77, 397–8). As discussed above, in setting aside the institutional authority of the papacy, Paraclete emphasizes the simple power of faith and devotion, which Lothair has always found so attractive. And the allegorical resonance of the scene is the direct result of Lothair's identification with the devout Syrian: "The heritage of Paraclete was among the oaks of Bashan, a lofty land, rising suddenly from the Jordan valley, verdant and well watered, and clothed in many parts with forest; there the host of Lothair resided among his lands and people, and himself dwelt in a stone and castellated building, a portion of which was of immemorial antiquity" (ch. 79, 403–4). The idealization of this passage suggests that the particular allusion, which obviously derives from Disraeli's nostalgic attachment to the Holy Land ever since the youthful days of his Eastern tour, has the unusual power of defining the political, religious, and historical continuities that are most important to the mature author and politician.

The fantasy structure of the novel, it should be noted, serves Disraeli not just as a compensation for, or rationalization of the recent political events, but also as an imaginative transcendence of defeat. Accordingly, the conclusion to the marriage theme is neither an implausible hope, nor a simple wish-fulfilling denial of reality. Disraeli does not expect Lord Bute to marry a Protestant, nor does he in reality fail to accept the result of the election. Rather, in making Lothair's growth to maturity the sequel to Tancred's quest for a divine sanction of his faith,[40] the defeat is transformed into victory through two complementary symbolic assertions: that in the hands of what might be termed "Young England," the constitution will retain its Protestant character; and that the papacy shall not lay its "hand ... upon the realm" (see above, ch. 14, 402). The relation between fantasy and reality in the construction of this allegorical romance is of particular interest for the way it shows that Disraeli's fictions are continuous with his politics. As was the case with *Tancred*, the fantasy structure of *Lothair* bears a striking similarity to the imaginative shaping of the political career at its most recent critical stage. Just as Disraeli's role as prime minister and his relationships with Manning, Gladstone, and the Queen were invested with elements of fantasy, so the novel is also a mixture of genres, incorporating into the conventions of romance a realism sufficient to the purpose of giving the work allegorical power. That realism lies in part in the accuracy of the satirical portraits and in part in the allusions to actual persons, historical events, and particular places.[41] Nevertheless, Disraeli has been criticized for the inaccuracy of his contextual detail in *Lothair*, most notably in the matter of Catholic rituals and ceremonies. For example, in his "Explanatory Notes" Bogdanor points out that several of the religious services differ from Disraeli's descriptions of them, though his objection to the description of a cardinal's robes as "pink" instead of scarlet is misguided, given that in English hunting circles scarlet jackets are known as "pink" coats. Somewhat paradoxically, any imprecision or carelessness with the facts on Disraeli's part seems to be a function of the allegorical purpose he has in mind, for, whether it is a matter of religious ardour or patriotic fervour, he often seems more intent upon expressing the emotional impact of scenes than upon establishing their authenticity.

Lothair, like the politics it comes to represent, is thus constituted by an imaginative mixture of Disraeli's public and private experience. Both contain the author's immediately discernible motives that are based upon rational thought, and both contain the powerfully compelling fantasies that derive from his crises of identity. Indeed, although the reader is asked to view Lothair as Disraeli sees himself – as the emblem of a constitutional struggle – the novel embodies not just the implications of Disestablishment dramatized in the romantic fate of its hero, but also the latest manifestation of the Catholic motif that had served as a disguise of Disraeli's ambivalence about his identity since the years of his adolescence. It is, therefore, not insignificant that there are a number of connections between *Lothair* and *The Young Duke*, the first of his novels to use the Catholic motif as the essence of a marriage plot. Like Lothair, the hero of the earlier novel is an orphan left to the care of two guardians, one of whom is a Catholic. Equally important, however, is the fact that the most positively portrayed of the Catholics in *Lothair*, the religiously devoted but tolerant "English gentleman," Lord St Jerome, appeared first in *The Young Duke*. There he is presented as the unprepossessing young rival of both the hero and Arundel Dacre for the hand of the Catholic heroine, May Dacre.[42] And in this early novel, inspired by the recent debate on Catholic Emancipation, the marriage plot is happily resolved with mixed marriages: eventually the Duke of St James marries May Dacre and Arundel marries Lady Caroline St Maurice, who is an Anglican, while from the later novel we learn that Lord St Jerome also married a Protestant, who had then "reverted to the ancient faith, which she professed with the enthusiastic convictions of a convert" (ch. 9, 35). These links between the two widely separated works support the claim that *Lothair* continues to embody Disraeli's ambivalence about Catholicism, even though the strong anticlericalism of the later novel would indicate that the underlying tensions of the Catholic disguise related to his Jewish heritage have been to some extent dissolved in the prime ministerial role of defender of Her Majesty's Protestant realm. Thus, for all the very real differences of tone and perspective between it and Disraeli's earlier fiction, *Lothair* is very much the sequel to the Young England trilogy, and yet another of his imaginatively autobiographical romances in which the themes of love, faith, and duty are powerfully blended.

16

"The Family Romance": Politics, Power, and Love in *Endymion*

Disraeli's last completed novel encapsulates the romance of politics that had been both the enduring concern of his earlier fiction and a shaping force of his political identity. Because *Endymion* was not completed and published until 1880, it might be thought to be retrospective of Disraeli's whole political career. But the first half of the novel was in fact written in the early 1870s, before Disraeli became prime minister for the second time, in 1874.[1] It should therefore be seen as a work that is in imaginative terms consecutive to *Lothair*, however much the two novels may at first seem to differ in their conceptions of politics.

Like Disraeli's earlier fictions, *Endymion* is an imaginatively autobiographical novel in which the central tensions of his personality, particularly the various emotional claims of "purity" and "success," play a significant role in shaping the story.[2] It is also a historical novel in which the fantasy of the hero's transcendent success is constructed from a mixture of history and romance. Both the plot and characterizations involve three types of narrative: that concerned with real persons and events; that involving imaginative transformations of real persons and events into fictional, but still recognizable portraits or descriptions taken from experience; and that formed by purely imaginary characters and topics. All of this is controlled by a narrator who is invested with both an emotional attachment to the eponymous hero and the political perspective of the author. The result is a dramatic and narrative version of the past that embodies idealizations, distortions, and suppressions of what is reductively called the literal truth. But it is also a story that once again allows Disraeli to explore and define the means to his deepest wish, a destiny in which power and love are perfectly blended.

As several critics have noted, *Endymion* seems in some ways to reflect Disraeli's statesmanly detachment from partisan political controversy, for, unlike *Coningsby, Sybil, Tancred,* and *Lothair,* this is a novel in which politics seems to be less a matter of ideological disputes than one of personal rewards. And in that respect Disraeli's eponymous hero finds his success, not with the conservative Tories, but with the liberal Whigs. This is, however, only one of many significant displacements that help create the vision of the past as it should have been. And, despite this change of colours, and perhaps not surprisingly, the career of Endymion Ferrars both directly and indirectly reflects the emotional crises of Disraeli's own rise to power.[3]

The most important relationship in Disraeli's myth of success is that of the protagonist and his twin sister, Myra. In many respects it is a relationship that is derived from the emotional intimacy between Disraeli and his sister, Sarah, but there are some significant differences as well. In the fiction, there is a displacement of feelings such that the passionate intensity of the bond between the siblings is expressed almost entirely in Myra's words. It is she, not Endymion, who is possessed by a ferocious ambition and a desire to restore their family's fortunes. And in the very idealization of making them twins, Disraeli obviously intends to exploit the narrative possibility of creating an alter-ego for his nominal hero. The story of their childhood is, in fact, another embodiment of the ambivalence Disraeli felt about his family heritage. The pride he took in his racial ancestry, which in his fictions had previously taken the form of a "natural aristocracy," and which had paradoxically manifested itself in his false account of the D'Israeli family's descent from Spanish Sephardic Jews, is here once again transformed into an English paradigm of superiority: the account of their parents' dazzling social and political success in the aristocratic world of Tory politics prior to the first Reform Bill. Indeed, the twins' father, Mr William Pitt Ferrars, as his father had been, is a Privy Counsellor, and is thought to have some prospect of becoming prime minister. But, just as it was in life, in the fiction the inheritance is dichotomous. The social stigma attached to Disraeli's Jewish ancestry is represented in the novel both by the children's sense of humiliation when, in the political crisis of 1832, the family is forced by relative poverty into a rustic exile from the world of fashion and power, and by the subsequent deaths of their parents – the mother's from hysterical illness and the father's by suicide.

This melodramatic turn of events suggests that the ambition and sense of alienation which shape the ensuing developments of the plot can be profitably seen in the light of Sigmund Freud's conception of "the family romance."[4] Fantasies concerning the relation to one's parents and siblings, which Freud saw as characteristic of highly gifted adolescents, typically have both an ambitious and an erotic aim embodied in the process of creating an identity that is independent of the parents' authority. The first evidence of such fantasies in Disraeli's imaginative life was the brief entry in an early diary covering the years of his early adolescence entitled, "Italian Story," in which the father, a popular religious painter, murders his wife, "the original of all his virgins," out of sexual jealousy.[5] These fantasies are subsequently reflected in the development of other early novels such as *Contarini Fleming* and *Henrietta Temple*.[6] It is hardly surprising that the very youthful Disraeli, caught up in the grip of gothic and Byronic enthusiasms, would incorporate the motifs of childhood alienation, imagined maternal sexual infidelity, retaliation, and revenge into his first attempts to create a fictional plot.[7] But it is striking that, more than fifty years later, his last completed novel also incorporates distinctive features of the family romance, as Disraeli again transforms the experience of his early years into the form of a novel.

The central fantasy of the family romance, in which the real parents, whose limitations the adolescent has come to recognize, are replaced by others of higher social standing, would seem to be the shaping power of the narrative that describes Endymion's and Myra's rise from an impoverished rustication to the centre of power and fame: the hero's to the position of prime minister of England, and his sister's, first to Lady Roehampton, wife of a powerful cabinet minister, and then to queen consort of a European monarch. Moreover, the twins' passionate relationship also incorporates the displacement of the incestuous desire between siblings in the family romance that Freud remarks upon, while their mutual success, in which Endymion gains the power denied to his father and Myra becomes the apotheosis of their mother's desire for social distinction, is the perfect symbolic representation of what Freud describes as the fantasy-builder's desire to recover the innocence and parental affection of his childhood.

To some extent the intense and lasting bond between Endymion and his sister is presented as a compensation for the traumatic losses of both family and status they suffer as children. But it clearly predates the collapse of the family's fortunes, which suggests that the sympathetic identification between them is meant to have a more profound significance. Indeed, the key to an understanding of that sympathy can be

found in the regressions that characterize the crises of their relationship. As spoiled young children they both indulge in visions of their
future greatness: Myra declares that she "should not think of marrying
anyone who was not in the House of Lords," and Endymion on the
same occasion replies complacently to one of his parents' aristocratic
dinner guests, "I shall go to Eton in two years ... and then I shall go to
Christchurch, and then I shall go into Parliament" (15). But when, some
years later, their parents face the ruin of their ambitions, the first elaboration of Myra's character is more revealing:

> That young lady was now thirteen, and though her parents were careful to
> say nothing in her presence which would materially reveal their real situ-
> ation, for which they intended very gradually to prepare her, the scrutinis-
> ing powers with which nature had prodigally invested their daughter
> were not easily baffled. She asked no questions, but nothing seemed to
> escape the penetrative glance of that dark blue eye, calm amid all the mys-
> tery, and tolerating rather than sharing the frequent embrace of her par-
> ents. After a while her brother came home from Eton, to which he was
> never to return. A few days before this event she became unusually rest-
> less, and even agitated. When he arrived, neither Mr. nor Mrs. Ferrars was
> at home. He knocked gaily at the door, a schoolboy's knock, and was hard-
> ly in the hall, when his name was called, and he caught the face of his sis-
> ter, leaning over the balustrade of the landing-place. He ran upstairs with
> wondrous speed, and was in an instant locked in her arms. She kissed him
> and kissed him again, and when he tried to speak, she stopped his mouth
> with kisses. And then she said, "Something has happened. What it is I can-
> not make out, but we are to have no more ponies." (39)

The incongruity displayed here – between the knowingness of the detached, thirteen-year-old daughter and the apparent childish ardour
with which she greets her brother in their parents' absence – is but the
first sign of a displaced ambivalence about the claims of power and
love, very similar to that which Disraeli had used to characterize earlier
protagonists of his fictions, most notably Contarini Fleming and David
Alroy. And as the story unfolds, it is soon clear that this projection is the
motive force of the plot, for it is Myra who continuously shapes both
Endymion's ambitions and her own in the name of their narcissistic
love for each other. In another displacement of the family romance, she
is the one whose resentment of their reduced circumstances issues in
contempt for the histrionic illness of their mother, and she is the one

who explicitly defines their goal in life to be the restoration of the family's fortunes. Somewhat later, she is the one who confesses that her marriage to Lord Roehampton, though it has brought her love and happiness, has been primarily a matter of advancing her brother's political prospects; she is the one who urges him to marry Adriana Neuchatel for the security of her fortune, and she is the one who, in the moment of their transcendent success, arranges the concluding scene in which Endymion, by then prime minister, goes with her to visit their former home on Hill Street:

> The queen visited all the principal rooms, and made many remarks appropriate to many memories. "But," she said, "it was not to see these rooms I came, though I was glad to do so, and the corridor on the second story whence I called out to you when you returned, and for ever, from Eton, and told you there was bad news. What I came for was to see our old nursery, where we lived so long together, and so fondly! Here it is; here we are. All I have desired, all I have dreamed, have come to pass. Darling, beloved of my soul, by all our sorrows, by all our joys, in this scene of our childhood and bygone days, let me give you my last embrace." (467–8)

The conclusion of the novel thus quite explicitly connects the triumphs of their respective power and fame with the poignant, intense intimacy of their childhood. Myra's crucial statement, "'All I have desired, all I have dreamed, have come to pass,'" may well be considered Disraeli's final tribute to Sarah's inspiring devotion, but it is also an idealization, not unlike that of *Lord George Bentinck*, that represents a purification by displacement of the real ambition within himself upon which his political success was built. In this novel, as in the earlier ones, that is the significance of the eponymous hero's passivity; in both love and politics it makes his remarkable success seem to be the inevitable reward of his innate purity and natural superiority.[8]

Endymion's docility extends as well to his relationships with the other women who take a strong interest in his career, Adriana Neuchatel, Lady Beaumaris, and Lady Montfort. For example, he accepts the £20,000 in Consols (sent anonymously by Adriana) as an altruistic gift of the independence necessary to stand for Parliament, without considering the potential claims it might entail. And he is equally gratified to accept the uncontested seat in the House of Commons, which is arranged by the influence of the Whig Lady Montfort and the Tory Lady Beaumaris upon their respective husbands. Even more notably, he is entirely passive in accepting Lady Montfort's control of every detail of their courtship after the death of her husband. These details of the controlling fantasy are grandiose versions of the influence Mary Anne Lewis had in helping Disraeli get elected in 1837 in her first husband's riding of Maidstone and in furthering Disraeli's subsequent career both before and after their marriage.

The impulse of imaginative autobiography also works pervasively in this novel to dissolve the conflicts of principle and expediency that characterized all of Disraeli's political life. For example, his quarrels with the Conservative prime minister, Sir Robert Peel in the 1840s are given the dignity of legitimate Opposition when they are displaced into Endymion's apprenticeship under Lord Roehampton, a fictional embodiment of Lord Palmerston. On 15 August 1843 Palmerston had inquired of the prime minister about treaties made between Russia and the Porte, and he had then moved for the production of papers connected with Servia. Peel replied that this was not possible because the transactions had not yet been brought to a close. Disraeli then followed with a provocative and flamboyant attack on his own party's Government, insisting that England should maintain "the independence and integrity of the Turkish empire," and remarking that the ministry's current "policy with respect to the East made them ... the laughing-stock of Europe."[9] In the novel, however, Lord Roehampton first prompts Endymion to ask a question on an important subject of foreign policy. And then after considering the ministerial answer, Roehampton adds, "'This must be followed up. You must move for papers. It will be a good opportunity for you, for the House is up to something being in the wind, and they will listen. It will be curious to see whether the minister follows you. If so, he will give me an opening'" (360). It is significant, too, that the effect of the hero's maiden speech in Parliament is noticeably different from that of Disraeli's almost disastrous one in 1837, in which he was laughed at for his rhetorical excesses and hooted to silence. Although Endymion is nervous as he rises to speak, his success is unquestioned: "His statement was lucid, his arguments were difficult to encounter, and his manner was modest. He sat down amid general applause" (361). The most important detail of this compensatory version of the first parliamentary performance is, however, that "the minister again followed him, and in an elaborate speech," even though he was "overwhelmed ... with the labours of his own department, the general conduct of affairs, and the leadership of the House." The subject, "in the opinion of the minister, was of too delicate and difficult a character to trust to a subordinate" (361).

The gratifications of such recognition are clearly both reflections and displacements of Disraeli's own pleasure in provoking Sir Robert Peel to take him seriously as an antagonist in the years of Young England's triumphs. Endymion, we are told, "habitually made inquiries, or brought forward motions, which were evidently inconvenient or embarrassing to the ministry; and the very circumstance, that he was almost always replied to by the Prime Minister, elevated him in the estimation of the House as much as the pertinence of his questions ... at the end of three sessions, he was a personage universally looked upon as one who was 'certain to have office'" (372–3). But these fictional gratifications are also, it would appear, an ironic transformation of Disraeli's specific success in his consular speech of 1842, in which he attacked Lord Palmerston's administration of the Foreign Office prior to 1841. He thought that the effect of that speech had been magnified because Palmerston had replied to him "with great pains & with as much effort as if he were answering Peel."[10] The fictional version of the first ministerial intervention is also a means of displacing Disraeli's vitriolic personal hostility to Peel. Endymion's friend, Waldershare, the Under-Secretary of the Foreign Office, is furious at this usurping of his responsibility, which, as the narrator points out, was a mistake that made "a personal enemy of one who naturally might have ripened into a devoted follower, and who from his social influence, as well as from his political talents, was no despicable foe" (362). The fantasy thus incorporates Peel's failure to recognize Disraeli's capacity for official duties in 1841, and yet through the narrator's perspective it displaces the anger that followed this "humiliation" onto the character who is the fictional embodiment of Disraeli's Young England colleague, George Smythe, who in 1846 had accepted Peel's offer of that same Under-Secretary's position.

The compensatory fictional displacement then continues in the form of Waldershare joining the Protectionists in principled resignation from the Conservative party over the issue of repealing the Corn Laws. What is most interesting about this process, however, is the division of motives and responsibilities within the imaginative recreation of the historical events. Waldershare, in moving "the amendment to the first reading of the obnoxious bill," carries the burden of Disraeli's altruistic Protectionist claims in opposing Peel's ministry, while Endymion's role within the Opposition temporarily supporting the Government is one of silent sympathy with the disaffected Tories: "Among these was Mr. Ferrars, who it was observed never opened his lips during the

whole session" (381). The disruptive side of Young England's opposition to Peel's Government is thus amusingly projected in the novel
onto the absurd pretensions of Mr Bertie Tremaine and his "Mountain,"
otherwise known as "the school of Pythagoras": "Mr. Bertie Tremaine
seconded the amendment of Waldershare, and took the occasion of expounding the new philosophy, which seemed to combine the principles
of Bentham with the practice of Lord Liverpool ... The debates during
the session were much carried on by the Pythagoreans, who never
ceased chattering. They had men ready for every branch of the subject,
and the debate was often closed by their chief in mystical sentences,
which they cheered like awe-struck zealots" (381). In somewhat maliciously turning himself into the image of Monckton Milnes, upon whom
Mr Bertie Tremaine seems in part to be modelled, Disraeli is acknowledging that in retrospect the Young England movement seemed to some
to be composed of a hilarious mixture of the sublime and the ridiculous.[11] But the more important effect of these displacements within the
larger fantasy is to make the hero's purity and success compatible.

The momentum of the plot then immediately returns to the account
of Endymion's seemingly fated success. When the Whigs resume office,
after the Tories have been "ignominiously defeated" in "the dark hour
of retribution," Lord Roehampton appoints Endymion (now his brother-in-law) as his Under-Secretary at the Foreign Office. As a consequence, although it may be fairly said that one of Disraeli's most
obvious themes in *Endymion* is the influence of women upon a man's
political career, the vision resulting from the dramatization of this influence (in this case Myra's) is one in which women, especially those in the
aristocracy, though debarred from holding political office themselves,
find a quite extraordinary fulfilment of their intellectual capacities and
emotional desires through the manipulation of men they have be-
friended, or to whom they are related. In this regard Disraeli invests
women with so much power that they can, if necessary, do for men
what men could never do for themselves – quite transcend the barriers
of social class and political parties. Indeed, the most remarkable aspect
of *Endymion* is that it displays a society in which the demarcations of
class are shown to be both arbitrary and permeable, and defined to a
very large extent by the ability of women to make their beauty and their
brains the key to change.[12]

Perhaps no other novelist of the Victorian period focuses as sharply
as does Disraeli upon the transformations of social identity made possible by accumulated wealth, individual talent, brains, or bravado. The

world of his imagination, for all that it seems to exalt the finer distinctions of rank, is a constant challenge to the boundaries of social intercourse that are usually thought to typify Victorian society. And *Endymion* in particular is a psychological romance that continuously contemplates and demonstrates the possibility of changing one's social position. The tragic deaths of Endymion's parents in madness and suicide, for example, are clearly related to the loss of their position in the fashionable upper-middle class and to their consequent mortification of having to accept a clerkship for him in a "second-rate government office" (73). But this precipitous descent into the world of lower-middle-class clerks is softened in part by Disraeli's or the narrator's nostalgia for the amusements and intellectual pretensions of Endymion's new companions and in part by the division of his working and domestic life into separate spheres. Because Endymion first lodges in London with Mr Rodney, his father's former valet and secretary, he is never deprived completely of his former identity, but rather finds it constantly reiterated in his landlord's obsessive testimonials.

On the other hand, the Rodneys exemplify social change of another sort. As the daughter of a fashionable dressmaker and then secretary-companion to Mrs Ferrars, Mrs Rodney has, like her husband, observed and assimilated the manners of the middle class. Thus, when set up as the managers of a stylish lodging house in Warwick Street that is owned by a wealthy tailor, Mr Vigo, they quite transcend their former lives in service. Their tenants are persons of quality. And Mrs Rodney's evening tea-table and champagne and lobster suppers attract a circle of admirers, among whom is the tenant of the second floor, a young man who "might some day even be a peer of the realm" (87). This youthful and capricious aristocrat is, indeed, Waldershare, the "only child of a younger son of a patrician house" (92), who at this point has just been returned as a Tory MP. He takes the fancy of educating Mrs Rodney's beautiful younger sister, Imogene, who after extensive private tutelage acquires the taste and social graces necessary to her eventual elevation to the aristocracy as Lord Beaumaris's wife.

But perhaps the two best images of this striking intermixture of social classes are the picnic excursion to the Derby, in which the Rodneys, Imogene, Waldershare, and Endymion are all the guests of a flamboyant young earl, and the dinner party at Mr Vigo's Thames-side Richmond villa, to which the same guests are invited. In the case of the former, Disraeli captures Endymion's exhilarating sense of transcendent personal freedom at "the Carnival of England," not just in the gaiety of the

luncheon and the excitement of the horse race, but also in the gratifications of being observed on the way home by his fellow clerks from
Somerset House who are returning in an omnibus: "Endymion felt as if
he were almost acting a distinguished part in some splendid triumph of
antiquity, as ... the four splendid dark chesnuts swept along, two of
their gay company playing bugles, and the grooms sitting with folded
arms of haughty indifference. There was a momentary stoppage, and ...
his quick eye could not avoid recognising the slightly surprised glance
of Trenchard, the curious amazement of Seymour Hicks, and the indignant astonishment of St. Barbe" (90). Equally emblematic of the power
of the unconventional is the description of Mr Vigo's banquet. In this
scene, as he does so frequently, Disraeli portrays the liberating sense of
social transgression in terms of individual taste and personal happiness.
Endymion is flattered to be the guest of a man who owns a "Palladian
mansion" with "chambers of majestic dimensions – lofty ceilings, rich
cornices, and vast windows of plate glass" (94–5). But it is the narrator,
just as much as the hero, who indulges in the sensory delights of the occasion: at each place, we are told, there were "turtle and venison and
piles of whitebait, and pine-apples of prodigious size, and bunches of
grapes that had gained prizes," while the "champagne seemed to flow
in fountains," and was only interrupted that one might "quaff Burgundy
or taste Tokay" (97). The most notable characteristic of this occasion is,
however, the eclectic nature of the invited party, which recalls the tone
of Lady Blessington's soireés at Seamore Place and Gore House in the
1840s. Apart from the circle of Endymion's friends in Warwick Street
(which again includes Waldershare and the young earl who so admires
Mrs Rodney and her sister), the guests include a sporting attorney, the
chief partner in a firm that imports Indian shawls, the first tenor of the
opera, a prima donna, celebrated actors and actresses, artists, a dan-
seuse, some literary men, "chiefly brethren of the periodical press," and
some members of either House of Parliament (96). Moreover, after dinner there are comic songs, operatic performances, cards, and dancing to
cap the panorama of pleasures. In such company the distinctions of social class are set aside as stifling and irrelevant, and Disraeli makes this
point explicit in the conversation of Waldershare and his noble friend:

"Well, Clarence ... was I right?'
    "By Jove! yes. It is the only life. You were quite right. We should indeed
be fools to sacrifice ourselves to the conventional." (97)

Endymion thus embodies much the same iconoclastic vision of society as does Disraeli's first novel, *Vivian Grey*, published fifty-four years earlier. But it is an empowering vision as well, for the social world described by the narrator offers acceptance and opportunity to Endymion and his sister at every turn. For example, it is Myra's response to the banker Neuchatel's advertisement for a companion for his daughter, Adriana, that becomes the entrée for them both to circles of wealth, power, and influence. Adriana's emotional dependence on her more accomplished and confident companion is the key to the twins' future, for once Myra and her brother are introduced to that world, their innate characteristics of intelligence and genteel temperament lead to even more extraordinary attachments. Lord Roehampton, who is thought to be courting Adriana in his visits to the Neuchatels' estate (a fictional version of the de Rothschilds' Gunnersbury) falls in love with Myra, while Lady Montfort, the most beautiful and ambitious of the novel's aristocratic young women, takes up Endymion as her protégé. Beyond the events of the controlling family romance, the society of the novel is equally a world where other characters find growing power and influence. Mr Vigo, the tailor, becomes a powerful railway magnate, and both he and Mr Rodney become members of Parliament, as does Job Thornberry, the radical son of farmer Thornberry at Hurstley. Mr Trenchard and Seymour Hicks, two of Endymion's fellow clerks from Somerset House, also in the end enter the House of Commons, while another, the vain and snobbish St Barbe (Disraeli's revenge for Thackeray's parodic "Codlingsby, by B. de Shrewsbury, Esq." in *Punch*)[13] finds a career of both literary and diplomatic success. But perhaps the most remarkable acquisition of power and influence in the novel, beyond the careers of Myra and Endymion, is that of Nigel Penruddock, the son of the rector at Hurstley, who first establishes a brilliant career in the Church of England and then converts to Roman Catholicism, soon becoming an archbishop and ultimately a cardinal. His rise is clearly modelled mostly on that of Henry Manning, whose successful career within the Church of England similarly terminated in a conversion to Rome in 1851, followed by his elevation to Archbishop of Westminster in 1865, and then to cardinal in 1875.

Archbishop Manning had also been the inspiration in *Lothair* for the charming but manipulative and Jesuitical Cardinal Grandison, who is bent on the eponymous hero's conversion. As chapter 15 has shown, that characterization and the foiling of the cardinal's ultramontane plots clearly reflect Disraeli's fear of papist conspiracies and his anger over Manning's betrayal of him in the Irish Church Disestablishment crisis of 1868. So it is significant that the climax of *Endymion* revolves around the issue of a Catholic conversion. This is especially so, given that in a number of his early novels, Disraeli had used the motif of Protestant versus Catholic identity as a disguise of his concern for his ambivalence about his Jewish heritage.[14] When after the death of Lord Roehampton, Myra accepts King Florestan's proposal, it necessarily entails her conversion to Catholicism, for in marrying him she will become the queen consort of his Catholic country. This seemingly astounding turn of events has been prefigured in the text. When Prince Florestan, living in exile in England under the name Colonel Albert, first meets Myra at the Neuchatels'estate, he is puzzled by her familiar appearance, not realizing that she is the twin sister of the young boy who had been his admiring fag at Eton. And on several other social occasions after his true identity is known, and before the death of her husband, the prince shows a marked preference for Lady Roehampton's conversation and companionship. Moreover, Endymion's early lessons in foreign affairs come not just from the tutelage of Lord Roehampton, but also from his conversations with the prince and the prince's retainer, Baron Sergius.

Myra's decision to accept Florestan's proposal is the most critical moment in the novel's family romance, for it complicates the twins' relation to one another, by providing the emotional as well as the physical terms of their ultimate separation. Indeed the decision troubles Endymion, when he is told of it, precisely because of what it implies about the psychological as well as the physical distance that now separates them. The traumatic effect on him of her news is suggested not just by the "constraint" he feels for the first time in her presence, but also by the narrator's description of his response: "It was a long interview, very long, and if one could judge by the countenance of Endymion, when he quitted the boudoir and hastened to his room, of grave import. Sometimes his face was pale, sometimes scarlet; the changes were rapid, but the expression was agitated rather than one of gratification" (419). The reader is already familiar with the matter of "grave import," having in an earlier chapter seen Florestan's letter to Myra, offering her his "heart" and "throne," and having seen, as well, her anticipation of "a future of such unexpected lustre and happiness" (398). And the next chapter begins with Lady Montfort's response to the news of the marriage, already communicated by Endymion: "'Well, something has happened at last ... it is too marvellous!'" Endymion then explains to Lady

Montfort the significance of religion in the arrangements that have been made: "'She enters the Catholic Church, the Archbishop of Tyre has received her. There is no difficulty and no great ceremonies in such matters. She was re-baptized, but only by way of precaution. It was not necessary, for our orders, you know, are recognised by Rome'" (419). And when Lady Montfort exclaims, "'And that was all!'" Endymion replies, "'All, with a first communion and confession. It is all consummated now; as you say, "It is too wonderful." A first confession, and to Nigel Penruddock, who says life is flat and insipid!'" Such a change in religious identity, which in the context of the Tractarian movement and John Henry Newman's 1845 conversion to Rome would have been a very contentious and controversial issue in mid-Victorian England, is here in the family romance at first simply accepted and subsumed in the wonder of his sister's apotheosis and their childhood friend's transformation.

Myra's marriage to King Florestan is directly linked to the topic of Endymion's future through the repetition of her insistence, on the point of his return to England, that he should marry Adriana Neuchatel as a matter of expediency for the security that connection would bring him within the world of politics. This, Endymion recognizes, has been "the only subject on which they had ever differed" and it leads back to the traumatic recognition of his loss:

> He felt he had crossed her there – that he had prevented the fulfilment of her deeply matured plans. Perhaps; had that marriage taken place, she would never have quitted England. Perhaps; but was that desirable? Was it not fitter that so lofty a spirit should find a seat as exalted as her capacity. Myra was a sovereign ... His heart was agitated, and his eyes were often moistened with emotion. He seemed to think that all the thrones of Christendom could be no compensation for the loss of this beloved genius of his life, whom he might never see again. (421–2)

Such separation anxieties, whether expressed in fantasy or conscious thought, tend to be especially intense for twins, but the more so in this fictional instance because Myra exerts the full force of her emotional influence upon her brother to counter his infatuation with Lady Montfort:

> Your present position, if you persist in it, is one most perilous. You have no root in the country; but for an accident you could not maintain the public

position you have nobly gained. As for the great crowning consummation of your life, which we dreamed over at unhappy Hurstley, which I have sometimes dared to prophesy, that must be surrendered. The country at the best will look upon you only as a reputable adventurer to be endured, even trusted and supported, in some secondary post, but nothing more. I touch on this, for I see it is useless to speak of myself and my own fate and feelings; only remember, Endymion, I have never deceived you. I cannot endure any longer this state of affairs. When in a few days we part, we shall never meet again. And all the devotion of Myra will end in your destroying her. (434)

It is consistent with the novel's myth of inevitable success that at this climactic moment, the projected "great crowning consummation" of Endymion's life is portrayed as a social eminence, but not as an acquisition of power for ideological or political purposes. The use of the word "adventurer" and the reference to the country's view of him are also telling in this context, for that was perhaps the word most often used to describe the young and even the mature Disraeli's political motivations, and it alludes to the struggle he had in the 1850s and 1860s to gain the leadership of the Conservative party against fierce and prejudiced opposition. But Myra's pragmatic argument for Endymion's success gives way to the regressive claims of their love for each other. It is her melodramatic threat of a permanent separation and her accusation that he will be responsible for her misery and destruction that are most revealing, for they suggest that the real cause of their separation from each other is indeed Endymion's love of another woman. This accusation breaks Endymion's resistance to her will and he immediately replies: "'My own, my beloved Myra, do with me what you like. If —.'" When, at this moment, Florestan interrupts their private conversation to announce Lord Montfort's death, Endymion is thus on the point of being completely absorbed by Myra's now imperious desire to protect the fantasy of his eventual political success, supported by expediency but sustained primarily by the intensity of their special bond. But the intrusion suspends the terms of the fantasy imposed by Myra and it is immediately replaced with the alternative of Endymion's conflicting desire.

From this point the novel moves quickly forward to complete the family romance as a fulfilment in which power and love are perfectly blended. For a while Endymion fears that the changed circumstances have left him bereft of all feminine support. He feels a tone of constraint in his communications with his sister and fears that it is occasioned as much by his refusal to marry Adriana as by the alteration in her position. As much to the point, however, he imagines that Lady Montfort's loss of prestige and wealth as a consequence of her husband's death will push her to fulfil her social ambitions in ways that will exclude his passionate feelings for her. Lady Montfort finds, however, that Lord Montfort has bequeathed to her his entire fortune, including all his personal wealth and property beyond the hereditary estates of Montfort Castle and Montfort House. And after the socially required period of mourning she permits Endymion to visit her in the company of her parents, while, with his help, she arranges for purchase and possession of a London mansion. The scene in which she shows him the room she has prepared for his study and so proposes that he should share her life in that mansion is the happy conclusion to the period of inertia that has been imposed upon him, as much by his own fears as by the requirements of social decorum. This again is a grandiose version of the arrangement by which Disraeli and Mary Anne lived at 1 Grosvenor Gate, the house overlooking Hyde Park owned by her first husband, Wyndham Lewis. Much the same sort of marvellous revelation then occurs in his political career, shortly after their marriage, when Endymion is offered the position of Foreign Secretary in the new administration, as the Whigs return to power under the leadership of Sidney Wilton, his father's former colleague and friend in the days before the disastrous decision to follow the Tories.

The motif of Catholic versus Protestant religious identity within the family romance is raised again in the novel when Disraeli links this change in Endymion's political fortunes directly to real political events in the years 1850 and 1851. In September 1850, without any reference to the hierarchy of the Church of England, Pope Pius IX proclaimed the restoration of Catholic sees in England and appointed Nicholas Wiseman first to the position of archbishop of Westminster and then, almost immediately, a cardinal. This caused a storm of religious and political controversy, best exemplified by Prime Minister Lord John Russell's notorious "Durham letter" denouncing the pope's pretensions of supremacy and the so-called papal aggression upon England's Protestantism as "insolent" and insidious."[15] The publication of Russell's letter, which had been written without any consultation with his colleagues, had the immediate effect of destabilizing the Government, for both the Irish members and the Peelites were furious and withdrew their support. Disraeli's correspondence from the time shows that he was less concerned with the religious issue than with the political ones, for in a public letter to Lord Carrington, the

Lord Lieutenant of the county of Buckingham (also published in *The Times*, 9 November 1850), he pointed out that "the whole question" had been previously "surrendered" and "decided in favour of the Pope" by the Government's and the Queen's recognition of the legitimacy of "the Romish Bishops of Ireland."[16]

In the novel these events are incorporated into the family romance through the conflationary device of having Nigel Penruddick named the cardinal who is to oversee the Vatican's restored episcopate. This has been anticipated in the plot when, at the time just prior to Myra's marriage, Endymion has a conversation with Penruddick. In contrast to his earlier seeming acceptance of his sister's conversion in the conversation with Lady Montfort, he tells the archbishop that Myra's '"secession ... from the Church of her fathers'" is to him '"by no means a matter of unmixed satisfaction.'" To which the cleric replies, '"The time will come when you will recognise it as the consummation of a Divine plan'" (426). The novel's linking of politics and personal identity suddenly crystallizes as the conversation continues in an argumentative strain more characteristic of *Lothair*. Endymion says that he is confident that his sister '"will never be the slave of superstition'" and that '"she will remember that the throne she fills has been already once lost by the fatal influence of the Jesuits.'" To this Penruddick responds, '"The influence of the Jesuits is the influence of Divine truth ... Before two years are past ... I foresee that the Jesuits will be privileged in England, and the hierarchy of our Church recognised'" (426). As the reference to the Jesuits implies, the device of constructing this fictional anticipation of the Catholic restoration has as much to do with Disraeli's retrospective view of Manning after 1868 as it does with his view of Wiseman in 1850, though neither of the priests was in fact a Jesuit. Its significance is that this is the only point in the novel where Endymion asserts himself in an active fashion to define the primary element of his identity. Otherwise he is characterized as a man who "always said and did the right thing" (453).

The narrator attributes the eventual collapse of the Whig ministry to the "anti-papal manifesto" of the prime minister, though in reality Lord Russell's Government, though seriously weakened by his controversial actions, survived until February of 1852, when it was defeated on an amendment to the Local Militia Bill and Lord Derby then formed a Conservative ministry. In the fictional version of these events, Endymion resigns his position as Under Secretary of the Foreign Office during the ministerial crisis of 1851 and then spends four years out of office, while enjoying a happy domestic life and a marked social success. And in the novel's account of the formation of the ensuing Conservative Government, the narrator refers, rather coyly, to Disraeli's appointment as chancellor of the exchequer: "a gentleman without any official experience whatever, was not only placed in the Cabinet, but was absolutely required to become the leader of the House of Commons, which had never occurred before, except in the instance of Mr. Pitt in 1782" (455). The narrative blending of the real and fictional worlds is particularly notable for the way in which the reiterated passive voice and the subordinate clause stress the remarkable nature of this elevation, while avoiding entirely the controversial political force of Disraeli's leadership of the Protectionists since the defeat of Sir Robert Peel's Government six years earlier. In effect then, the fiction presents not just an idealized family romance, but also a purified version of the historical reality.

Much the same effect is created by the attenuated account of Endymion's subsequent political career as a cabinet minister when the Whigs return to power with Sidney Wilton as prime minister: "There were years of war, and of vast and critical negotiations. Ferrars was equal to the duties, for he had much experience, and more thought, and he was greatly aided by the knowledge of affairs, and the clear and tranquil judgement of the chief minister" (458). The novel thus transfers the public version of the working relationship that Disraeli had with Lord Derby to the myth of success upon which the fiction is founded. But compared with the reality of Whig politics in the 1850s and 1860s, it is certainly a highly revisionist and somewhat sardonic account, with palpable hits at Russell, Palmerston, and Gladstone: "The ministry was strong and it was popular. There were no jealousies in it; every member was devoted to his chief, and felt that he was rightly the chief, whereas, as Lady Montfort said, the Whigs never had a ministry before in which there were not at least a couple of men who had been Prime Ministers, and as many more who thought they ought to be" (458). The only remaining description that refers to actual political events is equally misleading and attenuated, and leads directly to the putative climax of the family romance: "The ministry had lasted several years; its foreign policy had been successful; it had triumphed in war and secured peace. The military conduct of the troops of King Florestan had contributed to these results, and the popularity of that sovereign in England was for a foreigner unexampled" (464).

In writing his novel, Disraeli was, of course, under no obligation to create or refer to events with historical accuracy. The myth of inevitable success upon which Endymion's career is built is nothing more than a fantasy whose structure and details permit a reconstruction of the past in idealized form. In that world the conflicts of party and parliamentary politics are all dissolved in the gratifications of rank and position amid the splendours of aristocratic society. Accordingly the novel contains two chapters devoted to an idealized version of the day-long Eglinton mock medieval tournament that took place in 1839, while the complicated events and all the agonies of the Crimean War are reduced to less than a sentence. In the former, Endymion's love for the married Lady Montfort is deflected symbolically into the rituals of the tournament and expressed as the jealousy he feels for the Count of Ferroll, who claims her favours. In the latter the experience of being a senior cabinet minister, which in reality is the actual qualification for leading a political party, is subordinated to the simple passage of time. In short, the fantasy structure of the novel makes very few claims on political history, even as it asserts the historical importance of individual character in the political process.

When after his marriage to Lady Montfort and upon the retirement of the prime minister for reasons of health, Endymion receives the royal summons that is the prelude to being asked to form a Government, it can be seen as yet another projection of Disraeli's relation to Lord Derby in 1867 back on to the Whig politics of the fiction, ostensibly that of the mid-1850s. In the narration, however, there is no indication that the event comes through political struggle on Endymion's part. The emphasis is on the moment being the culmination of Lady Montfort's ambition to make her husband prime minister. This is Disraeli's penultimate tribute to the political influence of women, to be succeeded only by the final moments of regressive intimacy between the twins in their childhood nursery that have already been noted. Freud explicitly links his discussion of the dynamics of "the family romance" to his larger work, *The Interpretation of Dreams*[17] by pointing out the significance of royalty in the dreams of adults and the relation of their appearance to the "child's overvaluation of his parents" ("Family Romances," 241). In the case of *Endymion*, the twins' respective marriages, representing the apogee of social and political distinction, are in each case the perfect embodiment of love and power fused into single identities. But they also conform to the imperatives of the family romance. Myra's elevation to the position of Florestan's queen consort recaptures the twins' innocent trust in the parental power and distinction to which they thought they were born. It also works, as a fulfilment of destiny, to dissolve the impediment of her desire that has been hinted at in Myra's insistence that her brother marry Adriana Neuchatel for the sake of wealth and security. The significance of the concluding scene in the nursery at Hill Street is thus that it projects the permanent separation made possible by a transcendence of the struggle for both power and love. That scene also attests to the autobiographical nature of the novel, for Myra's farewell and "last embrace" in their old nursery (468) is an idealization that undoubtedly expresses Disraeli's wish that his sister had lived to share his ultimate political triumph.[18] The fantasy structure of the novel is thus a specific elaboration of the type of the imaginative activity that Freud would later see as typical of particularly gifted children and adolescents. As such, *Endymion* is, like all of the earlier novels, a psychological romance in which Disraeli both explores and revisits the relations and issues most important to his sense of himself.

17

The "Faery" Queen, the "Arch Villain," and the "Mephistopheles of Statesmanship"

Since his death on 19 April 1881, Disraeli's reputation as a politician has depended to a great extent on the achievements of his second ministry, from 1874 to 1880. In both domestic policy and foreign affairs those achievements were considerable, though when he became prime minister for the second time, after the general election of 1874, Disraeli seemed, to the surprise of his colleagues, not to have a strong legislative agenda already prepared.[1] But the Home Secretary, Richard Cross, and his cabinet colleagues soon brought forward a steady stream of social legislation that would eventually give Disraeli's Government a progressive character not matched by any Conservative Government since. As Paul Smith has pointed out, however, despite the Tory party's comfortable majority, there were both ideological and practical constraints on their ability to address social problems.[2] On the one hand, Conservatives often opposed the idea of any further intervention into commercial activity or paternalistic intrusion into private affairs, and there was a widespread preference within the party for necessary social improvements to be arranged at the local level. On the other hand, there was the awkward fact that social reforms were costly and could leave the Government vulnerable to charges of fiscal irresponsibility, whether the problem was dealt with directly or by compensations in lieu of local taxation. Nevertheless, within the first two years of its mandate, Disraeli's Government introduced and passed significant legislation improving regulations governing employment, public health (sanitation, adulteration of food, pollution), and housing for the working class. There were also bills establishing new regulations for licensing of public houses, Friendly Societies, merchant shipping, and primary education. As Smith has noted, these measures were not the result of a coherent Tory paternalism, but, rather, most often they arose as the consequence of royal commissions or select committees. In intent they were, as he says, a mixture of "paternalistic benevolence with empiricism and Peelite liberalism."[3]

Disraeli certainly played an important part in the successful passage of his Government's domestic legislation, mediating conflicts among his colleagues and finding compromises between opposing interests. But it is perhaps not surprising that he found his energies absorbed much more in these years by the conduct of diplomacy and the crises of foreign affairs. In this area the issues of Disraeli's identity and character continued to have a powerful public resonance and in a very real sense they came to define the convulsive struggle between liberalism and conservatism from 1875 to 1880 that manifested itself in the discussions about the Suez Canal, the opposition to the Royal Titles Bill, and the handling of the Eastern question. Disraeli's critics, then and since, have seen his actions in these matters as proof of his untrustworthiness and of his failure to take seriously the moral imperatives of constitutional government. Nowhere is this better illustrated, perhaps, than in the Opposition's view of Disraeli's relations with the Queen and in the way Gladstone reacted to the news of the Bulgarian atrocities. There is, however, plenty of evidence in Disraeli's correspondence that he did not himself confuse the matters of style and substance when it came to these topics. Rather, he quite consciously constructed his fantasies of the romance of politics as a strategy and an amusement, while keeping a shrewd and wary eye upon the realpolitik of each issue.

The so-called purchase of the Suez Canal in the fall of 1875 is often cited in biographies as an event of tremendous significance. Yet, at the time, in both public and private circles, its actual nature was often misrepresented. Kaiser Wilhelm II might write to his mother, the crown princess of Prussia, "I know you will be so delighted that England has bought the Suez canal,"[4] but that was not in fact what had happened. England had acquired the Khedive's shares in the Suez Canal Company, representing 44 per cent of the total. The exaggeration, which also caught the imagination of the general public in England, stemmed in large part from Disraeli's love of intrigue and melodrama, very evident in his letters about the matter. On 18 November, in a letter explaining his and the cabinet's actions, already well advanced, Disraeli told the Queen, "Tis an affair of millions; about four at least; but would give the possessor an immense, not to say preponderating, influence in the management of the Canal ... It is vital to your Majesty's authority and power at this critical moment, that the Canal should belong to England."[5] The next day she replied that she had "telegraphed her approval of the course he intends pursuing" and he in turn wrote again on the 20th to tell her that "the Cabinet are unanimous as to the policy, and have given *carte blanche* to Mr. Disraeli to carry it into effect." But it is significant that he adds, "Your Majesty's approbation greatly strengthens him." The language of the correspondence shows that while Disraeli was negotiating with the Khedive on his own initiative and with a strong sense of its strategic imperative, he was making a confidante of the Queen about matters of high drama and secrecy, even as he undertook his constitutional duty of keeping the monarch informed as to the Government's actions. The Queen's approbation was an important aspect of Disraeli's eventual explanation to the House of Commons for the expenditure of such a large sum without its authorization. But the rhetorical strategy of this correspondence is revealing in another way, for it flatters the Queen's sense of her power. On 24 November Disraeli exulted to the Queen, "It is just settled; you have it, Madam. The French Government has been out-generaled ... the entire interest of the Khedive is now yours,"[6] while to Selina, Lady Bradford, who had become his romantic confidante in virtually every aspect of his political life, he wrote to tell her "a great State secret ... the most important of this year, and not one of the least events of our generation":

> After a fortnight of the most unceasing labor and anxiety ... I have purchased for England the Khedive of Egypt's interest in the Suez Canal.
>
> We have had all the gamblers, capitalists, financiers of the world, organised and platooned in bands of plunderers, arrayed against us, and secret emissaries in every corner, and have baffled them all, and never been suspected.
>
> The day before yesterday, Lesseps,[7] whose Company has the remaining shares, backed by the French Government, whose agent he was, made a great offer. Had it succeeded, the whole of the Suez Canal would have belonged to France, and they might have shut it up!
>
> We have given the Khedive 4 millions sterling for his interest, and run the chance of Parliament supporting us. We could not call them together for the matter, for that would have blown everything to the skies, or to Hades.
>
> The Faery is in ecstacies about "this great and important event" – wants "to know all about it when Mr. D. comes down to-day."
>
> I have rarely been through a week like the last – and am to-day in a state of prostration – coma – sorry I have to go down to Windsor – still more sorry not to have had a line to-day, which would have soothed
>
> Your affectionate
> D
>
> P.S. – Though secret here, the telegraph will send the news from Egypt, I doubt not, to-day.[8]

Disraeli followed this letter with two others, one written at Windsor Castle the next day and one (also from Windsor Castle) on 30 November, in which he gave Lady Bradford all the details of his private audiences with the Queen: "A most hurried line to tell you that nothing could be more successful – I might say triumphant – than my visit. The Faery was most excited about Suez, said 'what she liked most was, it was a blow at Bismarck,' referring, I apprehend, to his insolent declarations that England had ceased to be a political power. This remark she frequently made, showing it was the leading idea of her mind."[9] It is not just the delight in secrecy and the imaginative construction of the baffled conspiracy – of outwitting the "plunderers" and "secret emissaries," the "gamblers, capitalists [and] financiers" – nor the misleading reference to the "remaining shares," which were in fact the majority, that are of interest in these letters. Equally important is the recognition that it would have been imprudent in the extreme to have the canal company owned entirely by the French government or French interests. Disraeli knew perfectly well that four fifths of the traffic through the canal was British shipping and that the canal was of strategic interest for the quicker access it gave to moving either material or troops to India. He was also aware that, when the canal was built in 1869, Gladstone, then prime minister, had declined to purchase the shares in the Suez Canal Company that had been offered to England. The Khedive's financial embarrassments were thus an opportunity to rectify what had come to seem a very short-sighted mistake. And Disraeli was certainly interested in seizing the chance to assert England's power in Europe, though his remark about the Queen's "leading idea" suggests some distance, if not differentiation in his own thinking. Apart from the danger of French control, he was perhaps less concerned about "a blow at Bismarck" than about a check to Russian aggrandizement, as is indicated by his other comments in the letter about Prince Gorchakov and the "amusing" consternation caused by the news.[10]

These letters are important for what they show about Disraeli's relationship with the Queen. Disraeli had long since established a special relationship with Victoria that was based on a most flattering sympathy on his part with the Queen's view that she was beset by burdens almost too heavy to bear. He approached the Queen not just as his sovereign, but as a woman, and he invested their conversations with highly sentimental expressions of chivalry and romance designed to assure her of his devotion and of his desire to serve her in both a personal and constitutional sense. As already mentioned (ch. 14, 406), Her Majesty took great delight in receiving his prime ministerial notes, often scribbled in the heat of debate in the Commons or composed after meetings of the cabinet. As Robert Blake has remarked, his notes and letters to the Queen had all the flavour of a novel, for they gave her a lively sense of the personalities and topics at issue,[11] so much so, indeed, that she believed that for the first time she "knew *everything*" about what was going on within the councils of her Government.[12]

This was, of course, not so. However much Disraeli himself enjoyed the romance of politics, his relationship with the Queen was fraught with strategic considerations. Their tussles over clerical appointments in 1868 had shown him just how difficult a matter it could be to please the Queen while pursuing his own political objectives. And though her actual constitutional role was by this time quite circumscribed by the powers of Parliament, she was apt to take her royal supremacy seriously and it would not have been good policy to challenge or confront her directly in that regard. In the case of the Suez Canal shares, Disraeli's critics, Gladstone in particular, suspected him of abusing the prerogative of a minister to act without the support of Parliament. By working secretly with Baron Lionel de Rothschild to finance the purchase of the Suez shares, and doing so with royal approval, Disraeli seemed to forestall any objections and cover the boldness of his actions with Her Majesty's sanction. The danger Gladstone and others feared was that such an action encouraged the Queen to take a more literal and unrealistic view of her powers than was warranted. George Buckle argued that there really was no substance to the charge of straining the ministerial prerogative. However much Disraeli used courtly language that seemed to invest the Queen with ownership of the Government's policies, he "never forgot that constitutionally the responsibility was his."[13] Still, from the outset of his second ministry even some of Disraeli's cabinet colleagues saw the danger of giving the Queen the impression that the Government would defer to her wishes. Lord Derby wrote to his chief (in a note from the Foreign Office, marked "Private"), "Nobody can have managed the lady better than you have; but is there not just a risk of encouraging her in too large ideas of her personal power, and too great indifference to what the public expects? I only ask; it is for you to judge."[14] And there were, indeed, times when Disraeli had to take a very firm position in direct opposition to the Queen's wishes, though he always stressed the pain it gave him to do so.[15] In many matters, however, he recognized that Queen Victoria did, through the network of her extended family and aristocratic household connections, have sources of information independent of the prime minister and the Government. And he also recognized that her experience over such a long reign had given her a uniquely informed perspective on some topics. For all of these reasons Disraeli adopted the rhetorical posture of reiterating his dependence on Her Majesty's wisdom and experience and his need for her advice, even when, as these and other letters show, he found the exercise irksome.[16]

Disraeli also found personal attendance on the Queen at Windsor, Balmoral, or Osborne a tiresome duty that took time away from more important business or prevented him from getting badly needed rest. And, as some letters show, he also found the Queen's views on various matters to be provocations. It would, however, be a mistake to conclude that the chivalric form of Disraeli's address to her was insincere or hypocritical. The romance of the Faery Queen he constructed contained his own role as well as hers. His extravagant compliments and flattery may well have had their purpose, but they also broke through the severe etiquette and strict formal protocol of the royal household and established a sense of intimacy both enjoyed. This made his wit more effective, for much of it was satiric, implying (as satire always does) a shared superiority and sense of command. Moreover, their relationship was in general marked by mutual respect, sympathy, admiration, and affection. Still, by referring to the Queen as "the Faery" and quoting her conversation in the letters to Lady Bradford, her sister, Lady Chesterfield, and others, Disraeli was asserting bold and imaginative claims to his own power, perhaps the more so for the danger that the telling of such secrets might be read as satire. Had she known the full scope of Disraeli's romance, and the extent to which she was a character in its other narrative forms, it is almost certain that the Queen would not have been amused.[17]

I

The passage of the Royal Titles Bill in 1876 is another instance of the way in which Disraeli's imagination shaped the conduct of parliamentary business during his second ministry. As early as the summer of 1857, at the time of the Indian Rebellion, Disraeli had suggested using the image of the Queen to create a stronger identification with the monarchy in the minds of the people of India and thereby establish British rule more securely. It was, he thought, England's duty to protect the property, the customs, and the religion of the Indian population, not to impose Western values and institutions upon them. In a three-hour speech in the House of Commons on 27 July, he deprecated the Whig Government's policy of appropriation and annexation and their reliance on military force to suppress the forces of rebellion, arguing that the native discontent with British rule in India was far more extensive and justified than the specific events of the mutiny seemed to suggest.[18] Disraeli's views were certainly Orientalist, in the sense that Edward Said has defined, but they were unusual for the time in that, when most people were outraged and calling for vengeance, he could imagine the feelings of the native opinion and see how they might be altered. His views on the situation in India in 1857 were as bold and insightful as his views of the situation in Ireland had been in 1844: "You ought at once … to tell the people of India that the relation between them and their real Ruler and Sovereign, Queen Victoria, shall be drawn nearer. You must act upon the opinion of India on that subject immediately; and you can only act upon the opinion of Eastern nations through their imagination." And after suggesting that a royal commission be sent out to inquire into the grievances of the various classes of the Indian population, Disraeli went on to indict the Government's policy by emphasizing the importance of the Queen's persona: "You ought to issue a royal proclamation to the people of India declaring that the Queen of England is not a Sovereign who will countenance the violation of treaties; that the Queen of England is not a Sovereign who will disturb the settlement of property; that the Queen of England is a Sovereign who will respect their laws, their usages, their customs, and, above all, their religion." Doing this in a way that would attract "universal attention" would, Disraeli argued, "do as much as all your fleets and armies can achieve."[19]

Disraeli also mentioned his ideas about the role of the monarch in India to the Queen herself. In a letter dated 24 June 1858, reporting that the India Bill had been read a second time, without division, he said that though it was "a wise & well digested measure," it was "only the antechamber of an imperial Palace": "Yr Majesty would do well to deign to consider the steps, wh: are now necessary to influence the opinions, & affect the imagination, of the Indian populations. The name of Yr Majesty ought to be impressed upon their native life. Royal Proclamations, Courts of Appeal in their own land, & other institutions[,] forms & ceremonies, will tend to this great result."[20] In essence what Disraeli wanted to do was "identify the symbolism of the monarchy with the symbolism of Empire,"[21] which in 1858 was an urgent matter of stabilizing British rule in India. By

1876 that had been largely accomplished, but there was now the threat posed by Russian expansion in central Asia. Moreover, the Queen by this time was firmly set upon the idea of assuming the title, Empress of India. Disraeli had raised the topic with her shortly after he took office in 1874 and she was entirely receptive to the idea.[22] The tsar was an emperor and so was Kaiser Wilhelm, in Germany, so the matter of their international precedence rankled not a little. Indeed, the initiative for the Government's bill in 1876 seems to have come from Victoria, as Disraeli's letters to Lord Cairns and Lord Salisbury show. To the former he wrote: "The Empress-Queen demands her Imperial Crown. Since our conference at Hatfield, I have avoided touching on the matter, but can do so no longer."[23] Four days later, he suggested to Lord Salisbury that he was "pressed much by the Empress about her Crown" and that the announcement of the Royal Titles Bill should be placed in the Queen's speech for the imminent session of Parliament immediately after a paragraph about the Prince of Wales's forthcoming visit to India: "What then might have been looked upon as an ebullition of individual vanity, may bear the semblance of deep and organised policy: connected, as it will be, with other things."[24]

Gladstone and many other Liberals, as well as a few dissident Conservatives, were outraged at the idea of what they assumed was an inevitable supplanting of the English title, King or Queen, with that of Emperor or Empress, associated as it had been, even recently, so strongly with foreign lands such as France and Mexico. And, as Richard Shannon has pointed out, the proposal's "semblance of deep and organised policy" was "precisely what was urged against it: it seemed to connect only too deeply Suez with Besika Bay."[25] Gladstone, in particular, was reported to be much exercised by the bill, and on three evenings (9, 20, and 23 March) he raised objections to it, though in each case he felt constrained to avoid a direct confrontation with the central point and tried instead to find tangential arguments of resistance, such as the bill's failure to address the status of other British colonies.[26]

From the first introduction of the bill, however, Disraeli seems to have enjoyed Gladstone's discomfiture. Writing to Lady Bradford, after the first night of debate, about his own success in conciliating the House, he described his rival's frustration: "I was told when I sate down, that certain members on the other side of influence and independence, thought that there ought to be now no division; and the Speaker afterwards told me that Lord Hartington was of that opinion too. But that would not satisfy Mr. Gladstone who was brimful, took the reins in his own hands and, after a speech of vituperative casuistry, imagining every combination which could never happen, fled from his own Motion and left his party in a ditch."[27] Eleven days later, when the bill had cleared committee, Disraeli gloated again: "Gladstone ... gave us as much trouble as he could, being all the night in one of his white rages and glancing looks at me, which would have annihilated any man who had not a good majority and a determination to use it. Never was such a triumphant evening. I carried the Bill through Committee without a single amendment, though many were tried and more threatened."[28] Gladstone's speeches, as reported in *The Times* (10, 21, 24 March 1876), do not, in fact, read as if he were in a state of white rage when he delivered them. They seem, rather, to reflect his sense that he is powerless to stop a bill that he thinks is unwise but yet, he fears, will increase both Disraeli's favour with the Queen and his popularity with the general public. And the leader in *The Times* on the 24th, though by no means dispassionate, described Gladstone's tone as one of "calm, and almost despairing solemnity."[29] So Disraeli's account to Lady Bradford is a melodramatic exaggeration, but one whose significance should not be underestimated. It certainly tells us how Disraeli characterized his relationship to Gladstone within the dynamics of their parliamentary political theatre. And in all likelihood he gave a similarly dramatic account of these debates to the Queen in his audiences with her. His letter to the Queen, dated 1 April 1876, does, in describing the opposition to the bill (especially in newspapers hostile to the Government), use the word "vituperation" as something he is inured to. He also refers to their "insolence," when he describes the speculations in the hostile press that he may be forced to resign as a result of having led the Queen and his colleagues into a political "imbroglio." In this context the word "insolence," as do other phrases in the letter, seems to have the effect of aligning his feelings with Her Majesty's: "Mr. Disraeli is to be expelled as having been a mere Court sycophant ... Yr. Majesty knows, that this is not so, & tho' Mr. Disraeli never wishes to conceal, that he is bound to Yr. Majesty by feelings of personal devotion, which is not strange as he owes his position entirely to Yr. Majesty & has received great sympathy from Yr. Majesty in his domestic life, his conscience assures him, that he has ever been to Yr. Majesty a faithful Minister, & ever looked to Yr. Majesty's honor, & the welfare of Your Realm."[30] Indeed, although the debates on the Royal Titles Bill are not seen by Gladstone's biographers as having much significance, they undoubtedly intensified the Queen's dislike of him. On 22 March she had written to Disraeli what he termed "a most impassioned letter as to the conduct of the Opposition – 'personal' to herself; she will 'resent' it, etc. etc."[31] And, as R.C.K. Ensor has said, "Queen Victoria was deeply galled by the Opposition's attitude. It helped to fix the anti-liberal bias of her later years."[32] In Disraeli's mind, and probably in the Queen's, the defining spirit of this opposition was the "Arch-Villain" of the prime minister's comic melodrama: "Gladstone is quite mad and I have no doubt that by next Thursday he will have prepared blowing-up materials equal to Guy Fawkes. I understand that it is to be something dreadful, but my friends are firm and Harry Chaplin is going to give us a speech out of love for me and hatred of G."[33]

When the Royal Titles Bill passed through committee and on to the third reading without amendments, Disraeli told Lady Bradford that he looked upon it as having "proved more than anything the strength of the Ministry," and, he added, "I see no rocks ahead now and am going down to the House for the first time this Session without the tension of the nervous system which I have had since Parliament met."[34] This was a delusion, for when the bill reached the Lords, the opposition to it was renewed, and the press, especially *The Times*, became vociferous again. On 31 March, the prime minister confessed to Lady Chesterfield that he was "living in a fiery furnace": "There never was such a factious Opposition … The great struggle is on Monday, and I hope the faction will be overthrown. The insolence of the Duke of Somerset surpasses belief. I will some day greatly chastise him."[35] On the Sunday evening Disraeli wrote to Lady Bradford: "To-morrow is the great battle of Armageddon when it will be decided who governs England, I or the newspapers." He encouraged her not to be frightened by "the *Times* and all the rest" and declared his resolve not to compromise on the matter of the title of "Empress": "If you want to govern the world you must know how to say Bo to a goose. And what is the use of Power if you don't make people do what they don't like?"[36] And then before the vote on the Monday, he wrote again to Lady Bradford, adding: "as far as the *Times* is concerned, it is a question who shall rule the country: the Queen's Minister or Printing House Square. I think it will be the Queen's Minister."[37]

At the heart of the opposition to the Royal Titles Bill was the issue of Disraeli's character. It was reasonable enough of the Opposition to fear that behind the title, Empress, were the associations of military conquest and despotic rule that were easily attached to the masculine form of Emperor. It was equally reasonable to doubt that the use of the title could be excluded from England and confined only to India, and to deprecate the unilateral extension of direct sovereignty over all of India in the person of the Queen. But there was, beyond those reasons, a widespread suspicion in Liberal and even some Tory quarters that Disraeli was manipulating both the Queen and Parliament for deeper purposes. Gladstone made this explicit in the debate on 23 March when he said, "In the proceedings of government you must allow much for the weakness, much for the fluctuation of the public mind, and not a little for the designs and intrigues of evil-minded men; and if you do not guard against these designs and intrigues, though you may not share with these evil-minded men the guilt which they bear, you will share the responsibility for what ensues."[38] This sense of there being something sinister in Disraeli's intentions was echoed in several other speeches that night. Robert Lowe, for example, complained that the prime minister was playing with and mocking the House of Commons by providing only "miserable frivolity and drivelling" in support of the bill while concealing his real arguments for it until it was too late to debate them: "It is as though he were pulling out one by one the slides of a magic lantern, instead of developing the policy of a great nation."[39] This was in response to Disraeli's comment that Russia's expansion of influence in Central Asia left them only a few days march from India's northern frontier – hardly, Lowe and others pointed out, a strategic matter that could be countered by the symbolic action of making Queen Victoria an empress.

Throughout this period the rhetoric of the opposition, both in the debates and in the leaders of *The Times*, was infused with such words as "designs," "intrigues," "secret," "scheme," "manipulation," "veil," "beguiled," "corrupt," "parasitical," and "parvenue." The cumulative effect of such language is to suggest that Disraeli, through the mechanism of the Royal Titles Bill, is engaged in a subversion of the constitution for nefarious, if unclear, ends. The climax of these suspicions was the speech of the Duke of Somerset when the bill was first debated in the House of Lords. He began by saying that he desired "to raise the veil of Asiatic mystery, which has been drawn over this proposition, and to exhibit … [it] as it appears when unadorned by any such contrivance."[40] The duke believed that the bill was "contrary to the spirit of the Constitution," but his allusion to "the veil of Asiatic mystery" immediately places Disraeli's actions and motives in the context of the reactions to *Tancred; or the New Crusade*, and in particular, perhaps, recalls the characterization of the adventurer, Fakredeen, whose flattery and intrigues hide a vaunting ambition. That would seem to be the import of the duke's continuation when he said: "The Prime Minister is a man of brilliant genius and a man of Oriental imagination ... given to vagaries of a wild and poetical character." But the accusation that Disraeli and the Queen resented was the charge that he had "become intoxicated by the atmosphere of the Court, and, desirous of paying to Her Majesty a great compliment, he thought nothing would do so well as to make her an Empress." However proud he was of *Tancred* at the time he wrote it, and however much the politics of 1876 took the form of a romance in his imagination, Disraeli no doubt found it irritating to have the affairs of state and his role as the Queen's devoted minister some thirty years later seen in the reductive light of the of his most extravagant fiction. Yet for those who in 1876 were suspicious of Disraeli's motives, *Tancred* contains a scene that seems a startling, if bizarre vision of "the greatest empire that ever existed." In chapter 3 of Book 4 the ever conspiring Fakredeen tells Tancred:

> "the game is in our hands, if we have energy. There is a combination which would entirely change the whole face of the world, and bring back empire to the East ... the Queen will listen to what you say; especially if you talk to her as you talk to me. ... You will magnetise the Queen as you have magnetised me ... one thing is clear, it is finished with England ... The game is up ... Now see a *coup d'etat* that saves all ... quit a petty and exhausted position for a vast and prolific empire. Let the Queen of the English collect a great fleet, let her stow away all her treasure, bullion, gold plate, and precious arms; be accompanied by all her court and chief people, and transfer the seat of her empire from London to Delhi. There she will find an immense empire ready made ... In the meantime I will arrange with Mehemet Ali. He shall have Bagdad and Mesopotamia and pour Bedoueen cavalry into Persia. I will take care of Syria and Asia Minor ... We will acknowledge the Empress of India as our suzerain, and secure for her the Levantine coast. If she like, she shall have Alexandria as she now has Malta: it could be arranged ... the only difficult part, the conquest of India, which baffled Alexander, is all done!"[41]

As chapter 12 has shown, Disraeli's characterization of Fakredeen is satirical. So from the authorial perspective this "combination" that makes Victoria the empress of India is just romantic hyperbole. Long before the end of the novel Fakredeen is shown to be an untrustworthy and delusional opposite of the noble, eponymous hero. The difficulty is that this conspiratorial alter-ego of the protagonist is recognizably an extravagant version of one side of his author's youthful personality. Thus in 1876 the allusions to this "curious" passage from *Tancred* in both Parliament and *The Times*[42] helped express the deep distrust of Disraeli by those who had all along seen him as an unscrupulous "adventurer." Even as satire, a Disraelian hero magnetizing the Queen seemed in retrospect a most dangerous idea, the more so because the author was now himself prime minister. The most fearful members of the Opposition were thus convinced that Disraeli was "the Mephistopheles of statesmanship."[43]

II

The third notable instance of the way in which Disraeli's imagination shaped the conduct of parliamentary business after 1874 is his handling of what became known as the Eastern question. This comprised the English reaction to the Bulgarian atrocities in 1876, the Government's attempts to defend British interests in the Russo-Turkish war that followed, and Disraeli's role in the Congress of Berlin. His opponents at the time, and unsympathetic historians since, believed that the British Government's response to the Turks' savage suppression of the rebellion of their Christian subjects in the Balkans in the summer of 1875 was largely shaped by the prime minister's love of Eastern exoticism. Their presumption was that his youthful expressions of admiration of the Turks' despotic rulers, first developed during his Mediterranean tour of 1830–1, had been carried forward as a disinclination to believe the brutal reality of the atrocities committed by Turkish mercenaries as the rebellion of the Slavic populations of Herzegovina and Bosnia spread throughout the Balkan states. But Disraeli's response to these events was nothing so simple or reductive. In the spring of 1875 he had been much concerned with the belligerence toward Belgium and France shown by Germany's Chancellor Bismarck. It was, he thought, essential to counteract the influence of the Dreikaiserbund (the alliance of the Governments in St Petersburg, Vienna, and Berlin) and so prevent the possibility of another European war. In early May, months before the Balkan controversy erupted, he had written to Lord Derby, the Foreign Secretary, "My own impression is that we should construct some concerted movement to preserve the peace of Europe, like Pam did when he baffled France and expelled the Egyptians from Syria. There might be an alliance between Russia and ourself for this special purpose; and other powers, as Austria, and perhaps Italy might be invited to accede."[44] As this suggests, Disraeli was anxious to have England take an active role in the affairs of Europe and so protect those British commercial and strategic interests that would be threatened by war.

In this context the state of the Ottoman Empire had been of concern for some time. It was becoming clear that the Porte was on the verge of bankruptcy with large debts held by British investors. At that time Turkish rule extended well into Europe, including what is now Bulgaria, Albania, Serbia, Montenegro, Bosnia, and northern Greece. As Blake notes, in 1875 the Turks' rulers had "the spiritual authority of the popes, combined all too often with the moral outlook of the more deplorable Roman emperors." As a result, the "cruelty and corruption of the ré-gime were tempered only by incompetence."[45] The misrule was at its worst in the European part of the Turkish Empire, for there Christians were treated as inferior subjects, fit only for exploitation. These Orthodox Christians were mostly Slavic people, who naturally looked to Russia for a sense of common ethnic identity. Thus, when the rebellion broke out in Herzegovina in July and quickly spread to Bosnia and later Bulgaria, and attempts to suppress it failed, the British Government was faced with the prospect that Russia and her partners would interfere to settle the matter of the sultan's Balkan possessions among themselves. From Disraeli's perspective, even though he could contemplate Britain's cooperation with Russia to preserve the peace, the danger of any attempt to break up the Turkish Empire was not just that war would be disruptive. He thought that it would increase the likelihood of Russian expansion that could, in some alarmist scenarios, threaten Britain's control of India. Fears of this sort, that Russian control of Constantinople could lead to their interference with the Suez Canal, for example, were quite unrealistic given the distances and terrain involved. But the belief that the Ottoman Empire was a bulwark against Russia's ambitions, and that its integrity must be maintained, was still, more than twenty years after the Crimean War, the strongest tenet of Conservative Eastern foreign policy. And it was this reasoning, as well as a general desire to reassert Britain's influence and diplomatic independence, that guided Disraeli's initial responses to the Eastern question in 1875 and 1876.

When the news of the massacres of Christians that came to be called "the Bulgarian atrocities" was first published in the *Daily News* towards the end of June 1876, there was not, at first, much reaction. Certainly Gladstone, who had resigned the leadership of his party and retreated to his estate at Hawarden after his Government's defeat in 1874, had no immediate sense of a significant political opportunity. Nor had Disraeli or Lord Derby any sense of how events in the Balkans would affect the English electorate and soon create an impending crisis for the Government. In May 1876 Disraeli's assertive foreign policy, including the outright rejection of the Imperial Powers' Berlin Memorandum and the sending of a British fleet to Besika Bay, had enjoyed wide public support. These moves, diplomatic and military, were Disraeli's way of insisting that England would not accept a subsidiary role in the sorting out of the mess that Turkey had continued to make of her empire since the end of the Crimean War and the Treaty of Paris, and that England was prepared to use all means at her command to defend her interests in the region. Not the least of these interests in Disraeli's view was thwarting any hopes Russia had of expanding her sphere of influence. The Berlin Memorandum, drawn up by Austria, Germany, and Russia without prior consultations with England, France, and Italy, called for an armistice in the Balkans fighting, financial relief and reconstruction of the destroyed villages, and the implementation of various administrative reforms similar to those that had been suggested in the so-called Andrássy Note of December 1875. The danger perceived by Disraeli was that the memorandum also threatened Turkey with "efficacious measures" should the armistice expire without the objects of the powers being obtained. The note of explanation he drew up and read to the cabinet of 16 May 1876 makes clear how pragmatic his concerns at the time were. He believed, he said, that it was "impossible for the Sultan to reconstruct the houses and churches of the insurgents, or to find food for the refugees." The distribution of relief by such a means as the commission the memorandum proposed would, he thought, be "a huge system of indiscriminate almsgiving totally beyond the power of the Porte to effect" and thus "utterly demoralising." The concentration of troops in certain places, designed to avoid unnecessary clashes with residents, Disraeli added, "would be delivering up the whole country to anarchy," and the proposed "consular supervision" would "reduce the authority of the Sultan to a nullity." Finally, he concluded, when "the hope of restoring tranquillity by these means" proved "groundless," the "efficacious measures in the interests of peace" would turn out to be measures "to break up the Empire."[46] So rather than sanction the Dreikaiserbund in "putting a knife to the throat of Turkey," Disraeli proposed, if Turkey agreed, to recommend an armistice and a European Conference based upon "the territorial *status quo*." Disraeli's critics would later argue that the cabinet's unanimous decision not to adhere to the proposals in the Berlin Memorandum was a serious mistake, but at the time the Government's action was accepted by the country and the leaders of the Opposition (Lords Hartington and Granville) as a "prudent and dignified course."[47]

The sensational accounts in the *Daily News*[48] of the massacre of many thousands of Bulgarian men, women, and children, with horrific details of widespread rape, sodomy, torture, and arson, excited a strong revulsion in England. Many people, but especially non-conformists, responded to the news in the light of their Christian conscience and High Victorian moral sensibility. Almost immediately there was a spread of agitation in the country to provide relief for Christian victims still alive and to condemn publicly the Turks' immoral brutality and the British Government's support for the Ottoman Empire. As Shannon has pointed out, the "crisis of conscience" that ensued arose from the perception that the Government's attempt to protect Turkey from the coercions of the European powers had made England an accessory to the atrocities. Disraeli was suspicious of the *Daily News* because of its political and personal hostility, and, as he told Lady Bradford, he was inclined to believe that the accounts of the "horrors," which appeared in that paper alone, were "to a great degree, inventions" whose object was "to create a cry against the Government."[49] The situation was made worse when Disraeli relied on incorrect assurances from Henry Elliot, the ambassador in Constantinople, and played down the seriousness of events in Bulgaria. He even went so far as to say that he doubted that "torture has been practised on a great scale among oriental people who seldom … resort to torture, but generally terminate their connection with culprits in a more expeditious manner."[50] And when, in the House of Commons debate of 31 July, Gladstone accused the Government of withholding a consular report on the atrocities, Disraeli replied that the statistics it contained were unreliable and exaggerated, and that he had "never adopted that coffee-house babble brought by a Bulgarian to the Vice-Consul as authentic information which we ought to receive."[51] Richard Millman's detailed discussion of the situation in Bulgaria, and of the various diplomatic reports from the region,[52] indicates that the numbers of people allegedly killed were in fact exaggerated, unreliable estimates often based on faulty assumptions about the population of the villages and usually taken from one side or the other. There were, he points out, murders and outrages committed by both sides, and in some cases the most inflammatory reports of atrocities proved to be inventions. Millman also quotes Walter Baring's report to Elliot (1 August) to the effect that the Russian vice-consul in the area had played a significant role in starting the Christian insurgency.[53] But at the time, even in context, Disraeli's remarks seemed to many to be deplorably flippant and when repeated and taken out of context, they could be interpreted as callous by those who were alarmed by the horrifying accounts of the massacres in the newspapers.

Most of Gladstone's speech on 31 July did not focus on the question of the atrocities, except as they suggested to him that the Government had a moral duty to act in concert with the European powers to coerce the Turks into granting their Christian subjects religious and administrative autonomy. He tried to use the Crimean War and its results as a parable from which he could assert Britain's moral responsibility to use "the weight of authority" rather than "friendly advice" in this regard, but in the end he did little more than express his distrust of both the Turks and the Conservative Government: "The principles of civil society as they are understood in Europe are not understood in Turkey, are not embraced in the Ottoman faith ... I have come to the conclusion that the administration of its provinces on the old footing is a task which ... we must now ... admit the Porte is incompetent to fulfil ... It was an error to reject the [Berlin] Memorandum instead of making it the basis of communication with the Powers."[54] The prime minister was then able to reply with a detailed summary of the Government's actions, going over again the reasons for their responses to the Andrássy Note and the Berlin Memorandum, denying that in sending the fleet to Besika Bay his intention had been to signal his unqualified support for Turkey, and insisting that his purpose was, rather, to "maintain the interests of England and the British Empire." Britain's actions, he said, had brought the other powers to adopt the Government's policy of non-interference and neutrality, and they were now prepared to act with Britain, when the opportunity arose, to establish peace and work towards the improvement of the population living under Turkish rule. Apart from his unwise use of the phrase, "coffee-house babble," and a repetition of the absurd claim that "secret societies and revolutionary committees" were "unceasingly at work in these affairs," Disraeli closed the debate on what seemed a triumphant note.[55]

Any sense of gratification to be drawn from this conclusion was, however, short-lived. Baring, who had been sent out to the Balkans to investigate the "atrocities" sent in a preliminary report in early August, which made it clear that there had indeed been appalling massacres in the region, with an estimated 12,000 victims.[56] Meanwhile, Disraeli was not in good health and was finding the burden of leading the Government in the House of Commons too much to bear. The Queen insisted that he should accept a peerage, and so Disraeli became the Earl of Beaconsfield when the parliamentary session ended, and henceforth led the Government from the House of Lords. It is interesting, especially in recalling the allusion in the title of the *Vindication of the English Constitution in a letter to a noble and learned Lord,* that the title he chose is the same one that King George III had wanted to confer on Edmund Burke. Disraeli's last speech in the Commons on 11 August was a reiteration of the theme of Britain's imperial destiny, but the agitations throughout the country did not subside. The meetings of protest, stimulated by the newspaper reports, grew larger and more frequent; the cabinet was divided on the subject of foreign policy; and the situation in Constantinople was unstable. At the end of the month the new sultan was deposed in favour of his notoriously tyrannical half-brother; and the Turkish armies were proving unexpectedly victorious in the war with Serbia, thus making the Porte intransigent about reforms and raising the likelihood of Russian intervention. Disraeli, far from being perturbed at that prospect, now anticipated that there would eventually be a joint invasion by Russia and Austria-Hungary, and he contemplated a leading role for England in bringing about peace and determining the resultant partition of territories among the European powers.[57]

It was in this context that Gladstone suddenly awoke to the realization that, as he put it, "the game was afoot and the question yet alive," and "that the iron was hot and the time to strike had arrived."[58] On 29 August he told Lord Granville: "Good ends can rarely be attained in politics without passion: and there is now, the first time for a good many years, a virtuous passion." Shannon has argued that this, rather than the horror of the atrocities themselves, was what "excited Gladstone most profoundly," because he saw that it could restore "the moral rapport between himself and the masses which the defeat of 1874 had snapped."[59] Certainly, Granville and his Liberal co-leader, Lord Hartington, were less than enthusiastic about the idea of Gladstone's political crusade, for they thought that he and his friends were "'rather exaggerating' the government's share of responsibility for the atrocities."[60] But Gladstone was heedless of their caution and launched into the writing of a pamphlet, *Bulgarian Horrors and the Question of the East,* which he completed in five days and published on 5 September.[61] It was a sensational success: 40,000 copies were sold in the first week, and by the end of September the total had reached an astounding 200,000.

Despite the excitement, the central argument it contained was nothing new. As his comments to Henry Broadhurst and Lord Granville indicate, Gladstone's intention was to exploit and politicize the atrocities agitation in England. His avowed aim was to focus public opinion on the need to get the Government to reverse its course and act in concert with the other European powers to remove the Turks' administrative control of Bulgaria. But Gladstone's language was often violent, clearly a reflection of how the reports of the atrocities had captured his mind, and of how his excitable nature responded to the opportunity he now saw of wresting the initiative on foreign policy out of the hands of the "Evil Genius" (58).[62] Indeed, two rhetorical features of the pamphlet stand out. The first is the extent to which Gladstone's indignation was stimulated by the reports of widespread rape of Christian women occurring as part of the general mayhem and slaughter and no doubt meant as an instrument of demoralization. Gladstone repeatedly characterizes the Turks as "the one great anti-human specimen of humanity" (13) and he does this with sexual language that links the massacres and rapes in Bulgaria to the stereotypical fantasy of "the lustful Turk": they are men of "abominable and bestial lust" (33), "of unbounded savagery ... [and] unbridled and bestial lusts" (53), who indulge in "fell Satanic orgies" (53).[63] This kind of language has much in common with the anti-Turk fulminations of Thomas Carlyle going back as far as the Crimean War, though it is also worth noting that Carlyle's letter to the press (24 November 1876) giving his views on the Eastern question is clearly indebted for some of its phrases to Gladstone's pamphlet.

Gladstone's desire to end Turkish control of Bulgaria was reasonable enough, but he gets carried away when he phrases this as compelling the Turks to "one and all, bag and baggage ... clear out from the province they have desolated and profaned" (61). This "thorough riddance" and "most blessed deliverance" he then describes as "the only reparation ... [the British] can make," not just to "those heaps and heaps of dead," but also to "the violated purity alike of matron, of maiden, and of child" (62). And perhaps it is not entirely paradoxical that the word he uses to describe the Turkish government's inability to fulfil its promises of reform is "impotent" (63). There is warrant in Gladstone's character for recognizing such language as yet another manifestation (like his rescue work with prostitutes and its attendant self-flagellations) of his public sexual excitability. Such words also suggest that the emotionally violent language of this pamphlet, however much it is consciously meant to intensify the reader's outraged response to the terrible news from Bulgaria, is itself an imaginatively displaced form of his own aggression. This was widely recognized at the time by those who, from either temperament or political perspective, resisted the pull of Gladstone's rhetoric.

However much Gladstone said he loathed the "bestial" Turk, the real and immediate object of his hostility was the prime minister, and this is the second rhetorical feature of his pamphlet. Again and again it returns to an indictment of Disraeli and his Government. The most potentially damaging of Gladstone's accusations is the one that derives from the universal revulsion occasioned by the news of the atrocities: that in the "moral and material support ... afforded to the Turkish government," Disraeli has led the English people into a "moral complicity with the basest and blackest outrages upon record within the present century, if not within the memory of man" (12, 9). But Gladstone's desire to punish Disraeli for this moral failure led him to other accusations that reflect the narrow, partisan, political motives behind the pamphlet. Disraeli, he thought, had, through denials and delays, manipulated Parliament in order to deprive the House of Commons of its "legitimate share of influence" and "jurisdiction in the case." In making this accusation Gladstone characterized the public agitation as the nation taking "its most sacred duties ... primarily into its own hands," rather than see them "unperformed" (11). The nation, he said, "must ... teach its Government, almost as it would teach a lisping child, what to say. *Then* will be taken out of the way of an united Europe the sole efficient obstacle to the punishment of a gigantic wrong" (11). On 9 September, while addressing a large crowd at Blackheath, Gladstone used language similar to that of the pamphlet in repeating his accusations. There he spoke of "the floodgates of lust" and the Turks' "dire refinements of cruelty," and said that there could be no end to the agitation against the Government "until atonement had been made, until punishment had descended, until justice had been vindicated" by driving out "those armies of Asiatic hordes that are now desolating Servia."[64] Such language suggests not only the personal and political motives behind Gladstone's attacks, but also the extent to which they are a compensation for his sense of political helplessness prior to his sudden awakening and since. Indeed, he would later admit that his belated leadership in the agitation was entirely motivated by a desire to dislodge his rival's hold on power: "for the last 18 months I may be said to have played the part of an agitator ... My purpose ... has been ... to the best of my power ... day and night, week by week, month by month, to counterwork as well as I could what I believe to be the purpose of Lord Beaconsfield."[65] Not surprisingly Disraeli read this simply as jealousy. The next day he would write to Lady Bradford from 10 Downing Street: "I am glad you had time to read Gladstone's speech. What an exposure! The mask has fallen and instead of a pious Christian, we find a vindictive fiend who confesses he has, for a year and a half, been dodging and manoeuvring against an individual – because he was a successful rival!"[66]

Disraeli's view of Gladstone was the obverse of Gladstone's view of him. His sense that Gladstone was exploiting the public's horror at the Bulgarian atrocities (with its attendant religious and sexual *frissons*) for personal political gains found expression in his repeated characterization of him as a hypocrite, "a ceaseless Tartuffe."[67] But, as Disraeli well knew, the dynamic of governing was very different from that of leading the Opposition and he had more to worry about than their mutual distrust of one another. Three other aspects of Britain's response to the Eastern question were more significant and posed deeper challenges to Disraeli's Government. The first was the fact that the cabinet was seriously divided as to both general policy and strategic initiatives, as the threat of a European war grew larger. Disraeli's intention was to defend "the permanent interests of England," which, he was convinced, would be endangered if the Ottoman Empire suddenly collapsed and the European powers took advantage of the moment to expand their own territories and influence. In this respect Disraeli felt that it was essential to prevent Russia's expansion, and, especially to prevent her from gaining control of Constantinople, which he saw as potentially a direct threat to Britain in the Mediterranean and hence to England's control of the Suez route to India. Sceptics then and since have argued that even if Russia had occupied Constantinople she would not have posed a military threat to the Suez Canal, but Disraeli had good reason to fear that Russia had designs on both the Bosphorous and Dardanelles as well as on the European states under Turkish rule. He knew from reliable diplomatic sources that General Nicholas Ignatieff, Russia's ambassador to Constantinople, had been actively fomenting the revolts in Serbia, Montenegro, Bosnia, and Bulgaria, and that Ignatieff favoured a policy of threatening war, not only against Turkey, but also other European countries, if necessary, in order to achieve Russia's complete control of the Balkan states.[68]

Disraeli believed there were two paramount issues in foreign policy: that it was essential to prevent the other European powers from excluding Britain from any settlement of the Eastern question, and that it was essential to thwart any plans that Russia had to occupy Constantinople and to dominate the Balkans. In his view the first of these goals required an active and aggressive policy in which Britain insisted on a central role for herself in stopping the Balkan conflicts, while the latter required that Britain be prepared to threaten Russia with war in the event that she took actions that undermined British interests. Disraeli was willing to consider an alliance with Austria, or even with Russia herself, if it would further his objectives, but also to go beyond diplomatic overtures and use the Mediterranean fleet and garrisons to signal his firm resolve, if the situation warranted such moves. And all the while there was the complicated matter of trying to persuade the Turks that they must accept the necessity of taking decisive actions to remove the grievances of their Christian subjects, and not count on British support should they fail to do so and so precipitate a war with either Austria or Russia, or both. The difficulty was that Lord Derby, the Foreign Secretary, preferred a minimalist policy and refused to take any diplomatic initiatives of an aggressive kind, while some other members of the cabinet, especially Lord Carnarvon, were equally opposed to any decisions or measures that they thought might lead Britain towards war.

In this context, Disraeli was faced not only with having his difficulties "aggravated" by, what he called, "the treasonable conduct of that wicked maniac Gladstone,"[69] but also with the extraordinary situation in which Lady Derby, with her husband's knowledge and tacit consent, if not encouragement, pursued a peace policy directly at odds with the strategy of the prime minister by repeatedly revealing the dissensions of the cabinet to the Russian ambassador in London, Count Schuvalov, with whom she had developed friendly relations. Disraeli thus had to take into account the fact that Prince Gorchakov, the Russian Foreign Minister in St Petersburg, was fully informed about the internal conflicts over Britain's Eastern policy almost as soon as they arose. This leaking of confidential information became notorious and was eventually the subject of explicit comment, both within the cabinet and by the Queen. But through all of 1876 and 1877, despite a continuous sense of being thwarted by his Foreign Secretary, Disraeli felt it was essential to keep Lord Derby in the cabinet to avoid an open and probably disastrous splitting of his party.

With the collapse of the Constantinople Conference in January 1877 and the beginning of Russia's war against Turkey the following April, the question of what Britain was prepared to do to forestall the Russians occupying the Turkish capital and gaining control of the Bosphorous

and Dardanelles became an urgent matter. Even before the Russo-
Turkish war began, there were well-placed fears in England that Russia
and Austria had secretly agreed to a compact of mutual support in the
event of war. Disraeli had no doubt that the Russian army would eventually defeat the Turks and, meanwhile, he found it frustrating in the
extreme to conduct diplomatic negotiations with Austria, Germany,
and Russia without a unified cabinet behind a decisive policy. He
thought that the only way of containing Russia's expansion was to
issue a direct warning that Britain would fight to protect her interests in
the region, coupled with suitable military demonstrations of her willingness to do so. The cabinet, however, for many months could not be
brought to agree on anything like such a step. In this context it is interesting to see how Disraeli's relationship with Queen Victoria played a
significant and determining role in the resolution of diplomatic paraly-
sis that had afflicted the Government over the past eighteen months.

Disraeli's opponents and enemies thought it probable that his flattery of the Queen would produce serious mischief by giving her an
unreasonable sense of her own powers. But the narrative of the minister entirely devoted to the wishes of his royal mistress that shapes
Disraeli's correspondence and conversations with Victoria suggests
that he never lost sight of the distinction between the fiction and the
reality and that the chivalric romance served his own strategic purposes. It is certainly true that Disraeli kept the Queen informed about the
conflicts in the cabinet and the strategies of parliamentary debate in
more dramatic, gossipy detail than any of his predecessors had done,
but he did so, in large measure, to ensure the alignment of her sympathies with his policies. He intuitively understood that, as both monarch
and woman, she would respond well to the drama of beleaguered patriotism and the expressions of empathy that they could share. He
understood that, though the Queen's constitutional powers were much
diminished from those of her ancestors, and much less than she might
like to imagine, there was a great advantage to having her as an ally in
his political struggles, both within the Conservative party and against
his political opponents, as well as in conducting diplomatic negotiations with other countries. Disraeli's relationship with the Queen was
the very antithesis of Gladstone's. Where he was personal and sympathetic, Gladstone was formal and distant, and perhaps even condescending. The Queen famously complained that Gladstone always
addressed her as if she were a public meeting.[70] But her dislike of
Gladstone was not merely a matter of tactless tone and style. She had

resented his opposition to the Royal Titles Bill, and now she was "infuriated" by his moral crusade and his neglect of what Disraeli, in his speech at Aylesbury during the Bucks by-election, had called "the permanent and important interests of England."[71] The Queen shared fully her prime minister's suspicion of Russia's intentions, as well as his view that Gladstone's words and actions were reckless in their disregard of the Government's attempts to prevent a European war.

Queen Victoria's political support for Disraeli can be illustrated not just by their correspondence and the accounts of their conversations in his letters to Lady Bradford, but in the way Her Majesty's influence was brought to bear on the fractious cabinet. In the spring of 1877, as war between Russia and Turkey seemed inevitable and the cabinet seemed incapable of reaching a consensus, the Queen became passionately consumed with the threat that Russia posed to British interests. The situation was inflamed, just a month before the outbreak of war, when General Ignatieff concluded his tour of European capitals with a visit to London in mid-March and was invited to Hatfield by Lord Salisbury, who had been his counterpart at the Constantinople Conference. Much to the Queen's dismay the general and his very handsome and flirtatious wife also found a ready welcome among those of Gladstonian views. Disraeli told Lady Bradford that he was receiving "telegrams and letters" from "Head Quarters" about the visit "every hour."[72] By the middle of April, with the situation continuing to deteriorate, and just days before Russia's declaration of war on Turkey, the Queen decided (whether with Disraeli's concurrence, or at his suggestion, is not clear) to compose a letter that was to be read to the cabinet at its next meeting. In both its tone and substance it is a remarkable document.

Her Majesty began by insisting that the "present moment ... of great gravity" must be met with "calmness, firmness and complete unanimity" for "any difference of opinion, if known, would encourage the Opposition in their harassing, tho' hitherto fruitless, attacks on the Government." But the Queen's concern was really Britain's vital interests and welfare, so it was necessary, she thought, not to carry caution and prudence so far as to give "the appearance of feebleness and vacillation":

> The Queen appeals to the feelings of patriotism which she knows animate her Government, and is certain that every member of it will feel the absolute necessity of showing a bold and united front to the enemy in the country as well as outside it.

No time should be lost or wasted in deliberating on the best steps to be taken in this momentous crisis.

It is not the question of upholding Turkey; it is the question of Russian or British supremacy in the world![73]

Such a coercive letter, with its characterization of the parliamentary Opposition as the "enemy in the country," and with its didactic assertion of the "absolute necessity" of a bold policy and cabinet unity, all in the name of patriotism, took the Queen well beyond both the conventions of parliamentary government and her constitutional authority. Disraeli told her that the reading of her letter "produced a marked effect," as no doubt it did. But in some cases it was not the effect intended, for some of Disraeli's colleagues did not respond well to the royal initiative. But it is nevertheless clear that the Queen's articulation of the crisis as a climactic struggle with Russia for world supremacy was the epitome of Disraeli's belief that the Russians had to be contained within what Britain would define as their legitimate sphere of influence, which did not include the Mediterranean Sea or the Balkan States.

The Queen's letter had no discernible effect on the dissensions within the cabinet; indeed, over the next six months they got worse. Lords Derby, Carnarvon, and Salisbury continued to oppose Disraeli's idea of sending the Mediterranean fleet to the Dardanelles or Constantinople as a signal of Britain's determination to prevent Russia's domination of the area, while other members of the cabinet hoped for the support of Austria or the consent of Turkey before agreeing to take such action. At the heart of the disagreements about what Britain should do was a difference in reading Russia's intentions and a difference of opinion about whether clarity and firmness on Britain's part was more likely, or less likely, to lead her into a war with Russia. Disraeli understood that such differences in Britain were the parallel of similar ones in Russia, where the tsar was receiving conflicting advice from doves and hawks about what Russia should do and whether Britain would risk a repetition of the Crimean conflict. Ambassador Schuvalov, in London, was reassuring about Russia's peaceful intentions, but Disraeli and the Queen feared the influence and duplicity of General Ignatieff, surmising correctly that he would exploit any weakness or inability to act on England's part.[74]

Disraeli also knew that the cabinet's indecisiveness could lead to political defeat, especially if their disagreements led to resignations. On 25 May he wrote to Lord Derby, echoing the views of Hugh Cairns, the Lord Chancellor: "It is quite apparent, that Russia is trying to bridge over the few weeks, which will make her safe against any action of ours. She will then be potentially master of Constantinople and will arrange the passage of the Straits, as she and Germany please, and will snap her fingers at us. Then the Opposition will turn upon us, and our friends will join them."[75] In his reply the next day, Derby said that he did not at all share this sense of an impending crisis. For the moment, as he knew, the Opposition was as divided as the cabinet and Gladstone had found that his desire to attack the Government through a series of parliamentary resolutions had little support within the Liberal party. Moreover, the agitation over the Bulgarian atrocities had largely subsided and public opinion was shifting round to support of the Government's Eastern policy. But from Disraeli's point of view, the fact that there was also a noticeable Russophobia in the country suggested that the danger of public anger should Russia overwhelm the Turkish Empire and gain complete control of the Balkans was quite real. As a result, Disraeli felt that he had to take extraordinary measures to overcome Lord Derby's passivity. He wrote in secret and by "a trusty hand" to the new British ambassador to the Porte, Austen Henry Layard, suggesting that he attempt to get the sultan to invite Britain (without altering her official neutrality) to send her fleet to Constantinople and to occupy the Gallipoli peninsula as a "material guarantee of existing treaties," but with the promise "to evacuate this position at the termination of the war."[76]

Meanwhile the Queen, with Disraeli's encouragement, was also active in talking to individual cabinet ministers and ambassadors about her concerns and fears. Her Majesty's support was, however, something of a mixed blessing. Because she was "in the know" more than she had ever been and yet she was not really able to control or shape her ministers' decisions, her anxieties became obsessive. Disraeli found that he was the recipient of more royal advice than he needed or wanted and he also found that his political romance involved the constant burden of patiently responding to the Queen's sense of frustration. She would often write more than once a day and send telegrams as well. It was not just the frequency, but also the extremity of her anti-Russian views that were of concern, both to him and other members of the cabinet, some of whom were convinced that the Queen wanted war. Her letters to Disraeli over the next eight months do contain phrases that could give that impression. She refers, for example, to "Russia's false, hypocritical intrigues" and to "Russia's monstrous treachery," and at one point she confides to him: "Oh, if the Queen were a man, she would like to go and give those Russians, whose word one cannot believe, such a beating! We shall never be friends again till we have it out."[77] Her Majesty also frequently recurs to the theme of the country's honour, or lack of it, and her disgust at the opposition to strong measures within the cabinet. The policy of neutrality, she thought, was "fatal."[78] On several occasions she suggests in quite melodramatic language that if the situation were to continue, "her own first impulse would be to throw everything up, and to lay down the thorny crown": "She feels she cannot, as she before said, remain the Sovereign of a country that is letting itself down to kiss the feet of the great barbarians, the retarders of all liberty and civilisation that exists."[79] Such comments are, of course, not to be taken literally. What they reflect are the tensions within a constitutional monarchy, where the real power lies beyond the sovereign's command.

Disraeli, meanwhile, was pursuing a policy of realpolitik. He presciently assumed that, while Russia was at war with Turkey, any material assistance to Britain from Austria was unlikely. He also knew that formal military cooperation with Turkey was not possible, both because the Turks were suspicious of Britain's declared neutrality and because, in the light of the atrocities, an alliance with them would be repugnant to most Britons. The Russo-Turkish war posed a real threat to British interests, but Disraeli saw that his Government's formal neutrality was not just a liability, but could also be the basis for England brokering the terms of peace at its conclusion, provided that Russia could be stopped short of a total victory. The key to the Eastern question thus became a matter of getting the cabinet to define clearly what the British interests in the region were and of issuing a credible threat to Russia that if she harmed those interests Britain would declare war. Disraeli knew that if Russia miscalculated England's intentions there was a real chance that there would be another European war, but he believed that it was the lack of a firm stance on Britain's part in 1854 that had precipitated the Crimean conflict and all its suffering.

In the fall of 1877 it became clear that it was only a matter of time until the Turks would capitulate to the Russian army. The imminent possibility of such a collapse began to shape the sense of crisis among Disraeli's colleagues. There were further memoranda from the Queen urging the cabinet to adopt a unified, bold course,[80] but Disraeli concluded that he would eventually have to accept the resignations of Lord Derby and Lord Carnarvon. It was, however, essential, he thought, to keep the fracture to that minimum and keep Lord Salisbury in the Government. Salisbury, who had, on religious grounds, initially been favourably disposed to Russian administration of the Balkans, gradually came to see things from Disraeli's perspective: that Russian control of the straits was unacceptable and that it would be necessary to make the issue a *causus belli* to prevent it. Before that, however, Disraeli was able to get the cabinet to agree that Parliament should be recalled to vote the funds for military preparations that would render Britain's position credible, while at the same time he explained to the Queen that the timing of Lord Derby's departure had to be managed within the crisis so that there would be no other defections (beyond Carnarvon's) and no public dissatisfaction that would give the Opposition grounds for attacking his ministry. An armistice between the Russian and Turkish armies was signed on 31 January 1878, but, as Disraeli suspected they would, the Russians continued to advance for another week, eventually stopping just short of the Turkish capital. Disraeli told the Queen that "the whole affair of the armistice is a comedy" and the news on 7 February that Russian troops were on the outskirts of Constantinople produced a panic on the London Stock Exchange.[81] The same day Disraeli reported that the approaches to Westminster were "thronged with excited crowds cheering him as he made his way through them from Downing Street to the House of Lords."[82] The parliamentary opposition to the six-million-pound vote of credit collapsed and the cabinet finally agreed to order a division of the fleet to Constantinople to "protect the life and property of British subjects" in the event of turmoil in the Turkish capital. Meanwhile, with a popular music-hall refrain, the British public's patriotic fervour and support for the Government found its voice in jingoism: "We don't want to fight, but by Jingo, if we do, / We've got the ships, we've got the men, we've got the money too!"

Despite the swing of public opinion in favour of the ministry, Disraeli found that his Government's situation with regard to Russia remained perilous for the next two weeks. For fear of angering the Russians, the Turks were unwilling to provide any sanction for the movements of the British fleet, and the Russians threatened to send troops into Constantinople, if the British fleet moved into position there. Meanwhile the British Government was attempting to gain the support of Italy, France, and Austria for some concerted naval action. Russia, of course, interpreted the idea of protecting "the life and property of British subjects" as no more than a weak excuse for Britain's real intentions, about which they continued to be informed by Count Schuvalov's reports of what Lady Derby told him. In an exchange of diplomatic notes Britain tried to convince the Russians that their fleet posed no threat, but that any movement of Russian soldiers into Constantinople or toward Gallipoli would force Britain to abandon her neutrality.[83] Meanwhile the cabinet was meeting every day and Britain's plans for sending an expeditionary force to Turkey, if it should be necessary, went ahead. It was a game of bluff that could easily have ended in a war that neither side really wanted. That it did not was, ironically, in part the result of the friendship between Lord Derby and Count Schuvalov and in part the effect of the action taken on their own authority by Ambassador Layard and Admiral Hornby at the scene of dispute. Because they both wanted to maintain peace and trusted and liked one another, Derby and Schuvalov were able to work together to, as Millman puts it, "douse," what they took to be "the ardour for war in London and St. Petersburg." For his part Schuvalov "dwelt on the financial embarrassments of his own Government" and "the absence of any desire on the part of Russia to go to war with England." Derby in turn bolstered the known determination of Disraeli and the Queen with the argument that in the event of such a war, Austria might well decide to side with Britain. There was no certainty of this, but both men hoped to convince their principals that it would be unwise to take any step that would provoke the other. At the same time, responding to threats from Russia, the Porte pleaded with Layard to have the fleet removed some ten miles farther away from Constantinople, an action that he and the admiral took on their own responsibility.

On the afternoon of 16 February, after a private conversation with Count Schuvalov, Lord Derby, in the form of a telegram to his embassies that was to be conveyed to the respective Governments, revived the idea of a European conference to settle the terms of peace between Russia and Turkey. "The immediate assembling of the Conference seemed to Her Majesty's Government," he said, "to promise the only satisfactory issue from the present political complications" and he urged "that all the neutral Powers should join without delay in pressing on the Russian Government that it should be forthwith convened."[84] France, Italy, and Austria all promptly agreed and pressed the Russian Government to accept the convening of a congress on neutral ground. Russia's response, however, was indirect and came in the form of a telegram from Prince Gorchakov to Lord Derby to the effect that "the Imperial Cabinet maintains its promise not to occupy Gallipoli nor to enter the lines of Bulair," and that it "expects, in return that no British troops should be landed on the Asiatic or European coast [of the Straits]."[85] When the British cabinet agreed to accept this quid pro quo, the possibility of war seemed for the moment to have been significantly lessened, but when the Russian army continued to advance and then moved to set up their headquarters in the fishing village of San Stefano, just five miles from Constantinople, it seemed that Disraeli's suspicions of Russia were all too justified.

Indeed, the British fears of Russian duplicity were much exacerbated when the nature of Russia's demands from the Turks became known. General Ignatieff was in charge of Russia's negotiations with the Porte and this, too, led to considerable paranoia within the British diplomatic and military establishment, as it became clear that Russia proposed to take complete control of the Balkan states as well as of the Bosphorous and Dardanelles. Such an outcome, it was widely felt, would character-ize the British Government as powerless and would leave the Queen feeling humiliated. Disraeli's letters to Her Majesty in these weeks re-flect his awareness of this danger, which would almost certainly have political repercussions, but he writes to her less often at this time, even though he knows that she is feeling neglected. The sharp decline in the number of letters Disraeli writes to the Queen, from thirteen in January to only seven in February, in part simply reflects the pressure of events on his time, but it is also, in part, strategic, because he is working in se-cret, and on his own initiative, to try and arrange a concerted European response to the danger posed by Russia's aggressive posture.[86] The change, however, did not go unremarked, as is indicated in the follow-ing extract from one of his letters in which he pleads his exhaustion:

> "sometimes, Lord Beaconsfield feels that he can scarcely stem the torrent. It truly makes him miserable, that your Majesty should ever feel yourself neglected, and yet he is conscious all day, that, notwithstanding his heart and brain are at your Majesty's service, your Majesty must be sensible of some difference in the frequency and fulness of his communications. He humbly hopes your Majesty will be indulgent to him in this respect. He feels there is no devotion that your Majesty does not deserve, and he only wishes he had youth and energy to be the fitting champion of such an in-spiring Mistress as your Majesty."[87]

As is so often the case in his relations with the Queen, Disraeli here acknowledges her expectations, as monarch, to be fully informed. He does this, as he has done before, through the chivalric romance of the Faery Queen with all its mutual sense of their empathic connection, while at the same time he preserves his own political independence through secrecy and clandestine action, which are at the same time, for him, both prudential and psychological. By early March he is prepared to be more forthcoming and to take the Queen more fully into his plans. Several of the letters he then writes about the results of his "unofficial" negotiations with Austria, Italy, Greece, and France carry the heading "Secret," or "Most Secret," as if, indeed, to make the Queen belatedly his co-conspirator. On 2 March, after an audience at Windsor the day before, Disraeli even tells her, no doubt with delight at the suggestion of melodrama, "The plot thickens."[88] Four days later he writes again to tell her that he "hopes to bring about a league of Mediterranean powers to secure the independence of that sea. But this is a secret of secrets, and its success greatly depends on inviolable confidence. It must be managed, a great deal, by private communications with colleagues, and not be brought, at least, at present, before the entire Cabinet."[89] It is clear from this comment that Disraeli adopted private and secret discussions and diplomacy primarily as a means of overcoming his colleagues' dissent and preventing the Russians from knowing his plans. The secrecy extended not just to the proposed concerted action of a League of Mediterranean Powers, but also to negotiations with Count Andrássy for the mobilization of Austrian troops, to the possibility of purchasing ironclad ships from the Turkish navy and maintaining the navigability of the straits, and to the acquisition of another military base in the Mediterranean.

III

When the terms of the Treaty of San Stefano ending the war between Russia and Turkey became known at the beginning of March, the Russophobia in Britain ran dangerously high. Even in late February there had been violent clashes of demonstrators in Hyde Park and Gladstone's residence was the target of stone-throwing mobs. It now appeared that Ignatieff had scored a victory in his internal struggle with Gorchakov for influence with the tsar, and that, in addition to gaining new territory in Asia, Russia would indeed acquire or dominate all of the Balkan states through the creation of a great Bulgaria and have control of the Bosphorous and Dardanelles. For England these were unacceptable terms. The Government's supporters saw a "Big

Bulgaria" as likely to be soon converted to a "Little Russia"[90] and the public reaction was nasty. Lord Derby and his wife became the victims of much verbal abuse. Even some Conservative MPs engaged in the shameful behaviour of libelling Lady Derby with ribald verses charging her with infidelity to her husband with Count Schuvalov.[91] Perhaps needing to counter Ignatieff's influence and sensing that the situation could easily drift into a new war, Gorchakov moved to get the European powers to hold the previously suggested Congress at Berlin, to which they all quickly agreed. Disraeli knew, however, that it was essential to define the mandate of that congress in advance, lest, under Russian duress, it only ratify the terms of the peace that had been coerced from Turkey. Accordingly, he persuaded the cabinet that Britain's participation should be conditional on the whole Treaty of San Stefano being submitted to the Congress for its discussion and approval of any territorial changes in the Ottoman Empire.

Gorchakov and Bismarck had proposed to bring to the Congress only those parts of the treaty which affected the previous treaties of Paris in 1856 and London in 1871. And for several weeks in March, there was much confusion and speculation as to what Britain's refusal to meet under those terms would mean. Initially Disraeli tried to persuade the Queen and his colleagues that in such a case Russia would open direct negotiations with Britain, but once it became clear that Russia would reject these conditions, Disraeli knew that the whole matter of the Eastern question had reached a critical and decisive stage. It was his firm conviction that attempts at conciliation with Russia would be a drift towards war, and that peace could only be secured through a demonstration of Britain's strength. The idea of a League of Mediterranean Powers had not proved workable, nor had the negotiations with Austria led to any definite commitments of support, so at a series of cabinet meetings in mid- to late March Disraeli insisted that his colleagues authorize several steps to assert Britain's interests and power. These included "calling out the Reserves" as part of the preparations to mobilize an expeditionary force, the transfer of a large number of troops in India to staging areas in the Persian Gulf and the Mediterranean, and the acquisition of one or more new military stations ("new Gibraltars") that would facilitate any actions by land or sea in the region that British forces might be called upon to undertake.[92] When, on 27 March, the cabinet agreed to take these steps, Lord Derby resigned as Foreign Secretary[93] and was replaced by Lord Salisbury, who, after an earlier period of sharing Derby's and Lord Carnarvon's resistance to Disraeli's views, had come to agree with the prime minister that Britain should now take active measures to circumscribe Russia's influence and territorial ambitions.

Disraeli wanted to ensure that the steps the cabinet had agreed upon would have the maximum psychological effect at St Petersburg, so he insisted that for the moment the decision to move troops from India to the Mediterranean should be kept secret. Nonetheless, from Derby's conversations with Count Schuvalov, the Russians were aware that the Foreign Secretary's resignation had been the result of "measures resolved on by the Cabinet which he was not at liberty to tell the ambassador."[94] With a unified cabinet, and the active prosecution of his policy at the foreign office, Disraeli found that the very things that had been so problematic for his Government at the time of the atrocities agitation now worked in his favour. The majority of the press and public opinion were now strongly supportive of his Eastern policy. That and the Queen's known belligerence toward Russia, as well as the recognition of the cabinet's new unity, all had the effect of giving Russia the impression that Britain would indeed take whatever actions were necessary to defend her interests. At this point Disraeli used both publicity and secrecy in tandem to increase the pressure on Russia. The action of calling up the army reserves was announced to Parliament on the same day that Derby announced his resignation, 28 March, which, from a general sense of the insufficiency of his stated motive, led many people to speculate about the cabinet's other decisions and to assume that a declaration of war was imminent. For example, on information gleaned at the Russian embassy, the Rev. Malcolm MacColl, canon of Ripon and friend and ardent defender of Gladstone, wrote to the editor of the *Daily News* that Lord Derby had resigned because of the Government's decision to seize "a strategic point belonging to Turkey, possibly Gallipoli or Mitylene."[95] Meanwhile, General Ignatieff, who had gone to Vienna for the purpose, had had no more success than Disraeli in trying to get the Austrians to commit to an alliance. And when Salisbury sent a circular defending the British position on the Congress to all the European powers, and to the newspapers in their capitals, it was favourably received. The Russian Government thus found itself on the defensive and concluded that the only alternative to a war they could not win was direct negotiation with Britain over the terms on which the Congress would be held.

Disraeli's determination to force a drastic revision of the terms of the Treaty of San Stefano was underlined by the announcement on 17 April, just as Parliament was about to recess, that 7,000 troops would be moved from India to Malta. The strategy of keeping the decision secret until that moment was to increase the psychological pressure on the Russians as direct negotiations were developing and to avoid any lessening of that effect from criticism by the Opposition in Parliament. As Lord Derby's notes from the cabinet meeting of 27 March indicate, Disraeli suspected that the Russians were in no shape to fight another war, for their finances were in terrible shape and their army was weakened by disease and exhaustion.[96] By mid-April it was also beginning to seem that Ignatieff's success in extracting the harsh conditions of peace from the Turks was in fact a great mistake. As Blake put it, moderate people "began to see the Treaty of San Stefano not as a triumph of Panslav policy, but as the reckless seizure of a position which Russia could not relinquish without humiliation, but could not in the long run hold without a war against England and possibly Austria-Hungary, too."[97] Moreover, Serbia, Greece, and Montenegro were as unhappy with the treaty's creation of a huge Bulgaria stretching south to the Aegean and west to Albania as were the major European powers. And when Ignatieff failed to get Andrássy to commit to an Austrian alliance, it became clear that some accommodation with Britain was required.

The result of the direct negotiations, conducted on the Russian side by Schuvalov and on the English by Salisbury and Disraeli, was a series of agreements known as the Anglo-Russian Conventions. Russia realized that she would not be allowed to control the Straits and gave way to all the British concerns about Bulgaria, which was to be smaller and divided into two parts, a northern autonomous one and a southern one ruled by Turkey under strict guidelines. In return, after secret negotiations with the sultan about an Anglo-Turkish defensive alliance had led to the British acquisition of Cyprus, Britain conceded that Russia would keep most of the additional territories in Asia agreed to at San Stefano. It was also agreed, as Britain had insisted, that there could be no alterations in the terms of previous European treaties of Paris in 1856, and London in 1871, without the endorsement of the Congress. Thus, when, with Bismarck's mediation, both Russia and Britain agreed that they would withdraw from the immediate vicinity of Constantinople, the threat of war seemed to diminish, even though Gorchakov strung out the negotiation of the details of that withdrawal for several weeks while he still attempted to reach an alliance with Austria.[98]

In the face of Disraeli's and Salisbury's aggressive diplomacy and Britain's continuing preparations for war, those in opposition who favoured a policy of peace, rather than what they took to be provocation, found themselves hampered by the strength of public opinion now supporting the Government. And, as Millman points out, there were also those in the Liberal ranks who feared that the only real alternative to Disraeli's Government would be one led by Gladstone, whose overt absence of patriotism in the midst of the crisis they took to be a "lack of sanity."[99] In effect such an attitude towards Gladstone by some of those in his own party was a recognition by the official Liberal leaders, Hartington and Granville, that Disraeli's Government could not be successfully challenged on its foreign policy and that the domestic agitation over the atrocities that Gladstone had tried to exploit had lost its purchase as the result of the Russo-Turkish war and the Pan-Slav ambitions revealed by the terms of the Treaty of San Stefano. For his part Gladstone had welcomed the war as a sure sign that the end of Turkish misrule was imminent. The Russians, he thought, were doing God's work and he described the Treaty of San Stefano as a "glorious result." In Parliament there were not many Liberals who would go that far, and Gladstone often felt that there he was struggling alone against the "evil" of Disraeli's policy. Outside of Parliament, however, there were a group of Gladstonians quite willing to support his view of the Russians and take up the task of agitation. Among the most prominent of these were J.A. Froude and W.T. Stead, the latter of whom considered himself Gladstone's northern lieutenant. Their opinions of Disraeli were quite as extreme as Gladstone's and their language was less restrained. Stead, for example, characterized West-end London society, which was staunch in its support of the Government, as a "synagogue of Satan." And some of the minor figures in the Gladstonian circle, men such as E.A. Freeman, were even more overtly anti-Semitic, referring constantly to "the Jew and his tricks."

Stead, like Gladstone, was in regular correspondence with Madame Olga Novikoff,[100] who was determined to act as an unofficial emissary of the Russian Government. When she was in England, Madame Novikoff used all of her social skills to support Gladstone and to influence the British press to take a favourable view of Russia's actions and intentions. Her frequent letters to *The Times* and other newspapers, and her book, *Is Russia Right?* (published in London during the Russo-Turkish war), were extraordinary interventions into British politics. So much so, that Disraeli once sardonically referred to her as "the M.P. for Russia."[101] When she was in Moscow among her Pan-Slav enthusiasts, Madame Novikoff used all the information sent to her by her English

Liberal correspondents to persuade the Russian Government that they must give Disraeli no excuse for war. In so propagating the Gladstonian point of view in Russia, in particular the characterization of Disraeli as dangerous and intent on war, she no doubt unintentionally strengthened Disraeli's hand in the negotiations prior to the Congress. And it is hardly surprising, in the light of Gladstone's friendly interactions and correspondence with both Count Schuvalov and Madame Novikoff, that the patriotic or "Jingo Press" concluded that he had also been "working incessantly" in Russia's interests and thereby undermining the British Empire.[102] Indeed, while chairing a public meeting on 10 January 1878, the Duke of Sutherland, the son of Gladstone's old friend and confidante, Harriet, the Dowager Duchess, had publicly described him as a Russian agent.[103] This was also a view expressed in the forty or fifty abusive letters Gladstone received every day and at the dozens of raucous pro-Government meetings held throughout the country in February, at many of which effigies of "Gladstone the Traitor" were burned.[104] These patriotic "ebullition[s] of popular feeling in favour of the Government" Stead attributed to "a liberal allowance of torchlight processions, brass bands, bonfires, beer, and 'Rule Britannia.'"[105]

For his part Gladstone considered Disraeli's strategy reckless and wicked, but there was little he could do in a parliamentary way to thwart it once it was clear that the major European powers had all agreed to hold the Congress in Berlin. What Gladstone did do was continue his counter-work by attempting to sway public opinion with his pen. After reading the latest in the series of nasty, anti-Semitic attacks on Disraeli, entitled "The Political Adventures of Lord Beaconsfield," that had been appearing in the *Fortnightly Review*,[106] Gladstone began in the latter part of May to compose a piece for the *Nineteenth Century* entitled, "Liberty in the East and West."[107] The focus of the article was the Government's decision to move seven thousand Indian troops to the Mediterranean as a preparation for war. In Gladstone's view this move was "the very rashest measure that ever was adopted by a British Government" and, not at all surprisingly, his denunciation of it took the form of accusations that the Government had committed an "assault" on "the common law of England" and on "the Constitution" by using Indian soldiers as a standing army without the consent of Parliament. The "monstrous theory" that the Crown was free to use Indian troops in European wars was, he argued, a despotic "stretch of power" such that the House of Commons became "the tool and plaything of the Minister."[108] In Gladstone's view the relationship between Britain and

India ought to be that of a guardian and his ward, though he conceded that it was in reality that of a master and his subordinate. In the consideration of the likely military results and the financial implications of the Government's policy, he concluded that the "effusion of blood" and the misappropriation of Indian revenues would be "a gross and monstrous injustice" and that "those who are parties to its perpetration must prepare for the results to which injustice leads." Here, as in so many of his attacks on Disraeli, Gladstone's language is extreme, but in asking "Will India be content? Can India be content? Ought India to be content?" he seemed to the Government's supporters to be on the verge of inciting rebellion.[109]

Gladstone's frame of mind in the weeks before the Congress of Berlin continued to be much disturbed by the conviction that the prime minister was also violating Britain's constitution in his relations with the Queen. It was widely known that the very subject of Russia's intentions would provoke expressions of extreme hostility from Her Majesty and Gladstone was convinced that Disraeli was manipulating her feelings on the subject to his own advantage. The Queen's suspicions of Russia were, however, of much longer standing than the current crisis; indeed they went back to her conversations with Prince Albert at the time of the Crimean War. And in that regard they were not dissimilar to those absorbed and expressed by Disraeli as early as the 1840s in, for example, his conversations with King Louis Philippe during the visits to Paris, and in the words spoken by Sidonia in *Coningsby*. It is nonetheless true that in the crisis of 1878 Disraeli encouraged the Queen to think of herself as playing an active, central role that Gladstone and his supporters found profoundly disturbing. The day before he finished this article for the *Nineteenth Century*, Gladstone's diary records under the heading "Secret" a conversation he had that day with Lord Carnarvon on the subject of the Queen's interference in the affairs of government: "It has happened repeatedly not only that Cabinet ministers have been sent for to receive 'wiggings' from the Queen ... but communications have from time to time been made to the Cabinet warning it off from certain subjects and saying she could not agree to this and could not agree to that ... I said that such an outrage as this was wholly new, totally unknown in every Cabinet in which I had served, and that the corruption must be regarded as due to Lord Beaconsfield ... "[110] It was not surprising then that the unauthorized publication of a summary of the Anglo-Russian agreement between Schuvalov and Salisbury in the *Globe* on 30 May and the announcement five days later that Britain's plenipotentiaries at the Congress were to be Disraeli and Lord Salisbury caused much consternation among the members and supporters of the Liberal Opposition. The general fear was that, should questions of deep and momentous importance need to be decided, Disraeli, the "adventurer," could not be trusted not to let his "Semitic" or Turkophile prejudices prevail. In Parliament, the concern expressed by Lords Granville, Hartington, and Grey[111] was that such an unprecedented arrangement would deprive other members of the cabinet of their collective responsibility for foreign policy, or, more likely, of their power to restrain their prime minister. In reply Disraeli made short work of these objections by pointing out that the other members of the cabinet and the Queen had concurred in the choice of plenipotentiaries, that no one but he and Lord Salisbury had sufficient knowledge of the recent negotiations with the other powers, and that the chief ministers of Russia, Germany, and Austria would all be representing their countries.

The reality was that Disraeli fully understood that, despite his age and ill health, it was incumbent upon him to attend the Congress because no one else could speak with final authority as to what Britain would be prepared to concede and what she would insist were her non-negotiable interests. He also knew that in the eyes of the leaders of the other countries he was a man of mystery, power, and fascination and that, as a consequence, his presence would prevent any possibility of there being a Russian retreat from previous agreed upon commitments. Something of this can be seen in Prince Bismarck's famous remark: "Der alte Jude, das ist der Mann," and in the fact that Disraeli soon became the "lion of the Congress."[112] His letters from Berlin to Queen Victoria and to Lady Bradford describe a nightly social whirl of private meetings, dinners, and receptions that would have exhausted a man in the prime of life, but somehow Disraeli found the energy to attend almost all of them. And though he left the hard work of negotiating the details to Lord Salisbury, his role at the Congress was also substantive. As Blake states, Disraeli "concentrated primarily on three matters left open by the Anglo-Russian Conventions: first, that the sultan should have full military rights in the southern of the two Bulgarias; second, that the Balkan frontier should be so drawn that the Turks controlled the vital mountain passes; and third, that the province should be called Eastern Roumelia, not Southern Bulgaria, so as to strike a blow at any subsequent moves for unification."[113] From the very opening of the discussions Disraeli adopted a posture and rhetoric of intransigence on these matters and let it be known that he was prepared to break up the Congress if the Russians did not agree to these points.[114] That uncompromising tone was also established by delivering his opening address in English, not French, though his motive for doing so, as Blake suggests, may also have been his very poor command of the diplomatic language. It nonetheless offended the Russians, as, perhaps, it was intended to do, and in the end Disraeli got his way over Bulgaria. He was less successful in the matter of Batum, a seaport on the Black Sea. Britain had promised in the Anglo-Russian Conventions not to make the Russians' annexation of Batum a cause of war. But when the text of those conventions was leaked to the *Globe* by a foreign office copy clerk and published on 14 June, just as the Congress was getting under way, Disraeli found his position on this issue somewhat weakened, for he was intent on still keeping Britain's compensation, the occupation of Cyprus, a secret. Back in England the Government's jingoist supporters were quickly alarmed and fearful that Disraeli and Salisbury would give away too much, and their commentary in the press was something of an irritation, especially for Salisbury, who was carrying the burden of steering British negotiations through the complicated maze of vested interests represented in Berlin. The strategy that he and the prime minister had followed in Berlin was to rely on Austria's assistance in eliminating or cutting down Russian influence in the Balkans in return for agreeing later to the idea that Austria should be allowed to occupy and administer both Bosnia and Montenegro. Most of the important boundary issues in the various Balkan states were handled in this fashion with the result that virtually all of Russia's Pan-Slav ambitions in Europe were whittled away.

On the matter of Batum itself, Disraeli met privately with Gorchakov and conceded Russia's claim to the port, settling for an assurance that it would remain "essentiellement commercial." But just as the matter of Batum's status was being resolved, on 8 July *The Daily Telegraph* published the text of the agreement with Turkey over the acquisition of Cyprus. The timing was exactly what Disraeli had wanted, for it created a sensation at the Congress, in Britain, and throughout Europe, throwing every other topic into the background. In the House of Commons that same day, the Marquess of Hartington asked Richard Cross, the Home Secretary and Acting Foreign Secretary, whether that morning's report in the press was accurate. The reply was interesting for the way it revealed what had been the Government's strategy both before and during the Congress:

In view of the retention by Russia of a portion of the Asiatic territories of the Porte, a conditional convention on the 4th of June last was entered into between Her Majesty and the Sultan to the following effect:– "If Batoum, Ardahan, Kars, or any of them, shall be retained by Russia, and if any attempt shall be made at any future time by Russia to take possession of any further portion of the Asiatic territories of the Sultan as fixed by the definitive Treaty of Peace, England engages to join the Sultan in defending them by force of arms. In return the Sultan promises to England to introduce necessary reforms (to be agreed upon between the two Powers) into the government of the Christian and other subjects of the Porte in those territories. And in order to enable England to make necessary provision for executing her engagement, the Sultan further consents to assign the island of Cyprus to be occupied and administered by England. (Cheers.) If the Government of Russia should at any time surrender to the Porte the territory it acquired in Asia by the recent war, the stipulations in the Convention will cease to operate and the island will be evacuated" ... a Firman has been issued by the Porte authorising the transfer of Cyprus to England ... Her Majesty has been pleased to appoint Sir Garnet Wolseley to administer the government of the island. (Cheers.)[115]

Such a reply does several things: it puts to rest the jingoists' fears that Britain has given away too much and failed to contain the Russians' ambitions; at the same time it makes it clear that Britain's engagement to defend Turkish territory is conditional and would only become operative should Russia violate the boundaries set by the congress. Equally significant, however, is the sultan's promise to introduce necessary, mutually agreed upon reforms into the government of his Christian subjects, for this undermines the Gladstonian objection that Disraeli's Government has been indifferent to the issue of Turkish misrule. In addition, the announced willingness on Britain's part to evacuate Cyprus, should the Russians return to Turkey the territories they had seized in the recent war, is a refutation of the charge that Disraeli had all along been scheming to augment permanently British possessions as part of some larger imperialist agenda. Such a conditional announcement did not, of course, allay Gladstone's suspicions and hostility, and it might, indeed, have only intensified them, for it pointed to a most unlikely scenario, and the royal personifications of the Government's actions at the beginning and end of the Home Secretary's statement were undoubtedly, in Gladstone's view, but further evidence of Disraeli's wickedness in co-opting the monarchy.

For the prime minister the drama of the Congress had transcended the partisan manoeuvres within Parliament. The real political issue, as he knew, was the struggle to shape public opinion through the agency of the press. In that regard, as the events of the preceding two years had shown, both Disraeli and Gladstone knew that emotions played a dominant role in the public's response to the Eastern question. Whether it was the result of Liberal moral indignation at the Bulgarian atrocities or Conservative patriotic fervour for the Queen and her empire, it was clear that in the public sphere ideology was a function of affect. Accordingly, the terms of the agreement with Turkey were a great success. And the delay of its announcement was an important strategic matter, as negotiations at the Congress were still in a sensitive state and the Government tried to ensure that the news would have the strongest possible impact. On 27 June Salisbury had telegraphed Ambassador Layard at Constantinople: "Do all you can to keep issue of Firman secret. We are very anxious to keep things quiet a few days longer." And on 3 July he told Sir Stafford Northcote in London, "Our torpedo must explode in a very few days. I trust we may avoid Saturday – in deference to your instructions." When the news broke, *The Times* reported that the most widely repeated exclamation among the delegates to the Congress, was "Quel magnifique coup de théâtre!" It also noted that there was a general sense that by this "daring stroke ... English diplomacy enjoyed a *prestige* such as it has not enjoyed for a long time."[116] Despite the note of surprise in the reactions of many of the delegates in Berlin, some of the foreign Governments either knew or suspected earlier that an arrangement between Britain and Turkey had been concluded. France was formally advised of the details the day before the Convention was published in the *Daily Telegraph* and Lord Salisbury had previously told the Russian ambassador, Schuvalov, that Britain would have to take counter-measures if Russia kept Batum, Kars, and other Asiatic territories gained in their war with Turkey.

The Times reported, as well, that the newspapers in the European capitals were full of comments about the Anglo-Turkish Treaty. The *Neue Freie Presse* in Vienna, for example, thought that it was "a stroke directed against the Congress and against Russia." From Disraeli's perspective it was certainly both. His "grand surprise" had made it clear to the delegates in Berlin that Britain would act independently to secure her interests, which necessarily included containing Russia's plans to expand her sphere of influence.[117] But equally important, it had made it clear to the British public that Disraeli's Government had acted boldly and decisively both to forestall the threats of Russian Pan-Slav imperialism and to avoid having its own policies be the subject of ratification by other European powers. The Queen had felt both of these dangers intensely, as the anger and fears of humiliation expressed in her correspondence at this time show.[118] Britain's success at Berlin was thus in her mind of such a sublime magnitude that it warranted making Disraeli a marquess or a duke.[119] Something of her rapturous feelings on the subject can be inferred from the messages she received from him and from her uncle, King Leopold of Belgium. On the day that the treaty was signed Disraeli wrote from Berlin to tell her of the details of the occasion and to say "how deeply and finely he feels the privilege of being the trusted servant of a Sovereign whom he adores!" The next day King Leopold added to this his message of "most sincere and ... warmest congratulations on the occasion of the great triumph of English policy": "Bright pages have been added to the history of a splendid reign. Honour to Lord Beaconsfield, honour to you, dear Cousin, who have sustained and encouraged him and have given him the necessary support to render immense services to your Empire."[120] Quite sensibly the prime minister declined the Queen's offer of a dukedom or marquessate, but he accepted the Order of the Garter on the condition that Salisbury receive it too. This was only just, for Salisbury and his staff had done most of the hard work in Berlin of negotiating and settling the great many territorial and boundary questions. And, as Salisbury himself had told his wife at one point, Disraeli's age, poor health, and very limited command of French had often left him with only "the dimmest idea" of what was going on in the day to day deliberations.[121] Disraeli was, nonetheless, the lion of the Congress and the vision and strategy that led to the British triumph there were essentially his.

18

The Conquering Hero / *Falconet*

The British plenipotentiaries' return from the Congress to London was a triumph worthy of a Caesar. Crowds of enthusiastic Conservative supporters were organized to meet Disraeli and Salisbury upon their arrival at Dover and also when their train reached London. At Dover, after a local band had played "Home, Sweet Home," there were addresses to the prime minister by the mayor and the Dover Working Men's Constitutional Association. The rhetoric of the speeches suggests that careful thought was given to the opportunity for propaganda that the occasion supplied:

> by the blessing of God, you have, by your great intellect and firm demeanor, aided so materially in the restoration of the peace of Empires and the assertion of England's might and position among nations. We have hailed with intense satisfaction the wise and farseeing policy adopted by Her Majesty's Government during the terrible and devastating struggle which is now happily at and end; and, as firm upholders of the Constitution, we pray that your Lordship and your colleagues may long be spared to counsel and assist our beloved Sovereign in her happy and beneficent ruling of the people of her Empire.[1]

This expression of nationalist sentiment, it is clear, was really meant to be a broad public appeal, and it was deliberately crafted in partisan terms of loyalty to the constitution and the Queen as a preemptive strike at Gladstonian opposition. Similar thought was given to the visual aspects of the moment, for *The Times* reported as well that when the prime minister had thanked the speakers and acknowledged his pleasure at such a reception, his way to the waiting train was "carpeted with crimson cloth, and a body of little girls dressed in the Conservative colours strewed his path with flowers." As the train pulled out the crowd sang "Auld Lang Syne."

In London a much grander reception awaited their Lordships, which Salisbury for his part found more than a little distasteful. *The Times* reported that a "vast concourse of people ... assembled [on the railway platform] to do honour to the Ministers." To give colour and fragrance to the scene," there was a gigantic floral display, consisting of 10,000 plants, provided by John Wills, florist to the Queen. And an "old world pomp was given to the ceremony by the appearance of the Lord Mayor and Sheriffs in their most gorgeous array, with chains of office and gilded and scarlet robes, who were the first to greet the Earl of Beaconsfield as he stepped from the train." In the same report *The Times* listed the names of all the members of the aristocracy and the other distinguished persons who had come to hail the conquering heroes, and went on to describe the setting in great detail:

> the station itself was very beautifully decorated. The carriages of those who came to welcome the Prime Minister drove in over pavement bright with fresh gravel between high masts decorated with flags and past a crimson barrier to where the carriage way entered the station under an arch, above the keystone of which a trophy blazed with the flags of all the nations that attended the Congress. The arch within the station was decorated in a like manner ... and in the midst of the Congress flags, placed higher than the rest, was the Union Jack, entwined with bay leaves as a sign of bloodless victory.

After the most important persons had been introduced to the prime minister, he and Salisbury were escorted to a carriage by Lady Abergavenny and Lady Northcote and more cheering crowds thronged the streets from Charing Cross to 10 Downing Street from whence at a window Disraeli was able to reiterate what he had said at Dover: that they had brought them "a peace with honour."[2]

So great a project was this triumphal return that eight hundred Metropolitan Police constables and officers were required to control the crowds and traffic. These demonstrations of enthusiasm, had been organized by Lord Henry Lennox, working with local Conservative associations. In writing to Montagu Corry in Berlin on 1 July, he had said that he planned to organize "something which will enable the working men to join in, which shall startle Europe and be the grandest reception

ever given to a subject in this Country ... something which will rever-
berate through the Empire from one end to another." Accordingly he
suggested that the arrival at Charing Cross should be at "the best Hour
for a monster Gathering."[3] When they first learned of Lennox's plans
the returning plenipotentiaries, especially Lord Salisbury, were taken
aback at the idea of such public displays of enthusiasm and at first tried
to damp them down. But the plans had gone too far ahead for that, and
in the end Corry had to agree with the organizers in London that it
would not do to offend or thwart the staunch party supporters who
were behind the arrangements: "see that no 'brusquerie' is committed
towards our friends! ... let the conceived plans be executed. It won't do
to be rude to zealous friends."[4]

There was no shortage of zealous friends when, on Saturday, 27 July,
five hundred Conservative peers and members of the House of Commons attended a magnificent testimonial dinner to pay tribute to Lords
Beaconsfield and Salisbury at the Duke of Wellington's Riding School in
Knightsbridge. The large hall was decorated with flags, banners, and
Conservative mottoes, conspicuous among which was "Peace With
Honour." As the guests took their seats amid loud and continued plau-
dits, the band played "See the Conquering Hero Comes," which set a
notably military tone for the evening, which featured toasts to the army,
the navy, and the reserves, all of which were replied to with ardent
speeches. The widespread sense that Disraeli had achieved a great victory for England at the Congress was the more intense from the contrast
with the sense of defeat and humiliation among the Pan-Slav activists in
Russia, which had been reported in *The Times* the previous week. In a
speech at Moscow when the Congress was nearing its climax, the prominent Slavophil leader, Ivan Aksakoff had described their feelings:
"Blushing with shame we are struck dumb with astonishment at what
we hear. Can it be true that victorious Russia allows herself to be degraded, to play the role of the defeated party[?] ... Have we been beaten
by the Turks? ... Are we the party routed, and has the Turk gained the
upper hand?" In answering his own rhetorical questions, Aksakoff
tried to diminish, but in fact reinforced the sense of Disraeli's power:
"Nothing of the kind is the case. All that has occurred is this: Lord
Beaconsfield has frowned and stamped the ground with his foot.
Russian diplomacy has been frightened by the angry ebullition of the
great foreigner, and is making concessions ... In other words, Lord
Beaconsfield has had no hesitation in telling us that [the] Congress is
neither more nor less than a conspiracy against the Russian people."[5]

Disraeli's speech at the Conservative dinner played up to the audience's desire to celebrate England's triumphant victory over the Russians, but it also reflected the prime minister's desire to vanquish his great parliamentary rival. From the very moment that the terms of the Anglo-Turkish treaty were made public, Gladstone had been in a state of furious anger, and on 20 July, in a public speech at Southwark, he had attacked Disraeli for his whole handling of the Eastern question. The Anglo-Turkish agreement was, he said, "an insane covenant," and the negotiation of it "an act of duplicity of which every Englishman should be ashamed" for "British engagements had been enormously extended, and British taxation vastly increased, without British assent, even without British knowledge." No despotic power, he said, would have dared to do what Lord Beaconsfield had done.[6] Disraeli's response to the substance of Gladstone's complaints was to deny them altogether by pointing out that had Russia's movement into Asia Minor not been constrained by the Cypress Convention, England would have sooner or later had to fight a war to "arrest the course" of that expansion or face unacceptable threats to her empire in the East. Moreover, Disraeli argued, the result of the Berlin Congress had been to prove that neither the Crimean war nor the Russo-Turkish war would have taken place if England had spoken with the necessary firmness before they began. In other words, the only real guarantee of the terms of European peace established by the Treaty of Berlin was Britain's willingness to fight to enforce them.

These statesmanly arguments were a repetition of the ones Disraeli made to the House of Lords shortly after his return from Berlin. But in the partisan atmosphere of the Conservative party's dinner he could not resist the chance of mocking his opponent, and in doing so he descended to the very "personalities" that he found so irritating when directed at himself. In remarking on Gladstone's phrase, "an insane covenant," he said that he could not pretend to be "as competent a judge of insanity" as his opponent, but he would put the question to an English jury: "which do you believe most likely to enter an insane convention, a body of English gentlemen honoured by the favour of their Sovereign and the confidence of their fellow subjects, managing your affairs for five years, I hope with prudence, and not altogether without success, or a sophistical rhetorician, inebriated with the exuberance of his own verbosity, and gifted with an egotistical imagination that can at all times command an interminable and inconsistent series of arguments to malign an opponent and to glorify himself.'"[7] It would appear that for the purpose of amusing his listeners Disraeli was trying to imitate and mock Gladstone's habit of accumulating his indignation by means of extended sentences. And amid the warmth of the occasion it was certainly effective, as the thunderous and sustained cheers for both Disraeli and Salisbury testified. But in the sober light of Monday's newspapers the language of Disraeli's conclusion seemed marked by as much animus as anything Gladstone had said and it was the subject of some unflattering commentary.

Just how much Disraeli and Gladstone felt the force of each other's rhetoric is suggested by their continued sparring over words. On 30 July Gladstone wrote to Disraeli requesting to be supplied with a list of epithets he was alleged to have applied, not merely to "Lord Beaconsfield's measures, but to his person and character." Moreover, Gladstone decided to read his letter to the House of Commons that same evening, claiming that, though it was a "repulsive subject," he felt obliged to do so as a matter of honour.[8] Given the extreme nature of his own language over the previous two years, this was unwise, for Disraeli was able to produce a forcible reply. He began by pointing out that in his Oxford speech, Gladstone had confessed to have been "counter-working 'by day and night, week by week, and month by month' the purpose of Lord Beaconsfield." Disraeli went on to quote several specific examples of such personal attacks, starting with the remark in the same Oxford speech, that "when he [Gladstone] spoke of the Government, he meant Lord Beaconsfield, who was alone responsible, and by whom 'the great name of England had been degraded and debased.'" Disraeli also referred to the recent speech at Southwark in which Gladstone had charged him with "an act of duplicity of which every Englishman should be ashamed" and added the remark that perhaps "Such an act … might be expected from a Minister who, according to Mr. Gladstone, had 'sold the Greeks.'" Then in conclusion Disraeli took some pleasure in manners and wit:

> With regard to the epithet "devilish" which Lord Beaconsfield used in the House of Lords, he is informed that it was not Mr. Gladstone at Hawarden who compared Lord Beaconsfield to Mephistopheles, but only one of Mr. Gladstone's friends, kindly enquiring of Mr. Gladstone how they were "to get rid of this Mephistopheles": but as Mr. Gladstone proceeded to explain the mode, probably the Birmingham caucus, Lord Beaconsfield may perhaps be excused for assuming that Mr. Gladstone sanctioned the propriety of the scarcely complimentary appellation.[9]

Such a reply, exquisitely formal and polite, yet mischievously full of fun would have irritated Gladstone immensely, as no doubt it was intended to do. It points to the antithetical nature of the two men's sense of themselves. As Richard Shannon has said, Gladstone's politics had become "sublimely self-centred." Questions that he conceived as turning on a moral issue excited his imagination and turned his struggles into a righteous cause: "His subjectivity ... was complemented powerfully by the conviction that he was, in a direct and special way, however unworthy, an instrument of God's will."[10] This does much to explain his frustration and his reaction to Disraeli's success at the Congress and to the public response upon the plenipotentiaries' return. Even before the Congress ended, the Conservative chief whip, W.H. Dyke, had written privately to Disraeli in Berlin, saying that "Gladstone is rabid, and looks as if he must tear something or somebody in pieces or expire with rage."[11] This is neither a disinterested nor an objective comment, but it suggests that Gladstone would have been unable to see anything humorous in the situation and that he would have found it very hard to bear his rival's flippant public or private remarks, which failed to take seriously the opposing claims of rectitude and righteousness. In the end the Treaty of Berlin was endorsed in the House of Lords without a division and in the House of Commons the Government had a decisive and most satisfying majority of 143, which led the leader-writer in *The Times* to comment upon the demoralization of the Opposition and the complete failure of their tactics in the debate.[12]

After receiving Disraeli's reply to his letter, Gladstone no doubt felt some consolation for his sense of injury and some sense of justification for his position when the next day he read the fourth in the series of scurrilous articles in the *Fortnightly Review* entitled, "The Political Adventures of Lord Beaconsfield." It began with the Gladstonian sentiment that "The sensible public is never blinded by the vulgar glitter of stars and garters ... Englishmen with good memories see under this new blue riband the political bravo who struck at Peel."[13] The article went on to describe the results of the Berlin Congress, particularly the "protectorate over Asia Minor" as a piece of "gigantic charlatanism" and "Lord Beaconsfield's triumphant entry into London, and the theatrical procession from Charing Cross," as "a bit of harlequinade from which, one would have thought, the self-respect and reserve of an English statesman and gentleman would have shrunk" (251). Then, after an unflattering comparison of the prime minister's character to that of "his feminine counterpart," Thackeray's unscrupulous Becky

Sharp, the article went on to a lengthy discussion of Disraeli's career in English politics between 1852 and 1878, involving frequent invidious contrasts with that of Gladstone, "the greater and better man" (253). And having raised again the Liberal objections to the growing influence of the monarch and the prime minister's "unconstitutional" evasions of parliamentary control, the article, in its conclusion, moved to xenophobic abuse, characterizing Disraeli as nothing more than "a grotesque foreign accident in our English political history" (269). As support for this prejudice, the author revived the evidence to be drawn from the novels, especially *Tancred*. Disraeli's statesmanship over the Eastern question seemed to be, he said, "the product rather of an Oriental imagination than of a European intelligence. He has introduced the wild dreams and projects of his Eastern heroes into the practical politics of the West" (267). And having once again quoted Fakredeen's proposal that Tancred should "magnetize" the Queen and persuade her to establish the capital of her empire at Delhi, the article equates the evident satire of 1847 with the realpolitik of 1878 by suggesting that the secret of his "wildest freaks of policy" can be found in the "most grotesque passages" of his old novels.

> Already the Emir Beaconsfield has given effect to a large part of the scheme of the Emir Fakredeen. We have an Empress of India. The convention with Turkey gives England the protectorate and the reversion of the sovereignty of the Levant, and, indeed, the whole of Asiatic Turkey ... The capital of the empire has not yet been transferred from London to Delhi; but Indian troops have been summoned to fight our battles in Europe, and the first step has been taken towards making England, in a military sense, dependent upon what used to be her dependency of India. Above all, the Emir Beaconsfield has done something to get rid of the embarrassment of the English Chambers, and the Chambers have acquiesced in a series of unconstitutional invasions and evasions of their legitimate authority ... (269)

From such a passage it is clear that there are intensely paranoid elements in the Gladstonian reactions to Disraeli's success. Every detail of the Government's policies and actions seems to confirm for those who fear and loathe him the coherence of the conspiracy that has allegedly lain dormant in his imagination until he achieved power. The plausibility in their minds does, however, also derive from the fact that the characterization of Fakredeen in *Tancred* reflects parts of Disraeli's youthful public and private persona. As a young man his life had been sufficiently scandalous that much was known about his debts, his various attempts to get into Parliament, and his personal and social indiscretions. And with sufficient animus, born of prejudice or conflict, it proved easy for his enemies to ignore the humour of his fantasies in fiction and so misread the text in such a way that Fakredeen's hyperbolic ideas become his author's heroic ideal.

The appearance of the latest issue of the *Fortnightly Review* at the beginning of August had, however, little dampening effect on the general response to Disraeli's success in thwarting Russia's Pan-Slav ambitions and securing peace. On Saturday, 3 August, there was a ceremony and banquet at the Guildhall at which the prime minister and Lord Salisbury were the honoured guests and were given "the freedom of the City." More than three thousand people were invited to watch all or part of the splendid ancient ceremony and three hundred of them were invited to the dinner at the Mansion House afterwards. This was, as even Gladstone would later admit, the high point of Disraeli's fame and political fortune. As the prime minister, wearing the broad blue riband of the Garter, rode in a carriage from Downing Street to the Guildhall, the streets were again thronged with cheering crowds. The press of well-wishers at the open window of the landau was so great that from Charing Cross onward the forward motion was slowed to a foot-pace and police constables had to walk before and alongside the carriage to prevent it being halted entirely. As Disraeli would later tell the Queen, this display of public enthusiasm was "quite spontaneous"; this time there had been "no organisation, no committee work,"[14] though the occasion had certainly been anticipated, for extra excursion trains had been laid on to accommodate the thousands of people coming in from the suburbs.[15]

The sense of a great political triumph had now continued for weeks and Disraeli reported to Lady Bradford on 6 August that "Nearly a thousand Conservative Associations, represented by 700 Deputies, waited on Salisbury and myself at [the] F[oreign].O[ffice]. today, and we had to shake hands with every one as they passed."[16] Some of these Conservative Associations presented formal addresses to the prime minister, and in reply to them he defended the contrived nature of the original demonstrations of political enthusiasm: "'Public opinion loses nothing of its genuineness and sincerity when organised; I wish to impress upon you that organisation is absolutely essential – that organisation is perfectly consistent with the highest sentiments of patriotism, and that although you may be acting under the influence of the most excited feelings at times, that is no reason why you should relax your discipline.'"[17] Four years into the term of his Government and with the timing of the next dissolution already being discussed by his closest advisors, such an emphasis on organisation and party discipline was quite natural, though it is possible that Disraeli also wished to counter the sneering criticism in Liberal circles of his attempts "to manage public opinion": "The whole thing was mountebank to the last degree; but it was not the less in harmony with the career of the Cagliostro-Chatham who was its principal figure"[18]

The images here of the charlatan, clown, and foreign impostor are striking in their own right, but would have been especially so for Gladstone, who went on the very day of Disraeli's triumphant reception at the Guildhall to admire the almost finished portrait of himself being painted by Sir John Everett Millais – "surely a very fine work" – a most handsome image of a man of noble and serious purpose.[19] And a week later, as he slowly recovered at Hawarden from the "exhaustion" and "confusion" he had felt at the end of the parliamentary session, Gladstone no doubt found yet more consolation for his recent frustrations when he took up for leisure reading an anonymous work entitled *Beaconsfield: A Mock-Heroic Poem and Political Satire*. Disraeli is here described as "A very Moses in the House of Lords" and as someone whose "craftiness of race" is "emblematic."[20] The *Westminster Review* found this 51-page pamphlet as lacking any satirical edge and described its lines as "lame, clumsy, and lumbering."[21] But it was nonetheless a sign of the times, for this was one of many such satirical attacks on Disraeli published in the 1870s, most of which were deeply anti-Semitic, and many of which, as Stanley Weintraub has pointed out, can be found among Gladstone's papers.[22] As Anthony Wohl has shown, the expressions of racial prejudice directed at Disraeli during his second ministry were far more widespread and dangerous than the instances of such hostility during the earlier years of his career. For his most vehement critics, what had previously been seen as a part of his identity became the whole of his identity; what had been just "un-English" became sinister; the "Jew d'esprit" became the "loathsome Jew."[23]

It was characteristic of Gladstone's earnestness that he could miss the satirical humour in Disraeli's novels, but had no difficulty in appreciating satirical portraits of him. Both effects were also a reflection of the deep revulsion Gladstone felt at the thought of his rival's success, a feeling caught in his use of such words as "degradation" and "corruption" when referring to the consequences in England of the

Government's Eastern policy. But although Gladstone's rhetoric in
public speeches and parliamentary debates could be extreme, and
though it would seem he took obsessive pleasure in the most hateful
images of his rival, he did not articulate his racial prejudice (linked as
it is in his case to both religious belief and sexual morality) in the kind
of despicable virulent language that many of his followers used.
William Crosbie, for example, saw Disraeli's Eastern policy as "a vulgar parody of the ancient Jewish dream" and called it a "diseased ex-
crescence."[24] Gladstone did, however, believe that "the real motivation
behind Disraeli's Eastern diplomacy was his Judaism."[25] On one occasion he was more explicit when he wrote that "the fountainhead" of
Disraeli's "strange and inexplicable proceedings on the Eastern
Question" was "race antipathy, that aversion, which the Jews, with a
few honourable exceptions, are showing so vindictively toward the
Eastern Christians." And to this he added: "though he [Disraeli] has
been baptised, his Jew feelings are the most radical and the most real,
and so far respectable, portion of his profoundly falsified nature."[26]
Gladstone claimed to "admire the conduct of English Jews in the discharge of their civil duties," but at the same time he did say, "I deeply
deplore the manner in which what I may call Judaic sympathies, beyond as well as within the circle of professed Judaism, are now acting
in the question of the East."[27] Such statements from such a leader would
and did provide some justification to followers eager to see a conspiracy behind Disraeli's use of power; they also seemed, to them at least,
to license the utterance of their hatred in obnoxious epithets – "the
Hebrew conjuror," "Lord Beaky," etc. And while Gladstone did not
overtly encourage such ugly anti-Semitism, he was in constant contact
with people who did, and it is clear that he shared to some degree their
suspicions and their feelings.

I

Almost from the moment of the plenipotentiaries' triumphant return
from Berlin, there were signs that the Conservative Government faced a
deteriorating economic situation. The deepening agricultural depression
and related commercial distress ate away at the Government's popularity in country constituencies and their political situation was further
weakened by blunders in military foreign affairs that resulted in the
onset of the second Afghan war and the Zulu massacre of British forces
at Isandhlwana in South Africa. By 1879 too, in obvious counterpoint,

Disraeli's health continued to falter, while Gladstone found renewed energy and moral fervour with which to oppose the Conservatives out of doors with the monster rallies of the second Midlothian campaign. The result was that in the election of the spring of 1880 there was a complete reversal of the parties' popular standing: the formerly demoralized and disorganized Liberals had a decisive victory, while the Tories' triumph in the Congress of Berlin collapsed into devastating defeat.

It was clear that, though Gladstone was not the official leader of the Liberal party at the time of the election, the Liberal victory was in very large measure the result of his campaign. And there was immediate speculation in the newspapers about who would be asked to form the new ministry. The general public consensus was that Gladstone ought to have the first refusal of the premiership, but that was certainly not the Queen's first reaction. The Queen was in Baden Baden in early April, when the final election results were known, and the various letters and memoranda at that time to and from her private secretary, Sir Henry Ponsonby, show that her personal feelings might well have disrupted the smooth transition to a new Government. A few weeks earlier, while denying that she was a "partizan," she had made it clear that she was "*deeply* grieved over & [had] been *indignant* at the *blind & destructive* course pursued by the *Opposition* wh wd *ruin* the country."[28] On 4 April, having received Disraeli's letter announcing the outcome of the election and his intention to retire from office without facing Parliament, the Queen made it clear just how painful and bitter was the prospect of change: "The grt alarm in the country is Mr. Gladstone, the Queen perceives, & she will sooner *abdicate* than send for or have any *communication* with *that half-mad fire-brand* who wd soon ruin everything & be a *Dictator*. Others but herself *may submit* to his democratic rule, but *not the Queen*."[29] Ponsonby thus had the difficult task of overcoming such feelings and gradually suggesting to Her Majesty the "imperative" of her constitutional duty. Gladstone for his part recognized that the threat of abdication was "the greatest power the Sovereign possessed ... for the position of a Minister who forced it on would be untenable." But, as Ponsonby said to his wife in a letter dated 12 April, the consequences would be equally terrible were the Queen to prevent a leader who had won a majority in the House of Commons from taking office.[30]

In a letter on 15 April, Ponsonby replied to an enquiry by the Queen by advising her that the Liberal leaders, Hartington and Granville, would find it "nearly impossible to form a Government unless it is publicly known that Mr. Gladstone declines office." He also pointed out that if she sent for either Lord Granville or Lord Hartington they would be obliged to ask leave to consult him. Ponsonby went on to express his anxiety about the future and suggested that it would be better to have Gladstone in the cabinet rather than out of it, because in the Government he would be "invested with responsibility, advised by his colleagues and influenced by Your Majesty," adding that he [Gladstone] is "loyal and devoted to the Queen who can control him" and that he would in fact be a "strong barrier against the movements of factious men" and could "keep the Liberal party in order." But "out of the Cabinet," Ponsonby argued, Gladstone "would have power without responsibility, he would exercise an undue influence over Ministers, and he would be thrown into the arms of designing men who would make him unconsciously and unwillingly their leader."[31] These arguments seem to have had some influence on the Queen, with the exception of the claim that Gladstone was loyal and devoted to her. In her sharp reply the next day she insisted: "He is *neither*; for *no one* CAN be, who spares no means ... to vilify – attack – accuse of every species of iniquity a Minister who had most difficult times & questions to deal with – & who showed a most unpardonable & disgraceful spite & personal hatred to Lord Beaconsfield who has restored England to the position she had lost under Mr. Gladstone's Govt ... Such conduct is unheard of & the only excuse is – that he is not quite sane."[32] Notwithstanding this outburst of displeasure, and much to Ponsonby's pleasant surprise, when the Queen met Lord Hartington a week later, she made no resistance to his advice that she should send for Gladstone and ask him to form the next Government. In the end the Queen understood that she could not allow her personal feelings to intervene and she was determined to perform her duty as the constitution and precedent required. Moreover, once Gladstone was again her prime minister, to the surprise of those who knew of her opinions, the Queen made a point of inviting him to Windsor as appropriate occasions came up. The Queen's relationship with Gladstone was, however, never warm, or more than civil. Her letters continued to reflect her regret that she could not communicate openly with him and her fear that his Government would prove both radical and dangerous. In that regard, almost a year later, Gladstone commented to Ponsonby privately on the subject of the monarchy in words that recalled the Secretary's prescient advice to the Queen at the time of the 1880 election, while at the same time reiterating the Liberal view of Disraeli's relationship to her.

Formerly I saw no reason why Monarchy should not have gone on here
for hundreds of years, but I confess that the way in which Monarchy has
been brought to the front in political and foreign affairs by the late
Government has shaken my confidence and I dread any shock that may
weaken the power of the Crown with the rising mass of politicians. Some
– and those you live with probably accuse me of being a radical. I am not.
But I believe I have the confidence – possibly far more than I deserve of
those who are extreme radicals – but who as long as I am here pay me that
respect of following me in most of what I do – even tho' they do not think
I am advanced enough.[33]

Such a self-conscious remark, whether prompted or spontaneous,
clearly reflects Gladstone's awareness of the Queen's views, but it also
suggests that he has come to see his own political role as an alternative
romance: the mediation between radical democracy and traditional institutions, which it is his special mission to accomplish. As the phrase
"the rising mass of politicians" suggests, Gladstone, especially in his
despondent moments, could foresee that his heroic romance involved a
struggle with dangerous and powerful domestic political forces that
was just as compelling as Disraeli's determination to thwart Russia's
Balkan expansion. The Irish question would be for Gladstone what the
Eastern question had been for his rival.

II

For Disraeli the electoral defeat in 1880 was effectively the end of his
remarkable political career. But the romance of politics lost none of its
attractions for him. In May he took up again the manuscript of his half
completed novel, *Endymion*, that he had begun in the early 1870s. And
when that novel was published in the fall, he immediately began writing another one, *Falconet*, which seems in its preliminary chapters to be
developing the shape of a satire. In the slightly more than nine short
chapters extant the reader is introduced to the evangelical middle-class
society of the Clapham sect, the *beau-monde* of Lady Bertram and Lady
Clanmorne, and the mysterious world of a family of German bankers
with exotic foreign connections. All of this suggests that the novel will
be a mix of amusing and instructive scenes in much the same way as its
predecessors were. There are even passing references to earlier Disraelian
characters, Lothair and Hugo Bohun, and the tone is persistently one of
gentle mockery.

The fragment of the manuscript is too short to be sure of Disraeli's full intentions, but the narrator's description of the protagonist, Joseph Toplady Falconet, is such that most readers have followed Philip Guedalla's suggestion that he is a fictional version of the "Arch Villain," Gladstone, rather than of Thomas Babbington Macaulay, as was argued by Wilbur L. Cross.[34] It is true that the parallels between the details of Macaulay's childhood and youth and those of Falconet are strong: the family home near Clapham Common; the precocious childhood manifesting itself in astonishing "feats of memory," a disputatious temper, and "incessant talk far beyond his years"; and the reputation as "the unrivalled orator" of the "mimic Parliament" of the Cambridge Union. But there are other details in the description of the novel's youthful protagonist that suggest that the Clapham setting may have been something of a blind and that the "A.V." may have been the more powerful inspiration for Disraeli's last piece of fiction. Rather like Gladstone, at least in his public persona, Falconet, the narrator says, had "a complete deficiency in a sense of humour, of which he seemed quite debarred." This would not be an accurate description of Macaulay, whose wit was often on display. Moreover, Falconet leaves the university in "a blaze of glory as Senior Wrangler," which, despite the nomenclature, is more consistent with Gladstone's brilliant, double First at Oxford in Literae Humaniores and Mathematics than with Macaulay's failure to obtain an honours degree at Cambridge because of his poor showing in Mathematics, occasioned, his father thought, by his self-indulgent reading of novels. Moreover, the narrator's description of Falconet as "Firm in his faith in an age of dissolving creeds," is a slightly sardonic echo of Gladstone's narcissistic conception of his role as he began his career in politics: "he wished to believe that he was the man ordained to vindicate the cause of religious truth. With these ardent hopes, he had renounced the suggestion which he had once favoured of taking Orders. It was as the lay champion of the Church that he desired to act, and believed that in such a position his influence would be infinitely greater than in that of a clergyman whatever his repute" (474–5).

As is the case with Falconet, Gladstone's and Macaulay's entry into the House of Commons was a matter of patronage. Both were nominated to unreformed boroughs, the former by the Tory Duke of Newcastle in 1832, the latter by the Whig Lord Lansdowne two years before. And both men had early recognition of their superior abilities. Macaulay immediately showed himself to be an effective speaker and he played a significant role in the Reform Bill debates, which brought him much praise. Gladstone, on the other hand, showed so much promise that at the age of twenty-five he was appointed a junior Lord of the Treasury at the outset of Sir Robert Peel's abortive Conservative Government of 1834–5; and only a month later he was promoted to be Under-Secretary of the War and Colonial Office when that position became unexpectedly vacant. There he made such a sharp and profound impression upon Peel and the other leaders of the party that it ensured his further promotion to the cabinet when the Conservatives next resumed office. What is interesting, though, is the contrast in their responses to these successes. Macaulay's letters to his family describing the social world of Reform politics and the debates themselves are often lively and witty, sometimes even taking the form of jocular verse,[35] while the focus of Gladstone's sober earnestness is on more abstruse political topics. In 1838 he produced his first book, *The State in Its Relations with the Church*, an entirely serious work that defined the state as a divine ordinance morally bound to pursue the ends of the Church by establishing peace, order, and the temporal well-being of man. But only through a unity of belief and consistency of practice, Gladstone argued, could the Government in the persons of its ministers make moral choices that rest upon the truth or the nearest approximation to it. Implicitly the work is an exploration of the limits and powers of conscience for individuals pursuing political careers, and, as such, it is a justification of his own choices. This was followed in 1840 by a companion volume, *Church Principles Considered in Their Results*, which, with its complex discussion of the Church of England's theological doctrines and lengthy discussion of its historical positions through time, was unsuited to a wide readership and had little impact beyond ecclesiastical circles. Most of Gladstone's friends thought that he was likely to ruin his political career with the publication of such works; his opponents simply thought him priggish.

In *Falconet*, by contrast, Disraeli places his protagonist's moral seriousness in the midst of social satire. Claribel, Countess Bertram, while engaged in banter with her cynical stepson, Lord Gaston, insists that "'Mr. Falconet has none but the most exalted ideas. His life is devoted to the vindication and the triumph of religious truth'" (487). That seems to be so, and yet there is a hint that he is also infatuated with his aristocratic hostess. In the next chapter the narrator adds that "On a certain day in every week it came to be understood that Mr. Joseph Toplady Falconet would probably be drinking a cup of tea at Bertram House and expounding his schemes of regeneration for a society which he was resolved to save" (490). The mocking juxtaposition of the social call with moral fervour is then followed by an account of how, by taking up the Sabbatarian question in the House of Commons, Falconet had gathered a number of supporters, who, though respectable men, were "quite incapable of grappling with the great questions that touch the convictions and consciences of nations." These men, the reader is told, "hailed with satisfaction a commanding expounder of opinions which in their hands they felt would have assumed a character of feebleness which they were persuaded was undeserved." The narrator's gentle mockery then quickly turns sharp and corrosive: "He gathered other allies. With all his abilities and acquirements, Joseph Toplady Falconet was essentially a prig, and among prigs there is a freemasonry which never fails. All the prigs spoke of him as of the coming man" (490–1). The reiteration of the full name, with its satiric allusions to Sheridan's Joseph Surface and to Augustus Toplady, the author of the hymn "Rock of Ages," reinforces the suggestion of sexual scandal linked to religious piety, something for which Gladstone's intense relationship with the reformed courtesan, Laura Thistlewaite, and his rescue work with prostitutes had made him notorious. *Falconet*, as far as it goes, is thus completely consistent with its author's expressed view of Gladstone as a religious hypocrite. Had he lived long enough, Disraeli would have no doubt been amused by Gladstone's choice of a title for his 1890 collection of his essays, reprinted from *Good Words*: *The Impregnable Rock of Holy Scripture*.

It was clear at the time of their rivalry that the political careers of Disraeli and Gladstone were to a large extent symbiotic. This was not just a matter of ideology, but also of psychology. Gladstone's conception of himself as the champion of Christian political morality was the antithesis of everything he took Disraeli to be: an alien Jew, unprincipled, untrustworthy, and immoral. Whereas Gladstone saw himself as righteously rational in his attempts to accommodate both change and tradition, he saw Disraeli as an insincere and wicked schemer, pursuing fantasies of self-glorification without regard for either the legality or constitutionality of his actions. Conversely, by the 1870s Disraeli's conception of himself as the pragmatic champion of England's imperial power, and of her rightful influence in the councils of Europe, was the antithesis of everything he took Gladstone to be: an egotistical and reckless moral hypocrite. Whereas Disraeli saw himself as defending England and her empire from the dangers of Russian expansion through the exercise of realpolitik, he believed that Gladstone was in the grip of a dangerous mania, so caught up in the violent expression of his obsessions as to be unable to distinguish between treason and legitimate means and ends. The implicit stories from these points of view are reciprocal romances in which the heroes and villains change places. It is evident that both narratives are shaped by a paranoid conviction that the villainous opponent has a devious or secret plan. And it is equally evident that in both romances Queen Victoria played a major role: Gladstone suspected that she was being manipulated, if not "magnetized," by the "oriental wizard," who had become her favourite prime minister; Disraeli knew that his expressions of devotion and royal servitude helped to ensure that his "Faery Queen" was a powerful and useful political ally, but he also knew that the romance of their mutual sympathies was necessarily subordinate to the constitutional powers of his own office.

The fulfilment of Disraeli's ambitions in his handling of the Eastern question, embodied as it is in the romance of the Faery Queen, would seem to be the perfect culminating example of the way in which the imaginative shaping of his political career bears a striking resemblance to the recurring fantasy structure of his novels. As I suggested in the introduction, from *Vivian Grey* to *Endymion* and *Falconet* the writing of the fiction at its most conscious level offered a form of compensation for failure or defeat by imagining transcendent success. The analyses in foregoing chapters have shown that it also served, perhaps less consciously, as a means of self-discovery and self-realization, a way of working out the consequences of his imaginative choices. It is also clear now that the journalism, pamphlets, speeches, diaries, and letters reveal that Disraeli's political career embodied the same themes and that his sense of his political identity was shaped by the same fantasies. Accordingly, Disraeli's novels are not just a gloss on his politics or the politics an explanation for the fiction. Rather, as I suggested at the outset, both are enactments of the same urgencies and purposes.

Such a claim raises interesting, larger questions about the dynamics of political culture in the Victorian era. It was then, when political leaders were first becoming intensely aware of the need to shape as well as respond to public opinion, that the rapidly expanding realm of political journalism and the extensions of the franchise rendered the relation between their private and public senses of the self ever more problematic. In Disraeli's rise to "the top of the greasy pole" we begin to see the defining reciprocal powers of political ideology and the imaginative life of individuals, which have become ever more significant in the age of mass media.

Notes

Introduction

1 Blake, *Disraeli* (1966), is still the most detailed political biography. See also Bradford, *Disraeli* (1983), Vincent, *Disraeli* (1990), Weintraub, *Disraeli* (1993), and Ridley, *Young Disraeli* (1995), each of which has its own particular emphasis and interest. Paul Smith's *Disraeli* (1996) is an excellent brief interpretation of Disraeli's ideas.
2 Blake, *Disraeli*, 3–4.
3 Ibid., 12.
4 Disraeli, *Vivian Grey*, vol. 1 of *The Novels and Tales of Benjamin Disraeli*, Bradenham Edition, 18. Unless otherwise indicated, references to the novels and tales are given in this edition

1. *The Representative* Affair

1 An earlier version of portions of chapters 1–4 was published as "The Autobiographical Nature of Disraeli's Early Fiction" in *Nineteenth-Century Fiction* 31.3 (December 1976): 253–84 (Copyright The Regents of the University of California); or as "Disraeli's Early Careers" in *Queen's Quarterly* 90.3 (fall 1983): 676–87.
2 See Blake, *Disraeli*, 25.
3 "The Chevalier" is Sir Walter Scott, Lockhart's father-in-law. I have indicated whenever I have added italics or emphasis within a quotation. If I have not so indicated with "italics added" or "emphasis added," the italics are in the original. "M" is Lockhart. "+" may have been Canning. To John Murray, [21] September [1825], *Benjamin Disraeli Letters*, vol. 1 (#28), 37–40. Hereafter all references to this edition are given as *Disraeli Letters* and cited by volume, letter number, and pages.

4 Monypenny and Buckle, *The Life of Benjamin Disraeli*, 1:32–3. The first
   two volumes and part of the third were written by Monypenny. After his
   death, Buckle completed the biography. Hereafter this work is cited as
   Monypenny and Buckle, *Life*, by volume and page number.
5 This letter is printed in Appendix III of Scott, *Familiar Letters*, 2:406.
6 William Wright to J.G. Lockhart, 3 October 1825; quoted in Lang, *The Life
   and Letters of John Gibson Lockhart*, 1:367–8.
7 Monypenny and Buckle, *Life*, 1:70–1.
8 John Murray to J.G. Lockhart, 23 November 1825; printed in Appendix III
   of Scott, *Familiar Letters*, 2:414–15.
9 To John Murray, 23 November 1825, *Disraeli Letters*, 1 (#39), 52–3.
10 To J.G. Lockhart, [24] November 1825, *Disraeli Letters*, 1 (#41), 55.
11 Ibid.
12 John Murray to Mr Sharon Turner, 16 October 1826. See Smiles, *A Publisher
   and His Friends, Memoir and Correspondence of the Late John Murray*, 2:217–18.
13 Ibid., 215–16.
14 To Murray, [21] September [1825], *Disraeli Letters*, 1 (#28), 38. See also
   Smiles, *A Publisher and His Friends*, 2:190–3.
15 Maria D'Israeli to John Murray, 21 May 1826, *Disraeli Letters*, 1: 64, n. 4. See
   Blake, *Disraeli*, also, 45–6.
16 *Vivian Grey* (volumes 1 and 2 [Part 1]) was issued anonymously by Henry
   Colburn on 22 April 1826. Almost at once there appeared a "Key to *Vivian
   Grey*," purporting to identify the persons depicted in this roman-à-clef.
   The sensational popularity of the work may be gauged from the fact that
   by 1827, when volumes 3–5 [Part 2]) appeared, there had been three
   editions of the novel and ten editions of the "Key."
17 In 1819, when he was the London publisher for *Blackwood's Magazine* and
   Lockhart was a contributor, Murray had repeatedly complained to William
   Blackwood about the satirical young man's slanderous "personalities,"
   which were often directed at the *Quarterly*'s most cherished authors. In the
   end, Murray felt his own character was impugned by association, and was
   so offended by Blackwood's failure to restrain Lockhart that he withdrew
   from the joint publishing arrangement. See Smiles, *A Publisher and His
   Friends*, 1:477–96.
18 In his very fine discussion of this novel, Daniel Schwarz raises two other
   aspects of the ambivalence in Vivian Grey's characterization, that embodied in his response to his father, and that of the narrator's sympathy and
   judgment. See above (p. 26) and Schwarz, *Disraeli's Fiction*, 8–21.
19 To Isaac and to Sarah, 9 August – 15 October 1826, *Disraeli Letters*, 1 (#50–8),
   67–94.

20　See Blake, *Disraeli*, 52–3.

21　The most notable example was that of William Ewart Gladstone, ultimately to be Disraeli's great antagonistic rival for political power. See Blake, *Disraeli*, 53.

22　Browning, *Letters of Robert Browning and Elizabeth Barrett Barrett, 1845–1846*, ed. Elvan Kintner, 1:49–52. It is interesting to note as well that "Violet Fane" was the chosen pseudonym of the young poet Mary Montgomerie Lamb (1843–1905).

23　Schwarz, *Disraeli's Fiction*, 19–21.

24　Blake, *Disraeli*, 57–8.

25　Disraeli, *The Young Duke*, 17, 14.

26　For an excellent discussion of Byron's love of Venice, see Foot, *The Politics of Paradise*.

2. The Byronic Legacy

1　An earlier version of the discussion of "Ixion in Heaven" in Part III of this chapter was published in the *Disraeli Newsletter* 1.1 (spring 1976): 14–26.

2　Blake, *Disraeli*, 53. See also Richmond and Post, "Disraeli's Crucial Illness," in *The Self-Fashioning of Disraeli*, ed. Richmond and Smith, 66–89.

3　Blake, *Disraeli*, 51.

4　To Isaac D'Israeli, 1 July [1830], *Disraeli Letters*, 1 (#90), 129. The family letters from this tour were originally published as *Home Letters Written by the late Earl of Beaconsfield in 1830 and 1831*, ed. Ralph Disraeli (London: Murray, 1885; reprinted New York: Kraus, 1970), but the many errors and conflations in this edition make it unreliable for scholarly purposes.

5　Gregory, *An Autobiography*, 96.

6　To Isaac, 14 July 1830, *Disraeli Letters*, 1 (#92), 134, 135–6.

7　To Maria D'Israeli, 1 August 1830, *Disraeli Letters*, 1 (#94), 141. See p. 140, editorial comment: "The greater part of the letter was inserted in *Contarini Fleming* part v chs 6 and 7. Indeed there is scarcely a sentence in those chapters not drawn from this letter."

8　To Isaac, 25 (cont'd. 27) August 1830, *Disraeli Letters*, 1 (#97), 155.

9　To Isaac, 1 July 1830, *Disraeli Letters*, 1 (#91), 133.

10　Entry for 29 March 1830; quoted in Monypenny and Buckle, *Life*, 1:124.

11　Monypenny and Buckle, *Life*, 1:125. Cf. "Beaconsfield," *Encyclopaedia Britannica*, 10th ed.where the description is attributed to Henry Bulwer. For the best discussion of the reciprocal influence and mutual admiration between Disraeli and Bulwer, see Ellen Moers, *The Dandy* (New York: Viking, 1960).

12 Blake, *Disraeli*, 59.

13 Monypenny and Buckle, *Life*, 1:155.

14 To Ralph D'Israeli [17] September [1830], *Disraeli Letters*, 1 (#99), 162.

15 To Isaac, 25 October 1830, *Disraeli Letters*, 1 (#101), 169–70.

16 Blake, *Disraeli*, 59.

17 To Isaac, 25 October 1830, *Disraeli Letters*, 1 (#101), 171–2.

18 To Isaac, 1 July 1830, *Disraeli Letters*, 1 (#91), 132.

19 To Isaac, 10 October 1830, *Disraeli Letters*, 1 (#100), 164.

20 "He affects all the affable activity of a European Prince, mixes with his subjects, interferes in all their pursuits and taxes them most unmercifully … After all his defeats, he has now sixty thousand regular infantry excellently appointed and well disciplined. They are certainly not to be compared to the French or English line – but they would as certainly beat the Spanish or the Dutch, and many think with fair play, the Russians. Fair play their monarch certainly had not during the last campaign. Its secret history wo[ul]d not now interest, but it was by other means than military prowess that the Muscovites advanced so successfully. The Sultan had to struggle against an unprecedented conspiracy the whole time, and the morning that Adrianople was treacherously delivered up, the streets of Stamboul were filled with the dead bodies of detected traitors." To Isaac, 11 January 1831, *Disraeli Letters*, 1 (#109), 184.

21 To Isaac, [23? December 1830], *Disraeli Letters*, 1 (#105), 177. See also n. 1.

22 To Sarah, 20 March 1831, *Disraeli Letters*, 1 (#110), 187–9.

23 To Sarah, 28 May 1831, *Disraeli Letters*, 1 (#111), 189ff.

24 Monypenny and Buckle, *Life*, 1:177.

25 Disraeli, *Vindication of the English Constitution in a letter to a noble and learned Lord*), reprinted in Hutcheon, *Whigs and Whiggism*. See Hutcheon, *Whigs and Whiggism*, 171.

26 To Isaac, 20 July 1831, *Disraeli Letters*, 1 (#112), 197.

27 The words are those of Sir Philip Rose; quoted by Blake, *Disraeli*, 70.

28 To Sarah, 20 July 1831, *Disraeli Letters*, 1 (#114), 201.

29 Disraeli's later dedication in Sarah's copy of *Alroy*, in which he describes her as his own "gazelle," suggests that his "brother's love" did indeed contain a sublimation of his deepest conflicts of identity. See *Disraeli Letters*, 1 (# 251), n. 4, 339 and below, ch. 4, 94–5, which discuss the use of the gazelle motif in *Contarini Fleming*, *Alroy*, "The Consul's Daughter," and *Henrietta Temple*.

30 To Sarah, 2 April 1832, *Disraeli Letters*, 1 (#169), 257.

31 To Sarah, [April 1833], *Disraeli Letters*, 1 (#270), 356.

32 The words are attributed to Mr Raymond Mortimer; quoted in Blake, *Disraeli*, 75.

33 Published by John Murray (London: 1832); hereafter cited as *Gallomania*.

34 To Sarah, [22 February 1832], *Disraeli Letters*, 1 (#141), 228; Disraeli to Murray, [30 March 1832], *Disraeli Letters*, 1 (#163), 251. See also Disraeli to Murray, [2 April 1832], *Disraeli Letters*, 1 (#168), 255, n. 1, in which the editors note that a draft of pages 57–141 of the *Gallomania* is in Baron de Haber's hand.

35 To Sarah, [20 February 1832], *Disraeli Letters*, 1 (#140), 227.

36 To Murray, [30 March 1832], *Disraeli Letters*, 1 (#163), 251; (#161), 249.

37 To Murray, [19 March 1832], *Disraeli Letters*, 1 (#156), 244.

38 Blake, *Disraeli*, 85; To Isaac, 25 (29) August 1830, *Disraeli Letters*, 1 (#97), 156.

39 To Sarah, 28 May 1831, *Disraeli Letters*, 1 (#111), 191.

40 To Murray, [30 March 1832], *Disraeli Letters*, 1 (#163), 251.

41 Blake, *Disraeli*, 85; Letter from Isaac and Sarah, Thursday, postmarked 20 April 1832, Disraeli Papers A/I/i/29.

42 *Gallomania*, 13.

43 To Benjamin Austen, [2 June 1832], *Disraeli Letters*, 1 (#198), 285. Note that the flippant phrase was previously used to describe the reactionary "coadjutors" of the *Gallomania* in the letter to Murray, 30 March 1832.

44 Sarah to Disraeli, 11 May 1832; quoted in *Disraeli Letters*, 1:272, n. 1.

45 Monypenny and Buckle, *Life*, 1:213–14.

46 Jerman, *The Young Disraeli*, 159–60; also Blake, *Disraeli*, 89.

47 Disraeli, "Ixion in Heaven," in *Popanilla and Other Tales*, Bradenham Edition., 110. Hereafter cited as "Ix" with page numbers in the text. See Graves, *The Greek Myths*, 1:208, and The *Oxford Companion to Classical Literature*, which give much the same account, stressing Ixion's treachery and his gross ingratitude to Zeus.

48 The phrase is Byron's; quoted in *Medwin's Conversations of Lord Byron*, ed. Lovell, 168.

49 To Murray, 27 May 1830, *Disraeli Letters*, 1 (#86), 124.

50 See Disraeli's letter to Murray, 10 February 1832, *Disraeli Letters*, 1 (#135), 223.

51 Blake, *Disraeli*, 80, 81.

52 The most obnoxious passages were deleted from the 1853 and subsequent editions.

53 Murray to Sharon Turner, 16 October 1826; quoted by Blake, *Disraeli*, 47.

54 To Anne Murray, 21 May 1826, *Disraeli Letters*, 1 (#48), 63.

55 Jerman, *The Young Disraeli*, 159.

56 See Sadleir, *Blessington-D'Orsay*. Sadleir suggests that D'Orsay was
    impotent, and that he and Lady Blessington were not guilty of much they
    were accused of doing.

57 Bulwer Lytton to Lady Blessington, 23 October 1834; quoted in Sadleir,
    Blessington-D'Orsay, 244.

3. Virtues and Vanities

1   Monypenny and Buckle, *Life*, 1:217–19.
2   Blake, *Disraeli*, 90.
3   *The Times*, 10 November 1832; *The Times*, 13 November 1832, rpt *Disraeli
    Letters*, 1 (#219), 308.
4   *The Times*, 10 November 1832, 3.
5   Clara Bolton to Disraeli, 19 November 1832, Disraeli Papers, Box 13/A/
    IV/G/8.
6   Monypenny and Buckle, *Life*, 1:218–19 and n. 1. This is from a speech
    recorded in the *Wycombe Sentinel*, 30 November 1832, a weekly campaign
    publication of which there were eight numbers issued gratis.
7   Jerman (*The Young Disraeli*, 169) uses this first phrase without attribution in
    discussing the parallel response to *Vivian Grey*. *Blackwood's Magazine*, July
    1826, called the author "an obscure person for whom nobody cares a
    straw." J.G. Lockhart commented on *Coningsby* in 1844: "That Jew scamp
    has published a very blackguard novel." See Lang, *Life and Letters of J.G.
    Lockhart*, 2:199. Jerman's phrase would thus seem to reflect the tone of
    much current opinion. Jews were excluded from Parliament until 1858
    unless they were ready to take the necessary oath "on the true faith of a
    Christian." At least four men of the "Jewish race" who were members of
    the Anglican Church had entered Parliament between 1770 and 1819. See
    Blake, *Disraeli*, 10.
8   Mutilated Diary, Disraeli Papers, Box 11/A/III/C/21–2.
9   Monypenny and Buckle, *Life*, 1:196.
10 The extent to which charges of inconsistency, insincerity, hypocrisy, and
    expediency affected Disraeli can be gauged by reading the political
    pamphlets and satires that are discussed in the next chapter.
11 Disraeli, *The Wondrous Tale of Alroy*, vol. 5 of the Bradenham Edition, 9.
    Compare a passage from the original edition of *The Young Duke* (1831)
    with similar import: "But where are now my deeds and aspirations ... My
    life has been a blunder and a blank ... I keenly feel myself what indeed I
    am – far the most prostrate of a fallen race" (Bk 4, ch. 3, 22, and Bk 3, ch. 18,
    218–19). These remarks are part of a pervasive Byronic exaggeration that

characterizes the intrusions of the implied author. Their autobiographical significance stems from the fact that Disraeli found this authorial mode attractive.

12 Blake, *Disraeli*, 15–16.

13 This ambivalence is also manifested in Disraeli's shifting attitude toward Catholicism amid the political events of the 1830s. See chapter 6 below, which provides a detailed account of Disraeli's violent anti-Catholic prejudice at the time of the Municipal Corporations Reform Bill (1835) and assesses this prejudice in the context of Disraeli's involvement with the Ultra-Tory faction of the Conservative party and his campaign in the Taunton by-election.

14 Disraeli, *The Rise of Iskander*, in *Popanilla and Other Tales*, Bradenham Edition, 221. David H. Curnow, my friend and colleague so learned in the history of the Middle East, pointed out to me that "Iskander" is the Turkish form of "Alexander." For more information, see Kovic, *Disraeli and the Eastern Question*.

15 "Cherry and Fair Star" [Benjamin and Sarah Disraeli]. *A Year at Hartlebury or The Election* (London: Saunders and Otley, 1834. All citations are to the only modern edition published by the University of Toronto Press, 1983.

16 This similarity of titles and character was first pointed out by Graham, "Emma's Three Sisters." The further details of comparison have not been previously discussed.

17 "Agitate – agitate – agitate" was a popular radical slogan of the 1830s, but the words were first used by the Marquess of Anglesey as a recommendation to the Irish people as the best means of effecting Catholic Emancipation. Quoted in "The Mary-Le-Bone Election," *The Northern Star*, vol. 1: no. 17, 10 March 1838, 1.

18 To Sarah, [14 January 1834], *Disraeli Letters*, 1 (#304), 389–90: "Do what you like with the end. I will have nothing to do with suicide or anything else. Poetical justice is all stuff. I think you will spoil the book, but you are Lady Paramount."

4. Henrietta: A Love Story

1 Disraeli Papers, Box 13/A/IV/H. Both B.R. Jerman and Robert Blake provide excellent accounts of the Sykes affair, to which I am greatly indebted.

2 Disraeli Papers, Box 13/A/IV/H/85.

3 Disraeli Papers, Box 27/A/XI/A/8.

4 Disraeli Papers, Box 13/A/IV/H/1.

5 Aubrey Bohun's libertine past in the eastern Mediterranean would seem to be a reflection of Disraeli's. In her biography Sarah Bradford reports that "it is very likely that, under Clay's expert auspices, he had his first sexual initiation in the brothels of Constantinople." *Disraeli*, 40–1.

6 To Sarah Disraeli, *Disraeli Letters*, 1 (#s 273, 275, 276), 357–62.

7 Disraeli, "The Consul's Daughter," in *Popanilla and Other Tales*, Bradenham Edition, 313–44.

8 Cirlot, *A Dictionary of Symbols*, 110.

9 Disraeli, *Henrietta Temple: A Love Story*, Bradenham Edition.

10 *"What Is He?"* published in April 1833, was one of Disraeli's first attempts to rationalize the apparent political inconsistency and expediency with which he was charged by his political opponents. The pamphlet is reprinted in *Whigs and Whiggism*, ed. Hutcheon, 16–22. See the next chapter for an analysis of this pamphlet in the context of Disraeli's attempts to enter Parliament from 1832 to 1837.

11 Nineteen letters of "Runnymede" appeared in *The Times* from 19 January to 16 May 1836. Two additional letters appeared on 13 February and 17 April 1837.

12 Examination of the manuscript reveals, contrary to what has been assumed by every previous critic, that the portion of the text written in 1833 consists of Book 1 and part of the first chapter of Book 2, but not the whole of the first of three volumes in which it was published. Disraeli's comment in the Mutilated Diary – that the first "volume" of the novel was written three years before its publication – is therefore misleading. Ms. of *Henrietta Temple*, Disraeli Papers, Box 219/E/I/12. Cf. Mutilated Diary, Disraeli Papers, Box 11/A/III/C/49. At the point where the ms. breaks off there are some notes indicative of Disraeli's future intentions: "remains 3 yrs. more at Malta / conduct and situation described. / Travels in Italy and Greece. / Grandfather dies & leaves his whole / fortune to Kate his cousin // F. returns home & engages himself / to his cousin at Bath. / The Grandisons about to visit Arm. / F. obliged to visit London on military business / arrives at Arm: a week before their / expected arrival. Embraces Glast.y, they / dine tog.r & sit up nearly all night / talking over his prospects: delight of Gl.y."

13 "Beautiful, brilliant, and ambitious, his eccentricities and love of fame made him a soldier of fortune respectively in the 'Imperial Service … the Turkish Army,' and revolutionary France; but when he was condemned to death on the guillotine for supposedly betraying the Jacobin cause, he left the once vast and free Armine estates so entailed that his son and heir, Sir Ratcliffe, was reduced to a life of poverty."

14 Early Notebook, Disraeli Papers, Box 11/ A/Ill/E/I.
15 Disraeli's letters to Mrs Lewis during the period of their courtship reveal that he cast her in a maternal role in much the same way that he had done with Henrietta Sykes. Simply being twelve years his senior Mrs Lewis may have been better suited than Lady Sykes for the role in which Disraeli wished to place his lover, but she also seems to have been more temperamentally suited to indulging his imagination than was the excitable and demanding Henrietta. See *Disraeli Letters*, vol. 3 (1838–41); the original copies are in the Bodleian Library, Disraeli Papers, Box 1/ A/I/ A/34b, 44.
16 A public letter to Daniel O'Connell [5 May 1835] inserted in the press (*The Times*, 6 May 1835); *Disraeli Letters*, 2 (# 398), 37.
17 Blake, *Disraeli*, 143–4.
18 Disraeli Papers, Box 11/A/III/C/49; 53–4.
19 Disraeli Papers, Box 11/A/III/C/44.
20 "To Sir Robert Peel" ("The Letters of Runnymede," V), *The Times*, 26 January 1836; *Disraeli Letters*, 2 (Appendix II), 358–61.
21 To William Pyne, [21 July 1836], *Disraeli Letters*, 2 (# 515), 175.
22 Blake, *Disraeli*, 143.
23 Jerman, *The Young Disraeli*, 277–8.
24 The pamphlet was subtitled, "By the Author of Vivian Grey," a testimony to the fact that Disraeli's political identity was at this time seen by the voting public as an extension of his authorial persona.

5. What Is He? The Crisis Examined

1 An earlier version of the discussion of *The Revolutionary Epick* in Part I of this chapter was published in the *Disraeli Newsletter* 2.1 (spring 1977): 24–42.
2 B.R. Jerman was the first to explore the complicated manoeuvres of Disraeli's financial escapades, *The Young Disraeli*, chs 4–8, but much more has come to light with the publication of the first eight volumes of the *Disraeli Letters*.
3 See Monypenny and Buckle, *Life*, 1:218, and Blake, *Disraeli*, 90.
4 *Disraeli Letters*, 1 (#215), 303–5. The best study of Bolingbroke is Isaac Kramnick's *Bolingbroke and His Circle*. Cf. also, Bolingbroke, *Remarks on the History of England* (1730–1) and *A Letter on the Spirit of Patriotism* (1736).
5 *Disraeli Letters*, 1 (#221), 309–10. Bolingbroke refers to the "fabric" of the constitution in *A Dissertation Upon Parties* (1735) and is clearly an apologist for the gentry in much of his writing.
6 *Disraeli Letters*, 1 (# 263), 348–9.
7 Blake, *Disraeli*, 91.

8 Disraeli, *"What Is He?"* reprinted in *Whigs and Whiggism*, ed. Hutcheon, 16–22.

9 Monypenny and Buckle, *Life*, 1:211.

10 Blake, *Disraeli*, 78.

11 See also *Contarini Fleming*, 364.

12 See Isaac Kramnick, *Bolingbroke and His Circle*, ch. 1.

13 Bolingbroke, *The Works of the Late Right Honourable Henry St. John, Lord Viscount Bolingbroke*, 8 vols. (London: J. Johnson *et al.*, 1809), 4: 327–34. This is the edition of Bolingbroke's *Works* in the library at Hughenden. It was in all probability part of Isaac D'Israeli's collection later transferred there from Bradenham.

14 Quoted in Monypenny and Buckle, *Life* 1:227. This letter is one of the many that Monypenny and Buckle had access to and that have subsequently disappeared, for it is no longer among the Disraeli Papers.

15 *The Wondrous Tale of Alroy*, 75; published a month earlier, March 1833.

16 Blake, *Disraeli*, 114.

17 Ibid., 273.

18 Preface to *The Revolutionary Epick*, i–ii. Subsequent references to this poem are cited from *"The Revolutionary Epick" and Other Poems.*, reprinted from the Original Edition and Edited by W. Davenport Adams.

19 To Sara Austen, 1 December 1833, *Disraeli Letters*, 1 (# 297), 380, and to Benjamin Austen, [23 March 1834], *Disraeli Letters*, 1 (# 316), 399–400.

20 To Sara Austen, 1 December 1833, *Disraeli Letters*, 1 (# 297), 380.

21 Monypenny and Buckle, *Life*, 1:245.

22 Ibid., 1:244–5.

23 Entries from The Mutilated Diary for 1833–4, *Disraeli Letters*, 1, Appendix III, 447.

24 The Mutilated Diary, *Disraeli Letters*, 1, Appendix III, 447.

25 Cf. Pope, *An Essay on Man*; Epistle I, lines 171–2, 247–58, 281–94; Epistle II, lines 249–52; Epistle III, lines 295–302; Epistle IV, lines 49–62; *The Poems of Alexander Pope*, vol. 3.

26 See Kramnick, *Bolingbroke and His Circle*, ch. 4, 84–110.

27 Woodring, *Politics in English Romantic Poetry*.

28 Shelley, *Prometheus Unbound*, Act I, lines 53ff.

29 See the letter to John Murray, already cited, about the deletion of high-Tory sentiments from the *Gallomania* [30 March 1832], *Disraeli Letters*, 1 (# 163), 251.

30 To Sara Austen, [1 December 1833], *Disraeli Letters*, 1 (# 297), 380.

31 *Rev. Epick*, 110. To the Duke of Wellington, 3 March 1834, *Disraeli Letters*, 1 (# 312 and n. 1), 396–7.

32 Maître, *Disraeli*, 250.

33 Blake, *Disraeli*, 113, 153.

34 Torrens, *Memoirs of William Lamb*, 275. Also quoted in Monypenny and Buckle, *Life*, 1:255. "Disraeli never forgot this curious conversation. Forty years later he told Lord Rowton that he could still repeat every word that Melbourne had said." Blake, *Disraeli*, 114.

35 Lasswell, *Psychopathology and Politics*, provides a good discussion of the way private motives are displaced and rationalized in the formation of political ideology.

36 The following summary of political events is drawn from Kitson Clark, *Peel and the Conservative Party*, chs 3–4, pp. 91–192.

37 To Sarah Disraeli, [28 May; 2, 4, 7, 9, 16, 19 June 1834], *Disraeli Letters*, 1 (#s 322, 323, 324, 325, 326, 329, 331), 404–15.

38 To Sarah Disraeli, [2 June 1834], *Disraeli Letters*, 1 (# 323), 405–6.

39 To Sarah Disraeli, [4 June 1834], *Disraeli Letters*, 1 (# 324), 406.

40 Disraeli, "The Infernal Marriage," *Popanilla and Other Tales*, vol. 3 of the Bradenham Edition, 143–212.

41 "The Infernal Marriage," 157–8; Blake, *Disraeli*, 99–100, 113.

42 To Isaac D'Israeli, [23 December 1830], *Disraeli Letters*, 1 (# 105), 177. Disraeli used the same phrase a few days later in letters to Benjamin Austen and Edward Lytton Bulwer: *Disraeli Letters*, 1 (# 106 and 107), 178, 180.

43 For a more detailed account of this relationship, see Blake, *Disraeli*, 114–19, from which the foregoing summary is drawn.

44 Kitson Clark, *Peel and the Conservative Party*, 175–88.

45 Letter to Lord Aberdeen, 23 August 1834, privately printed in *Aberdeen Correspondence, 1832–1834*, 14; quoted in Kitson Clark, *Peel and the Conservative Party*, 190.

46 To Lady Blessington, 15 August [1834], *Disraeli Letters*, 1 (# 346), 426.

47 To Benjamin Austen, 24 October 1834, *Disraeli Letters*, 1 (# 351), 431.

48 [To Sarah Disraeli] [4 November 1834], *Disraeli Letters*, 1 (# 352), 432.

49 A memorandum inscribed over the date "Hughenden, 1863" but written at Bradenham in 1836. Disraeli Papers, Box 11/A/III/D/ii/a/6. Hereafter cited as the Bradenham Memo.

50 Kitson Clark, *Peel and the Conservative Party*, 194.

51 Bradenham Memo, Disraeli Papers, Box 11/A/III/D/ii/a/12–13.

52 Kitson Clark, *Peel and the Conservative Party*, 195–8.

53 To Lord Durham, 17 November [1834], *Disraeli Letters*, 1 (# 353), 434.

54 Ibid., n. 4.

55 To Sarah Disraeli, [24 November 1834 and 29 November 1834], *Disraeli Letters*, 1 (# 354, 355), 435.

56 To Sarah Disraeli, [8 December 1834], *Disraeli Letters*, 1 (# 357), 437.

57 *The Crisis Examined*, in *Whigs and Whiggism*, ed. Hutcheon, 23–40.

58 Kitson Clark, *Peel and the Conservative Party*, 210.

59 Disraeli, *Coningsby; or the New Generation*, vol. 8 of the Bradenham Edition, 104.

60 "To the ELECTORS of the BOROUGH of TAMWORTH," in *Memoirs by the Right Honourable Sir Robert Peel*, Part 2, 62. Hereafter cited by pages in the text or as "Tamworth Manifesto."

61 Monypenny and Buckle, *Life*, 1:268–9.

62 Norman Gash, *Politics in the Age of Peel*, 436.

63 To Lord Durham, [30 December 1834], *Disraeli Letters*, 1 (# 361), 441.

64 Woodward, *The Age of Reform*, 84. Cf. also the letter to Sarah, 4 June 1834, *Disraeli Letters*, 1 (# 324), 406, in which Disraeli reports that Durham is demanding a further "extension of the Constituency."

65 Blake, *Disraeli*, 123.

6. Prejudice

1 Sir Robert Peel, *Memoirs*, 32, 33–4.

2 Croker, *The Croker Papers*, 2:248; Kitson Clark, *Peel and the Conservative Party*, 203.

3 Kitson Clark, *Peel and the Conservative Party*, 205 ff.

4 Ibid., 239–41.

5 To the Duke of Wellington, [7 January 1835], *Disraeli Letters*, 2 (# 363), 5.

6 To Sarah Disraeli, 24 May [1832], *Disraeli Letters*, 1 (# 192), 279.

7 To Sarah Disraeli, [20 February 1835], *Disraeli Letters*, 2 (# 377), 16.

8 To Isaac Disraeli, 1 April 1835, *Disraeli Letters*, 2 (# 386), 25.

9 To Sarah Disraeli, 4 April 1835, *Disraeli Letters*, 2 (# 387), 26.

10 To Isaac Disraeli, Good Friday [17 April] 1835, *Disraeli Letters*, 2 (# 389), 28–9.

11 Bradenham Memo, Disraeli Papers, Box 11/A/III/D/ii/a. The account of this intrigue given in the memo is essentially the same, though more restrained in tone, as one would expect with a retrospective view of two years.

12 *Pen and Ink Sketches of Poets, Preachers, and Politicians* (London, 1846), quoted in Monypenny and Buckle, *Life*, 1:281–2.

13 Sadleir, *Blessington-D'Orsay: A Masquerade*, 49 ff. Cf. d'Aurevilly, "Du Dandysme et de George Brummell," 667–773.

14 Baudelaire, *Le Peintre de la Vie Moderne*, quoted in Sadleir, *Blessington-D'Orsay*, 50.

15 See Monypenny and Buckle, *Life*, 1:282, quoting a letter from Count D'Orsay, and especially n. 2 about the Westminster Club.

16 Monypenny and Buckle, *Life*, 1:282–4.

17 To Sarah Disraeli, [26 April] 1835, *Disraeli Letters*, 2 (# 391), 30.

18 To Sarah Disraeli, [28] April 1835, *Disraeli Letters*, 2 (# 393), 31–2.

19 *Pen and Ink Sketches*, quoted in Monypenny and Buckle, *Life*, 1:284–5.

20 Monypenny and Buckle, *Life*, 1:285–6.

21 To Sarah Disraeli, [20 February 1835], *Disraeli Letters*, 2 (# 377), 16.

22 *Dorset County Chronicle*, 30 April 1835; reprinted in *Selected Speeches of the Late Right Honourable the Earl of Beaconsfield*, ed. Kebbel, 1:25–31. Cf. Blake, *Disraeli*, 124, and Monypenny and Buckle, *Life*, 1:286.

23 *Courier*, 6 May 1835, quoted in Monypenny and Buckle, *Life*, 1:287–8. Disraeli first saw these remarks in *The Times*, 5 May 1835.

24 To Daniel O'Connell, 5 May 1835, *Disraeli Letters*, 2 (#398), 37.

25 To the Electors of Taunton, 12 May 1835, *Disraeli Letters*, 2 (#403), 43.

26 For the point and the elegant phrase I am indebted to Donald J. Gray.

27 See the "Summary of Political events from 1826–36" in two small notebooks written at Bradenham in 1836, Disraeli Papers, Box 11/A/III/D/1–11a; rpt. as Appendices IV and V, *Disraeli Letters*, 2:419–28.

28 The essential points of this discussion are drawn from Kitson Clark, *Peel and the Conservative Party*, 262–90.

29 To Sarah Disraeli, [11 August 1835], *Disraeli Letters*, 2 (# 416), 87.

30 To Sarah Disraeli, [4 August 1835], *Disraeli Letters*, 2 (#413), 73–4.

31 Kitson Clark, *Peel and the Conservative Party*, 275.

32 To Sarah Disraeli, [4 and 11 August 1835], *Disraeli Letters*, 2 (# 413, 416), 73–4; 87–8.

33 "Summary of Political Events from 1826–36," Appendix IV, *Disraeli Letters*, 2:422.

34 See, for example, a letter from the Marquess of Londonderry to the Duke of Buckingham, 10 August 1835: "There will be no schism in the party, and hopes are strongly held out that our large majority will enable us to make it a Conservative arrangement, which Lyndhurst has pledged himself to do. We could not take the leap of total rejection. If it be an entire new Bill, the H. of C. will be those who reject it, not us." Buckingham and Chandos, *Memoirs of the Courts and Cabinets of William IV and Victoria*, 2:198.

35 Kitson Clark, *Peel and the Conservative Party*, 278–9.

36 On 17 August Londonderry wrote to Buckingham again, "It sometimes occurs to me, if Melbourne retired, and Peel would not take the helm, whether L******** would accept if called upon by the King and party … Peel supporting, of course, the arrangement." *Memoirs of the Courts and Cabinets of William IV and Victoria*, 2:199.

37 Greville, *The Greville Memoirs, 1814–1860*, 3:248.

38 Kitson Clark, *Peel and the Conservative Party*, 290, quoting Lord Wharncliffe.
39 Campbell, *Lives of Lord Lyndhurst and Lord Brougham*, 104; quoting *Hansard*, 3rd ser., vol. 29, 3 August 1835, c. 1399.
40 Greville, *The Greville Memoirs, 1814–1860*, 3:253, 256.
41 Campbell, *Lives of Lord Lyndhurst and Lord Brougham*, 104; quoting *Hansard*, 3rd ser., vol. 29, 3 August 1835, c. 1389.
42 Monypenny and Buckle, *Life*, 1:305.
43 *Morning Post*, 22 August 1835. This series of articles was reprinted as "Peers and People," in *Whigs and Whiggism*, 42–110. See 46–7.
44 *The Greville Memoirs*, 3:256.
45 *Morning Post*, 22 August 1835; *Whigs and Whiggism*, 48–9.
46 *Morning Post*, 28 August 1835; *Whigs and Whiggism*, 69.
47 *Morning Post*, 25 August 1835; *Whigs and Whiggism*, 54–5, 70–1.
48 *Morning Post*, 28 August 1835; *Whigs and Whiggism*, 69–70. See 70, n. 2 for the case of James Naylor, "a Quaker religious enthusiast, who (in 1656) … was arrested and examined by a committee of the House of Commons, and was sentenced … to be whipped, to be branded, and to have his tongue bored with a hot iron."
49 Jupp, "Disraeli's Interpretation of English History," 151. In the same volume there is a brief, but cogent analysis of Disraeli's political ideas as they are expressed in his early writings and novels. See Paul Smith, "Disraeli's Politics," 152–73.
50 *Morning Post*, 22 August 1835; *Whigs and Whiggism*, 43–4.
51 *Morning Post*, 22 August 1835; *Whigs and Whiggism*, 45. Thomas Attwood was the MP for Birmingham and the father of the Political Unions.
52 *Morning Post*, 24 August 1835; *Whigs and Whiggism*, 50–1. 51, n. 2: "He who hangs behind – who opens the door and receives the money – is conductor, or, in the vulgar tongue, cad," *Penny Magazine*, 31 March 1837. Joseph Hume, MP for Middlesex; Henry Warburton, MP for Bridport; Thomas Wakley, MP for Finsbury.
53 *Morning Post*, 29 August 1835; *Whigs and Whiggism*, 77.
54 *Morning Post*, 29 August 1835; *Whigs and Whiggism*, 78–9.
55 *Morning Post*, 31 August 1835; *Whigs and Whiggism*, 85, 87.
56 *Morning Post*, 31 August 1835; *Whigs and Whiggism*, 88–9.
57 Campbell, *Lives of Lord Lyndhurst and Lord Brougham*, 118.
58 *Whigs and Whiggism*, 88, n. 1. Though Campbell places Lyndhurst's "alarm" in the context of events in 1837, the editor, William Hutcheon, records it as occurring in 1835, quite probably a reasonable backward extrapolation.
59 Campbell, *Lives of Lord Lyndhurst and Lord Brougham*, 118.
60 Froude, *The Earl of Beaconsfield*, 64. Cf. Monypenny and Buckle, *Life*, 1:351–3; Blake, *Disraeli*, 134; and Jerman, *The Young Disraeli*, chs 7–8.

61 *Morning Post*, 31 August 1835; *Whigs and Whiggism*, 89–90.

62 *Morning Post*, 26 August 1835; *Whigs and Whiggism*, 57–8. The phrase "perjured Papists" is an allusion to the MPs' oath of allegiance, which Disraeli believes the Irish members in the House of Commons to have violated and in deference to which, he alleges, the Catholic peers had declined to vote on the matter.

63 *Morning Post*, 22 August 1835; *Whigs and Whiggism*, 43. The phrase "Popish rebels" occurs in the articles of 24, 27, 28, 29, 31 August and 2 September.

64 *Morning Post*, 27 and 29 August 1835; *Whigs and Whiggism*, 65, 73.

65 *Morning Post*, 28 August 1835; *Whigs and Whiggism*, 69.

66 *Morning Post*, 29 August 1835; *Whigs and Whiggism*, 72–3. The Radical newspaper was probably the *Courier*.

67 *Morning Post*, 31 August and 2 September; *Whigs and Whiggism*, 85, 96.

68 *Morning Post*, 26 August 1835; *Whigs and Whiggism*, 44, 59–60.

69 *Morning Post*, 27 August 1835; *Whigs and Whiggism*, 62–4.

70 *Morning Post*, 4 September and 27 August 1835; *Whigs and Whiggism*, 102, 64.

71 *Morning Post*, 4 September 1835; *Whigs and Whiggism*, 103–4.

72 *Morning Post*, 31 August 1835; *Whigs and Whiggism*, 87.

73 *Morning Post*, 3 September 1835; *Whigs and Whiggism*, 98, 100.

74 To Sarah Disraeli, [11 August 1835], *Disraeli Letters*, 2 (# 416), 87–8.

75 *Morning Post*, 22 August 1835; *Whigs and Whiggism*, 46.

76 *Morning Post*, 24 August and 26 August 1835; *Whigs and Whiggism*, 49, 57.

77 *Morning Post*, 26 August 1835; *Whigs and Whiggism*, 59.

78 *Morning Post*, 31 August 1835; *Whigs and Whiggism*, 80–1. Cf. Kitson Clark, *Peel and the Conservative Party*, 278.

79 "What Is He?" in *Whigs and Whiggism*, 22.

80 *Morning Post*, 31 August 1835; *Whigs and Whiggism*, 81.

81 *Morning Post*, 1 September 1835; *Whigs and Whiggism*, 90–1.

82 *Morning Post*, 2 September 1835; *Whigs and Whiggism*, 93–4.

83 *Morning Post*, 3 September 1835; *Whigs and Whiggism*, 97–100.

84 *Morning Post*, 7 September 1835; *Whigs and Whiggism*, 110.

85 *Morning Post*, 4 September 1835; *Whigs and Whiggism*, 102–4; *Morning Post*, 5 September 1835; *Whigs and Whiggism*, 106.

7. Vindication

1 Kitson Clark, *Peel and the Conservative Party*, 294–5.

2 *Morning Post*, 7 September 1835; *Whigs and Whiggism*, 107.

3 Kitson Clark, *Peel and the Conservative Party*, 295.

4 Ibid.

5 Disraeli the Younger, *Vindication of the English Constitution*. Hereafter cited as *Vindication* with chapter and page references to the reprinted text in *Whigs and Whiggism*, ed. Hutcheon, 111–232.

6 Monypenny and Buckle, *Life*, 1:308.

7 Stewart, *Benjamin Disraeli*, 55. An invaluable bibliography.

8 Blake, *The Conservative Party*, 3.

9 Faber, *Beaconsfield and Bolingbroke*.

10 Blake, *The Conservative Party*, 20.

11 Among the other members were Alexander Pope, Jonathan Swift, Dr Arbuthnot, John Gay, Lord Chesterfield, and William and Daniel Pulteney.

12 *Morning Post*, 7 September 1835; *Whigs and Whiggism*, 108–9.

13 *Vindication*, chs 2–3; *Whigs and Whiggism*, 114–21.

14 Kramnick, *Bolingbroke and His Circle*, 96.

15 Ibid., 96–7, 89–92.

16 This and the following summary of Bolingbroke's ideas are drawn from Kramnick's excellent discussion, 92–103.

17 Ibid., 95.

18 Ibid., 94, 102.

19 Ibid., 102–3.

20 Ibid., 102.

21 Ibid., 103.

22 Bolingbroke, *On the Spirit of Patriotism*, in *The Works of ... Lord Viscount Bolingbroke*, 4:187–9.

23 *Vindication*, ch. 5; *Whigs and Whiggism*, 124–5.

24 Ibid., 125.

25 Kramnick, *Bolingbroke and His Circle*, 102.

26 In the *Vindication* Disraeli elaborates this argument with a discussion of the history of the formation of the Commons through a merger of the burgesses and the Estate of the Knights in the thirteenth century. See chs 12–14; *Whigs and Whiggism*, 148–61.

27 Kramnick, *Bolingbroke and His Circle*, 104.

28 Ibid., 37, 101, 97.

29 *Vindication*, chs 23 and 24; *Whigs and Whiggism*, 198–9.

30 See Isaac D'Israeli, *Commentaries on the Life and Reign of Charles I*.

31 *Vindication*, chs 19 and 20; *Whigs and Whiggism*, 177–9.

32 See Bolingbroke, *Remarks on the History of England*, in *Works*, 2:109–424; and *A Dissertation Upon Parties*, in *Works*, 3: 3–312. Cf. Disraeli, *Vindication*, chs 19 and 20, 175–83.

33 *Morning Post*, 7 September 1835; *Whigs and Whiggism*, 108.

34 *Vindication*, ch. 24; *Whigs and Whiggism*, 229.

35　Bolingbroke, *The Idea of a Patriot King*, in *Works*, 4:281; henceforth cited as *Patriot King*.

36　Ibid., 271.

37　Ibid., 322, 315.

38　Kramnick, *Bolingbroke and His Circle*, 6–7.

39　Monypenny and Buckle, *Life*, 1:282–6.

40　Faber, *Beaconsfield and Bolingbroke*, 81.

41　*Vindication*, ch. 31; *Whigs and Whiggism*, 218–19.

42　To Sarah Disraeli, 9 January 1836, *Disraeli Letters*, 2 (# 464), 128.

43　*Vindication*, ch. 32, 221–2.

44　Blake, *The Conservative Party*, 3–8. Cf. Faber, *Beaconsfield and Bolingbroke*, 70–7.

45　Blake, *The Conservative Party*, 8.

46　Faber, *Beaconsfield and Bolingbroke*, 73.

47　Ibid., 82.

48　Lasswell, *Psychopathology and Politics*, 74–5. Lasswell's theory rests upon the clinical evidence of the many pathological manifestations of political behaviour he treated in psychiatric patients, but it is not intended to be restricted to the realm of the abnormal.

49　Monypenny and Buckle, *Life*, 1:306.

50　Letter from Isaac, Wednesday, nd, Disraeli Papers, A/I/C/62. *Disraeli Letters*, 2 (# 450), n. 4, gives the date of Isaac's letter as 23 December 1835. See also Monypenny and Buckle, *Life*, 1:306–7.

51　See, for example, the text of a lecture by Richard Garnett, "Shelley and Lord Beaconsfield," printed by The Shelley Society (London, 1887), and R.A. Duerksen, "Disraeli's Use of Shelley," *Victorian Newsletter* 26 (1964): 19–22

52　*Venetia* is in vol. 7 of the Bradenham Edition of *The Novels and Tales of Benjamin Disraeli*.

53　Bradford, *Disraeli*, 92–3.

54　As most of Disraeli's readers in 1837 would know, some of the details of this episode are drawn from Lady Caroline Lamb's infatuation with Byron, which led her to disguise herself as a page or servant in the hope of gaining entrance to his company long after he had tired of her passion.

8. Young England / *Coningsby*

1　Earlier versions of portions of this chapter were published as "The Arts of a Designing Person" in the *Proceedings of the Disraeli Colloquium* (Queen's University, spring 1979): 98–115; or as "Disraeli's *Coningsby*: Political

Manifesto or Psychological Romance?" in *Victorian Studies* 23.1 (fall 1979): 57–78. Copyright Indiana University Press.

2 Mutilated Diary, Disraeli Papers, A/III/C/49.

3 To Sarah Disraeli, [16 March 1838], *Disraeli Letters*, 3 (# 747), 36–8.

4 Disraeli's brother James was a spectator in the House of Commons that night.

5 To Sarah Disraeli, [26 April 1838], *Disraeli Letters*, 3 (# 766), 51–2.

6 To Sarah Disraeli, [25? February 1839], *Disraeli Letters*, 3 (# 897), 148–9.

7 To Sarah Disraeli, [1 March 1839], *Disraeli Letters*, 3 (# 900), 151–2.

8 To Sarah Disraeli, [9 March 1839], *Disraeli Letters*, 3 (# 904), 155.

9 To Sarah Disraeli, 21 June 1839, *Disraeli Letters*, 3 (# 941), 180–1. See also n. 1: "'Thick as autumnal leaves that strow the brooks/ In Vallombrosa,' *Paradise Lost*, I, 302–3."

10 To Sarah Disraeli, [13 July 1839], *Disraeli Letters*, 3 (# 965), 197.

11 To Sarah Disraeli, [9 August 1839], *Disraeli Letters*, 3 (# 978), 205.

12 To Sarah Disraeli, 10 August 1839, *Disraeli Letters*, 3 (# 980), 206.

13 Monypenny and Buckle, *Life*, 2:89. See also *Disraeli Letters*, 3 (# 1036), 252, n. 1.

14 To Sarah Disraeli, 15 May 1841, *Disraeli Letters*, 3 (# 1156), 334–5.

15 To Sarah Disraeli, [23 January 1840], *Disraeli Letters*, 3 (# 1036), 251–2.

16 To Sarah Disraeli, [18 March 1841], *Disraeli Letters*, 3 (# 1140), 325; [22 March 1841], *Disraeli Letters*, 3 (# 1143), 327.

17 See the letter to Sarah Disraeli, 15 May 1841, *Disraeli Letters*, 3 (# 1156), 334, n. 1; To Sir Robert Peel, 6 June 1841, *Disraeli Letters*, 3 (# 1160), 338.

18 To Sarah Disraeli, [24 July 1841], *Disraeli Letters*, 3 (# 1174), 350.

19 To Sarah Disraeli, [27 and 29 July 1841], *Disraeli Letters*, 3 (# 1175, 1176), 351; to Sarah Disraeli, [19 August 1841], *Disraeli Letters*, 3 (# 1179), 353.

20 To Mary Anne Disraeli, [24 August and 2 September 1841], *Disraeli Letters*, 3 (# 1181 and 1185), 354, 355; to Sarah Disraeli, [31 August? 1841], *Disraeli; Letters*, 3 (# 1184), 355.

21 To Sir Robert Peel, 5 September 1841, *Disraeli Letters*, 3 (# 1186), 356.

22 To Sarah Disraeli, 6 September 1841, *Disraeli Letters*, 3 (# 1188), 357.

23 Gash, *Sir Robert Peel*, 267.

24 Brit. Mus. Add. Mss. 40486, f. 7.

25 To Sir Robert Peel, 17 August 1841, *Disraeli Letters*, 3 (# 1178), 352.

26 To Sir Robert Peel, 5 September 1841, *Disraeli Letters*, 3 (# 1186), 356.

27 Sir Robert Peel to Benjamin Disraeli, 7 September 1841, cited in Peel, *Sir Robert Peel from His Private Papers*, 2:487–8.

28 To Sir Robert Peel, 8 September 1841, *Disraeli Letters*, 3 (# 1189), 358.

29 Blake, *Disraeli*, 165–6.

30 To Mary Anne Disraeli, [25 February 1842], *Disraeli Letters*, 4 (# 1217), 17–18.

31 To Mary Anne Disraeli, 9 March 1842, *Disraeli Letters*, 4 (# 1224), 25–6. This phrase would become part of a scenario in Disraeli's last completed novel, where Endymion has a similar triumph.

32 To Mary Anne Disraeli, [10 March 1842], *Disraeli Letters*, 4 (# 1226), 28–30.

33 To Mary Anne Disraeli, [11 and 13 March 1842], *Disraeli Letters*, 4 (# 1229 and 1231), 31, 34–5.

34 To Mary Anne Disraeli, [13 March 1842], *Disraeli Letters*, 4 (# 1231), 35: "I think it wo[ul]d be as well for me if, in consequence of a cause, which thank God no longer exists, domestic anxiety were to take me into the country – rather suddenly – & so not go down to the House tomorrow." Cf. the letter to Mary Anne Disraeli, 15 March [1842], *Disraeli Letters*, 4 (# 1233), 39: "I kept from the house, because Vyvyan, as I was informed, was going to attack Peel, & oppose the progress of the Corn Bill ... I believe there is to be a grand row on Friday – but I shall steal off in the morning before, & all the better, as affairs political are very queeer" [*sic*].

35 Blake, *Disraeli*, 171.

36 Bolingbroke, "A Letter on the Spirit of Patriotism," in *The Works of the Late Right Honourable Henry St. John, Lord Viscount Bolingbroke*, 4:213.

37 Blake, *Disraeli*, 174.

38 Whibley, *Lord John Manners and His Friends*, 1:143–4.

39 Alexander Baillie-Cochrane to Lord John Manners, nd, quoted in Whibley, *Lord John Manners and His Friends*, 1:148–9.

40 Appendix III, *Disraeli Letters*, 4, 371–3. A rough draft of this memorandum is in the Disraeli Papers and a more or less accurate transcription of it is also printed as an Appendix to vol. 2 of Monypenny and Buckle, *Life*, 409–13.

41 To Lord John Manners, 3 December 1842, quoted in Whibley, *Lord John Manners and His Friends*, 1:141

42 Quoted in Whibley, *Lord John Manners and His Friends*, 1:149, 153.

43 Quoted in Whibley, *Lord John Manners and His Friends*, 1:174.

44 Bolingbroke was also familiarly known as "Harry." The best modern study of Bolingbroke's writings (including *The Spirit of Patriotism* and *A Dissertation Upon Parties*) is Kramnick, *Bolingbroke and His Circle*.

45 Blake, *Disraeli*, 190. Cf Langdon-Davies, introduction to *Coningsby*, xxviii: "Disraeli has created a new type. The novel is essentially political, written to expound a political creed."

46 Both prefaces are cited by Blake, *Disraeli*, 193–4. *Coningsby* was first published by Henry Colburn; the Collected Edition of 1870 was published by Longmans.

47 Monypenny and Buckle, *Life*, 2:199.
48 Book, chapter, and page references are to vol. 8 of the Bradenham Edition.
49 Disraeli first met the baron's nephew, Anthony de Rothschild, several years earlier at a dinner party in London.
50 Isaac D'Israeli, *Curiosities of Literature with a View of the Life and Writings of the Author by his Son*, 3 vols., 14th ed. (London: Moxon, 1849), 1:xx–xxi. See also below, ch. 11, and the letter to Robert Shelton Mackenzie, 26 February 1845, *Disraeli Letters*, 4 (# 1395), 158–9.
51 *"What Is He?"* in *Whigs and Whiggism*, ed. Hutcheon, 19.
52 *Coningsby*, Bk 6, ch. 7, and *Henrietta Temple*, Bk 2, chs 5 and 9. Cf. *The Wondrous Tale of Alroy*, Part 5, ch. 6.
53 *Coningsby*, Bk 6, ch. 8 and Bk 7, ch. 1; *Henrietta Temple*, Bk 2, ch. 9.
54 Cf. *Henrietta Temple*, Bk 2, chs 11 and 13.
55 Cf. *Henrietta Temple*, Bk 3, ch. 1.
56 Appendix III, *Disraeli Letters*, 4:371–3.

9. Sir Robert Peel and the Apotheosis of Young England

 1 Monypenny and Buckle, *Life*, 2:245–6.
 2 Monypenny and Buckle, *Life*, 2:245.
 3 *Hansard*, 3rd ser., vol. 71, 15 August 1843, c. 839.
 4 Monypenny and Buckle, *Life*, 2:179, n. 1: "During Disraeli's stay in Paris, Louis Philippe had lamented '*l'insouciance avec laquelle l'Autriche et l'Angleterre laissaient tomber l'Empire Ottoman sous le bon vouloir de la Russie.*'"
 5 *Hansard*, 3rd ser., vol. 71, 15 August 1843, c. 835. Cf. the report of this speech in *The Times*, 16 August 1843, 5, which in paraphrase entirely misses the sarcasm of Disraeli's words.
 6 Sir James Graham to John Wilson Croker, 22 August 1843, in Croker, *The Croker Papers*, 3:9.
 7 Sir James Graham to Sir Robert Peel, 21 December 1843, in Peel, *Sir Robert Peel, from His Private Papers*, 3:424.
 8 Sir Robert Peel to Sir James Graham, 22 December 1843, in Peel, *Sir Robert Peel, from His Private Papers*, 3:425.
 9 Sir Robert Peel to Croker, 22 April 1845, in Croker, *The Croker Papers*, 3:32.
10 Disraeli to Peel, 4 February 1844, *Disraeli Letters*, 4 (# 1337), 116–18; Peel to Disraeli, 6 February 1844, *Disraeli Letters*, 4:118, n. 6.
11 *Hansard*, 3rd ser., vol. 72, 16 February 1844, c. 1014.
12 *The Times*, 17 February 1844, 3. Cf. *Hansard*, 3rd ser., vol. 72, 16 February 1844, c. 1016.

13 *Hansard*, 3rd ser., vol. 190, 16 March 1868, c. 1791.

14 *Hansard*, 3rd ser., vol. 72, 16 February 1844, c. 1016. Cf. *The Times*, 17 February 1844, 3.

15 *Hansard*, 3rd ser.,vol. 72, 16 February 1844, c. 1012. Cf. *The Times*, 17 February 1844, 3.

16 *Hansard*, 3rd ser., vol. 72, 16 February 1844, c. 1015. Cf. *The Times*, 17 February 1844, 3.

17 Monypenny and Buckle, *Life*, 2:242, Blake, *Disraeli*, 180; *Hansard*, 3rd ser., vol. 75, 17 June 1844, c. 1030. Cf. *The Times*, 18 June 1844, 3–4.

18 Benson and Esher, *The Letters of Queen Victoria*, 2:16 (18 June 1844). In Queen Victoria's opinion Peel's resignation would have been "*a great calamity*," for, she said, "*we cannot* have a better and a *safer* Minister … Our present people are all *safe*, and not led away by impulses and reckless passions" (16–17).

19 To Sarah Disraeli, 9 July 1844, *Disraeli Letters*, 4 (# 1362), 132–4. John Walter was the editor of *The Times*.

20 To Mary Anne Disraeli, 27 August 1844, *Disraeli Letters*, 4 (# 1370), 139–41.

21 To Mary Anne Disraeli, 28 August 1844, *Disraeli Letters*, 4 (# 1371), 141–2.

22 To Mary Anne Disraeli, 27 August 1844, *Disraeli Letters*, 4 (# 1370), 139.

23 To Mary Anne Disraeli, 28 August 1844, *Disraeli Letters*, 4 (# 1371), 141.

24 *The Times*, 5 October 1844, 5. Dickens had presided at the meeting of the previous year.

25 *The Times*, 5 October 1844, 6. Cf. Whibley, *Lord John Manners and His Friends*, 1:175–6.

26 *The Times*, 5 October 1844, 6. Cf. Whibley, *Lord John Manners and His Friends*, 1:176–7.

27 Whibley, *Lord John Manners and His Friends*, 1:172–3. Cf. "Birmingham Athenic Institution," and the "Editorial comment – Abridged from the *Birmingham Journal*," *The Times*, 4 September 1844, 5.

28 *The Times*, 5 October 1844, 6. Cf. Whibley, *Lord John Manners and His Friends*, 1:177–8.

29 Whibley, *Lord John Manners and His Friends* 1:178. Cf. *The Times*, 5 October 1844, 6. It is necessary to use caution in citing quotations in Whibley, for he sometimes conflates phrases and sentences and he occasionally appropriates metaphors from other speakers to enhance the point at issue.

30 *The Times*, 5 October 1844, 6.

31 Smythe to Disraeli, 2 July 1852, Disraeli Papers, B/XXI/S/652. Cf. an earlier letter, which gives an indication of how Smythe's thoughts were particularly focused on Disraeli's leadership on the occasion of the speech at Manchester: "I … never shall forget how you found me low abused in

my own esteem and that of others, morbidly debating my own powers, and how you made a man of me and set me on my legs at Manchester, and have ever been to me the kindliest and gentlest of councillors." Smythe to Disraeli, 16 January 1846 (erroneously dated 16 December), Disraeli Papers, B/XXI/S/650.

32 *The Times*, 5 October 1844, 6.
33 Monypenny and Buckle, *Life*, 2:247–8.
34 To Sarah Disraeli, 19 Janaury 1845, quoted in Monypenny and Buckle, *Life*, 2:249. Cf. *Disraeli Letters*, 4:154, n. 1.
35 To Sarah Disraeli, 20 January 1845, *Disraeli Letters*, 4 (# 1389), 154: "You have heard of our sudden expedition to Stowe, and its brilliant success; Her Majesty, Peel, Aberdeen, and all equally distinguishing us by their courtesy."
36 *The Times*, 21 February 1845, 4. Cf. *Hansard*, 3rd ser., vol. 77, 20 February 1845, c. 906 and Monypenny and Buckle, *Life*, 2:311–12.
37 *The Times*, 22 February 1845, 4. Cf. *Hansard*, 3rd ser., vol. 77, 21 February 1845, c. 998.
38 Blake, *Disraeli*, 185. Cf. George Smythe's Manchester Athenaeum speech (above, 282–3): "Remember how in high life his views were thwarted, his spirit cowed, his heart broken – how he was hasted to his grave ... "
39 To Robert Shelton Mackenzie, 26 February 1845, *Disraeli Letters*, 4 (# 1395), 158–9, and n. 1.
40 *The Times*, 1 March 1845, 5. Cf. *Hansard*, 3rd ser., vol. 78, 28 February 1845, cc. 154–5.
41 "Mr. B. Disraeli," *Fraser's Magazine* 35 (February 1847), 205.
42 *Fraser's Magazine* 35 (February 1847), 205.
43 *The Times*, 1 March 1845, 5. Cf. *Hansard*, 3rd ser., vol. 78, 28 February 1845, cc. 155–6.
44 G. Smythe to Mary Anne Disraeli, quoted in Monypenny and Buckle, *Life*, 2:317–18.
45 To Sarah Disraeli, [3 March 1845], *Disraeli Letters*, 4 (# 1396), 159.
46 *Hansard*, 3rd ser., vol. 78, 13 March 1845, cc. 785–810.
47 *Hansard*, 3rd ser., vol. 78, 13 March 1845, cc. 810–20; 818.
48 *Hansard*, 3rd ser., vol. 78, 17 March 1845, c. 1028. Cf. *The Times*, 18 March 1845, 4, which in this case gives a very poor summary of Disraeli's speech. It is interesting and perhaps significant that on this issue Smythe supported the Government.
49 Blake, *Disraeli*, 183.
50 *Hansard*, 3rd ser., vol. 79, ll April 1845, cc. 555–69, 561, 567; Cf. *The Times*, 12 April 1845, 4.

51 *The Times*, 12 April 1845, 4. Cf. *Hansard*, 3rd ser., vol. 79, ll April 1845, cc. 568–9.

52 Thomas Babington Macaulay, *Hansard*, 3rd ser., vol. 79, 14 April 1845, c. 657. Cf. *The Times*, 12 April 1845, 4. See also, Monypenny and Buckle, *Life*, 2:330, n. 1.

53 Disraeli, *Lord George Bentinck*, 7–8.

54 To Sarah Disraeli, [19 July 1845], *Disraeli Letters*, 4 (# 1428), 178.

55 To Sarah Disraeli, [6 September 1845], *Disraeli Letters*, 4 (# 1441), 189–90.

56 To Sarah Disraeli, [8 September 1845], *Disraeli Letters*, 4 (# 1443), 190–1.

57 To Sarah Disraeli, 26 October 1845, *Disraeli Letters*, 4 (#1446), 195–6: "I have been able to write very regularly, & made better progress than usual, wh: is encouraging."

58 To Lord John Manners, 17 December [1845], *Disraeli Letters*, 4 (# 1455), 207–8: "What is going to happen? After living three months in profound solitude in a Flemish wilderness … I arrived here a fortnight ago, & found myself in a political atmosphere of fever heat." See also, Whibley, *Lord John Manners and His Friends*, 1:195.

59 Sarah to Disraeli, mid-October 1845, quoted in Monypenny and Buckle, *Life*, 2:334.

60 Peel, *Memoirs*, vol. 2, part 3, 105–8. See also Blake, *Disraeli*, 222.

61 Blake, *Disraeli*, 222.

62 Disraeli, *Lord George Bentinck*, 34.

63 Croker, *The Croker Papers*, 3:44.

64 Wellington to Croker, 29 December 1845, *The Croker Papers*, 3:45.

65 Croker to Peel, 16 December 1845, *The Croker Papers*, 3:39.

66 Peel, *Memoirs*, vol. 2, part 3, 203. Cf. Lord Ripon to Sir Robert Peel, 29 November 1845, ibid., 195–7: "the crisis is one of immense magnitude; and … I cannot look without the greatest apprehension upon the evils which may fall upon the Queen and the country if you are withdrawn from the guidance of public affairs … I catch at any idea which may possibly afford the means of preventing the occurrence of the calamity which I so much dread."

67 "To Sir Robert Peel," signed "'Runnymede,' January 26, 1836," *The Times*, 27 January 1836, 2: "You are summoned now, like the Knight of Corinth in Schiller's heroic ballad, as the only hope of a suffering people. In your chivalry alone is our hope. Clad in the panoply of your splendid talents and your spotless character, we feel assured that you will subdue this unnatural and unnational monster … Rescue your Sovereign from an unconstitutional thraldom – rescue an august Senate which has already fought the battle of the people – rescue our national church … our

venerable constitution ... but, above all ... rescue THE NATION."
Reprinted in Disraeli, *The Letters of Runnymede*, where the "Knight of
Corinth" has become the "Knight of Rhodes" and "a suffering people" has
become "a suffering island."

68 Peel, *Memoirs*, vol. 2, part 3, 155: "The Minister who foresaw ... that there
would be 'cruel distress' in Ireland from the scarcity of food, might surely
advise the removal of restrictions on its import without justly incurring
the reproach of treason and perfidy to his party connections." Cf. Lord
Stanley to Peel, 2 November 1845, ibid., 161: "I foresee that this question,
if you persevere in your present opinion, must break up the Government
one way or the other; but I shall greatly regret indeed if it should be
broken up, not in consequence of our feeling that we had proposed
measures which it properly belonged to others to carry, but in consequence of differences of opinion among ourselves."

69 Cabinet Memorandum, 29 November 1845, in Peel, *Memoirs*, vol. 2, part 3,
193: "suppose there should be real scarcity in the spring; suppose there
should be disease as the consequence of it; suppose there should be a
turbulent spirit or actual violence: shall we not be enabled to act with
greater energy and decision in repressing violence?"

70 The Duke of Wellington, for example, justified his support of Peel's new
policy and cabinet in a letter to Croker, 6 January 1846, *The Croker Papers*,
3:51, 53: "I am the *retained* servant of the Sovereign of this empire ... But I
will not be instrumental in placing the Government in the hands of the
League and the Radicals."

71 See, for example, Henry Goulbourn to Peel, 30 November 1845, in Peel,
Memoirs, vol. 2, part 3, 202: "I fairly own that I do not see how the repeal
of the Corn Law is to afford relief to the distress with which we are
threatened."

72 Much of the weight of Peel's explanations in these memoranda falls on the
"ultimate and not remote extinction of protective duties." Cabinet
Memorandum, 2 December 1845, *Memoirs*, vol. 2, part 3, 219.

73 To Sarah Disraeli, 5 December 1845, *Disraeli Letters*, 4 (# 1452), 202–3; to
Baron Lionel de Rothschild, 3 December 1845, *Disraeli Letters*, 4 (# 1451),
201–2; to Lord John Manners, 17 December [1845], *Disraeli Letters*, 4
(# 1455), 207–9.

74 To Lord Palmerston, 14 December 1845, *Disraeli Letters*, 4 (# 1453), 204–6.

75 Ibid., 205.

76 Ibid., 206.

77 Ibid.

78 Ibid., 204, 338; to Lord John Manners, 17 December 1845, *Disraeli Letters*, 4
(# 1455), 209. Cf. the letter to Sarah Disraeli, 10 November 1845, *Disraeli*

Letters, 4 (# 1447), 197: "tho' I can scarcely believe Sir R. will call Pt. tog[ethe]r. When[eve]r he does, I trust to his confusion."

79 Disraeli to Manners, 17 December [1845], *Disraeli Letters*, 4 (# 1455), 209. In fact Russell did not actually give up his attempt to form the government until 19 December. In the meantime Palmerston had sent a reply to Disraeli on the 18th, thanking him for his interventions with Guizot and the king and authorizing him to "speak in the same sense on the subject to any-body with whom you may converse upon it." Lord Palmerston to Disraeli, 18 December 1845, Monypenny and Buckle, *Life*, 2:341.

80 Lord Palmerston to Disraeli, 18 December 1845, Monypenny and Buckle, *Life*, 2:341.

10. *Sybil*: Two Nations, Or One? An Allegorical Romance

1 An earlier version of this chapter was published as "Two Nations or One? Disraeli's Allegorical Romance" in *Victorian Studies* 30.2 (winter 1987): 211–34. Copyright Indiana University Press.

2 *Coningsby*, like *Vivian Grey*, inspired the publication of unofficial "Keys," intended to inform those not in the know about the real identities of the various characters.

3 Book, chapter, and page citations are to the Bradenham Edition, vol. 8. Among the best discussions of *Sybil* are Levine, *Benjamin Disraeli*; Brantlinger, *The Spirit of Reform*; Schwarz, *Disraeli's Fiction*; and Braun, *Disraeli the Novelist*. Donald Stone, *The Romantic Impulse in Victorian Fiction*, has a good essay, "Benjamin Disraeli and the Romance of the Will."

4 The best essays on Disraeli's sources are Sheila M. Smith, "Willenhall and Wodgate," and Fido, "'From His Own Observation.'" Chief among Disraeli's sources are the Children's Employment Commission's Blue Books (1842–3), Thomas Tancred's *First Report from the Midland Mining Commissioners, South Staffordshire* (1843), William Dodd's *The Factory System* (1842), Edwin Chadwick's *Report of the Sanitary Condition of the Labouring Population of Great Britain* (1842), William Cobbett's *A History of the Protestant Reformation in England and Ireland* (1824), Gilbert Burnet's *History of My Own Times* (1724–34), and Isaac D'Israeli's *Commentaries on the Life and Reign of Charles I* (1828–30).

5 Disraeli subtitled *Contarini Fleming* "A Psychological Romance." Here I use the term in much the same sense he did, and, accordingly, an allegorical romance in this case is a love story whose plot and characters can be seen to embody the struggle of various social, political, and religious values within Victorian society.

6 General Preface to the collected edition of the novels (London: Longmans, 1870); reprinted in vol. 1 of the Bradenham Edition, x. A more convenient citation is Blake, *Disraeli*, 193–4.

7 Brantlinger, *The Spirit of Reform*, 97.

8 Ibid., 104.

9 In his speeches in 1839 and 1840 Disraeli criticized the centralization of relief inherent in the New Poor Law, advocating instead the traditional system of local responsibility for the poor. He also voted against a bill advancing money for a police force in Birmingham and he spoke against the harsh sentences given to Chartist leaders convicted of felonies. See Blake, *Disraeli*, 161–2. Disraeli was, in fact, sympathetic to individual Chartists and their grievances without ever endorsing essentially democratic ideas.

10 Brantlinger, *The Spirit of Reform*, 100.

11 General Preface, x.

12 "Industry" in this context means "the spirit of labour"; see the *Oxford English Dictionary*.

13 The best previous treatments of religion in *Sybil* are Levine, *Benjamin Disraeli*, 107–14, and Schwarz, *Disraeli's Fiction*, 111–14.

14 See the notes by Thom Braun to the Penguin edition of *Sybil* (Harmondsworth, 1980), 505–9, 514–15.

15 Schwarz, *Disraeli's Fiction*, 111, 114, 120.

16 Lilies are often associated with the Virgin Mary and appear symbolically in many paintings of the period. In the Tate Gallery's catalogue, *The Pre-Raphaelites* (London: Penguin, 1984), for example, the notes to Dante Gabriel Rossetti's *Ecce Ancilla Domini!* (1849–50) read in part: "the dove, symbolising the Holy Spirit, and the lily, with one bud still to break … are the instruments of conception" (73). See Charles Allston Collins's "Convent Thoughts" (1850–1) in the same catalogue: "The inscription at the top of the frame, 'Sicut Lilium,' is from the Song of Solomon 2.2, 'Sicut lilium inter spinas' ('As the lily among thorns'), an image applied frequently to the Virgin Mary" (87).

17 Disraeli, *Lord George Bentinck*, 507. Lord John Russell's motion to remove the Jewish disabilities was made on 16 December 1847. Disraeli's unorthodox views gave consternation to his friends, who preferred to argue the case on the basis of tolerance.

18 Not the least curious feature of this development in *Sybil* is the underlying similarity it suggests between Disraeli's ideas on the ideal relation between politics and religion and Gladstone's. Of course, the differences between the two men are many and obvious. While Disraeli's Young

England ideas were laced with Byronic recklessness, Gladstone's Tractarian sympathies were well diluted with evangelical probity. And Disraeli was increasingly estranged from the Conservatism of Sir Robert Peel which Gladstone idolized. Further, Gladstone would have found Disraeli's claims of Hebrew superiority repugnant, even though he shared the strong sense of continuity in the historical development of Judaic-Christian theology. In light of such comparisons, it is interesting to speculate on what the conception of *Falconet* might have shown about Disraeli's awareness of the similarity. The protagonist of the last, unfin-ished novel, Joseph Toplady Falconet, is clearly a caricature of Gladstone.

19 Surrogate portraits with both romantic and spiritual associations are also used in *Contarini Fleming* and *Coningsby*. See above, chs 1 and 8.

20 Brantlinger recognizes that Disraeli puts the theory of the Two Nations in the mouth of "a godless Owenite," but sees it as part of a genuine paradox (*The Spirit of Reform*, 102). Schwarz describes the author of the Two Nations concept as Egremont's "amoral, agnostic, and paranoid rival," but concludes that this is merely "a curiosity of *Sybil*" (*Disraeli's Fiction*, 120).

21 Book 3, ch. 4. Disraeli's exaggeration of some of the conditions at Willenhall is discussed by Sheila M. Smith in "Willenhall and Wodgate." Thom Braun summarizes her points in *Disraeli the Novelist*, 98.

22 The best previous discussion of social class and irony in *Sybil* is that of Brantlinger, *The Spirit of Reform*, 96–107.

23 *Hansard*, 3rd ser., vol. 49, 246–52.

24 See the "Advertisement" to *Sybil*, May 1845 (London: Colburn, 1845).

25 General Preface to the *Collected Edition of the Novels and Tales by the Right Honorable B. Disraeli* (London: Longmans, 1870), 1:xii; reprinted in the Bradenham Edition of the novels, 1:xiii, and quoted by Blake, *Disraeli*, 193–4.

26 After the triumph of Young England at the meeting of the Manchester Athenaeum on 3 October 1844, Disraeli and his wife made an extended round of visits in the north of England to the homes of friends and sympathizers. While visiting the Ferrands at Bingley, Disraeli made a speech that outlines his political ideas at the time he was writing *Sybil*: "We are asked sometimes what we want. We want in the first place to impress upon society that there is such a thing as duty. We don't do that in any spirit of conceit or arrogance; we don't pretend that we are better than others; but we are anxious to do our duty, and, if so, we think we have a right to call on others, whether rich or poor, to do theirs. If that principle of duty had not been lost sight of for the last fifty years, you would never have heard of the classes into which England is divided" (Monypenny and

Buckle, *Life*, 2:247–8). It is only presumptive evidence that Disraeli had
one, not two nations in mind when he began to work on *Sybil*, but in *The
Croker Papers* the editor, Louis J. Jennings, describes the Young Englanders'
speeches at the Manchester Athenaeum: "They went to Manchester (in
1844) and attended meetings of the operatives, and Mr. Disraeli showed
how strongly he held the opinions which he afterwards developed in
'Sybil, or the New Nation,' as the book was at first called, the sub-title
being afterwards changed to 'The Two Nations'" (*The Croker Papers*, 3:9).
Although *Sybil* was never published with such a subtitle, it fits with the
earlier work, *Coningsby; or, the New Generation*, and the later, *Tancred; or, the
New Crusade*.

11. Rhetoric, Principles, and Expediency:
The Corn Law Debate of 1846 and the Politics of Protection

1 Blake, *Disraeli*, 221–2.
2 Disraeli, *Lord George Bentinck*, 48–52. The following citations in the text are
   to this book.
3 *Hansard*, 3rd ser., vol. 83, 22 January 1846, cc. 113–14. Cf *The Times*, 23
   January 1846, 5. The text of this speech given in *Hansard* is reprinted in
   Disraeli, *Selected Speeches of the Late Right Honourable Earl of Beaconsfield*,
   1:98–110. It is also quoted at length in Monypenny and Buckle, *Life*,
   2:351–7, whose account interpolates the listeners' reactions.
4 *The Times* of July and August 1839 carried almost daily accounts of the
   situation in the Levant under the heading of foreign correspondence from
   Constantinople, Aleppo, Alexandria, and Paris. Disraeli seems to be basing
   his version of events in large part upon his memory of these columns.
5 *Hansard*, 3rd ser., vol. 83, 22 January 1846, c. 95; *The Times*, 23 January 1846, 4.
6 To Lord John Manners, 17 December 1845, *Disraeli Letters*, 4 (# 1455),
   207–9.
7 *Hansard*, 3rd ser., vol. 83, 22 January 1846, cc. 115–16. Cf. *The Times*, 23
   January 1846, 5; Monypenny and Buckle, *Life*, 2:352.
8 *The Times*, 23 January 1846, 5. Cf. *Hansard*, 3rd ser., vol. 83, 22 January 1846,
   c. 116. In this instance the wording in *The Times* seems preferable because
   of its immediacy, even though the correspondent admits that at times the
   speaker was "very imperfectly heard in the gallery."
9 *Hansard*, 3rd ser., vol. 83, 22 January 1846, c. 118. Cf. *The Times*, 23 January
   1846, 5; Monypenny and Buckle, *Life*, 2:354.
10 *Hansard*, 3rd ser., vol. 83, 22 January 1846, c. 119. Cf. *The Times*, 23 January
   1846, 5. Shakespeare, *Henry IV, pt 2*, 5. 5.46; *Henry V*, 4.1.45; Milton, "Lycidas."

11 *Hansard*, 3rd ser., vol. 83, 22 January 1846, cc. 122–3. Cf. *The Times*, 23 January 1846, 5; Monypenny and Buckle, *Life*, 2:356.
12 Disraeli, *Lord George Bentinck*, 38.
13 Ibid., 37; and a letter from Lord George Bentinck to Lord Stanley, 21 January 1846 [?], quoted in Monypenny and Buckle, *Life*, 2:360.
14 Monypenny and Buckle, *Life*, 2:359–60.
15 The ostensible winner of the race, "Running Rein," was subsequently proved to be a four-year-old horse and therefore disqualified.
16 Greville, *The Greville Memoirs 1814–1860*, vol. 5 (Jan. 1842–Dec. 1847), 185.
17 Monypenny and Buckle, *Life*, 2:360.
18 *Lord George Bentinck*, 1–3.
19 Ibid., 38–9.
20 *Hansard*, 3rd ser., vol. 86, 15 May 1846, c. 673.
21 *The Times*, 16 May 1846, 4; *Hansard*, 3rd ser., vol. 86, 15 May 1846, c. 677.
22 *Coningsby*, Bk. 8, ch. 2, 425–6; ch. 4, 438–9.
23 *Hansard*, 3rd ser., vol. 86, 15 May 1846, cc. 689–90.
24 *Hansard*, 3rd ser., vol. 86, 15 May 1846, cc. 707–9.
25 To Sir Robert Peel, 5 September 1841, *Disraeli Letters*, 3 (# 1186), 356.
26 Sir Robert Peel to Disraeli, 7 September 1841, quoted in Monypenny and Buckle, *Life*, 2:119.
27 To Sir Robert Peel, 8 September 1841, *Disraeli Letters*, 3 (# 1189), 358.
28 The more sympathetic reading of Disraeli's situation in 1841 and 1846 was first suggested by Professor Wiebe in response to a paper I delivered at Queen's University, and it has since been further developed in private correspondence
29 To Sarah, 19 August, 21 August, 25 August, and 31 August 1841; to Mary Anne, 24 August, 28 August, and 2 September 1841, *Disraeli Letters*, 3 (# 1179–85), 353–55.
30 Mary Anne Disraeli to Sir Robert Peel, [4 September 1841], *Disraeli Letters*, 3, 356, n. 2.
31 To Sarah, 6 September 1841, *Disraeli Letters*, 3 (# 1188), 357.
32 Blake, *Disraeli*, 237.
33 To Sir James Graham, 20 December 1843, *Disraeli Letters*, 4 (# 1332), 113. A similar, slightly less acerbic letter was sent to Lord Stanley, 6 December 1843, Disraeli *Letters*, 4 (# 1331), 112. Cf. #1260, 16 September 1842, 4:56.
34 Quoted in *Disraeli Letters*, 4:113, n. 1.
35 Monypenny and Buckle, *Life*, 2:121–2.
36 *Morning Post*, 18 May 1846, 4.
37 *Morning Post*, 30 June 1846, 4.
38 *Morning Post*, 27 June 1846, 4.

39 The *Nonconformist*, Wednesday, 20 May 1846, 349.

40 The *Spectator*, Saturday, 27 June 1846, 614, 613.

41 The *Observer*, Sunday, 17 May 1846, 4; this item was reprinted the next day in the issue of Monday, l8 May.

42 *Douglas Jerrold's Weekly Newspaper*, No. 5, Saturday, 15 August 1846, 97.

43 *The Times*, 19 May 1846, 6.

44 Blake, *Disraeli*, 237–8.

45 See chs 1 and 10 for Disraeli's identification with George Canning.

46 Dixon, *George Canning*, 280–1. This view is expressed in a letter from Earl Grey to Lord Holland, 14 April 1827, Grey Papers, University of Durham, Box 35:2.

47 *Lord George Bentinck*, 230, 234–5.

48 Ibid., 235.

49 Ibid., 240–4.

50 Ibid., 248; Monypenny and Buckle, *Life*, 2:395.

51 *Lord George Bentinck*, 253; *Hansard*, 3rd ser. vol. 87, 8 June 1846, c. 182.

52 *Lord George Bentinck*, 253–4; *Hansard*, 3rd ser., vol. 87, 8 June 1846, c. 182.

53 *Lord George Bentinck*, 254; *Hansard*, 3rd ser., vol. 87, 8 June 1846, c. 183.

54 *Lord George Bentinck*, 254–5; *Hansard*, 3rd ser., vol. 87, 8 June 1846, cc. 183, 184.

55 *The Times*, Saturday, 13 June 1846, 5; *Hansard*, 3rd ser., vol. 87, Friday, 12 June 1846, c. 430; *Lord George Bentinck*, 265.

56 *The Times*, Saturday, 13 June 1846, 5.

57 *Hansard*, 3rd ser., vol. 87, Friday, 12 June 1846, c. 437. For a cogent discussion of the difficulties of using *Hansard* and the newspapers of the day to determine what Members of Parliament actually said, see Robson, *What Did He Say?*

58 The words are Disraeli's, in his account of Peel's speech in *Lord George Bentinck*, 267.

59 *Hansard*, 3rd ser., vol. 87, 15 June 1846, c. 526. Cf. *The Times*, Tuesday, 16 June 1846, 4.

60 *Hansard*, 3rd ser., vol. 87, 15 June 1846, c. 528; *The Times*, Tuesday, 16 June 1846, 4.

61 Charles James Fox, quoted by Disraeli, *Hansard*, 3rd ser., vol. 87, 15 June 1846, c. 528; *The Times*, Tuesday, 16 June 1846, 4.

62 *Hansard*, 3rd ser., vol. 87, 15 June 1846, c. 529; *The Times*, Tuesday, 16 June 1846, 4

63 *Hansard*, 3rd ser., vol. 87, 15 June 1846, c. 531.

64 *Hansard*, 3rd ser., vol. 87, 15 June 1846, cc. 536–7; *The Times*, Tuesday, 16 June 1846, 4.

65 *Hansard*, 3rd ser., vol. 87, 19 June 1846, c. 710.

66 *Hansard*, 3rd ser., vol. 87, 19 June 1846, c. 730.

67 *Greville Memoirs*, vol. 5, 11 May 1846, 321. In several previous entries Greville had commented that the Protectionists, in their desire for revenge, had no object but to drive Peel from office.

68 *The Times*, Saturday, 20 June 1846, 6. "Curiosities of Literature" is the title of a popular work by Isaac D'Israeli.

69 *Greville Memoirs*, vol. 5, 19 June 1846, 327–8.

70 *The Croker Papers*, 3:103.

71 Lord George Bentinck to Lord John Manners, quoted in Whibley, *Lord John Manners and His Friends*, 1:283. Disraeli's role in the 1847–8 campaign to remove Jewish disabilities has only recently come to light with the discovery that he was anonymously, but extensively involved with his friend, Lionel de Rothschild in the writing and publication (15 January 1848) of a pamphlet on the question, now republished as Appendix VI of the *Disraeli Letters*, 8:419–24.

72 To James Crossley, 17 July 1845, *Disraeli Letters*, 4 (# 1427), 176–7.

73 In this regard, it is interesting to note that Robert Browning refers a number of times to *Vivian Grey* in the famous courtship correspondence with Elizabeth Barrett during the spring and summer of 1845. See *The Letters of Robert Browning and Elizabeth Barrett Barrett 1845–1846*, ed. Kintner, 1:49–50, 51, 54.

74 To Philip Rose, 28 April 1846, *Disraeli Letters*, 4 (# 1484), 226.

75 To Mary Anne Disraeli, 7 August 1846, *Disraeli Letters*, 4 (# 1506), 243.

76 To Sarah Disraeli, [12 December 1846], *Disraeli Letters*, 4 (# 1528), 265.

12. *Tancred* and the Politics of Identity: Principles, Expediency, and Trust

1 To Lord John Manners, 19 September 1846, *Disraeli Letters*, 4 (# 1519), 259.

2 To Thomas Bailey, 6 September 1846, *Disraeli Letters*, 4 (# 1518), 257. Cf. the letter to Lady Londonderry, 1 September 1846, *Disraeli Letters*, 4 (# 1515), 256.

3 Disraeli Papers, E/I/2.

4 Lord John Manners to Disraeli, 25 March 1847, Disraeli Papers, E/VI/Q/7; quoted in *Disraeli Letters*, 4:275, n. 3.

5 Isaac's response to the novel is given in two letters, one from Sarah to Disraeli, 19 March 1847, and one from Isaac written in Sarah's hand, [21] March 1847: Disraeli Papers, D/III/A/120 and A/I/C/78; quoted in *Disraeli Letters*, 4:275, n. 3.

6 Leslie Stephen, "Mr. Disraeli's Novels," *Fortnightly Review* 22, new ser. 16 (October 1874), 430–50.

 7 Milnes, "Review of *Tancred* and *Die Judenfrage* by Bruno Bauer."
 8 See Monypenny and Buckle, *Life*, 3:55–66, especially 59.
 9 Monypenny and Buckle, *Life*, 3:50.
10 Blake, *Disraeli*, 194.
11 Ibid., 194, 209, 201, 215, 201, 202, 215.
12 Levine, *Benjamin Disraeli*, 118.
13 Ibid., 129
14 Ibid., 123.
15 Schwarz, *Disraeli's Fiction*, 81, 99.
16 Ibid., 99.
17 Ibid., 101.
18 Ibid., 103.
19 To Mary Anne Disraeli, 29 June 1846, *Disraeli Letters*, 4 (# 1499), 236.
20 Ridley, *Young Disraeli 1804–1846*, 315.
21 Paul Smith, *Disraeli: A Brief Life*, 88–9.
22 Clausson, "'Picturesque Emotion' or 'Great Asian Mystery'?"
23 Schwarz, *Disraeli's Fiction*, 103.
24 Schwarz, *Disraeli's Fiction*, 103–4. To Robert Carter, 9 November 1870; see
    Hoeltje, "Benjamin Disraeli's Letters to Robert Carter."
25 Said, *Orientalism*, 192.
26 To Sarah Disraeli, 10 November 1845, *Disraeli Letters*, 4 (# 1447), 197.
27 George Smythe, at his father's urging, had in early 1846 accepted the position
    of Under-Secretary of State for Foreign Affairs in Peel's administration.
28 "Mr. Disraeli's Novels," *Fortnightly Review* 22; new ser. 16 (October 1874),
    430–50.
29 Isaac and Sarah to Disraeli, 20 April 1832 [postmark], Disraeli Papers,
    A/I/i/29.
30 *Tancred; or The New Crusade*, vol. 10 of the Bradenham Edition, Bk 2, ch. 9,
    111–13.
31 *Tancred*, Bk 3, ch. 4, 196. Cf. Matthew 27:25.
32 *Tancred*, Bk 3, ch. 4, 201.
33 See, for example, the pragmatic arguments of Sidonia in *Coningsby*. Cf.
    Lord George Bentinck, ch. 24.
34 Monypenny and Buckle, *Life*, 3:34.
35 The doctrine of "theocratic equality" asserts the brotherhood of all
    mankind under God. The angel of Arabia also reassures Tancred that
    "power is neither the sword nor the shield, for these pass away, but ideas
    which are divine." *Tancred*, Bk 4, ch. 7, 299.
36 Blake, *Disraeli*, 70.

37 Mutilated Diary, Disraeli Papers, A/III/C/21–2.

38 It is also interesting to note that names such as "Emir Bescher" and Pascha "Effendi," as well as place-names such as "Aleppo," occur prominently both in the novel and in the accounts of the "war in the Levant" published in *The Times* of July and August, 1839, from which Disraeli clearly derived his 1846 anecdote of the Lord High Admiral's treason.

39 *Tancred*, Bk 2, ch. 4, 74.

40 *Tancred*, Bk 6, ch. 4, 446

41 For an interesting discussion of the conception of the "grandiose self," its relation to narcissism, and its importance in the formation of a coherent sense of identity, see two works by Kohut: *The Search for the Self*, and *The Restoration of the Self*.

42 Lady Blessington to Disraeli, 22 March 1847, Disraeli Papers, E/VI/Q/36; rpt in Stewart, *Disraeli's Novels Reviewed*, 238.

43 Millar, *Disraeli's Disciple*, 195–205.

44 Warburton, *The Crescent and the Cross*, 2:324–5.

45 Cf. Warburton, *The Crescent and the Cross*, 2:270–1, 281–7, and *Tancred*, Bk 5, ch. 5; Bk 4, ch. 12, and Bk 5, ch. 2.

46 To [Eliot Warburton], 23 May 1845, *Disraeli Letters*, 4 (# 1412), 170.

47 *Tancred*, Bk 6, ch. 11, 497.

48 Bivona, "Disraeli's Political Trilogy and the Antinomic Structure of Imperial Desire."

49 For an exception, see the introduction to the fourth volume of the *Disraeli Letters*, where John Matthews finds the last sentence of the novel to be "unexpectedly momentous in its implications" (xlix).

50 *Tancred*, Bk 6, ch. 12, 501.

51 Bivona, "Disraeli's Political Trilogy," 318.

52 To Lady Londonderry, 26 December 1846, *Disraeli Letters*, 4 (# 1530), 266–8.

13. Leadership

1 Blake, *Disraeli*, 247.

2 Bentinck to John Wilson Croker, 28 December 1847, *The Croker Papers*, 3:163.

3 Bentinck to Lord John Manners, nd [December 1847]: "I don't like letting Disraeli vote by himself apart from the party: otherwise I might give in to the prejudices of the multitude ... I am just starting for London, and I feel like a condemned felon going to Botany Bay"; quoted in Charles Whibley, *Lord John Manners and His Friends*, 1:283.

4 A vivid account of his decision to resign is given in Bentinck's letter to Croker, 26 December 1847. See *The Croker Papers*, 3:156–8. Cf. the earlier letters of W.B. Baring and J.G. Lockhart to Croker on the subject of "the 'Jew' and the 'Jockey,'" 3:103.

5 Ibid., 157.

6 See also letters to Prince Metternich, 30 September 1848, 12 October 1848, 30 October 1848, 3 January 1849, *Disraeli Letters*, 5 (# 1722, 1725, 1737, 1760), 88–9, 91–3, 99–101, 122–3; also to Mary Anne Disraeli, 7 January 1849, ibid. (# 1763), 127–8.

7 The full text of Lord Stanley's letter is given in Monypenny and Buckle, *Life*, 3:121–4.

8 To Lord Stanley, 26 December 1848, *Disraeli Letters*, 5 (# 1755), 118–19.

9 Lord Stanley to Charles Newdegate, 25 December 1848; Monypenny and Buckle, *Life*, 3:126.

10 Lord Henry Bentinck to Disraeli [2 January 1849]; for a partial transcription see note 3, *Disraeli Letters*, 5 (# 1761), 124.

11 To Mary Anne Disraeli, 5 January 1849, *Disraeli Letters*, 5 (# 1761), 123–6. The references are to Sir John Trollope, the Marquis of Granby, and Lord Mandeville.

12 To Mary Anne Disraeli [8 January 1849], *Disraeli Letters*, 5 (# 1764), 128–9. The references are to Samuel Phillips and John Delane, editor of *The Times*.

13 See note 1, *Disraeli Letters*, 5 (#1755), 118.

14 To Mary Anne Disraeli [9, 10 January 1849], *Disraeli Letters*, 5 (# 1766, 1767), 129–30.

15 To Mary Anne Disraeli, [20 January 1849]; to Sarah Disraeli, [20 January 1849]; to Mary Anne Disraeli, 22 January 1849; to Mary Anne Disraeli, 24 January 1849, *Disraeli Letters*, 5 (# 1772, 1773, 1774, 1777), 132–6.

16 To Lord John Manners, 29 January 1849, *Disraeli Letters*, 5 (# 1781), 139–41.

17 *Disraeli Letters*, 5, 140, n. 3.

18 Ibid., n. 4.

19 Gregory, *An Autobiography*, 92. In the light of such prejudice, Disraeli's fanciful claims to be the descendant of Sephardic Jews who left Spain at the time of the Inquisition rather than give up their religion under the threat of persecution would seem to embody an element of compensation and defiance. Such an account of his family's history, including the assertion that the name D'Israeli was adopted at that time as a mark of pride in their origin, was published in his introduction to his father's collected works in 1849.

20 To Mary Anne Disraeli, [31 January 1849], *Disraeli Letters*, 5 (# 1782), 141–2.

21 *Disraeli Letters*, 5:141, n. 1.

22 To Sarah Disraeli, [6 February 1849], *Disraeli Letters*, 5 (# 1784), 142–3 and n. 2.
23 Disraeli Papers, A/X/A/52. See also the letter to Lady Londonderry, 12 March 1849, *Disraeli Letters*, 5 (# 1796), 153, n. 3.
24 Gregory, *An Autobiography*, 104–5.
25 Blake, *Disraeli*, 278–84.
26 To Lord Henry Lennox, 18 July 1852, *Disraeli Letters*, 6 (# 2335), 94.
27 To Queen Victoria, [15 March 1852], *Disraeli Letters*, 6 (# 2255), 37–8.
28 To Queen Victoria, [22 March 1852], *Disraeli Letters*, 6 (# 2260), 42.
29 To Queen Victoria, [30 March 1852], *Disraeli Letters*, 6 (# 2266), 45. The Opposition argued that the present system of open polling was "conducive to extravagance, disorder and drunkenness," while the Government responded that "concealment provided more opportunities for fraud, bribery, intimidation and other evils." See n. 1.
30 To Queen Victoria, 2 April [1852], *Disraeli Letters*, 6 (# 2267), 46.
31 The best discussion of Disraeli's role in the establishment and management of *The Press* is still that in Monypenny and Buckle, *Life*, 3:489–506. After 1851 "Lord Stanley" is the son of the 14th Earl of Derby.
32 *The Press*, 4 June 1853, quoted in Monypenny and Buckle, *Life*, 5:499–500.
33 To Sarah Brydges Willyams, 10 October 1853, *Disraeli Letters*, 6 (# 2567), 269–70.
34 To Lady Londonderry, 7 August 1854, *Disraeli Letters*, 6 (# 2669), 354.
35 See the letter to Lord Henry Lennox, 13 January 1854, *Disraeli Letters*, 6 (# 2614), 310–11, n. 1.
36 To Lord Stanley, 10 August 1858, *Disraeli Letters*, 7 (# 3177), 228 and n. 2.
37 To William Gladstone, 25 May 1858, *Disraeli Letters*, 7 (# 3128), 192–4. For Gladstone's reply see 194, n. 7. The original of Gladstone's letter is in the Disraeli Papers, B/XX/G/100.
38 Blake, *Disraeli*, 456–77.
39 Viscount Cranborne, *Hansard*, 3rd ser., vol. 188, 15 July 1867, 1539; Robert Lowe, *Hansard*, 3rd ser., vol. 186, 8 April 1867, 1315.
40 Cowling, *1867 Disraeli, Gladstone and Revolution*, 48–9.
41 Cowling, *1867 Disraeli, Gladstone and Revolution*, 50–4.
42 Monypenny and Buckle, *Life*, 4:600.

14. On Top of the Greasy Pole: The Disestablishment Crisis of 1868

1 *Pall Mall Gazette*, 3 March 1868, quoted in Monypenny and Buckle, *Life*, 5:3.
2 Disraeli Papers, B/IX/A/1.
3 Manning to Disraeli, 13 April 1867, Disraeli Papers, B/XXI/M/160.
4 Manning to Disraeli, 4 May 1867, Disraeli Papers, B/XXI/M/161.

5 Manning to Disraeli, 21 May 1867, Disraeli Papers, B/XXI/M/163.
6 Manning to Disraeli, 20 August 1867, Disraeli Papers, B/XXI/M/165.
7 Manning to Disraeli, 6 December 1867, Disraeli Papers, B/XXI/M/166.
8 Manning to Disraeli, 22 December 1867, Disraeli Papers, B/XXI/M/167.
9 Manning to Disraeli, 27 December, 1867, 15 January 1868, 19 February 1868, Disraeli Papers, B/XXI/M/168, 169, 170.
10 Manning to Disraeli, 26 February 1868, quoted in Monypenny and Buckle, *Life*, 5:6–7.
11 See Manning's autobiographical note, numbered 41, printed in Purcell, *Life of Cardinal Manning*, 2:518–19.
12 Quoted in Leslie, *Cardinal Manning*, 91.
13 Manning to Disraeli, 15, 16 March 1868, Disraeli Papers, B/XXI/M/171, 172.
14 Disraeli Papers, B/IX/A/17a.
15 These letters are in the Gladstone Papers in the British Library. This passage is quoted in McClelland, *Cardinal Manning*, 167.
16 Lytton Strachey's essay on Manning in *Eminent Victorians* remains the most unsympathetic portrait of his motives and actions. The discussion focuses more on church than parliamentary politics and Strachey, following Purcell's *Life*, characterizes Manning as ruthless and cruel in the service of religious imperatives. The best biography is Gray, *Cardinal Manning*.
17 Quoted in Leslie, *Cardinal Manning*, 86.
18 The details of Manning's argument are summarized concisely in McClelland, *Cardinal Manning*, 169–70, though he mistakenly describes the political context as "after the accession of Gladstone to power." A fuller description of the pamphlet can be found in Gwynn, "Manning and Ireland," 111–35.
19 McClelland, *Cardinal Manning*, 171. Part of Manning's strategy was to appeal to Gladstone's idealism. A week after the resolutions had been announced, for example, Manning wrote to Gladstone that Disestablishment was "no question of religion, but of political justice." Manning to Gladstone, 24 March 1868, quoted in Leslie, *Cardinal Manning*, 86.
20 Best, *Shaftesbury*, 61–2.
21 The words are the ones Gladstone spoke when informed by telegram that General Grey would arrive at Hawarden shortly to convey the Queen's request that he form the next Government. See Morley, *The Life of William Ewart Gladstone*, 2:252.
22 Lasswell, *Psychopathology and Politics*, 74–7.
23 O'Kell, "William Ewart Gladstone," 102.
24 Manning to Disraeli, 2 December 1868, Disraeli Papers, B/XXI/M/173.

25 J. Pope Hennessey to Lord Mayo, 19 May 1870, quoted in Purcell, *Life of Cardinal Manning*, 2:516–17.

26 Disraeli Papers, B/IX/A/42b-42c. This unsigned pencilled note, obviously written sometime later, confuses the details of the specific occasion, but the general import is correct: "The Catholic Party rejected this scheme eventually, & voted against Mr. D in '68. It was for this reason that Mr. D. told Card Manning (coming as one of a Dep' to Gro Gate) that he had 'been stabbed in the back.'"

27 Manning to Disraeli, 7 May 1870, Disraeli Papers, B/XXI/M/174; also quoted in Purcell, *Life of Cardinal Manning*, 2:518.

28 See, for example, the speeches of the Earl of Mayo and Mr G. Cavendish Bentinck, *Hansard*, 3rd ser., vol. 191, 3 April and 27 April 1868, cc. 881, 1383.

29 *Hansard*, 3rd ser., vol. 171, 9 June 1863, c. 642–55; rpt as "On Act of Uniformity" in Disraeli, *Selected Speeches of the Late Right Honourable The Earl of Beaconsfield*, 2:581–95; see 590–1.

30 "The Future Position of the Church" [speech delivered at a public meeting in aid of the Oxford Diocesan Society for the Augmentation of Small Benefices, held at High Wycombe, Thursday, 30 October 1862], rpt Disraeli, *Selected Speeches*, 2:567–80; 580. Cf. "The Present Position of the Church" [speech delivered at the annual meeting of the Oxford Diocesan Church Societies, held at Aylesbury, 14 November 1861], ibid., 555–66. Cf. also, "Church Policy" [speech delivered at Oxford at a meeting for the Augmentation of Small Benefices, 25 November 1864], ibid., 596–613.

31 "Church Policy," in Disraeli, *Selected Speeches*, 2:601.

32 "The Present Position of the Church, 1861," in Disraeli, *Selected Speeches*, 2:563.

33 *Hansard*, 3rd ser., vol. 191, 3 April 1868, cc. 923–4.

34 Disraeli to the Rev. Arthur Baker, [9 April] 1868, quoted in Monypenny and Buckle, *Life*, 5:25.

35 Gladstone, *Hansard*, 3rd ser., vol. 191, 3 April 1868, c. 924.

36 *Hansard*, 3rd ser., vol. 191, 30 April 1868, c. 1672. Disraeli is here referring to the argument of his Rt Hon. friend, Spencer Walpole, who had spoken earlier in the evening: "They [the people] claim at your hands perfect freedom from sacerdotal tyranny on the one hand, and from wild fanaticism on the other" (ibid., c. 1641).

37 Lord Derby to Disraeli, 3 April 1868, quoted in Monypenny and Buckle, *Life*, 5:27; Gathorne Hardy to Disraeli, 5 April 1868, Hardy, *Gathorne Hardy, First Earl of Cranbrook*, 1:274–5.

38 Disraeli to Queen Victoria, 23 March 1868, Royal Archives, D23/58.
39 Disraeli to General Grey, 19 March 1868, Royal Archives, D23/51. In this letter he outlines the basis on which the Government "could consistently, and constitutionally, decline to act on … [Gladstone's] motion," thus obliging him to "make another move."
40 Disraeli to Queen Victoria, 20 April and 1 May 1868, Royal Archives, D24/24 and A37/17.
41 Ibid., 1 May.
42 *Hansard*, 3rd ser., vol. 191, 7 May 1868, c. 1943.
43 *British Quarterly Review* 48 (July 1868), 181.
44 *Fraser's Magazine for Town and Country* 77 (April 1868), 525–44; (May 1868), 666–78. The notes in *The Gladstone Diaries*, 6 (1861–8), conflate the two articles and attribute them to the March issue. See the entries for 30 March 1868, 587, n. 6; and for 30 April 1868, 593, n. 15.
45 See *The Wellesley Index to Victorian Periodicals* 2:473 (4861), 474 (4870). Hayward had a distinct animus with respect to Disraeli and the Jewish question, feeling apparently that his career as both novelist and politician had done the Jews more harm than good.
46 Hayward, "The Caucasian Administration in Trouble," 671, 677.
47 Disraeli to Queen Victoria, 22 April 1868, Royal Archives D24/29. This is an account of the Lord Chancellor's remarks to the cabinet, which Disraeli had orchestrated beforehand with a view to pre-empting any discussion of resignation.
48 Blake, *Disraeli*, 490–4.
49 Lady Augusta Stanley to Lord Clarendon. See Maxwell, *Life and Letters of George William Frederick, Fourth Earl of Clarendon*, 2:346.
50 *The Gladstone Diaries*, 6, 28 February 1868, 579.
51 Hardy, *Gathorne Hardy, First Earl of Cranbrook*, 2:275.
52 Hardy, *The Diary of Gathorne Hardy, later Lord Cranbrook, 1866–1892: Political Selections*, 6 May 1868, 72.
53 Disraeli was, of course, not the first prime minister to do so. It is interesting in the light of what follows to note that in 1857 Gladstone had violently objected to Palmerston's use of Church patronage for secular ends. For example, in an essay entitled, "The New Parliament and Its Work" (April 1857), Gladstone denounces the partisan policy of excluding the High and favouring the Low in dividing "the spoils of the Church," and he angrily accuses Palmerston of using political influence rather than merit or the needs of the Church as the criterion in the recent choice of four prelates, some of whom, he says, do not even "come up to the standard of intellectual mediocrity" (551–4).

54 Quoted in Monypenny and Buckle, *Life*, 5:19. Disraeli sent much the same witty account to the Queen, 21 March 1868, Royal Archives, D23/56.

55 Queen Victoria to Disraeli, 27 March 1868; Prince of Wales to his mother, 27 March 1868; General Grey to Disraeli, 30 March 1868; Disraeli to Queen Victoria, 31 March 1868; Queen Victoria to Disraeli, 31 March 1868; Royal Archives, A37/13, D1/67, D1/68, D1/69, D1/70.

56 Disraeli to Lord Beauchamp, 1 April 1868. This letter remains in the Beauchamp archives, but there is a copy in the files of the Disraeli Project and it will appear in vol. 9 of the *Benjamin Disraeli Letters*.

57 Disraeli to Queen Victoria, 24 April 1868, Royal Archives, D1/72.

58 Disraeli to Queen Victoria, 3 May 1868, Royal Archives, D1/75.

59 Monypenny and Buckle, *Life*, 5:59. Perhaps it is significant that Dr Woodford later became bishop of Ely upon Gladstone's recommendation.

60 Disraeli to Queen Victoria, 4 June 1868, Royal Archives, A37/38 (CAB 41/1/10): "Mr. Birch has accepted the Canonry with overflowing gratitude, & evidently some surprise. Mr. Disraeli confesses he was a little disappointed, as he would have liked, in Yr. Majesty's name, to have made the Whippingham hearth happy. However, if things go well, Yr. Majesty will have other opportunities of doing so." The Queen's wish to promote Mr Prothero, the rector of Whippingham, was fulfilled in October, when he was offered the position of canon of St Paul's vacant upon the preferment of Canon Champneys as dean at Lichfield. At Mr Prothero's request, he was instead preferred canon of Westminster. See Victoria, *The Letters of Queen Victoria*, 2nd ser., 1:531, 542–3, 554.

61 Disraeli to Queen Victoria, 14 August 1868, Royal Archives, D1/79.

62 Sir Thomas Biddulph to Disraeli, 16 August 1868; Disraeli to Queen Victoria, 19 August 1868, Royal Archives, D1/81, D1/82.

63 Disraeli to Queen Victoria, 21 August 1868, Royal Archives, A37/49.

64 Lady Ely to Disraeli [copy], 7 September 1868, Royal Archives, D1/84.

65 Dean Wellesley to the Princess Louise, 1 September 1868, *The Letters of Queen Victoria*, 2nd ser., 1:536–7. Cf. the conversation recorded in the diary of Bishop Samuel Wilberforce, 28 November 1868, in Ashwell and Wilberforce, *Life of the Samuel Wilberforce*, 3:268–9.

66 Disraeli to Queen Victoria, 10 September 1868, Royal Archives, D1/87. Cf. the very fine account of the situation given by Meacham in *Lord Bishop: The Life of Samuel Wilberforce*, 282ff., in which he points out that the Low Church *Record* of 17 August had warned the prime minister against "the machinations of 'The Bishop of Oxford,'" 285.

67 Queen Victoria to Disraeli, 18 September 1868, quoted in Monypenny and Buckle, *Life*, 5:64; *The Letters of Queen Victoria*, 2nd ser., 1:537.

68 Disraeli to Lord Derby, 18 September 1868, Monypenny and Buckle, *Life*, 5:65.

69 Samuel Wilberforce to Disraeli, 11 September 1868, Ashwell and Wilberforce, *Life of Samuel Wilberforce*, 3:260–1.

70 Dean Wellesley to Queen Victoria, nd [10 September], Royal Archives, D1/89. See also, Blake, *Disraeli*, 511.

71 Disraeli to Montagu Corry, 21 September 1868, Monypenny and Buckle, *Life*, 5:66.

72 *The Times*, 29 October 1868, 9.

73 Dean Wellesley to Queen Victoria, nd [30 October 1868], *The Letters of Queen Victoria*, 2nd ser., 1:545–7.

74 Disraeli to Queen Victoria, 4 November 1868, Royal Archives, D1/112. Disraeli consistently misspells "embarrassment."

75 Disraeli to Lord Derby, 2 November 1868, Monypenny and Buckle, *Life*, 5:67–8; Lord Derby to Disraeli, 3 November 1868, Monypenny and Buckle, *Life*, 5:68–9.

76 Dean Wellesley to Queen Victoria, nd [30 October 1868], *The Letters of Queen Victoria*, 2nd ser., 1:545–7.

77 Disraeli to Lord Derby, 12 November 1868, Monypenny and Buckle, *Life*, 5:69. Disraeli first suggested Christopher Wordsworth, canon of Westminster, and nephew of the poet, for preferment to London, but the Queen objected on the grounds of both his inexperience and the better qualifications of some of the other bishops. As a result Wordsworth became bishop of Lincoln, succeeding Jackson.

78 Royal Archives, D1/112.

79 Queen Victoria to Disraeli, 6 November 1868, Royal Archives, D1/115.

80 Ashwell and Wilberforce, *Life of Samuel Wilberforce*, 3:267; also quoted in Monypenny and Buckle, *Life*, 5:70.

81 General Grey to Disraeli, 10 November 1868, Royal Archives A37/64.

82 Disraeli to Queen Victoria, 20 November 1868; Dean Wellesley to Queen Victoria, 21 November 1868, *The Letters of Queen Victoria*, 2nd ser., 1:554–5.

83 Ashwell and Wilberforce, *Life of Samuel Wilberforce*, 3:267.

84 Extracts from Wilberforce's diary, 28 November 1868, ibid., 3:268–9.

85 Samuel Wilberforce to Sir Charles Anderson, 16 November 1868, Ashwell and Wilberforce, *Life of Samuel Wilberforce*, 3:270: "Disraeli has done exactly as I expected with his Church preferments. The appointment of Canterbury was, I believe, pressed on him by the Queen. But Lincoln to London is all his own to please the 'Record'… Tait was quite heartily warm about my succeeding him. I am afraid my dear children and friends will be disappointed. For myself, I really thank God; it very little disturbs me. I in my

reason apprehend that by the common rule in such matters I had no right to be so treated; but I am really thankful in feeling so cool about it."

86 Extract from Wilberforce's diary, 20 November 1868; Wilberforce to Sir Charles Anderson, 26 November 1868, Ashwell and Wilberforce, *Life of Samuel Wilberforce*, 3:270–1.

87 Extract from Wilberforce's diary, 11 December 1868; Samuel Wilberforce to Ernest Wilberforce, 12 December 1868; Samuel Wilberforce to Sir Charles Anderson, 15 December 1868; ibid., 3:271–2.

88 W.F. Hook to Sir Charles Anderson, 30 October 1868, ibid., 3:265.

89 A note on the back of the previously cited letter from Hook to Anderson, 30 October 1868; cited by Meacham, in *Lord Bishop: The Life of Samuel Wilberforce*, 288, n. 64, is in the Wilberforce Papers, Bodleian Deposit, I, C192. See also Ashwell and Wilberforce, *Life of Samuel Wilberforce*, 3:254–5.

90 See Meacham, *Lord Bishop: The Life of Samuel Wilberforce*, 288–9, where he cites Disraeli's remark as recorded in Hamilton's Diary, 11 January 1894, British Museum Add. Mss. 48662.56.

91 Extract from Wilberforce's diary, 29 August 1868; Letters to Ernest Wilberforce, 24 October 1868, Ashwell and Wilberforce, *Life of Samuel Wilberforce*, 3:257–8.

15. *Lothair*: The Politics of Love, Faith, and Duty

1 Blair, *John Patrick, Third Marquess of Bute, K.T.*, 70.

2 Disraeli Papers, B/XX/Co/45. Corry's source was Sir James Fergusson, MP for Ayrshire, who had served as Lord Bute's guardian for the last seven years of his minority, and who was the curator of his Ayrshire estate. As it turned out, the impending conversion led to the breaking off of this projected marriage to Albertha Frances Anne, the sixth daughter of the Duke and Duchess of Abercorn. See Blair, *John Patrick*, 58 and below.

3 The *Glasgow Herald*, quoted in Blair, *John Patrick*, 81.

4 Thomas Longman to Disraeli, 6 May 1870, quoted by Monypenny and Buckle, *Life*, 5:165; ibid., 165–7.

5 Quoted in Monypenny and Buckle, *Life*, 5:164.

6 *Atlantic Monthly* 26 (August 1870), 249–51; rpt R.W. Stewart, *Disraeli's Novels Reviewed*, 255–9.

7 George Russell, quoted in Monypenny and Buckle, *Life*, 5:168; [G.W. Dasent], *Quarterly Review* 129 (July 1870), 63–87; Frederic Harrison, *Fortnightly Review* new ser. 13 (June 1870), 654–67.

8 Monypenny and Buckle, *Life*, 5:152.

9 Painting, "Disraeli and the Roman Catholic Church."

10 Blake, *Disraeli*, 518–19; Froude, *Lord Beaconsfield*, 231, 218.

11 Schwarz, *Disraeli's Fiction*, 126, 128.

12 Frederic Harrison, *Fortnightly Review* new ser. 13 (June, 1870), 654–7.

13 Sir Leslie Stephen, quoted by Monypenny and Buckle, *Life*, 5:157.

14 Monypenny and Buckle, *Life*, 5:150; Froude, *Lord Beaconsfield*, 227.

15 Monypenny and Buckle, *Life*, 5:163–4.

16 Disraeli, *Lothair*, vol. 11 of the Bradenham Edition, title page. There is also a modern edition with an introduction by Vernon Bogdanor. See pp. 1 and xii.

17 For a brief but cogent discussion of Terence's play, see Douglass Parker's introduction to *The Eunuch*, 147–52.

18 Monsignor Talbot to Archbishop Manning, 21 January 1868: "Regarding Scotland, I see the absolute necessity of creating a hierarchy, notwithstanding the protest of Lord Clarendon, who has somehow got to hear of the project"; quoted in Purcell, *Life of Cardinal Manning*, 2:399–400. Ironically, two days earlier Manning had written to Talbot: "I write one line, too late I fear, to put you on your guard lest Lord Clarendon should be urging the endowment of the Catholic clergy in Ireland. This is done with the avowed intention of gaining a hold over them … I suspect that some expressions of yours have been written home by Lord Clarendon. He is one to whom you may apply your warning *Cavete ab hominibus*" (ibid., 2:399).

19 Blair, *John Patrick*, 26–7.

20 Ibid., 63–4.

21 Monsignor Capel to Mrs. Scott Murray, 31 May 1868, quoted in Blair, *John Patrick*, 67–8.

22 Blair, *John Patrick*, 68.

23 Ibid., 70.

24 Vincent, *Disraeli, Derby and the Conservative Party*, 8 February 1868, 328.

25 Lord Bute to Mrs Scott Murray, 16 December 1868, quoted in Blair, *John Patrick*, 71–2.

26 Schwarz, *Disraeli's Fiction*, 130–1.

27 Goldwin Smith to Thomas Longman, 25 May 1870, quoted in Monypenny and Buckle, *Life*, 5:166.

28 In 1868 Goldwin Smith had published a pamphlet, *The Reorganisation of the University of Oxford*, in which he advocated the abolition of religious tests for entry to the university.

29 Disraeli's inspiration for Lothair's involvement in Garibaldi's campaign was clearly Amelia B. Edwards's novel, *Half a Million of Money* (1866), from which he transposed characters such as Signora Colonna and several events in the plot.

30 Both the substance and the tone of Grandison's words echo those of Archbishop Manning's discussions of the pope's infallibility and temporal

power as bulwarks against the revolutionary forces of Europe. See Manning, *The Temporal Power of the Vicar of Jesus Christ*, and Drexler, *The Authority to Teach*, 80–4.

31 Gladstone's *Address on the Place of Ancient Greece in the Providential Order of the World*, a lecture delivered at the University of Edinburgh, 3 November 1865 and subsequently published as a pamphlet, anticipates many of the specific points of Mathew Arnold's *Culture and Anarchy* (1869), including the contrast of the Hebraic and Hellenic cultures. See O'Kell, "William Ewart Gladstone," 99.

32 Bogdanor, "Explanatory Notes," in Disraeli, *Lothair*, 385–6.

33 Archbishop Manning to Monsignor Talbot, quoted in Purcell, *Life of Cardinal Manning*, 2:398. "Gladstone is coming to Rome in October. *Show him all the kindness you can*. I am anxious about him. He has been driven and goaded into extremes, and may become very dangerous. But for a long time he has been *silent about Rome* and the Temporal Power. And he has been helping us … I have had *strong* battle with Gladstone. He promises to avoid bad company, and I believe he will. I also promised to write to Cardinal Antonelli. Gladstone is *much* softened. He fully holds that the Holy Father must be *independent*. But his head is full of schemes. I think he will do nothing *hostile*. Towards us in England and towards Ireland he is the most just and fargoing of all our public men. Be kind to him. He is very susceptible of any kindness, and his *sympathies* and *respect* religiously are all with us … He does not come as an enemy, and may be made friendly, or he might become on his return most dangerous."

34 Morley, *The Life of William Ewart Gladstone*, 2:217.

35 *The Gladstone Diaries*, 31 December 1866, 6:489.

36 The audience with the pope is described in the diary entry for 22 October 1866 (ibid., 6:472–5). There was some discussion of Ireland in the context of deploring the Fenian outrages and with reference to the "University question." Otherwise most of the conversation was about the situation in Italy and the possibility of some form of peaceful unification.

37 *The Times*, 10 November 1866, 9a.

38 *The Times*, 12 November 1866, 10a: "Mr. Gladstone has written a letter to the official journal denying the account of his interview with the Pope published by the Corriere Italiano and other journals." The next day *The Times* reported that "Intelligence received here from Rome states that it has been decided at a secret consistory, that if the Pope be obliged to quit Rome he will seek an asylum in Malta," 13 November 1866, 9b.

39 See above, ch. 14, 380; quoted in Monypenny and Buckle, *Life*, 5:65. Some readers of Disraeli's letters may find such an allusion to Psalm 22

distressingly flippant, but it does invoke the great anguish of the Psalmist nevertheless.

40 In the explanatory note to "Page 111," Bogdanor points out that "In the manuscript, 'Tancred' is written in place of 'Lothair' at this point – a good indication of the connections operating in Disraeli's mind at the time," 380–1.

41 Bogdanor's "Explanatory Notes" to the text are the most reliable key to the historical allusions and the minor characters' real identities: Theodora as Jessie White Mario; Mr Phoebus as Lord Leighton; Captain Bruges as General Cluseret, etc.

42 *The Young Duke*, Bk 2, ch. 3. Dacre is an ancestral family name of the Duke of Norfolk, Earl of Arundel, who by royal warrant in 1832 added Fitzalan to his own family name of Howard. Lord Bute's marriage to his grand-daughter in 1872 can thus be seen in imaginative terms as an alternative, ironic conclusion to Disraeli's plot.

16. "The Family Romance": Politics, Power, and Love in *Endymion*

1 The complex chronology of the novel's composition has been fully discussed by Blake in "The Dating of *Endymion*." See also Weintraub, *Disraeli*, 630ff.

2 Citations of the novel are by pages in vol. 12 of the Bradenham Edition of *The Novels and Tales*.

3 The name is itself significant, for "Endymion" recalls not just Keats's poem (1818), but also the young Disraeli's interests in Greek mythology, manifest in such tales as his "Ixion in Heaven" (1832–3) and "The Infernal Marriage" (1834). Ferrars is a name borrowed from Jane Austen's *Sense and Sensibility*, which can be presumed deliberate, given the many allusions to Austen's *Emma* in *A Year at Hartlebury or The Election* (1834). Disraeli also used a similar name, "Ferrers," in his short story, "The Consul's Daughter" (1836).

4 Freud, "Family Romances," in *The Standard Edition*, 9:236–41.

5 "Early Diary," nd, Disraeli Papers, Box 11/A/III/E/3.

6 O'Kell, "The Autobiographical Nature of Disraeli's Early Fiction."

7 See O'Kell, "The Psychological Romance."

8 Many critics have commented on Endymion's inert character and his "fatally successful" career. See, for example, A.G. Sedgwick whose review appeared in *The Nation*.

9 *Hansard*, 3rd ser., vol. 71, 15 August 1843, c. 839.

10 To Mary Anne Disraeli, 9 March 1842, *Disraeli Letters*, 4 (#1224), 25–6.

11 Mr Bertie Tremaine and his brother, Tremaine Bertie, are also partly an allusion to the Bulwer brothers, Edward Bulwer Lytton and William Henry Lytton Bulwer.

12 For an excellent discussion of the power and influence that some women had in Victorian politics, as hostesses, confidantes and go-betweens, see Reynolds, *Aristocratic Women and Political Society in Victorian Britain*. It is also worth noting the similar roles that women often play in Anthony Trollope's Palliser novels.

13 *Punch; or the London Charivari* 12 (1847), 166, 198–9, 213–14, 223.

14 Isaac D'Israeli had his children baptized in the Church of England, after he left the Congregation of Bevis Marks synagogue in 1817. Cecil Roth and Robert Blake have noted that the baptisms of Benjamin (31 July) and Sarah (28 August) were later than those of their younger brothers, James and Ralph (11 July), and they speculate that there may have been some resistance from the older children to being included on the first occasion. Roth, *The Earl of Beaconsfield*, 12–13, and Blake, *Disraeli*, 11.

15 The bishop of Durham had written to the prime minister seeking to know the Government's views on the pope's actions. Russell's letter in reply, dated 4 November, was printed in *The Times* on 7 November 1850.

16 To Lord Carrington, 8 November 1850, *Disraeli Letters*, 5 (#2057), 371.

17 Freud, *The Interpretation of Dreams*, in *The Standard Edition*, 5:353.

18 Sir Philip Rose, recalling the occasion when Disraeli first became prime minister, remembered saying to him: "If only your sister had been alive [now] to witness your triumph, what happiness it would have given her." Disraeli replied, "Ah! poor Sa! poor Sa! we've lost our audience, we've lost our audience" (Monypenny and Buckle, *Life*, 1:180; Blake, *Disraeli*, 425).

17. The "Faery" Queen, the "Arch Villain," and the "Mephistopheles of Statesmanship"

1 Blake, *Disraeli*, 543, and Paul Smith, *Disraelian Conservatism*, 199, quote Cross's *A Political History*, 25.

2 The best account of the Government's legislative program from 1874 to 1880 is still that of Paul Smith, *Disraelian Conservatism and Social Reform*.

3 Ibid., 258.

4 Bradford, *Disraeli*, 329.

5 To Queen Victoria, 18 November 1875, The National Archives, CAB 41/6/33; quoted in Monypenny and Buckle, *Life*, 5:443–4.

6 To Queen Victoria, 24 November 1875, The National Archives, CAB 41/6/36; quoted in Monypenny and Buckle, *Life*, 5:448–9.

7 The Suez Canal was constructed and operated by a private company, the majority of whose shares were owned by a French syndicate, whose chief was Ferdinand de Lesseps. The Khedive of Egypt owned approximately 44 per cent of the shares. In 1874 Disraeli had sent a private emissary to Paris to see if de Lesseps would sell his shares to the British Government, but he was not interested in doing so. In mid-November 1875 the Khedive was negotiating with two rival French syndicates for the sale of his shares, but without the French Government's sanction, neither was able to raise the necessary funds. A week later the Khedive agreed to sell his shares to England. See Blake, *Disraeli*, 581–7 for the story of how Disraeli got Baron Lionel de Rothschild to advance the required £4 million on very short notice.

8 To Lady Bradford, 25 November 1875, in Disraeli, *The Letters of Disraeli to Lady Bradford and Lady Chesterfield*, 1:305–6. (Henceforth cited as Disraeli, *The Letters … to Lady Bradford and Lady Chesterfield*).

9 To Lady Bradford, 26 November 1875, ibid, 1:306–7. Cf. the second letter, 30 November 1875, ibid., 1:308: "The Faery was in the tenth Heaven, having received a letter of felicitations from the King of the Belges on 'the greatest event of modern politics'; 'Europe breathes again,' etc. etc."

10 Ibid.,1:308. "It seems that Prince Gortchakoff had arranged to call at Berlin on his way home and just catch Prince Bismarck after his five months' retirement, and then confer together and settle the Eastern question. It must have been during this meeting, or the day before it took place, that the great news arrived which – as it is supposed they were going to settle everything without consulting England – was amusing!"

11 Blake, *Disraeli*, 491.

12 Maxwell, *Life and Letters of George William Frederick, Fourth Earl of Clarendon*, 2:346.

13 Monypenny and Buckle, *Life*, 6:457.

14 Lord Derby to Benjamin Disraeli, 4 May 1874, Monypenny and Buckle, *Life*, 5:414.

15 See, for example, his very blunt letter of 30 August 1879, giving his reasons for recalling Lord Chelmsford from Africa after the disastrous events in the Zulu war. Monypenny and Buckle, *Life*, 6:459.

16 Both the importance and difficulties of attending to the Queen's wishes are illustrated by other passages in the letter to Lady Bradford, written at Windsor on 26 November 1875: "I got here at a quarter to 6, and was summoned to the presence exactly at 6. She received me almost with caresses, absolutely said she never saw me looking so well and all sorts of things. When I could get to general business, though I had an awful catalogue of demands and suggestions they were comparatively soon

exhausted – no difficulties made, everything granted, nothing but smiles and infinite *agaceries* ... The *Times* has only got half the news and very inaccurate, but it is evidently staggered. I believe the whole country will be with me. The Faery thinks so." To Lady Bradford, 26 November 1875, Disraeli, *The Letters ... to Lady Bradford and Lady Chesterfield*, 1:306–8.

17 The first and perhaps only use of the word "Faery" in Disraeli's letters to the Queen occurs in one dated 25 February 1875, in which he thanks her for her personal gift of a bouquet of fresh flowers:

> Yesterday eve, there appeared, in Whitehall Gardens, a delicate looking case, with a royal superscription, which, when he opened, he thought, at first, that your Majesty had graciously bestowed upon him the stars of your Majesty's principal orders. And, indeed, he was so impressed with this graceful illusion, that, having a banquet, where there were many stars and ribbons, he could not resist the temptation, by placing some snowdrops on his heart, of showing that he, too, was decorated by a gracious Sovereign.
>
> Then, in the middle of the night, it occurred to him, that it might all be an enchantment, and that, perhaps, it was a Faery gift and came from another monarch: Queen Titania, gathering flowers with her Court, in a soft and sea-girt isle, and sending magic blossoms, which, they say, turn the heads of those who receive them.
>
> They certainly would turn Mr. Disraeli's, if his sense of duty to your Majesty did not exceed, he sincerely believes, his conceit.
> (Quoted in Monypenny and Buckle, *Life*, 6:463–4)

18 The administration of affairs in India was until 1858 the direct responsibility of the East India Company, but, as Blake has pointed out, the policies creating discontent were in effect those of the Government. Before his Government was defeated, Palmerston indicated his intention to abolish the East India Company, but the India Bill of 1858 doing so was chiefly the work of Disraeli and Lord Stanley in Lord Derby's following Conservative ministry. See Blake, *Disraeli*, 377–81.

19 *Hansard*, 3rd ser., vol. 147, 27 July 1857, c. 479.

20 To Queen Victoria, 24 June 1858, *Disraeli Letters*, 7 (# 3157), 215.

21 Martin, "The Victorian Monarchy," 384.

22 To Queen Victoria, 14 April 1874, quoted in Monypenny and Buckle, *Life*, 5:457.

23 To Lord Cairns, 7 January 1876, Monypenny and Buckle, *Life*, 5:457.

24 To Lord Salisbury, 11 January 1876, Monypenny and Buckle, *Life*, 5:457–8.

25 Shannon, *The Age of Disraeli*, 278.

26 *The Times*, 21 March 1876, 7. Gladstone was also concerned about the constitutionality of unilaterally extending the British administration to all of India and about the possibility that the Imperial title would be conferred on other members of the royal family. Disraeli assured the House of Commons that the title of Empress would refer only to the Queen's position in India and that no other colonies or persons would be affected by the provisions of the bill.

27 To Lady Bradford, 10 March 1876, Disraeli, *The Letters ... to Lady Bradford and Lady Chesterfield*, 2:23.

28 To Lady Bradford, 21 March 1876, Disraeli, *The Letters ... to Lady Bradford and Lady Chesterfield*, 2:26.

29 *The Times*, 24 March 1876, 9.

30 To Queen Victoria, 1 April 1876, Cabinet Papers, The National Archives, CAB 41/7/6.

31 To Lady Bradford, 23 March 1876, Disraeli, *The Letters ... to Lady Bradford and Lady Chesterfield*, 2:27.

32 Ensor, *England, 1870–1914*, 39.

33 To Lady Bradford, 13 March 1876, Disraeli, *The Letters ... to Lady Bradford and Lady Chesterfield*, 2:24.

34 To Lady Bradford, 21 March 1876, ibid., 2:26.

35 To Lady Chesterfield, 31 March 1876, ibid., 2:30.

36 To Lady Bradford, 2 April, 1876, Disraeli, ibid., 2:31.

37 To Lady Bradford, 3 April 1876, Disraeli, ibid., 2:32.

38 *Hansard*, 3rd ser., vol. 228, 23 March 1876, c. 491. Cf. *The Times*, 24 March 1876, 6.

39 *Hansard*, 3rd ser., vol. 228, 23 March 1876, c. 514–15. Cf. *The Times*, 24 March 1876.

40 *Hansard*, 3rd ser., vol. 228, 30 March 1876, cc. 831–3; *The Times*, 31 March 1876, 6.

41 *Tancred; or the New Crusade*, vol. 10 of the Bradenham Edition of *The Novels and Tales of Benjamin Disraeli*, 270–1.

42 *The Times*, 31 March 1876, 9.

43 Clayden, *England Under Lord Beaconsfield*, 233. It is interesting that during the debates on the Royal Titles Bill the Duke of Argyll persuaded Gladstone to read *Tancred*. See Blake, *Disraeli*, 601. The prejudicial image of Disraeli as Mephistopheles was quite popular among his sceptics and detractors. Cf., for example, Conway, *Autobiography Memories and Experiences of Moncure Daniel Conway*, 1:69: "no one could look at him without seeing that his natural place was to be acting Mephistopheles in

Her Majesty's Theatre rather than that of the political cynic in Her Majesty's House of Commons."

44 To Lord Derby, 6 May 1875, Monypenny and Buckle, *Life*, 5:422. As Richard Shannon has noted with great acuity, Disraeli's "Palmerstonian mode" of conducting foreign policy was a dubious strategy, for it was too often a matter of opportunism, drift, or default, rather than actions based on well thought out, long-term goals. See *The Age of Disraeli, 1868–1881*, 270–2.

45 Blake, *Disraeli*, 575–6.

46 This note for the cabinet of 16 May 1876 is given in full in Monypenny and Buckle, *Life*, 6:24–6.

47 Monypenny and Buckle, *Life*, 6:26–7.

48 23 June and 8 July 1876. The author of these reports was Edwin Pears, the correspondent of the *Daily News* in Constantinople.

49 To Lady Bradford, 13 July 1876, Disraeli, *The Letters ... to Lady Bradford and Lady Chesterfield*, 2:58.

50 *Hansard*, 3rd ser., vol. 230, 10 July 1876, cc. 1181–2.

51 *The Times*, 1 August 1876, 8–9. Cf. *Hansard*, 3rd ser., vol. 231, 31 July 1876, c. 203. See, also, n. 55.

52 Millman, *Britain and the Eastern Question*, 146ff.

53 Ibid., 153

54 *Hansard*, 3rd ser., vol. 231, 31 July 1876, cc. 172–202.

55 *Hansard*, 3rd ser., vol. 231, 31 July 1876, cc. 202–16. Cf. Disraeli to Lady Bradford, 13 July 1876, Disraeli, *The Letters ... to Lady Bradford and Lady Chesterfield*, 2:58.

56 On 22 August Mr Eugene Schuyler, the notably anti-Turk American Consul General in the area, would report to his Government that 15,000 was the lowest estimate of those killed. A preliminary account of that report was published in the *Daily News*, 29 August 1876.

57 Disraeli (now Earl of Beaconsfield) to Sir Stafford Northcote, 2 September 1876 and to Lord Derby, 4 September 1876, Monypenny and Buckle, *Life*, 6:51–3.

58 Shannon, *Gladstone and the Bulgarian Agitation, 1876*, 100. Shannon cites the original sources respectively as Gladstone Papers, Add. MSS 44790, ff. 112–14, and Gladstone to [Henry] Broadhurst, 20 September 1896, Broadhurst Papers, L.S.E., vol. 5, no. 1.

59 Gladstone to Lord Granville, 29 August 1876, quoted in Shannon, *Gladstone and the Bulgarian Agitation, 1876*, 106–7; see also, p. 92.

60 Ibid., 107.

61 Gladstone, *Bulgarian Horrors and the Question of the East*.

62 Gladstone uses this phrase to describe the image he thinks England has acquired by following Disraeli's policies.

63 *The Lustful Turk* was an epistolary pornographic novel, first published anonymously in 1828, in which the virginal English heroine is raped by the Turkish Dey of Algiers, but the stereotypical fantasy is of longer standing. See Marcus, *The Other Victorians*, 197–216.

64 *The Times*, 11 September 1876, 10.

65 "Mr. Gladstone at Oxford. Great Meeting," *The Times*, 31 January 1878, 10.

66 To Lady Bradford, 1 February 1878, Disraeli, *The Letters … to Lady Bradford and Lady Chesterfield*, 2:158.

67 To Lady Bradford, 3 October 1877, quoted in Monypenny and Buckle, *Life*, 6:180–1. Cf. Disraeli's comment a fortnight after Gladstone's speech at Blackheath: "If we succeed in carrying a satisfactory treaty, I think the Greenwich Tartuffe will have a long face." To Lady Bradford, 25 September 1876, Disraeli, *The Letters … to Lady Bradford and Lady Chesterfield*, 2:76.

68 For a candid and colourful account of General Ignatieff's diplomatic career, see Ignatieff, *The Russian Album*, 54–60.

69 To Lady Chesterfield, 12 October 1876, Disraeli, *The Letters … to Lady Bradford and Lady Chesterfield*, 2:79.

70 Weintraub, *Disraeli*, 477.

71 20 September 1876, quoted in Monypenny and Buckle, *Life*, 6:65.

72 To Lady Bradford, 16 March 1877, Disraeli, *The Letters … to Lady Bradford and Lady Chesterfield*, 2:108.

73 From Queen Victoria, 19 April 1877, quoted in Monypenny and Buckle, *Life*, 6:132–3.

74 See Blake's summary and succinct analysis of the situation. Blake, *Disraeli*, 607–10.

75 To Lord Derby, 25 May 1877, quoted in Monypenny and Buckle, *Life*, 6:141.

76 To Austen Henry Layard, *Secret*, 6 June 1877, quoted in Monypenny and Buckle, *Life*, 6:142.

77 From Queen Victoria, 7 February 1878, quoted in Monypenny and Buckle, *Life*, 6:243; from Queen Victoria, 10 January 1878, quoted in Monypenny and Buckle, *Life*, 6:217.

78 From Queen Victoria, 10 February 1878, quoted in Monypenny and Buckle, *Life*, 6:217.

79 From Queen Victoria, 9 February 1878, quoted in Monypenny and Buckle, *Life*, 6:245; from Queen Victoria, 10 January 1878, quoted in Monypenny and Buckle, *Life*, 6:217.

80 From Queen Victoria, 11 January 1878, read to the cabinet the next day, quoted in Monypenny and Buckle, *Life*, 6:218; from Queen Victoria,

7 February 1878, referred to in Disraeli's letter to Queen Victoria, 9 February 1878, quoted in Monypenny and Buckle, *Life*, 6:244; The National Archives, CAB 41/10/17: "He conveyed to the Cabinet the contents of Your Majesty's last letter, and read in detail the extracts from his own correspondence … and then he called upon the Cabinet to fulfill their engagement to their Sovereign."

81 Millman, *Britain and the Eastern Question*, 369–71; Monypenny and Buckle, *Life*, 6:242.

82 To Lady Bradford, 7 February 1878, Disraeli, *The Letters … to Lady Bradford and Lady Chesterfield*, 2:159; also quoted in Monypenny and Buckle, *Life*, 6:242.

83 Millman, *Britain and the Eastern Question*, 392–3, quotes the text of the British Government's warning that Derby provided to Count Schuvalov, verbally on 13 February and in writing on 15 February 1878.

84 Quoted in ibid., 395–6.

85 Quoted in ibid., 396.

86 To Queen Victoria, 16 February 1878, quoted in Monypenny and Buckle, *Life*, 6:248–9; The National Archives, CAB 41/10/19.

87 To Queen Victoria, 16 February 1878, quoted in Monypenny and Buckle, *Life*, 6:248–9; The National Archives, CAB 41/10/19. Cf. To Queen Victoria, 19 March 1878, The National Archives, CAB 41/11/5: "He regrets that Yr. Majesty shd. think for a moment Yr. Majesty's letters were ever neglected … " At this time Disraeli's much trusted confidential secretary, Montagu Corry had broken down under the stress of his many responsibilities, including the negotiations with the Austrian ambassador in the hope of securing a promise of military assistance.

88 To Queen Victoria, 2 March 1878, quoted in Monypenny and Buckle, *Life*, 6:253–4; The National Archives, CAB 41/10/22.

89 To Queen Victoria, 6 March 1878, quoted in Monypenny and Buckle, *Life*, 6:254; The National Archives, CAB 41/10/23.

90 *Daily Telegraph*, 23 March 1878; Cf. *The Times*, which acknowledged that Bulgaria "would easily become a kind of Russian province and all the minor states in the Peninsula would simply cluster round." See Seton-Watson, *Disraeli, Gladstone, and the Eastern Question*, 345, 348.

91 Millman, *Britain and the Eastern* Question, 404, citing A.J. Mundella.

92 To Queen Victoria, 16 March 1878, quoted in Monypenny and Buckle, *Life*, 6:259; The National Archives, CAB 41/11/5. In addition, the admiral commanding the British fleet had been making plans in the event of war to force his ships' way through the Bosphorous and interrupt Russian supply lines in the Black Sea. To Queen Victoria, 8 March 1878, quoted in Monypenny and Buckle, *Life*, 6:255; The National Archives, CAB 41/10/25.

93 Lord Derby had first submitted his resignation with that of Carnarvon two months earlier, on 24 January, when the fleet was first ordered to Constantinople. But when a draft of the Russians' peace terms was received by telegraph from Ambassador Layard, and with some uncertainty in London about both how that might affect the parliamentary response to the Government's request for funds and what the political fallout of Derby's resignation would be, it was decided that the fleet should return to Besika Bay and Disraeli persuaded the Foreign Secretary to remain at his post.

94 Millman, *Britain and the Eastern* Question, 413.

95 MacColl, *Memoirs and Correspondence*, 57; quoted in Millman, *Britain and the Eastern Question*, 592, n. 19. The Reverend MacColl had himself written several pamphlets on the Eastern question. See, for example, *Mr. Gladstone and Oxford: A Vindication of Mr. Gladstone's Political Consistency by Scrutator* [i.e., Malcolm MacColl] (London, 1865); *The Eastern Question: Its Facts and Fallacies* (London, 1877); *Three Years of the Eastern Question* (London, 1878).

96 As was his usual practice, Lord Derby made notes of what was said as the meeting took place and later added an entry to his diary. Both documents are quoted by Monypenny and Buckle, *Life*, 6:264–6.

97 Blake, *Disraeli*, 643.

98 The negotiations before the opening of the Congress between London, St Petersburg, Vienna, and Berlin were more complex than indicated here. The best discussion of the many issues and personalities involved is that of Millman, *Britain and the Eastern* Question, 403–51.

99 Ibid., 420.

100 Madame Novikoff's husband had been killed while fighting as a volunteer during the rebellion in Serbia.

101 The Gladstonians were quite flattered by the description and W.T. Stead later took it as the title of his book, *The M.P. for Russia*.

102 *Daily Telegraph*, 23 March 1878. For Gladstone's awareness of the dangers of his correspondence with Madame Olga Novikoff, see Stead's *The M.P. For Russia*, 1:356.

103 *The Times*, 11 January 1878, 8.

104 Estelle W. Stead, *My Father, Personal and Spiritual Reminiscences*, 80. Gladstone estimated that in all he had received about three thousand such letters, usually containing "quotations from *The Daily Telegraph*'s leaders and correspondents, with paragraphs relating to the Russians underlined and garnished with expletives"(ibid.); Cunningham, "Jingoism in 1877–78," 448.

105 W.T. Stead, *The M.P. for Russia*, 1:450.

106 [Hill], "The Political Adventures of Lord Beaconsfield."

107 Gladstone, "Liberty in the East and West."

108 Ibid., 1160–3.

109 Ibid., 1164–5. The result was a notice of motion by Mr Robert William Hanbury, MP for North Staffordshire, to censure Gladstone for language "calculated to create sedition in Her Majesty's Indian Empire." *Hansard*, 3rd ser., vol. 240, 3 June 1878, cc. 1069–70; quoted in *The Times*, 4 June 1878, 6. Two weeks later the intended motion was withdrawn since the desired effect of calling attention to Gladstone's extreme language had been achieved.

110 26 May 1878, *The Gladstone Diaries*, 9:317.

111 Gladstone, whose sense of outrage can be imagined, was temporarily absent from the House of Commons, attending the funeral of the Duchess of Argyll.

112 Sumner, *Russia and the Balkans*, 505; quoted by Blake, *Disraeli*, 646.

113 Blake, *Disraeli*, 648.

114 See Montagu Corry's letter to Lady Ilchester, which gives an account of Disraeli's ultimatum, Monypenny and Buckle, *Life*, 6:326.

115 *Hansard*, 3rd ser., vol. 241, 8 July 1878, cc 965–6; *The Times*, 9 July 1878, 6.

116 *The Times*, 10 July 1878, 5.

117 For a detailed account of the Congress, see Sumner, *Russia and the* Balkans, ch. 18, 501–53.

118 See, for example, Queen Victoria to Lord Beaconsfield, 9 February 1878, Monypenny and Buckle, *Life*, 6:245.

119 Monypenny and Buckle, *Life*, 6:346; Queen Victoria to Lord Beaconsfield, 17 July 1878, Monypenny and Buckle, *Life*, 6:347.

120 To Queen Victoria, 13 July 1878, Monypenny and Buckle, *Life*, 6:344; King Leopold to Queen Victoria, 14 July 1878, ibid.

121 To Lady Salisbury, in Lady Gwendolen Cecil, *Life of Robert, Marquis of Salisbury*, 2:287.

18. The Conquering Hero / *Falconet*

1 Address by the Dover Working Men's Constitutional Association, *The Times*, 17 July 1878, 5.

2 Ibid.

3 Lord Henry Lennox to Montagu Corry, 1 July 1878, Disraeli Papers, B/XX/lx/530; quoted in Swartz, *The Politics of British Foreign Policy*, 97–8.

4 Swartz, *The Politics of British Foreign Policy*, 98. Salisbury's vexation at the demonstrations of public excitement were not just a matter of personal

distaste, though that was certainly strong. According to his daughter, he felt that this popular reception "would emphasize those sensational features of the Government policy whose existence he was anxious to minimize and which he was convinced were fundamentally antipathetic to the temper of his fellow countrymen. The wirepullers were making a great blunder, he declared." Cecil, *The Life of Robert, Marquis of Salisbury*, 296.

5 *The Times*, 20 July 1878, 10.
6 *The Times*, 22 July 1878, 10.
7 *The Times*, 29 July 1878, 9.
8 *Hansard*, 3rd ser., vol. 242, 30 July 1878, cc. 671–2; Cf. *The Times*, 31 July 1878, 6.
9 To W.E. Gladstone, 30 July 1878, quoted in Monypenny and Buckle, *Life*, 6:537. For a discussion of satirical cartoons in which Disraeli was represented as the devil, see Wohl, "'Ben JuJu.'"
10 Richard Shannon, *Gladstone and the Bulgarian Agitation, 1876* , 12.
11 W.H. Dyke to Lord Beaconsfield, 9 July 1878, Disraeli Papers B/XX/D/480.
12 *The Times*, 5 August 1878, 9.
13 *The Gladstone Diaries*, 1 August 1878, 9:334–5. [Hill], "The Political Adventures of Lord Beaconsfield."
14 To Queen Victoria, 6 August 1878, quoted in Monypenny and Buckle, *Life*, 6:361.
15 "The Ministers in the City," *The Times*, 5 August 1878, 9.
16 Disraeli, *The Letters … to Lady Bradford and Lady Chesterfield*, 2:180.
17 Cunningham, "Jingoism in 1877–78," 448, citing the National Union of Conservative and Constitutional Associations, Publication No. 36.
18 *Fortnightly Review* 30 (August 1878), 251.
19 *The Gladstone Diaries*, 3, 6, 9 August 1878, 9:335, 336, 337. Millais's portrait is reproduced opposite p. 350.
20 Anonymous, *Beaconsfield: A Mock-Heroic Poem and Political Satire* (London: Abel Heywood, 1878), 23.
21 *Westminster Review* 110 (new ser. 54) (Oct. 1878), 566.
22 Weintraub, *Disraeli: A Biography*, 601–8.
23 E.A. Freeman to James Bryce, 23 November 1876, Bryce Papers, Bodleian Library, quoted by Millman, *Britain and the Eastern Question*, 524, n. 63: "There is a nation [Russia] in the freshness of a new life, burning to go on the noblest of crusades and our loathsome Jew wants to stop them." See Wohl, "'Dizzi-Ben-Dizzi,'" 380. Cf. also Wohl's discussion of political cartoons from the period, "'Ben JuJu.'"

24 William Crosbie, *The Beaconsfield Policy: An Address* (London: 1879), quoted by Feldman, *Englishmen and Jews*, 113.

25 Quoted by Lord Halifax in a letter to Lord Grey, 11 October 1876; cited in Millman, *Britain and the Eastern Question*, 524, n. 63.

26 Quoted by Wohl in "'Dizzi-Ben-Dizzi,'" 399.

27 W.E. Gladstone to Leopold Gluckstein, 6 October 1876, quoted in *The Gladstone Diaries*, 9:161, n. 4.

28 From the Queen, 13 March 1880. Ponsonby, *Henry Ponsonby Queen Victoria's Private Secretary*, 183.

29 Ibid., 184.

30 Ibid., 187.

31 Ibid.

32 Ibid., 188.

33 28 March 1881, ibid., 190.

34 Philip Guedalla, "A Note on 'Endymion' and 'Falconet,'" in *Endymion and Falconet*, vol. 12 of the Bradenham Edition , xiii; Cross, "Falconet Not Gladstone?" 8.

35 For Macaulay's parody of the nursery song, "Twenty Pounds Shall Marry Me," see Clive, *Thomas Babbington Macaulay*, 156: "What though now opposed I be? / Twenty peers shall carry me. / If twenty won't, thirty will, / For I'm his Majesty's bouncing Bill."

Bibliography

Primary Sources

Manuscript Collections

British Museum, Add. Mss, The British Library, London
Disraeli Papers, Bodleian Library, Oxford
Disraeli Project, Queen's University, Kingston, Ontario, Canada
The National Archives (Public Record Office), Kew.
Royal Archives, Windsor Castle.

Printed Sources of Disraeli's Works

Benjamin Disraeli Letters.
    8 + vols. Toronto: University of Toronto Press, 1982–present.
"The Consul's Daughter." In *Book of Beauty*, ed. Lady Blessington, 1836.
The Crisis Examined, by Disraeli the Younger. London: Saunders and Otley, 1834;
    reprinted in *Whigs and Whiggism*, ed. William Hutcheon, 23–40.
England and France; or, A Cure for the Ministerial Gallomania. London: Murray,
    1832.
Home Letters Written by the late Earl of Beaconsfield in 1830 and 1831. Ed. Ralph
    Disraeli. London: Murray, 1885; reprinted New York: Kraus, 1970.
"The Infernal Marriage." In *Popanilla and Other Tales*. Vol. 3 of the Bradenham
    Edition. NewYork: Knopf, 1934.
The Letters of Disraeli to Lady Bradford and Lady Chesterfield. Edited by the
    Marquis of Zetland. 2 vols. London: Ernest Benn, 1929.
The Letters of Runnymede. London: Macrone, 1836; reprinted as Appendix II,
    Disraeli Letters, Vol. 2.

Lord George Bentinck: A Political Biography. London: Colburn, 1852.

Lothair. Ed. Vernon Bogdanor. London: Oxford University Press, 1975.

The Novels and Tales of Benjamin Disraeli, 1st Earl of Beaconsfield. Bradenham Edition. 12 vols. London: Peter Davies, 1926–7; New York: Knopf, 1934.

"Peers and People." In *Whigs and Whiggism*, ed. William Hutcheon, 42–110.

The Revolutionary Epick. London: Moxon, 1834.

"The Revolutionary Epick" and Other Poems reprinted from the Original Edition and Edited by W. Davenport Adams. London: Hurst and Blackett, 1904.

Selected Speeches of the Late Right Honourable the Earl of Beaconsfield. Ed. T.E. Kebbel. 2 vols. London: Longmans, Green, 1882.

Sybil or The Two Nations. Ed. Thom Braun. Harmondsworth: Penguin, 1980.

Vindication of the English Constitution in a letter to a noble and learned Lord. London: Saunders and Otley, 1835; reprinted in *Whigs and Whiggism*, ed. William Hutcheon, 111–232.

Vivian Grey. London: Henry Colburn, 1826; reprinted in *The Early Novels of Benjamin Disraeli*. Vol. 1. Ed. Michael Sanders. London: Pickering & Chatto, 2004.

"What Is He?" London: James Ridgway, 1833; reprinted in *Whigs and Whiggism*, ed. William Hutcheon, 16–22.

Whigs and Whiggism: Political Writings by Benjamin Disraeli. Ed. William Hutcheon. London: Murray, 1913.

A Year at Hartlebury or the Election. London: Saunders and Otley, 1834; republished by the University of Toronto Press, 1983.

The Young Duke. 3 vols. London: Henry Colburn and Richard Bentley, 1831.

Secondary Sources

Aldous, Richard. *The Lion and the Unicorn: Gladstone vs. Disraeli*. London: Hutchinson, 2006.

Aronson, Theo. *Victoria and Disraeli: The Making of a Romantic Partnership*. London: Cassell, 1977.

Ashwell, A.R., and Reginald G. Wilberforce. *Life of the Right Reverend Samuel Wilberforce*. 3 vols. London: Murray, 1880–2.

Barbey d'Aurevilly, Jules. "Du Dandysme et de George Brummell." In *Oeuvres Romanesque Complètes*, ed. Jacques Petit, 2:677–733. Editions Gallimard. Paris: Bibliothèque de la Pléiade, 1966.

Baudelaire, Pierre Charles. *Le Peintre de la Vie Moderne*. Paris, 1868.

Beaconsfield: A Mock-Heroic Poem and Political Satire. London: Abel Heywood, 1878.

Berlin, Isaiah. "Benjamin Disraeli, Karl Marx and the Search for Identity." In
Isaiah Berlin, *Against the Current*, ed. Henry Hardy, 252–86. London:
Pimlico/ Random House, 1997.

Best, G.F.A. *Shaftesbury*. London: Batsford, 1964.

Bivona, Daniel. "Disraeli's Political Trilogy and the Antinomic Structure of
Imperial Desire." *Novel: A Forum on Fiction* 22.3 (1989): 305–25.

Blair, David Hunter. *John Patrick, Third Marquess of Bute, K.T.* New York:
Longmans, Green, 1921.

Blake, Robert. *The Conservative Party from Peel to Churchill*. London: Eyre &
Spottiswoode, 1970.

– "The Dating of *Endymion*." *Review of English Studies* ns 17 (May 1966): 177–82.

– *Disraeli*. London: Eyre & Spottiswoode, 1966.

Blessington, Countess of (Marguerite Gardiner). *Book of Beauty*. London, 1836.

Bodenheimer, Rosemarie. *The Politics of Story in Victorian Social Fiction*. Ithaca,
NY: Cornell University Press, 1988.

Bolingbroke, Viscount (Henry St John). *The Works of the Late Right Honourable
Henry St. John, Lord Viscount Bolingbroke*. 8 vols. London: J. Johnson et al.,
1809.

– *A Dissertation upon Parties*, Vol. 3, 1–312.

– *The Idea of a Patriot King*, Vol. 4, 223–334.

– *A Letter on the Spirit of Patriotism*, Vol. 4, 187–222.

– *Remarks on the History of England*, Vol. 2, 107–424.

Bowle, John. *Politics and Opinion in the Nineteenth Century*. London: Jonathan
Cape, 1963.

Bradford, Sarah. *Disraeli*. New York: Stein and Day, 1983.

Brantlinger, Patrick. "Disraeli and Orientalism." In *The Self Fashioning of
Disraeli, 1818–1851*, ed. Richmond and Smith, 90–105.

– "Nations and Novels: Disraeli, George Eliot, and Orientalism." *Victorian
Studies* 35.3 (1992): 255–75.

– *The Spirit of Reform: British Literature and Politics, 1832–1867*. Cambridge,
MA: Harvard University Press, 1977.

Braun, Thom. *Disraeli the Novelist*. London: Allen and Unwin, 1981.

Browning, Robert, and Elizabeth Barrett Barrett. *The Letters of Robert Browning
and Elizabeth Barrett Barrett, 1845–1846*. Ed. Elvan Kintner. 2 vols.
Cambridge, MA: Harvard University Press, 1969.

Buckingham and Chandos, Duke of. *Memoirs of the Courts and Cabinets of
William IV and Victoria*. 2 vols. London: Hurst and Blackett, 1861.

Burke, Edmund. *A Letter from the Right Honourable Edmund Burke to a Noble
Lord*. London, 1796.

Byron, Lord (George Gordon). *Medwin's Conversations of Lord Byron*. Ed. E.J. Lovell. Princeton: Princeton University Press, 1966.

Campbell, Lord John. *Lives of Lord Lyndhurst and Lord Brougham*. London: Murray, 1869.

Cecil, Lady Gwendolen. *The Life of Robert, Marquis of Salisbury*. 4 vols. London: Hodder and Stoughton, 1921.

Cirlot, J.E. *A Dictionary of Symbols*. Trans. J. Sage. New York: Philosophical Library, 1962.

Clausson, Nils. "Interpretation, Genre, Revaluation: The Conventions of Romance and the Romance of Religion in Benjamin Disraeli's *Lothair*." *Dickens Studies Annual* 43 (2012): 187–208.

– "'Picturesque Emotion' or 'Great Asian Mystery'? Disraeli's *Tancred* as an Ironic *Bildungsroman*." *Critical Survey* 16.1 (2004): 1–19.

Clayden, P.W. *England under Lord Beaconsfield: The Political History of Six Years from the End of 1873 to the Beginning of 1880*. Intro. E.J. Feuchtwanger. Richmond, U.K.: Richmond Publishing, 1971.

Clive, John. *Thomas Babbington Macaulay: The Shaping of the Historian*. London: Secker and Warburg, 1973.

[Colburn, Henry]. *Key to Vivian Grey*. [London: Colburn, 1826].

Conway, Moncure Daniel. *Autobiography Memories and Experiences of Moncure Daniel Conway*. 2 vols. London: Cassell; Boston and New York: Houghton Mifflin, 1904.

Cottret, Bernard, ed. *Bolingbroke's Political Writings*. London: Macmillan. 1997.

Courthope, W.J. "The Crown and the Constitution." *Quarterly Review* 145 (April 1878): 277–328.

Cowling, Maurice. *1867 Disraeli, Gladstone and Revolution: The Passing of the Second Reform Bill*. Cambridge: Cambridge University Press, 1967.

Croker, John Wilson. *The Croker Papers: The Correspondence and Diaries of J.W. Croker*. Ed. L.J. Jennings. 3 vols. London, 1885.

Crosby, Travis L. *The Two Mr. Gladstones: A Study in Psychology and History*. New Haven and London: Yale University Press, 1997.

Cross, Richard. *A Political History*. Printed for Private Circulation, 1903.

Cross, Wilbur L. "Falconet Not Gladstone?" *The New York Times*, 8 February 1905, 8.

Cunningham, Hugh. "Jingoism in 1877–78." *Victorian Studies* 14.4 (June 1971): 429–53.

Davis, R.W. "Disraeli, the Rothschilds and Antisemitism." In *Disraeli's Jewishness*, ed. Endelman and Kushner, 162–79.

Dellamora, Richard. *Friendship's Bonds: Democracy and the Novel in Victorian England*. Philadelphia: University of Pennsylvania Press, 2004.

D'Israeli, Isaac. *Commentaries on the Life and Reign of Charles I*. 5 vols. London: Colburn and Bentley, 1828–31.

– *Curiosities of Literature with a View of the Life and Writings of the Author by his Son*. 3 vols. 14th ed. London: Moxon, 1849.

Dixon, Peter. *George Canning: Politician and Statesman*. New York: Mason/ Charter, 1976.

Drexler, Charles H. *The Authority to Teach: A Study in the Ecclesiology of Henry Edward Manning*. Washington, DC: University Press of America, 1979.

Duerksen, R.A. "Disraeli's Use of Shelley," *Victorian Newsletter* 26 (1964): 19–22.

Edgeworth, Maria. *Harrington*. Ed. Susan Manly. Peterborough, ON: Broadview, 2004.

Edwards, Amelia B. *Half a Million of Money*. [London], 1866.

Encyclopaedia Britannica. 10th ed. London, 1902.

Endelman, Todd M. "Benjamin Disraeli and the Myth of Sephardi Superiority." In *Disraeli's Jewishness*, ed. Endelman and Kushner, 23–39.

Endelman, Todd M., and Tony Kushner, eds. *Disraeli's Jewishness*. London & Portland, OR: Vallentine Mitchell, 2002.

Ensor, R.C.K. *England 1870–1914*. Oxford: Clarendon Press, 1966,

Erikson, Erik. *Childhood and Society*. 2nd ed. New Work: Norton, 1964.

– *Identity: Youth and Crisis*. New York: Norton, 1968.

Faber, Richard. *Beaconsfield and Bolingbroke*. London: Faber and Faber, 1961.

– *Young England*. London: Faber and Faber, 1987.

Feldman, David. *Englishmen and Jews: Social Relations and Political Culture 1840–1914*. New Haven: Yale University Press, 1994.

Feuchtwanger, E.J. *Disraeli, Democracy and the Tory Party: Conservative Leadership and Organisation after the Second Reform Bill*. Oxford: Clarendon Press, 1968.

– "'Jew Feelings' and Realpolitik: Disraeli and the Making of Foreign and Imperial Policy." In *Disraeli's Jewishness*, ed. Endelman and Kushner, 180–97.

Fido, Martin. "'From His Own Observation': Sources of Working Class Passages in Disraeli's *Sybil*." *Modern Language Review* 72 (1977): 268–84.

Fitzsimons, John, ed. *Manning: Anglican and Catholic*. London: Burns Oates, 1951.

Flavin, Michael. *Benjamin Disraeli: The Novel as Political Discourse*. Brighton: Sussex Academic Press, 2005.

Foot, Michael. *The Politics of Paradise: A Vindication of Byron*. London: Collins; New York: Harper & Row, 1988.

Freud, Sigmund. "Family Romances." In *The Standard Edition of the Complete Psychological Works of Sigmund Freud*, ed. James Strachey, 9:236–41. London: Hogarth Press, 1959.

– *The Interpretation of Dreams*. In *The Standard Edition of the Complete Psychological Works of Sigmund Freud*, ed. James Strachey, 5:339–627. London: Hogarth Press, 1959.

Froude, J.A. *The Earl of Beaconsfield*. London: Dent, 1905.

– *Lord Beaconsfield*. London: Sampson Low, Marston, Searle, & Rivington, 1890.

Gallagher, Catherine. *The Industrial Reformation of English Fiction: Social Discourse and Narrative Form, 1832–1867*. Chicago: University of Chicago Press, 1985.

Garnett, Richard. *Shelley and Lord Beaconsfield*. London: Shelley Society, 1887.

Gash, Norman. *Politics in the Age of Peel*. London: Longmans, Green, 1953.

– *Sir Robert Peel: The Life of Sir Robert Peel after 1830*. Totawa, NJ: Rowman & Littlefield, 1972.

Gladstone, William Ewart. *Address on the Place of Ancient Greece in the Providential Order of the World*. A lecture delivered at the University of Edinburgh, 3 November 1865.

– *Bulgarian Horrors and the Question of the East*. London: Murray, 1876.

– *The Gladstone Diaries*. Ed. M.R.D. Foot and H.C.G. Matthew. 14 vols. Oxford: Clarendon Press, 1968–94.

– "Liberty in the East and West." *The Nineteenth Century* 3 (June 1878): 1154–74.

– "The New Parliament and Its Work." *Quarterly Review* 101 (April 1857): 551–4.

Gopnick, Adam. "Life of the Party: Benjamin Disraeli and the Politics of Performance." *New Yorker*, 3 July 2006, 72–8.

Graham, Peter W. "Emma's Three Sisters." *Arizona Quarterly* 43.1 (spring 1987): 39–52.

Graves, Robert. *The Greek Myths*. 2 vols. Harmondsworth: Penguin, 1964.

Gray, Robert. *Cardinal Manning*. London: Weidenfeld & Nicolson; New York: St Martin's Press, 1985.

Gregory, Sir William. *An Autobiography*. Ed. Lady Gregory. London: Murray, 1894.

Greville, Charles. *The Greville Memoirs, 1814–1860*. Ed. Lytton Strachey and Roger Fulford. 8 vols. London: Macmillan, 1938.

Gwynn, Denis. "Manning and Ireland." In *Manning: Anglican and Catholic*, ed. John Fitzsimons, 111–35. London: Burns Oates, 1951.

Hardie, Frank. *The Political Influence of Queen Victoria, 1861–1901*. London: Frank Cass, 1963.

Hardy, Gathorne. *The Diary of Gathorne Hardy, later Lord Cranbrook, 1866–1892: Political Selections*. Ed. Nancy E. Johnson. Oxford: Clarendon Press, 1981.

– *Gathorne Hardy, First Earl of Cranbrook: A Memoir*. Ed. Alfred E. Gathorne-Hardy. 2 vols. London: Longmans, Green, 1910.

Hayward, Abraham. "The Caucasian Administration and the Irish Difficulty." *Fraser's Magazine for Town and Country* 77 (April 1868): 525–44.

– "The Caucasian Administration in Trouble." *Fraser's Magazine for Town and Country* 77 (May 1868): 666–78.

[Hill, Frank Harrison]. "The Political Adventures of Lord Beaconsfield." *Fortnightly Review* 29, 30 (1878); Part I, 29 (April 1878): 477–93; Part II, 29 (May 1878): 691–709; Part III, 29 (June 1878): 867–88; Part IV, 30 (August 1878): 250–70.

Hilton, Boyd. *The Age of Atonement: The Influence of Evangelicalism on Social and Economic Thought, 1795–1865*. Oxford: Clarendon, 1988.

– "Peel: A Reappraisal." *The Historical Journal* 22.3 (Sept. 1979): 585–614.

Hoeltje, Hubert H. "Benjamin Disraeli's Letters to Robert Carter." *Philological Quarterly* 31.1 (January 1952): 17–26.

Ignatieff, Michael. *The Russian Album*. Toronto: Penguin Canada, 2009.

James, Henry. "Review of *Lothair*." *Atlantic Monthly* 26 (August 1870): 249–51.

Jerman, B.R. *The Young Disraeli*. Princeton: Princeton University Press, 1960.

Jupp, Peter. "Disraeli's Interpretation of English History." In *The Self-Fashioning of Disraeli, 1818–1851*, ed. Richmond and Smith, 131–51.

Kennedy, Padraic C. "'Underhand Dealings with the Papal Authorities': Disraeli and the Liberal Conspiracy to Disestablish the Irish Church." *The Parliamentary History Yearbook, 2008*, 19–29.

Key to "Vivian Grey." London: William Marsh, 1827.

Kirsch, Adam. *Benjamin Disraeli*. New York: Schocken, 2008.

Kitson Clark, George. *Peel and the Conservative Party*. 2nd ed. London: Frank Cass, 1964.

Kohut, Heinz. *The Restoration of the Self*. New York: International Universities Press, 1977.

– *The Search for the Self*. Ed. Paul H. Ornstein. 2 vols. New York: International Universities Press, 1978.

Kovic, Milos. *Disraeli and the Eastern Question*. Oxford: Oxford University Press, 2010.

Kramnick, Isaac. *Bolingbroke and His Circle*. Cambridge, MA: Harvard University Press, 1968.

Kreilkamp, Ivan. *Voice and the Victorian Storyteller*. Cambridge: Cambridge University Press, 2005.

Kuhn, William. *The Politics of Pleasure: A Portrait of Benjamin Disraeli*. London: Free Press, 2006.

Lang, Andrew. *The Life and Letters of John Gibson Lockhart*. 2 vols. London: J.C. Nimmo, 1897.

Langdon-Davies, Bernard. Introduction to *Coningsby* by Benjamin Disraeli. New York: Capricorn, 1961.

Langley, Helen, ed. *Benjamin Disraeli Earl of Beaconsfield: Scenes from an Extraordinary Life*. Oxford: Bodleian Library, 2003.

Lasswell, Harold. *Psychopathology and Politics*. New ed. New York: Viking, 1960.

Leslie, Shane. *Cardinal Manning: His Life and Labours*. New York: P.J. Kennedy, 1954.

Levine, Richard A. *Benjamin Disraeli*. New York: Twayne, 1968.

MacColl, Malcolm. *Memoirs and Correspondence*. London: Smith, Elder, 1914.

Maître, Raymond. *Disraeli: Homme de Lettres*. Paris: Didier, 1963.

Manly, Susan. Introduction to *Harrington* by Maria Edgeworth. Peterborough, ON: Broadview, 2004.

Manning, Henry Edward. *The Temporal Power of the Vicar of Jesus Christ*, 2nd ed. London: Burns and Lambert, 1862.

Marcus, Steven. *The Other Victorians: A Study of Sexuality and Pornography in Mid-Nineteenth-Century England*. New York: Basic Books, 1964.

Martin, Kingsley. "The Victorian Monarchy." *Edinburgh Review* 243.496 (April 1926): 365–84.

Maxwell, H. *Life and Letters of George William Frederick, Fourth Earl of Clarendon*. 2 vols. London: Edward Arnold, 1913.

McClelland, Vincent Alan. *Cardinal Manning: His Public Life and Influence, 1865–1892*. London: Oxford University Press, 1962.

Meacham, Standish. *Lord Bishop: The Life of Samuel Wilberforce*. Cambridge, MA: Harvard University Press, 1970.

Millar, Mary. *Disraeli's Disciple: The Scandalous Life of George Sydney Smythe*. Toronto: University of Toronto Press, 2006.

Millman, Richard. *Britain and the Eastern Question 1875–1878*. Oxford: Clarendon Press, 1979.

Milnes, Richard Monckton. "Review of *Tancred* and *Die Judenfrage* by Bruno Bauer." *Edinburgh Review* 86 (July 1847): 138–55; rpt in *Disraeli's Novels Reviewed, 1826–1868*, ed. Robert Stewart, 222–6. Metuchen, NJ: Scarecrow, 1975.

Moers, Ellen. *The Dandy*. New York: Viking, 1960.

Monypenny, William Flavelle, and George Earle Buckle. *The Life of Benjamin Disraeli*. 6 vols. London: Murray, 1910–20.

Morley, John. *The Life of William Ewart Gladstone*. 3 vols. London and New York: Macmillan, 1909.

Nickerson, Charles C. "O! Venetia . . . Byron, Shelley, and Miss Havisham." *TLS* (28 March 2008), 14–15.

O'Kell, Robert. "'The Arts of a Designing Person'? Disraeli, Peel, and Young England." In *Proceedings of the Disraeli Colloquium*, 22–3 April 1978, Queen's University (Supplement to the *Disraeli Newsletter* (spring 1979)): 98–115.

– "The Autobiographical Nature of Disraeli's Early Fiction." *Nineteenth-Century Fiction* 31.3 (December 1976): 253–84.

– "Disraeli's *Coningsby*: Political Manifesto or Psychological Romance." *Victorian Studies* 23.1 (autumn 1979): 57–78.

– "Ixion in Heaven: The Representative Hero." *Disraeli Newsletter* 1 (spring 1976): 14–26.

– "The Psychological Romance: Disraeli's Early Fiction and Political Apprenticeship." PhD dissertation, Indiana University, 1974. Xerox University Microfilms, 75-8994.

– "The Revolutionary Epick: Tory Democracy or Radical Gallomania?" *Disraeli Newsletter* 2 (spring 1977): 24–42.

– "Two Nations, or One? Disraeli's Allegorical Romance." *Victorian Studies* 30.2 (winter 1987): 211–34.

– "William Ewart Gladstone." In *Dictionary of Literary Biography: Victorian Prose Writers After 1867*, ed. William B. Thesing, 57. Detroit: Gale, 1987.

Painting, David E. "Disraeli and the Roman Catholic Church." *Quarterly Review* 304 (1966): 17–25.

Parker, Douglass. Introduction to *The Eunuch* in *The Complete Comedies of Terence: Modern Verse Translations* by Palmer Bovie, Constance Carrier, and Douglass Parker, ed. Palmer Bovie, 147–52. New Brunswick, NJ: Rutgers University Press, 1974.

Parris, Leslie, ed. *The Pre-Raphaelites* (reprinted with corrections). London: Tate Gallery Publications, 1994.

Peel, Robert. *Memoirs by the Right Honourable Sir Robert Peel*. 3 Parts. London: Murray, 1856–7; reprinted New York: Krause, 1969.

– *Sir Robert Peel from His Private Papers*. Ed. C.S. Parker. 3 vols. London: Murray, 1899.

Pen and Ink Sketches of Poets, Preachers, and Politicians. London, 1846.

Ponsonby, Arthur. *Henry Ponsonby, Queen Victoria's Private Secretary: His Life from His Letters*. London: Macmillan, 1943.

Pope, Alexander. *The Poems of Alexander Pope*. Twickenham edition. Ed. John Butt. 11 vols. Vol. 3, ed. Maynard Mack. London: Methuen; New Haven: Yale University Press. 1950.

Punch. Benjamin Disraeli. Earl of Beaconsfield, K.G.: In Upwards of 100 Cartoons from the Collection of "Mr. Punch." London: *Punch* Office, 1878.

Purcell, Edmund Sheridan. *Life of Cardinal Manning.* 2 vols. New York & London: Macmillan, 1896.

Ragussis, Michael. *Figures of Conversion: "The Jewish Question" and English National Identity.* Durham: Duke University Press, 1995.

Reynolds, K.D. *Aristocratic Women and Political Society in Victorian Britain.* Oxford & New York: Clarendon Press, 1998.

Richmond, Charles. "Disraeli's Education." In *The Self-Fashioning of Disraeli, 1818–1851,* ed. Richmond and Smith, 16–41.

Richmond Charles, and Jerrold M. Post. "Disraeli's Crucial Illness." In *The Self Fashioning of Disraeli, 1818–1851,* ed. Richmond and Smith, 66–89.

Richmond, Charles, and Paul Smith, eds. *The Self-Fashioning of Disraeli, 1818–1851.* Cambridge: Cambridge University Press, 1998.

Ridley, Jane. *Young Disraeli 1804–1846.* London: Sinclair-Stevenson, 1995.

Robson, John. *What Did He Say? Editing Nineteenth-Century Speeches from Hansard and the Newspapers.* F.E.L. Priestley Lecture Series. Lethbridge, AB: University of Lethbridge Press, 1987.

Roth, Cecil. *The Earl of Beaconsfield.* New York: Philosophical Library, 1952.

Saab, Ann Pottinger. "Disraeli, Judaism, and the Eastern Question." *International History Review* 10.4 (1988): 559–78.

Sadleir, Michael. *Blessington-D'Orsay: A Masquerade.* London: Constable, 1933.

Said, Edward. *Orientalism.* London: Routledge & Kegan Paul, 1978.

Schmidt, James, ed. *Moses Mendelssohn: The First English Biography and Translations.* Bristol: Thoemmes, 2002.

Schwarz, Daniel R. *Disraeli's Fiction.* London: Macmillan, 1979.

– "Disraeli's Romanticism: Self-fashioning in the Novels." In *The Self-Fashioning of Disraeli, 1818–1851,* ed. Richmond and Smith, 42–65.

– "'Mene, Mene, Tekel, Upharsin': Jewish Perspectives in Disraeli's Fiction." In *Disraeli's Jewishness,* ed. Endelman and Kushner, 40–61.

Scott, Walter. *Familiar Letters of Sir Walter Scott.* 2 vols. Edinburgh: Douglas, 1894.

Sedgwick, A.G. "*Endymion.*" In *The Nation* 31 (9 December 1880): 413–14; rpt in *Disraeli's Novels Reviewed,* ed. Stewart, 274–7.

Seton-Watson, R.W. *Disraeli, Gladstone, and the Eastern Question.* New York: Norton, 1972.

Shannon, Richard. *The Age of Disraeli, 1868–1881: The Rise of Tory Democracy.* London and New York: Longman, 1992.

– *Gladstone and the Bulgarian Agitation 1876.* London: Nelson and Sons, 1963.

Shelley, Percy Bysshe. *Shelley's Prometheus Unbound: A Variorum Edition.* Ed. Lawrence John Zillman. Seattle: University of Washington Press, 1959.

Smiles, Samuel. *A Publisher and His Friends: Memoir and Correspondence of the Late John Murray*. 2 vols. London: Murray, 1891.

Smith, Goldwin. *The Reorganisation of the University of Oxford*. Oxford and London: J. Parker, 1868.

Smith, Paul. *Disraeli: A Brief Life*. Cambridge: Cambridge University Press, 1996.

– *Disraelian Conservatism and Social Reform*. London: Routledge & Kegan Paul; Toronto: University of Toronto Press, 1967.

– "Disraeli's Politics." In *The Self-Fashioning of Disraeli, 1818–1851*, ed. Richmond and Smith, 152–73.

Smith, Sheila M. "Willenhall and Wodgate: Disraeli's Use of Blue Book Evidence." *Review of English Studies* ns 13 (1962): 368–84.

Stead, Estelle W. *My Father: Personal and Spiritual Reminiscences*. London: Heinemann, 1913.

Stead, W.T., ed. *The M.P. for Russia: Reminiscences & Correspondence of Madame Olga Novikoff*. 2 vols. London: Andrew Melrose, 1909.

Stephen, Leslie. "Mr. Disraeli's Novels." *Fortnightly Review* 22 ns 16 (October 1874): 430–50.

Stewart, Robert. *The Politics of Protection: Lord Derby and the Protectionist Party, 1841–1852*. Cambridge: Cambridge University Press, 1971.

Stewart, R.W. *Benjamin Disraeli: A List of Writings by Him, and Writings about Him, with Notes*. Metuchen, NJ: Scarecrow Press, 1972.

– ed. *Disraeli's Novels Reviewed, 1826–1868*. Metuchen, NJ: Scarecrow Press, 1975.

– "The Publication and Reception of Disraeli's *Vivian Grey*." *Quarterly Review* 298 (1960): 409–17.

Stone, Donald. *The Romantic Impulse in Victorian Fiction*. Cambridge, MA: Harvard University Press, 1980.

Strachey, Lytton. *Eminent Victorians*. London: Chatto and Windus, 1979.

Sumner, B.H. *Russia and the Balkans, 1870–1880*. Oxford: Oxford University Press, 1937; rpt Hamden, CT: Archon Books, 1962.

Swartz, Marvin. *The Politics of British Foreign Policy in the Era of Disraeli and Gladstone*. New York: St Martin's Press, 1985.

Thackeray, William Makepeace. "'Codlingsby,' by B. de Shrewsbury, Esq." *Punch; or the London Charivari* 12 (1847): 166, 198–9, 213–14, 223.

Torrens, W.M. *Memoirs of William Lamb, Second Viscount Melbourne*. London: Ward, Lock, 1890.

Victoria, Queen. *The Letters of Queen Victoria: A Selection from Her Majesty's Correspondence between the Years 1837 and 1861*. Ed. Arthur Christopher Benson, and Viscount Esher. 3 vols. London: Murray, 1908.

– *The Letters of Queen Victoria, 2nd Series: A Selection from Her Majesty's Correspondence between the Years, 1862 and 1878*. Ed. George Earle Buckle, 2 vols. London: Murray, 1926.

Vincent, J.R., ed. *Disraeli, Derby and the Conservative Party: Journals and Memoirs of Edward Henry, Lord Stanley 1849–1869*. Hassocks, U.K.: Harvester Press, 1978.

Voskuil, Lynn M. "A Political Masquerade: Disraeli, Victoria and the Royal Titles Bill." In *Acting Naturally: Victorian Theatricality and Authenticity*, 140–81. Charlottesville: University of Virginia Press, 2004.

Warburton, Eliot. *The Crescent and the Cross*. 2 vols. London: Colburn, 1845.

Warren, Allen. "Disraeli, the Conservatives and the National Church, 1837–1881." *Parliamentary History* 19.1 (2000): 96–117.

Weintraub, Stanley. *Disraeli: A Biography*. New York: Truman Talley Books/ Dutton, 1993.

The Wellesley Index to Victorian Periodicals. Ed. Walter E. Houghton. 5 vols. Toronto: University of Toronto Press; London: Routledge & Kegan Paul, 1966–89.

Whibley, Charles. *Lord John Manners and His Friends*. 2 vols. Edinburgh & London: Blackwood, 1925.

White, William. *The Inner Life of the House of Commons*. Ed. with a preface by Justin McCarthy. New intro. by E.J. Feuchtwanger. Richmond, U.K.: Richmond Publishing, 1973.

Wohl, Anthony. "'Ben JuJu': Representations of Disraeli's Jewishness in the Victorian Political Cartoon." *Jewish History* 10.2 (fall 1996): 89–134.

– "'Dizzi-Ben-Dizzi': Disraeli as Alien." *Journal of British Studies* 34.3 (July 1995): 375–411.

Woodring, Carl. *Politics in English Romantic Poetry*. Cambridge, MA: Harvard University Press, 1970.

Woodward, Llewellyn. *The Age of Reform*. 2nd ed. Oxford: Clarendon Press, 1962.

Zlotnick, Susan. *Women, Writing, and the Industrial Revolution*. Baltimore and London: Johns Hopkins University Press, 1998.

Index